Along These Lines

Writing Paragraphs and Essays

with Writing from Reading Strategies

Eighth Edition

John Sheridan Biays, Professor Emeritus of English
Broward College

Carol Wershoven, Professor Emerita of English
Palm Beach State College

330 Hudson street, New York, NY 10013

Vice President, Portfolio Management:
 Chris Hoag
Editorial Assistant: Andres Maldonado
Vice President, Product Marketing:
 Roxanne McCarley
Field Marketing Manager: Michael Coons
Product Marketing Coordinator: Erin
 Rush
Managing Editor: Joanne Dauksewicz
Development Editor: Nancy Doherty
 Schmitt

**Project Coordination, Text Design,
 and Electronic Page Makeup:** Integra
 Software Services
Cover Designer: Pentagram
Cover Illustration: Christopher DeLorenzo
Manufacturing Buyer: Roy L. Pickering, Jr.
Printer/Binder: LSC Communications Willard
Cover Printer: LSC Communications

Acknowledgments of third-party content appear on page 633, which constitutes an extension of this copyright page.

Library of Congress Cataloging-in-Publication data on file at the Library of Congress.

1 18

www.pearsonhighered.com

Annotated Instructor's Edition
ISBN 10: 0-134-77173-7
ISBN 13: 978-0-13477173-1

Student Edition
ISBN 10: 0-134-75890-0
ISBN 13: 978-0-13475890-9

Loose-leaf Edition
ISBN 10: 0-134-77661-5
ISBN 13: 978-0-13477661-3

Contents

MN 11.13.2018 1400

Grammar for Writers   373

Preface for Instructors

Students need more help than ever in becoming proficient writers and effective communicators. We applaud your ongoing commitment to helping developing writers become confident learners, and we remain extremely grateful for your ongoing trust in our work.

Along These Lines: Writing Paragraphs and Essays with Writing from Reading Strategies, 8/e, retains the intensive coverage of the writing process that adopters have praised, and the self-contained chapters provide a flexible framework that can accommodate a host of learning styles and instructional preferences. Many caring reviewers have offered insightful, practical, and creative revision suggestions, and thanks to their collective wisdom, this updated edition is the most engaging and visually appealing text to date. We hope you'll agree and that this updated edition serves you well in your quest to educate those students who aspire for a college degree and the promise that it offers.

NEW FEATURES AND ENHANCEMENTS IN THE EIGHTH EDITION

- **Significant improvements have been made to the Readings**, including the incorporation of many new readings on current and interesting topics and a larger number of readings than in the last edition. A selection from literature has been added, as well as new readings from diverse perspectives, and there are three essays written by students.

- **Improved questions and writing prompts have been added to support the Readings**. These new questions and writing prompts better differentiate between reading comprehension and opportunities for discussion.

- **New, current, and engaging exercises and writing prompts** on topics interesting to students have been added to every chapter.

- **More critical thinking boxes have been added to the writing chapters** to encourage students to develop the role critical thinking plays in writing and reading.

- **Enhanced Topics for Critical Thinking and Writing** at the end of each writing chapter offer students prompts and activities to extend their thinking.

- **Grammar chapters have been clarified and streamlined** where needed.

- **Additional questions have been added to Chapter Tests** at the end of each grammar chapter to provide more practice for students.

- **New instruction on evaluating online sources** for credibility and trustworthiness when researching has been added to the chapter "Using Research to Strengthen Essays."

- **Coverage of MLA style has been totally reorganized and rewritten** to reflect online research and changes in MLA style, Eighth Edition.

POPULAR FEATURES RETAINED

Based on positive feedback from current users and new reviewers, the following popular and distinctive features have been retained:

The Writing Chapters

- The writing process approach, supported by a model paragraph or essay that is developed throughout the entire chapter from outline, and drafts, to the final version.
- The key roles of revision, editing, and proofreading during the writing process are reinforced, and differences between basic revision strategies and in-text editing are clearly distinguished.
- Visually appealing and easy-to-follow checklists and "Info Boxes" provide quick reference and reinforcement of key terms and ideas.
- A "Walk-Through" assignment in each chapter guides students, step-by-step, through the stages of the writing process.

The Grammar Chapters

- The three types of grammar exercises, **Practice** (simple reinforcement), **Collaborate** (partner or group work), and **Connect** ("in context" identification of grammatical errors to strengthen editing skills), provide structure to each chapter's instruction.
- Grammar concepts taught in a step-by-step fashion, as in "Two Steps to Check for Fragments."
- A Chapter Test, ideal for class review or quick quizzes, anchors each grammar chapter.

Reading Instruction and Selections

- Easily applied prereading procedures and quick summarizing techniques.
- Carefully selected readings reflecting a broad range of timely, high-interest themes.
- Numerous writing options, including critical-thinking topics, inspired by a selection's content and designed to encourage careful analysis and independent thought.

Throughout the Text

- Engaging teaching tips, including ones tailored for English language learners, in the *Annotated Instructor's Edition*.

WRITING RESOURCES AND SUPPLEMENTS

Annotated Instructor's Edition for Along These Lines: Writing Paragraphs and Essays with Writing from Reading Strategies
ISBN 0134771737 / 9780134771731

Instructor's Resource Manual for Along These Lines: Writing Paragraphs and Essays with Writing from Reading Strategies
ISBN 0134771729 / 9780134771724

Test Bank for Along These Lines: Writing Paragraphs and Essays with Writing from Reading Strategies
ISBN 0134772636 / 9780134772639

PowerPoint Presentation for Along These Lines: Writing Paragraphs and Essays with Writing from Reading Strategies
ISBN 0134772555 / 9780134772554

Answer Key for Along These Lines: Writing Paragraphs and Essays with Writing from Reading Strategies
ISBN 0134772563 / 9780134772561

Reach Every Student by Pairing This Text with MyLab Writing

MyLab™ is the teaching and learning platform that empowers you to reach *every* student. By combining trusted content with digital tools and a flexible platform, MyLab personalizes the learning experience and improves results for each student. When students enter your developmental writing course with varying skill levels, MyLab can help you identify which students need extra support and provide them targeted practice and instruction outside of class. Learn more at www.pearson.com/mylab/writing.

- **Empower each learner**: Each student learns at a different pace. Personalized learning pinpoints the precise areas where each student needs practice, giving all students the support they need — when and where they need it — to be successful.
  - MyLab Writing diagnoses students' strengths and weaknesses through a pre-assessment known as the **Path Builder**, and offers up a personalized **Learning Path**. Students then receive targeted practice and multimodal activities to help them improve over time.

- **Teach your course your way**: Your course is unique. So whether you'd like to build your own assignments, teach multiple sections, or set prerequisites, MyLab gives you the flexibility to easily create *your* course to fit *your* needs.

- **Improve student results**: When you teach with MyLab, student performance improves. That's why instructors have chosen MyLab for over 15 years, touching the lives of over 50 million students.

ACKNOWLEDGMENTS

We are indebted to the following professionals for their comprehensive reviews, practical advice, and creative suggestions regarding the *Along These Lines* series:

Stephanie Alexander	Mountwest Community and Technical College
Elizabeth Andrews	South Florida State College
Elizabeth Barnes	Daytona State College
Iris Chao	Saddleback College
Patty Crockett	Bishop State Community College
Mellisa Dalton	Lanier Technical College
Linda Hasty	Motlow State Community College
Gregg Heitschmidt	Surry Community College
Johnnerlyn Johnson	Sandhills Community College

Therese Jones	Lewis University
Cassi Lapp	Northwest Arkansas Community College
Ann Moore	Florence-Darlington Technical College
Deana Pendley	Copiah-Lincoln Community College
Sandra Valerio	Del Mar College

The updates and additions to this text would not have been possible without the help, support, and collaboration of a great many people. We are greatly indebted to the outstanding professionals at Pearson and Ohlinger Studios for the work they put into and the guidance given to making this edition a reality. We also thank the reviewers, whose comments helped to shape the most recent edition:

Kristina Beckman-Brito	Pima Community College
Scott Hopkins	Lake-Sumter State College
Therese Jones	Lewis University
Jean Miller	McCook Community College
John Nordlof	Eastern University
Cheryl Weller-Anderson	Pima Community College

We extend our deepest gratitude to Steven Jolliffe and Richard McCarthy for taking on the lion's share of revisions. Steve selected the new readings and wrote new questions and writing prompts to accompany them. Steve and Richard updated the text, wrote new exercise items and writing prompts throughout the text, and wrote new critical thinking boxes for the writing chapters. Steve and Richard are creative and knowledgeable instructors—they excel at inspiring student interest and at knowing just where to add a subtle change that makes all the difference. We also thank Steve for his dedicated partnering throughout the editing and production stages.

We are grateful for Nancy Doherty Schmitt, Development Editor, for her keen eye, her thoughtful suggestions, and her vision and guidance. There have been many hands who have contributed to this text throughout many editions, but Nancy has brought new clarity and unity to this completely updated edition.

We also want to pay tribute to all the unsung heroes in the classroom who help struggling students overcome adversity, find their voice, and reach their potential. We are humbled by your dedication and resilience, and you exemplify effective teaching at its best.

Finally, and most importantly, we send heartfelt thanks to the thousands of students who have intrigued, impressed, and inspired us through the years. You have taught us far more than you can ever imagine, and you have made our journey extraordinary along *all* lines.

Writing in Stages: The Process Approach

Learning by Doing

Writing is a skill, and like any skill, writing improves with practice. This book provides you with ample practice to improve your writing through a variety of individual and group activities. Whether you complete assignments at home or in the classroom, just remember that *good writing takes practice*: you can learn to write well by simply writing.

Steps Make Writing Easier

Writing is easier if you *do not try to do too much at once*. To make the task of writing easier, *Along These Lines* breaks the process into stages:

PREWRITING

In this stage, you think about your topic, and you *gather ideas*. You *react* to your own ideas and add even more thoughts. You can also react to other people's ideas as a way of expanding your own.

PLANNING

In this stage, you *examine your ideas* and begin to *focus* them around one main idea. Planning involves combining, dividing, and even eliminating some ideas. Placing your specific details in a logical order often involves *outlining*.

DRAFTING AND REVISING

In this stage, the thinking and planning begin to take shape as a piece of writing. You complete a draft of your work, a *rough version* of the finished product. Then you examine the draft and consider ways to *revise* it, a process that may require writing and reworking several versions of your original draft.

EDITING AND PROOFREADING

In this stage, you give your latest revised draft one last, careful *review* when you are rested and alert. You concentrate on refining your style and identifying and correcting any mistakes in sentence structure, word choice, spelling, or punctuation you may have overlooked. This stage is the *final check* of your work to make your writing the best it can be.

These four stages in the writing process—*prewriting, planning, drafting and revising*, and *editing and proofreading*—may overlap. You may be changing your plan even as you work on the draft of your paper. Throughout this book, you will have many opportunities to become familiar with the stages of effective writing. Working individually and with your classmates, you can become a better writer along *all* lines.

Writing a Paragraph

Jumping In

*Where do you get your ideas for writing? Do they seem to come at you all at once? Working with a jumble of ideas is often part of the writing process, and a key step is sorting through these ideas. By sorting, you will be working toward one **paragraph** that focuses on one idea or point.*

Learning Objectives

In this chapter, you will learn how to:

1. Prewrite to generate a topic.
2. Recognize and write a clear topic sentence.
3. Write a paragraph that is unified, supported with detail, and coherent.

WHAT IS THE ROLE OF A PARAGRAPH?

Usually, students write because they have a writing assignment requiring them to write on some topic or choice of topics, and the writing is due by a certain day. So assume that you get such an assignment and it calls for one paragraph. You might wonder, "Why a paragraph? Why not something large, like a two- or three-page paper? After all, many classes will ask for papers, not just paragraphs."

For one thing, all essays are a series of paragraphs. If you can write one good paragraph, you can write more than one. The **paragraph** is the basic building block of any essay. It is a group of sentences focusing on *one idea* or one point. Keep this concept in mind: *one idea to a paragraph.* Focusing on one idea or one point gives a paragraph **unity**. If you have a new point, start a new paragraph.

You may ask, "Doesn't this mean a paragraph will be short? How long should a paragraph be, anyway?" To convince a reader of one main point, you need to make it, support it, develop it, explain it, and describe it. There will be shorter and longer paragraphs, but for now, you can assume your paragraph will be somewhere between seven and twelve sentences long.

This chapter guides you through each stage of the writing process:

- **Prewriting**—how to generate and develop ideas for your paragraph
- **Planning**—how to organize your ideas
- **Drafting and Revising**—how to create and revise
- **Editing and Proofreading**—how to review and make one final check

We give extra emphasis to the prewriting stage in this chapter to give you some extra help in getting started.

PREWRITING   A PARAGRAPH

1 Prewrite to generate a topic.

Suppose your instructor asks you to write a paragraph about your favorite city or town. Writing about your favorite city or town is your general **topic**, but you must choose one city or town to make the topic more specific. With this topic, you already know your **purpose**—to write a paragraph that makes some point about the city or town. You have an **audience** because you are writing this paragraph for your instructor and classmates. Often, your purpose is to write a specific kind of paper for a class. Occasionally, you may have to write with a different purpose or audience, such as writing instructions for a new employee at your workplace, a letter of complaint to a manufacturer, or a short biographical essay for a scholarship application. Knowing your audience and purpose is important in writing effectively.

Freewriting, Brainstorming, and Keeping a Journal

Once you have identified your purpose and audience, you can begin by finding some way to *think on paper*. You can use the techniques of freewriting, brainstorming, or keeping a journal to gather ideas and potential details.

Freewriting Give yourself fifteen minutes to write whatever comes into your mind on your subject. If your mind is a blank, write, "My mind's a blank. My mind's a blank," over and over until you think of something else. The main goal here is to *write without stopping*. Do not stop to tell yourself, "This is stupid," or "I can't use any of this in a paper." Do not stop to correct your spelling or punctuation. Just write. Let your ideas flow. Write *freely*. Here is an example:

Freewriting about a Favorite City or Town

Favorite city or town. City? I like New York. It's so big and exciting. Haven't been there much, though. Only once. My hometown. I like it. It's just another town but comfortable and friendly. Maybe St. Augustine. Lots of fun visits there. Grandparents there. Hard to pick a favorite. Different places are good for different reasons.

Brainstorming This technique is like freewriting because you write whatever comes into your head, but it is a little different because you can pause

---

Brainstorming about a Favorite City or Town

Favorite place

City or town

What's the difference between a city and a town?

Doesn't matter. Just pick one. Cities are bigger.

How is city life different from town life?

Cities are bigger. More crowded, like Atlanta.

Which do you like better, a city or a town?

Sometimes I like cities.

Why?

There is more to do.

So, what city do you like?

I like New York and St. Augustine.

Is St. Augustine a city?

Yes. A small one.

Do you like towns?

I loved this little town in Mexico.

---

to ask yourself questions that will lead to new ideas. When you **brainstorm** alone, you "interview" yourself about a subject. You can also brainstorm and ask questions within a group.

If you feel like you are running out of ideas in brainstorming, try to form a question out of what you've just written. *Go where your questions and answers lead you.* For example, if you write, "There is more to do in cities," you could form these questions:

> *What is there to do? Sports? Entertainment? Outdoor exercise? Meeting people?*

You could also make a list of your brainstorming ideas, but remember to *do only one step at a time.*

Keeping a Journal   A **journal** is a notebook of your personal writing, a notebook in which you write *regularly and often. It is not a diary, but it is a place to record your experiences, reactions, and observations.* In it, you can write about what you have done, heard, seen, read, or remembered. You can include sayings that you would like to remember, news clippings, snapshots—anything that you would like to recall or consider. A journal provides an enjoyable way to practice your writing, and it is a great source of ideas for writing.

Journal Entry about a Favorite City or Town

I'm not going south to see my grandparents this winter. They're coming here instead of me going to St. Augustine. I'd really like to go there. I like the warm weather. It's better than months of snow, ice, and rain here in Easthampton. I'll miss going there. I've been so many times that it's like a second home. St. Augustine is great around Christmastime.

Finding Specific Ideas

Whether you freewrite, brainstorm, or consult your journal, you end up generating ideas. Follow those first ideas, and see where they can take you. You are looking for specific ideas, each of which can focus on the general topic you started with. At this point, you do not have to decide which specific idea you want to write about. You just want to *narrow your range* of ideas.

You might think, "Why should I narrow my ideas? Won't I have more to say if I keep my topic big?" But remember that a paragraph has one idea; you want to state it clearly and with convincing details for support. If you try to write one paragraph on city life versus town life, for example, you will probably make so many general statements that you will say very little, or you will bore your reader with big, sweeping statements. General ideas are big, broad ones. Specific ideas are smaller, narrower ones. If you scanned the freewriting example on a favorite city or town, you might underline many specific ideas as possible topics:

> *Favorite city or town. City? I like <u>New York</u>. It's so big and exciting. Haven't been there much, though. Only once. <u>My hometown</u>. I like it. It's just another town but comfortable and friendly. Maybe <u>St. Augustine</u>. Lots of fun visits there. Grandparents there. Hard to pick a favorite. Different places are good for different reasons.*

Consider the underlined terms. They are specific places. You could write a paragraph about any one of these places. Or you could underline specific places in your brainstorming questions and answers:

> *Favorite place*
> *City or town*

> **What's the difference between a city and a town?**
> *Doesn't matter. Just pick one. Cities are bigger.*

> **How is city life different from town life?**
> *Cities are bigger. More crowded, like <u>Atlanta</u>.*

> **Which do you like better, a city or a town?**
> *Sometimes I like cities.*

> **Why?**
> *There is more to do.*

> **So, what city do you like?**
> *I like <u>New York</u> and <u>St. Augustine</u>.*

> **Is St. Augustine a city?**
> *Yes. A small one.*

> **Do you like towns?**
> *I loved this <u>little town in Mexico</u>.*

Each of these specific places could be a topic for your paragraph.

If you reviewed the journal entry on a favorite city or town, you would also be able to underline specific places:

> *I'm not going south to see my grandparents this winter. They're coming here instead of me going to <u>St. Augustine</u>. I'd really like to go there. I like the warm weather. It's*

better than months of snow, ice, and rain here in Easthampton. I'll miss going there. I've been so many times that it's like a second home. St. Augustine is great around Christmastime.

Remember: Following the steps can lead you to specific ideas.

Critical Thinking and the Writing Process

As you know by now, one of the popular methods of prewriting is called *brainstorming*, the practice of asking yourself key questions that can lead you to new ideas and directions related to your writing topic. During your college career, you will find that such questioning can enable you to engage in **critical thinking**, a type of reasoning that has several meanings and practical uses. For now, just remember that any time you evaluate the relevance of supporting details, determine their order of importance, and attempt to justify their inclusion, you are making judgments that are considered *critical*. Making such judgments will become more common for you as you tackle college writing assignments.

You will soon appreciate the crucial role critical thinking plays in effective writing, whether you are comparing and contrasting ideas, identifying a trend's causes and effects, arguing rationally for or against a proposal, or questioning what you read. Additionally, whenever you evaluate a piece of writing based on such criteria as unity, support, coherence, and intended audience, you will be sharpening your critical thinking skills.

Critical thinking and writing options can be found at the end of each writing chapter and at the end of each reading selection in this book. These topics may require you to take a stand, defend a choice, imagine a certain scenario, or examine a trend. Whether you discuss these topics with peers or decide to write about them, keeping an open mind will help you become a better writer and a stronger critical thinker.

Selecting One Topic

Once you have a list of specific ideas that can lead you to a specific topic, you can pick one topic. Let's say you decided to work with the list of places you gathered through brainstorming:

> Atlanta
> New York
> St. Augustine
> a little town in Mexico

Looking at this list, you decide you want to write about St. Augustine as your favorite city.

Exercise 1 **Practice: Creating Questions for Brainstorming**

Following are several topics. For each one, brainstorm by writing at least four questions related to the topic that could lead you to further ideas. The first topic is done for you.

1. topic: social media

Question 1:   Why is social media popular with young adults?

Question 2:   Which social media apps are most popular?

Question 3: What type of person uses social media apps the most? _____

Question 4: Which is better for viewing social media: a desktop or a

smartphone? _____

2. topic: running

Question 1: _____

Question 2: _____

Question 3: _____

Question 4: _____

3. topic: vacation

Question 1: _____

_____

Question 2: _____

Question 3: _____

Question 4: _____

Exercise 2   Practice: Finding Specific Details in Freewriting

Two samples of freewriting follow. Each is a written response to a different topic. Read each sample, and then underline any words and phrases that could become the focus of a paragraph.

Freewriting Reaction to the Topic of Winter

A lot of my friends complain about winter. It is too cold. It lasts too long. Others say they like snow, but are happy to see spring when it arrives. I like winter. I like to ski. Being the first one on the lift and skiing untracked trails makes me happy. Getting outside in the winter is really important. It helps me maintain a sense of balance.

Freewriting Reaction to the Topic of Online Shopping

I love shopping online. I know a lot of people talk about the dangers of being too impulsive while online shopping. I like the fact that I can browse as long as I like without buying anything. I get anxious when I shop in stores. I don't like the crowds. Plus, many online stores offer convenient shipping and return policies. You also get better deals online.

Exercise 3   Practice: Finding Specific Details in a List

Several lists of words or phrases follow. In each list, one item is a general term, and the others are more specific. Underline the words or phrases that are more specific. The first list is done for you.

1. chocolate cake
   raspberry torte
   desserts
   tapioca pudding
   cheesecake
   peanut butter cookies

2. Instagram
   Facebook
   Snapchat
   Twitter
   social media

3. mathematics
   psychology
   academics
   French
   composition class
   sociology

4. transportation
   high speed rail
   subway
   bus
   autonomous automobiles
   airline

Collaborate

Exercise 4 **Collaborate: Finding Topics through Freewriting**

The following exercise must be completed with a partner or a group. Several topics follow. Pick one and freewrite on it for ten minutes. Then read your freewriting to your partner or group. Ask your listener(s) to jot down any words or phrases from your writing that could lead to a specific topic for a paragraph.

Your listener(s) should read the jotted-down words or phrases to you. You will be hearing a collection of specific ideas that came from *your* writing. As you listen, underline the words in your freewriting.

Freewriting topics (pick one):

1. future goals
2. overcoming an obstacle
3. a celebratory moment in life

Freewriting on (name of topic chosen): _____

_____

_____

_____

CRITICAL THINKING

When adding more detail to your topic, consider the 5Ws and I H questions that begin with *Wh* and *H*. Ask ...

What?	*Who?*	*Where?*
When?	*Why?*	*How?*

Adding Details to a Specific Topic

You can develop the specific topic you picked in a number of ways.

1. *Check your list* for other ideas that seem to fit with the specific topic you've picked.

2. *Brainstorm*—ask yourself more questions about your topic, and use the answers as details.

3. *List* any new ideas you have that may be connected to your topic.

One way to add details is to go back and check your brainstorming for other ideas about St. Augustine:

I like St. Augustine.
a small city

Now you can brainstorm some questions that will lead you to more details. The questions do not have to be connected to each other; they are just questions that could lead you to ideas and details:

What's so great about St. Augustine?

People can go to the beach nearby.

Is it a clean, big beach?

Sure. And the water is a clear blue.

What else can people do in St. Augustine?

There's lots of history.

Like what?

A fort. The oldest schoolhouse. Old houses.

Another way to add details is to list any ideas that may be connected to your topic. The list might give you more specific details:

grandparents live there
warm in winter
grandparents feed me
I use their car

If you had tried all three ways of adding detail, you would end up with this list of details connected to the topic of a favorite city or town:

a small city	*clear blue water*
no freeways	*lots of history*
no skyscrapers	*a fort*
not millions of people	*oldest schoolhouse*
thousands of visitors every day	*grandparents live there*
can always visit family for free	*warm in winter*
beach nearby	*grandparents feed me*
clean, big beach	*I use their car*

INFO BOX **Beginning the Prewriting: A Summary**

The prewriting stage of writing a paragraph enables you to gather ideas. This process begins with several steps.

1. **Think on paper and write down any ideas that you have about a topic.** You can do this by freewriting, by brainstorming, or by keeping a journal.

2. **Scan your writing for specific ideas that have come from your first efforts.** List these specific ideas.

3. **Pick one specific idea.** Then, by reviewing your early writing, by questioning, and by thinking further, you can add details to the one specific idea.

This process may seem long, but once you have worked through it several times, it will become nearly automatic. When you think about ideas before you try to shape them into a paragraph, you are off to a good start. Confidence comes from having something to say, and once you have a specific idea, you will be ready to begin shaping and developing details that support your idea.

Exercise 5   **Practice: Adding Details to a Topic by Brainstorming**

Two topics follow. Each has two or three details listed. Brainstorm more questions, based on the existing details, that can lead to more details.

1. topic: advantages of carpooling to school

details: better for the environment

saves gas money

Question 1: _____

Question 2: _____

Question 3: _____

Question 4: _____

2. topic: issues associated with going to school and having a full-time job

details: time management issues

fewer hours of sleep per night

fewer opportunities for relaxation

Question 1: _____

Question 2: _____

Question 3: _____

Question 4: _____

Exercise 6   **Practice: Adding Details by Listing**

Following are three topics for paragraphs. For each topic, list details that seem to fit the topic.

1. topic: online shopping

details: a. _____   c. _____

b. _____   d. _____

2. topic: renting an apartment for the first time

details: a. _____ c. _____

b. _____ d. _____

3. topic: buying a car

details: a. _____ c. _____

b. _____ d. _____

Focusing the Prewriting

The next step of writing is to *focus your ideas around some point*. Your ideas will begin to take a focus if you reexamine them, looking for *related ideas*. Here are two techniques that you can use:

- marking a list of related ideas
- mapping related ideas

Listing Related Ideas

To develop a marked list, take another look at the list we developed under the topic of a favorite city or town. The same list is shown here, but you will notice some of the items have been marked with symbols that show related ideas.

N marks ideas about St. Augustine's natural good points.
H marks ideas about St. Augustine's history.
F marks ideas about family in St. Augustine.

Here is the marked list of ideas related to the topic of a favorite city or town:

a small city	N clear blue water
no freeways	H lots of history
no skyscrapers	H a fort
not millions of people	H oldest schoolhouse
thousands of visitors every day	F grandparents live there
F can always visit family for free	N warm in winter
N beach nearby	F grandparents feed me
N clean, big beach	F I use their car

You have probably noticed that some items are not marked: a small city, no freeways, no skyscrapers, not millions of people, and thousands of visitors every day. Perhaps you can come back to them later, or you may decide you do not need them in your paragraph.

To make it easier to see what ideas you have, and how they are related, try *grouping related ideas*, giving each list a title, like this:

natural good points of St. Augustine

beach nearby clear blue water

clean, big beach warm in winter

history in St. Augustine

lots of history oldest schoolhouse
a fort

family in St. Augustine

can always visit family for free grandparents live there

grandparents feed me I use their car

Mapping

Another way to focus your ideas is to mark your first list of ideas, and then cluster the related ideas into separate lists. You can **map** your ideas, like this:

Whatever way you choose to examine and group your details, you are working toward *a focus, a point.* You are asking and beginning to answer the question, "Where do the details lead?" The answer will be the **topic sentence** of your paragraph. It will be the *main idea* of your paragraph.

② Recognize and write a clear topic sentence.

Forming a Topic Sentence

To form a topic sentence, you can do the following:

1. Review your details and see if you can form some general idea that can summarize the details.
2. Write that general idea as one sentence.

Your sentence that summarizes the details is the **topic sentence**. It makes a general point, and the more specific details you have gathered will support this point.

To form a topic sentence about your favorite city, St. Augustine, review the many details you have listed about the city. It is time to ask questions about those details. You could ask yourself, "What kind of details do I have? Can I summarize them?" You might then write the summary as the topic sentence:

I love St. Augustine because it has sun and sea, history, and family.

Check the sentence against your details. Does it cover the natural good points of St. Augustine? Yes. The topic sentence sums them up as *sun and sea.* Does it cover history and family? Yes. The topic sentence says the place has *history and family.*

Writing Good Topic Sentences

Be careful. *Topics are not the same as topic sentences. Topics are the subjects you will write about.* A topic sentence states the *main idea* you have developed on a topic. Consider the differences between these topics and the topic sentences:

> **topic:** why empathy is important
> **topic sentence:** Empathy allows people to understand and sympathize with the experiences and emotions of other people.
>
> **topic:** cars and their owners
> **topic sentence:** People purchase cars that are extensions of their personality.

Topic sentences *do not announce; they make a point.* Look at the sentences that follow, and notice the differences between the sentences that announce and the topic sentences.

> **announcement:** I will discuss the importance of routinely making your bed in the morning.
> **topic sentence:** Routinely making your bed in the morning can bring order into your life.
>
> **announcement:** An analysis of why recycling paper is important will be the subject of this paper.
> **topic sentence:** Recycling paper is important because it saves trees, money, and even certain animals.

Topic sentences can be too big to develop in one paragraph. A topic sentence that is *too broad* may take many paragraphs—even pages of writing—to develop. Look at the very broad sentences that follow, and then notice how they can be narrowed.

> **too broad:** Business executives get paid too much money. (This sentence is too broad because "business executives" could mean anything from local business leaders to the heads of *Fortune 500* companies; "too much money" could refer to salary, bonuses, or stock options.)
> **a narrower, better topic sentence:** Several Silicon Valley executives are paid significantly more than the computer programmers who work for them.
>
> **too broad:** I have changed a great deal since my last year of high school. (The phrase "changed a great deal" could refer to physical changes, intellectual changes, emotional changes, or just about any other change you can think of.)
> **a narrower, better topic sentence:** Since leaving high school, I have improved as a writer and researcher.

Topic sentences can be too small to develop in one paragraph. A topic sentence that is *too narrow* cannot be supported by detail. It may be a fact, which cannot be developed. A topic sentence that is too narrow leaves you with nothing more to say.

> **too narrow:** Brussel sprouts are healthy.
> **an expanded topic sentence:** Brussel sprouts are healthy for two reasons.

too narrow: It takes twenty minutes to get out of the school's parking lot.

an expanded topic sentence: Congestion is causing problems for students trying to exit the parking lot.

The prewriting stage begins with free, unstructured thinking and writing. As you work through the prewriting process, your thinking and writing will become more focused.

Focusing the Prewriting: A Summary

The prewriting stage of writing a paragraph enables you to develop an idea into a topic sentence and related details. You can focus your thinking by working in steps.

1. Try marking a list of related details, or try mapping to group your ideas.
2. Write a topic sentence that summarizes your details.
3. Check that your topic sentence is a sentence, not a topic. Make sure that it is not too broad or too narrow and that it is not an announcement. Check that it makes a point and focuses the details you have developed.

Exercise 7   **Practice: Grouping Related Items in Lists of Details**

Lists of details follow. In each list, circle the items that seem to fit into one group; then underline the items that seem to belong to a second group. Some items may not belong in either group. The first list is done for you.

1. **topic:**   online learning

lack of connection	freedom from school
convenient	saves time
feel isolated	no parking problem
no child care issues	need self-discipline
self-paced	procrastination anytime, anyplace

2. **topic:**   clothes

jeans	shirts
evening gown	silk tie
high heels	sneakers
underwear	tuxedo
sweatpants	flip-flops

3. **topic:**   fame

public admiration	media interviews
sudden riches	loss of privacy
false friends	photographers
nasty Internet rumors	personal power
famous athletes	stalkers

Exercise 8   **Practice: Writing Topic Sentences for Lists of Details**

Lists of details that have no topic sentence follow. Write an appropriate topic sentence for each one.

1. topic sentence: _____

_____

Latino families celebrate *quinceañera,* the fifteenth birthday of their daughters.

Jewish families celebrate the *bar mitzvah,* or coming of age of thirteen-year-old Jewish boys.

Jewish girls have their own similar ceremony, the *bat mitzvah.*

For many young American women, a Sweet Sixteen party is a tradition to mark a teen's growth into adulthood.

Every year, thousands of twenty-year-old Japanese men and women come together on one day.

They participate in a traditional ceremony, similar to a graduation ceremony, with speeches and celebrations.

In Korea, a coming-of-age party is held for young women at age fifteen and young men at age twenty. During the young man's celebration, he must lift a heavy rock over his head. Once he does, he is declared a man.

2. topic sentence: _____

_____

Emily Dominguez was the prettiest girl in my first-grade class.

She had long hair and wide eyes.

I used to watch her in class, admiring the way she held her pencil or raised her hand.

One day she caught me looking at her.

Emily smiled and turned her head.

Now I was truly in love because I believed Emily liked me.

For a few days, I lived in a dream in which Emily, the princess, chose me as her hero.

Then I saw her at recess, giggling with Tommy Malone on the playground.

I knew my dream would not come true.

3. topic sentence: _____

_____

My roommate Etienne is Haitian, so at first, I had a hard time understanding his English.

He also seemed very shy.

I didn't see him much, so I figured he was socializing with his own friends and didn't like me.

Then one night I had an important algebra test to study for.

I went to the tutoring center to get some help with my math.

Etienne was there, wrapped up in books.

Later, I learned he was there every night, studying English, but also tutoring other people in math.

Etienne and I are good friends now; I help him with English, and he teaches me algebra.

Exercise 9 **Practice: Turning Topics into Topic Sentences**

Some of the items in the list that follow are topic sentences, but some are topics. Put an *X* by the items that are topics. In the lines after the list, rewrite the topics into topic sentences.

1. _____ Two simple ways to lose weight without following a strict diet or taking diet pills.
2. _____ The happiest day in my life started out as a bad day.
3. _____ Having poor study habits and facing the consequences.
4. _____ Worrying about the future can become an obsession.
5. _____ How I met my husband.
6. _____ Why procrastinating is a destructive habit.
7. _____ One strong family can survive many tragedies.
8. _____ College classes are not what I expected.
9. _____ Volunteering at a nature preserve gives me a break from my worries.
10. _____ My ten-year-old niece is obsessed with makeup.

Rewrite the topics. Make each one into a topic sentence.

_____

_____

_____

_____

_____

_____

_____

_____

Exercise 10 **Practice: Revising Topic Sentences That Are Too Broad**

Some of the topic sentences that follow are too broad to support in one paragraph. Put an *X* by the ones that are too broad. Then, on the lines after the list, rewrite those sentences as a topic sentence, focusing on a limited idea, that could be supported in one paragraph.

1. _____ Childhood is a time of innocence.
2. _____ The best part of studying in the library is that I must turn my smartphone off and focus completely on my work.

3. _____ Trust is the most important factor in negotiations.

4. _____ Omar needs to be more realistic about his goals.

5. _____ Colin has two jobs so that he can afford to go to college next year.

6. _____ American teenagers are deeply troubled.

7. _____ Jie always loved drawing; she knew she wanted to enter a major that included art and that is why she is majoring in graphic design.

8. _____ When I finish my education, I want to do some meaningful work.

9. _____ My mother would have liked to be a stay-at-home mother.

10. _____ My life as a thirty-year-old student is nothing like the lives of college students in most movies.

Rewrite the broad sentences. Make each one more limited.

_____

_____

_____

_____

_____

_____

_____

_____

_____

_____

Exercise 11   **Practice: Making Announcements into Topic Sentences**

A list of sentences follows: some are topic sentences and some are announcements. Put an *X* by the announcements. Then, on the lines after the list, rewrite the announcements, making them into topic sentences.

1. _____ Sticking to a budget can be difficult for a college student.

2. _____ This paper will be about the loss of green space in our town.

3. _____ I want to become a nurse for many reasons.

4. _____ Flowers are a convenient, all-purpose gift, but they can be expensive.

5. _____ Why my brother is in prison is the subject of this essay.

6. _____ The need for more and better campus lighting is the area to be discussed.

7. _____ The smartest change I made all year was to put down my smartphone when I study.

8. _____ The topic of this paper will be the recent carjacking on Patriot Road.

9. _____ I will discuss the reasons for taking the bus to work.

10. _____ Arthur O'Malley deserves a reward for heroism.

Rewrite the announcements. Make each one a topic sentence.

_____

_____

_____

_____

_____

_____

_____

_____

_____

Exercise 12 **Practice: Revising Topic Sentences That Are Too Narrow**

A list of topic sentences follows: some of them are topics that are too narrow and they cannot be developed with details. Put an *X* by the ones that are too narrow. Then, on the lines after, rewrite those sentences as broader topic sentences that could be developed in one paragraph.

1. _____ My father has to sell my grandmother's house.

2. _____ Every night, I cook dinner for my children.

3. _____ Adrian Levine's people skills made him a good psychologist.

4. _____ Armando has a commercial pilot's license.

5. _____ The movie theater is across the street from the mall.

6. _____ Once classes got out for break, the campus was like a ghost town.

7. _____ Heavy flooding drove hundreds of people from their Kansas homes.

8. _____ There was a fire at the abandoned bowling alley on Dowling Road.

9. _____ Our first day of English class was full of surprises.

10. _____ Ted and I played basketball all Saturday afternoon and most of Sunday morning.

Rewrite the narrow sentences. Make each one broader.

_____

_____

_____

_____

_____

_____

_____

_____

_____

_____

_____

_____

_____

PLANNING   A PARAGRAPH

Checking Your Details

Once you have a topic sentence, you can begin working on an **outline** for your paragraph. The outline is a plan that helps you stay focused in your writing. The outline begins to form when you write your topic sentence and write your list of details beneath the topic sentence. You can now look at your list and ask yourself an important question: "Do I have **enough details** to **support** my topic sentence?" Remember, your goal is to write a paragraph of seven to twelve sentences.

Consider this topic sentence and list of details:

topic sentence:	People can be very rude when they shop in supermarkets.
details:	talk on phone
	express lane
	too many items

Does the list contain enough details for a paragraph of seven to twelve sentences? Probably not.

Adding Details When There Are Not Enough

To add details, try brainstorming. Ask yourself some questions like these:

Where else in supermarkets are people rude?
Are they rude in other lanes besides the express lane?
Are they rude in the aisles? How?
Is there crowding anywhere? Where?

By brainstorming, you might come up with this detail:

topic sentence:	People can be very rude when they shop in supermarkets.
details:	talk on phone
	too many items
	hit my cart with theirs in aisles
	block aisles while they decide
	push ahead in deli area
	argue with cashier over prices

Keep brainstorming until you feel you have enough details for a seven- to twelve-sentence paragraph. Remember that it is better to have too many details than too few because you can always edit the extra details later.

If you try brainstorming and still do not have many details, you can refer to your original ideas—your freewriting or journal—for other details.

Eliminating Details That Do Not Relate to the Topic Sentence

Sometimes, what you thought were good details do not relate to the topic sentence because they do not fit or support your point. Eliminate details that do not relate to the topic sentence. For example, the following list contains details that really do not relate to the topic sentence. Those details are crossed out.

topic sentence:	Waiters have to be very patient in dealing with their customers.
details:	customers take a long time ordering
	~~waiter's salary is too low~~
	waiters have to explain specials twice
	customers send orders back
	customers blame waiters for any delays
	waiters can't get angry if customer gets angry
	~~waiters work long shifts~~
	customers change their mind after ordering

From List to Outline

Take another look at the topic sentence and list of details on a favorite city or town:

topic sentence:	I love St. Augustine because it has sun and sea, history, and family.	
details:	a small city	clear blue water
	no freeways	lots of history
	no skyscrapers	a fort
	not millions of people	oldest schoolhouse
	thousands of visitors every day	grandparents live there
	can always visit family for free	warm in winter
	beach nearby	grandparents feed me
	clean, big beach	I use their car

After you scan that list, you are ready to develop the outline of the paragraph.

An outline is a plan for writing, and it can be a type of draft in list form. It sketches what you want to write and the order in which you want to present it. *An organized, logical list will make your writing unified because each item on the list will relate to your topic sentence.*

When you plan, keep your topic sentence in mind:

I love St. Augustine because it has <u>sun</u> and <u>sea</u>, <u>history</u>, and <u>family</u>.

Notice the underlined key words, which lead to three key parts of your outline:

> sun and sea
> history
> family

You can put the details on your list together so that they connect to one of these parts:

sun and sea

> beach nearby, clean, big beach, clear blue water, warm in winter

history

> lots of history, a fort, oldest schoolhouse

family

> can always visit family for free, grandparents live there, grandparents feed me, I drive their car

With this kind of grouping, you have a clearer idea of how to organize a paragraph.

Now that you have grouped your ideas with key words and details, you can write an outline.

An Outline for a Paragraph

topic sentence	I love St. Augustine because it has sun and sea, history, and family.
details	It is warm in the winter.
sun and sea	There is a beach nearby.
	It is big and clean.
	The water is clear blue.
history	It has lots of history.
	There is a fort.
	The oldest schoolhouse is there.
family	My grandparents live in St. Augustine.
	I stay at their house.
	They feed me.
	I use their car.

As you can see, the outline combined some of the details from the list. Even with these combinations, the details are very rough in style. As you reread the list, you will notice items that could be combined and that some ideas that need more explanation. Keep in mind that an outline is merely a very rough organization of your paragraph. You can review the following checklist as you work through the steps of devising an outline.

Checklist for an Outline

✓ **Unity:** Do all of the details relate to the topic sentence? If they do, the paragraph will be unified.

✓ **Support:** Do you have enough supporting ideas? Can you add to these ideas with even more specific details?

✓ **Coherence:** Are the details listed in the right order? If the order of points is logical, the paragraph will be coherent.

Coherence: Putting Your Details in Proper Order

Check the sample outline again, and you will notice that the details are grouped in the same order as the topic sentence: first, details about sun and sea; next, details about history; last, details about family in St. Augustine. Putting the details in an order that matches the topic sentence is a logical order for this paragraph.

Putting the details in logical order makes the ideas in your paragraph easy to follow. The most logical order for a paragraph depends on the subject of the paragraph. If you are writing about an event, you might use **time order** (such as telling what happened first, second, and so forth); if you are arguing some point, you might use **emphatic order** (such as saving your most convincing idea for last); if you are describing a room, you might use **space order** (such as from left to right, or from top to bottom).

The format of the outline helps to organize your ideas. The topic sentence is written above the list of details. This position helps you to remember that the topic sentence is the *main idea*, and the details that support it are written under it. The topic sentence is the most important sentence of the paragraph. You can easily check the items on your list, one by one, against your main idea. You can also develop the *unity* (relevance) and *coherence* (logical order) of your details.

When you actually write a paragraph, the topic sentence does not necessarily have to be the first sentence in the paragraph. Read the paragraphs that follow, and notice where each topic sentence is placed.

Topic Sentence at the Beginning of the Paragraph

<u>Watching a horror movie on the late show can keep me up all night</u>. The movie itself scares me to death, especially if it involves a creepy character sneaking up on someone in the dark. After the movie, I'm afraid to turn out all the lights and be alone in the dark. Then every little noise seems like the sound of a sinister intruder. Strange shapes seem to appear in the shadows. My closet becomes a place where someone could be hiding. There might even be a creature under the bed! And if I go to sleep, these strange invaders might appear from under the bed or in the closet.

Topic Sentence in the Middle of the Paragraph

The kitchen counters gleamed. In the spice rack, every jar was organized neatly. The sink was polished, and not one spot marred its surface. The stove burners were surrounded by dazzling stainless steel rings. <u>The chef kept an immaculate kitchen</u>. There were no finger marks on the refrigerator door. No sticky spots dirtied the floor. No crumbs hid behind the toaster.

Topic Sentence at the End of the Paragraph

On long summer evenings, we would play softball in the street. Sometimes we'd play until it was so dark we could barely see the ball. Then our mothers would come to the front steps of the row houses and call us in, telling us to stop our play. But we'd pretend we couldn't hear them. If they insisted, we'd beg for a few minutes more or for just one more game. It was so good to be outdoors with our friends. It was warm, and we knew we had weeks of summer vacation ahead. There was no school in the morning; there would be more games to play. <u>We loved those street games on summer nights</u>.

> **Note:** Many of your paragraph assignments will require a clear topic sentence, so be sure you follow your own instructor's directions about placement of the topic sentence.

CRITICAL THINKING

As you become more confident as a writer, you may want to experiment with the *effect* of shifting your topic sentence's position in your paragraph.

Placing your topic sentence at the beginning of a paragraph *telegraphs* the topic and main idea to your audience.

Placing your topic sentence at the end of a paragraph may create a *climactic* effect.

Exercise 13   **Practice: Adding Details to Support a Topic Sentence**

The topic sentences that follow have some—but not enough—details. Write sentences to add details to the list after each topic sentence.

1. **topic sentence:** A bad cold can be a miserable experience.

   a. No one wants to be around a person with a cold.

   b. My head hurts because of congestion.

   c. A constantly dripping nose makes it hard to do any work.

   d. _____

   e. _____

   f. _____

   g. _____

2. **topic sentence:** Unexpected time off can be a great gift.

   a. I used to love snow days when I was in elementary school.

   b. I could stay home, play in the snow, or watch television.

   c. _____

   d. _____

   e. _____

   f. _____

   g. _____

3. topic sentence: Anyone who has moved to a new place knows what loneliness means.

    a. There is no old friend to visit nearby.

    b. At work, everyone seems to have a closed group of friends.

    c. Those groups don't need a new person at the workplace.

    d. _____

    e. _____

    f. _____

    g. _____

Exercise 14 **Practice: Eliminating Details That Do Not Fit**

Topic sentences and lists of supporting details follow. Cross out the details that do not fit the topic sentence.

1. topic sentence: A gray and rainy day has a special kind of appeal for me.

    details: When I wake up on a dark, rainy morning, I appreciate my bed.

    It is warm and comfortable.

    I like to stay in bed for a few minutes and savor the sound of the rain.

    Unfortunately, I can't stay in bed forever.

    Drinking a hot cup of coffee and seeing the dripping trees outside, I feel safe and protected.

    Even when I have to drive to work in the rain, I enjoy the glistening streets and misty air.

    Everywhere I look, I see drivers racing through puddles and splashing poor pedestrians on the sidewalks.

2. topic sentence: A new seatbelt law has made me angry and upset.

    details: The old law allowed the police to check for a seatbelt violation only if they spotted another violation first.

    The new law says police can now randomly check for seatbelt violations.

    Last week, police officers stopped me and about forty other students just as we pulled out of the parking lot at our college.

    I was so busy trying to pull out of my parking space and slip into the long line of cars that I forgot to buckle up.

    Between classes, the parking lot is jammed with people coming and going.

    Instead of giving me a warning, an officer issued a ticket that costs more than a hundred dollars.

    I am furious about this unfair treatment.

    My mother says that the officer was trying to protect me, but she's just being silly.

Exercise 15 **Practice: Coherence: Putting Details in the Right Order**

These outlines have details that are in the wrong order. In the space provided, number the sentences in the right order: 1 would be the number for the first sentence, and so on.

1. topic sentence: Finding emergency day care for my son was difficult.

_____ Ryan, my four-year-old son, was a little grumpy at breakfast on Friday morning.

_____ Michelle said my son had a slight fever and a runny nose.

_____ By 8:00 AM, when I dropped him off at his regular day care facility, he seemed better.

_____ My second was to call my sister, but I reached her at my aunt's house, two hours away.

_____ Michelle wanted me to pick up Ryan immediately so that the other children would not be infected.

_____ My first option was to leave work and risk being fired.

_____ At noon, while I was at work, I got a call from Michelle, the owner of the day care facility.

_____ As I listened to Michelle, I examined my options.

_____ Finally, my brother, who works at night, brought Ryan home and stayed with him until I finished work.

2. topic sentence: My argument with Patrick was a silly quarrel between two stubborn people.

_____ Our quarrel ended when the theater ran out of tickets before we reached the ticket window.

_____ It started over a movie that we both wanted to see.

_____ We arranged to go to a nine o'clock showing.

_____ When we got to the theater, a huge line snaked around the building.

_____ At 9:20, we were still in line, and I wanted to leave.

_____ "You won't miss any of the movie," Patrick answered, "just the advertisements and the coming attractions."

_____ "I hate to miss any of the movie," I said, "so let's go and come back another time."

_____ Patrick's words irritated me, so I replied, "You go to the movie if you want to. I'll just wait in the car."

_____ "Fine," Patrick snarled, "you sit in the car for two hours."

DRAFTING AND REVISING   **A PARAGRAPH**

③ Write a paragraph that is unified, supported with detail, and coherent.

Drafting a Paragraph

The outline is a draft in list form. You are now ready to write the list in paragraph form, to "rough out" a draft of your assignment. This stage of writing is the time to draft, revise, and draft again. You may write several drafts in this stage, but don't think of this as an unnecessary chore or a punishment. It is a way of taking the pressure off yourself. By revising in steps, you are reminding yourself that the first try does not have to be perfect.

Review the outline on a favorite city or town on page 21. You can create a first draft of this outline in the form of a paragraph. (Remember that the first line of each paragraph is indented.) In the draft of the following paragraph, the first sentence of the paragraph is the topic sentence.

First Draft of a Paragraph

I love St. Augustine because it has sun and sea, history, and family. St. Augustine is warm in the winter. There is a beach nearby. It is clean and big. The water is clear blue. St. Augustine has lots of history. There is an old stone fort. The oldest schoolhouse is there. I can always visit my family for free. My grandparents live in St. Augustine. They feed me. I use their car.

Revising

Once you have a first draft, you can begin to think about revising it. **Revising** involves reviewing and changing your paper's organization, structure, and content. This often requires moving sentences around, as well as adding more information, including examples and details.

One way to begin revising is to read your work aloud to yourself. Listen to your words, and consider the questions in the following checklists.

Checklist for Revising Your Draft of a Paragraph

✓ Are all the sentences on topic and staying on my point? (No)

✓ Should I take out any ideas that do not relate? (Yes)

✓ Do I have enough to say about my point? (No)

✓ Should I add any details? (Yes. I could add more details about the schoolhouse or the beach.)

✓ Should I change the order of my sentences? (Maybe)

If your instructor agrees, you can work with your classmates. You can read your draft to a partner or a group. Your listener(s) can react to your draft by applying the questions on the checklist and by making notes about your draft as you read. When you are finished reading aloud, your partner(s) can discuss the notes about your work. **Remember that writing and revising several drafts may be necessary before you are satisfied with your paragraph content.**

Revised Draft of a Paragraph

(Note: Editing still needed to correct errors and improve style.)

added *Florida* to be more specific

added detail about the stone fort

added detail about the schoolhouse

connected my family to why I like St. Augustine

added more detail to why I love visiting my family

deleted sentences that appeared disconnected to topic

I love St. Augustine, <u>Florida</u> because it has sun and sea, history and family. St. Augustine is warm in the winter. There is a beach nearby. It is clean and big. The water is clear blue. St. Augustine has lots of history. There is an old stone fort. <u>It looks out over the ocean.</u> The oldest schoolhouse <u>in America</u> is there; <u>it is made of wood.</u> <u>My favorite part of St. Augustine is my family</u>. ~~I can always visit my family for free.~~ My grandparents live in St. Augustine. <u>They are my favorite relatives. They always make me feel welcome and take good care of me.</u> ~~They feed me. I use their car.~~ <u>When I visited them, my grandmother cooks wonderful meals, and my grandfather lets me use his car to see the sights.</u>

Exercise 16 **Collaborate: Adding Details to a Draft**

Collaborate

Complete this exercise with a partner or a group. The paragraph that follows lacks the kind of details that would make it more interesting. Working with a partner or a group, add the details to the blank spaces provided. When you are finished with the additions, read the revised paragraph to the class.

Paragraph to be revised:

Families often choose to vacation in Florida. The state offers a wide range of family-friendly activities. Families can travel to one of the many beaches to _____, _____, and _____. In addition to having fun at the beach, families can travel to a variety of amusement or theme parks. Spending a day or two at places like _____ or _____ provides a family with entertainment including _____, _____, and _____. Florida offers families a variety of options for lodging, and families can choose to stay in _____, _____, or condominiums. Some families even choose to camp in one of the state's many campgrounds, spending their evenings under the stars and sleeping in _____ or _____. No matter where families choose to stay, Florida is a wonderful place to make memories.

EDITING AND PROOFREADING   A PARAGRAPH

After you are satisfied with the latest revised draft of your paragraph, you are ready to edit. **Editing** often involves making improvements or correcting errors you may have overlooked during the revision process. Examining sentence patterns and length, checking appropriate word choice, and ensuring that specific details are aligned smoothly are all natural refinements during editing.

Checklist for Editing Your Revised Draft

✓ Is my choice of words appropriate? (Some wording is too informal.)

✓ Is my choice of words repetitive? (No)

✓ Are my sentences too long? Too short? (Some are too short.)

✓ Should I combine any sentences? (Yes)

✓ Am I running sentences together? (No)

✓ Am I writing in complete sentences? (Yes)

✓ Are my verb choices appropriate? (No)

✓ Can I link my ideas more smoothly? (Maybe)

Review the following edited version of the paragraph on a favorite city and compare it with the revised draft on page 27. Changes are labeled for easy reference.

Edited Version of a Revised Draft

added a comma before *because*

combined sentences that were too short

rewrote description of schoolhouse

corrected verb mistake of *visited*

I love St. Augustine, Florida, because it has sun and sea, history, and family. St. Augustine is warm in the winter, and has a big, clean beach with clear blue water. St. Augustine has a lot of history, including an old stone fort that looks out over the ocean. It also has the oldest schoolhouse in America, a tiny wooden building. My favorite part of St. Augustine is my family. My grandparents live in St. Augustine, and they are my favorite relatives. They always make me feel welcome and take good care of me. When I visit them, my grandmother cooks wonderful meals, and my grandfather lets me use his car to see the sights.

A side-by-side comparison of the first draft and the edited version reveals significant improvement in style and content thus far:

First Draft	Revised and Edited Paragraph
I love St. Augustine because it has sun and sea, history, and family. St. Augustine is warm in the winter. There is a beach nearby. It is clean and big. The water is clear blue. St. Augustine has lots of history. There is an old stone fort. The oldest schoolhouse is there. I can always visit my family for free. My grandparents live in St. Augustine. They feed me. I use their car.	I love St. Augustine, Florida, because it has sun and sea, history, and family. St. Augustine is warm in the winter, and has a big, clean beach with clear blue water. St. Augustine has a lot of history, including an old stone fort that looks out over the ocean. It also has the oldest schoolhouse in America, a tiny wooden building. My favorite part of St. Augustine is my family. My grandparents live in St. Augustine, and they are my favorite relatives. They always make me feel welcome and take good care of me. When I visit them, my grandmother cooks wonderful meals, and my grandfather lets me use his car to see the sights.

Exercise 17 Practice: Editing a Draft by Combining Sentences

The paragraph that follows has many short, choppy sentences, which are underlined. Wherever you see two or more underlined sentences clustered next to each other, combine the clustered sentences into one clear, smooth sentence. Write your revised version of the paragraph in the spaces above the lines.

Paragraph to be revised:

I have often claimed that I would love a rainy holiday. I swore that it would be a perfect time for me. It would be a time for me to relax. It would be a time for me to enjoy my solitude. I was wrong. Last week, because of the Memorial Day holiday, I had a free three-day weekend. The rain began on Saturday morning. I watched the water splatter the windows. It gushed from the gutters. "Fine," I thought. I planned to enjoy every minute of my freedom. I started with a leisurely cup of coffee. I spent some time calling all my friends. How wonderful it is to have all this time, I thought. By late afternoon, it was raining hard. I was bored. I did a few chores. I took a nap. I woke up to darkness and pouring rain. The rain continued on Sunday. Now I was feeling cheated of my great weekend. I could not play softball. I could not sunbathe in the park. I could not have a picnic or go for a walk. My friends did not want to get together in the nasty weather. By Monday, as the rain continued, I had to admit that rainy holidays do not put me in a holiday mood.

Proofreading

Once you have edited your latest draft to check for precise word choice, accurate spelling, coherent sentence structure, and appropriate punctuation, you are ready to **proofread** it. When you proofread, you make a clean copy of your work, and then check it for any careless errors in format, spelling, punctuation, and typing. You can then submit a clean, final version to your instructor for evaluation.

CRITICAL THINKING

There are many strategies to consider when proofreading your writing. Think about which strategy works best for you.

1. Read your writing to a peer *or* have a peer read your writing to you. Listen for errors or awkward wording.

2. Color code your paragraph. Highlight your topic sentence in one color, your supporting details in a second color, and transition words in a third color. Do your supporting details support your topic sentence? Are they in the proper order?

3. Put your essay aside for twenty-four hours before you proofread it a final time.

Giving Your Paragraph a Title

When you prepare the final version of your paragraph, you may be asked to give it a title. The title should be short and should fit the subject of the paragraph. For example, an appropriate title for the paragraph on a favorite city or town could be "My Favorite City" or "The City I Love." Check with your instructor to see if your paragraph needs a title. In this book, the paragraphs do not have titles.

The Final Version of a Paragraph

Even though the writer carefully revised and edited his paragraph, he found a few more ways to improve it as he prepared his final version. Notice that he added two specific details, refined some wording, and devised a concluding sentence to reemphasize the paragraph's main point.

Final Version of a Paragraph

(Note: Changes from the edited draft are underlined.)

    I love St. Augustine, Florida, because it has sun and sea, history, and family. St. Augustine is warm in the winter, and a <u>wide</u>, clean beach with clear blue water is <u>ten minutes away</u>. In addition, St. Augustine is <u>filled with</u> history, including an old stone fort that looks out on the water. It also has the oldest schoolhouse in America, a tiny wooden building <u>smaller than a two-car garage</u>. Best of all, my grandparents live in St. Augustine. They are my favorite relatives, and they make me feel very welcome. When I am in St. Augustine, I stay with them, enjoy their <u>delicious Spanish</u> food, and use their car. St. Augustine has the natural advantages, history, and family connections to make it my favorite city.

REVIEWING THE WRITING PROCESS

This chapter has taken you through four important stages in writing. As you become more comfortable with them, you will be able to work through them more quickly. For now, try to remember the four stages.

> **INFO BOX** **The Stages of the Writing Process**
>
> **Prewriting**: gathering and developing ideas, thinking on paper through free-writing, brainstorming, mapping, or keeping a journal
>
> **Planning**: planning the paragraph by combining and dividing details, focusing the details with a topic sentence, listing the supporting details in proper order, and devising an outline
>
> **Drafting and Revising**: writing and revising several drafts of the paragraph
>
> **Editing and Proofreading**: reviewing the latest revised draft of the paragraph to improve style and then checking for any careless errors in grammar, punctuation, spelling, and format

Exercise 18 **Practice: Proofreading to Prepare the Final Version**

Following are two paragraphs with the kind of errors it is easy to overlook when you prepare the final version of an assignment. Correct the errors by writing above the lines. There are eleven errors in the first paragraph and nine errors in the second paragraph.

1. Andrew is working hard, but is having a hard time coping with the pressures of his first semester in college. Andrew was not a very good student in High School because he had other intrests. He was friends with some ruff people and even got arrested 2 times. Andrew managed to get a high school diploma but really didn't know what to do next? After two years of working at jobs such as delivering pizza and washing cars, Andrew faced the reality. He knew he needed a better education so he could find more satisfying work. The decision was a huge first step in Andrew's journey to a better life. How ever, Andrew is not use to taking the small and difficult steps toward success in college. Concentrating in class is difficult for a man who never paid much attention in his high school classes. Homework seems to pile up and threatens to overwhelm him. Fortunately, he has an advisor who encourages him to be patience and take one small step, at a time.

2. Because I dont have a car, I depend on half a dozen people to get me to my job, my classes, the supermarket, and my mother's house. My cousin and I work in the same mall so I ride with him. Since our schedules are nearly identicle this plan works fairly well, especially because, I split the cost of gas with my cousin. Of course, if he misses a day of work, I have to find someone to get me to my job.

Then I beg one of my coworkers to take me home. Fortunately, I have a room mate who attends college, owns a car, and has several classes at times when I am also in class. My roommate also drive me to visit my mother because my mother cooks us fabulous dinners. Grocery shopping, visiting a pharmacy, or taking advantage of bargains at a big discount store, present problems. sometimes my sister takes me to a supermarket. I wish that I could afford a car or lived near a bus line, but I'm lucky to have a kind and generous support system of friends and families.

Lines of Detail: A Walk-Through Assignment

This assignment involves working within a group to write a paragraph.

Step 1: Read the three sentences that follow. Pick the one sentence you prefer as a possible topic sentence for a paragraph. Fill in the blank for the sentence you chose.

a. The best book I have ever read was

_____(fill in the title).

b. The absolute worst job in the world is

_____(fill in the name of the job).

c. People who hate crowded places should avoid

_____(fill in the name of the place).

Collaborate

Step 2: Join a group composed of other students who picked the same topic sentence you picked. In your class, you'll have "book" people, "job" people, and "place" people. Brainstorm in a group. Discuss questions that could be used to get ideas for your paragraph.

For the book topic, sample questions could include "What was the best part of the book?" or "What kind of book was it—a mystery, a horror story, or some other kind?" For the job topic, sample questions could include "Have you ever worked this job before?" or "Do you know anyone who has?" For the place topic, sample questions could include "Where have you experienced a crowded place before?" or "What was the experience like?"

As you discuss, write the questions, not the answers, below. Keep the questions flowing. Do not stop to say, "That's silly" or "I can't answer that." Try to devise **at least five questions**.

Five Brainstorming Questions:

1. _____

2. _____

3. _____

4. _____

5. _____

Step 3: Split up. Alone, begin to think on paper. Answer as many questions as you can, or add more questions and answers, or freewrite.

Step 4: Draft an outline of the paragraph. You will probably have to change the topic sentence to fit the details you have gathered. For example, your new topic sentence might be something like:

_____ was the most exciting

book I have ever read; it creates suspense by using

_____, _____, and

_____.

or

The worst job in the world is _____ because of

its poor pay, _____, and _____.

or

People who hate crowded places should avoid

_____ because _____ and

_____ make it a popular destination for others.

Remember to look at your details to see where they lead you. The details will help you to refine your topic sentence.

Step 5: Prepare the first draft of the paragraph.

Step 6: Read the draft aloud to your writing group, the same people who met to brainstorm. Ask each member of your group to make at least one positive comment and one suggestion for revision.

Step 7: Revise your draft extensively, considering the group's ideas and your own ideas for improvement.

Step 8: Edit your draft to improve style, and correct any serious errors or omissions.

Step 9: Prepare a final version, and proofread it carefully to spot and correct any careless spelling, punctuation, format, or typing errors.

Topics for Writing a Paragraph

When you write on any of these topics, follow the four basic stages of the writing process in preparing your paragraph.

Collaborate

1. Begin this assignment with a partner. The assignment requires an interview. Your final goal is to write a paragraph that will introduce a class member, your partner, to the rest of the class. In the final paragraph, you may design your own topic sentence or use one of the topic sentences that follow, filling in the blanks with the material you have discovered.

   There are several details you should know about

   _____ (fill in your partner's name).

   or

   Three unusual events have happened to _____ (fill in your partner's name).

   Before you write the paragraph, follow these steps:

   Step 1: Prepare to interview a classmate. Make a list of five questions you might want to ask. They can be questions like, "What's your favorite activity?" or "What's the biggest challenge you've faced?" List the questions on the following interview form, leaving room to fill in short answers later.

   Interview Form

   Question 1: _____

   Answer: _____

   Question 2: _____

   Answer: _____

   Question 3: _____

   Answer: _____

   Question 4: _____

   Answer: _____

   Question 5: _____

   Answer: _____

   Step 2: Meet and interview your partner. Ask the questions on your list. Jot down brief answers. Ask any other questions you think of as you are talking; write down the answers.

   Step 3: Change places. Let your partner interview you.

Step 4: Split up. Use the list of questions and answers about your partner as the prewriting part of your assignment. Work on the planning and drafting stages.

Step 5: Ask your partner to read the draft version of your paragraph, to write any comments or suggestions for improvement after the paragraph, and to mark any spelling or grammar errors in the paragraph itself.

Step 6: After you are satisfied with your latest draft, edit it to improve style.

Step 7: Prepare a final version, and proofread carefully to correct any careless errors. Then read your paragraph to the class.

2. Some topic sentences follow. Select one and use it to write a paragraph.

A student's experience with college applications can be _____.

My personal goal is to become a _____.

Most college students tend to be _____.

3. Write a paragraph on one of the topics that follow. Create your own topic sentence; explain and support it with specific details.

a favorite meal   a popular type   an important
                     of social media   relationship

4. Examine the photograph of a cultural celebration shown here. Next, consider your own culture and its celebrations. Do you have a picture of you or your family members taking part in one of these celebrations? Write a paragraph that begins with the statement,

Celebrations are an important part of culture.

Your photograph can provide you with some details, but come up with others on your own.

Topics for Critical Thinking and Writing

Note: College writing assignments will often require you to engage in *critical thinking*. Evaluating and questioning your own views and assumptions is a natural part of critical thinking and the writing process. The following topics will involve a careful analysis of some of your basic attitudes and opinions.

1. Do you make major decisions quickly, or do you take considerable time evaluating your options? Write about a major decision, perhaps a life-changing one, you have made. Include the factors that led to this decision and how pleased or dissatisfied you are with it.

2. Imagine that you could institute one new rule on your campus. What would the rule be? Explain the reasons you believe this rule is needed.

Note: Additional writing options can be found in the "Readings for Writers" appendix of this book.

Illustration

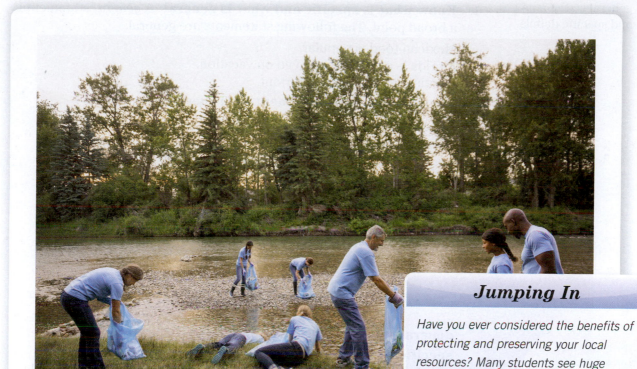

CHAPTER 2

Jumping In

*Have you ever considered the benefits of protecting and preserving your local resources? Many students see huge benefits in being stewards of their local community. Money is saved, the natural beauty that surrounds them is preserved, and opportunities for those in need arise. In addition, these students gain a feeling of satisfaction from helping out, from playing an active role in their local community. When you discuss the ways that everyone wins when people are better stewards of their local resources, you are developing a topic by **illustration**.*

Learning Objectives

In this chapter, you will learn how to:

1 Distinguish between general statements and specific details.

2 Prewrite to generate a topic for an illustration paragraph.

3 Write a clear topic sentence.

4 Write an illustration paragraph that uses transitions and details effectively.

WHAT IS ILLUSTRATION?

Illustration uses specific examples to support a general point. In your writing, you often use illustration because you frequently want to support a point by providing a specific example.

① Distinguish between general statements and specific details.

Hints for Writing an Illustration Paragraph

1. **Know what is specific and what is general.** A *general* statement is a broad point. The following statements are general.

    Mexican food is popular.
    Florida is a good place to go on vacation.
    Meeting deadlines is important.

2. **Support a general statement with specific examples.**

    general statement: Mexican food is popular.
    specific examples: The fastest-growing cuisine in the United States is Mexican food.
    Many cities boast a plethora of street carts that serve hot tamales and tacos.

    general statement: Florida is a good place to go on vacation.
    specific examples: The sandy beaches of the Gulf Coast are white quartz in color.
    The springtime weather in Florida is sunny and warm, inviting for those who live further north.

    general statement: Meeting deadlines is important.
    specific examples: If you miss a deadline for an important assignment, you may compromise your grade in the class.
    Managers are less likely to promote employees who struggle to meet their deadlines.

3. **Be careful to support a general statement with specific examples, not with more general statements.**

    not this—general statement: College is harder than I thought it would be.
    ~~more general statements:~~ ~~It is tough to be a college student.~~ ~~Studying takes a lot of my time.~~
    but this—general statement: College is harder than I thought it would be.
    specific examples: I have to balance my school work with my responsibilities at work.
    I often have multiple assignments in different classes due on the same day.

    If you remember to illustrate a broad statement with specific examples, you will have the key to this kind of paragraph.

CRITICAL THINKING

General statements are like umbrellas. They broadly cover topics, categories, or types of people. General statements need specific examples to clarify or explain. This is why specific examples are necessary in an illustration paragraph.

Exercise 1   **Practice: Recognizing Broad Statements**

Each list that follows contains one broad statement and three specific examples. Underline the broad statement.

1. The cost of owning a pet exceeds $1,200 dollars per year, on average.

   Many pets require daily exercise to maintain their health.

   Grooming your pet is time consuming and often messy.

   Owning a pet is a lot of work.

2. College students are often given generous credit lines that exceed their income.

   Credit cards can be dangerous.

   It is easy to lose track of how much you spend when you use a credit card.

   Owning a credit card opens a consumer up to potential identity theft.

3. Choosing a major is often a long process.

   I know many business majors.

   Computer science majors can work in the healthcare industry.

   Everyone tells me I should major in nursing.

4. People fill the movie theaters when rain spoils their plans for a holiday outdoors.

   Malls are popular places on a wet, hot, or snowy holiday.

   Bad weather on a holiday can mean big profits for certain businesses.

   When the weather gets too nasty, many people call a pizza delivery service.

Exercise 2   **Practice: Distinguishing the General Statement from the Specific Example**

Each general statement that follows is supported by three items of support. Two of these items are specific examples, but one is too general to be effective. Underline the one that is too general.

1. **general statement:**   Adolescent boys are very choosy about their footwear.

   support: They know that some shoes will make them outcasts at school.

   Shoes chosen by their parents make teenage boys cringe.

   They select their sneakers and other footwear according to strict standards.

2. **general statement:**   Vegan food choices are more popular than ever.

   support: More and more people are turning to vegan dishes.

   Today, veggie burgers are sold in almost every supermarket.

   Major restaurant chains have vegan meals on their menus.

3. **general statement:**   Many preteen girls adore the color pink.

   support: Many young girls dream of an all-pink bedroom.

   Pink handbags, shoes, and clothing dominate the aisles in the preteen sections of department stores.

   Many girls between the ages of two and twelve love pink.

Collaborate

Exercise 3   **Collaborate: Adding Specific Examples to a General Statement**

With a partner or group, add four specific examples to each general statement.

1. **general statement:**   Father's Day is associated with several popular gifts.

   examples: _____
   _____
   _____
   _____

2. **general statement:**   The sense of being ignored is a painful feeling.

   examples: _____
   _____
   _____
   _____

3. **general statement:**   People caught in a sudden rainstorm have creative ways to stay dry.

   examples: _____
   _____
   _____
   _____

2 Prewrite to generate a topic for an illustration paragraph.

WRITING THE ILLUSTRATION PARAGRAPH IN STEPS

PREWRITING   **ILLUSTRATION**

Suppose your instructor asks you to write a paragraph about some aspect of preserving local resources. You can begin by thinking about your subject to gather ideas and to find a focus for your paragraph. Looking through entries in your journal might lead you to the following underlined entry:

Journal Entry about Preserving Local Resources

Yesterday I <u>removed garbage from the riverbank</u>. It was a <u>messy job</u>. It made my day though, as I <u>value the natural beauty that surrounds our campus</u>. This event was <u>sponsored by the football team</u>. There are others in my community who are <u>good stewards of our local resources</u>. The <u>student leaders and various clubs all sponsor different events</u>. The events help to <u>build a sense of campus community</u>, and they help to <u>save money and resources</u>. They leave a <u>lasting impact</u> on our college community.

The underlined terms can lead you to a list:

removed garbage from the riverbank   *student leaders sponsor different events*
messy job   *various clubs sponsor different events*
value the natural beauty that surrounds   *build a sense of campus community*
*   our campus*   *save money and resources*
sponsored by the football team   *lasting impact*
good stewards of our local resources

Consider the underlined terms. Many of them are specific ideas about preserving local resources. You could write a paragraph about one item or about several related items on the list.

Adding Details to an Idea

Looking at the list of ideas above, you might decide you want to write something about the topic: being a better steward of local resources. To add details, you decide to brainstorm.

Who values stewardship in the local campus community?

The football team, the Electrical Engineering Club, students, and student leaders

What actions do they take to be better stewards of the school's resources?

Clean up the riverbank, compost food, install LED lighting, coordinate resources, save money that can be used for scholarships

What resources do they protect and preserve?

The local riverbank, school energy use, school expenses, the local landfill, local gardens

Who are the beneficiaries of campus stewardship?

The campus community, the local environment, students in need who receive scholarships

Why is it important to be a good steward of resources?

Saves energy, restores natural beauty, saves resources

Are there negative consequences of being a steward?

It can be messy

You now have this list of ideas connected to the topic of being a better steward of local resources:

removed garbage from the riverbank   *student leaders sponsor different events*
messy job   *builds a sense of community*
value the natural beauty that   *compost food waste*
*   surrounds our campus*   *install LED lighting*
sponsored by the football team   *campus community coordinates resources*
good stewards of our local resources   *campus community benefits*
student leaders play an active role   *school finances benefited*
the Electrical Engineering Club   *savings help students in need by funding*
*   volunteers*   *   scholarships*
saves money and resources   *local gardens benefit from compost*
lasting impact   *school energy use reduced*
local landfill benefits from less waste   *local environment*
various clubs sponsor different events   *restores natural beauty*

③ Write a clear topic sentence.

Creating a Topic Sentence

If you examine this list looking for *related ideas*, you can create a topic sentence. The ideas on the list include (1) details on who values stewardship on campus, (2) details about the actions stewards take, and (3) details about the benefits of stewardship on campus. Not all of the details fit into these three categories, but many do.

Grouping the related ideas into the three categories can help you focus your ideas into a topic sentence.

who values stewardship on campus

football team sponsors river cleanup
student leaders proposed ways to reduce food waste
the Electrical Engineering Club installed LED lights
campus community coordinates resources

actions stewards take

install LED lighting
clean up the local riverbank
save money and resources
compost food waste
school energy use reduced
school finances benefited

benefits of stewardship on campus

build a sense of community
lasting impact
more scholarship money available for students in need
restores natural beauty
local gardens benefit from compost
local landfill benefits from less waste

You can summarize these related ideas in a topic sentence:

When student groups value stewardship and protect and preserve the school's resources, the entire college community benefits.

Check the topic sentence against your details. Does it explain who values stewardship? Yes. It says that student groups value stewardship. Does it cover the actions that stewards take? Yes. It says that the students "protect and preserve the school's resources." Does it cover the benefits of stewardship? Yes. It explains "the entire college community benefits." The topic sentence has given you a focus for your illustration paragraph.

Exercise 4 **Practice: Finding Specific Ideas in Freewriting**

Following are two samples of freewriting. Each is a response to a broad topic. Read each sample, and then underline any words that could become a more specific topic for a paragraph.

Freewriting Reaction to the Topic of Vacations

I love vacation. I schedule my vacations well in advance. I select a place to visit. Then research the amount of money it will take to fund my vacation there. Then I plan the resources I will need. One of my favorite vacations was a trip to Yosemite National Park. The waterfalls and sheer rock faces were very impressive. It was also an inexpensive trip. I was able to borrow camping equipment and share a ride to the Park with a friend. It is very important to clean your campsite. The bears in Yosemite love human food.

Freewriting Reaction to the Topic of Reading for Pleasure

I don't get to read enough for pleasure. Chores. Duties, college writing assignments. All of these activities prevent me from reading for pleasure. I try to carve out time to read at night. Right before bedtime. But I always manage to fall asleep after reading only a few pages. The last book I read took me two months to finish. It was about living in Paris. The main character was a student studying abroad. It was great though. I would have to reread sections of the book because I had fallen asleep. Maybe I need to read sitting in a chair in the morning.

Exercise 5   **Practice: Finding Specific Ideas in Lists**

Following are two lists. Each is a response to a broad topic. Read each list, and then underline any words that could become a more specific topic for a paragraph.

1. **topic:** the environment

environmental issues	a community garden
water pollution	dangers of greenhouse gases
recycling at my workplace	saving rainwater in your yard
cloth shopping bags	endangered species
Environmental Protection Agency	wasting paper at home

2. **topic:** apps

games	share with friends
use apps for productivity	connect with people from all
learn a language	over the world
free vs. paid	using apps for entertainment
better on particular smartphone	run smoothly on tablet
protect identity theft	

Exercise 6   **Practice: Grouping Related Ideas in Lists of Details**

Following are lists of details. In each list, circle the items that seem to fit into one group; then underline the items that seem to fit into a second group. Some items may not fit into either group.

1. **topic:** courage

seeking treatment for depression	attending patriotic events
volunteering for military service	bullying a child
recovering from addiction	reading books about heroes
accepting one's mistakes	confronting a gang member
rescuing a drowning person	admitting an addiction

2. **topic:** living with a roommate

less loneliness	too little privacy
male or female	different concepts of neatness
risk of clashing personalities	international students
can share a social life	split the cost of rent
possible lifelong friendship	unauthorized borrowing

Exercise 7 **Practice: Writing Topic Sentences for Lists of Details**

Following are lists of details that have no topic sentences. Write an appropriate topic sentence for each one.

1. topic sentence: _____

_____

A salesperson who made a big sale may rush home to share the news with a loved one.

A worker who gets a promotion could celebrate with friends at a local restaurant.

A man who just became a father could react by telling everyone he knows.

A lottery winner may keep staring at the winning ticket, safely stashed away.

2. topic sentence: _____

_____

Posting negative comments about coworkers can cause problems.

Posting inappropriate pictures can send the wrong message.

Human Resources departments often look through social media sites to ensure employees are representing the company positively.

Not using proper security settings can give strangers access to private information.

3. topic sentence: _____

_____

Alexander Depree was born in Haiti in the same month that his father died.

Alexander and his mother struggled against the constant threat of starvation in their village.

When Alexander was ten, he and his mother were admitted to the United States as refugees.

Alexander and his mother knew only a few words of English.

Alexander struggled to survive in a school where almost all the students spoke English or Spanish.

After high school, he found a night job as a janitor in a large business complex; in the daytime, he attended the police academy.

Now a police officer, Alexander is respected by his fellow officers and a mentor to boys in the growing Haitian community.

Exercise 8 **Practice: Choosing the Better Topic Sentence**

Following are lists of details. Each list has two possible topic sentences. Underline the better topic sentence for each list.

1. possible topic sentence:

    a. High school can be a source of exciting memories.

    b. Reunions can be disappointing when one friend has grown up but the other hasn't.

Michael had the same best friend for all four years of high school.

He and Brian, his friend, were known for their carefree attitudes and crazy pranks.

After they finished high school, Michael joined the U.S. Navy.

Brian left their hometown in Virginia to look for work in California.

Michael lost touch with Brian but liked to remember their wild times.

Five years after their high school graduation, the two friends reunited.

Michael was home on leave from his Army base in Germany.

Brian was visiting his family and having another wild time.

Although Michael had looked forward to the reunion, he was saddened by the meeting.

Michael shared the adventures and struggles he had experienced in the military.

Brian had worked at a series of jobs, but none of the jobs had worked out, he said.

All Brian wanted to do was to relive their glory days in high school.

2. possible topic sentence:

a. Being popular sometimes means not being yourself.

b. Friendship can be strange and confusing.

My sister Tanya feels sorry for me because I'm not as popular as she is.

Her phone is always ringing, and she has hundreds of friends online and locally.

On the other hand, I have just a few friends.

Many of Tanya's friends are interested in parties and drinking.

I like sports, hiking, and nature.

I have tried to fit in with Tanya's friends.

However, I realized that, to fit in, I would have to pretend I liked socializing all night and getting drunk.

My group of friends doesn't go to huge parties or drink much.

They understand me.

I decided to be myself and enjoy my small circle of friends.

PLANNING   ILLUSTRATION

When you plan your outline, keep your topic sentence in mind.

When <u>student groups value stewardship</u> and <u>protect and preserve the school's resources</u>, <u>the entire college community benefits</u>.

Notice the three key phrases:

student groups value stewardship

> protect and preserve the school's resources
> the entire college community benefits

Assign each detail to **one** of the key phrases.

student groups value stewardship

the football team sponsors river cleanup
student leaders proposed ways to reduce food waste
the Electrical Engineering Club installed LED lights
campus community coordinates resources

protect and preserve the school's resources

LED lighting installed
local riverbank cleaned up
food waste composted
school energy use reduced
school finances benefited

the entire college community benefits

a sense of community created
lasting impact
money and resources saved
more scholarship money available for students in need
restores natural beauty
local gardens benefit from compost
local landfill benefits from less waste

With this kind of grouping, you have a clearer idea of how to organize a paragraph.

Outline for an Illustration Paragraph

topic sentence	When student groups value stewardship and protect and preserve the school's resources, the entire community benefits.
details	
Which student groups value stewardship?	The football team sponsors Cleanup the River Day. The Electrical Engineering Club installs LED lighting. Student government coordinates efforts.
How do they protect and preserve resources?	The football team helps to beautify the riverbank. LED lighting saves the school money. Student leaders have reduced waste.
How does the college community benefit?	People can enjoy the natural beauty of the riverbank. Money and resources saved. More scholarship money available. The environment benefits from less waste sent to the landfill. The campus experiences a real sense of community.

As you can see, the outline combined some of the details from the list. You can combine other details, avoid repetition, and add more details as you draft your paragraph.

Exercise 9   Collaborate: Adding Details to an Outline

Three partial outlines follow. Each has a topic sentence and some details. Working with a partner or group, add more details that support the topic sentence.

1. **topic sentence:** Sleeping habits vary a great deal.

   a. Some people like to sleep without a pillow.

   b. Others like to sleep with a pillow covering their face.

   c. Some people like to sleep with a window open, even in winter.

   d. _____

   e. _____

   f. _____

   g. _____

2. **topic sentence:** Choosing either a tablet for viewing an e-book or reading a paper book is a personal choice.

   a. Holding a book is important for many people.

   b. Many students often prefer carrying one tablet over five heavy textbooks.

   c. Reading with a tablet can be hard on your eyes after a while.

   d. _____

   e. _____

   f. _____

   g. _____

Exercise 10   Practice: Eliminating Details That Are Repetitive

In the following outlines, some details use different words to repeat an example given previously in the list. Cross out the repetitive details.

1. **topic sentence:** Lying may help a person in the short term, but it can be self-destructive in the long term.

   Lying as an excuse for lateness or for broken promises can work for a while.

   Eventually the excuses aren't believable and make a bad habit more obvious.

   People who lie about their money or background to impress others may gain admiration at first.

   Sooner or later, people will spot the lying braggart and become resentful or contemptuous.

   Telling too many elaborate stories about car problems, family emergencies, or illness does not work forever.

Lies of infidelity may get a husband or wife out of a difficult situation.

However, a cheating spouse can become entangled in too many lies.

Someone who creates a phony image of wealth is bound to be exposed and mocked.

2. **topic sentence:** Nosy neighbors can be helpful people, even lifesavers.

They may appear to be gossipy, nasty people.

However, they may be lonely and just want something to fill their time.

They will collect your mail when you are away.

If you are away for a few days, you can ask them to keep an eye on your house.

The neighbors who are not minding their own business could spot a crime such as a burglary in progress.

You can ask them to check your mailbox if you are going to be out of town.

People who observe the comings and goings of their neighbors can spot a change in someone's routine.

That change could involve someone who hasn't left the house for days.

A person who slipped or fell at home, can't walk, and can't crawl to a phone would welcome a rescue by a nosy neighbor.

A nosy neighbor acts like your own Neighborhood Crime Watcher.

He or she can be almost as good as a paramedic.

④ Write an illustration paragraph that uses transitions and details effectively.

DRAFTING AND REVISING   **ILLUSTRATION**

Review the outline on stewardship of local resources on page 46. You can create a first draft of this outline in the form of a paragraph. Then as you begin to revise your drafts, you can add details and transitions to link your ideas. You can use the following checklist.

Checklist for Revising an Illustration Paragraph

✓ Do I need more or better transitions?

✓ Should I add more details to support my points?

✓ Should some of the details be more specific?

Transitions

As you revise your illustration paragraph, you may find places where one idea ends and another begins abruptly. This problem occurs when you forget to add **transitions**, which are words, phrases, or sentences that connect one idea to another. Using transitions effectively will make your writing clear and smooth. When you write an illustration paragraph, you will need some transitions that link one example to another and other transitions to link one section of your paragraph to another section. Here are some transitions you may want to use in writing an illustration paragraph.

INFO BOX   **Transitions for an Illustration Paragraph**

another example	in the case of	other kinds
a second example	like	such as
for example	one example	the first instance
for instance	one instance	another instance
in addition	other examples	to illustrate
finally	as a result of	moreover
furthermore	ultimately	since then

Look carefully at the following draft of the paragraph on stewardship of resources, and note how it combines sentences, adds details, and uses transitions to transform the outline into a clear and developed paragraph. You can assume that the writer worked through several rough drafts to get to this point.

Revised Draft of an Illustration Paragraph

(Note: Editing and proofreading is still necessary to refine style and correct errors.)

topic sentence ———— When student groups value stewardship and protect and preserve the school's resources, the entire

transition ———— (community benefits. <u>One example</u> of this stewardship is the annual "Cleanup the River Day" sponsored by our campus football team. This year they

detail added ———— <u>removed over two-hundred pounds of trash</u> from the

transition added ———— riverbank. <u>A second example</u> is the work of the Electrical Engineering Club. They volunteered their

details added ———— free time to install <u>energy-efficient and cost-saving</u>

detail added ———— LED lighting fixtures <u>in the science and technology</u>

transition added ———— building. <u>Another example of stewardship</u> is the effort of student government to compost food waste

detail added ———— <u>from the school's cafeteria</u>. This <u>effort required a</u>

detail added ———— <u>coordination among student leaders, the school's</u> <u>administration, and the food service provider</u>. It seems our entire community wants to be a part of protecting and preserving our resources. We know that our school has been good to us. Moreover, we enjoy knowing that we have made a lasting impact

transition ———— on our community. <u>As a result of our actions</u>, every-

transition ———— one benefits. <u>For instance</u>, people can again enjoy the natural beauty of the riverbank and the school can use the money saved on electricity to better assist students in need, and also less food waste is

transition ———— sent to our local landfill. <u>Finally</u>, our effort have helped to build a real sense of community on our campus.

Collaborate

Exercise 11   Collaborate: Adding Details to a Draft

The paragraph that follows lacks the kind of details that would make it more interesting. Working with a partner or group, add details to the blank spaces provided. When you are finished, read the revised paragraph to the class.

People who need to cut back on their spending handle the challenge in different ways. One of the first cuts involves nonessential clothing purchases. Teens may buy fewer _____, _____, and _____. Their parents may decide not to buy any more of the _____, _____, and _____ they regularly wear to work. Some people decide to cut their spending on fuel. To save money on gasoline, they may limit their driving and avoid trips to _____ and _____. To save on gas or electric heating and cooling at home, residents will turn up the thermostat on their air conditioning, and _____.

Finally, food shopping changes when people are short of money. In good times, a food budget may leave room for a few luxuries such as _____, _____, and _____. In more challenging times, shoppers are likely to replace pricey goodies with cheaper treats such as _____, _____, and _____.

Exercise 12   Practice: Revising a Draft by Adding Transitions

The paragraph that follows needs some transitions. Add appropriate transitions (words or phrases) to the blanks.

Meeting people is difficult for me. I never know what to say after shaking hands or mumbling "Hi." Should I say "Nice to meet you"? Should I ask "How are you doing?"? Then there is the problem of eye contact. This problem has many facets. _____ making eye contact is supposed to indicate openness and good character. _____, eye contact shows that a person is confident. However, I am afraid to hold the eye contact for too long or too short a time. _____ I can remember a time when I felt myself looking

down at the floor too soon. I must have looked as if I were ashamed of something.

Other examples involve holding eye contact for too long. _____ I felt

as if I were invading the other person's space. _____ I felt uncom-

fortable because my lengthy eye contact made me look too needy. To cope with

my fears about meeting people, I pay close attention to television and movie

scenes where people meet. The actors always seem confident and suave. Actors

_____ Will Smith and Denzel Washington never seem nervous or

tongue-tied. Maybe I can learn to act confident even when I feel nervous.

EDITING AND PROOFREADING   ILLUSTRATION

After you are satisfied with your latest revised draft, you are ready to edit. As you begin to edit your paragraph, look for the correct verb forms, redundant words, ways to combine sentences, and any spelling mistakes. You can use the following checklist.

> ### Checklist for Editing Illustration Paragraph
> ✓ Are all the verb forms correct and consistent?
> ✓ Are any words redundant?
> ✓ Should some of the sentences be combined?
> ✓ Is everything spelled correctly?

Finally, proofread your writing. Read every word carefully to be sure that what you've written makes sense and is error free.

Final Version of an Illustration Paragraph

(Note: Changes from previous draft are underlined.)

When student groups value stewardship and protect and preserve the school's resources, the entire college community benefits. One example of this stewardship is the annual "Cleanup the River Day" sponsored by our campus football team. This year they removed over two-hundred pounds of trash from the riverbank. A second example is the work of the Electrical Engineering Club, which volunteered their free time to install energy-efficient and cost-saving LED lighting fixtures in the science and technology building.

sentences combined

spelling corrected

(Continued)

sentences combined

> <u>Another example of stewardship is the effort of student government to compost food waste from the school's cafeteria, an effort that required a coordination among student leaders, the school's administration, and the food service provider.</u> It seems our entire community wants to be a part of protecting and preserving our resources. We know that our school has been good to us. Moreover, we enjoy knowing that we have made a lasting impact on our community. <u>As a result of our actions, everyone benefits. For instance, people can again enjoy the natural beauty of the riverbank. The school can use the money saved on electricity to better assist students in need. Less food waste is sent to our local landfill.</u> Finally, our <u>efforts</u> have helped to build a real sense of community on our campus.

wording improved

noun form corrected: efforts

For your information: A sample illustration essay based on the same topic and following the same writing steps can be found in Chapter 12.

Exercise 13 Practice: Editing a Draft by Combining Sentences

The paragraph that follows has many short, choppy sentences, which are underlined. Wherever you see two or more underlined sentences clustered next to each other, combine them into one clear, smooth sentence. Write your revised version of the paragraph in the spaces above the lines.

My sister Patrice loves the color red. <u>She has red shoes. She has six pairs of them. They include bright red sneakers, tomato-colored platform heels, and scarlet boots.</u> Her love of red does not end with clothing. <u>Her hair is dyed crimson. It is not a natural shade.</u>

Of course, her nails are always painted bright red, and she never appears in public without a shiny red coating of lipstick. Patrice collects red purses and bags, too. <u>She haunts thrift shops in search of vintage bags in red. She hits the sales at the mall. She looks for designer handbags in red.</u> All this searching makes Patrice happy because she can survey her collection and know that she will never run out of red accessories. The greatest and most beloved item in her collection is not an item at all. <u>It is her dog Pepper. He is a red Irish setter.</u>

Exercise 14 **Practice: Editing and Proofreading to Prepare the Final Version**

The following is an illustration paragraph that has the kinds of errors that are easy to overlook when you prepare the final version of an assignment. Correct the errors by writing above the lines. There are ten errors in the paragraph.

Sleep is a precious gift, but not all sleep are equal. People with deep anxieties or sorrows can suffer thru a broken sleep that leaves them exhausted and trouble. Passengers in a car, bus, train, or plane often fall into a long doze interrupted by periods of semi-consciousness. They incorporate the sound of engines, the talk of other passenger, and the jolts of travel into their sleep. They wake up feeling, grimy, disoriented, and cramped. A person who has worked for too many hours without sleeping may finally fall into a exhausted sleep. However, that sleep is'nt alway's refreshing. The best sleep is a soft, gentle fall into peace and silence. Its' rare and valuable, and the people who enjoy it regularly should be greatful.

Lines of Detail: A Walk-Through Assignment

Your assignment is to write an illustration paragraph about music.

Step 1: Freewrite or brainstorm on this broad topic for ten minutes.

Step 2: Review your freewriting or brainstorming. Underline any parts that are a specific idea related to the broad topic of music.

Step 3: List all the specific ideas. Choose one as the narrowed topic for your paragraph.

Step 4: Add related ideas to your chosen, narrowed topic. Do this by reviewing your list for related ideas and by brainstorming for more related ideas.

Step 5: List all your related ideas and review their connection to your narrowed topic. Then write a topic sentence for your paragraph.

Step 6: Write a first draft of your paragraph.

Step 7: Revise your first draft. Be sure it has enough details and clear transitions, and work through several drafts if necessary. Combine any choppy sentences.

Step 8: Edit your latest draft to refine word choice, combine sentences, and correct serious errors.

Step 9: Prepare a final version, and proofread it to catch any spelling, punctuation, format, or typing errors.

Topics for Writing an Illustration Paragraph

When you write on any of these topics, follow the four basic stages of the writing process in preparing your illustration paragraph.

1. Adages are short statements that express a truth. Adages are synonymous with clichés, bromides, maxims, proverbs, and truisms. Consider the adage, "the pen is mightier than the sword," penned by Edward Bulwar-Lytton in 1839. Discuss the wisdom of this adage with a group of peers. Do you agree with your peer's opinions? Disagree?

   After discussing this adage with your peers, consider your own position. Then, write a paragraph that illustrates the truth expressed in that statement.

Collaborate

2. An expert in anything was once a novice. Write a paragraph that illustrates the steps you took on the road from novicehood toward expertise. You might consider the following topics:

driving a car	learning a new skill
mastering a game	learning to cook
building something	managing your money
interacting in crowds	staying fit
interviewing for a job	learning a new language

3. Select one of the topic sentences that follow. Write an illustration paragraph in which you support the topic sentence with several specific examples.

Social media has changed the way we have received news.	There never seems to be enough time in the day.	There are many ways to show you love someone.	America is a land of opportunity.
Living with your parents while in college isn't that bad.	Popular music is becoming more political.	Multitasking is necessary in today's workplace.	Surprises often come in many forms.
We live in the golden age of television.	There are ways to overcome stagefright.	I no longer trust the weatherman.	It is better to be loved than to be feared.

4. Consider the photo at the top of the next page. People are often inspired by elements of the natural world. Some people love the beach, others the mountains. Some are held captive by streams, lakes, and rivers, and still others are enamored by the stark beauty of the desert. Find a photograph of you in the natural world, and then write a paragraph that illustrates your experience in that place at the time the photo was taken and how that experience inspired you.

Topics for Critical Thinking and Writing

1. There are many people who chose not to participate in local, state, or national politics because they feel their voices will not be heard or their participation will not have an impact. Consider the ways in which individuals have voiced their opinions in the past and how their voices have impacted our society. You may wish to do some further research into the issue to explore the ways in which these individuals voiced their opinions.

    Then write a paragraph that illustrates ways in which an individual can be more engaged in local, state, or national politics.

2. Assume you are a member of your school's environmental stewardship society. Your responsibility is to design an advertising campaign to encourage peers to be better stewards of the environment. To kick the campaign off, you have been asked to write a brief editorial for the school's newspaper. Generate a potential list of ways students might conserve campus resources. Consider each suggestion's feasibility, and the implications of implementing each recommendation. Organize your list and prioritize those that are both feasible and easily implemented. Present them to your student body in your editorial. (It may want to share your initial list with your peers to elicit their feedback before composing your editorial.)

Note: Additional writing options suitable for illustration-related assignments can be found in the "Readings for Writers" appendix at the end of this book.

Description

Learning Objectives

In this chapter, you will learn how to:

1. Use specific words and phrases, including sense words.
2. Prewrite to generate a topic for a descriptive paragraph that supports a dominant impression.
3. Write a descriptive paragraph that uses specific details and transitions effectively.

WHAT IS DESCRIPTION?

Description shows a reader what a person, place, thing, or situation is like. When you write description, you try to *show, not tell about*, something. You want to make the reader see that person, place, or situation, and then, perhaps, to make the reader think about or act on what you have shown.

HINTS FOR WRITING A DESCRIPTIVE PARAGRAPH

1 Use specific words and phrases, including sense words.

Using Specific Words and Phrases

Using specific words and phrases will help the reader "see" what you are describing. If a word or phrase is *specific*, it is *exact and precise*. The opposite of specific language is language that is vague, general, or fuzzy. Think of the difference between specific and general in this way:

56

Imagine that you are browsing through a shoe department. A clerk approaches you.

> "Can I help you?" the clerk asks.
> "I'm looking for shoes," you say.
> "Well, what kind of shoes did you have in mind?" asks the clerk.
> "Comfortable ones," you say.
> "For work or play?" asks the clerk.
> "Not sure," you say.

The conversation could go on and on. You are being general in saying that you want shoes. The salesman is looking for specific details: What kind of shoes? What will they be used for?

In writing, if you use words like *good* or *nice* or *bad* or *interesting*, you will not have a specific description or an effective piece of writing. Whenever you can, try to use a more precise word instead of a general term. To find a more explicit term, ask yourself such questions as, "What type?" or "How?" The examples that follow show how a general term can be replaced by a more specific one.

> **general word:** shoes (Ask "What type?")
> **more specific words:** sneakers, boots, flip flops

> **general word:** textbook (Ask "What type?")
> **more specific words:** math, English, algebra

> **general word:** sleep (Ask "How?")
> **more specific words:** snoozed, crashed, dozed

> **general word:** nice (Ask "How?")
> **more specific words:** friendly, thoughtful, courteous

Exercise 1 Practice: Identifying General and Specific Words

Lists of words follow. Put an *X* by the one term in each list that is a more general term than the others. The first one is done for you.

List 1	List 2	List 3
_X_ science	_____ physical exercise	_____ blog
_____ botany	_____ lifting weights	_____ Internet
_____ biology	_____ hiking	_____ wiki
_____ chemistry	_____ swimming	_____ e-mail
_____ geology	_____ biking	_____ social networking

Exercise 2 Practice: Ranking General and Specific Items

Lists of items follow. In each list, rank the items, from the most general (1) to the most specific (4).

List 1	List 2	List 3
_____ car interiors	_____ advising	_____ money
_____ seats in cars	_____ major advising	_____ coins
_____ cars	_____ course advising	_____ quarters
_____ leather seats in cars	_____ academic advising	_____ silver-colored coins

Collaborate

Exercise 3   **Collaborate: Interviewing for Specific Answers**

To practice being specific, interview a partner. Ask your partner to answer the questions that follow. Write his or her answers in the spaces provided. When you have finished, change places. In both interviews, your goal is to find specific answers, so you should both be as explicit as you can in your answers.

Interview Questions

1. What is your favorite part about being a student?

   _____

   _____

2. What did you eat and drink for lunch yesterday?

   _____

   _____

3. What is your favorite sport and what is your favorite professional sports team?

   _____

   _____

4. If you could buy any car in the world, what car would you choose?

   _____

   _____

5. Would you rather read online or from an actual book?

   _____

   _____

6. When you think of a great friend, who comes to mind?

   _____

   _____

7. What smell reminds you of your favorite holiday?

   _____

   _____

8. If you wanted to boast about your city, what would you say?

   _____

   _____

Exercise 4 | **Practice: Finding Specific Words or Phrases**

List four specific words or phrases beneath the (underlined) general one in each list. List 1 is done for you.

List 1

general word: After dinner, we ate some <u>dessert</u>.

specific word or phrase: coconut cake

                          chocolate ice cream

                          flan

                          brownies

List 2

general word: Kenny was my <u>friend</u>.

specific word or phrase: _____

                          _____

                          _____

                          _____

List 3

general word: I need some <u>rest</u>.

specific word or phrase: _____

                          _____

                          _____

                          _____

Exercise 5 | **Practice: Identifying Sentences That Are Too General**

Lists of sentences follow. Put an *X* by one sentence in each group that is general and vague.

1. a. _____ I like excitement.

   b. _____ I enjoy action movies.

   c. _____ I get lonely if I stay home alone on the weekends.

2. a. _____ Jen's algebra teacher is helpful.

   b. _____ Jen's algebra teacher meets with students individually.

   c. _____ Jen's algebra teacher continually updates a class Web site where students can find explanations and extra practice.

3. a. _____ At the free concert, the crowd arrived early and stayed late.

   b. _____ Everyone had a nice time at the free concert.

   c. _____ Everyone danced and sang along with the music at the free concert.

Using Sense Words in Your Descriptions

One way to make your description specific and vivid is to *use* **sense words**. As you plan a description, ask yourself,

What does it **look** like?
What does it **sound** like?
What does it **smell** like?
What does it **taste** like?
What does it **feel** like?

The sense details can make the description vivid. Try to include details about the five senses in your descriptions. Often you can brainstorm sense details more easily if you focus on specific details that relate to each sense.

CRITICAL THINKING

Skillful writers make decisions about writing at the word level. They vary the generality or specificity of words according to the needs of their readers. When writing, think about the value of each word you select. Is it specific enough for your needs? Can it be more (or less) specific?

Collaborate

Exercise 6 **Collaborate: Brainstorming Sense Details for a Descriptive Paragraph**

Review the Info Box. Then, with a partner or a group, brainstorm the topic ideas for a paragraph by listing at least six questions and answers that could help you find sense details. Be prepared to read your completed exercise to another group or to the class.

INFO BOX **Devising Sense Details**

For the sense of	Think about
sight	colors, shapes, light and dark, shadows, or brightness
hearing	noise (soothing or grating), silence, whisper, shout
smell	fragrance, odors, degrees (overpowering, subtle, faint), scents, aromas, or perfume
taste	bitter, sour, sharp, sweet, or compare the taste of one thing to another
touch	the feel of things: texture, hardness, softness, roughness, smoothness, temperature

1. topic: The closet was a mess.
              Brainstorm questions and answers:

Q: _____

Q: _____

Q: _____

Q: _____

Q: _____

Q: _____

2. topic: The dessert was terrible.
            Brainstorm questions and answers:

Q: _____

Q: _____

Q: _____

Q: _____

Q: _____

Q: _____

Exercise 7   **Practice: Writing Sense Words**

Write sense descriptions for the items that follow.

1. Write four words or phrases to describe the texture of sand on a beach:

   _____

   _____

2. Write four words or phrases to describe what the ocean looks like:

   _____

   _____

3. Write four words or phrases to describe the sounds of traffic:

   _____

   _____

WRITING THE DESCRIPTIVE PARAGRAPH IN STEPS

PREWRITING   **DESCRIPTION**

Writing a descriptive paragraph begins with thinking on paper, looking for or recalling specific details and sense descriptions. It is almost like detective work because it forces you to consider all the "evidence" that you might have not paid much attention to because of your busy life. You can think by brainstorming, freewriting, or writing in a journal. For example, you might decide to write about the contents of someone's garage. Brainstorming might lead you to something like the following list of ideas.

2 Prewrite to generate a topic for a descriptive paragraph that supports a dominant impression.

Brainstorming a List for a Descriptive Paragraph

- *my husband*
- *Bradley's motorcycle*
- *cycle always in pieces*
- *his tools for the cycle, yard work, home repairs*
- *paint cans*
- *bulletin board with photos*
- *his little plastic containers of nails, screws*

(Continued)

- *dusty shelves on walls*
- *oil stains and smells on the floor*
- *Bradley's work bench*
- *musty smell of Bradley's boxes of junk on the floor*
- *noise of engine running*
- *bags of fertilizer*
- *garbage can smells*
- *gasoline smells*
- *Bradley's camping gear, a tent*
- *my collection of hand-painted ceramic bowls*

The Dominant Impression

When you think you have enough details, you can begin to think about focusing them. Look over these details and consider where they are taking you. If you were to look at the preceding list, you might identify ideas that keep appearing in the details:

- *my husband*
- *Bradley's motorcycle*
- *cycle always in pieces*
- *his tools for the cycle, yard work, and home repairs*
- *bulletin board with photos*
- *little plastic containers of nails, screws*
- *dusty shelves on walls*
- *oil stains and smells on the floor*
- *Bradley's work bench*
- *musty smell of Bradley's boxes of junk on the floor*
- *noise of engine running*
- *bags of fertilizer*
- *garbage can smells*
- *gasoline smells*
- *Bradley's camping gear, a tent*

Reading over this list, you realize that all the items and details connect to Bradley. The cycle, work bench, tools, and camping gear reflect his hobbies and interests. The garbage can and tools may relate to his chores. Therefore, the garage seems to be almost an extension of Bradley and his territory. This idea is the **dominant impression**, or the main point of the description. In a descriptive paragraph, the topic sentence conveys the dominant impression of the scene. For example, the topic sentence could be:

The garage is my husband's territory.

Once you have a dominant impression, you are ready to add more ideas to explain and support it. Now you need to add sensory detail to help it "come alive."

Exercise 8 **Practice: Adding Details to a Dominant Impression**

Following are sentences that could be used as a dominant impression in a descriptive paragraph. Some details to explain and support the dominant impression are already given. Add more details.

1. dominant impression: The car was destroyed.

    details: a. <u>The front and rear windshields were gone.</u>

                b. <u>The front bumper was almost wrapped around the</u>

                    <u>telephone pole.</u>

                c. _____

                d. _____

                e. _____

2. dominant impression: My toddler enjoyed the wrapping paper more than the gift inside it.

    details: a. _____

                b. _____

                c. He flung the bow into the air.

                d. _____

                e. _____

Exercise 9   **Practice: Creating a Dominant Impression from a List of Details**

Following are lists of details. For each list, write one sentence that could be used as the dominant impression created by the details.

    1. dominant impression: _____

    _____

    details: Clarice's hair was tangled. The hair on the back of her head was flat.

                She was wearing sweat pants and a t-shirt.

                She had her head on the breakfast table.

                She was barefoot.

                She grunted instead of talking.

    2. dominant impression: _____

    _____

    details: The salespeople pretty much refused to come out from behind the counters.

                They rolled their eyes when their manager spoke to them.

                They avoided looking at the shoppers browsing through the departments.

                When they made a sale, the clerks just said "Next" instead of saying "Thank you."

                After they completed the transaction, they stared at their phones.

3. dominant impression: _____

_____

details: My five-year-old son David begins to jump when he sees an ice cream cone in my hand.

He grabs it from me, crying, "Yum!"

First, he licks it from the top, pushing the soft ice cream out of the sides of the cone.

To get the last drops of ice cream out of the cone, he turns the cone upside down.

He licks the inside of the cone with gusto.

Finally, he crushes the cone, eats it, and grins.

PLANNING   DESCRIPTION

The sentence you created as the dominant impression can be the topic sentence for your outline. Beneath the topic sentence, list the details you have collected. Once you have this rough list, check the details by asking:

Do all the details relate to the topic sentence?
Are the details in logical order? Do they flow together in a way that conveys the sense of what is being described?

Following are the topic sentence and list of details for the paragraph describing the contents of the garage. The details that are crossed out don't "fit" the topic sentence.

topic sentence: The garage is my husband's territory.

- my husband
- Bradley's motorcycle
- cycle always in pieces
- his tools for the cycle, yard work, home repairs
- paint cans
- bulletin board with photos
- his little plastic containers of nails, screws
- dusty shelves on walls
- oil stains and smells on the floor
- Bradley's work bench
- musty smell of Bradley's boxes of junk on the floor
- ~~noise of engine running~~
- bags of fertilizer
- garbage can smells
- gasoline smells
- Bradley's camping gear, a tent
- ~~my collection of hand-painted ceramic bowls~~

Notice what is crossed out. The detail about the noise of the engine running doesn't fit because the paragraph is about the contents of the garage, not what happens in the garage. In addition, the detail about the wife's collection of ceramic bowls is not related to the topic sentence because the topic sentence focuses on the garage as Bradley's place. It is about his interests and responsibilities.

Remember that as you write and revise, you may decide to eliminate other ideas, to reinsert ideas you once rejected, or even to add new ideas. Changing your mind is a natural part of revising. Even though you like a specific idea or observation, it may not "fit" with all the other pieces.

Once you have decided on your best list of details, check their order. Remember, when you write a description, you are trying to make the reader *see*. It will be easier for the reader to imagine what you see if you put your description in a simple, logical order. You might want to put descriptions in order by **time sequence** (first to last), by **spatial position** (top to bottom, or right to left), or by **similar types** (for example, all about the flowers, then all about the trees in a park), or by **sensory relation** (smells together, sounds together, etc.).

If you are describing a car, for instance, you may want to start with the outside of the car and then describe the inside. You do not want the details to shift back and forth, from outside to inside and back to outside. If you are describing a pet, you might want to group all the details about its face before you describe its body.

Look again at the details describing the garage. It is logical to use these categories: from the bare floor, to the covered floor, and to the walls. Now look at the following outline and notice how this order works.

Outline for a Descriptive Paragraph

topic sentence	The garage is my husband's territory.
details	The area of bare floor is covered in oil stains.
bare floor	It smells like gasoline.
	This area is very small.
	Most of the garage floor is filled.
	Boxes of Bradley's junk give off a musty odor.
	Bradley's work bench is pushed into one corner.
covered floor	Bradley's camping gear and a tent fill another corner.
	His motorcycle, usually in pieces, fills one-third of the space.
	The garbage can smells of rotting food.
	The back and side walls are covered with dusty metal shelves.
	They contain tools for cycle repair, yard work, and home repair.
walls	Old, crusty paint cans are on the shelves.
	Bags of fertilizer are on the shelves.
	Dozens of small plastic containers of nails and screws are there.
	One wall has a bulletin board with photos.

You probably noticed that the outline has more details than the original list. These details help to make the descriptions more specific. You can add them to the outline and to the drafts of your paragraph.

Once you have a list of details focused on a topic sentence and arranged in some logical order, you can begin a draft of your descriptive paragraph.

CRITICAL THINKING

An essay's order of ideas is essential to the communication process. Your responsibility as a writer is to communicate your ideas as clearly as possible and to eliminate all *non sequiturs* and any *tangential ideas*. The term *non sequitur* in Latin means "does not follow." *Tangential* refers to ideas that are only loosely connected to a line of reasoning. When writing, you want to eliminate non sequiturs and tangential ideas to enhance clarity.

Exercise 10 Practice: Finding Details That Do Not Relate

Survey the following lists. Each includes a topic sentence and several details. In each list, cross out the details that do not relate to the topic sentence.

1. **topic sentence:** At my apartment building, the laundry facilities are inadequate and unreliable.

   details: Twenty apartments share two washers and two dryers.

   When I try to do laundry, the machines are full of someone else's clothes.

   The washers are medium-sized, so it takes twice as much money and twice as much time as it should.

   The washers break down at least once a week probably because people overfill them to save money.

   The ancient dryers are inefficient.

   The dryers spin my sheets or clothes into long, rope-like tangles that are still damp.

   I never remember to bring enough money to the laundry room.

   The laundry room shares a little hut with the mail boxes.

2. **topic sentence:** My academic advisor is a good listener.

   details: I can tell that he is genuinely interested in what I have to say because he asks me questions.

   He likes to sit in a quiet place.

   He never interrupts me with his opinions or criticism.

   He maintains eye contact, smiles, and nods his head.

   After I finish talking, he asks me follow-up questions to help focus the next move I should make with my courses.

   He can keep a secret.

3. topic sentence: The Bread Basket is a great restaurant for college students.

details: It has a wide choice of soups, salads, sandwiches, and bagels.

A big menu is posted on one wall.

It also offers the cookies, muffins, and brownies that students love and require for little "mind breaks."

For those who are in need of caffeine, the coffee and tea are excellent.

The prices are fair.

The parking lot is usually overcrowded.

Many students come to eat or hang out on the patio.

Others place their laptops on the wide tables and booths indoors, do their homework, and study in peace.

It is student friendly; no one pushes out the students who linger over their homework or conversation.

Exercise 11 Practice: Putting Details in Order

Following are lists that start with a topic sentence. The details under each topic sentence are not in the right order. Put the details in logical order by labeling them, with 1 being the first detail, 2 the second, and so forth.

1. topic sentence: My job interview at a local restaurant confused me. (Arrange the details in time order.)

details: _____ After fifteen minutes of waiting, the manager led me to a small table near the kitchen.

_____ When I came in, a hostess told me to wait because the manager was busy.

_____ Waiting, I heard some waitresses complaining about the customers.

_____ I struggled to hear the manager's words over the noise from the kitchen.

_____ I did my best to answer the manager's questions, but she was distracted by her staff three or four times when I was answering her questions.

2. topic sentence: The exterior of the candy store was designed to bring out the love of candy in all children and adults. (Arrange the details from the top of the store to the bottom.)

details: _____ Hanging from the bottom of the sign, a line of brightly lighted animal crackers hung.

_____ On either side of the store's entrance, huge windows displayed enormous piles of dark chocolate, milk chocolate, and white chocolate bonbons.

_____ The strangest part of the store was the roof, topped by a giant candy cane that was held by a gingerbread man.

_____ Directly below the roof, huge pink gumdrops spelled out the words "Candy Haven."

_____ Even the welcome mat at the store's entrance looked like a line of red and black licorice sticks.

3. topic sentence: As soon as Michelle and Liam saw the house, they dreamed of owning it. (Arrange the details from outside to inside.)

details: _____ A stone walkway began at the front gate.

_____ The walkway, bordered by brightly colored flowers, led to the front door.

_____ The small brick home was set back from the street and shaded by oak trees.

_____ Inside the front door, a small tiled hall opened up into a living room.

_____ The living room, which followed the hall, had a brick fireplace, hardwood floors, and large windows facing the sun.

Exercise 12 **Practice: Creating Details Using a Logical Order**

The following lists include a topic sentence and indicate a required order for the details. Write five sentences of details in the required order.

1. topic sentence: On the first day of class, my math instructor was intimidating.
(Describe the class from beginning to end.)

a. _____

_____

b. _____

_____

c. _____

d. _____

_____

e. _____

_____

2. **topic sentence:** The Student Center was noisy and bright.
   (Describe the noise; then describe the lighting.)

   a. _____

   b. _____

   c. _____

   d. _____

   e. _____

3. **topic sentence:** As my sister ran her first marathon, her expression changed.
   (Describe the changes from beginning to end.)

   a. _____

   b. _____

   c. _____

   d. _____

      _____

   e. _____

DRAFTING AND REVISING   DESCRIPTION

③ Write a descriptive paragraph that uses specific details and transitions effectively.

After you have an outline, the next step is creating a first rough draft of the paragraph. Your goal is simply to put your ideas in paragraph form so that you can see how they look, and you can check them to see what needs to be improved.

The first draft of a paragraph will not be perfect. If it were perfect, it wouldn't be a first draft. Once you have the first draft, check it using the following list.

Checklist for Revising a Descriptive Paragraph

✓ Are there enough details?

✓ Are the details specific?

✓ Do the details use sense words?

✓ Do the details create a purposeful flow and order?

✓ Is there a dominant impression?

✓ Do the details connect to the dominant impression?

✓ Have I made my point?

A common problem in writing description is creating a fuzzy, vague description. Take a look at the following fuzzy description:

The soccer fans were rowdy and excited. They shouted when their team scored. Some people jumped up. The fans showed their support by cheering and stomping. They were enjoying every minute of the game.

The description could be revised so that it is more specific and vivid:

> The soccer fans were rowdy and excited. They sang and chanted throughout the course of the entire game. When their team scored, they cheered and stomped their feet. Three fans, with faces painted the team colors of blue and white, were so thrilled they spilled their drinks on the teenagers seated below them. Every time a call went against their team, the fans shouted their disagreements with the officials. As people cheered, whooped, and woofed, they turned to grin at each other and thrust their clenched fists into the air.

The vivid description meets the requirements of the checklist. It has sufficient specific details describing what the fans looked and sounded like. The details also support a dominant impression of rowdy, excited fans.

As you revise the drafts of your essay, you will notice how the right details, sense words, and a focus on the dominant impression (the topic sentence) make your description more engaging and more accurate.

Exercise 13 Practice: Revising a Paragraph, Finding Irrelevant Sentences

Following are two descriptive paragraphs. In each, there are sentences that are irrelevant, meaning they do not have anything to do with the first sentence, the topic sentence. Cross out the irrelevant sentences in the paragraphs below.

1. The heavy snow made driving difficult. The snow was coming down so hard that that drivers could barely see. It was a typical early winter autumn storm. The huge flakes, falling fast and hard, covered the cars' windshields. Drivers could barely make out the shapes of the cars and trucks around them. Surrounded by a curtain of snow, the drivers inched their way down the road. A few impatient drivers created a hazard by racing past the cautious ones, kicking up swirls of snow as they passed. Anyone trying to get out of a parked car would be covered with snow in seconds. Within just one hour, the blizzard had left four inches of snow across the city.

2. My six-month-old nephew has the face of an angel. His soft, fuzzy hair barely covers his scalp, but it looks like a halo. I like to touch the strands of his hair because it is so different from mine. Benjamin's blue eyes are large and round, radiating innocence and joy. They always seem to show his surprise at the wonderful world he has entered. He has a perfect little snub nose. Finally, his small mouth is exactly like the mouths of the angels shown on valentines and Christmas cards. When he smiles, Benjamin looks a little more mischievous than an angel.

Exercise 14 **Practice: Revising a Paragraph for More Specific Details**

In the following paragraphs, the details that are underlined are not specific. Change the underlined sentences to more specific descriptions. Write the changes in the lines after each paragraph.

1. My bizarre Uncle Steve was dressed in an odd combination of clothing. On his head was a weird hat. He wore a red bandana around his neck and his shirt was made of faded cotton with a flower print. The sleeves were rolled up, and the ragged shirttails hung over a pair of expensive, neatly pressed khakis that were also rolled up. He wore white socks with a dark blue band around the top. His shoes, however, did not match the socks.

revisions: _____

_____

2. The plane taking us to Odessa represented air travel at its least glamorous. The roof of the aircraft was low enough to threaten each entering passenger with decapitation. After one step inside, passengers looked like rats who had taken a wrong turn in a maze. The interior of the plane smelled awful. The storage bins only had room for small bags or boxes, and the doors on the bins kept popping open. The hard, narrow seats imprisoned the passengers. There was hardly any leg room. Our in-flight beverage choice was warmish water or tepid coffee. In addition, those with window seats could barely see through the filthy windows.

revisions: _____

_____

Transitions

As you revise your descriptive paragraph, you may notice places in the paragraph that seem choppy or abrupt. That is, one sentence may end, and another may start, but the two sentences don't seem to be connected. Reading your paragraph aloud can help find weakness in the flow of ideas.

You can make the writing smoother and make the content clearer by using **transitions**, which are words or phrases that link one idea to another idea. They tell the reader what he or she has just read and what is coming next. Some transitions that you may want to use in writing a description follow.

> **INFO BOX**   **Transitions for a Descriptive Paragraph**
>
> **To show ideas brought together:**
>
> | | | |
> |---|---|---|
> | and also | in addition | next |
>
> **To show a contrast:**
>
> | | | | |
> |---|---|---|---|
> | although | however | on the contrary | unlike |
> | but | in contrast | on the other hand | yet |
>
> **To show a similarity:**
>
> | | | | |
> |---|---|---|---|
> | all | each | like | similarly |
> | both | | | |
>
> **To show a time sequence:**
>
> | | | | |
> |---|---|---|---|
> | after | first | next | then |
> | always | second (etc.) | often | when |
> | before | meanwhile | soon | while |
>
> **To show a position in space:**
>
> | | | | |
> |---|---|---|---|
> | above | between | in front of | over |
> | ahead of | beneath | inside | there |
> | alongside | beyond | near | toward |
> | among | by | nearby | under |
> | around | close | next to | up |
> | away | down | on | underneath |
> | below | far | on top of | where |
> | beside | here | outside | |

There are many other transitions you can use, depending on what you need to link your ideas. Take a look at a draft of the description paragraph of a garage. Compare it to the outline on page 65. A sentence of details has been added to the end of the paragraph; it gives specific details about another of Bradley's interests. You will also notice that more sense details have been added. Transitions have been added, too. Pay particular attention to the transitions in this draft.

Revised Draft of a Descriptive Paragraph

(Note: Editing and proofreading are still necessary.)

transition added —— The garage is my husband Bradley's territory. <u>Near</u> the

added details —— entrance to the garage is small <u>area of bare floor</u>. This area is covered in oil stains and smells like gasoline. <u>Next to</u> this

transition added —— patch of open floor is the <u>long, cluttered part of the floor</u>. <u>On</u>

details, transition added —— <u>one side</u>, boxes of Bradley's sweatshirts, rags, boots, and a motorcycle manual give off a musty odor. Bradley's work

transition added	bench is pushed into one corner. <u>In front of</u> it is Bradley's
	motorcycle. It is usually in pieces. The cycle fills one-third of the
transition added	space in the garage. Pushed <u>close to</u> the bench and the cycle,
	the garbage can smells of roting food. Dusty metal shelves cover
transition added	the back and side walls. The shelves <u>next to</u> the motorcycle
details	contain tools for motorcycle repair and <u>a few items</u> for home
transition added	repair and yard work. <u>On the opposite wall</u>, old, crusty paint
transition added	cans <u>share space with</u> dozens of small plastic container of nails
details added	and screws. <u>Heavy</u> bags of <u>lawn</u> fertilizer <u>cause the shelves of</u>
details added	<u>the back wall</u> to sag. Sitting on the <u>top shelf</u> of this wall, a <u>cork</u>
sentence of detail	board is covered with photographs. <u>Bradley's camping gear and</u>
added	<u>a small tent are stuffed in to the lower shelves of the back wall</u>.
	This garage gives a portrait of my husband as a man who
	maintains the house and the yard and who loves the outdoors.

Exercise 15   **Practice: Recognizing Transitions**

Underline the transitions in the paragraph that follows.

My college roommate and I found an apartment that is going to suit us very well. Nearby, there is a bus stop that serves the college campus. A huge supermarket a block away from our apartment should meet our needs for groceries and snacks; just up the street from the market is a coffee shop with free Wi-Fi. About a mile beyond our apartment, there is a jogging path and green space that will be a good spot to unwind. Here we could exercise, study, and relax. In addition, we could meet new people who might soon become friends.

EDITING AND PROOFREADING   DESCRIPTION

After you have revised your description, the next step is editing. At this point, you can check grammatical structures, sentence length and structure, word forms, punctuation, and spelling. Once you have revised your draft, you can check it using the following list.

Checklist for Editing a Descriptive Paragraph

✓ Are the verb forms correct and consistent?

✓ Are other grammatical structures correct?

✓ Can any sentences be combined?

✓ Did you correctly punctuate?

✓ Is everything spelled correctly?

Practice: Combining Sentences and Using Transitions

The following description has some choppy sentences that could be combined to create a smoother paragraph. Combine each pair of underlined sentences by revising them in the space above each pair and using appropriate transitions.

At Thanksgiving, my Uncle Chris—the worst cook in the world—insists on cooking dinner for kind-hearted people who cannot say "no." His entire family gathers for a meal that always begins with a fruit cocktail that he serves in tiny glass bowls with chunks of pears and peaches, and one or two red cherries. <u>All the fruit has come straight out of a can. It is swimming in the sugary sweet liquid that also came from the can.</u> Next is the main course. The side dishes are always the same. We guests have a choice of vegetables. <u>We can eat stringy green beans. They come from a can.</u> Corn is another choice. <u>It is not on the cob. It is corn kernels from a freezer bag.</u> Uncle Chris also serves potatoes. <u>These potatoes have been baked. They have not been baked long enough.</u> Nothing is worse than trying to eat a potato that is hard in the middle. The turkey arrives last. Unfortunately, Uncle Chris tends to burn the bird which is better than undercooking the bird. <u>The turkey may not be perfect. It is edible.</u> Finally, there is the dessert, and even Uncle Chris can't spoil a pumpkin pie from the local bakery and vanilla ice cream from the supermarket.

Practice: Proofreading to Prepare the Final Version

The following descriptive paragraph has the kinds of errors that are easy to overlook when you write the final version of an assignment. Correct the errors, writing above the lines. There are twelve errors in the paragraph.

At one shop in the mall, I feel like an intruder. The store is a clothing store, and it offers clothes for people my age. However, I do not feel comftable in the store. The windows draw me in with glimpses of attractive jeans, shirts, sweater, and jackets. Unfortunately, when I take a few steps inside the store, I sense that I do not belong. The store is unnaturaly quiet and too brightly lit. In addition, The racks of clothing are in perfect order. On the shelves, the color-coded shirts and sweaters are stacked in immaculate piles. On look at the price of a sweater tells me I cant afford the style, and fashion in this place. I leave before 1 of the salespeople approach me and

reconizes me as to broke, two sloppy, or too unfashionable to shop there.

Finally, proofread your writing. Read every word carefully to be sure that what you've written makes sense and is error free.

Final Version of a Descriptive Paragraph

(Note: Changes from the previous draft are underlined.)

The garage is my husband Bradley's territory. Near the entrance to the garage is a small area of bare floor. This area is covered in oil stains and smells like gasoline. Next to this patch of open floor is the long, cluttered part of the floor. On one side, boxes of Bradley's sweatshirts, rags, boots, and motorcycle manuals give off a musty odor. Bradley's work bench is pushed into one corner. In front of it is Bradley's motorcycle, which is usually in pieces. The cycle fills one-third of the space in the garage. Pushed close to the bench and the cycle, the garbage can smells of rotting food. Dusty metal shelves cover the back and side walls. The shelves next to the motorcycle contain tools for motorcycle repair and a few items for home repair and yard work. On the opposite wall, old crusty paint cans share space with dozens of small plastic containers of nails and screws. Heavy bags of lawn fertilizer cause the shelves of the back wall to sag. Sitting on the top shelf of this wall, a cork board is covered with photographs. Bradley's camping gear and a small tent are stuffed into the lower shelves of the back wall. This garage is a true reflection of my husband, a man who maintains the house and the yard and who loves the outdoors.

Annotations (left margin):
- the article *a* is added
- verb consistency—present time
- comma added
- spelling corrected: *rotting*
- need plural for *containers*
- *into* one word
- wording improved

For your information: A sample descriptive essay based on the same topic and following the same writing steps can be found in Chapter 12.

Lines of Detail: A Walk-Through Assignment

Your assignment is to write a paragraph describing your favorite place to eat. Follow these steps:

Step 1: To begin, freewrite about the restaurant, food truck, or café you want to consider.

Step 2: Read your freewriting. Underline all the words, phrases, and sentences of description.

Step 3: List everything you underlined, grouping the ideas in some order.

Step 4: After you've surveyed the list, write a sentence about the dominant impression of the details.

Step 5: Using the dominant impression as your topic sentence, write an outline. Add specific details where you need them. Concentrate on details that appeal to the senses.

Step 6: Write a first draft of your paragraph. Be sure to check the order of your details. Combine short sentences and add transitions.

Step 7: Revise your first draft version to be sure you have sufficient sensory details arranged in a logical sequence.

Step 8: Edit your latest draft to improve style and check for serious errors or omissions.

Step 9: Prepare a final version, and proofread carefully to spot and correct any careless errors in spelling, punctuation, format, and typing.

Topics for Writing a Descriptive Paragraph

When you write on any of the following topics, work through the stages of the writing process in preparing your descriptive paragraph. Be sure that your paragraph is based on a dominant impression, and put the dominant impression into your topic sentence.

1. Write a paragraph that describes one of the following items.

    the place you work   a coach
    a tattoo you want to get   an eccentric friend
    your favorite place to study   your first car
    the bookstore   an irritating relative
    a vacation spot   your favorite piece of jewelry
                                         an activity that energizes you

2. Describe a place that creates one of the following impressions.

    joy   tension   warmth
    anxiety   danger   pride

3. Describe a person who conveys one of the following impressions.

    faith   style   arrogance
    intelligence   curiosity   physical strength

4. Visit the Web site of your local newspaper, and find a photograph of a local event involving two or more individuals. Create a descriptive paragraph that uses the skills and methods that we have discussed in this chapter. Be sure your details relate to a dominant impression of the scene. After you have written the paragraph, read the actual news article that accompanied the photograph. Consider how your descriptive paragraph presents the news in a different manner. Attach the photograph and the news article to the completed paragraph.

Collaborate

5. Interview a partner so that you and your partner can gather details and then write a description paragraph with the title, "My Ideal Day Off."

First, prepare a list of at least six questions to ask your partner. Write down the answers your partner gives and use those answers to form more questions. For example, if your partner says her ideal day off would be to go to the beach, ask her what she would do there. If your partner says his ideal day off would be to spend time with his family, ask about his family.

When you've finished the interview, switch roles. Let your partner interview you. Feel free to add more questions or to follow up on previous ones.

Give your partner his or her interview responses. Take your own responses and use them as the basis for gathering as many details as you can on your perfect day off. If you have never experienced the place that you would like to go on that day off, go online to look at some pictures that might help you get some sensory images. Then go on to the outline, draft, and final version of your paragraph. Be prepared to read your completed paragraph to your partner.

6. Study the photograph. Then write a paragraph that describes and explains the dominant impression of this scene.

Topics for Critical Thinking and Writing

1. Have you ever heard the old saying, "Nothing is ever real until it is gone"? Do you agree with that statement? If so, describe a person or place that you might have taken for granted, but now appreciate more deeply. Recall the important sense details that you feel are important in conveying this remembrance.

2. Imagine that you had to create a brochure to convince a family member from another state to come visit. Make a list of some of your town's more memorable natural attractions, buildings, or landmarks. If the brochure had to focus on a specific sort of tourism (dining, museums, adventure, historical sites), which holds the most promise? Write a descriptive paragraph focusing on one of those specific types of tourism using as many sense details as possible.

> **Note:** Additional writing options suitable for description-related assignments can be found in the "Readings for Writers" appendix of this book.

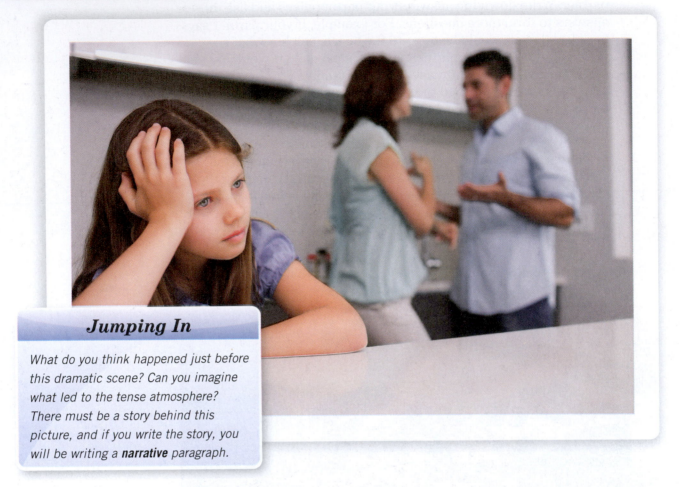

Learning Objectives

In this chapter, you will learn how to:

1. Recognize that a narrative paragraph needs a point.
2. Prewrite to generate a topic for a narrative paragraph.
3. Write a narrative paragraph that uses details and transitions effectively.

WHAT IS NARRATION?

You may have heard of a narrator; this just means the person or voice telling the story. Everybody tells stories; some people are better storytellers than others. **Narration** means telling a story. When you write a **narrative** paragraph, you can tell a story about something that happened to you or to someone else, or about something that you saw or read.

A narrative, like a description, relies on specific details, but it is also different from a description because it covers events in a time sequence. Although a description can be about a person, a place, or an object, a narrative is always about happenings: events, actions, incidents. A narrative will have a storyline—an arc—with a beginning, a middle, and an end.

Interesting narratives do more than just tell what happened; they help the reader become involved in the story by providing vivid details. These details come from your memory, your observation, or your reading. Using good details, you don't just tell the story; you *show* it.

Give the Narrative a Point

We all know people who tell long stories that seem to lead nowhere. These people talk on and on; they recite an endless list of activities and soon become boring. Their narratives have no point.

The difficult part of writing a narrative is making sure that it has a point. That point will be included in the topic sentence. The point of a narrative is the meaning of the incident or incidents you are writing about. To get to the point of your narrative, ask yourself questions like these:

What did I learn?
What is the meaning of this story?
What is my attitude toward what happened?
Did it change me?
What emotion did it make me feel?
Was the experience a good example of something (such as unfairness, kindness, generosity, or some other quality)?

The answers to such questions can lead you to a point. An effective topic sentence for a narrative is

not this: I'm going to tell you about the time I flunked my driving test. (This is an announcement; it does not make a point.)
but this: When I failed my driving test, I learned not to be overconfident.

not this: Yesterday I was late for an important family get-together. (This identifies the incident but does not make a point. It is also too narrow to be a good topic sentence.)
but this: When I walked into my family's house thirty minutes late, I was anxious and embarrassed.

The topic sentence, stating the point of your narrative paragraph, can be placed in the beginning, middle, or end of the paragraph. You may want to start your story with the point so that the reader knows exactly where your story is headed, or you may want to conclude your story by leaving the point until last. Sometimes the point can even fit smoothly into the middle of your paragraph.

Consider the narrative paragraphs that follow. The topic sentences are in various places.

Topic Sentence at the Beginning

<u>When I was five, I learned how serious it is to tell a lie</u>. One afternoon, my friend John asked me if I wanted to walk down the block to play ball in an empty lot. When I asked my mother, she said I couldn't go because it was too near dinner time. I wanted to go play, so I did. Yet as I played in the dusty lot, a dull buzz of guilt or fear distracted me. As soon as I got home, my mother confronted me. She asked me whether I had gone to the sandlot. I lied and said no. Something about my mother's tone of voice made me feel ashamed, so I told her that yes I had. I knew I had let her down.

Topic Sentence in the Middle

When I was little, I was afraid of diving into water. I thought I would smash my head on the bottom of the pool or go down and never come

① Recognize that a narrative paragraph needs a point.

back up. Then one day, my father took me to a pool where we swam, but he never forced me to try a dive. After about an hour of playing, I walked round and round the edge of the pool, trying to get the courage to dive in. Finally, I did it. <u>When I made that first dive, I felt blissful because I had done something I had been afraid to do.</u> As I came to the surface, I wiped the water from my eyes and looked around. Best of all, I saw my father looking at me with a smile. "You did it," he said. "Good for you! I'm proud of you."

Topic Sentence at the End

It seemed like I'd been in love with Reeza for years. Unfortunately, Reeza was always in love with someone else. Finally, she broke up with her boyfriend Nelson. I saw my chance. I asked Reeza out. After dinner, we talked and talked. Reeza told me all about her hopes and dreams. She told me about her family and her job, and I felt very close to her. We talked late into the night. When she left, Reeza kissed me. "Thanks for listening," she said. "You're like a brother to me." <u>Reeza meant to be kind, but she shattered my hopes and dreams.</u>

CRITICAL THINKING

Even though your topic sentence can be placed at different places within a paragraph, narrative paragraphs in general have a clear beginning, middle, and end. They also frequently involve tension or some form of conflict. This tension is introduced in the beginning, builds in the middle, and is often resolved in the end.

Exercise 1 **Practice: Finding the Topic Sentence in a Narrative Paragraph**

Underline the topic sentence in each narrative paragraph that follows.

Paragraph 1

After I finished high school, I wanted to have some fun because I was sick of studying and being told where to be and what to do. I spent the summer going to the beach and surfing with my friends. I kept my part-time job at a discount store (the same one I had worked at for two years) and lived at my parents' house so that I could afford to live a carefree life. Summer was great, and the days went by quickly. Soon it was fall, and I had this feeling that I should become more serious. Most of my friends had found full-time work, started college, or combined work and school. On a rainy day in October, I sat alone on a sand dune. I realized that it was time for me to grow up. My friends had moved on, and here I was, feeling anxious about my future. Soon after, I started looking for a full-time job. Then I spoke with a counselor at a local community college. She told me about early registration for the next term. We also discussed careers.

Paragraph 2

Hurting my knees gave me a small hint of what it means to be disabled or elderly. In a silly accident, I slipped on the wet pavement near my house. My knees were bloody, but I picked myself up and kept walking. At first, all that concerned me was the blood on my knees. Later, I felt an ache in my shoulders. Then my knees began to hurt whenever I sat or bent down. When I got out of bed the next morning, the pain was worse. Every time I bent my knees—stooping down or walking up stairs—my knees ached in pain. I was not used to having a body that did not simply do what I asked of it without complaining. I felt overcautious, constricted, and conscious of my weakness.

> **Exercise 2**   Practice: Writing the Missing Topic Sentences in Narrative Paragraphs

Following are two paragraphs. If the paragraph already has a topic sentence, write it in the lines provided. If it does not have a topic sentence, create one. (One of the paragraphs has no topic sentence.)

Paragraph 1

 I have never felt as much shame as the shame I felt after my one involvement in cheating. At eighteen, I was facing pressures I had never faced before. I was taking a few college courses, working, and helping my mom out at home. I really wanted to succeed, but felt so pressured at work and at home, I didn't put in the time and energy I needed to at school. One day my English instructor told me that my grades were quite low and if I didn't score high on my last essay, I would have to repeat the course. I was furious. So, I went to the library and started writing away. However, none of my ideas were very sharp. I went online to look at some sample essays on the topic. One essay had exactly the information that I needed and it was well written. I did a "copy/paste" and dropped the sentences into my essay. I finished the paper, and handed it in. The next class period Ms. Hubbs asked to see me after class. I knew I was in trouble. She asked if I had written everything in my paper. She told me to sit down beside her computer and she typed in those same three sentences and hit enter. The same Web site that I had used came up. She asked me if I remembered the discussion about plagiarism from the first week of class. She told me that copying from an uncited source is plagiarism. Next, she told me I would fail the paper and the course. I was so upset with myself.

If the paragraph already has a topic sentence, write it here. If it does not have a topic sentence, create one. _____

_____

_____

Paragraph 2

 My seventh birthday was here, and I was sure that I wouldn't celebrate it much. My father was living in a distant state, and he had stopped sending child support checks for me and my sisters several months earlier. I knew money was tight at home despite my mom working two jobs. At school, I thought of better birthdays when my folks had been together and money had not been such a problem. As I walked slowly home from school, I told myself, "A birthday is just a day; it doesn't need to be anything special. A birthday cake can be enough." However, I kept hoping that at least one small gift would be waiting for me. My little sisters, smiling, opened the door. My mother, trying to smile, stood by the kitchen table. On it were six chocolate cupcakes, each with a blue candle in the chocolate icing. "So this is it," I thought. I loved my mother and sisters, and they loved me. However, this wasn't much of a birthday celebration for a seven-year-old. Suddenly my five-year-old sister Rosalee began to jump up. "Look under the table!" she cried. There was a big box beneath the table. I picked it up, and it felt heavy, with the weight in it shifting from side to side. Inside the box was the most beautiful orange and white kitten I had ever seen. I named her Special.

If the paragraph already has a topic sentence, write it here. If it does not have a topic sentence, create one. _____

_____

_____

Hints for Writing a Narrative Paragraph

Everyone tells stories, but some people tell stories better than others. When you write a story, be sure to

- Be clear.
- Be interesting.
- Stay in order.
- Pick a topic that is not too big.

1. Be clear. Put in all the information the reader needs to follow your story. Sometimes you need to explain the time or place or the relationships of the people in your story to make the story clear. Sometimes you need to explain how much time has elapsed between one action and another. This paragraph is not clear:

> I've never felt so stupid as I did on my first day of work. I was stocking the shelves when Mr. Cimino came up to me and said, "You're doing it wrong." Then he showed me how to do it. An hour later, he told me to call the produce supplier and check on the delivery of fruit. Well, I didn't know how to tell Mr. Cimino that I didn't know where the phone was. I also didn't know how to get the phone number of the produce supplier. I felt really stupid asking these questions.

The narrative lacks some key information. Who is Mr. Cimino? Is he the boss? Is he a produce supervisor? And, more importantly, what kind of place is the writer's workplace? The reader knows the place has something to do with food, but is it a supermarket, a fruit market, or a warehouse?

2. Be interesting. A general narrative that does not give specific details can make even the greatest adventure sound a bit dull:

> I had a wonderful time at our family reunion. It was held at a big park. I saw relatives that I had not seen in many years. We played some games, talked, and ate a lot of food. It was a good day for my family.

Good specific details are the difference between an interesting story and a dull one. Whenever possible, use sense imagery (sight, sound, smell, taste, and touch) to help recreate the events. If done well, engaging the senses will engage the reader.

3. Stay in order. Put the details in a clear order so that the reader can follow your story. Usually, time order is the order you follow in narration. This narrative has a confusing order:

> My impatience cost me twenty dollars last week. There was an expensive pair of shoes I really wanted. I had wanted them for weeks. So, when payday came around, I went to the mall and checked the price on the shoes. I had been checking the price for weeks before. The shoes were expensive, but I really wanted them. On payday, a friend who works at the shoe store told me the shoes were about to go on sale. But I didn't want to wait so I bought them at full price, and three days later, the shoes were marked down twenty dollars.

There's a better approach. Tell the story in the order it happened: first, I saw the expensive shoes and wanted them; second, I checked the price for several weeks; third, I got paid; fourth, on the same day, I checked the price again; fifth, my friend at the store told me the shoes were about to go on sale; sixth, I paid full price right away; seventh, three days later the shoes went on sale. A clear time sequence helps the reader follow your narrative.

4. Pick a topic that is not too big. If you try to write about too many events in a short space, you run the risk of being superficial. You cannot describe anything well if you cover too much. This paragraph covers too much:

> Starting my junior year at a rival high school was a difficult experience. Because my family had just moved across town, I had to go to a school that I had spent the previous two years cheering against. I didn't know anybody at school, and I wasn't sure if I wanted to. On the first day of school, I sat by myself at lunch. Finally, two students at another table started a conversation with me. I thought they were just feeling sorry for me. They were nice, but I didn't tell them that I was from Calhoun High School. At the end of the first week, it seemed like the whole school was talking about exciting plans for the weekend. I spent Friday and Saturday night with my friends from my old school.

This paragraph would be better if it discussed one shorter time period in greater depth and detail. It could cover the first day at school, or the first lunch at school, or the difficulty of keeping information from people.

Using a Speaker's Exact Words in a Narrative

Some of the examples of narratives that you have already seen have included the exact words someone said. You may want to include part of a conversation in your narrative. To do so, you need to know how to punctuate speech.

A person's exact words get quotation marks around them. If you change the words, you do not use quotation marks.

exact words: "You're a pretty good dancer," he told me.
not exact words: He told me that I was a good dancer.

exact words: My sister said, "I think I left it on the bus."
not exact words: My sister said that she probably left it on the bus.

There are a few other points to remember about punctuating a person's exact words. Once you've started quoting a person's exact words, periods and commas generally go inside the quotation marks. Here are two examples.

Richard said, "That's not the way I would have done it."
"Be careful," my mother yelled at me from the bottom of the ladder.

When you introduce a person's exact words with phrases like *She said* or *The teacher told us*, put a comma before the quotation marks. Here are two examples.

She said, "You'd better call your parents."
The teacher told us, "This won't be on the final, but you had better know it any way."

> If you are using a person's exact words and have other questions about punctuation, read about the use of quotation marks in Chapter 28 in the grammar section of this book.

2 Prewrite to generate a topic for a narrative paragraph.

WRITING THE NARRATIVE PARAGRAPH IN STEPS

PREWRITING   **NARRATION**

Finding something to write about can be the hardest part of writing a narrative paragraph because it is usually difficult to think of anything interesting or significant that you have experienced. The prewriting stage is essential in generating ideas. Some people find success through freewriting, journaling, or mind-mapping. Others prefer to ask and answer questions.

Collaborate

Exercise 3   **Collaborate: Questionnaire for Gathering Narrative Topics**

Answer the questions that follow and list details in the spaces provided. Then read your answers to a group. The members of the group should then ask you follow-up questions. Write your answers on the lines provided; the answers will add details to your list.

Finally, ask each member of your group to circle one topic or detail on your questionnaire that could be developed into a narrative paragraph. Discuss the suggestions. Repeat this process for each member of the group.

Narrative Questionnaire

1. Have you ever lost something valuable (an item, a pet, or a person)? When? Write three details you remember about the occasion:

   a. _____

   b. _____

   c. _____

   Additional details, to be added after working with the group:

   _____

   _____

2. Have you ever had a pleasant surprise? Write three details about what happened before, during, and after:

   a. _____

   b. _____

   c. _____

   Additional details, to be added after working with the group:

   _____

   _____

3. Have you ever won anything (a game, a contest, a raffle, some other prize or competition)? Write three details about the experience:

   a. _____

   b. _____

   c. _____

   Additional details, to be added after working with the group:

   _____

   _____

Freewriting for a Narrative Topic

One good way to discover something to write about is to freewrite. For example, if your instructor asks you to write a narrative paragraph about something that changed you, you might begin by freewriting.

Freewriting for a Narrative Paragraph

Topic: Something that changed me

Something that changed me. I don't know. What changed me? Lots of things happened to me, but I can't find one that changed me. Graduating from high school? Everybody will write about that, how boring, and anyway, what was the big deal? I haven't gotten married. No big change there. Divorce. My parents' divorce really changed the whole family. A big shock to me. I couldn't believe it was happening. I was really scared. Who would I live with? They were really calm when they told me. I've never been so scared. I was too young to understand. Kept thinking they'd just get back together. They didn't. Then I got a stepmother. The year of the divorce was a hard time for me. Kids suffer in divorce.

Narrowing and Selecting a Suitable Narrative Topic

After you freewrite, you can assess your writing, looking for words, phrases, or sentences that you could expand into a paragraph. The sample writing has several ideas for a narrative:

high school graduation
learning about my parents' divorce
adjusting to a stepmother
the year of my parents' divorce

Looking for a topic that is not too big, you could use:

high school graduation
learning about my parents' divorce

Because the freewriting has already called graduation a boring topic, the divorce seems to be a more attractive subject. In the freewriting, you already have some details related to the divorce; add to these details by brainstorming. Follow-up questions and answers might include the following:

How old were you when your parents got divorced?

I was seven years old when my mom and dad divorced.

Are you an only child?

My sister was ten.

Where did your parents tell you? Did they both tell you at the same time?

They told us at breakfast in the kitchen. Both my folks were there. I was eating toast. I remember I couldn't eat it when they both started talking. I remember a piece of toast with one bite out of it.

What reasons did they give?

They said they loved us, but they couldn't get along. They said they would always love us kids.

If you didn't understand, what did you think was happening?

At first I just thought they were having another fight.

Did you cry? Did they cry?

I didn't cry. My sister cried. Then I knew it was serious. I kept thinking I would have to choose which parent to live with. Then I knew I'd really hurt the one I didn't choose. I felt so much guilt about hurting one of them.

What were you feeling?

I felt ripped apart.

Questions can help you form the point of your narrative. After brainstorming, you can go back and survey all the details. Do they lead you to a point? Try asking yourself the questions listed previously in this chapter: What did I learn? What is the meaning of this story? What is my attitude toward what happened? Did it change me? What emotion did it make me feel? Was the experience a good example of something (like unfairness, or kindness, or generosity)?

For the topic of the divorce, the details mention a number of emotions: confusion, pain, shock, disbelief, fear, guilt. The *point* of the paragraph cannot list all these emotions, but it could be started this way:

When my parents announced they were divorcing, I felt confused by all my emotions.

Now that you have a point and several details, you can move on to the planning stage of writing a narrative paragraph.

> **Exercise 4** **Practice: Distinguishing Good Topic Sentences from Bad Ones in Narration**

Some sentences follow that would make good topic sentences for a narrative paragraph. Others would not because they are too big to develop in a single paragraph, they are so narrow they can't be developed, or they make no point about an incident or incidents. Put an *X* by the sentences that would not make good topic sentences.

1. _____ At a ceremony at the courthouse, I watched my father become a U.S. citizen.

2. _____ Nothing has pleased me more than my husband's congratulations to me at my college graduation.

3. _____ My sister's obsession with social media is causing problems for our entire family.

4. _____ When I passed my driving test, I felt an enormous sense of freedom.

5. _____ Last Thanksgiving, I spent five hours waiting in a local hospital's emergency department.

6. _____ Being told to visit the writing lab was the best advice my English instructor ever gave me.

7. _____ I come from a small Midwestern town where everybody thinks they know everyone else, but they really don't.

8. _____ Years of working at a coffee shop made me hate the smell of coffee.

9. _____ Not knowing how to change a car tire cost me a job.

10. _____ After my last experience at Crescent Beach, I have a new respect for lifeguards.

> **Exercise 5**   **Practice: Developing a Topic Sentence from a List of Details**

Following is a list of details with an incomplete topic sentence. Read the details carefully; then complete the topic sentence.

> **topic sentence:** Backpacking alone in the wilderness taught me an important lesson about _____
>
> _____
>
> **details:** I planned my trip to Yosemite National Park for months in advance.
>
> One of the things I was worried about were bears.
>
> I learned that bears are attracted to scent and human food.
>
> To avoid bear encounters, I needed to keep a clean campsite and use a bear-proof food canister.
>
> Unfortunately, the bear canister was huge and barely fit into my backpack.
>
> Trying to get food in and out of the canister was inconvenient, and by my third day on the trail I started to keep snacks in my pack's top pocket.
>
> That evening I set up my tent overlooking a beautiful and peaceful mountain lake.
>
> I set up a cooking area 100 feet from my tent and prepared my meal.

Because I was so hungry and tired from hiking, the macaroni and cheese I had that night was the best ever.

Afterward, I cleaned my pot and dishes carefully and set them to dry next to the bear-proof food canister on a rock far away from my campsite.

I walked back to my tent, placed my backpack inside, and went to sleep.

Around 2:00 in the morning I was awakened by a loud grunting sound and a pawing at my tent.

I was scared silly, but remembered what experts said to do in case of a bear encounter.

I made a lot of noise and yelled at the bear.

Luckily, the bear ran off into the woods.

It wasn't until the next morning that I realized I had left food inside the top pocket of my backpack.

Thankfully, the bear was scared away before he destroyed me or my equipment.

PLANNING NARRATION

The topic of how an experience changed you has led you to a point and a list of details. You can now write a rough outline, with the point as the topic sentence. Once you have the rough outline, check it for the following qualities.

Relevance: Do all the details connect to the topic sentence?
Order: Are the details in a clear order?
Development: Does the outline need more details? Are the details specific enough?

Your revised outline might look like the following.

Outline for a Narrative Paragraph

topic sentence	When my parents announced that they were divorcing, I felt confused by all my emotions.
details	I was seven when my mom and dad divorced.
	My sister was ten.
	Both my folks were there.
background of the narrative	They told us at breakfast, in the kitchen.
	I was eating toast.
	I remember I couldn't eat anything when they started talking.
	I remember a piece of toast with one bite out of it.
	My parents were very calm when they told us.
	They said they loved us but couldn't get along.
story of the divorce announcement	They said they would always love us kids.
	It was a big shock to me.

---

my reactions at each stage

I couldn't believe it was happening.
At first I just thought they were having another fight.
I was too young to understand.
I didn't cry.
My sister cried.
Then I knew it was serious.
I kept thinking I would have to choose which parent to live with.
I knew I'd really hurt the one I didn't choose.
I felt so much guilt about hurting one of them.
I felt ripped apart.

Once you have a revised outline, you're ready to write a draft of the narrative paragraph.

Exercise 6   **Practice: Finding Details That Are Out of Order in a Narrative Outline**

The following outline has details that are out of order. Put the details in correct time order by numbering them 1, 2, and so forth.

topic sentence: A small surprise changed my attitude on Sunday.

details: _____ Sunday started as a rainy day.

_____ The rain matched my mood.

_____ Even if it had been sunny, I couldn't have gone outdoors because I had homework and chores.

_____ After two hours with my chemistry textbook, my brain decided it had had enough and was shutting down.

_____ I began by dealing with the worst part of the day: studying for a chemistry test.

_____ Working through the chapters I had previously failed to read, I felt doomed to fail.

_____ I decided to give my head a break and do some mindless chores.

_____ During this break, I began to sort the dirty laundry piled in my closet.

_____ Frustrated and irritated, I kicked the dirty clothes back into the closet.

_____ After I pulled all my dirty laundry out of the closet and dropped it on the floor, I realized that I was too broke to do my laundry.

_____ Grabbing a pair of dirty jeans still on the floor, I heard a clink.

_____ I shook the pants and heard that musical clink of coins in a pocket.

_____ After retrieving the coins, I checked the pockets of the jeans.

_____ I didn't find any more coins, but I did find a ten-dollar bill.

_____ Life no longer seemed so bleak; I pulled my new favorite jeans on and went out to get some pizza.

Exercise 7 Practice: Recognizing Irrelevant Details in a Narrative Outline

The following outline has details that are not relevant to the topic sentence. Cross out the details that do not fit.

topic sentence: Meeting my uncle led me to an important decision.

details: My Uncle Benjamin lives far away from us, so I first met him when I was twelve years old.

He is a cook in a famous restaurant in California, and he visited us to cook for my sister's engagement party.

My sister is the kind of person who enjoys elaborate parties.

Bored by the fancy celebration, I watched my uncle in the kitchen.

He prepared the kitchen efficiently, assembling bowls, utensils, pots, pans, and spices.

He chopped vegetables, sautéed garlic, onions, and capers, and sliced meat into thin strips.

It's not a big kitchen, but Uncle Benjamin was able to work efficiently in a small space.

When he began to cook, he expertly managed all four burners on the stove at once.

My uncle concentrated intently on managing complicated tasks and getting the timing right for all the dishes.

The guests in the living room were drinking toasts to my sister and her fiancé.

My uncle sautéed, he blended, he mixed sauces, and he added spices with precision.

His work was like an art.

Uncle Benjamin's talent and skill made me want to learn what he knew: the culinary art.

3 Write a narrative paragraph that uses details and transitions effectively.

DRAFTING AND REVISING   NARRATION

After you have a revised outline for your narration paragraph, you can begin working on a rough draft. As you write, attempt to combine some of the short sentences of the outline. Once you have a draft, check it for places you would like to improve. Remember that revising largely involves improving your structure and content as you organize your details as clearly and logically as possible. (Later, you can improve your style and correct mistakes during the editing and proofreading stage of the writing process.) The following checklist will help you as you revise your narrative.

Checklist for Revising Your Draft of a Narrative Paragraph

✓   Is my narrative vivid?

✓   Are the details clear and specific?

✓   Does the topic sentence relate to all of the details?

✓   Are the details written in a clear order?

✓   Do the transitions make the narrative easy to follow?

✓   Have I made my point?

Revising for Sharper Details

A good idea for a narrative can be made better if you revise for sharper details. In the paragraph that follows, the underlined words and phrases could be revised to create better details. In the following example, see how the second draft has more vivid details than the first draft.

First Draft: Details Are Dull

A woman at the movies showed me just how rude and selfish people can be. It all started when I was in line with <u>a lot</u> of other people. We had been waiting <u>a long time</u> to buy our tickets. We were outside, and it <u>wasn't pleasant</u>. We were impatient because time was running out and the <u>movie</u> was about to start. Some people were <u>making remarks</u>, and <u>others were pushing</u>. Then <u>a woman cut to</u> the front of the line. The cashier at the ticket window <u>told</u> the woman there was a line and she would have to go to the end of it. The woman <u>said she didn't want to wait because her son didn't want to miss the beginning of the movie</u>.

Second Draft: Better Details

A woman at the movies showed me just how rude and selfish people can be. It all started when I was in line with <u>forty or fifty other people</u>. We had been waiting to buy our tickets for <u>twenty minutes</u>. We were outside, <u>where the temperature was about 90 degrees and it looked like rain</u>. We were all getting impatient because time was running out and the movie was about to start. <u>I heard two people mutter about how ridiculous the wait was, and someone else kept saying, "Let's go!" The man directly behind me kept pushing me, and each new person at the end of the line pushed the whole line forward against the ticket window</u>. Then a woman <u>with a loud voice and a large purse thrust her purse and her body in front of the ticket window</u>. The cashier <u>politely</u> told the woman there was a line and she had to go to the end of it. But the woman answered <u>indignantly</u>. <u>"Oh no," she said. "I'm with my son Mickey. And Mickey really wants to see this martial arts movie. And he hates to miss the first part of any movie. So I can't wait. I've got to have those tickets now."</u>

Checking the Topic Sentence

As you have probably gathered by now, writing is a process of discovery; you seldom know where you will end up when you begin. Sometimes you think you have a good idea, a good topic sentence, and specific details, but when you write the draft of the paragraph, you realize the topic sentence does not quite relate to all of the details. When that happens, you can either revise the details or *rewrite the topic sentence*.

In the paragraph that follows, the topic sentence (underlined) does not quite fit all the details, so the topic sentence should be rewritten.

<u>I didn't know what to do when a crime occurred in front of my house.</u> At 9:00 pm, I was watching television when I heard a bang, like a garbage can that had fallen over. I looked out the window expecting to see a dog getting into the garbage cans, but I couldn't see anything because the street light in front of my house was broken. Then I heard at least two voices, and they sounded angry and threatening. I heard another voice, and it sounded like someone moaning. I was afraid. I pulled out my phone to call 911, but then I paused. What if the police came, and people got arrested? Would the suspects find out I was the one who had called the police? Would they come after *me*? I didn't want to get involved. So I went back to the couch and started watching television. In my mind, I kept picturing someone getting beaten. I couldn't stand it anymore. I called the police. When they came, they found a young teenager, badly beaten, in the street. They said my call may have saved his life.

The previous paragraph has good details, but the story has more of a point than "I didn't know what to do." The person telling the story did, finally, do something. Following is a better topic sentence that covers the whole story.

topic sentence rewritten: I finally found the courage to take the proper action when a crime occurred in front of my house.

Exercise 8 **Practice: Adding Better Details to a Draft of a Narrative**

The following paragraph has some details that could be more vivid. Rewrite the paragraph in the lines after it, replacing the underlined details with more vivid words, phrases, or sentences.

Even the most stubborn people have to admit they are sometimes wrong. My father is extremely <u>bad</u> when he drives to a new destination. He insists that he knows how to get to the place. He refuses to look at a map or at his cell phone's GPS before we all pile into the car. Then we watch him drive confidently in the wrong direction, but we hesitate to correct him. If we try to steer my father to the right route, he reacts <u>badly</u>. He says that he knows exactly where he is going. <u>Things</u> deteriorate when we passengers begin to notice certain landmarks appearing three or four times as my father blindly circles and recircles the wrong streets. Meanwhile, my father is getting <u>mad</u>, and we are getting <u>madder</u>. Eventually, my father does acknowledge that he is lost. We feel <u>good</u> now that my father is ready to take directions.

rewrite:

_____

_____

_____

_____

_____

_____

_____

_____

_____

_____

_____

_____

_____

_____

_____

Exercise 9   **Practice: Writing a Better Topic Sentence for a Narrative**

The paragraphs that follow could use better topic sentences. (In each paragraph, the current topic sentence is underlined.) Read each paragraph carefully, then write a new topic sentence for it in the lines after.

1. <u>Last week my brother told me a terrible story</u>. The problem started when he left work at the mall. He had just gotten someone to cover his Saturday shift so that he could go out with Nicole, his girlfriend. As my brother drove out of the parking lot, he wanted to share the good news with Nicole, so he had his phone out and was texting her. As the texts began to fly back and forth about plans for Saturday, my brother stopped paying attention to his driving. Suddenly, he felt a big jolt and the phone flew out of his hand. He looked up and saw that he had rear-ended a pickup truck. No one was injured, but he knew the accident was going to cost him some money to fix his car and his insurance was going to go up. If only he had waited to contact his girlfriend and had concentrated on driving.

new topic sentence: _____

_____

2. <u>Janelle and I saw a beautiful red fox recently</u>. We live in a typical suburban neighborhood, and the most exotic animals we see are the neighborhood cat prowling around and squirrels racing after each other. However, we do have a few wooded areas between the houses and

apartment buildings that make up our town. One day, Janelle and I were walking through our neighborhood when she grabbed my arm. "Look," she said, nodding her head toward an undeveloped area of trees and bushes. I saw what I initially thought was a dog with a really bushy tail standing at the edge of the property. "It's a fox," Janelle whispered. When we stood still, we were able to focus on its long legs, its red and white body, and its black nose. Then, in a flash, the fox turned and sprinted into the trees and bushes. Janelle and I looked at each other, stunned by the sight of a wild animal hiding and surviving in the middle of our civilized, regulated environment.

new topic sentence: _____

_____

Using Transitions Effectively in Narration

If you have ever been given directions from someone, you know how difficult it can be to follow what someone is telling you. When you tell a story, you have to be sure that your reader can follow you as you move through the steps of your story. One way to make your story easier to follow is to use transitions. Most of the transitions in narration relate to time so using transitions will help to clarify a story that may be clear to you but is new to another. A list of transitions writers often use in writing narration follows.

INFO BOX Transitions for a Narrative Paragraph

after	before	in the meantime	soon after
again	during	later	still
always	finally	later on	suddenly
at first	first	meanwhile	then
at last	second (etc.)	next	until
at once	frequently	now	when
at the same time	immediately	soon	while

A Revised Draft

Following is a revised draft of the paragraph on divorce. As you read it, you will notice some changes that are typical of narrative writing. Because telling a story (narrative) involves events in time order, a first draft tends to focus on simply putting those events in the correct sequence. However, once the time order is correct, a writer has to focus on two important issues: (1) making sure that the narrative is more than a list of the details, in time sequence, and (2) avoiding short, choppy writing. When you study this revised draft, you will notice the many **transitions** that help create a seamless shift from one stage of the divorce announcement to another. You will also notice several places where **sentences** from the outline have been **combined** for smoother, more logical connections. Finally, using the exact words of **dialogue** in part of the story adds realistic detail. (You can assume the writer worked through several drafts prior to the current revised draft.)

Revised Draft of a Narrative Paragraph

(Note: Changes from the outline are underlined; editing and proofreading are still necessary to refine style and correct errors.)

When my parents announced that they divorcing, I felt confusing by all my emotions. <u>At the time</u> of their announcement, <u>I was seven and my sister was ten</u>. Both my parents were there to tell us. They told us at breakfast in the kitchen. <u>I was eating toast, but I remember I couldn't eat anything when they started talking. In fact</u>, I remember staring at a piece of toast with one bite taken out of it. My parents were very calm when they told us. <u>"We love both of you very much," my dad said "but your mother and I aren't getting along."</u> They said they would always love us. <u>The announcement was such a shock to me that I couldn't believe it was happening</u>. At first I just thought they were having another fight. <u>Because I was too young to understand I didn't cry. Suddenly, my sister started to cry, and then I knew it was serious</u>. I kept thinking I would have to chose which parent to live with. <u>I knew I'd really hurt the one I didn't choose, so I felt terrible guilt about hurting one of them</u>. I felt riped apart.

Margin labels:
- transition
- sentences combined
- sentences combined and transition added
- dialogue added
- sentences combined
- sentences combined and transition added
- sentences combined and transition added

Exercise 10   **Practice: Recognizing Transitions in a Narrative Paragraph**

Underline the transitions in the following paragraph.

A little time spent with my mom delivering meals to elderly people in the neighborhood made me realize that "man does not live by bread alone." My mother has always loved to help people, and I always thought it was neat that she brought meals to people in the neighborhood. Frequently, she would ask me to come along with her, but I usually found a good excuse—sports, friends, or homework—to avoid having to go along. Finally, I agreed. After picking up the meals at the food pantry, we drove from house to house delivering the meals. Initially, I had expected the people to grab the food and turn back into their homes. However, at every stop, the people asked us to come in for a visit. Each time, my mother apologized and stated that "things were too busy today," but she would certainly make the time next week. Every one of the people smiled and hugged her before we left.

Eventually my curiosity got the better of me, and I asked, "Why does everyone want to ask us into their homes? I mean, they got the food so why not just go and eat it?" My mother smiled, and then said, "Man does not live by bread alone."

Exercise 11 Practice: Adding the Right Transitions to a Narrative Paragraph

In the following paragraph, circle the correct transition in each of the pairs.

When /After I was ten, I had my first infatuation, which was a blend of elation and pain. My beloved was a singer on the Disney Channel, and I watched his performances faithfully. Now/ Soon I was recording the shows and rewatching them so the two of us "could spend more time together." Until/ Then I discovered his Web site, and my heart beat faster. Awkwardly aware of the age and distance between he and I, frequently /during I would study the boys in school to see who looked the most like him. The problem was that none of them did. As a result, I created elaborate fantasies in which my loved one met me and was immediately /still stricken with a burning love. These dreams sustained me through months of the ordinary days of a ten-year-old at school and home. Suddenly /Before my fantasies became nightmares. Pictures of my hero with a beautiful teenage girl began to appear online. The two seemed to be in love. At first /Always I was overcome by a sense of loss. Immediately/ Later my grief began to subside. However, I can finally/ still remember the strong and often terrible emotions of my fantasy romance.

EDITING AND PROOFREADING   NARRATION

After you have revised your narration, the next step is editing. At this point, you can look at grammatical structure, sentence length and structure, word forms, punctuation, and spelling. Once you have revised your draft, you can check it using the following list.

Checklist for Editing a Narrative Paragraph

✓ Are the verb forms correct and consistent?

✓ Are other grammatical structures correct?

✓ Can any sentences be combined?

✓ Did you correctly punctuate?

✓ Is everything spelled correctly?

Exercise 12   **Practice: Combining Sentences in a Draft of a Narrative**

The following paragraph contains some short, choppy sentences, which are underlined. Wherever you see two or more underlined sentences clustered next to each other, combine them into one clear, smooth sentence. Write your revised version of the paragraph in the spaces above the lines.

Mother Nature pulled me out of a dark mood this morning. I was driving to work in the rain during rush hour and I was checking my watch every two minutes. I began making a mental list of all my worries. In addition to being afraid of getting to work late, I was worried about being broke. My last credit card bill had been astronomical. I couldn't afford to get caught in a cycle. The cycle would be dangerous. The cycle would involve high interest rates and increasing debt. School was another worry. I had a quiz coming up in my accounting class. I was nervous about it. I was afraid that I wouldn't pass the quiz. All these fears and the frustration of a slow ride in heavy traffic made me feel that I was drowning in misery. Then I looked up. Beyond the rain was a beautiful sight. I saw a bright, clear rainbow. It curved across the horizon like an arch of glowing colors. I felt that the rainbow was a sign. The sign told me to be cheerful. Almost against my will, I began to feel better.

Final Version of Your Narrative Paragraph

The final version of your narrative paragraph should reflect your best writing efforts. In the sample that follows, notice the crucial role final proofreading plays in correcting errors.

Final Version of a Narrative Paragraph

(Note: Corrections from the previous draft are underlined.)

verb added: were ———

spelling corrected: confused

comma added ———

comma after *said* ———

When my parents announced that they <u>were</u> divorcing, I felt <u>confused</u> by all my emotions. At the time of their announcement, I was seven and my sister was ten. Both my parents were there to tell us. They told us at breakfast<u>,</u> in the kitchen. I was eating toast, but I remember I couldn't eat anything when they started talking. In fact, I remember staring at a piece of toast with one bite taken out of it. My parents were very calm when they told us. "We love both of you very much," my dad said<u>,</u> "but your mother and I aren't getting along." They said they would

(Continued)

comma added —————

comma added —————

spelling corrected: *choose* —

spelling corrected: *ripped* —

always love us. The announcement was such a shock to me that I couldn't believe it was happening. At first, I just thought they were having another fight. Because I was too young to understand, I didn't cry. Suddenly, my sister started to cry, and then I knew it was serious. I kept thinking I would have to <u>choose</u> which parent to live with. I knew I'd really hurt the one I didn't choose, so I felt terrible guilt about hurting one of them. I felt <u>ripped</u> apart.

> **For your information:** A sample narrative essay based on this topic and following the same writing steps can be found in Chapter 12, "Different Essay Patterns: Part One."

Exercise 13   **Practice: Proofreading to Prepare the Final Version**

The following narrative paragraph has the kinds of errors that are easy to overlook when you prepare the final version of an assignment. Correct the errors, writing above the lines. There are ten errors.

I discovered a new passion when a friend dragged me, to a lecture on the star's. I had no thing to do last Tuesday nite and my best friend texted me about a lecture at the college planetarium. It was an extra credit field trip and the teacher said he could bring a friend. I didn't want to spend the evening sitting in my room doing nothing, I decided to meet him there. Form the outside, the building was impressive. It had a curved dome and astrological signs lit up on the side of the building. Inside, we passed telescopes and cases with chunks of meteorites as we made our way to a Theater with stadium seating. When the lecture began, the lights dimmed, the speaker pressed a button, an the ceiling disappeared. A glass dome took it's place. Beyond it, we could see the stars; it looked like black paper with pin holes in it. Soon, the lecture began with a sound and light show, with thrilling music spectacular close-ups, and dramatic language. After the presentation, my friend and me left the building and immediately looked up at the night sky.

Lines of Detail: A Walk-Through Assignment

Write a paragraph about an incident in your life that embarrassed, amused, frightened, saddened, or angered you. In writing the paragraph, follow the following steps.

Step 1: Begin by freewriting. Then read your freewriting, looking for both the details and focus of your paragraph.

Step 2: Brainstorm for more details. Then write all the freewriting and brainstorming as a list.

Step 3: Survey your list. Write a topic sentence that makes a point about the details.

Step 4: Write an outline. As you write the outline, check that your details fit the topic sentence and are in clear order. As you revise your outline, add details where they are needed.

Step 5: Write and revise a draft of your paragraph. Revise until your details are specific and in a clear order and your transitions are smooth.

Step 6: Edit your latest draft for better style by combining choppy sentences.

Step 7: Prepare a clean copy, and proofread it carefully to spot and correct any careless errors in spelling, punctuation, format, or typing.

Topics for Writing a Narrative Paragraph

When you write on any of the following topics, be sure to work through the stages of the writing process in preparing your narrative paragraph.

1. Write about the kindest thing someone other than a family member has ever done for you. Begin by freewriting. Then read your freewriting, looking for both the details and the focus of your paragraph.

   Collaborate

   If your instructor agrees, ask a writing partner or group to (a) listen to you read your freewriting, (b) help you focus it, and (c) help you add details by asking questions.

2. Write a narrative paragraph about a mistake in judgement that you made about a person. Include how that mistake came about and how it proved to be a valuable lesson.

3. Interview an older family member or friend. Ask him or her to tell you an interesting story about his or her past. Ask questions as the person speaks. Take notes. If you have a phone, ask the person if you can record it or film it so that you can refer back to it during the drafting process for details.

   When you've finished the interview, review the information with the person you've interviewed. Ask the person if he or she would like to add anything. If you wish, ask follow-up questions.

   Next, on your own, find a point to the story or a perspective that considers how you now have a better understanding of the person. Work through the stages of the writing process to turn the interview into a narrative paragraph.

4. Visit the Web site of your local newspaper and find a news article about a crime that involved a sequence of events leading to a confrontation, arrest, or escape. Write the details of the story in time order, and be sure to use effective transitions. Your topic sentence should state what type of crime occurred as well as the outcome

of it. (As you take notes from the article, be aware that newspaper accounts are not written in time order, so you will have to do some reordering of events.) Include a copy of the article with your paragraph.

5. Consider the following photograph. Write a narrative about the moments leading up to, during, or after the scene depicted in the following photograph. Be sure to use specific details to bring life to your narrative.

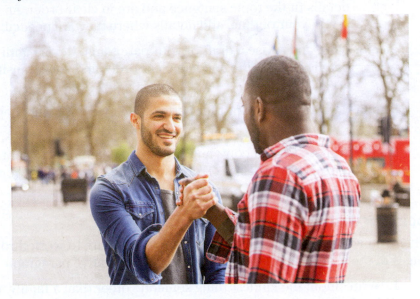

Topics for Critical Thinking and Writing

1. Becoming an adult is more than just an accumulation of years; it is a series of steps and understandings. Recall a specific event that you would consider to be one of the most important steps toward you becoming an adult. Write a narrative paragraph about this event, but write it from the perspective of someone close to you who would have been aware of the event and would have noticed the change. For example, how would a parent, sibling, or close friend describe the changes in you after you got a driver's license, your own apartment, or enrolled in college?

2. If your job involves dealing with the public, write a narrative about one of your best or worst experiences with a customer or client. Next, imagine that you are the customer, and write a narrative from his or her perspective that would develop after he or she has left your presence. Use the same verb tense and sequence of events for both versions. Share your narratives with your classmates to see which version they prefer.

> **Note:** Additional writing options suitable for narration-related assignments can be found in the "Readings for Writers" appendix at the end of this book.

Jumping In

*Finding the right apartment takes planning and careful investigation. What should you do before, during, and after the process to ensure a successful move? How would you share what you've learned about finding a great apartment? Understanding the steps in a **process** helps us share our experiences with others who face similar challenges.*

Learning Objectives

In this chapter, you will learn to:

1 Recognize the difference between directional and informational processes.

2 Prewrite to generate a topic for a process paragraph.

3 Write a process paragraph that uses transitions and correct grammatical person.

WHAT IS PROCESS?

1 Recognize the difference between directional and informational processes.

Process writing explains how to do something or describes how something happens or is done. When you tell the reader how to do something (a **directional process**), you speak directly to the reader, giving clear, specific instructions about performing some activity. Your purpose is to explain an activity so that a reader can do it. For example, you may have to leave instructions telling a new employee how to log in to a system or use the copier. A directional process uses the word *you*, or in the way it gives directions, the word *you* is understood.

When you describe how something happens or is done (an **informational process**), your purpose is to explain an activity without telling a reader how to do it. For example, you can explain how a boxer trains for a fight or how a special effect for a movie was created. Instead of speaking directly to the reader, an informational process speaks about *I*, *he*, *she*, *we*, *they*, or about a person by his or her name.

A Process Involves Steps in Time Order

Whether a process is directional or informational, it describes something that is done in steps, and these steps are in a specific order, a *time order*. The process can involve steps that are followed in minutes, hours, days, weeks, months, or even years. For example, the steps in changing a tire may take minutes, whereas the steps taken to lose ten pounds may take months.

You should keep in mind that a process involves steps that *must follow a certain order*, not just a range of activities that can be placed in any order. This sentence *signals a process:*

> Learning to post photos on social media is easy if you follow a few simple directions. (Sharing photos online involves following steps in order; that is, you cannot share anything until you have turned on the device you wish to use.)

This sentence *does not signal a process:*

> There are many options when it comes to finding affordable meals for college students. (Each option is separate; there is no time sequence here.)

Telling a person, in a conversation, how to do something or how something is done gives you the opportunity to add important points you may have overlooked or to throw in details you may have skipped at first. Your listener can ask questions if he or she does not understand you. Plus, you can read the listener's body language to see if he or she understands your communication. Writing a process, however, is more difficult. Your reader is not there to stop you, to ask you to explain further, or to question you. In writing a process, you must be organized, well-structured, and clear.

Hints for Writing a Process Paragraph

1. In choosing a topic, find an activity you know well. If you write about something familiar to you, you will have a clearer paragraph.

2. Choose a topic that includes steps that must be done in a specific time sequence.

> **not this:** I am pretty good at being productive on the weekends.
> **but this:** I have a system for using my time wisely on a weekend.

3. Choose a topic that is fairly small. A complicated process cannot be covered well in one paragraph. If your topic is too big, the paragraph can become vague, incomplete, or boring.

> **too big:** There are many steps to becoming a registered nurse.
> **smaller and manageable:** Will power and support were the most important elements in my struggle to quit smoking.

4. Write a topic sentence that makes a point. Your topic sentence should do more than announce. Like the topic sentence for any paragraph, it should have a point. As you plan the steps of your process and gather details, ask yourself some questions: What point do I want to make about this process? Is the process hard? Is it easy? Does the process require certain tools? Does the process require certain skills, like organization, patience, or endurance?

> **an announcement:** This paragraph is about how to change a shower fixture in your house.
> **a topic sentence:** You do not have to be a plumber to change the shower fixture in your bathroom, but you will need a few tools and some patience.

5. **Include all of the steps.** If you are explaining a process, you are writing for someone who does not know the process as well as you do. Keep in mind that what seems clear or simple to you may not be clear or simple to the reader, and be sure to tell what is needed before the process starts. For instance, what ingredients are needed to cook the dish? Or what tools are needed to assemble the furniture?

6. **Put the steps in the right order.** If you have ever been given poor directions, you know how frustrating that can be. Nothing is more irritating to a reader than trying to follow directions that skip back and forth because the writer did not have a clear picture of what he or she was saying. Careful planning, drafting, and revising can help you get the time sequence right.

7. **Be specific in the details and steps.** To be sure you have sufficient details and clear steps, keep your reader in mind. Put yourself in the reader's place. Could you follow your own directions or understand your steps? Are there some steps that are more serious (making sure to turn off the breaker when changing an electrical fixture) or more dangerous (connecting "positive" to "positive" when jumping a car battery) than the others?

If you remember that a process explains how to do something or how something is done, you will focus on being clear. Now that you know the purpose and strategies of writing a process, you can begin the prewriting stage.

Exercise 1   Practice: Recognizing Good Topic Sentences for Process Paragraphs

If a sentence is a good topic sentence for a process paragraph, put *OK* on the line provided. If a sentence has a problem, label that sentence with one of these letters:

> A This is an announcement; it makes no point.
> B This sentence covers a topic that is too big for one paragraph.
> S This sentence describes a topic that does not require steps.

1. _____   You can use a simple procedure to remove stains from a carpet.

2. _____   When I became a babysitter, I discovered a simple way of getting and holding a child's attention.

3. _____   This essay is about the way to wash a car so that it gleams in the sunshine.

4. _____   Many things contribute to giving a dynamic speech in front of a business organization.

5. _____ Selling items on e-Bay is a business that grew over several years.

6. _____ Finding the right Valentine's Day gift for a loved one demands some creative thinking and strategic shopping.

7. _____ Several tips can help you to get a good deal on a laptop.

8. _____ The process of training for a career in nursing is not for those without a true commitment to quality, compassionate care.

9. _____ How a security system in a twenty-four-hour food mart works is the subject of this paper.

10. _____ If you know how to bargain, you can get a good deal on used furniture at a garage sale.

Collaborate

Exercise 2 **Collaborate: Including Necessary Materials in a Process**

Two possible topics for a process paragraph follow. For each topic, work with a partner or a group and list the items (e.g., materials, ingredients, tools, utensils, supplies) the reader would have to gather before he or she began the process. When you've finished the exercise, compare your lists with another group's list to see if you've missed any items.

1. **topic:** giving your dog a bath

   needed items: _____

   _____

2. **topic:** gift wrapping an object

   needed items: _____

2 Prewrite to generate a topic for a process paragraph.

WRITING THE PROCESS PARAGRAPH IN STEPS

PREWRITING **PROCESS**

The easiest way to start writing a process paragraph is to pick a small topic, one that you can cover well in one paragraph. Then you can gather ideas by listing or freewriting or both.

If you decide to write about how to find the right apartment, you might begin by freewriting.

Then you might check your freewriting, looking for details that have to do with the process of finding an apartment. You can underline those details, as in the example that follows.

Freewriting for a Process Paragraph

Topic: Finding the right apartment

You have to <u>look around. Don't pick the first apartment you see</u>. Sean did that, and he ended up with a dump. <u>Look at a bunch</u>. But <u>not too many</u>, or you'll get confused. <u>The lease</u>, too. <u>Check it carefully. How much is the security deposit? How many bedrooms do you want? Friends can help</u> if they know of any nice apartments. I found my place that way. Maybe somebody you know lives in <u>a good neighborhood</u>. A <u>convenient location can be more expensive</u>. But <u>can save you money on transportation.</u>

Next, you can put what you've underlined into a list, in correct time sequence:

before the search

How many bedrooms do I want?
Friends can help.
a good neighborhood
A convenient location can be more expensive.
can save you money on transportation

during the search

look around
Don't pick the first apartment you see.
Look at a bunch.
not too many

after the search

Check the lease carefully.
How much is the security deposit?

Check the list. Are some details missing? Yes. A reader might ask, "What other ways (besides asking friends) can help you find apartments? What else should you do before you search? When you're looking at apartments, what should you be looking for? What questions should you ask? After the search, how do you decide which apartment is best? And what, besides the security deposit, should you check on the lease?" Answers to questions like these can give you the details needed to write a clear and interesting directional process.

CRITICAL THINKING

You do not need to be an expert in something to compose an excellent process paragraph. Just think about all the processes you go through each day!

Consider your own routines, your survival tips, or your strategies for attacking everyday chores and events!

Just ask yourself: what processes do I undergo on a daily basis? There are bound to be many.

Writing a Topic Sentence for a Process Paragraph

Freewriting and a list can now help you focus your paragraph by identifying the point of your process. You already know what the subject of your paragraph is: finding the right apartment. But what's the point? Is it easy to find the right apartment? Is it difficult? What does it take to find the right apartment?

Maybe a topic sentence could be

Finding the right apartment takes planning and careful investigation.

Once you have a topic sentence, you can think about adding details that explain your topic sentence and you can begin the planning stage of writing.

Exercise 3 **Practice: Finding the Steps of a Process in Freewriting**

Read the following freewriting, then reread it, looking for all the words, phrases, or sentences that relate to steps. Underline all those items. Then once you've underlined the freewriting, put what you've underlined into a list of specific steps.

How to Cut Back on Complaining: Freewriting

Cut back? Wouldn't it be better just to stop complaining? Everybody complains. Maybe it's impossible to stop complaining. After you've started counting complaints, notice what you complain about. Decide that you will make a conscious effort to reduce the number of times you complain. Start by noticing how often you complain. Next, focus on changing your conversations. As soon as you hear yourself starting to complain, change the subject or cut off your whining. Try to shift your dark mood to a lighter one. It's tough to shift from a negative attitude to a positive one; you may feel a little bit phony. However, if you focus on the positive, you'll eventually feel better and make others feel better, too.

Your List of Steps in Time Sequence

1. _____

_____

2. _____

_____

3. _____

_____

4. _____

_____

5. _____

_____

6. _____

_____

7. _____

_____

PLANNING **PROCESS**

Using the freewriting and topic sentence on finding an apartment, you can make an outline. Then you can revise it, checking the topic sentence and the list of details, improving them where you think they could be better. A revised outline on finding the right apartment is shown.

CRITICAL THINKING

Process paragraphs need to include *what* and *how* for each *when*. Example:

The *when*: Before the search
The *what*: Decide what you want.
The *how*: Check the advertisements.

Outline for a Process Paragraph

topic sentence	Finding the apartment you want takes planning and careful investigation.
details	Decide what you want.
	Ask yourself, "Do I want a one-bedroom?" "What can I afford?"
	A convenient location can be expensive.
before the search	It can also save you money on transportation.
	Friends can help you with names of nice apartments.
	Maybe somebody you know lives in a good neighborhood.
	Check the advertisements in the newspapers and online.
	Look around.
	Don't pick the first apartment you see.
	Look at several.
	But don't look at too many.
during the search	Check the cleanliness, safety, plumbing, and appliances of each one.
	Ask the manager about the laundry room, additional storage, parking facilities, and maintenance policies.
	Compare the two best places you saw.
after the search	Consider the price, location, and condition of the apartments.
	Check the leases carefully.
	Check the requirements for first and last month's rent deposits.

The following checklist may help you revise an outline for your own process paragraph.

Checklist for Revising a Process Outline

✓ Is my topic sentence focused on some point about the process?

✓ Does it cover the whole process?

✓ Do I have all of the steps?

✓ Are they in the right order?

✓ Have I explained the steps clearly?

✓ Do I need better details?

Exercise 4   **Practice: Revising the Topic Sentence in a Process Outline**

The topic sentence that follows doesn't cover all the steps of the process. Read the outline several times; then write a topic sentence that covers all the steps of the process and has a point.

topic sentence: You can train your dog to sit and stay.

details: First, put your dog on a leash and lead it outside.

Go to a grassy space that is away from distractions and loud noises.

Stand in front of your dog and then kneel down so that you are face to face with it.

Put one hand under the collar and the other on the dog's rear end just above the tail.

Speak in a positive, soothing way to the dog.

Gently, but firmly, push down on the dog's rear while pushing back and slightly up with the collar hand.

Use the command *SIT* with a firm voice. Don't ask, tell.

Hold the dog in that sitting position for about five to ten seconds while you repeat the command sit.

Say *OK* and allow the dog to stand up again. Praise the dog.

Repeat this process in brief sessions (five times in a row) approximately four times a day.

Once the dog sits without the pressure on the collar or rear end, switch to giving the command while the dog is walking beside you on the leash. A slight tension on the leash upward might be necessary.

State the commands firmly and always praise success.

revised topic sentence: _____

_____

_____

Exercise 5   **Practice: Revising the Order of Steps in a Process Outline**

The steps in each outline are out of order. Put numbers in the spaces provided, indicating what step should be first, second, and so on.

1. topic sentence: Whenever my brother sits down to study, he gets sidetracked in a process that defeats him.

details: _____   As he places his books, a notebook, pencils, and his laptop on the table, he seems focused and serious.

_____   Mike starts the process with good intentions.

_____ His first mistake is to turn on his computer before he looks at his textbooks or checks his assignments.

_____ Once his laptop is on, Mike does a quick check of his e-mail.

_____ The quick check of the e-mail takes time because Mike is popular.

_____ Checking the e-mail leads Mike to deleting some of the e-mail and replying to most of it.

_____ Once Mike has finished dealing with his e-mail, he makes his second big mistake.

_____ By the time he has checked his Facebook and shared a few more with his friends, an hour has passed.

_____ The second mistake is his decision to check his social media.

_____ After an hour of sitting at his desk, Mike feels hungry.

_____ He decides to head to the kitchen to check out his snacking options.

_____ Most of the time, Mike decides to eat his snack in front of the television, and he never gets around to studying.

2. topic sentence: Sal's Sports Center has survived for twenty years because Sal, the owner, has a perfect system for making his customers feel free to roam but never ignored.

details: _____ A bell rings as soon as a customer enters Sal's Sports Center.

_____ Most customers say, "No thanks; I'm just looking around."

_____ Once he hears the bell, Sal approaches and says, "Can I help you with anything?"

_____ Sal knows how to respond to "No thanks"; he just goes back to the counter and leaves the customer to roam the aisles.

_____ Usually, Sal's customers, grateful for his relaxed attitude, leave with a purchase.

_____ Every ten or fifteen minutes, Sal walks through the store, stocking or straightening the shelves.

_____ "Have a great day!" Sal says, as another satisfied customer leaves with a purchase.

_____ On these periodic trips, Sal is available to answer questions or give help, but he never pushes himself on a shopper.

Exercise 6   **Practice: Listing All of the Steps in an Outline**

Following are two topic sentences for process paragraphs. Write all the steps needed to complete an outline for each sentence. After you've listed all the steps, number them in the correct time order.

1. **topic sentence:** You can make restaurant-quality garlic bread at home with a few simple ingredients, some basic kitchen supplies, and very little skill.

steps: _____

_____

_____

_____

_____

_____

_____

_____

_____

_____

_____

_____

_____

_____

_____

_____

_____

_____

2. **topic sentence:** When attending a free outdoor concert with small children, a few simple steps will help you to make the most of the event.

steps: _____

_____

_____

_____

_____

_____

_____

_____

_____

DRAFTING AND REVISING   **PROCESS**

You can take the outline and write it in paragraph form, and you'll have a first draft of the process paragraph. As you write the first draft, you can combine some of the short sentences from the outline. Then you can review your draft and revise it for organization, details, and clarity.

 3 Write a process paragraph that uses transitions and correct grammatical person.

CRITICAL THINKING

As you organize, draft, and revise your paragraph, consider how your reader might feel about the topic and the process you are conveying. If the topic is about getting your first apartment or changing the oil in your car, the reader may be experiencing some anxiety. Keep your audience in mind and ensure that you have included all the necessary steps to confidently and safely complete the process.

Using Transitions Effectively

As you revise your draft, you can add transitions. Transitions are particularly important in a process paragraph because you are trying to show the steps in a *specific sequence*, and you are trying to show the *connections* between steps. Effective transitions will also keep your paragraph from sounding like a choppy, boring list.

Following is a list of some of the time transitions you can use in writing a process paragraph. Be sure that you use transitional words and phrases only when it is logical to do so, and try not to overuse the same transitions in a paragraph.

INFO BOX   Transitions for a Process Paragraph

after	during	last	the second step, etc.
afterward	eventually	later	then
as	finally	meanwhile	to begin
as he (or she) is	first	next	to start
as soon as	second, etc.	now	until
as you are	first of all	quickly	when
at last	gradually	sometimes	whenever
at the same time	in the beginning	soon	while
before	immediately	suddenly	while I am …
begin by	initially	the first step	

When you write a process paragraph, you must pay particular attention to clarity. As you revise, keep thinking about your audience to be sure your steps are easy to follow. The following checklist can help you revise your draft.

> ## Checklist for Revising a Process Paragraph
>
> ✓   Does the topic sentence cover the whole paragraph?
>
> ✓   Does the topic sentence make a point about the process?
>
> ✓   Is any important step left out?
>
> ✓   Should any step be explained further?
>
> ✓   Are the steps in the right order?
>
> ✓   Have I used transitions effectively?

Exercise 7   **Practice: Revising Transitions in a Process Paragraph**

The transitions in this paragraph could be better. Rewrite the underlined transitions directly above each one so that the transitions are smoother.

Walking in snow or on icy walkways can be treacherous if you're not prepared and vigilant. <u>First</u>, wear sensible footwear. "Sensible" means shoes or boots with some traction on the soles, not flip-flops or high heels. <u>Second</u>, as you walk, concentrate on walking. That is, don't be distracted by your phone or your worries. Focus on the process of walking on slippery terrain by taking short, sturdy steps. <u>Third</u>, be careful about hazards such as steps, curbs, or piles where someone has shoveled or pushed the snow. <u>Fourth</u>, look ahead for patches of ice that can lead you into a sudden slide onto your knees or back. <u>Fifth</u>, do not let down your guard until you are safely indoors in a dry, not slippery, hallway or room. <u>Six</u>, you can relax and take off your winter boots.

A Revised Draft

The following is a revised draft of the process paragraph on finding an apartment. This draft has more details than the outline on page 107, and you can assume that the writer has worked through several drafts already. You may see that new transitions and additional details make this directional process authoritative and complete. (You may also notice that this revised draft still has a few spelling and grammatical errors that can be corrected during the editing and proofreading stage.)

Revised Draft of a Process Paragraph

(Note: Changes from the outline are underlined; editing and proofreading are still necessary.)

transition added ——————

Finding the apartment you want takes planning and investigation. <u>First of all</u>, you must decide what you want. Ask yourself, "Do I want a added detail and transition ———— one-bedroom apartment?" or "<u>Do I want a studio apartment?</u>" <u>Most important</u>, ask yourself, "What can I afford?" <u>A convenent location can be expen-</u>

added detail and transition ———— <u>sive. On the other hand, that location can save you money on transportation</u>. <u>Before</u> I start looking for a place, do some research. Freinds can help you with the names of nice apartments. Be sure to check the advertisements in the newspaper and

transition added ———— online. <u>Once</u> you begin your search, don't pick the first place you see. You should look at several

detail added ———— places. But <u>looking at too many can make your search confusing</u>. Just remember to check each apartment's clean, safety, plumbing, and appli-

transition added ———— ances. <u>Then</u> ask the manager about the laundry room, additional storage, parking facility, and

transition added ———— maintenance policies. <u>After</u> you've completed your search, compare the two best places you saw. Consider each one's price, location, and condition.

detail added ———— Carefully checking each lease, <u>studying the amount of the security</u> deposit, the deposit for first

detail added ———— and last months' rent, <u>and the rules for tenants</u>. When you've completed your comparison, you're ready to chose the apartment you want.

Using the Same Grammatical Person

Remember that the *directional* process speaks directly to the reader, calling him or her *you*. Sentences in a directional process use the word *you*, or they imply it.

> **directional:** *You* need a flathead screwdriver to get started. Begin by making a list. (*You* is implied in the second sentence.)

Remember that the *informational* process involves somebody doing the process. Sentences in an informational process use words like *I*, *we*, *he*, *she*, *they*, or a person's name.

> **informational:** *Chip* needed a flathead screwdriver to get started. First, *I* can make a list.

One common error found in process papers is shifting from describing how someone did something to telling someone how to do an activity. You must decide whether your process paragraph will be directional or informational.

In grammar, the words *I* and *we* are considered to be in the *first person. You* is in the *second person*, and *he, she, it*, and *they* are in the *third person*. If these words refer to one, they are *singular*; if they refer to more than one, they are *plural*. It is important to keep both the "person" and the "number" consistent in your piece of writing. An error in this structure is called a **shift in person** or **shift in number**. The following list may help you remember singular and plural subject pronouns:

> **INFO BOX** A List of Subject Pronouns
>
> | | |
> |---|---|
> | First person singular: | I |
> | Second person singular: | you |
> | Third person singular: | he, she, it, or a person's name |
> | First person plural: | we |
> | Second person plural: | you |
> | Third person plural: | they, or the names of more than one person |

Examples of a shift in person and a shift in number follow; study how each shift is corrected.

shift in person: After *I* preheat the oven to 350 degrees, *I* mix the egg whites and sugar with an electric mixer set at high speed. *Mix* until stiff peaks form. Then *I* put the mixture in small mounds on an ungreased cookie sheet. If the oven is ready, *put* the cookie sheet in the oven. ("Mix until stiff peaks form" and "put the cookie sheet in the oven" are a shift to the *you* person.)

shift corrected: After *I* preheat the oven to 350 degrees, *I* mix the egg whites and sugar with an electric mixer set at high speed. *I* mix until stiff peaks form. Then *I* put the mixture in small mounds on an ungreased cookie sheet. If the oven is ready, *I* put the cookie sheet in the oven.

shift in number: *A salesperson* has to be careful when a customer tries on clothes. *The clerk* can't hint that a suit may be a size too small. *They* can insult a customer with a hint like that. (The sentences shifted from singular, "a salesperson" and "a clerk," to plural, "they.")

shift corrected: *A salesperson* has to be careful when customers try on clothes. *The clerk* can't hint that a suit may be a size too small. *He or she* can insult a customer with a hint like that.

EDITING AND PROOFREADING PROCESS

After you have revised your process paragraph, the next step is editing.

At this point, you can check grammatical structure, sentence length, word form, punctuation, and spelling. Once you have edited your draft, you can double-check it using the following list.

> **Checklist for Editing a Process Paragraph**
>
> ✓ Are the verb forms correct and consistent?
>
> ✓ Have you used the same person throughout the paragraph to describe the process?
>
> ✓ Have you used the same number with your pronouns?
>
> ✓ Should any sentences be combined?
>
> ✓ Did you punctuate correctly?
>
> ✓ Is everything spelled correctly?

Exercise 8 **Practice: Correcting Shifts in Person in a Process Paragraph**

A paragraph that shifts from being an informational to a directional process in several places follows. Those places are underlined. Rewrite the underlined parts directly above the original ones so that the whole paragraph is an informational process.

My sister Colleen has a system for getting the most out of a bottle of shampoo. As soon as she stands in the shower and opens a new bottle of shampoo, she is careful to pour only a tiny portion of the liquid into the palm of her hand. She knows the temptation to slap a huge glop of shampoo right onto your head. Pouring on the shampoo is wasteful, and it also saturates her hair with too many soapy suds. Colleen carefully takes the liquid from the palm of her hand and smears it onto the top of her head. Then she carefully adds a little water to the shampoo on her head. Now you can massage the mixture into her hair and scalp. She doesn't waste shampoo or water on a rinse followed by a second shampooing. Instead, she simply rinses her hair thoroughly once. Then you cap the shampoo so that it will not drip or collect dripping water. Next, you must place the shampoo bottle in a safe part of the shower so that the bottle will not fall, pop open, and leak. When she is near the end of her bottle of shampoo, add a little water to the bottle and you can get enough shampoo to last a week or more.

Exercise 9 **Practice: Combining Sentences in a Process Paragraph**

The following paragraph has many short, choppy sentences, which are underlined. Wherever you see two or more underlined sentences clustered next to each other, combine them into one clear, smooth sentence. Write your revised versions of those sentences in the space above the original.

My dog has a clever way of telling me that she needs a bedtime visit outdoors. First, her bedtime is not my bedtime. If it were, my dog's system for getting outside would not be necessary. However, my dog gets restless about half an hour before I want to turn off the television and go to bed. Her routine always begins at the same time. I am watching a contest or a drama. It is about to reach its peak. Just as the winner is about to be announced or the criminal exposed, my dog begins to stir. She wakes up from her nap. <u>She has been dozing on the couch. She begins to look around</u>. This is my first clue that my dog is nearly ready to travel outdoors. <u>Soon, she begins licking my hand. She also licks my face</u>. When these forms of persuasion do not work, she resorts to her final tactic. <u>She jumps onto the floor. Then she starts to moan</u>. Now I begin to think that she needs to go outside immediately. When I open the door to the backyard, my dog runs out happily. <u>She sniffs the bushes. She explores the area beneath the trees. She checks for any animal intruders</u>. Finally, she relieves herself and runs inside for her nighttime dog biscuit. While I have been waiting at the open door and have missed the climax of the television show, my dog has gotten just what she wanted.

Preparing Your Final Version

After you have edited your latest draft, prepare a clean copy and proofread it carefully. Reading your paragraph aloud can help you identify and correct any careless errors in punctuation and spelling, and you may even catch some missing words or typos. Your goal is to make your work error free. As you review the sample final version, compare these editing and proofreading changes to the draft on pages 112–113.

- *Convenient* is now spelled correctly.
- Sentences are now combined in two places.
- Subject pronoun *I* is replaced by *you* for pronoun consistency.
- *Friends* is now spelled correctly.
- *Cleanliness* now appears instead of the incorrect *clean*.
- *Facilities* is now in the plural form.
- *Check* is now in the correct verb form.
- *Choose* is now spelled correctly.

Final Version of a Process Paragraph

(Note: Changes from editing and proofreading are underlined.)

Finding the apartment you want takes planning and investigation. First of all, you must decide what you want. Ask yourself, "Do I want a one-bedroom apartment?" or "Do I want a studio apartment?" Most important, ask yourself, "What can I afford?" A <u>convenient location can be expensive; on the other hand, that location can save you money on transportation</u>. Before <u>you</u> start looking for a place, do some research. <u>Friends</u> can help you with the names of apartments. Be sure to check the advertisements in the newspaper and online. Once you begin your search, don't pick the first place you see. <u>You should look at several places, but looking at too many can make your search confusing</u>. Just remember to check each apartment's <u>cleanliness</u>, safety, plumbing, and appliances. Then ask the manager about the laundry room, additional storage, parking <u>facilities</u>, and maintenance policies. After you've completed your search, compare the two best places you saw.

Consider each one's price, location, and condition. Carefully <u>check</u> each lease, studying the amount of the security deposit, the deposit for first and last months' rent, and the rules for tenants. When you've completed your comparison, you're ready to <u>choose</u> the apartment you want.

> **For your information:** A sample process essay based on this topic and following the same writing steps can be found in Chapter 12, "Different Essay Patterns: Part One."

Exercise 10   **Practice: Proofreading to Prepare the Final Paragraph**

The following process paragraph has the kind of errors it is easy to overlook when you prepare the final version of an assignment. Correct the errors, writing above the lines. There are nine errors in the paragraph.

Sooner or later, every one gets a cold, so I dealing with a cold by preparing for it,and accepting it. To prepare for a cold, I stock up on supplies. I make sure that I have tea, honey, and chicken noodle soup in my kitchen When I feel a cold begining, I decide to give in to it. Instead of trying to endure my stuffy head, sneezing, and general misery at work and school; I stay home. I can sleep as long as I need to, and I can sneeze without spreading my germs at work or in class. Once I get out of bed, I do not force myself to eat when I feel sick. Instead, I do what I can to make myself feel comftable. I lay on the couch, and cover my self with a blanket. I watch videos or television Until I fall asleep again. If I am feeling energetic, I get up to make myself some soothing tea with honey or a bowl of soup.

Lines of Detail: A Walk-Through Assignment

Your assignment is to write a paragraph on how to plan a special day. Follow these steps:

Step 1: Focus on one special day. If you want to, you can begin by using your own experience. Ask yourself such questions as, Have I ever planned a birthday party? A baby or wedding shower? A surprise party? A picnic? A reunion? A barbecue? A celebration of a religious holiday? Have I ever seen anyone else plan such a day? If so, how would you teach a reader about planning for such a day?

Step 2: Once you have picked the day, freewrite. Write anything you can remember about the day and how you or someone else planned it.

Step 3: When you've completed the freewriting, read it. Underline all the details that refer to steps in planning that event. List the underlined details in time order.

Step 4: Add to the list by brainstorming some essential and related questions. Ask yourself questions that can lead to more details. For example, if an item on your list is "Send out invitations early," ask questions like "How early?" and "How do you decide whom to invite?"

Step 5: Survey your expanded list. Then write a topic sentence that makes some point about your planning for this special day. To reach a point, think of questions like these: "What makes a plan successful?" or "If you are planning for a special day (birthday, barbecue, surprise party, and so forth), what must you remember?"

Step 6: Use the topic sentence to prepare an outline. Be sure that the steps in the outline are in the correct time order.

Step 7: Write a draft of the paragraph and revise it extensively, adding and reordering details as necessary. Work through several drafts if necessary.

Step 8: Edit your draft for better style by combining sentences and using effective transitions.

Step 9: Prepare a clean copy, and proofread carefully; correct any careless errors in spelling, punctuation, typing, or format.

Topics for Writing a Process Paragraph

When you write on one of these topics, be sure to work through the stages of the writing process in preparing your process paragraph. Also, be sure to write from your own experience.

1. Write a *directional* or *informational process* about one of these topics:

preparing for an essay
   test
participating in a cultural
   ritual
cleaning a kitchen
video chatting online
preparing your favorite
   meal
avoiding social media while
   out with friends

getting out of the house efficiently
   in the morning
setting up a social-networking
   account
performing a family ritual
setting up a good workout
   schedule and program
efficiently doing your laundry
   at a laundromat
preparing for a job interview

2. Write about the worst (or best) way to pick a college to attend. Try to generate ideas from your personal experience or the stories that you have heard from peers.

3. Interview one of the counselors at your college. Ask the counselor to tell you the best steps for deciding on a major. Take notes or record the interview.

    After the interview, write a paragraph explaining the process for selecting a college major. Your explanation is directed at a freshman in college.

4. Interview someone who you know has many responsibilities and yet always seems to manage his or her time wisely. Ask that person to tell you the steps involved in prioritizing responsibilities and organizing his or her day. Take notes or tape the interview. After the interview, make a list of *your* responsibilities and compare these with the tasks of the person you interviewed. Next, write a paragraph explaining how to create a schedule or daily planning system that would work best for you.

5. Make a couple of visits to your college's cafeteria (once during peak hours and once during a lull) and examine both the food options and the traffic patterns that seem to occur. Understanding that you cannot always eat during a lull, write a paragraph that explains the most-efficient process for getting the food items you need during peak hours. Your paragraph should be addressed to an incoming student.

6. Examine the photograph of the basketball player, and then write a paragraph on how an athlete can focus his or her concentration for maximum benefit.

Topics for Critical Thinking and Writing

1. What steps do you follow when you decide to purchase a new piece of technology such as a phone, tablet, or laptop? Do you consult others to help you make a choice? Do you seek information that will clarify your choices and help you weigh the pros and cons of your options? Have you made purchases impulsively, leading you to believe that you should follow a clearer process? Identify the steps involved in your decision making and write a process paragraph about a recent technology purchase you have made since becoming an adult. Be sure to provide specific details for each of the steps you cover, including why or how you undertook each step.

2. Many students have to commute to college. Your daily commute to school can be restful or a bit hectic. Recall two different commuting options (car, bus, carpool, walk, or bike) and the route/course that each takes you from your usual point of departure to your classroom. Make two lists—one for a commute that goes as expected, and one for a commute that is the result of some difficulty or chaos that has come into your day—that take the reader on a step-by-step process of you getting to class. Then write a process paragraph detailing the commute from point A to point Z. For each paragraph, have the same reader in mind (for example, your professor or the person that helped create the difficulty).

> **Note:** Additional writing options suitable for process-related assignments can be found in the "Readings for Writers" appendix at the end of this book.

Comparison and Contrast

CHAPTER 6

Jumping In

*Clearly, there are differences between commuting to work or school on a bicycle or in a car. Can you think of several differences? Are there any similarities? Examining similarities and differences is a way of **comparing** and **contrasting**.*

Learning Objectives

In this chapter, you will learn to:

1. Recognize the difference between comparing and contrasting.
2. Organize your comparison or contrast paragraph subject by subject or point by point.
3. Prewrite to generate a topic for a comparison or contrast paragraph.
4. Write a comparison or contrast paragraph using either a point-by-point or subject-by-subject pattern.

WHAT IS COMPARISON? WHAT IS CONTRAST?

1. Recognize the difference between comparing and contrasting.

To **compare** means to point out *similarities*. To **contrast** means to point out *differences. When you compare or contrast, you need to come to some conclusion.* It's not enough to say, "These two things are similar" or "They are different." Your reader will be asking, "So what? What's your point?" You may be showing the differences between two restaurants to explain which is the better buy:

If you like Mexican food, you can go to either Café Mexicana or Juanita's, but Juanita's has lower prices.

Or you may be explaining the similarities between two family members to explain how people with similar personalities can clash.

My cousin Bill and my brother Karram are both so stubborn they can't get along.

Hints for Writing a Comparison or Contrast Paragraph

1. Limit your topic. When you write a comparison or contrast paragraph, you might think that the easiest topics to write about are broad ones with many similarities or differences. However, if you make your topic too large, you will not be able to cover it well, and your paragraph will be full of large, boring statements.

Here are some topics that are too large for a comparison or contrast paragraph: two countries, two periods in history, two kinds of addiction, two wars, two economic or political systems, two presidents.

2. Avoid the obvious topic. Some people think it is easier to write about two items if the similarities or differences between them are obvious; but with an obvious topic, you will have nothing new to say, and you will risk writing a boring paragraph.

Here are some obvious topics: the differences between high school and college, the similarities between *Game of Thrones* and *Vikings*. If you are drawn to an obvious topic, *try a new angle* on the topic. Write about the unexpected, using the same topic. Write about the similarities between high school and college, or the differences between *Game of Thrones* and *Vikings*. You may have to do more thinking before you come up with ideas, but your ideas may be more interesting to write about and to read.

CRITICAL THINKING

Comparing and contrasting often involves evaluating the positive and negative features of two different but similar items or concepts. When evaluating, be sure to make word choices that carry strong meanings, such as *reliable*, *loyal*, *committed*, and *passionate*.

3. Make your point in the topic sentence of your comparison or contrast paragraph. Indicate whether the paragraph is about similarities or differences in a topic sentence like this:

Because he is so reliable and loyal, Michael is a much better friend to me than Stefan. (The phrase "much better" indicates differences.)
My two biology teachers share a love of the environment and a passion for protecting it. (The word "share" indicates similarities.)

4. Do not announce in the topic sentence. The sentences that follow are announcements, not topic sentences.

This paper will explain the similarities between my two biology teachers.
Let me tell you how Michael is a different kind of friend than Stefan.

5. Make sure your topic sentence has a focus. It should indicate similarities or differences; it should focus on the specific kind of comparison or contrast you will make.

> **not focused:** My old house and my new one are different.
> **focused:** My new home is bigger, brighter, and more comfortable than my old one.

6. In the topic sentence, cover both subjects to be compared or contrasted.

> **covers only one subject:** The beach at Santa Lucia was dirty and crowded.
> **covers both subjects:** The beach at Santa Lucia was dirty and crowded, but the beach at Fisher Bay was clean and private.

Be careful. It is easy to get so carried away by the details of your paragraph that you forget to put both subjects into one sentence.

> **Exercise 1** Practice: Identifying Suitable Topic Sentences for a Comparison or Contrast Paragraph

Following is a list of possible topic sentences for a comparison or contrast paragraph. Some would make good topic sentences. The ones that wouldn't make good topic sentences have one or more of these problems: they are announcements, they don't indicate whether the paragraph will be about similarities or differences, they don't focus on the specific kind of comparison or contrast to be made, they cover subjects that are too big to write about in one paragraph, or they don't cover both subjects.

Mark the problem sentences with an *X*. If a sentence would make a good topic sentence for a comparison or contrast paragraph, mark it *OK*.

1. _____ Both expensive jeans and bargain-priced jeans appeal to a wide range of ages, offer a variety of styles, and can be worn almost anywhere.

2. _____ Driving in heavy rain and driving in heavy snow require similar precautions.

3. _____ On the one hand, there are Hollywood movies; on the other, there are Bollywood movies.

4. _____ Child actors and child singers can become rich, famous, and loved by audiences.

5. _____ Online shopping gives you more choice and bigger savings, without the crowd.

6. _____ Forest Park College and Richmond State College have demanding academic programs, caring teachers, and various extracurricular activities.

7. _____ This essay will discuss the similarities between my first summer job and my first summer at band camp.

8. _____ Bollywood and Hollywood movies are dramatic, entertaining, and extremely popular around the world.

9. _____ On the one hand, there are expensive jeans; on the other hand, there are bargain-priced jeans.

10. _____ Texting is more convenient, saves more time, and is less of an interruption than phoning.

② Organize your comparison or contrast paragraph subject by subject or point by point.

Organizing Your Comparison or Contrast Paragraph

Whether you decide to write about similarities (to compare) or differences (to contrast), you will have to decide how to organize your paragraph. You can choose between two patterns of organization: subject by subject or point by point.

Subject-by-Subject Organization In the subject-by-subject pattern, you support and explain your topic sentence by first writing all your details on one subject and then writing all your details on the other subject. If you choose a subject-by-subject pattern, be sure to discuss the points for your second subject *in the same order* as you did for the first subject. For example, if your first subject is an amusement park, and you cover (1) the price of admission, (2) the long lines at rides, and (3) the quality of the rides, when you discuss the second subject, another amusement park, you should write about its prices, lines, and quality of rides *in the same order*.

Look carefully at the outline and comparison paragraph that follow for a subject-by-subject pattern.

Comparison Outline: Subject-by-Subject Pattern

topic sentence

Once I realized that my brother and my mother are very much alike in temperament, I realized why they don't get along.

details

subject 1, James—temper

My brother James is a hot-tempered person.
It is easy for him to lose control of his temper.

unkind words

When he does, he often says things he later regrets.

stubbornness

James is also very stubborn.
In an argument, he will never admit he is wrong.
Once we were arguing about baseball scores.
Even when I showed him the right score printed in the paper, he wouldn't admit he was wrong.
He said the newspaper had made a mistake.
James's stubbornness overtakes his common sense.
James has inherited many of his character traits from our mother.

subject 2, mother—temper

She has a quick temper, and anything can provoke it.
Once, she got angry because she had to wait too long at a traffic light.

unkind words

She also has a tendency to use unkind words when she's mad.

stubbornness

She never backs down from a disagreement or concedes she was wrong.
My mother even quit a job because she refused to admit she'd made a mistake in taking inventory.
Her pride can lead her into foolish acts.
After I realized how similar my brother and mother are, I understood how such inflexible people are likely to clash.

Comparison Paragraph: Subject-by-Subject Pattern

subject 1,
James—temper

unkind words

stubbornness

subject 2,
mother—temper

unkind words

stubbornness

Once I realized that my brother and my mother are very much alike in temperament, I realized why they don't get along. My brother James is a hot-tempered person. It is easy for him to lose control of his temper, and when he does, he often says things he regrets. James is also very stubborn. In an argument, he will never admit he is wrong. I remember one time when we were arguing about baseball scores. Even when I showed him the right scores printed in the newspaper, he wouldn't admit he was wrong. James insisted that the newspaper must have made a mistake in printing the score. As this example shows, sometimes James's stubbornness overtakes his common sense. It took me a while to realize that my stubborn brother James has inherited many of his traits from our mother. Like James, she has a quick temper, and almost anything can provoke it. She once got angry because she had to wait too long at a traffic light. She also shares James's habit of saying unkind things when she's angry. And just as James refuses to back down when he's wrong, my mother will never back down from a disagreement or concede she's wrong. In fact, my mother once quit a job because she refused to admit she'd made a mistake in taking inventory. Her pride is as powerful as James's pride, and it can be just as foolish. After I realized how similar my mother and brother are, I understood how such inflexible people are likely to clash.

Look carefully at the paragraph in the subject-by-subject pattern, and you'll notice the following:

- It begins with a topic sentence about both subjects—James and his mother.
- It gives all the details about one subject—James.
- It then gives all the details about the second subject—his mother, in the same order.

Point-by-Point Organization   In the point-by-point pattern, you support and explain your topic sentence by discussing each point of comparison or contrast, switching back and forth between your subjects. You explain one point for each subject, then explain another point for each subject, and so on.

Look carefully at the outline and the comparison paragraph that follows for the point-by-point pattern.

Comparison Outline: Point-by-Point Pattern

topic sentence

Once I realized that my brother and my mother are very much alike in temperament, I realized why they don't get along.

details

point 1, temper James and mother

My brother James is a hot-tempered person.
It is easy for him to lose control of his temper.
My mother has a quick temper, and anything can provoke it.
Once she got angry because she had to wait too long at a traffic light.

point 2, unkind words James and mother

When my brother gets mad, he often says things he regrets.
My mother has a tendency to use unkind words when she's mad.
James is very stubborn.
In an argument, he will never admit he is wrong.
Once we were arguing about baseball scores.
Even when I showed him the right score printed in the newspaper, he wouldn't admit he was wrong.
He said the newspaper had made a mistake.

point 3, stubbornness James and mother

James's stubbornness overtakes his common sense.
My mother will never back down from a disagreement or admit she is wrong.
She even quit a job because she refused to admit she'd made a mistake in taking inventory.
She was foolish in her stubbornness.
After I realized how similar my mother and brother are, I understood how such inflexible people are likely to clash.

Comparison Paragraph: Point-by-Point Pattern

point 1, temper James and mother

point 2, unkind words James and mother

point 3, stubbornness James and mother

Once I realized that my brother and my mother are very much alike in temperament, I realized why they don't get along. My brother is a hot-tempered person, and it is easy for him to lose control of his temper. My mother shares James's quick temper, and anything can provoke her anger. Once, she got angry because she had to wait too long at a traffic light. When my brother gets mad, he often says things he regrets. Similarly, my mother is known for the unkind things she's said in anger. James is a very stubborn person. In an argument, he will never admit he's wrong. I can remember one argument we were having over baseball scores. Even when I showed him the right score printed in the newspaper, he wouldn't admit he had been wrong. He simply insisted the paper had made a mistake. At times like that, James's stubbornness overtakes his common sense. Like her son, my mother will never back down from an argument or admit she was wrong. She even quit a job because she refused to admit she'd made a mistake in taking inventory. In that case, her stubbornness was as foolish as James's. It took me a while to see the similarities between my brother and mother. Yet after I realized how similar these two people are, I understood how two inflexible people are likely to clash.

Look carefully at the paragraph in the point-by-point pattern, and you'll note that it

- begins with a topic sentence about both subjects—James and his mother;
- discusses how both James and his mother are alike in these points: their quick tempers, the unkind remarks they make when they are angry, and their often foolish stubbornness;
- switches back and forth between the two subjects.

The subject-by-subject and point-by-point patterns can be used for either a comparison or contrast paragraph. But whatever pattern you choose, remember these hints.

1. Be sure to use the same points to compare or contrast two subjects. If you are contrasting two cars, you can't discuss the price and safety features of one, then the styling and speed of the other. You must discuss the price of both, or the safety features, styling, or speed of both.

You don't have to list the points in your topic sentence, but you can include them, like this: "My old Ford turned out to be a cheaper, safer, and faster car than my boyfriend's new Mazda."

2. Be sure to give roughly equal space to both subjects. This rule doesn't mean you must write the same number of words—or even sentences—on both subjects. It does mean you should be giving fairly equal attention to the details of both subjects.

Because you will be writing about two subjects, this type of paragraph can involve more details than other paragraph formats. Thus, a comparison or contrast paragraph may be longer than twelve sentences.

Using Transitions Effectively for Comparison or Contrast

How and when you use transitions in a comparison or contrast paragraph depend on the answers to two questions.

1. Are you writing a comparison or contrast paragraph?

   - When you choose to write a *comparison* paragraph, you use transitional words, phrases, or sentences that point out *similarities*.
   - When you choose to write a *contrast* paragraph, you use transitional words, phrases, or sentences that point out *differences*.

2. Are you organizing your paragraph in the point-by-point or subject-by-subject pattern?

   - When you choose to organize your paragraph in the *point-by-point* pattern, you need transitions *within* each point *and between points*.
   - When you choose to organize in the *subject-by-subject pattern,* you need *most of your transitions* in the *second half* of the paragraph, to remind the reader of the points you made in the first half.

Here are some transitions you can use in writing comparison or contrast. Many others you may think of will also be appropriate for your ideas.

> **INFO BOX**   **Transitions for a Comparison or Contrast Paragraph**
>
> **To show similarities:**
>
> | | | | |
> |---|---|---|---|
> | additionally | both | in the same way | similar to |
> | again | each of | just like | similarly |
> | also | equally | like | so |
> | and | furthermore | likewise | too |
> | as well as | in addition | | |
>
> **To show differences:**
>
> | | | | |
> |---|---|---|---|
> | although | even though | instead of | though |
> | but | except | nevertheless | unlike |
> | conversely | however | on the other hand | whereas |
> | despite | in contrast to | otherwise | while |
> | different from | in spite of | still | yet |

Writing a comparison or contrast paragraph challenges you to make decisions: Will I compare or contrast? Will I use a point-by-point or a subject-by-subject pattern? Those decisions will determine what kind of transitions you will use and where you will use them.

Exercise 2   **Practice: Writing Appropriate Transitions for a Comparison or Contrast Paragraph**

Pairs of sentences follow. First, decide whether each pair shows a comparison or contrast. Then combine the two sentences into one, using an appropriate transition (either a word or a phrase). You may have to rewrite parts of the original sentences to create one smooth sentence. The first pair is done for you.

1. My mother loves to go out dancing.

   My father only danced at his wedding.

   combined: My mother loves to go out dancing, yet my father only

   danced at his wedding.

2. Young children should go to bed at the same time each night.
   Young children should have regularly scheduled meal times.

   combined: _____

   _____

3. A steady job can be tiring and stressful.
   Unemployment can be painful and terrifying.

   combined: _____

   _____

4. Playing chess with my uncle taught me to think deeply and plan my next move.
   When I was a member of a high school football team, I learned about the importance of strategy.

   combined: _____

   _____

WRITING THE COMPARISON OR CONTRAST PARAGRAPH IN STEPS

PREWRITING **COMPARISON OR CONTRAST**

One way to get started on a comparison or contrast paragraph is to list as many differences or similarities as you can on one topic. Then you can see whether you have more similarities (comparisons) or differences (contrasts), and decide which approach to use. For example, if you are asked to compare or contrast two restaurants, you could begin with a list like the one that follows.

③ Prewrite to generate a topic for a comparison or contrast paragraph.

List for Two Restaurants: Victor's and The Garden

similarities
both offer lunch and dinner
very popular
nearby

differences

Victor's	*The Garden*
formal dress	*informal dress*
tablecloths	*placemats*
food is bland	*spicy food*
expensive	*moderate*
statues, fountains, fresh flowers	*dark wood, hanging plants*

Getting Points of Comparison or Contrast

Whether you compare or contrast, you are looking for points of comparison or contrast—items you can discuss about both subjects.

If you surveyed the list on the two restaurants and decided you wanted to contrast the two restaurants, you'd see that you already have these points of contrast:

    dress   food
    decor   prices

To write your paragraph, start with several points of comparison or contrast. As you work through the stages of writing, you may decide you don't need all the points you've jotted down, but it is better to start with too many points than with too few.

Exercise 3 Collaborate: Developing Points of Comparison or Contrast

Do this exercise with a partner or a group. Some topics that could be used for a comparison or contrast paragraph follow. Underneath each topic, write three points of comparison or contrast. Be ready to share your answers with another group or with the class. The first topic is done for you.

Collaborate

1. topic: Compare or contrast two cars.
    points of comparison or contrast:
    a. gas mileage
    b. seating capacity
    c. resale value

2. **topic:** Compare or contrast two smartphones.
   points of comparison or contrast:

   a. _____

   b. _____

   c. _____

3. **topic:** Compare or contrast two fast-food restaurants.
   points of comparison or contrast:

   a. _____

   b. _____

   c. _____

Exercise 4 **Practice: Finding Differences in Subjects That Seem Similar**

Following are pairs of subjects that seem similar but have differences. List three differences for each pair.

1. subjects: laptops and desktops

differences: a. _____

b. _____

c. _____

2. subjects: online research and library research

differences: a. _____

b. _____

c. _____

3. subjects: coffee and energy drinks

differences: a. _____

b. _____

c. _____

Exercise 5 **Practice: Finding Similarities in Subjects That Seem Different**

Following are pairs of subjects that are different but have some similarities. List three similarities for each pair.

1. subjects: traveling alone and traveling with a group

similarities: a. _____

b. _____

c. _____

2. subjects: becoming an older adult and becoming a teenager

similarities: a. _____

b. _____

c. _____

3. subjects: earthquakes and tornados

similarities: a. _____

b. _____

c. _____

Adding Details to Your Points

Once you have some points, you can begin adding details to them. The details may lead you to more points. If they do not, they will still help you develop the ideas of your paragraph. If you were to write about the differences in restaurants, for example, your new list with added details might look like this:

List for a Contrast of Restaurants

Victor's	The Garden
dress—formal	informal dress
men in jackets, women in dresses	everyone in jeans
decor—pretty, elegant	placemats, on table is a card
statues, fountains	listing specials, lots of dark wood
fresh flowers on tables	and brass, green hanging plants
tablecloths	
food—bland tasting	spicy and adventurous
traditional, broiled fish or	pasta in tomato sauces, garlic
chicken, steaks,	in everything, curry,
appetizers like shrimp cocktail,	appetizers like tiny tortillas,
onion soup	ribs in honey-mustard sauce
price—expensive	moderate
everything costs extra,	price of dinner includes
like appetizer, salad	appetizer and salad

Reading the list about restaurants, you might conclude that some people may prefer The Garden to Victor's. Why? There are several hints in your list. The Garden has cheaper food, better food, and a more casual atmosphere. Now that you have a point, you can put it into a topic sentence. A topic sentence contrasting the restaurants could be:

> *Some people would rather eat at The Garden than at Victor's because The Garden offers better, cheaper food in a more casual environment.*

Once you have a possible topic sentence, you can begin working on the outline stage of your paragraph.

CRITICAL THINKING

Developing writers strategically apply skills and strategies learned from other writing assignments and other modes of writing. Consider how the strategies you have used with other writing assignments can enhance your ability to draw a clear comparison or contrast. Remember, *show, don't tell about* something. Use *sense details* when possible. Be *specific* to help your reader see what you are describing.

Exercise 6   **Practice: Writing Topic Sentences for Comparison or Contrast**

Lists of details follow. Some lists are for comparison paragraphs; some are for contrast paragraphs. Read each list carefully; then write a topic sentence for each list.

1. topic sentence: _____

_____

List of Details

cat training	dog training
litter box training	housebreaking
using a scratching post	walking on a leash
jumping on kitchen counters	behaving around people or pets
	obeying commands

benefits of personality	benefits of personality
affectionate	loving
mysterious	unpredictable
amusing	always entertaining
intuitive	sympathetic

examples of spontaneous behavior	examples of spontaneous behavior
curling up in bed	sneaking into bed
greeting owner	joyfully jumping on owner
playing with a cat toy	playing fetch

2. topic sentence: _____

_____

List of Details

baseball popularity	basketball popularity
people collect baseball cards	people compare playoff brackets
youth baseball is popular in rural and urban areas	many homes, neighborhoods, and schools have basketball hoops

many movies feature baseball in the storyline	basketball players are featured in product commercials
fun to watch	**fun to watch**
homeruns are exciting	slam dunks are entertaining
crowd participation during seventh inning stretch is communal	half-time shows can be extravagant
the completion of a double play is thrilling	a pass made behind the back is thrilling
fun to play	**fun to play**
you can practice hitting in a batting cage	you can practice shooting baskets alone or with peers
you can play games at picnics or in parks	pick-up games at the local court are fun
playing catch with a friend is an easy way to spend time together	it is easy to learn the rules

PLANNING   COMPARISON OR CONTRAST

With a topic sentence, you can begin to draft an outline. Before you can write an outline, however, you have to make a decision: What pattern do you want to use in organizing your paragraph? Do you want to use the subject-by-subject or the point-by-point pattern?

The following is an outline of a contrast paragraph in point-by-point form. (A sample subject-by-subject outline appears later in this chapter.)

Outline of a Contrast Paragraph: Point-by-Point Pattern

topic sentence Some people would rather eat at The Garden than at Victor's because The Garden offers better, cheaper food in a more casual environment.

details Food at Victor's is bland tasting and traditional.
The menu has broiled fish, chicken, and traditional steaks.
The spices used are mostly parsley and salt.
The food is the usual American food with a little French food on the list.
Appetizers are the usual things like shrimp cocktail or onion soup.

point 1, food Food at The Garden is more spicy and adventurous.
There are many pasta dishes in tomato sauce.
There is garlic in just about everything.
The Garden serves four different curry dishes.
It has all kinds of ethnic food.
Appetizers include items like tiny tortillas and hot, honey-mustard ribs.

(Continued)

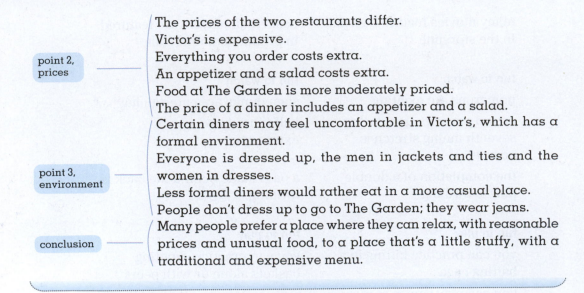

point 2, prices

The prices of the two restaurants differ.
Victor's is expensive.
Everything you order costs extra.
An appetizer and a salad costs extra.
Food at The Garden is more moderately priced.
The price of a dinner includes an appetizer and a salad.

point 3, environment

Certain diners may feel uncomfortable in Victor's, which has a formal environment.
Everyone is dressed up, the men in jackets and ties and the women in dresses.
Less formal diners would rather eat in a more casual place.
People don't dress up to go to The Garden; they wear jeans.

conclusion

Many people prefer a place where they can relax, with reasonable prices and unusual food, to a place that's a little stuffy, with a traditional and expensive menu.

Once you've drafted an outline, check it. Use the following checklist to help you review and revise your outline.

Checklist for an Outline of a Comparison or Contrast Paragraph

✓   Do I have enough details?

✓   Are all of my details relevant?

✓   Have I covered all the points on both sides?

✓   If I'm using a subject-by-subject pattern, have I covered the points in the same order for both subjects?

✓   Have I tried to cover too many points?

✓   Have I made my main idea clear?

Using this checklist as your guide, compare the outline with the prewriting list on page 131. You may notice several changes:

- Some details on decor in the list have been omitted because there were too many points.
- A concluding sentence has been added to reinforce the main idea.

Exercise 7   **Practice: Adding a Point and Details to a Comparison or Contrast Outline**

The following outline is too short. Develop it by adding a point of comparison and details to both subjects to develop the comparison.

topic sentence: People who wear caps and those who wear hats often choose them for similar reasons.

details: Caps and hats both make a statement.

Caps are often marked with the name of a tractor company, a football team, or a college, so they indicate an affiliation or interest.

Hats often indicate a person's interests, hobbies, or employment.

Fishing hats are worn by people who fish for fun or profit.

Cowboy hats appear on the heads of working ranchers and people on vacation.

Caps and hats can be a way for people to fit in.

Most people at a football or basketball game want to be seen with their team's insignia on their caps.

New students at a college like to wear the college's name on a cap.

In some places of worship, women like to wear elaborate hats on special occasions.

People who attend country music concerts like to come in cowboy hats.

Add a new point of comparison, and details, about caps and hats:

_____

_____

_____

_____

_____

_____

_____

_____

| Exercise 8 | **Practice: Finding Irrelevant Details in a Comparison or Contrast Outline** |

The following outline contains some irrelevant details. Cross out the details that don't fit.

topic sentence: Fibs and lies are quite different in intention, consequences, and in the nature of fibbers and liars.

details: Fibs tend to be small distortions of the truth.

When people have to choose between hurting another person's feelings by telling the truth and sparing that person some pain, they tell a fib.

"Your haircut looks great," a fibber will say.

Hair is a very sensitive subject with some people.

Lies are larger falsehoods.

Some people lie about being faithful to a partner.

So that they will not get caught cheating, they may say they were working late.

Many people are unemployed these days.

The consequences of telling a fib are not likely to be as serious as the consequences of lying.

Because a fib is about a small matter, it has a fairly small impact.

A fib told to avoid hurting another person may not be kind in the long run, but it isn't cruel.

It would be difficult for an average person to count all the fibs he or she has told.

Lies, on the other hand, can create great harm.

Lies about infidelity can poison a marriage.

The unsuspecting partner can sense a painful distance growing between the spouses.

The cheater is caught in a web of guilt.

Cheating is often portrayed on television as funny, but it is not.

Essentially, fibbers and liars are different types of people.

Young children may sense that fibbing is wrong, but their fibs are meant to save themselves, not to hurt others.

In the same way, adults who fib usually mean to avoid an awkward situation, but the fibs are not intentionally cruel.

Liars are most often adults, and their lies can be toxic.

Although unfaithful partners tell themselves they are not hurting anyone, they know better.

Their lies are both selfish and dangerous.

Everyone is human and therefore flawed, but fibbers are far less dangerous than liars.

Exercise 9   Practice: Revising the Order in a Comparison or Contrast Outline

Following is an outline written in the subject-by-subject pattern. Rewrite the part of the outline that is in italics so that the points in the second half follow the order of the first half. You do not have to change any sentences; just rearrange them.

topic sentence: Carl and Sean could not have been more different, yet they were college roommates who became best friends.

details: Carl was a country boy.

Carl's family lived on a ten-acre property fifteen miles from the nearest mall.

Carl had two horses, which he cared for himself.

He was used to seeing foxes, snakes, and possum in his back yard.

Carl loved football.

He had been a star player at his high school.

He drove two hours to attend every football game at the nearest university.

On his satellite television, he watched every professional game he could find.

Carl also loved country music.

When he wasn't watching football on television, he turned to country music channels.

The only concerts he attended featured country music superstars.

Sean loved hip-hop.

Hip-hop blasted from his bluetooth speakers.

Clubs that offered hip-hop entertainment were Sean's favorite hangouts.

Sean was a typical suburban teen.

He and his family lived in a three-bedroom house with a two-car garage and a small back yard.

Sean had never had a pet, but his mother had a Yorkshire terrier.

The creatures that lived in his yard were likely to be crows, squirrels, and worms.

He lived within a ten-minute drive to two huge malls, ten restaurants, and a multiplex movie theater.

A major part of Sean's life was basketball.

He had played basketball in high school.

He attended all the games at the nearby college.

He regularly drove half an hour to a nearby sports center where he watched nationally known teams play.

rewritten order: _____

_____

_____

_____

_____

_____

_____

_____

_____

_____

_____

_____

_____

_____

4   Write a comparison or contrast paragraph using either a point-by-point or subject-by-subject pattern.

DRAFTING AND REVISING   COMPARISON OR CONTRAST

When you've revised your outline, you can write the first draft of the restaurant paragraph. As you work through several drafts, you may decide to rearrange your points or refine your topic sentence. Adding vivid details and linking them effectively can make your paragraph more than a mere list of comparisons or contrasts. Remember that some sentences can serve as transitional links from one point of contrast (or comparison) to another.

CRITICAL THINKING

There are many things you can compare or contrast. The list is endless. As you develop your analytical skills, you will want to go beyond simply identifying similarities and differences between things. You will seek to explain the differences and the similarities and communicate to your audience why they are important.

As you write and revise your own comparison or contrast writing assignments, consider how can you revise your topic and concluding sentences to touch upon the importance or value of the comparison or contrast you are making.

A Sample Revised Draft

When you study the sample revised draft that follows, you'll notice changes from the outline on pages 133–134. The order of some details in the outline has been changed, and a few transitions have been added. Additional refinements and corrections are still necessary during the editing and proofreading stage, but you will still see considerable improvement. You can assume the writer worked through prior drafts to get to this point.

Revised Draft of a Contrast Paragraph: Point-by-Point Pattern

(Note: Changes from the outline are underlined; editing and proofreading are still necessary.)

Some people would rather eat at The Garden than at Victor's because The Garden offers better, cheap food in a more casual environment. The food at Victor's is bland tasting and traditional. The menu has broiled fish, chicken, and steaks. The food is the usual American food with a little French food on the list. Appetizers are the usual things like shrimp cocktail and onion soup. The spices used are mainly parsly and salt. Food at The

transition — Garden, <u>however</u>, is more spicy and adventurous. <u>The restaurant</u>

sentence order changed — <u>has all kinds of ethnic food</u>. There are many pasta dishes with tomato sauce. The menu has five kinds of curry on it. The appetizers include items like tiny tortillas and hot, honey-mustard ribs.

transitional phrase — <u>And if parsley is the spice of choice at Victor's</u>, garlic is the favor-

transition — ite spice at The Garden. The prices at the restaurants differ, <u>too</u>. Victor's is expensive because everything you order costs extra. An appetizer or a salad costs extra. Food at The Garden, <u>in contrast, is more moderately priced if a dinner includes an appetizer and a salad. Price and menu are important, but the</u>

transitional sentences — <u>most important difference between the restaurants has to do with environment</u>. Certain diners may feel uncomfortable at Victor's, which has a formal kind of atmosphere. Everyone is dressed up, the men in jackets and ties and the women in dresses. <u>Less formal dinners would rather eat in a more casual place. People don't dress up for The Garden; they wear jeans</u>. Many people prefer a place where they can relax, with reasonable prices and unusual food, to a place that is a little stuffy, with a traditional and expensive menu.

transitional sentences

The following checklist may help you revise your own draft:

Checklist for Revising Your Draft of a Comparison or Contrast Paragraph

✓ Did I include a topic sentence that covers both subjects?

✓ Are the paragraph's details arranged in a clear order?

✓ Does it stick to one pattern, either subject by subject or point by point?

✓ Are both subjects given roughly the same amount of space?

✓ Do all the details relate to the topic sentence?

✓ Are the details specific and vivid?

✓ Are transitions (and transitional sentences) used effectively?

✓ Have I made my point?

Exercise 10 **Practice: Revising the Draft of a Comparison or Contrast Paragraph by Adding Vivid Details**

You can do this exercise alone, with a writing partner, or with a group. The following contrast paragraph lacks the vivid details that could make it interesting. Read it; then rewrite the underlined parts in the space above them. Replace the original words with more vivid details.

I had always planned on getting a dog, but when I finally got one, the experience was not at all what I had expected. First of all, I had always imagined myself visiting the local animal shelter where I would find the largest dog in the place. He would be a great watchdog and know how to <u>do a lot of things</u>. After I selected him, I would take him back to <u>my place</u>, and he would <u>fit right in</u>. I felt sure that the dog would soon <u>learn the rules and be cool</u>. Finally, I dreamed of a dog that would love to <u>have all kinds of fun</u>. However, the reality of getting a dog was nothing like my fantasy. First, I didn't find my dog; she found me. I saw her on campus, and her tongue was hanging out. After I gave her some water, she followed me all day. She even tried to follow me into <u>some places at college</u>. When I had to leave at the end of the day, I picked her up and put her in my car. She was easy to pick up because, unlike the dog of my dreams, she <u>was not big</u>. When I took her to my apartment, she didn't exactly conform to my fantasies of a pet. Instead of fitting in, she took over my territory. Within the first ten minutes of her arrival, she had jumped on the sofa, chewed one of my old sneakers, and eaten part of a roll of toilet paper. Finally, I discovered that my idea of fun is not hers. She does not want to catch a ball, and she does not want to learn any tricks. However, she is fearless and loves to <u>do some wild stuff</u>. My dog is not the fantasy pet I expected to own, but she is a real dog with a courage and a joy for living that is all her own.

EDITING AND PROOFREADING   COMPARISON OR CONTRAST

Contrast Paragraph: Point-by-Point Pattern

When you edit your latest draft of your comparison or contrast paragraph, you can check whether any short sentences should be combined for smoother style. You can also determine if any word choices need improvement. When you are ready to proofread a clean copy of your paragraph, you can check for any careless errors in spelling, punctuation, or format. The following checklist will help you edit effectively.

Checklist for Editing a Compare or Contrast Paragraph

✓ Do all sentences have a subject and a verb?

✓ Are verb forms consistent?

✓ Can short sentences be combined?

✓ Are punctuation marks used correctly?

✓ Does each sentence begin with a capital letter?

✓ Is everything spelled correctly?

- *Cheap* has been corrected to *cheaper.*
- The repetitive use of *usual* has been replaced by the synonym *typical and standard.*
- *Onion soup* has been changed to *French* onion soup.
- The spelling of *parsley* has been corrected.
- "Everything *you* order" has been corrected to "everything *a person* orders."

- A *formal kind of atmosphere* has been changed to a *formal environment.*
- Two sentences have been combined, referring to some diners' preference for a less formal restaurant and casual attire.

In the following final version of a contrast paragraph in a point-by-point pattern, you may notice the following changes and corrections from the sample draft on pages 138–139.

Final Version of a Contrast Paragraph: Point-by-Point Pattern

(Note: Changes from the draft are underlined.)

Some people would rather eat at The Garden than at Victor's because The Garden offers better and <u>cheaper</u> food in a more casual environment. The food at Victor's is bland tasting and traditional. The menu has broiled fish, chicken, and steaks. The food is <u>typical</u> American food with a little French food on the list. Appetizers are <u>standard</u> things like shrimp cocktail and <u>French</u> onion soup. The spices are mostly <u>parsley</u> and salt. Food at The Garden, however, is more spicy and adventurous. The restaurant has all kinds of ethnic food. There are many pasta dishes with tomato sauce. The menu has four kinds of curry on it. The appetizers include items like tiny tortillas and hot, honey-mustard ribs. And if parsley is the spice of choice at Victor's, garlic is the favorite spice at The Garden. The prices at the restaurants differ, too. Victor's is expensive because everything <u>a person orders</u> costs extra. An appetizer or a salad costs extra. Food at The Garden, in contrast, is more moderately priced because the price of a dinner includes an appetizer and a salad. Price and menu are important, but the most important difference between the two restaurants has to do with environment. Certain diners may feel uncomfortable at Victor's, which has a <u>formal environment</u>. Everyone is dressed up, the men in jackets and ties and the women in dresses. <u>Less formal diners would rather eat in a more casual place like The Garden, where everyone wears jeans.</u> Many people prefer a place where they can relax, with reasonable prices and unusual food, to a place that is a little stuffy, with a traditional and expensive menu.

For your information: A sample point-by-point contrast essay based on this topic and following the same writing steps can be found in Chapter 12, "Different Essay Patterns: Part One."

Exercise 11 **Practice: Editing a Draft by Combining Sentences**

The paragraph that follows has many short, choppy sentences, which are underlined. Whenever you see two or more underlined sentences clustered next to each other, combine them into one smooth, clear sentence.

Whenever I visit a doctor, I feel as if I were going to prison. First, there is the weird atmosphere of the doctor's waiting room. The room is unusually quiet. It is full of people. <u>They are sitting. They are staring ahead. They are awaiting their doom.</u>

The staff behind the glass partition reminds me of a group of prison guards who keep the latest prisoners in order until the big door opens and incarceration begins. At long intervals, each patient's name is called. Each time, I look up. I hope the name is mine so that, like a prisoner, I can begin my ordeal and soon end it. On the other hand, I dread entering the space behind the big door. <u>That space contains another kind of waiting room. This is the solitary waiting area. Here I generally sit on a chair or on the edge of an examination table. Here I can dwell on what is wrong with me.</u> In a similar way, prisoners are supposed to use their incarceration to think about what they have done wrong. <u>I sit alone in the small, cell-like room. I fear the arrival of the doctor.</u> I have gone to the doctor to find out what is wrong. <u>However, I feel that I have committed some crime. Maybe I have eaten too much fatty food. Maybe I have skimped on exercise.</u> As I wait for the doctor to examine me, I feel as if a warden were about to enter, study me critically, and frown. Like a prisoner, I am unable to escape.

The Same Contrast Paragraph: Subject-by-Subject Pattern

To show you what the same paragraph contrasting restaurants would look like in a subject-by-subject pattern, an outline, sample draft, and final version follow.

Outline: Subject-by-Subject Pattern

topic sentence	Some people would rather eat at The Garden than at Victor's because The Garden offers better, cheaper food in a more casual environment.
details	Food at Victor's is bland tasting and traditional.
	The menu has broiled fish, chicken, and steaks.
	The spices used are mostly parsley and salt.
	The food is the usual American food with a little French food on the list.
subject 1, Victor's: food, prices, atmosphere	Appetizers are the usual things like shrimp cocktail and onion soup.
	Victor's is expensive.
	Everything you order costs extra.
	An appetizer or salad costs extra.
	Certain diners may feel uncomfortable at Victor's, which has a formal environment.
	Everyone is dressed up, the men in jackets and ties and the women in dresses.

subject 2, The Garden: food, prices, atmosphere

Food at The Garden is more spicy and adventurous.
There are many pasta dishes in tomato sauce.
There is garlic in just about everything.
The Garden serves four different curry dishes.
It has all kinds of ethnic food.
Appetizers include items like tiny tortillas and hot, honey-mustard ribs.
Food at The Garden is moderately priced.
The price of a dinner includes an appetizer and a salad.
The Garden is casual.
People don't dress up to go there; they wear jeans.

conclusion

Many people prefer a place where they can relax, with reasonable prices and unusual food, to a place that's a little stuffy, with a traditional and expensive menu.

Draft: Subject-by-Subject Pattern

(Note: Changes from the outline are underlined; editing and proofreading are still necessary.)

Some people would rather eat at The Garden than at Victor's because The Garden offers better, cheaper food in a more casual environment. The food at Victor's is bland tasting and traditional. The menu has broiled fish, chicken, and steaks on it. The food is the usual American food with a little French food on the list. Appetizers are the usual things like shrimp cocktail and onion soup.

sentence order changed, sentences combined

At Victor's, the spices are mostly parsley and salt. Eating traditional food at Victor's is expensive, since everything you order costs

transition

extra. An appetizer or a salad, for instance, costs extra.

transitional sentence

Victor's prices make some people nervous, and the restaurant's formal environment makes them uncomfortable. At Victor's, everyone is dressed up, the men in jackets and ties and the women in dresses.

transitional sentence

The formal atmosphere, the food, and the prices attract some diners, but others would rather go to The Garden for a meal. The food at The Garden is more spicy and adventurous than the offerings at Victor's. The place has all kinds of ethnic food.

sentences combined

There are many pasta dishes in tomato sauce, and The Garden serves four different curry dishes. Appetizers include items like tiny tortillas and hot, honey-mustard ribs.

transitional phrase

If Victor's relies on parsley and salt to flavor its food, The Garden sticks to garlic, which is in just about everything. Prices are lower at The Garden than they

transition

are at Victor's. The Garden's meals are more moder-

transition

ately priced because, unlike Victor's, The Garden includes an appetizer and a salad in the price of a

transition

dinner. And in contrast to Victor's, The Garden is a

(Continued)

casual restaurant. People don't dress up to go to The Garden; everyone wears jeans. Many people prefer a place where they can relax, with unusual food at reasonable prices, to a place that's a little stuffy, with a traditional and expensive menu.

Final Version: Subject-by-Subject Pattern

(Note: Minor editing changes from the draft are underlined.)

Some people would rather eat at The Garden than at Victor's because The Garden offers better, cheaper food in a more casual environment. The food at Victor's is bland tasting and traditional. The menu has broiled fish, chicken, and steaks on it. The food is typical American food, with a little French food on the list. Appetizers are the <u>standard</u> things like shrimp cocktail and <u>French</u> onion soup. At Victor's, the spices are mostly parsley and salt. Eating traditional food at Victor's is expensive, since everything <u>a person</u> orders costs extra. An appetizer or a salad, for instance, costs extra. Victor's prices make some people nervous, and the restaurant's formal environment makes them uncomfortable. At Victor's, everyone is dressed up, the men in jackets and ties and the women in dresses. The formal <u>environment</u> and the prices attract some diners, but others would rather go to The Garden for a meal. The food at The Garden is more spicy and adventurous than the offerings at Victor's. The place has all kinds of ethnic food. There are many pasta dishes in tomato sauce, and The Garden serves four different curry dishes. Appetizers include items like tiny tortillas and hot, honey-mustard ribs. If Victor's relies on parsley and salt to flavor its food, The Garden sticks to garlic, which is in just about everything. Prices are lower at The Garden than they are at Victor's. The Garden's meals are moderately priced because, unlike Victor's, The Garden includes an appetizer and a salad in the price of a dinner. And in contrast to Victor's, The Garden is a casual restaurant. People don't dress up to go to The Garden; everyone wears jeans. Many people prefer a place where they can relax, with unusual food at reasonable prices, to a place that's a little stuffy, with a traditional and expensive menu.

> **For your information:** A sample contrast essay based on this topic and following the same writing steps can be found in Chapter 12, "Different Essay Patterns: Part One."

Exercise 12 **Practice: Proofreading to Prepare the Final Version**

The following paragraph has the kinds of errors that are easy to overlook in a final copy of an assignment. Correct the errors, writing your corrections above the lines. There are fourteen errors in the paragraph.

My car is an old Toyota Camry that used to belong to my Mother, and I was

thrilled when I get the chance to drive my uncle's newer BMW for a few weeks

while he was out of town. However, I was surprised that my life did not change very much when I get the newer, sportier car. First, I axpected to attract more attention when I drove the BMW. No one looks twice at an old Camry in need of a paint job, so I always felt invisible when I drove it. People did look more closely at the BMW, but they didnt look at me. Another disappointment was related to the excessories and upgrades in my uncles car. At first, the BMW was like a great toy for me, with every automotive option, every entertainment choice, and every comfort I could imagine. It took me several days to learn what I could do, and how I could do it in this luxury car. It was wonderful to try out the satellite radio, the temperature controls, and all the other options in the car. Unfortunately, learning how to play with these gadgets and remembering how to use the upgrades becomes irritating after a while, especially when I couldn't get them to work. My greatest disappointment related to the car as a driving machine. At first, I enjoy the power of the BMW. I could weave in and out of Traffic, turn corners easily, and feel the car respond instantly when I stepped on the gas. But once I had been driving the car for a week, I felt less of a sense of adventure. After all, driving fast on the highway and burning to much gas is thrilling for only a short time. I loved my uncle's car, and I'm glad I got to drive it. However, I'm quite satisfied to be back in my old Camry. I'v learned that a car with a glamorous image, great accessories, and a terrific engine are fun, but the car doesn't make a new person out of the driver.

Lines of Detail: A Walk-Through Assignment

Write a paragraph that compares or contrasts any experience you've heard about with the same experience as you lived it. For example, you could compare or contrast what you heard about starting college with your actual experience of starting college. You could compare or contrast what you heard about falling in love with your experience of falling in love, or what you heard about a job during the interview process with your own experience working at that job. To write your paragraph, follow these steps:

Step 1: Choose the experience you will write about; then list all the similarities and differences between the experience as you heard about it and the experience as you lived it.

Step 2: To decide whether to write a comparison or contrast paragraph, survey your list to see which has more details, the similarities or the differences.

Step 3: Add details to your comparison or contrast list. Survey your list again, and group the details into points of comparison or contrast.

Step 4: Write a topic sentence that includes both subjects, focuses on comparison or contrast, and makes a point.

Step 5: Decide whether your paragraph will be in the subject-by-subject or point-by-point pattern. Write your outline in the pattern you choose.

Step 6: Write a draft of your paragraph and revise it extensively by checking the order of the points, the number of details, and the relevance and vividness of the details.

Step 7: Edit your draft for better style by combining short, choppy sentences and using effective transitions.

Step 8: Prepare a clean copy of your paragraph, and proofread carefully to spot and correct any careless errors in spelling, punctuation, typing, or format.

Topics for Writing a Comparison or a Contrast Paragraph

When you write on one of these topics, be sure to follow the stages of the writing process in preparing your comparison or contrast paragraph.

1. Compare or contrast what is most important in your life now to what was most important to you as a child. You may want to brainstorm about your values then and now before narrowing your focus to specific similarities or differences.

2. Compare or contrast any of the following:

two places to live	two friends	two characters in a book
two late night shows	two online news sites	two grocery stores
two film remakes	two weddings	two friends' Instagram pages

   If your instructor agrees, you may want to brainstorm points of comparison or contrast with a writing partner or a group.

3. Compare or contrast your taste in music, television shows or movies, social media, news sources, shopping habits, leisure time, or professional sports with a friend or relative's taste. Do these differences in taste impact your relationship? Under what circumstances?

Collaborate

4. Imagine that you have won a million dollars. How would you use the money? Now, choose a partner and interview him or her about the plans he or she made for the million dollars. Compare and contrast the plan that you have for your winnings with the plans of your partner. You might want to consider differences in saving versus spending, whether you or your partner are planning to give any portion of the money to charity or a friend or loved one, and what large purchases, if any, you are each planning to make.

5. Look carefully at the photograph of the children and their surroundings on the next page. Write a paragraph contrasting the mood of the children with the atmosphere of the background.

Topics for Critical Thinking and Writing

1. An epiphany is a sudden illuminating moment. Some epiphanies might include the moment you realized the career you wanted to pursue or a time when you realized the depth of your feelings for another person. Think of a time in your life when you have had an epiphany. Compare and contrast your mind-set and actions before and after the epiphany.

2. Although we are often shaped and influenced by the people closest to us, as we mature our beliefs and values may begin to differ from those of our family and close friends. Select a personal belief or value you have that differs from the beliefs or values of your family or close friends. Compare and contrast your differing beliefs and explain how they have impacted your relationship.

> **Note:** Additional writing options suitable for comparison or contrast–related assignments can be in the "Readings for Writers" appendix at the end of this book.

Classification

Learning Objectives

In this chapter, you will learn to:

1. Organize details into appropriate categories.
2. Prewrite to generate a topic for a classification paragraph.
3. Write a classification paragraph using transitions effectively.

WHAT IS CLASSIFICATION?

When you **classify**, you divide something into different categories, and you do it according to some basis. For example, you may classify the people in your neighborhood into three types: those you know well, those you know slightly, and those you don't know at all. Although you may not be aware of it, you have chosen a basis for this classification. You are classifying the people in your neighborhood according to *how well you know them.*

Hints for Writing a Classification Paragraph

1. Divide your subject into three or more categories or types.
If you are thinking about classifying Blu-ray players, for instance, you might
think about dividing them into cheap players and expensive players. Your
basis for classification would be the price of Blu-ray players. But you would
need at least one more type—moderately priced players. Using at least three
types helps you to be reasonably complete in your classification.

2. Pick one basis for classification and stick with it. If you are
classifying Blu-ray players by price, you cannot divide them into cheap,
expensive, and Chinese. Two of the categories relate to price, but
"Chinese" does not.

In the following examples, notice how one item does not fit its classification and has been crossed out.

fishermen

fishermen who fish every day
weekend fishermen
~~fishermen who own their own boat~~

(If you are classifying fishermen on the basis of how often they fish, "fishermen who own their own boat" does not fit.)

tests

essay tests
objective tests
~~math tests~~
multiple choice tests

(If you are classifying tests on the basis of the type of questions they ask,
"math tests" does not fit because it describes the subject being tested.)

> **1** Organize details into appropriate categories.

CRITICAL THINKING

Classifying involves evaluation. Evaluate potential topics for a common thread
or characteristic.

---

3. Be creative in your classification. Although it is easy to classify
drivers according to their age, your paragraph will be more interesting if
you choose another basis for comparison, such as how drivers react to a
slow driver in front of them.

4. Have a reason for your classification. You may be classifying to
help a reader understand a topic or choose something, or you may be trying to attack, criticize, or prove a point.

A classification paragraph must have a unifying reason behind it, and
the detail for each type should be as descriptive and specific as possible.
Determining your audience and deciding why you are classifying can help
you stay focused and make your paragraph more interesting.

Exercise 1   **Practice: Finding a Basis for Classifying**

Write three bases for classifying each of the following topics. The first topic is done for you.

1. **topic to classify:** famous vacation locations
   You can classify on the basis of

   a. location
   b. weather
   c. activities

2. **topic to classify:** bicycles
   You can classify bicycles on the basis of

   a. _____
   b. _____
   c. _____

3. **topic to classify:** water bottles
   You can classify water bottles on the basis of

   a. _____
   b. _____
   c. _____

Exercise 2   **Practice: Identifying What Does Not Fit the Classification**

In each list that follows, one item does not fit because it is not classified on the same basis as the others on the list. First, determine the basis for the classification. Then cross out the one item on each list that does not fit.

1. **topic:** pizza
   basis for classification: _____
   list: pepperoni pizza
             medium pizza
             mushroom pizza
             black olive pizza

2. **topic:** scary movies
   basis for classification: _____
   list: special effects movies
             alien invasion movies
             slasher movies
             zombie movies

3. **topic:** teachers
   basis for classification: _____
   list: psychology teachers
             junior high teachers
             high school teachers
             college teachers

Exercise 3   **Practice: Finding Categories That Fit One Basis**
                        for Classification

In the lines under each topic, write three categories that fit the basis of classification that is given. The first one is done for you.

> 1. **topic:** cartoons on television
>
>   **basis for classification:** when they are shown
>
>   **categories:**
>
>   a. Saturday morning cartoons
>
>   b. weekly cartoon series shown in the evening
>
>   c. cartoons that are holiday specials
>
> 2. **topic:** domestic pets
>
>   **basis for classification:** types of animals
>
>   **categories:**
>
>   a. _____
>
>   b. _____
>
>   c. _____
>
> 3. **topic:** food
>
>   **basis for classification:** types of food commonly eaten without utensils
>
>   **categories:**
>
>   a. _____
>
>   b. _____
>
>   c. _____

WRITING THE CLASSIFICATION PARAGRAPH IN STEPS

PREWRITING   CLASSIFICATION

First, pick a topic for your classification. The next step is to choose some basis for your classification.

2 Prewrite to generate a topic for a classification paragraph.

Brainstorming a Basis for Classification

Sometimes the easiest way to choose one basis is to brainstorm about different types related to your topic and to see where your brainstorming leads you. For example, if you were to write a paragraph classifying phone calls, you could begin by listing anything about phone calls that occurs to you.

phone calls

sales calls at dinner time	people who talk too long
short calls	calls I hate getting
calls in the middle of the night	wrong numbers
calling plans	waiting for a call

The next step is to survey your list. See where it is leading you. The list on phone calls seems to have a few items about *unpleasant phone calls:*

sales calls at dinner time
wrong numbers
calls in middle of night

Maybe you can label these "Calls I Do Not Want," and that will lead you toward a basis for classification. You might think about calls you *do not* want and calls you *do* want. You think further and realize that you want or do not want certain calls because of their effect on you.

You decide to use the effect of the calls on you as the basis for classification. Remember, however, that you need at least three categories. If you stick with this basis for classification, you can come up with three categories:

> calls that please me
> calls that irritate me
> calls that frighten me

By brainstorming, you can then gather details about your three categories.

Added Details for Three Categories

calls that please me

from boyfriend

good friends

catch-up calls—someone I haven't talked to for a while

make me feel close

calls that irritate me

sales calls at dinner time

wrong numbers

calls that interrupt

invade privacy

calls that frighten me

emergency call in middle of night

break-up call from boyfriend

change my life, indicate some bad change

Matching the Points within the Categories

As you begin thinking about details for each of your categories, try to write about the same points in each type. For instance, in the list on phone calls, each category includes some details about who made the call:

> calls that please me—from good friends, my boyfriend
> calls that irritate me—from salespeople, unknown callers
> calls that frighten me—from the emergency room, my boyfriend

Each category also includes some details about why you react to them in a specific way:

> calls that please me—make me feel close
> calls that irritate me—invade privacy
> calls that frighten me—indicate some bad change

You achieve unity by covering the same points for each category.

Writing a Topic Sentence for a Classification Paragraph

The topic sentence for a classification paragraph should do two things:

1. It should mention what you are classifying.
2. It should indicate the basis for your classification by stating the basis or by listing your categories, or both.

Consider the details on phone calls. To write a topic sentence about the details, you should do the following:

1. Mention what you are classifying: phone calls.
2. Indicate the basis for classifying by (a) stating the basis (their effect on me) or (b) listing the categories (calls that please me, calls that irritate me, and calls that frighten me). You may also state both the basis and the categories in the topic sentence.

Following these guidelines, you can write a topic sentence like this:

I can classify phone calls according to their effect on me.

or

Phone calls can be grouped into the ones that please me, the ones that irritate me, and the ones that frighten me.

Both of these topic sentences state what you're classifying and give some indication of the basis for the classification. Once you have a topic sentence, you are ready to begin the planning stage of writing the classification paragraph.

Exercise 4 Collaborate: Creating Questions to Get Details for a Classification Paragraph

Collaborate

Do this exercise with a partner or group. Each list that follows includes a topic, the basis for classifying that topic, and three categories. For each list, think of three questions that you could ask to get more details about the types. The first list is done for you.

1. **topic:** sports fans expressing support for a team

   basis for classification: how supportive they are

   categories: loyal fans, extremely loyal fans, fanatic fans

   questions you can ask:

   a. How will team support be expressed on each type's car?

   b. How much team-related clothing will each type wear to a game?

   c. How will each type's support be reflected in body decoration?

2. **topic:** college students waiting in line to register for classes

   basis for classification: how stressed they are

   categories: the calm, the mildly stressed, and the overstressed

   questions you can ask:

   a. _____

   b. _____

   c. _____

3. **topic:** boats

   basis for classification: How many people they can carry?

   categories: single person, 2–3 people, 4 or more people

   questions you can ask:

   a. _____

   b. _____

   c. _____

Exercise 5   **Practice: Writing Topic Sentences for a Classification Paragraph**

Review the topics, bases for classification, and categories in Exercise 4. Then, using that material, write a good topic sentence for each topic.

Topic Sentences

for topic 1: _____

_____

for topic 2: _____

_____

for topic 3: _____

_____

PLANNING   **CLASSIFICATION**

Effective Order in Classifying

After you have a topic sentence and a list of details, you can create an outline. Think about which category you want to write about first, second, and so on. The order of your categories will depend on what you're writing about. If you're classifying ways to meet people, you can save the best for last. If you're classifying three habits that are bad for your health, you can save the worst one for last. The order in which you present your categories will influence the final impact of your piece.

If you list your categories in the topic sentence, list them in the same order you will use to explain them in the paragraph.

Following is an outline for a paragraph classifying phone calls. The details have been put into categories. The underlined sentences have been added to clearly define each category before the details are given.

CRITICAL THINKING

To determine the best order of categories, you will need to evaluate each category's importance. As a writer, it is important to understand how sequence of your information will affect the reader. Do you want to begin with a shock, or slowly build so that your last category leaves the most lasting impression?

Outline for a Classification Paragraph

topic sentence   Phone calls can be grouped into the ones that please me, the ones that irritate me, and the ones that frighten me.

<u>There are some calls that please me</u>.
They make me feel close to someone.
I like calls from my boyfriend, especially when he calls just

category 1, details   to say he is thinking of me.
I like to hear from good friends.
I like catch-up calls.
These are calls from people I haven't talked to in a while.

<u>There are some calls that irritate me</u>.
These calls invade my privacy.
Sales calls always come at dinner time.

category 2, details   Most are recorded and offer me help with my credit card bills.
I get at least four wrong-number calls each week.
All these calls irritate me, and I have to interrupt what I'm doing to answer them.

<u>There are some calls that frighten me</u>.
They are the calls that tell me about some bad change in my life.

category 3, details   I once got a call in the middle of the night.
It was from a hospital emergency room.
The nurse said my brother had been in an accident.
I once got a call from a boyfriend.
He said he wanted to break up.

You can use the following checklist to help you revise your own classification outline.

Checklist for Revising the Classification Outline

✓   Do I have a consistent basis for classifying?

✓   Does my topic sentence mention what I am classifying and indicate the basis for classification?

✓   Do I have enough to say about each category in my classification?

✓   Are the categories presented in the most effective order?

✓   Am I using clear and specific details?

With a revised outline, you can begin writing your draft.

Exercise 6   Practice: Recognizing the Basis for Classification within the Topic Sentence

The topic sentences that follow do not state a basis for classification, but you can recognize the basis nevertheless. After you've read each topic sentence, write the basis for classification on the lines provided. The first one is done for you.

1. **topic sentence:** People at the supermarket can be classified into those who qualify for the express lane, those who push a moderately filled cart, and those who drag overloaded carts.

   basis for classification: <u>how much they have in their carts</u>

2. **topic sentence:** Used car purchases fall into three categories: the great deal, the fair deal, and the total waste of money.

   basis for classification: _____

   _____

3. **topic sentence:** There are three types of waiters and waitresses: the professional, the capable, and the terrible.

   basis for classification: _____

Collaborate

Exercise 7 **Collaborate: Adding Details to a Classification Outline**

Do this exercise with a partner or group. In this outline, add details where the blank lines indicate. Match the points covered in the other categories.

topic sentence: Talkers in my family can be classified into the non-stop conversationalists, the moderately talkative, and the silent minority.

details: My little brother is a nonstop conversationalist.

He has just started kindergarten.

He comes home full of excitement.

He wants to tell me about his day.

He is full of stories about his activities, his classmates, and even the pet turtle in his classroom.

My mother is less talkative.

She works in a dentist's office.

She is tired when she comes home.

_____

_____

My father, unlike my little brother and my mother, rarely talks unless he must.

_____

_____

He doesn't want to talk about his job, where he is under constant stress.

He will answer "yes" and "no" if I ask him a direct question.

I know the members of my family well, and I understand the reasons behind each one's level of communication.

DRAFTING AND REVISING   CLASSIFICATION

③ Write a classification paragraph using transitions effectively.

You can transform your outline into a first draft of a paragraph by writing the topic sentence and the details in paragraph form. As you write, you can begin adding details and inserting transitions.

Transitions in Classification

Various transitions can be used in a classification paragraph. The transitions you select will depend on what you are classifying and the basis you choose for classifying. For example, if you are classifying salsa according to how spicy it is, you can use transitions like, "*one mildly spicy salsa,*" and "*another, spicier kind,*" and "*the spiciest kind.*" In other classifications you can use transitions like, "the first type," "another type," or "the final type." In revising your classification paragraph, use the transitions that most clearly connect your ideas.

As you write your own paragraph, you may want to refer to a "kind" or a "type." For variety, try such other words as *class, group, species, form,* or *version* if it is logical to do so.

After you have a draft of your paragraph, you can revise it. The following checklist may help you with your revisions.

Checklist for Revising the Draft of a Classification Paragraph

✓   Does my topic sentence state what I am classifying?

✓   Does it indicate the basis of my classification?

✓   Do my transitions clearly connect my ideas?

✓   Should I add more details to any of the categories?

✓   Are the categories presented in the most effective order?

Following is a draft of the classification paragraph on phone calls. Compare these changes to the outline on page 155.

- An introduction has been added, in front of the topic sentence, to make the paragraph smoother.
- Some details have been added.
- Transitions have been added.
- A final sentence has been added so that the paragraph makes a stronger point.

Draft of a Classification Paragraph

(Note: Changes from the outline are underlined; editing and proofreading are still necessary.)

introduction added — I get many phone calls, but most of them fit into three types. Phone calls can be grouped into the ones that please me, the ones that irritate me, and the ones that frighten me. There are some calls that please me. They make me feel close to someone. I like calls from my boyfriend, especially when he called just to say he is thinking of me. I like to hear from my good friends. I like

(Continued)

added detail —— catch up calls. The calls from people I haven't talked to in a while. <u>They fill me in on what they have been doing.</u>

transition —— There are <u>also</u> calls that irritate me because they invade my privacy. Sales calls that feature recorded voices offer me help with my credit card bills always come at dinner

transition —— time. <u>In addition</u>, I get at least four wrong-number calls each week. All these calls irritate me, and I have to interrupt what I'm doing to answer them. <u>The more serious</u>

added detail —— <u>calls</u> are the ones that frighten me. They are the calls that tell me about some bad change in my life. I once got a midnight call from a hospital emergency room. It

transition —— informed me my brother had been in an accident. <u>Another time,</u> a boyfriend called to tell me he wanted to break up.

final sentence added —— When I get bad news by phone, I realize that the telephone can bring frightened calls as well as friendly or irritating ones.

Exercise 8 **Practice: Identifying Transitions in a Classification Paragraph**

Underline all the transitions in the paragraph. The transitions may be words or groups of words.

Insects that sneak into my house can be classified into the ones I expect to find, the ones that startle me, and the ones that horrify me. The first type, the ones I expect to find, are mainly ants. I am used to seeing trails of ants in my kitchen. These ants make their way across the floor when I have spilled a few drops of a sugary drink or a few crumbs of a cookie. It is easy to get rid of these insects. I simply spray a bit of insect spray or wipe up the ants with a wet paper towel. There is another kind of insect that appears in my house frequently but still makes me cringe. This group of bugs includes all species of roaches, especially the ones that fly. Roaches are sly, and they can be large. When they fly, I feel as if they are trying to bomb me. I hate to kill a roach by stepping on it or swatting it with a newspaper because the roach may not die, or worse, it may die and leave a gooey mess. As a result, I waste about half of a can of insecticide on one roach. The final kind of intruder insect is rare. However, I am now on the lookout for it. This species showed up just outside my back door recently. It was a three-inch, fat, brown, and shiny centipede. The idea that this form of garden pest was waiting to enter my house sent me into shock. In this case, I called on my friend to deal with the scary creature. However, I continue to think about the possibility that, barefoot, I could

have stepped out the back door and onto this latest version of an insect intruder.

EDITING AND PROOFREADING   CLASSIFICATION

Once you are satisfied with your latest draft, it is time to edit. You can begin by combining short sentences and refining word choice. Then you can check for any grammar, spelling, and punctuation errors. The following checklist may help you with your editing.

Checklist for Editing the Draft of the Classification Paragraph

✓ Should any of the sentences be combined?

✓ Are the verb forms consistent in tense?

✓ Are the word choices appropriate?

✓ Is the spelling correct?

✓ Is the punctuation correct?

If you compare the draft of the paragraph on pages 157–158 to the final version, you'll notice these improvements:

- Two sentences have been combined into *There are some calls that please me because they make me feel close to a person I care about.*
- Three sentences have been combined into *I like catch-up calls, the calls from people I haven't talked to in a while that fill me in on what friends have been doing.*
- The verb form *offer* has been corrected to *offering.*
- Two sentences have been combined into *I once got a midnight call from a hospital emergency room informing me that my brother had been in an accident.*
- *Frightened* has been corrected to *frightening.*
- *My* has been added to the second sentence to be more specific.
- The word choice has been refined: *someone* has been changed to *a person I care about* to make the detail more precise, and a reference to *irritate* has been changed to *annoy* to avoid repetition. The phrase *bad change in my life* has been replaced by *some crisis in my life,* a more precise description.

Final Version of a Classification Paragraph

(Note: Changes from the draft are underlined.)

I get many phone calls, but most of them fall into one of three types. <u>My</u> phone calls can be grouped into the ones that please me, the ones that irritate me, and the ones that frighten me. <u>There are some calls I want to receive because they make me feel close to a person I care about.</u> I like calls from my boyfriend, especially when he <u>calls</u> just to say he is thinking of me. I like to hear from my good friends.

(Continued)

I like catch-up calls, the calls from people I haven't talked to in a while that fill me in on what friends are doing. There are also calls I don't want because they invade my privacy. Sales calls that feature recorded voices offering me help with my credit card bills always come at dinner time. In addition, I get at least four wrong-number calls each week. All these calls annoy me, and I have to interrupt what I'm doing to answer them. The more serious calls are the ones I really don't want to receive. They are the calls that tell me about some crisis in my life. I once got a midnight call from a hospital emergency room informing me that my brother had been in an accident. Another time, a boyfriend called to tell me he wanted to break up. When I get bad news by phone, I realize that the telephone can bring frightening calls as well as friendly or irritating ones.

> **For your information:** A sample classification essay based on this topic and following the same writing steps can be found in Chapter 13, "Different Essay Patterns: Part Two."

Exercise 9   **Practice: Combining Sentences for a Better Classification Paragraph**

The paragraph has some short sentences that would be more effective if they were combined. Combine each pair of underlined sentences into one sentence. Write the new sentence in the space above the old ones.

The three types of worries in my life are brief worries, nagging little worries, and deep, serious worries. Brief worries are frequent. They don't bother me for long. A brief worry may occur when I notice that I need air in my left front tire. For a moment, I have a vision. I see myself stranded on the highway. I am stranded because my left front tire is completely flat. As soon as I make a mental note to put air in the tire the next time I use the car, the worry goes away. Nagging little worries are different. They are minor concerns. They keep returning. For instance, I know that I need to lose some weight. I can push this concern to the back of my mind. I can even keep this worry out of my awareness for days. It still comes back. Until I make a real effort to get more exercise, I will continue to worry about my weight. The worst kind of worry is the dark and serious kind. For example, I lost a cousin last year. He was an innocent bystander. He happened to be near a drive-by shooting. Now I fear for the safety of all the people I love. However, I am working hard. I want to accept the loss of my cousin. I would also like to live my life as fully as I can in spite of my fear.

Exercise 10 **Practice: Proofreading to Prepare the Final Version**

The following classification paragraph has the kind of errors it is easy to overlook when you prepare the final version of an assignment. Correct the errors, writing above the lines. The paragraph has twelve errors.

People who do not own a car have several options for getting from

one place to another; and these options include taking a bus, riding a bicycle,

and walking. Each of the options have its advantages. For example riding a bus

keeps a person out of rain, snow, and other, bad weather. In addition, riding a

bus is generally a safe and reliable way to get around. Another advantage is that

passengers on a bus have time to read, study, call their friends, or make new

friends with other passengers. For other reasons, ridding a bike is attractive. One

great reason is the healthy exercise that bike riding provides. Also, a person who

owns a bike owns transportation that is always available as long as they takes

minimal care of the bike. Best of all, bikeriders can weave their way around traffic

jams and often reach their destination faster than car's and buses can. Walkers

enjoy unique benefits, to. They don't have to pay bus fair, so they can save money.

They don't have to maintain a bicycle find a place to put it, or worry about

someone stealing it. Walkers rely souly on their bodies to get them where they

want to go. Walking is an uncomplicated way to travel.

Lines of Detail: A Walk-Through Assignment

Write a paragraph that classifies bosses on the basis of how they treat their employees. To write the paragraph, follow these steps:

Step 1: List all the details you can remember about bosses you have worked for or known.

Step 2: Survey your list. Then list three categories of bosses, based on how they treat their employees.

Step 3: Now that you have three categories, study your list again, looking for matching points for all three categories. For example, all three categories could be described by this matching point: where the boss works.

Step 4: Write a topic sentence that (a) names what you are classifying and (b) states the basis for classification or names all three categories.

Step 5: Write an outline. Check that your outline defines each category, uses matching points for each category, and puts the categories in an effective order.

Step 6: Write a draft of the classification paragraph. Revise it until it has sufficient details linked logically within each category.

Step 7: Edit your paragraph to improve style by using effective sentence combining and checking for precise word choice.

Step 8: Prepare a clean copy of your paragraph, and proofread it carefully to identify and correct any careless errors in punctuation, spelling, word choice, or format.

Topics for Writing a Classification Paragraph

When you write on any of these topics, be sure to work through the stages of the writing process in preparing your classification paragraph.

Collaborate

1. Write a classification paragraph on any of the topics listed. As a first step, you will need to narrow the topic. For example, instead of classifying all cars, you can narrow the topic to *sports* cars, or food to *food at a barbecue*. If your instructor agrees, brainstorm with a partner or a group to come up with (1) a basis for your classification, (2) categories related to the basis, and (3) points you can make to give details about each of the categories.

TV commercials	coffee shops	haircuts
tattoos	dogs	fast food
romantic movies	cars	social networks
snacks	politicians	dancers
students	diets	friendships
class assignments	salespeople	apologies
coaches	shoes	colleges

Collaborate

2. Some topics follow. Each one already has a basis for classification. Write a classification paragraph on one of these choices. If your instructor agrees, work with a partner or group to brainstorm categories, matching points and details for the categories.

   Classify the Following:
   a. Home repairs on the basis of how *difficult they are*
   b. Weekends on the basis of how *busy they are*
   c. Pizza spots on the basis of how *affordable they are*
   d. Breakfasts on the basis of how *quick they are*
   e. Jobs on the basis of *how difficult they are for you*
   f. Vacations on the basis of *how memorable they are to you*
   g. Local parks on the basis of *how clean they are*

3. Look carefully at the photograph on the next page. Then use its details to write a classification paragraph with this topic sentence:

   College students can be classified according to how well they work with others in a group.

Topics for Critical Thinking and Writing

1. Make a list or freewrite about your major goals and then see if you can classify them according to a single basis. For example, you might group them according to how long it will take to fulfill them (immediate, mid range, and long term), or you might group them according to quality-of-life goals (such as career, relationship, and humanitarian goals). You may even have several secret goals that you do not share with many people. After you have determined the basis for classifying these goals, be sure your details about each goal relate to your basis of classification.

2. Music is an integral part of many people's lives, and some individuals believe that it plays a crucial role in coping with or celebrating life itself. Consider how important music is to people you know and classify them on the basis of how much they depend on music in their lives.

Note: Additional writing options suitable for classification-related assignments can be found in the "Readings for Writers" appendix at the end of this book.

CHAPTER 8

Definition

Jumping In

*Can you define the expression on this child's face in one word? Why did you use that word? What does that word mean to you? By exploring such questions, you are now working toward a personal **definition**.*

Learning Objectives

In this chapter, you will learn how to:

1 Identify a word or phrase that has a personal meaning.
2 Prewrite to generate a topic for a definition paragraph.
3 Write a definition paragraph that uses transitions effectively.

1 Identify a word or phrase that has a personal meaning.

WHAT IS DEFINITION?

A **definition** paragraph is one that explains *what a term means to you*. You can begin thinking about what a term means by consulting the dictionary, but your paragraph will include much more than a dictionary definition. It will communicate a personal definition.

You can select several ways to explain the meaning of a term. You can give examples, you can tell a story, or you can contrast your term with another term. If you were writing a definition of empathy, for example, you could do one or more of the following: You could give examples of people you know who are empathetic, you could tell a story about someone who showed empathy, or you could contrast empathy with another quality, like contempt. You could also write about times when empathy is most needed or about the rewards of being empathetic.

Hints for Writing a Definition Paragraph

1. Pick a word or phrase that has a personal meaning for you and that allows you room to develop your idea. Remember that you will be writing a full paragraph on this term. Therefore, a term that can be defined quickly, in only one way, is not a good choice. For example, you would not have much to say about terms like "baking soda" or "toothbrush" unless you have strong personal feelings about baking soda or toothbrushes. If you don't have such feelings, your paragraph will be short.

When you think about a term to define, you might think about some personal quality you admire or dislike. If some quality provokes a strong reaction in you, you will probably have something to write about that term.

2. The topic sentence should have three parts. Include these items:

- the *term* you are defining
- the broad *class* or *category* into which your term fits
- the specific *distinguishing characteristics* that make the term different from all the others in the class or category

Each of the following topic sentences could be a topic sentence for a definition paragraph because it has the three parts.

      term   category   distinguishing characteristics
Resentment is the *feeling* that *life has been unfair.*

        term   category   distinguishing characteristics
A *clock watcher* is a *worker* who *is just putting in time, not effort.*

3. Select an appropriate class or category when you write your topic sentence.

not this: Resentment is a thing that makes you feel life has been unfair. (*Resentment* is a feeling or an attitude. Say so.)

not this: Resentment is when you feel life has been unfair. (*When* is a word that refers to a time, like noon or 7:00 PM. *Resentment* is a feeling, not a time.)

not this: Resentment is where a person feels life has been unfair. (*Where* is a word that refers to a place, like a kitchen or a beach. *Resentment* is not a place; it is a feeling.)

but this: Resentment is the feeling that life has been unfair.

4. Express your attitude toward the term you are defining in the "distinguishing characteristics" part of the topic sentence. Make that attitude clear and specific.

not this: Resentment is the feeling that can be bad for a person. (Many feelings can be bad for a person. Hate, envy, anger, and impatience, for instance, can all be bad. What is special about resentment?)

not this: Resentment is an attitude of resenting another person or a circumstance. (Do not define a word with another form of the word.)

but this: Resentment is the feeling that life has been unfair.

5. Use specific and concrete examples to explain your definition.
Concrete terms refer to things you can see, hear, smell, taste, or touch. Using concrete terms and specific examples will make your definition interesting and clear.

You may be asked to define an *abstract* idea like happiness. Even though an abstract idea cannot be seen, heard, smelled, tasted, or touched directly, you can give a personal definition of it by using concrete terms and specific examples.

> **not this:** Happiness takes place when you feel the joy of reaching a special goal. ("Joy" and "special goal" are abstract terms. Avoid defining one abstract term by using other abstract terms.)

> **but this:** I felt happiness when I saw my name at the top of the list of athletes picked for the team. Three months of daily, six-hour practices had paid off, and I had achieved more than I had set out to do. (The abstract idea of happiness is linked to a specific, concrete example of feeling happiness.)

If you remember to *show, not tell*, your reader what your term means, you'll have a better definition. Be especially careful not to define a term with another form of that term.

Exercise 1   Practice: Recognizing Abstract and Concrete Words

In the list that follows, put an *A* by the abstract words and a *C* by the concrete words.

1. _____ tolerance   9. _____ accountant

2. _____ chaos   10. _____ romance

3. _____ hubcap   11. _____ adventure

4. _____ peace   12. _____ poem

5. _____ anxiety   13. _____ faith

6. _____ mountain   14. _____ necklace

7. _____ smartphone   15. _____ fog

8. _____ delight   16. _____ knowledge

Exercise 2   Practice: Completing a Topic Sentence for a Definition Paragraph

Following are unfinished topic sentences for definition paragraphs. Finish each sentence so that the sentence expresses a personal definition of the term and has the three requirements for a definition's topic sentence.

1. A penny pincher is a person who grabs _____

_____

2. A game plan is a strategy for _____

_____

3. Tailgating is the traffic offense of _____

_____

4. A selfie _____

_____

5. A sore loser is a competitor who _____

_____

6. Nitpicking is the habit of _____

_____

7. A lemon is a car that _____

_____

8. Cybercrime is a term for illegal activity that _____

_____

Exercise 3   **Practice: Recognizing Problems in Topic Sentences for Definition Paragraphs**

Review the three components that should be included in the topic sentence for a definition paragraph. Then read the topic sentences that follow, put an *X* next to each sentence that has a problem, and underline the part of the sentence that is faulty. Then correct each of the problematic sentences in the space above the underlined problem.

1. _____ A sense of fun is a gift for enjoying the humor in everyday situations.

2. _____ An amusement park is a place where people go to amuse themselves.

3. _____ Rage is when a person feels uncontrollable anger at another person or about a situation.

4. _____ Emotional stability is where someone feels in control of his or her emotions.

5. _____ Doubt is the inability to trust another person or oneself.

6. _____ Adolescence is the thing that all teenagers struggle to endure.

7. _____ A crisis is a sudden situation that creates fear and extreme stress.

8. _____ A temper tantrum is a loud and juvenile expression of anger.

Exercise 4   **Collaborate: Writing Examples for Definition Paragraphs**

Collaborate

Incomplete statements from definition paragraphs follow. Complete them in the spaces provided by writing specific examples. When you have completed the statements, share your work with a group. After each group member has read his or her examples aloud, discuss the examples. Which examples did you like best? Which are the clearest and most specific? Do some examples lead to a different definition of a term than other examples do?

The first part of each sentence has been started for you.

1. I first experienced bullying when _____

_____

_____

Another example of bullying took place at _____ and the victim was _____

_____

_____

2. One person who was extremely generous to me was my older brother. He gave me _____

when _____

_____

Some people are generous to family members; others perform acts of generosity to total strangers. For example, _____

_____

_____

3. A time when a person must learn to forgive is when _____

_____

_____

I saw forgiveness in action when _____

_____

_____

_____

2 Prewrite to generate a topic for a definition paragraph.

WRITING THE DEFINITION PARAGRAPH IN STEPS

PREWRITING **DEFINITION**

To pick a topic for your definition paragraph, begin with some personality trait or type of person. For instance, you might define "the insecure person." If you listed your first thoughts, your list might look like this:

the insecure person
someone who is not emotionally secure
wants (needs?) other people to make him or her feel good
lacks self-esteem

CRITICAL THINKING

Selecting a topic involves differentiating meaning. Words often have different meanings for different cultural or social groups. Analyze and evaluate your topic based on one group's meaning.

Using Questions to Get Details

Often, when you look for ideas to define a term, you get stuck with big, general statements or abstract words, or you simply cannot come up with enough to say. If you are having trouble getting ideas, think of questions about your term. Jot these questions down without stopping to answer them. One question can lead you to another question. Once you have five or more questions, you can answer them, and the answers will provide details for your definition paragraph.

If you were writing about the insecure person, for example, you could begin with questions like these:

What are insecure people like?
What behavior shows a person is insecure?
How do insecure people dress or talk?
What makes a person insecure?
How do insecure people relate to others?
Does insecurity hurt the insecure person? If so, how?
Does the insecure person hurt others? If so, how?
What do insecure people do to mask their insecurity?

By scanning the questions and answering as many as you can, you can add details to your list. Once you have a longer list, you can review it and begin to group the items on the list. Following is a list of grouped details on the insecure person.

Grouped Details on the Insecure Person

wants (needs?) other people to make him or her feel important
lacks self-esteem

insecure people have to brag about everything
a friend who brags about his car
they tell you the price of everything
a friend who talks about salary and money

they put others down
saying bad things about other people makes insecure people feel better

insecure people can never relax inside
can never enjoy being with other people
other people are always their competitors
must always worry about what others think of them

The Topic Sentence

Grouping the details can help you arrive at several main ideas. Can they be combined and revised to create a topic sentence? Following is a topic sentence on the insecure person that meets the requirements of naming the term, placing it in a category, and distinguishing the term from others in the category:

| term | category | distinguishing characteristics |

The *insecure person* is *someone* who *needs other people to make him or her feel respected and important.*

Once you have a topic sentence, you can begin working on the planning stage of the paragraph.

Exercise 5 **Practice: Designing Questions to Gather Details**

Following are terms that could be defined in a paragraph. For each term, write five questions that could lead you to details for the definition. The first one has been done for you as an example.

1. **term:** arrogance

   questions: a. Do I know anyone who displays arrogance? _____

   b. Is there any celebrity I think is arrogant? _____

   c. What is an arrogant action? _____

   d. What kind of remark is an example of arrogance? _____

   e. Why are people arrogant? _____

2. **term:** a gossiper

   questions: a. _____

   b. _____

   c. _____

   d. _____

   e. _____

3. **term:** flexibility

   questions: a. _____

   b. _____

   c. _____

   d. _____

   e. _____

Exercise 6 **Practice: Grouping Related Ideas for a Definition Paragraph**

Following is a list of ideas for a definition paragraph. Read the list several times; then group all the ideas on the list into one of the three categories shown. Put the letter of the category next to each idea.

Categories:

   G = how secrecy can be **good**
   B = how secrecy can be **bad**
   D = **dealing** with secrecy

List

1. _____ Too much secrecy can poison a marriage or other close relationship.

2. _____ A surprise birthday party can be a wonderful secret.

3. _____ To protect national security, some countries have to keep certain weapons programs a secret.

4. _____ A shameful family secret can poison generations who try to hide the truth.

5. _____ Trusting a friend or sibling can mean allowing that person the privacy of small secrets such as the content of his or her e-mail.

6. _____ Spying to discover a secret is rarely a good idea unless life-or-death matters are involved.

7. _____ Secret codes or ID numbers protect consumers' credit.

8. _____ Children should be allowed the privacy of having a secret, imaginary friend.

9. _____ In most cases, if a friend confides a secret pain or sorrow to another friend, the listener should keep the secret.

10. _____ A bank that hides the reality of its failing investments puts the well-being of thousands in jeopardy.

PLANNING   DEFINITION

To make an outline for a definition paragraph, start with the topic sentence and list the grouped details. Often, a first outline does not have many examples or concrete, specific details. A good way to be sure you put specific details and concrete examples into your paragraph is to include shortened versions of them in your revised outline. If you compare the following outline to the grouped list of details on page 169, you will see how specific details and concrete examples have been added.

Outline for a Definition Paragraph

topic sentence	The insecure person is someone who needs other people to make him or her feel respected and important.
details	Insecure people have to brag about everything.
	An insecure friend may brag about his car.
	An insecure person talks about money and salary.
added detail	Insecure people wear expensive jewelry and tell you what it costs.
added detail	They brag about their expensive clothes.
added detail	They make sure they wear clothes with trendy labels, another kind of bragging.
added example	When some friends were talking about Susan's great new job, Jill had to make mean remarks about Susan. Jill hated having Susan look like a winner.
	Insecure people can never relax inside.
	They can never enjoy being with other people.
	Other people are always their competitors.

(Continued)

added example —————(Luke can't enjoy any game of basketball unless he is the star.

concluding sentence —————(Insecure people must always worry about what others think of them.

When you prepare your own definition outline, use the following checklist to help you revise.

Checklist for Revising a Definition Outline

✓   Does my topic sentence include a category and the characteristics that show how my term is different from others in the category?

✓   Have I defined my term so that it is different from any other term?

✓   Am I being concrete and specific in the details?

✓   Do I have enough examples?

✓   Do my examples relate to the topic sentence?

✓   Are my details in the most effective order?

With a revised outline, you are ready to begin writing a rough draft of your definition paragraph.

Exercise 7   Practice: Rewriting a Topic Sentence for a Definition Paragraph

An outline in which the topic sentence does not make the same point as the rest of the outline follows. Rewrite the topic sentence so that it relates to the details.

topic sentence: A sixth sense is a strange sense.

details: My aunt believes that her sixth sense changed the course of her life.

At seventeen, my aunt was engaged to be married to a man she had known all her life.

He was compassionate, attractive, and hardworking.

A month before the wedding, she met a new man, John, at a cousin's party.

John was an awkward, introverted man with few social skills.

Although my aunt thought John was quite strange and awkward, she could not stop thinking about him.

A week later, she canceled her wedding to her fiancé.

John and my aunt soon married and have been happy together for more than thirty years.

I never believed in a sixth sense until recently.

I have taken the same route to work for years.

It involves crossing an old bridge.

One day last month, I was approaching the bridge when I had a sick feeling.

I decided to turn around and take a different way to work.

Later that day, a portion of the old bridge collapsed into the water.

Two drivers were seriously hurt.

Even animals seem to have a sixth sense.

I recently read the story of a mutt and his family.

At 4:00 AM, the dog began whining, trying to wake up the mother and father.

Then the dog began running to the baby in her crib.

The father got up to push the dog outside.

Outside, the dog began to cry.

At last, the father opened the door and the dog ran inside, still crying.

Finally, both parents looked inside the crib.

The baby was unconscious and had a dangerously high fever.

In the emergency room, a doctor said the dog had saved the baby's life.

rewrite the topic sentence: _____

_____

Exercise 8   **Practice: Revising an Example to Make It More Concrete and Specific**

The following outline contains one example that is too abstract. In the lines provided, rewrite the example that is too abstract, using more specific, concrete details.

topic sentence: Culture shock is an extreme reaction to a new way of living.

details: I first experienced culture shock when I was sent
example 1 away to summer camp.

At first I was horrified by the living conditions at the camp.

I and five other boys had to sleep in a rustic cabin with rickety bunk beds.

The bathrooms were primitive and there was no privacy.

We went to bed early and were awakened before sunrise.

The food was tasteless, and there was no place to buy snacks.

It took me a week of misery before I adjusted to the campers' lifestyle.

example 2   A weekend visit to Los Angeles was my next experience of culture shock.

I could not believe the constant traffic on the freeways.

I tried hard to keep with the flow of traffic, particularly as other drivers confidently and aggressively changed lanes.

The crush of travelers on the freeway made me nervous.

At my grandfather's Los Angeles apartment, I could see and hear the constant flow of traffic on the freeway. I couldn't see how he could live in such a chaotic place.

example 3   Culture shock also struck on my first days on a college campus.

Students looked different than they did in high school.

Classes were different, too.

My schedule seemed so easy.

I felt a little confused because the rules seemed looser than those in high school.

On the other hand, I was nervous about messing up.

revised example: _____

_____

_____

_____

_____

_____

_____

_____

_____

_____

_____

_____

_____

_____

3 Write a definition paragraph that uses transitions effectively.

DRAFTING AND REVISING   DEFINITION

To write the first draft of your definition paragraph, you can rewrite the outline in paragraph form, combining some of the short sentences and adding more details. Remember that your purpose in this definition paragraph is to explain your personal understanding of a term. Therefore, you want to be sure that your topic sentence is clear and that your explanation connects your details to the topic sentence. Careful use of transitions will link your details to your topic sentence.

Transitions

Because you can define a term in many ways, you can also use many transitions. If you are listing several examples in your paragraph, you can use transitions like *first, second,* and *finally.* If you are contrasting your term with another, you can use transitions like *on the other hand* or *in contrast.* You may want to alert or remind the reader that you are writing a definition paragraph by using phrases like *can be defined as, can be considered as, means that,* or *implies that.*

Because many definitions rely on examples, the transitions listed here are ones you may want to use.

INFO BOX **Transitions for a Definition Paragraph**

a classic case of _____ is _____	in fact	another time
another case	in one case	sometimes
for example	in one instance	specifically
for instance	one time	similarly

A Sample Draft

Following is a draft of the definition paragraph on the insecure person. When you read it, you'll notice several changes from the outline on pages 171–172.

- Transitions have been added in several places. Some transitions let the reader know an example is coming, some transitions link one point about the topic to another point, and other transitions connect an example to the topic sentence.
- Examples have been made concrete and specific.

You may also spot some careless errors that can be corrected during the editing and proofreading stage.

Draft of a Definition Paragraph

(Note: Changes from the outline are underlined; editing and proofreading are still necessary.)

transition / specific details / transition / added detail, transition / transition

The insecure person is someone who needs other people to make him or her feel respected and important. The insecure person loves to brag about everything. <u>For instance</u>, a friend may brag about his car. <u>He tells everyone he meets that he drives a Mercedes</u>. He may talk about money and salary. An insecure person tells you the price of everything. He wears expensive jewelry and tells you what it costs, <u>like</u> the person who always flashes his <u>Rolex</u> watch. <u>Another</u> insecure person will brag about her expensive cloth or make sure she always wears clothes with trendy labels, <u>another kind</u> of bragging.

(Continued)

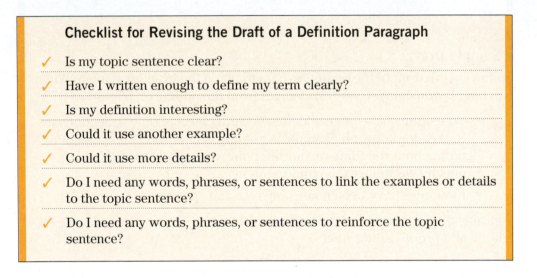

transitional
sentence — Bragging is not the only way an insecure person tries to look good; he or she may put other people down. Saying bad things about other people can put the insecure person on top.

transition — For instance, some friends were recently talking about another friend, Susan, who had just started a great new job. Jill had to add some mean remarks about how lucky Susan had been to get the job since Susan really wasn't qualified for it. Jill hated

added details — to have Susan look like a winner. The insecure person can hurt

transition — others but also suffers inside. Such a person can never relax because he or she always sees other people as competitors. An example of this attitude is seen in Luke, a college acquaintance

added details — who always plays pickup basketball games. Even though the games are just for fun Luke can't enjoy any game unless he is the star. Luke is a typically insecure person, for he must always worry about what others think of him.

The following checklist may help you revise the draft of your own definition paragraph.

Checklist for Revising the Draft of a Definition Paragraph

✓ Is my topic sentence clear?

✓ Have I written enough to define my term clearly?

✓ Is my definition interesting?

✓ Could it use another example?

✓ Could it use more details?

✓ Do I need any words, phrases, or sentences to link the examples or details to the topic sentence?

✓ Do I need any words, phrases, or sentences to reinforce the topic sentence?

Exercise 9 **Practice: Adding Examples to a Draft of a Definition Paragraph**

Two of the following paragraphs need examples with concrete, specific details to explain their points. Where the lines indicate, write an example with concrete, specific details. Each example should be at least two sentences long. The first paragraph is done for you.

1. Listlessness is the feeling that nothing is worth starting. After a hectic

week, I often wake up on Saturday morning feeling listless. I just do not have the

energy to do the things I intended to do. I may have planned to wash my car, for

example, but I cannot bring myself to get going. I cannot put together the bucket, detergent, brushes, and window cleaner I need to start the process. I tell myself, "Why wash the car? It will probably rain anyway." Another time I feel listless is when I am faced with a big assignment. For instance, I hate to start a term paper because there is so much to do. I have to think of a topic, do research, read, take notes, plan, write, and revise. When I am faced with so many things to do, I don't do anything. I tell myself it is not worth starting because I will probably get a bad grade on the paper anyway. I put off getting started. I let listlessness get the better of me.

2. Tact is the ability to express oneself without needlessly hurting another person's feelings. My boss at the clothing store where I work is a very tactful person. Customers often ask my boss how they look in an item they are trying on. My boss must be tactful in her answer. _____

_____

_____

_____ I have tried to be tactful in declining an invitation.

_____

_____

_____

_____

Of course, there are times when there is no way to be both tactful and honest.

_____

_____

_____

Although tact cannot always prevent others from feeling embarrassment or pain, tact is a great tool in many situations.

3. A clock watcher is a person who always wants to leave a place early. Clock watchers are commonly seen in the workplace. _____

_____

_____

_____

Clock watchers have a hard time sitting still in a classroom. _____

_____

_____

Clock watchers sometimes obsess about leaving a large sports or social event

early. _____

_____

_____

_____ Clock watchers cannot really experience the present

moment because they are preoccupied with getting away from it.

CRITICAL THINKING

When revising a definition paragraph (or any paragraph for that matter), switch roles. Instead of playing the role of the writer, consider the role of the reader. What details in your paragraph are most helpful to a reader? Which ones are not helpful? What words are too vague and unclear? Which ones are precise and specific? Remember, as a writer, your primary goal is to communicate clearly to your audience. Play the role of the reader to identify your essay's strengths and weaknesses. If changing roles is too difficult, consider listening to a recording of someone else reading your paragraph.

Exercise 10 **Practice: Identifying the Words That Need Revision in a Definition Paragraph**

The following paragraph has too many vague, abstract words. Underline the words that you think should be replaced with more specific or concrete words or examples.

Chronic complainers are people who rarely appreciate what they have or

where they are and who like to share their dissatisfaction. A chronic complainer

might have a nice car, but he will always note its flaws. For example, he will

remind others that his car doesn't get the best gas mileage or doesn't have other

stuff. Chronic complainers are also likely to be unhappy with their jobs or finan-

cial situation. A chronic complainer who works in a bank, for example, may whine that she is only a teller when she should be higher up by now. Another chronic

complainer will spend hours moaning that he cannot afford anything because

his boss is unfair. Eventually, friends and relatives tend to spend less time with a

chronic complainer. It is not fun to be around someone who can poison any social

event, even a conversation over a cup of coffee, with bitterness, anger, and

whatnot. Sooner or later, a chronic complainer will be unhappy about losing

friends.

Exercise 11 **Practice: Adding the Right Transitions to a Definition Paragraph**

In the following paragraph, circle the correct transition in each of the pairs.

Calm is a state of mind in which a person can think clearly. Words such

as *agitated*, *upset*, *elated*, or *thrilled* describe the opposite of calm. Neither

emotional lows nor highs are a good background for making a major decision.

For instance / In one case, people making choices about getting a job, leaving

college, or starting a relationship must be able to weigh the positive and negative

aspects of their choice. In one instance / Specifically, when they reach a decision,

people need to rely on their ability to reason rather than on a momentary high or

low mood. That is, they must reach a level of calm. One way that people can rec-

ognize a calm state of mind is to be sure that they do not feel rushed into making

a decision. Sometimes / In another case, people refer to "calm seas," and the term

refers to a good time to sail. In calm seas, ships may not sail as fast, but they are

not tossed about by rough waves. In the same way, calm people are not tossing up

and down emotionally. One time / In fact, calm people are slowly but confidently

moving to a choice.

EDITING AND PROOFREADING   DEFINITION

Once you are satisfied with your latest draft, it is time to edit. You can
begin by combining short sentences and refining word choice. Then you
can review your draft for grammar, spelling, and punctuation errors. The
following checklist may help you edit effectively.

> ### Checklist for Editing the Draft of the Definition Paragraph
>
> ✓ Should any of the sentences be combined?
>
> ✓ Are the verb forms correct and consistent?
>
> ✓ Are the word choices appropriate?
>
> ✓ Is the spelling correct?
>
> ✓ Is the punctuation correct?

If you compare the draft on pages 175–176 to the following final version of the paragraph on the insecure person, you will see these changes:

- The transition phrase, *To get* respect, has been added.
- To keep the paragraph consistent in person, the word *you* has been dropped.
- The fourth and fifth sentences have been combined.
- *Jewlery* has been corrected to *jewelry*.
- *Cloth* has been corrected to *clothes*.
- *Criticize* replaced *put other people down*, and *criticizing* replaced *saying bad things*.
- A comma has been added after the subordinating clause *Even though the games are just for fun*.
- The wording has been improved so that it is more precise.

Final Version of a Definition Paragraph

(Note: Changes from the draft are underlined.)

The insecure person is someone who needs other people to make him or her feel respected and important. <u>To get respect</u>, the insecure person loves to brag about everything. For instance, a friend may brag about his car. He tells everyone he meets that he drives a Mercedes <u>and often talks</u> about money and salary. An insecure person tells <u>people</u> the price of everything. He wears expensive <u>jewelry</u> and tells <u>people</u> what it costs, like <u>the man</u> who always flashes his Rolex watch. Another insecure person will brag about her expensive <u>clothes</u> or make sure she wears clothes with trendy labels, another kind of bragging. Bragging <u>isn't</u> the only way an insecure person tries to look good; he or she may also <u>criticize</u> other people. <u>Criticizing</u> others can put the insecure person on top. For instance, some friends were recently talking about another friend, Susan, who had just started a great new job. Jill had to add some mean remarks about how lucky Susan had been to get the job since Susan really wasn't qualified for it. Jill <u>couldn't stand</u> to have Susan look like a winner. The insecure person <u>like Jill</u> can hurt others but also suffers inside. Such a person can never relax because he or she always sees other people as competitors. An example of this attitude can be seen in Luke, a college acquaintance who always plays pick-up basketball games. <u>Even though the games are just for fun</u>, Luke can't enjoy any game unless he is the star. Luke is a <u>typical</u> insecure person, for he must always worry about what others think of him.

For your information: A sample definition essay based on this topic and following the same writing steps can be found in Chapter 13, "Different Essay Patterns: Part Two."

CRITICAL THINKING

Adding sentence variety is an effective way to make your writing livelier and more powerful. Too many long, complicated sentences can be tedious and monotonous to read. Too many short sentences sound choppy. Try varying your sentence types for effect. Short sentences are sometimes referred to as *telegraphic sentences* and can be used for emphasis. Longer sentences are more complex, signaling introspection and thought.

Exercise 12   **Practice: Combining Sentences in a Definition Paragraph**

The following definition paragraph has some short, choppy sentences that could be combined. These pairs or clusters of sentences are underlined. Combine each pair or cluster into one smooth sentence, and write the new sentence in the space above the original ones.

A peacemaker is a socially gifted person who knows how to resolve conflicts. My mother is a peacemaker. She has a natural skill. Her skill enables her to detect a family conflict. It is a family conflict that is about to begin. She can resolve it. She can resolve it quickly. She coaxes the unhappy family members into conversing honestly and calmly. Soon, what could have been a hot argument has cooled down. My high school hockey coach was a peacemaker, too. However, he was different from my mother. He was a tough, often physically involved settler of arguments. Hockey can be a brutal game. My coach could sense anger brewing between players. Before it started and spread, he did something. He grabbed the unhappy players. He scolded, shouted, and threatened them. His talent was his ability to push the players face to face before they created a chaotic situation. In a less physical way, some diplomats can bring nations together. A diplomat can do this by convincing hostile countries to send their representatives. Each country's representatives meet at a neutral location. There the representatives and the diplomats talk calmly. In the neutral atmosphere, things can happen. Treaties can be written. Trade agreements can be reached. Peacemaking can be global, or it can be personal. Either way, a special person has to initiate it.

Exercise 13 **Practice: Correcting Errors in the Final Version of a Definition Paragraph**

The following definition paragraph has the kinds of errors that are easy to overlook in a final version. Correct the errors by writing above the lines. There are eleven errors in the paragraph.

A luxury is a pleasant experience that a person does not usally have a chance to enjoy. For example, to a person who works 8 or ten hours a day at a demanding job, getting out of work two hrs early is, a luxury. It gives that person time to do anything he or she choses, from catching up on chores to spending time with a friend. A millionaire whose schedule allows his more freedom may think a luxury is a trip to the Seychelles Islands for sun and scuba diving. On the other hand, a child who doesn't spend much time with his busy parents' will feel that a whole day spent with his mother or father is a luxury. One Strange aspect of luxury is that something that was once a luxury may lose it's appeal if it is experience regularly. For example, the worker who becomes accustomed to leaving work early may gradually take the new schedule for granted. Similarly, a rich woman who can travel anywhere may become bored by cruises and sightseeing. However, lonely children who gets to spend more time with a parent may no longer consider that time a luxury, but they will never become sick of the attention.

Lines of Detail: A Walk-Through Assignment

Write a paragraph that gives a personal definition of the secure person. To write the paragraph, follow these steps:

Step 1: List all your ideas about a confident person.

Step 2: Write at least five questions that can add details about a confident person. Answer the questions as a way of adding details to your list.

Step 3: Group your details; then survey your groups.

Step 4: Write a topic sentence that includes the term you are defining, puts the term into a category, and distinguishes the term from others in the category.

Step 5: Write an outline. Begin by writing the topic sentence and the groups of details. Then add more details and specific examples.

Step 6: Write a draft of your paragraph. To revise, check that you have enough examples, that your examples fit your definition, and that the examples are in an effective order and linked logically. Remember that careful revision may involve writing several rough drafts before you are satisfied.

Step 7: Edit your latest draft by focusing on improving your sentence structure, word choices, and transitions. Also, correct any serious spelling or grammatical errors.

Step 8: Proofread a clean copy of your work to check for missing words and any careless errors in spelling, punctuation, format, or typing.

Topics for Writing a Definition Paragraph

When you write on any of these topics, be sure to work through the stages of the writing process in preparing your definition paragraph.

1. Define an abstract term using concrete, specific details. Choose from the following list. You can begin by looking up the term in a dictionary to be sure you understand the dictionary meaning. Then write a personal definition.

   Collaborate

   You can then start freewriting. If your instructor agrees, you can read your freewriting to a group for reactions and suggestions. If you prefer, you can start by brainstorming a list of questions to help you define the term. Again, if your instructor agrees, you can work with a group to develop brainstorming questions. Here is the list of abstract terms:

beauty	hope	wisdom
charity	humor	friendship
compassion	talent	infatuation
elegance	patience	relief
enthusiasm	trust	faith
tolerance	liberty	skill

2. Write a definition of a type of person. Develop your personal definition with specific, concrete details. You can choose one of the following types or choose your own type.

   Collaborate

   Freewriting on the topic is one way to begin. If your instructor agrees, you can read your freewriting to a group for reactions and suggestions. You can also begin by brainstorming a list of questions to help you define your term. If your instructor agrees, you can work with a group to develop brainstorming questions. Following is the list of types.

the rebel	the dead weight	the Internet troll
the innovator	the lone wolf	the confidante
the conspiracy theorist	the politician	the sympathizer
the optimist	the debater	the inconsiderate friend
the computer wizard	the manipulator	the sports fanatic
the pragmatist	the judge	the debutante

3. Think of one word that best defines you. In a paragraph, define that word, using yourself as a source of examples and details. To begin, you may want to freewrite about several words that define you; then you can select the most appropriate one.

4. Each year the Oxford University Press, publisher of the *Oxford Dictionary*, announces words (or phrases) of the year. In 2016, this word was *un-truth*. In the past, words such as *selfie, unfriend, locavore, podcast, carbon footprint,* and *credit crunch* were selected.

   Choose a word of the year, either from Oxford University Press or another major dictionary (i.e. *Merriam-Webster*). Write an essay that defines the term and provides specific details that go beyond a typical dictionary definition.

5. Study the photograph of the soldiers in battle. Then write a paragraph that defines (1) teamwork or (2) courage under fire.

Topics for Critical Thinking and Writing

1. Think of a word or phrase that has different meanings to different groups (age groups, political groups, people in different levels of socioeconomic status, and so on). For example, the word *freedom* means something different to a person in prison than it means to a teen who has a curfew. Choose an abstract word and write at least three meanings of it. Be sure to assign each meaning to a specific group or type of individual.

2. Too often, people resort to using stereotypes when they describe a group or even a type of person. For example, the word *politician* is a derogatory term when it is spoken with a condescending tone of voice in certain circumstances, but not all those who choose a career in public service are the same. As another example, "a free spirit" can be described as someone who is either highly creative and independent or unpredictable and erratic. Consider three terms that are commonly used today as quick, stereotypical definitions for complicated issues. In addition, explain how each term has alternate meanings.

> **Note:** Additional writing options suitable for definition-related assignments can be found in the "Readings for Writers" appendix at the end of this book.

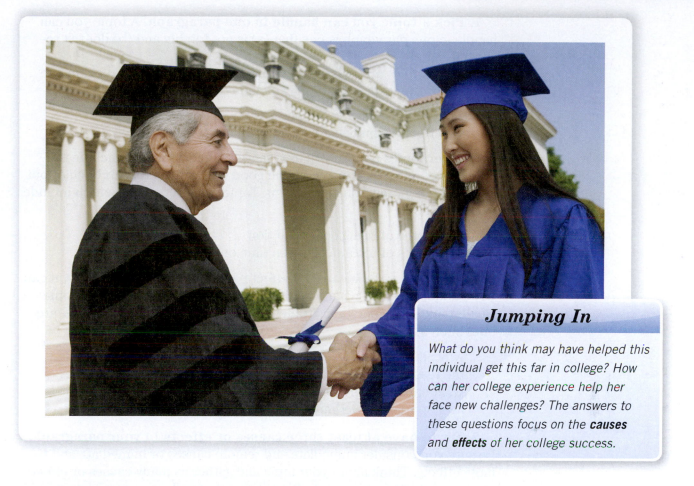

Jumping In

*What do you think may have helped this individual get this far in college? How can her college experience help her face new challenges? The answers to these questions focus on the **causes** and **effects** of her college success.*

Learning Objectives

In this chapter, you will learn how to:

1. Identify immediate and long-range cause and effect.
2. Prewrite to generate a topic for a cause or effect paragraph, deciding on the best order in which to present details.
3. Write a cause or effect paragraph that incorporates transitions and details effectively.

WHAT IS CAUSE AND EFFECT?

Almost every day, you consider the causes or effects of events so that you can make choices and take action. In writing a paragraph, when you explain the **reasons** for something, you are writing about **causes**. When you write about the **results** of something, you are writing about **effects**. Often in writing, you consider both the causes and effects of a decision, an event, a change in your life, or a change in society, but in this chapter, you will be asked to *concentrate on either causes (reasons) or effects (results).*

1. Identify immediate and long-range cause and effect.

Hints for Writing a Cause or Effect Paragraph

1. **Pick a topic you can handle in one paragraph.** A topic you can handle in one paragraph is one that (a) is not too big and (b) doesn't require research.

Some topics are so large that you probably can't cover them in one paragraph. Topics that are too big include ones such as:

why some people experience anxiety or depression
the effects of bullying on teenagers

Other topics require you to research the facts and to include the opinions of experts. They would be good topics for a research paper but not for a one-paragraph assignment. Topics that require research include ones such as:

the causes of rising college tuition
the effects of too much screen time on children

When you write a cause or effect paragraph, choose a topic you can write about by using what you already know. That is, make your topic smaller and more personal. Topics that use what you already know are ones such as:

why children love spending time on playgrounds
the reasons for my academic success
what enlistment in the marines did for my sister
how sports changed my life

2. **Try to have at least three causes or effects in your paragraph.** Be sure you consider immediate and remote causes or immediate and remote effects. Think about your topic and gather as many causes or effects as you can *before* you start drafting your paragraph.

An event usually has more than one cause. Think beyond the obvious, the **immediate cause**, to more **remote causes**. Although the immediate cause of your car accident might be the other driver who hit the rear end of your car, the more remote causes might include the weather conditions or the condition of the road.

Situations can have more than one effect, too. If you take Algebra I for the second time and you pass the course with a "C," an **immediate effect** (result) is that you fulfill the requirements for graduation. But there may be **long-range effects** (also called **remote results**). Your success in Algebra I may help to change your attitude toward mathematics courses, may build your confidence in your ability to handle college work, or may lead you to sign up for another course taught by the same teacher.

3. **Make your causes and effects clear and specific.** If you are writing about why short haircuts are popular, don't write, "Short haircuts are popular because everybody is getting one," or "Short haircuts are popular because they are a trend." If you write either of those statements, you have really said, "Short haircuts are popular because they are popular."

Think further. Have any celebrities been seen with this haircut? Write the names of actors, athletes, or musicians who have the haircut, or the name of the movie and the actor that started the trend. Is short hair easier to maintain?

Is it more professional looking? By giving specific details that explain, illustrate, or describe a cause or effect, you help the reader understand your point.

4. Write a topic sentence that indicates whether your paragraph is about causes or effects. You should not announce, but you can *indicate*.

> **not this:** The effects of my winning the scholarship are going to be discussed. (an announcement)
> **but this:** Winning the scholarship changed my plans for college. (indicates effects will be discussed)

You can *list* a short version of all your causes or effects in your topic sentence, like this:

> The high price of concert tickets has enriched a few performers and promoters, excluded many fans, and threatened the future of live entertainment.

You can just *hint* at your points by summarizing them, like this:

> The high price of concert tickets has brought riches to a few but hurt many others.

Or you can use words that *signal* causes or effects.

> **words that signal causes:** reasons, why, because, motives, intentions
> **words that signal effects:** results, impact, consequences, changed, threatened, improved

---

Exercise 1   **Practice: Selecting a Suitable Topic for a Cause or Effect Paragraph**

A list of topics follows. Some are suitable for a cause or effect paragraph. Some are too large to handle in one paragraph, some would require research, and some are both too large and would require research. Put an *X* next to any topic that is not suitable.

1. _____ the effects of alcoholism on the children of alcoholics

2. _____ the impact of technological advancements on the agricultural workforce

3. _____ the reasons I was accused of plagiarism

4. _____ my mother's motives for seeking a college degree

5. _____ how a stranger's kindness changed one baby's fate

6. _____ the media's impact on contributing to racial bias

7. _____ the causes of political disagreements

8. _____ how too much screen time changes cognition

CRITICAL THINKING

When devising a topic and developing a paragraph, think carefully about immediate causes and effects as well as remote causes and long-range effects. Think of a row of dominoes. Touching the first one affects the last one as well.

Exercise 2 Practice: Recognizing Cause and Effect in Topic Sentences

In the list that follows, if the topic sentence is for a cause paragraph, put *C* next to it. If the sentence is for an effect paragraph, put *E* next to it.

1. _____ Once my brother left home, he developed more mature attitudes toward earning, spending, and saving money.

2. _____ Chloe's trip to the Dominican Republic had a surprising impact on her career plans.

3. _____ I broke up with my boyfriend to escape his constant criticism, make my own friends, and reconnect with my family.

4. _____ Dr. Menendez has three reasons for opening a free clinic near the farm workers' camp.

5. _____ One successful semester at college changed my mother's hopes, ambitions, and self-esteem.

6. _____ Moving out of my parents' house allowed me to experience personal freedom, to demonstrate responsibility, and to live within a strict budget.

7. _____ Enrolling in an advanced psychology class changed my career choice.

8. _____ One way to explain the impact of social networking on our lives is to examine how people regularly use it.

WRITING THE CAUSE OR EFFECT PARAGRAPH IN STEPS

❷ Prewrite to generate a topic for a cause or effect paragraph, deciding on the best order in which to present details.

PREWRITING CAUSE OR EFFECT

Once you've picked a topic, the next—and very important—step is getting ideas. Because this paragraph will contain only causes *or* effects and details about them, you must be sure you have enough causes or effects to write a developed paragraph.

Freewriting on a Topic

One way to get ideas is to freewrite on your topic. Because causes and effects are so clearly connected, you can begin by freewriting about both and then you can choose one, causes or effects, later.

If you were thinking about writing a cause or effect paragraph on owning a car, you could begin by freewriting something such as:

Freewriting on Owning a Car

A car of my own. Why? I needed it. Couldn't get a part-time job without one. Because I couldn't get to work. Needed it to get to school. Of course I could have taken the bus to school. But I didn't want to. Feel like a grown-up when you have a car of your own. Freedom to come and go. I was the last of my friends to have a car. Couldn't wait. An old Ford. But I fixed it up nicely. Costs a lot to maintain. Car payments, car loan. Car insurance.

Now you can review the freewriting and make separate lists of the causes and effects you wrote down:

causes (reasons)

needed to get a part-time job
needed to get to school
my friends had cars

effects (results)

feel like a grown-up
freedom to come and go
costs a lot to maintain
car payments
car loan
car insurance

Because you have more details on the effects of owning a car, you decide to write an effects paragraph.

Your list of effects can be used several ways. You can add to it if you think of ideas as you are reviewing your list. You can begin to group ideas in your list and then add to it. Following is a grouping of the list of effects; grouping helps you see how many effects and details you have.

effects of getting my own car

effect 1:	*I had to pay for the car and related expenses.*
details:	*costs a lot to maintain*
	car payments
	car loan
	car insurance
effect 2:	*I had the freedom to come and go.*
details:	*none*
effect 3:	*I felt like a grown-up.*
details:	*none*

Will these effects work in a paragraph? One way to decide is to try to add details to the ones that have no details. Ask questions to get those details.

effect 2: I had the freedom to come and go.

What do you mean?

Well, I didn't have to beg my father for his truck anymore. I didn't have to get rides from friends. I could go to the city when I wanted. I could ride around just for fun.

effect 3: I felt like a grown-up.

What do you mean, "like a grown-up"?

Adults can go where they want, when they want. They drive themselves.

If you look carefully at the answers to the questions, you'll find that the two effects are really *the same*. By adding details to both effects, you'll find that both are saying that owning a car gives you the adult freedom to come and go.

So the list needs another effect of owning a car. What else happened, how else did things change when you got your car? You might answer:

I worried about someone hitting my car.
I worried about bad drivers.
I wanted to avoid the scratches you get in parking lots.

With answers like these, your third effect could be:

I became a more careful driver.

Now that you have three effects and some details, you can rewrite your list. You can add details as you rewrite.

List of Effects of Getting My Own Car

effect 1:   *I had to pay for the car and related expenses.*
details: *costs a lot to maintain*
                 car loans
                 car insurance
effect 2:   *I had the adult freedom to come and go.*
details: *didn't have to beg my father for his truck*
                 didn't have to get rides from friends
                 could go to the city when I wanted
                 could ride around for fun
effect 3:   *I became a more careful driver.*
details: *worried about someone hitting the car*
                 worried about bad drivers
                 wanted to avoid the scratches cars get in parking lots

---

Devising a Topic Sentence

With at least three effects and some details for each effect, you can create a topic sentence. The topic sentence for this paragraph should indicate that the subject is the *effects* of getting a car. You can summarize all three effects in your topic sentence, or you can just hint at them. A possible topic sentence for the paragraph can be:

Owning my own car cost me money, gave me freedom, and made me more careful about how I drive.

or

Once I got a car of my own, I realized the good and bad sides of ownership.

With a topic sentence and a fairly extensive list of details, you are ready to begin the planning stage in preparing your paragraph.

Collaborate

Exercise 3   **Collaborate: Devising Questions for a Cause or Effect Paragraph**

Four topics for cause or effect paragraphs follow. For each topic, write five questions that could lead you to ideas on the topic. (The first one is completed for you.) After you've written five questions for each topic, give your list to a member of your writing group. Ask him or her to add one question to each topic and then to pass the exercise on to the next member of the group. Repeat the process so that each group member adds to the lists of all the other members.

Later, if your instructor agrees, you can answer the questions (and add more questions and answers) as a way to begin writing a cause or effect paragraph.

1. **topic:** the effects of cell-phone cameras on crime

   questions that can lead to ideas and details:

   a. <u>Are unsuspecting people photographed and blackmailed?</u>

   b. <u>Can the cameras be used to photograph confidential documents?</u>

   c. <u>Are the cameras being used by Peeping Toms?</u>

   d. <u>Can criminals use the camera-phones to photograph banks?</u>

   e. <u>Can citizens photograph a crime in progress?</u>

   additional questions: <u>Can citizens photograph a suspect or perpetrator?</u>

   <u>Can police use the cameras in surveillance?</u>

2. **topic:** the effects of late-night cramming for an exam

   questions that can lead to ideas and details:

   a. _____

   b. _____

   c. _____

   d. _____

   e. _____

   additional questions: _____

   _____

3. **topic:** why many adults drink beverages full of sugar

   questions that could lead to ideas and details:

   a. _____

   b. _____

   c. _____

   d. _____

   e. _____

   additional questions: _____

   _____

Exercise 4   **Practice: Creating Causes or Effects for Topic Sentences**

For each of the following topic sentences, create three causes or effects, depending on what the topic sentence requires. The first one is completed for you.

1. **topic sentence:** Keeping a daily planner has both improved and complicated my life.

   a. <u>I do not miss as many important appointments as I used to.</u>

   _____

  b. I am better able to budget my time, particularly around busy periods in my life.

  _____

  c. Keeping an accurate daily planner requires additional time and diligence.

  _____

2. **topic sentence:** Studying with a friend can be a useful way to prepare for a test.

  a. _____

  _____

  b. _____

  _____

  c. _____

  _____

3. **topic sentence:** There are several reasons people enjoy outdoor concerts.

  a. _____

  _____

  _____

  b. _____

  _____

  _____

  c. _____

  _____

  _____

PLANNING   **CAUSE OR EFFECT**

With a topic sentence and a list of causes (or effects) and details, you can draft an outline of your paragraph. Once you have a rough outline, you can work on revising it. You may want to add to it, to take out certain ideas, to rewrite the topic sentence, or to change the order of the ideas. The following checklist may help you revise your outline.

> **Checklist for Revising the Outline of a Cause or Effect Paragraph**
>
> ✓ Does my topic sentence make my point?
>
> ✓ Does it indicate whether my paragraph is about causes or effects?
>
> ✓ Does the topic sentence relate to the rest of the outline?
>
> ✓ Have I included enough causes or effects to make my point?
>
> ✓ Have I included enough details?
>
> ✓ Should I eliminate any ideas?
>
> ✓ Is the order of my causes or effects clear and logical?

The Order of Causes or Effects

Looking at a draft outline can help you decide on the best order for your causes or effects. There is no single rule for organizing causes or effects. Instead, you should think about the ideas you are presenting and decide on the most logical and effective order. For example, if you are writing about some immediate and some long-range effects, you might want to discuss the effects in a **time order**. You might begin with the immediate effect, then discuss what happens later, and end with what happens last of all. If you are discussing three or four effects that are not in any particular time order, you might save the most important effect for last, for an **emphatic order**. If one cause leads to another, then use the **logical order** of discussing the causes.

Compare the following outline on owning a car to the list of effects on page 190. Notice that, in the outline, the carefree side of owning a car comes first, and the cares of owning a car, the expense and the worry, come later. The topic sentence follows the same order.

Outline for an Effects Paragraph

revised topic sentence	Owning my own car gave me freedom, cost me money, and made me careful about how I drive.
effect 1 details	I had the adult freedom to come and go. I didn't have to beg my father for his truck. I didn't have to get rides from my friends. I could go to the city when I wanted. I could ride around for fun.
effect 2 details	I had to pay for the car and related expenses. A car costs a lot to maintain. I had a car loan to pay. I had car insurance.
effect 3 details	I became a more careful driver. I worried about someone hitting the car. I worried about bad drivers. I wanted to avoid the scratches cars can get in a parking lot.

Once you have a revised outline of your cause or effect paragraph, you are ready to begin writing your draft.

Exercise 5 **Practice: Writing Topic Sentences for Cause or Effect Outlines**

The following outline has no topic sentence. Read the outline carefully several times. Then write a topic sentence.

topic sentence: _____

_____

details: Many of my high school friends were planning to attend Lyndon Community College.

As a result, I would have people to socialize with at the college.

I wouldn't feel as lonely as I would at a college full of strangers.

Lyndon Community College offered two-year degrees in Nursing, and I was thinking of becoming a nurse.

I like the idea of learning a marketable skill in two years.

Location was my main reason for choosing to attend Lyndon Community College.

The college was only fifteen minutes away from my parents' house.

I could save money on rent and food by continuing to live at home.

I could save on transportation costs, too.

Exercise 6   **Practice: Revising the Order of Causes or Effects**

Following are topic sentences and lists of causes or effects. Reorder each list according to the directions given at the end of the list. Put "1" by the item that would come first, and so forth.

1. **topic sentence:** Going on a diet changed my father's life.

   _____ He learned the difference between healthy and unhealthy food.

   _____ After eating right for a year, my father was better able to control his blood pressure.

   _____ Once my father began to choose more healthy foods such as fruits, vegetables, and fish, he began to have more energy.

   Use this order: Time order

2. **topic sentence:** Reducing my work hours so that I could attend college has had negative and positive effects on me.

   _____ I cannot spend much money on entertainment now.

   _____ I can see the future financial benefits of attending college.

   _____ I am able to focus more on my classes.

   Use this order: The order indicated by the topic sentence, from bad to good.

CRITICAL THINKING

When determining the most effective ordering of items, you will need to evaluate the time sequence and importance of each item.

Exercise 7   **Practice: Developing an Outline**

The following outline needs one more cause or effect and details for that cause or effect. Fill in the missing parts.

> **topic sentence:** People give many reasons for taking a gap year before attending college.

cause 1:	Some say gap years allow them to mature more before attending college.
details:	They say they are not ready to decide about their future.
	They believe they are not ready to live on their own responsibly.
	They feel they are not emotionally ready for college.
cause 2:	Others say gap years help to ignite a passion.
details:	Some say work experience can help them choose a field of study.
	Others claim service work sparks a desire to pursue careers that help other people.
	Others find interests through traveling and seeing the world.
cause 3:	_____
	_____

details (at least two sentences): _____

_____

_____

_____

_____

DRAFTING AND REVISING   CAUSE OR EFFECT

Once you have an outline in good order, with a sufficient number of causes or effects and a fair amount of detail, you can write a first draft of the paragraph. When the first draft is complete, you can read and reread it, deciding how you'd like to improve it. The following checklist may help you revise.

3 Write a cause or effect paragraph that incorporates transitions and details effectively.

Checklist for Revising the Draft of a Cause or Effect Paragraph

✓ Does my topic sentence indicate cause or effect?

✓ Does it relate to the rest of the paragraph?

✓ Do I have enough causes or effects to make my point?

✓ Do I have enough details for each cause or effect?

✓ Are my causes or effects explained clearly?

✓ Is there a clear connection between my ideas?

✓ Have I shown the links between my ideas?

✓ Do I need an opening or closing sentence?

Linking Ideas in Cause or Effect

When you write about how one event or situation causes another, or about how one result leads to another, you have to be clear in showing the connections among events, situations, or effects.

One way to be clear is to rely on transitions. Some transitions are particularly helpful in writing cause and effect paragraphs.

INFO BOX Transitions for a Cause or Effect Paragraph

For cause paragraphs:

because	for	for this reason	since
due to			

For effect paragraphs:

as a result	hence	so	therefore
consequently	in consequence	then	thus

Making the Links Clear

Using the right transition is not always enough to make your point. Sometimes you have to write the missing link in your line of thinking so that the reader can understand your point. To write the missing link means writing phrases, clauses, or sentences that help the reader follow your point.

> **not this:** Many mothers are working outside the home. Consequently, microwave ovens are popular.
>
> **but this:** Many mothers are working outside the home and have less time to cook. Consequently, microwave ovens, which can cook food in minutes, are popular.

The hard part of making clear links between ideas is that you have to put yourself in your reader's place. Remember that your reader cannot read your mind, only your paper. Connections between ideas may be clear in your mind, but you must spell them out on paper.

CRITICAL THINKING

It is important that writers clearly communicate to their audience—their readers. Communication breaks down when there are missing links in writing. When we eliminate these missing links, we *build bridges* that help to restore clear communication.

Revising the Draft

Assume that the following paragraph is a revised draft of the paragraph on owning a car. When you read it, you'll notice many changes from the outline on page 193.

- The details on "car payments" and "a car loan" said the same thing, so the repetition has been cut.
- Some details about the costs of maintaining a car and about parking have been added.
- The order of the details about the costs of a car has been changed. Now, paying for a car comes first; maintaining it comes after.
- Sentences have been combined.
- Transitions have been added.

You may spot some careless errors that can be corrected during the editing and proofreading stage.

Draft of an Effects Paragraph

(Note: Changes from the outline are underlined; editing and proofreading are still necessary.)

transition

Owning my own car gave me freedom, cost me money, and made me more careful about how I drive. <u>First of all</u>, my car gives me the adult freedom to come and go. I didn't have to beg my father for his truck. I didn't have to ask for rides from my friends anymore. I could go to the city or even ride around

transition

for fun when I wanted. <u>On the negative side</u>, I had to pay for the car and related expenses. I had to pay for the car loan. I

order of details changed

also had to pay for the car insurance. <u>A car costs a lot to maintain, too. I paid for oil changes, tune-ups, tires, belts and</u>

added details

<u>filters</u>. <u>With so much of my money put into my car</u>, I became a

transitional phrase

more careful driver. I worried about someone hitting the car and watched out for bad drivers. <u>In addition</u>, I wanted to avoid

transition

the scratchs a car can get in a parking lot, so I always parked far away from other cars.

Exercise 8   **Practice: Making the Links Clear**

Following are ideas that are linked, but their connection is not clearly explained. Rewrite each pair of ideas, making the connection clear.

1. It's been raining all week. As a result, I've been taking an allergy pill every day.

   rewritten: _____

   _____

   _____

   _____

   (Hint: What is the connection between your allergies and rain?)

2. Alex wanted a real Cuban dish of beans and rice. Therefore, he went home for the weekend.

   rewritten: _____

   _____

   _____

   _____

   (Hint: Can someone at home make Alex a real Cuban dish of beans and rice?)

3. The first dog I saw at the animal shelter had a long, thick coat of red hair. Consequently, I chose a brown dog with shorter hair.

rewritten: _____

_____

_____

_____

(Hint: Were you worried about the amount of hair the first dog would shed?)

Exercise 9 **Practice: Revising a Paragraph by Adding Details**

The following paragraph is missing details. Add at least two details as you extend the paragraph by two additional sentences.

Being diagnosed with diabetes had a tremendous impact on me. When the doctor told me the news, I was horrified. My first thoughts focused on losing a limb or dying young. In addition, the misery of constantly monitoring my blood sugar levels, giving myself frequent injections, and rigidly following a limited diet scared me. Once I became more informed and rational about the challenges I faced, I was angry. I could not understand why I had the bad luck of developing diabetes. I cursed my situation and wallowed in self-pity. Learning to eat healthy foods, to control my blood sugar, and to avoid infections seemed like punishments I did not deserve. When I finally accepted my situation, I understood that the doctor's diagnosis had been a gift of life. _____

_____

_____

_____

_____

Once I let go of misery, fear, and anger, I found a new gratitude for being alive.

EDITING AND PROOFREADING **CAUSE OR EFFECT**

Once you are satisfied with your latest draft, it is time to edit. As you strive to improve your style and check for mistakes, the following checklist will help you edit effectively.

> **Checklist for Editing a Draft of a Cause or Effect Paragraph**
>
> ✓   Should any sentences be combined?
>
> ✓   Are the verb forms correct and consistent?
>
> ✓   Are the word choices appropriate?
>
> ✓   Is the spelling correct?
>
> ✓   Is the punctuation correct?

As you check your latest draft for errors in sentence length, grammar, spelling, or preparation, you can also look out for small improvements in the style and continuity of the paragraph. When you contrast the final version with the draft on page 197, you'll notice several changes:

- An introductory sentence has been added.
- The verb form *gives* has been corrected to *gave*.
- The sentence *I didn't have to beg my father for his truck* has been combined with *I didn't have to get rides from my friends anymore*.
- The sentence *I had to pay for the car loan* has been combined with *I had to pay for car insurance*.
- A comma has been added after *belts*.
- The transitional phrase *to avoid dangers in the parking lot as well as on the road* has been added for better style.
- The spelling of *scratches* has been corrected.
- Some words have been changed so that the language is more precise.

Changes in style, word choice, and transitions can all be made before you decide on the final version of your paragraph. You may also want to add an opening or closing sentence to your paragraph.

Final Version of an Effects Paragraph

(Note: Changes from the draft are underlined.)

When I bought my first car, I wasn't prepared for all the changes it made in my life. Owning my own car gave me freedom, cost me money, and made me careful about how I drive. First of all, my car gave me the adult freedom to come and go. I didn't have to beg my father for his truck or get rides from my friends anymore. I could go to the city or even ride around for fun when I wanted. On the negative side, I had to pay for the car and related expenses. I had to pay for both the car loan and car insurance. A car costs money to maintain, too. I paid for oil changes, tune-ups, tires, belts, and filters. With so much of my money put into my car, I became a more careful driver. I worried about someone hitting the car and watched out for bad drivers. To avoid dangers in the parking lot as well as on the road, I always parked my car far away from other cars, keeping my car safe from scratches.

> **For your information:** A sample effects essay based on this topic and following the same writing steps can be found in Chapter 13, "Different Essay Patterns: Part Two."

Exercise 10 **Practice: Editing a Draft by Combining Sentences**

Combine the underlined sentences in the following paragraph. Write your combinations in the space above the original sentences.

Quitting smoking changed me in some unexpected ways. First, it gave me a real sense of power. I had been sure that quitting would be impossible for me. I was smoking a pack a day. At that time, I decided to try cutting back. My initial goal was to cut my smoking in half. I was able to do this. It did not take much effort. It took me about three months. When I had achieved this goal, I aimed to push ahead. I tried hard to cut my cigarette habit to five cigarettes per day. Eventually I succeeded in limiting myself to five a day. Then I tried four a day. Next I cut my limit to three. The hardest part was giving them up entirely, but I did it. Once I quit, I changed in another way. I developed a new understanding of the reasons that nonsmokers avoid smokers. I realized that rooms do absorb the smell of cigarettes. The clothes that smokers wear smell, too. Smokers also have bad breath. Suddenly I became someone who avoided smoke-filled people and rooms. Finally, breaking the smoking habit led me to make another big change. I stopped drinking. During the time when I was cutting back on cigarettes, I became aware that nothing made me crave a cigarette more than drinking a beer or mixed drink. In my final days as a smoker, I avoided any temptation to smoke. As a result, I stopped drinking. Now I am determined to stay nicotine-free. I am alcohol-free as well. I have broken two habits. I am twice as healthy as I expected to be.

Exercise 11 **Practice: Correcting a Final Copy of a Cause or Effect Paragraph**

Following are one cause and one effect paragraph with the kind of errors it is easy to overlook when you prepare the final version of an assignment. Correct the errors, writing above the lines. There are twelve errors in the first (cause) paragraph; there are twelve errors in the second (effects) paragraph.

Paragraph 1

I got my job at a Discount Appliance store for three reason's. First, I used my imagination and asked myself, "Who would want to hire me"? I didn't have much experience because I had spent the last three years at one job. That job was unpacking merchandise at my uncle's dollar store. When he had to close his store, I started thinking about my skills. I was able to carry heavy loads, I was careful not to break the merchandise, and I knowed how to make the best use of storage space. When, I realized that I did have some skills, I kept looking for a place that needed them. After any employer turned me down, I checked with him or her several more times. Soon I became a familiar, face. I smiled, and learned the names of the boss and the staff at each place of work. However, I also learned not to a nuisance. The last reason that I eventually found work was the more important. I swore that I was willing to work for a low wage. I was not to proud to accept any offer. I now have a job at the delivery entrance to a large household appliance store. I unload and fit large boxes of Refrigerators, stoves, washers, and dryers into tight storeage areas. By selling my skills, persevering, and accepting a minimum wage, I found employment.

Paragraph 2

When I was younger, I had a mania for clothes shopping and the crazyness hurt me in several way. First, I shopped in a state of elation, and I lost my common sense. The first item that caught my eye became irresistible. I felt that bying it, would, change my life. I knew that I had to have it. After I bought it, some shoes or jeans or a jacket seemed to be calling me. I craved them, too. In such an irrational state, I bought some hideous clothes. Second, I never truely enjoyed the experience of buying the items because the endless shopping was a compulsion. In every store, I acted like a robot. Hours after I returned home, I look at my purchases and felt disappointed. The new clothes hadn't changed much about my life. In fact; all the new purchases have done was to change my bank balance. The worse affect of my mania was the constant worry about paying for my shopping spree's. This fear became overwhelming as the bills kepped coming. My mania brought me three emotions: a rush of elation, inevitable disappointment, and endless fear.

Lines of Detail: A Walk-Through Assignment

Write a paragraph on this topic: Why Many Adults Drink Beverages Full of Sugar. To write your paragraph, follow these steps:

Step 1: Go back to Exercise 3 on pages 190–191. Topic 3 is the same topic as this assignment. If you have already done that exercise, you have five or more questions that can lead you to ideas and details.

Step 2: Use the answers to your questions to prepare a list of ideas and details. Put the items on your list into groups of causes and related details. Add to the groups until you have at least three causes (and related details) for the similarity in many college students' wardrobes.

Step 3: Write a topic sentence that fits your causes.

Step 4: Write an outline. Check that your outline has sufficient details and that you have put the causes in the best order.

Step 5: Write a rough draft of your paragraph and revise it until you have enough specific details to explain each cause. Your details should be logical, clearly stated, and ordered effectively. You may have to work through several drafts until you are satisfied.

Step 6: Edit your work extensively to improve style and correct any serious mistakes. Decide if your paragraph needs an opening sentence or a concluding sentence for better structure.

Step 7: Prepare a clean copy of your paragraph and proofread it carefully to spot and correct any careless spelling, punctuation, typing, or format errors.

Topics for Writing a Cause or Effect Paragraph

When you write on any of the following topics, be sure to work through the stages of the writing process in preparing your cause or effect paragraph.

1. Write a cause paragraph on one of the following topics. You create the topic by filling in the blanks.

   Why People Love _____
   Why People Prevent _____
   Why People Argue _____
   Why People Keep _____

Collaborate

2. Many schools and colleges design short marketing videos to promote their schools. Imagine your class has been asked by your school's marketing department to design new promotional videos they hope to post on YouTube. The video and the reasons you give to attend your school will hopefully result in increased enrollment.

   In a small group, brainstorm the reasons why a perspective student should attend your school. Organize these reasons so that the most important reason is stated last. Write a script for the promotional video and be sure to include at least three compelling reasons why a perspective student should attend your school.

Afterward, if there is time, you may want to create the actual promotional video from your script. Use the script as a background (a voice over) for the visual depictions of your reasons for attending your school.

3. Think of a current fad or trend. The fad can be a popular style of clothing, type of movie, style of music, a sport, a pastime, a kind of food or drink, an athlete, a gadget, an invention, an appliance, and so on. Write a paragraph on the causes of this fad or trend or the effects of it.

Collaborate

   If your instructor agrees, begin by brainstorming with a group. Create a list of three or four fads or trends. Then create a list of questions to ask (and answer) about each fad or trend. If you are going to write about **causes**, for example, you might ask questions like these:

> What changes in society have encouraged this trend?
> Have changes in the economy helped to make it popular?
> Does it appeal to a specific age group? Why?
> Does it meet any hidden emotional needs? For instance, is it a
>   way to gain status, to feel safe, or to feel powerful?

   If you are going to write about **effects**, you might ask questions like these:

> Will this trend last?
> Has it affected competitors?
> Is it spreading?
> Is the fad changing business, education, or the family?
> Has it improved daily life?

4. Write a paragraph that summarizes the effects of relying on a computer for composing most, if not all, of your writing assignments. Remember that the effects may be both positive and negative, so you will need to brainstorm or freewrite first. Be sure your final version of the paragraph reflects logical organization of details and appropriate transitions.

5. After looking at the photograph, write a paragraph on why joining an exercise group can have social benefits.

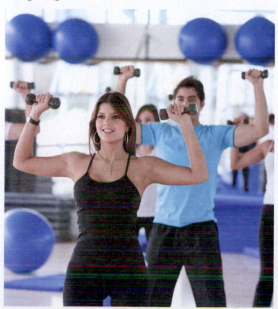

Topics for Critical Thinking and Writing

1. Why do you think so many Americans do not register or even bother to vote? Pose this question to some of your peers and friends to gather as many reasons as you can for so much voter apathy. Determine three main causes and use emphatic order (least to most significant) as you explain each cause.

2. Applying the same techniques suggested in topic 1, ask friends, peers, and family members who are registered voters why they feel voting is so important. Determine three main causes and use emphatic order as you explain each cause.

3. Before the Internet and cable television, many Americans received their news from network television or radio broadcast. Because there were relatively few choices in sources of news, news stations sought to attract large, diverse audiences. Today, however, Americans have countless sources of news information. These sources include social media, cable, and online news sources. This shift in the way Americans receive their news is a shift from broadcasting to narrowcasting. News stations are now attracting smaller, but more specific audiences.

   Consider this shift in the way Americans receive their news. What are the effects, both positive and negative, of this shift from broadcast to narrowcast news? Be sure to spend some time brainstorming potential effects. Consider creating a poll using a site like Survey Monkey. Then ask your friends and family to rate which of the effects are most beneficial and most negative. Use this information to identify and write about at least three effects of this shift.

Note: Additional writing options suitable for cause- or effect-related assignments can be found in the "Readings for Writers" appendix at the end of this book.

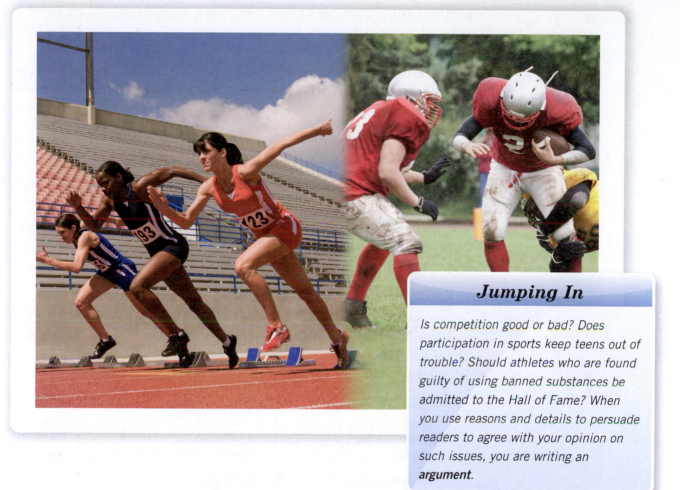

Jumping In

Is competition good or bad? Does participation in sports keep teens out of trouble? Should athletes who are found guilty of using banned substances be admitted to the Hall of Fame? When you use reasons and details to persuade readers to agree with your opinion on such issues, you are writing an **argument**.

Learning Objectives

In this chapter, you will learn how to:

1. Recognize the argument's targeted audience.
2. Prewrite to generate a topic for an argument paragraph, grouping ideas and ordering reasons.
3. Write a convincing argument paragraph that incorporates transitions effectively.

WHAT IS ARGUMENT?

A written **argument** is an attempt to *persuade* a reader to think or act in a certain way. When you write an argument paragraph, your goal is to get people to see your point so that they are persuaded to accept it and perhaps to act on it.

In an argument paragraph, you take a stand. Then you support your stand with reasons. In addition, you give details for each reason. Your goal is to persuade your reader by making a point that has convincing reasons and details.

① Recognize the argument's targeted audience.

Hints for Writing an Argument Paragraph

1. Pick a topic you can handle. Your topic should be small enough to be covered in one paragraph. For instance, you can't argue effectively for world peace in just one paragraph.

2. Pick a topic you can handle based on your own experience and observation. Topics like legalizing drugs, gun control, capital punishment, or climate change require research into facts, figures, and expert opinions to make a complete argument. They are topics you can write about convincingly in a longer research paper, but for a one-paragraph argument, pick a topic based on what you've experienced yourself.

> **not this topic:** organized crime
> **but this topic:** starting a crime watch program in my neighborhood

3. Do two things in your topic sentence: name the subject of your argument and take a stand. The following topic sentences do both.

> subject   takes a stand
> The college cafeteria should serve healthier snacks.

> subject   takes a stand
> High school athletes who fail a course should not be allowed to play on a school team.

You should take a stand, but *don't* announce it:

> **not this:** This paragraph will explain why Madison needs more bicycle lanes.
> **but this:** Madison should expand the number of bicycle lanes throughout the city. (This is a topic sentence with a subject and a stand.)

4. Consider your audience. Consider why your audience should support your points. How will they be likely to object? How will you get around these objections? For instance, you might want to argue to the residents of your community that the intersection of Hawthorne Road and Sheridan Street needs a traffic light. Would anyone object? If they would object, how might you address their objections?

At first, you might think, "No. Why would anyone object? The intersection is dangerous. There's too much traffic there. People risk major accidents getting across the intersection." However, if you think further about your audience, which is the people in your community, you might identify these objections: (1) Some town residents may not want to pay for a traffic signal, and (2) some drivers may not want to spend extra time waiting for a light to change.

There are several ways to handle objections:

- You can *refute* an objection. To refute means to prove that an objection isn't valid, or that it isn't true. For instance, if someone says that a light wouldn't do any good, you might say that a new light has already worked in a nearby neighborhood.
- Sometimes it's best to admit the other side has a point. You have to *concede* that point. For instance, traffic lights do cost money, and waiting for a light to change does take time.
- Sometimes you can *turn an objection into an advantage.* When you acknowledge the objection and yet use it to make your own point, you show that you've considered both sides of the argument.

For instance, you might say that the price of a traffic signal at the intersection is well worth the expense because that light will buy safety for all the drivers who try to cross Hawthorne Road and Sheridan Street. As an alternative, you might say that waiting a few moments for the light to change is better than waiting many minutes for an opening in the heavy traffic of the intersection.

5. Be specific, clear, and logical in your reasons. As always, think before you write. Think about your point and your audience. Try to come up with at least three reasons for your position.

Be careful that your reasons do not overlap. For instance, you might write the following:

topic sentence:	College students should get discounts on movie tickets.
audience:	Owners of movie theaters
reasons:	1. Many college students can't afford current ticket prices.
	2. The cost of tickets is high for most students.
	3. More people in the theater means more popcorn and candy sold at the concession stand.

But reasons 1 and 2 overlap; they are really part of the same reason.

Be careful not to argue in a circle. For instance, if you say, "One reason for having an after-school program at Riverside Elementary School is that we need one there," you've just said, "We need an after-school program because we need an after-school program."

Finally, be specific in stating your reasons.

not this: One reason to start a bus service to and from the college is to help people.

but this: A bus service to and from the college would encourage students to leave their cars at home and use travel time to study.

CRITICAL THINKING

If you are looking for inspiration for topic selection, consider reading the opinion or letters-to-the-editor page of your local newspaper. You might also conduct a quick Internet search of national periodicals or listen to a local talk-show radio program or streaming podcast. The key component to writing an argument paragraph is to be invested in your topic and to write with conviction. Some of the best ideas for an argument paragraph are right in front of us.

Exercise 1 **Practice: Recognizing Good Topic Sentences for an Argument Paragraph**

Some of the topic sentences that follow are appropriate for an argument paragraph. Some are for topics that are too large for one paragraph, and some are for topics that would require research. Some are announcements. Some do not take a stand. Put *OK* next to the sentences that would work well in an argument paragraph.

1. _____ Residents of the Whispering Pines neighborhood must not let their dogs run loose.

2. _____ We must ensure that all Americans have access to high-speed Internet.

3. _____ Our community needs a local noise ordinance forbidding excessively loud sound systems in cars and trucks.

4. _____ Something must be done about cost of health insurance.

5. _____ Students should be required to be up-to-date on all vaccinations before being allowed to attend school.

6. _____ More online courses should be available to juniors and seniors at Emerson High School.

7. _____ The local quick mart should expand its hours to better serve our local community.

8. _____ Quality First, the largest employer in the county, needs an on-site child care center for the children of its employees.

Collaborate

| Exercise 2 | **Collaborate: Recognizing and Handling Objections**

The topic sentences of arguments follow. Working with a group, list two possible objections to each argument that might come from the specific audience identified. Then think of ways to handle each objection, by refuting it, conceding it, or trying to turn it to your advantage. On the lines provided, write the actual sentence(s) you would use in a paragraph.

1. **topic sentence:** The downtown area of Carsonville needs a network of bicycle lanes.

   audience: The residents of Carsonville

   possible objections from this audience:

   a. _____

   _____

   b. _____

   _____

   answering objections:

   a. _____

   _____

   b. _____

   _____

2. **topic sentence:** Large commercial moving vans should not be allowed to park on the streets of Bayside overnight.

   audience: Residents of Bayside who are planning to move and need to use a van

   possible objections from this audience:

   a. _____

   _____

b. _____

_____

answering objections:

a. _____

_____

b. _____

_____

WRITING THE ARGUMENT PARAGRAPH IN STEPS

② Prewrite to generate a topic for an argument paragraph, grouping ideas and ordering reasons.

PREWRITING   **ARGUMENT**

Imagine that your instructor has given you this assignment:

> Write a one-paragraph letter to the editor of your local newspaper. Argue for something in your town that needs to be changed.

One way to begin is to **brainstorm** for some specific thing that you can write about.

> *Is there a part of town that needs to be cleaned up?*
> *Should something be changed at a school?*
> *What do I notice on my way to work or school that needs improvement?*
> *What could be improved in my neighborhood?*

By answering these questions, you may come up with one topic, and then you can list ideas on it.

topic
Cleaning up Roberts Park

ideas
dirty and overgrown
benches are all cracked and broken
full of trash
could be fixed up
people work nearby
they would use it

CRITICAL THINKING

The argument mode of writing dates back to Ancient Greece. Two key structural components include *refutation* and *concession*, which show the speaker has thoughtfully considered opposing viewpoints, anticipated objections, and allowed as much of the opposing viewpoints as possible without weakening the thesis. This contributes to the *ethos* of the speaker, which is basically an appeal to the audience to trust the speaker as someone who is credible and trustworthy.

You can consider your audience and possible objections:

audience
people of all ages who read the local paper

possible objections from this audience
would cost money
more important things to spend money on

answering objections
Money would be well spent to beautify the downtown.
Cleaning up the park will bring more people downtown.
City children could play there in the fresh air and in nature; workers could eat lunch there.

Grouping Your Ideas

Once you have a list, you can start grouping the ideas on your list to develop an argument with clear reasons and supporting details. You should consider how your answers to possible objections help you to identify key reasons to be used in your argument. In other words, by answering objections, you can come up with the key reasons that best support your point.

In many successful arguments, writers also directly state and address their opponents' argument(s). They anticipate and explicitly mention their audience's possible objections and then respond to them. This is called *refutation*. You might consider when grouping your ideas which objection you might explicitly state and how you would refute it.

Following is a list with a point to argue, three supporting reasons, some supporting details about cleaning up Roberts Park, an objection to the point, and an answer to that objection.

List for an Argument Paragraph

point: We should fix up Roberts Park.
reason: Improving the park would make the downtown area more attractive to shoppers.
details: Shoppers could stroll in the park or rest from their shopping.
               Friends could meet in the park for a day of shopping and lunch.
reason: City children could play in the park.
details: They could get fresh air.
               They could play in a natural setting.
reason: Workers could eat lunch outdoors.
details: Several office complexes are nearby.
               Workers would take a break outdoors.
objection: The cost of fixing the park will impact the city's budget.
refutation: The money spent on beautifying the park will bring more people downtown. They will, in turn, spend money at local establishments and experience more civic pride.

With three reasons and some details for each, you can draft a topic sentence. Remember that your topic sentence for an argument should (1) name your subject and (2) take a stand. A topic sentence about Roberts Park that does both follows.

       subject   **takes a stand**
Roberts Park should be cleaned up and improved.

With a topic sentence, you are ready to move on to the planning stage of preparing an argument paragraph.

Exercise 3 Practice: Distinguishing between Reasons and Details

The following list has three reasons and details for each reason. Put *reason 1*, *reason 2*, and *reason 3* next to the points on the following list. Then put *detail for 1*, *detail for 2*, or *detail for 3* by the items that give details about each reason. There may be more than one sentence of detail connected to one reason.

topic sentence: Crystal Lake needs a weekly farmers' market.

_____ Many people want fresh, locally grown produce, plants, crafts, and baked goods.

_____ Small, local farmers need local outlets for their produce.

_____ Seasonal vegetables and fruits straight from the fields taste better than supermarket produce.

_____ Small family farms can bring their products to a nearby market and save money on shipping costs.

_____ Neighbors meet at the market, talk, and share coffee and homemade muffins.

_____ Fresh produce is healthier than food treated with preservatives and other chemicals.

_____ Farmers' markets bring a community together.

_____ Those who regularly shop at the market become friends with the merchants.

_____ Many supermarket chains deal only with agricultural conglomerates and don't sell local produce.

_____ When a farmer can tell a customer how to prepare a vegetable or how to use a fruit in a salad, the farmer is likely to make a sale.

Exercise 4 Practice: Finding Reasons and Refuting Objections to Support an Argument

Consider the point of the following two arguments. Give three reasons to support each point. Then, identity a specific objection your audience might have to your argument and how you would refute it. In each case, the readers of your local newspaper will be the audience for an argument paragraph.

1. point: The city of Saugus needs regular bus service on the weekends, not just on the weekdays.

reasons: a. _____

_____

b. _____

_____

c. _____

_____

objection: _____

_____

refutation: _____

_____

_____

2. **point:** Backpacks should be banned at elementary schools.

reasons: a. _____

b. _____

c. _____

_____

objection: _____

_____

refutation: _____

_____

_____

PLANNING   **ARGUMENT**

With a topic sentence and a list of reasons and details, you can draft an outline. Then you can review it, making whatever changes you think it needs. The following checklist may help you to review and revise your outline.

Checklist for Revising an Argument Outline

✓ Does my topic sentence make my point? Does it state a subject and take a stand?

✓ Have I considered the objections to my argument so that I am arguing intelligently?

✓ Have I refuted objections?

✓ Do I have all of the reasons I need to make my point?

✓ Do any reasons overlap?

✓ Are my reasons specific?

✓ Do I have enough details for each reason?

✓ Are my reasons in the most effective order?

The Order of Reasons in an Argument

When you are giving several reasons, it is a good idea to keep the most convincing or most important reason for last. Saving the best for last is called using **emphatic order**. For example, you might have these three reasons to tear down an abandoned building in your neighborhood: (1) The building is ugly.

(2) Drug dealers are using the building. (3) The building is infested with rats. The most important reason, the drug dealing, should be used last, for emphatic order.

Following is an outline on improving Roberts Park. When you look at the outline, you'll notice several changes from the list on page 210:

- Because the safety of children at play is important, it is put as the last reason.
- Some details have been added.
- A concluding sentence has been added to the end of the outline. It explains why improving the park is a good idea for all members of the community.

Outline for an Argument Paragraph

topic sentence	Roberts Park should be cleaned up and improved.
reason	Improving the park would make the downtown area more attractive to shoppers.
details	Shoppers could stroll through the park or rest there after shopping. Friends could meet at the park for a day of shopping and lunch.
reason	Workers from nearby offices and stores could eat lunch outdoors.
details	Several office complexes are nearby. An hour outdoors is a pleasant break from work.
reason	City children could play there.
details	They would get fresh air. They would play on grass, not on asphalt. They would not have to play near traffic.
objection	The cost of fixing the park will impact the city's budget.
refutation	The money spent on beautifying the park will bring more people downtown. They will, in turn, spend money at local establishments and experience more civic pride.
concluding sentence: benefit	An attractive park improves the city, and all residents benefit when the community is beautified.

Exercise 5   **Practice: Working with the Order of Reasons in an Argument Outline**

Following are topic sentences and lists of reasons. For each list, put an *X* by the reason that is the most significant, the reason you would save for last in an argument paragraph.

1. topic sentence: Door-to-door sales of candy, raffle tickets, or other fundraising items should be outlawed.

   reason 1: _____ The solicitations are annoying.

   reason 2: _____ Opening a door to a stranger can lead to a crime.

   reason 3: _____ People feel pressured to buy overpriced items.

2. **topic sentence:** Students at the local college need an emergency health center near the campus.

reason 1: _____ A nearby health center would make a campus epidemic less likely.

reason 2: _____ Many college students think they are invincible and ignore the symptoms of an illness.

reason 3: _____ Flu and other highly contagious illnesses spread quickly on college campuses.

Exercise 6 **Practice: Recognizing Reasons That Overlap**

Following are topic sentences and lists of reasons. In each list, two reasons overlap. Put an *X* by the two reasons that overlap.

1. **topic sentence:** The salad bar at Kiki's Pizza needs improvement.

a. _____ There is little variety in the offerings.

b. _____ The lettuce is limp, and the leaves often have a brown edge.

c. _____ There are mushy chunks of cucumbers.

d. _____ The salad always contains the same items: lettuce from a bag, soft pieces of tomatoes, and shredded carrots.

2. **topic sentence:** The Student Action Club should hold a coat give away each fall.

a. _____ Cold weather hits hard at the homeless and others who are struggling.

b. _____ Children are especially vulnerable to illnesses caused by the cold.

c. _____ Many people have old coats and jackets they would be willing to give away.

d. _____ Boys and girls need the protection of warm clothing.

Exercise 7 **Practice: Identifying a Reason That Is Not Specific**

For each of the following lists, put an *X* by the reason that is not specific.

1. **topic sentence:** All cell phones should be turned off in movie theaters.

a. _____ Movies theaters are filled with strangers who must be considerate of other audience members if they are all to enjoy the film.

b. _____ Ringing phones or phone conversations distract and annoy many people in the audience.

c. _____ Being aware of the feelings and rights of others is always a good policy.

d. _____ When strangers in a theater become irritated by phone conversations, complaints, and insults can escalate into violence.

2. topic sentence: Crystal River Mall needs more than two maps of the mall inside the complex.

    a. _____ Shoppers want to have a pleasant experience as they walk through the mall.

    b. _____ Every shop in the mall wants potential customers to be able to locate its store quickly.

    c. _____ With four main entrances to the mall, but only two maps, many shoppers wander around until they become frustrated and leave.

    d. _____ The design of the mall is complicated, with twists, turns, and dead ends.

Exercise 8 **Practice: Adding Details to an Outline**

Following is part of an outline. It includes a topic sentence and three reasons. Add at least two sentences of details to each reason. Your details may be examples or descriptions.

    topic sentence: Students in evening classes at Crescent State College deserve the same services that students in day classes enjoy.

    reason: Students in evening classes may have jobs or other responsibilities during the day, but, like all students, they need to see counselors.

    details: _____

    _____

    details: _____

    _____

    reason: Students in evening classes may be on a tight schedule and may need to grab a quick snack on campus.

    details: _____

    _____

    details: _____

    _____

    reason: Darkness makes it important for every night student to be as safe as a day student.

    details: _____

    _____

    details: _____

    _____

DRAFTING AND REVISING **ARGUMENT**

Once you are satisfied with your outline, you can write the first draft of your paragraph. When you have completed it, you can begin revising the draft so that your argument is as clear, logical, and convincing as it can be. The following checklist may help you with your revisions.

3 Write a convincing argument paragraph that incorporates transitions effectively.

Checklist for Revising a Draft of an Argument Paragraph

✓ Have I left out a serious or obvious reason?

✓ Should I change the order of my reasons?

✓ Do I have enough details?

✓ Are my details specific?

✓ Do I need to explain the problem or issue I am writing about?

✓ Do I need to link my ideas more clearly?

✓ Do I need a concluding sentence that reinforces my point?

Checking Your Reasons

Be sure that your argument has covered all the serious or obvious reasons. Sometimes writers get so caught up in drafting their ideas that they forget to mention something basic to the argument. For instance, if you were arguing for a leash law for your community, you might state that dogs who run free can hurt people and damage property. But don't forget to mention another serious reason to keep dogs on leashes: Dogs who are not restrained can get hurt or killed by cars.

One way to see if you have left out a serious or obvious reason is to ask a friend or classmate to read your draft and to react to your argument. Another technique is to put your draft aside for an hour or two and then read it as if you were a reader, not the writer.

Explaining the Problem or the Issue

Sometimes your argument discusses a problem so obvious to your audience that you do not need to explain it. On the other hand, sometimes you need to explain a problem or issue so that your audience can understand your point. If you tell readers of your local paper about teenage vandalism at Central High School, you probably need to explain what kind of vandalism has occurred and how often. Sometimes it is wise to describe the seriousness of a situation by providing a few examples so that readers will be more interested in your argument.

Transitions That Emphasize Your Reasons and Introduce Opposing Viewpoints

In writing an argument paragraph, you can use any transition, depending on how you arrange your reasons and details. However, no matter how you present your reasons, you will probably want to *emphasize* one of them. Some transitions that can be used for emphasis follow.

INFO BOX **Transitions to Use for Emphasis**

above all	finally	most important	most significant
especially	mainly	most of all	primarily

For example, by saying, "*Most important*, broken windows at Central High School are a safety problem," you put the emphasis for your audience on this one idea.

You can also use a transitional phrase to introduce opposing viewpoints or arguments you plan to refute. Examples include "opponents argue" or "some people believe." Because you will refute these viewpoints, a transition word such as *however* is often used to introduce your refutation.

Revising a Draft

Following is a draft of the argument paragraph on Roberts Park. When you read it, you'll notice these changes from the outline on page 213:

- A description of the problem has been added.
- Details have been added.
- Transitions, including two sentences of transition, have been added. *Most important*, *Best of all*, and *Opponents argue*—transitions that show emphasis and introduce opposing viewpoints—have been included.

You may also notice some careless errors that can be corrected during the editing and proofreading stage.

Draft of an Argument Paragraph

(Note: Changes from the outline are underlined; editing and proofreading are still necessary.)

description of the problem	Roberts Park was once a pretty little park, but today it is overgrown with weeds and cluttered with trash and rusty benches. Roberts Park could be cleaned up and improved. Improving the park would make the downtown area more attractive to shoppers. Shopers could
added detail	stroll through a renovated park or rest there after shop-
transition	ping. Friends could also meet there for a day of shop-
transitional sentence	ping and lunch. Shoppers are not the only ones who could enjoy the park. Workers from nearby offices and stores could eat lunch outdoors. Several office complex
added details	is near the park, and workers from these offices could bring their lunch to work and eat outside in good weather. I think many people would agree that an hour
transition	spent outdoors is a pleasant break from work. Most important, city children could play in an improved Roberts Park. They would get fresh air. They can play on
transition	grass, not asphalt. Best of all, they would not have to
transition	play near traffic. Opponents argue the cost of fixing the park will impact the city's budget negatively. However, the money spent on beautifying the park will bring more people downtown, who will, in turn, spend money at local establishments and experience more civic pride.
transitional sentence	Children, shoppers, and workers would benefit from a clean-up of Roberts Park, but so would others. An attractive park improves the city and all residents benefit when a community is beautified.

Exercise 9   **Practice: Adding an Explanation of the Problem to an Argument Paragraph**

This paragraph could use an explanation of the problem before the thesis. Write a short explanation of the problem in the lines provided.

_____

_____

_____

_____

_____

The local drivers' license bureau needs a larger, better furnished, and electronically updated waiting area. For the applicants who have come to renew, reinstate, or be tested for a license, a large room would help them to feel less stressed. The increased size would reduce the anxiety of being crushed in a crowd of people, all waiting for an item as important as a driver's license. Finally, better furniture in the new area would encourage the applicants to feel welcome and respected rather than unwelcome and annoyed. Adequate seating would allow people to wait in some comfort and a calmer atmosphere. Finally, waiting would be more bearable if a clock or electric sign posted the estimated wait time. Applicants who arrived on a break from work would know whether to wait or return later. Posting the wait time would also eliminate the many questions about time that the staff must handle. These changes to the waiting room could reduce the irritation, misery, and even resentment of a necessary but unpleasant chore.

Exercise 10   **Practice: Recognizing Transitions in an Argument Paragraph**

Underline all the transitions—words, phrases, or sentences—in the paragraph that follows. Put a double line under any transitions that emphasize reasons.

On Saturdays, the entrance to many local supermarkets shelters boys or girls accompanied by several caring adults who are the parent sponsors of the children's group. The group can be an athletic team, a school club, or a chapter of a national boys' or girls' club. The children are selling something—cookies, popcorn, chocolate bars—to raise money for their school, team, or charitable organization. Although it is easy to walk past the children, we should support their efforts. First of all, the children are nervous, and they need encouragement. If a child can make a sale while other children and the adults are watching, that child feels proud and empowered. More important, all the children are learning about working hard for a cause. They may be raising money for a club, a school team, or a national organization that helps children. However, each child is collecting money for something bigger than him- or herself. The process brings them pleasure and pride in working for others. Most important, if we buy the item, we become part of something larger than ourselves. By spending a few dollars on chocolate or cookies, we join a circle of giving. The children's parents give their time, support, and protection, the children give their efforts and courage, and the buyers give their money to a needy organization. As a result, each small purchase does a small world of good.

EDITING AND PROOFREADING   ARGUMENT

Once you are satisfied with your latest draft, it is time to edit. You can begin by combining short sentences and refining word choice. Then you can check for spelling and punctuation lapses. The following checklist may help you with your revisions.

Checklist for Editing a Draft of an Argument Paragraph

✓ Should any sentences be combined?

✓ Are the verb forms consistent?

✓ Are the word choices appropriate?

✓ Is the spelling correct?

✓ Is the punctuation correct?

Following is the final version of the argument paragraph on Roberts Park. It includes several improvements since preparation of the draft on page 217. As you review this version, you will notice the following refinements:

- The first sentence has been changed so that it is more descriptive and uses a parallel pattern for emphasis.
- *Could* has been changed to *should*.

- *Shoppers* has been correctly spelled.
- *Renovated* has been changed to *restored*, for clarity.
- *Several office complex is* has been corrected to *Several office complexes are*.
- The sentence *They would get fresh air* has been combined with the sentence *They can play on grass, not asphalt*.
- The sentence *Opponents argue* has been combined with the sentence *However, the money spent*. Note that in combining these two sentences, the transition word *However* is no longer necessary,—because the initial sentence has been changed to a clause that begins with *While*.
- A comma has been added after *city* (in the last line).

Final Version of an Argument Paragraph

(Note: Changes from the draft are underlined.)

Roberts Park was once a pretty little park, but today it is overgrown with weeds, littered with trash, and cluttered with rusty benches. Roberts Park should be cleaned up and improved. Improving the park would make the downtown area more attractive to shoppers. Shoppers could stroll through a restored park or rest there after shopping. Friends could also meet at the park for a day of shopping and lunch. Shoppers are not the only ones who could enjoy the park. Workers from nearby offices and stores could eat lunch outdoors. Several office complexes are near the park, and workers from these offices could bring their lunch to work and eat outside in good weather. I think many people would agree that an hour spent outdoors is a pleasant break from work. Most important, city children could play in an improved Roberts Park. They would get fresh air while they played on grass, not asphalt. Best of all, they would not have to play near traffic. While opponents argue the cost of fixing the park will impact the city's budget negatively, the money spent on beautifying the park will actually bring more people downtown to spend money at local establishments and experience civic pride. Children, shoppers, and workers would benefit from a clean-up of Roberts Park, but so would others. An attractive park improves the city, and all residents benefit when a community is beautified.

> **For your information:** A sample argument essay based on this topic and following the same writing steps can be found in Chapter 13, "Different Essay Patterns: Part Two."

Exercise 11 Practice: Editing a Draft by Combining Sentences

In the following paragraph, combine each cluster of underlined sentences into one clear, smooth sentence. Write your combinations in the space above the original sentences.

Nicholson College has an impressive campus of nine large buildings set in

green grass, large trees, and open spaces. It is beautiful. It presents a challenge for

most people. These people include current students, new students, and applicants.

Nicholson College needs more signs on every building. Current students are likely to become bad-tempered at the beginning of a new term. On the first day of class, they check their printed copies of their class schedules. <u>At that moment, they realize their next class is scheduled for a building. The building is one that is far away. The building is one they have never entered</u>. They rush to find the building, but they are lost. At Nicholson College, each structure has its name in one place, on one wall. <u>The sign is impressive. However, even longtime students may not find it. They may be approaching the building from the wrong direction</u>. As a result, these students wander on the outskirts of one, two, or three buildings that they don't know well. New students suffer near panic as they struggle to find their classes. New students have many worries. <u>They worry about arriving late to class. They worry about looking ridiculous in front of a room full of seated students. They are afraid of irritating a professor</u>. Roaming the halls and sidewalks is not a good way to begin a term. However, the worst impact of insufficient signs hits applicants to the college. <u>Applicants may be visiting the campus for the first time. They may be unsure whether the place is right for them. They may be considering several colleges</u>. Anyone new to the college is likely to become irritated and frustrated as he or she wanders aimlessly. College maps are no help if the visitor cannot find signs on the buildings. A first-time visitor may decide to look somewhere else to start his or her college career or give up on college altogether. Nicholson College has much to offer, but it needs to offer clear directions to old, new, and aspiring students.

Exercise 12 Practice: Proofreading to Prepare the Final Version

The following paragraph has the kinds of errors that are easy to overlook when you prepare the final version of an assignment. Correct the errors, writing above the lines. There are fifteen errors in the paragraph.

Not all college students have access to computers at the homes. Most colleges have technology labs where students can use the computers to work on writing assignments or research projects. Unfortunately, the branch campuss where I attend college does not offer much access to technology. Eastside

business College need to offer more computers and more hours for students to use

them. Today, the college has only 1 computer lab for students' use. Unfortunately,

the lab fills up at 7:30 a.m., and most students have to stand in line for access. It is

also difficult to concentrate in a glass-walled room while inpatient students line

up outside the windows. Meanwhile, the students outside are wasting their time.

Another reason that access is poor involves the computer lab's hours. The lab

closes at 9:00 p.m. on weekdays, 5:00 p.m. on Saturdays, and is not open on

Sundays. The students who takes evening classes and has a full-time day job

rarely gets access to the lab unless they come to the College on Saturday

mornings. Saturday afternoons at the lab are especially crowded. Finally, many

of the student's who rely on the college's one lab are already struggling to stay

focused on college. Most likely, they, cannot afford there own computers. Many

of them have very little free time to commute to campus on Saturdays. Eastside

Business College must consider it's students' needs, and goals. It must offer wider

and better access to basic technology.

Lines of Detail: A Walk-Through Assignment

Write a one-paragraph letter to the editor of your local newspaper. Argue
for some change you want for your community. You could argue for a traffic
light, turn signal, or stop sign at a specific intersection. Or you could argue
for bike paths in certain places, a recycling program, more bus service, or
for any other specific change you feel is needed. To write your paragraph,
follow these steps:

Step 1: Begin by listing all the reasons and details you can about your
topic. Survey your list and consider any possible objections.
Answer the objections as well as you can, and see if the objections can lead you to more reasons.

Step 2: Group your reasons, listing the details that fit under each reason. Add details where they are needed and check to see if
any reasons overlap.

Step 3: Survey the reasons and details and draft a topic sentence.
Make sure that your topic sentence states the subject and
takes a stand.

Step 4: Write an outline; then revise it, checking that you have enough
reasons to make your point. Also check that your reasons are
specific and in an effective order. Make sure that you have

sufficient details for each reason. Check that your outline includes answers to any significant objections.

Step 5: Write a draft of your argument. Revise the draft until it includes any necessary explanations of the problem being argued, all serious or obvious reasons, and sufficient specific details. Also check that the most important reason is stated last. Add necessary transitions to link your reasons and details.

Step 6: Edit your latest draft to refine word choice, combine short sentences, and correct serious mistakes. Also, be sure that your transitions are logical and effective.

Step 7: Prepare a clean copy of your paragraph, and decide whether you need a final sentence to reinforce your point. Proofread carefully to spot and correct any careless errors in spelling, punctuation, format, or typing.

Topics for Writing an Argument Paragraph

When you write on any of the following topics, be sure to work through the stages of the writing process in preparing your argument paragraph.

1. Write a paragraph for readers of your college student newspaper, arguing for one of the following:

   a. A campus-wide ban on E-cigarette use

   b. Support for online courses as an alternative to face-to-face learning

   c. The need for school libraries

   d. The school cafeteria should offer locally sourced foods to support local farmers and food producers.

2. In a paragraph, argue one of the following topics to the audience specified. If your instructor agrees, brainstorm your topic with a group before you start writing. Ask the group to "play audience" by reacting to your reasons, raising objections, and asking questions.

   Collaborate

   topic a: Early-morning classes should be abolished at your college.

   audience: The dean of academic affairs

   topic b: College students should get discounts at movie theaters.

   audience: The owner of your local movie theater

   topic c: Your college should provide a day-care facility for students with children.

   audience: The president of your college

   topic d: Businesses should hire more student interns.

   audience: The president of a company (name it) you'd like to work for

3. Write a paragraph for or against any of the following topics. You will need to consider the potential local audience for each of the topics.

For or Against

a. The police should be required to wear body cameras.

b. Grades are the best indicators of a student's future success in the workforce.

c. Colleges should ban the use of alcohol on campus.

d. Cheating is getting worse on campus.

e. College students should be required to take physical education classes.

4. Some educators and parents are very concerned about the potentially harmful effects of violent video games on children. Using a search engine such as Google, type in the words "video games" and "action." See if you can find the manufacturer's description of a video game you have played, and find the targeted age range. Using this information, argue for or against this point: (*Name of the video game*) is suitable for children ages _____ to _____.

5. Study the photograph of the traffic jam. One way to relieve such congestion is for employers to offer telecommuting (working from home via a computer connected to a company's main office). Write an argument for more telecommuting jobs and be sure to include specific benefits to the employees and employers.

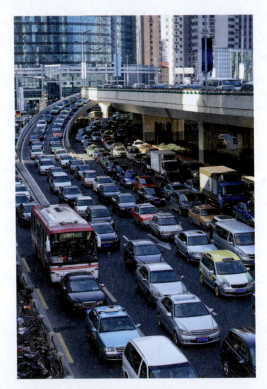

Topics for Critical Thinking and Writing

1. Many drivers often complain about dangerous street conditions and the high rate of accidents and fatalities near their neighborhood. Commonly proposed solutions involve traffic calming, a way of slowing down impatient drivers and reducing the number of deadly collisions. Traffic-calming methods include traffic circles

("roundabouts") and narrower lanes to discourage drivers from passing in a turn lane. Argue for or against a particular traffic-calming method and consider how it would or would not be practical for alleviating dangerous driving conditions on your commute to work or school. You may need to research the principles and practices of traffic calming and imagine how various methods apply to your local roadways.

2. Assume that a university wants to build a research center in your area of the state. You live in a region that is home for some major corporations but also has thousands of acres of farmland. Argue in favor of establishing either an agricultural-related research center or a business-related research center based on the most pressing needs of your region.

Note: Additional writing options suitable for argument-related assignments can be found in the "Readings for Writers" appendix at the end of this book.

CHAPTER 11

Writing an Essay

Jumping In

A quality home often reflects logical design, solid foundation and support, and careful attention to finishing touches. Similarly, an effective **essay** stems from careful preliminary work (prewriting and outlining techniques), well-constructed body paragraphs for thesis support (through drafting and revising), and meticulous attention to final details (editing and proofreading).

Learning Objectives

In this chapter, you will learn how to:

1. Identify the basic parts of an essay.
2. Recognize the difference between a topic sentence and a thesis statement.
3. Prewrite to narrow your topic.
4. Write a multi-paragraph essay with sufficient supporting details and effective transitions.

1 Identify the basic parts of an essay.

WHAT IS AN ESSAY?

You write an essay when you have more to say than can be covered in one paragraph. An **essay** can consist of one paragraph, but in this book, we take it to mean a writing of more than one paragraph. An essay has a main point, called a **thesis statement** (or **thesis**), supported by subpoints. The subpoints are the **topic sentences**. Each paragraph in the **body**, or main part, of the essay has a topic sentence. In fact, each paragraph in the body of the essay is like the paragraphs you've already written because each one makes a point and then supports it.

Comparing the Single Paragraph and the Essay

Read the paragraph and the essay that follow, both about Bob, the writer's brother. You will notice many similarities.

A Single Paragraph

I think I'm lucky to have a brother who is two years older than I am. For one thing, my brother Bob fought all of the typical child–parent battles, and I was the real winner. Bob was the one who made my parents understand that sixteen-year-olds shouldn't have an 11:00 p.m. curfew on weekends. He fought for his rights. By the time I turned sixteen, my parents had accepted the later curfew, and I didn't have to fight for it. Bob also paved the way for me at school. He was such a great athlete that I benefited from his reputation. When I tried out for the basketball team, I had an advantage before I hit the court. I was Bob Cruz's younger brother, so the coach thought I had to be pretty good. At home and at school, my big brother was a big help to me.

An Essay

Some people complain about being the youngest child or the middle child in the family. These people believe older children get all of the attention and grab all the power. I'm the younger brother in my family, and I disagree with the complainers. I think I'm lucky to have a brother who is two years older than I am.

For one thing, my brother Bob fought all the typical child–parent battles, and I was the real winner. Bob was the one who made my parents understand that sixteen-year-olds shouldn't have an 11:00 p.m. curfew on weekends. He fought for his rights, and the fighting wasn't easy. I remember months of arguments between Bob and my parents as Bob tried to explain that not all teens on the street at 11:30 are punks or criminals. Bob was the one who suffered from being grounded or who lost the use of my father's car. By the time I turned sixteen, my parents had accepted the later curfew, and I didn't have to fight for it.

Bob also paved the way for me at school. Because he was so popular with the other students and the teachers, he created a positive image of what the boys in our family were like. When I started school, I walked into a place where people were ready to like me, just as they liked Bob. I remember the first day of class when the teachers read the new class rolls. When they got to my name, they asked, "Are you Bob Cruz's brother?" When I proudly replied, "Yes, I am," they smiled. Bob's success opened doors for me in school sports, too. He was such a great athlete that I benefited from his reputation. When I tried out for the basketball team, I had an advantage before I hit the court. I was Bob Cruz's younger brother, so the coach thought I had to be pretty good.

I had many battles to fight as I grew up. Like all children, I had to struggle to gain independence and respect. In my struggles at home and at school, my big brother was a big help to me.

If you read the two selections carefully, you noticed that they make the same main point, and they support that point with two subpoints.

main point: I think I'm lucky to have a brother who is two years older than I am.

subpoints: 1. My brother Bob fought all the typical child–parent battles, and I was the real winner.
2. Bob also paved the way at school.

You also noticed that the essay is longer because it has more details and examples to support the points. You may have also noticed that each supporting point is its own paragraph.

② Recognize the difference between a topic sentence and a thesis statement.

ORGANIZING AN ESSAY

When you write an essay of more than one paragraph, the **thesis** (also called the **thesis statement**) is the focus of your entire essay; it is the major point of your essay. The other important points that relate to the thesis are within topic sentences.

> **thesis:** Working as a waiter has changed my character.
> **topic sentence:** I have learned patience.
> **topic sentence:** I have developed the ability to listen.
> **topic sentence:** I have become better at multi-tasking.

Notice that the thesis expresses a bigger idea than the topic sentences that follow it, and it is supported by the topic sentences. The essay has an introduction, a body, and a conclusion.

1. **Introduction:** The first paragraph is usually the introduction. The thesis is included in this paragraph.
2. **Body:** This central part of the essay is the part where you support your main point (the thesis). Each paragraph in the body of the essay has its own topic sentence.
3. **Conclusion:** Usually one paragraph long, the conclusion reminds the reader of the thesis.

Writing the Thesis

There are several characteristics of a thesis:

1. It is expressed in a sentence. A thesis is *not* the same as the topic of the essay or the title of the essay.

> **topic:** quitting smoking
> **title:** Why I Quit Smoking
> **thesis:** I quit smoking because I was concerned for my health, and I wanted to prove to myself that I could break the habit.

2. A thesis *does not announce*; it makes a point about the subject.

> **announcement:** This essay will explain the reasons why older people should continue to exercise.
> **thesis:** Older adults should continue to exercise so they can live healthy lives today and prevent future health problems.

3. A thesis *is not too broad*. Some ideas are just too big to cover well in an essay. A thesis that tries to cover too much can lead to a superficial or boring essay.

> **too broad:** People all over the world should work on solving their interpersonal communication problems.
> **acceptable thesis:** As a Southerner, I had a hard time understanding that some New Yorkers think slow speech is ignorant speech.

4. A thesis *is not too narrow*. Sometimes, writers start with a thesis that looks good because it seems specific and precise. Later, when they try to support such a thesis, they can't find anything to say.

too narrow: My sister pays forty dollars a week for a special formula for her baby.

acceptable thesis: My sister had no idea what it would cost to care for a baby.

Hints for Writing a Thesis

1. Your thesis can mention the specific subpoints of your essay. For example, your thesis might be as follows:

> I loved the movie *La La Land* because the film's screenplay was well-written, its actors were relatable, and its choreography was impeccable.

With this thesis, you have indicated the three subpoints of your essay: *La La Land* has a well-written screenplay, relatable actors, and impeccable choreography.

2. You can make a point without listing your subpoints. For example, you can write a thesis like this:

> I loved *La La Land* because of the care that went into its production.

With this thesis, you can still use the subpoints stating that the movie had a well-written screenplay, relatable actors, and impeccable choreography. You just don't have to mention all of your subpoints in the thesis.

Exercise 1   **Practice: Recognizing Good Thesis Sentences**

Following is a list of thesis statements. Some are acceptable, but others are too broad or too narrow. Some are announcements; others are topics, not sentences. Put a *G* next to the good thesis sentences.

1. _____ Fighting a speeding ticket involved me in plenty of frustration and drama.

2. _____ My landlord is evicting the family in the apartment next to mine.

3. _____ Movies that glorify violence are desensitizing viewers to the realities of suffering around the world.

4. _____ Why too much sugar is unhealthy for adults and children.

5. _____ Learning a second language was more difficult than I had expected.

6. _____ Rising unemployment rates affect every age group and social class.

7. _____ By the time I got married, I had learned three important rules about apologizing.

8. _____ School shootings are less likely to occur when all students feel safe and cared for.

9. _____ When impulsive purchases can keep a person from financial success.

10. _____ How the cost of electricity is causing local residents to change their ways.

> ### CRITICAL THINKING
> If you are going to identify the specific subpoints, make certain to use parallel structure. Parallel structure of subpoints means that you use the same pattern and grammar structure for all the subpoints.

Exercise 2 Practice: Selecting a Good Thesis Sentence

For each of the following pairs of thesis statements, put a *G* next to the good one.

1. a. _____ I am going to explain how global water shortages threaten to change the face of the earth in our lifetime.

   b. _____ Residents in Santa Elisa can adopt three simple ways to save water.

2. a. _____ Excessive sunbathing leads to leathery skin, wrinkles, and skin cancer.

   b. _____ The dangers of excessive sunbathing are the subject to be discussed in this essay.

3. a. _____ I found the perfect roommate through sheer luck.

   b. _____ How I found the perfect roommate is the topic of this essay.

4. a. _____ There are many sports that help to keep a person young.

   b. _____ The best sports to keep a person young are soccer, swimming, and Frisbee.

Exercise 3 Practice: Writing a Thesis That Relates to the Subpoints

Following are lists of subpoints that could be discussed in an essay. Write a thesis for each list. Remember that there are two ways to write a thesis: you can write a thesis that includes the specific subpoints, or you can write one that makes a point without listing the subpoints. As an example, the first one is done for you, using both kinds of topic sentences.

1. **one kind of thesis:** If you want a pet, a cat is easier to care for than a dog.

   _____

   another kind of thesis: Cats make better pets than dogs because cats don't

   need to be walked, don't mind being alone, and don't make any noise.

   subpoints: a. Cats don't have to be walked and exercised like dogs do.

   b. Cats are independent and don't mind being home alone, but a dog gets lonely.

   c. Cats are quieter than dogs.

2. **thesis:** _____

   _____

subpoints: **a.** A professional athlete risks permanent damage from injuries such as concussions or broken bones.

b. The pressure to perform at a high level often temps professional athletes to use steroids or painkillers.

c. Often, media attention is quick to pry into the lives of professional athletes.

3. thesis: _____

_____

subpoints: **a.** Many high school graduates will long remember the most popular song of their senior year.

b. Married couples reminisce about the song played for the first dance of their wedding celebration.

c. Parents remember the song they sang to help their baby fall asleep.

WRITING THE ESSAY IN STEPS

In an essay, you follow the same steps you learned in writing a paragraph—prewriting, planning, drafting and revising, and editing and proofreading—but you adapt them to the longer essay form.

PREWRITING AN ESSAY

❸ Prewrite to narrow your topic.

Often you begin by *narrowing a topic*. Your instructor may give you a large topic so that you can find something smaller, within the broad one, that you would like to write about.

Some students think that because they have several paragraphs to write, they should pick a big topic, one that will give them enough to say. But big topics can lead to boring, superficial, general essays. A smaller topic can challenge you to find the specific, concrete examples and details that make an essay effective. As explored in the previous chapters, good writing comes from a clear focus and specific detail.

If your instructor asked you to write about college, for instance, you might *freewrite* some ideas as you narrow the topic:

narrowing the topic of college

what college means to me—topic is too big, and it could be dull
college versus high school—everyone might choose this topic
college students—too big
college students who have jobs—better!
problems of working and going to college—OK!

In your freewriting, you can consider your *purpose*—to write an essay about some aspect of college—and *audience*—your instructor and classmates. Your narrowed topic will appeal to this audience because many students hold jobs and instructors are familiar with the problems of working students.

Listing Ideas

Once you have a narrow topic, you can use whatever process works for you. You can brainstorm by writing a series of questions and answers about your topic, you can freewrite on the topic, you can list ideas on the topic, or you can do any combination of these processes.

Following is a sample listing of ideas on the topic of the problems of working and going to college:

problems of working and going to college

early classes	weekends only time to study
too tired to pay attention	no social life
tried to study at work	apartment a mess
got caught	missed work for makeup test
got reprimanded	get behind in school
slept in class	need salary for tuition
constantly racing around	impatient with customers
no sleep	girlfriend ready to kill me
little time to do homework	

Clustering the Ideas

By clustering related items on the list, you'll find it easier to see the connections between ideas. The following items have been clustered (grouped), and they have been listed under a subtitle:

Problems of Working and Going to College: Ideas in Clusters

problems at school	**problems at work**
early classes	tried to study at work
too tired to pay attention	got caught
slept in class	got reprimanded
little time to do homework	missed work for makeup test
get behind in school	rude to customers

problems outside of work and school

weekends only time to study
no social life
apartment a mess
girlfriend ready to kill me

When you surveyed the clusters, you probably noticed that some of the ideas from the original list were left out. These ideas—constantly racing around, not getting enough sleep, and needing tuition money—could fit into more than one place or might not fit anywhere. You might come back to them later.

When you name each cluster by giving it a subtitle, you move toward a focus for each body paragraph of your essay. And by beginning to focus the body paragraphs, you start thinking about the main point, the thesis of the essay. Concentrating on the thesis and on focused paragraphs helps you to *unify* your essay.

Reread the clustered ideas. When you do so, you'll notice that each cluster is about problems at a different place. You can incorporate that concept into a thesis with a sentence like this:

Students who work while they attend college face problems at school, at work, and at home.

Once you have a thesis statement and a list of details, you can begin working on the planning part of your essay.

Exercise 4 **Collaborate: Narrowing Topics**

Collaborate

Working with a partner or a group, narrow these topics so that the new topics are related, but smaller and suitable for short essays between four and six paragraphs long. The first topic is narrowed for you.

1. **topic:** summer vacation
   smaller, related topics:

   a. how to get along on a long car trip

   b. the benefits of camping or staying at a hotel

   c. my vacation job

2. **topic:** luck
   smaller, related topics:

   a. _____

   b. _____

   c. _____

3. **topic:** music
   smaller, related topics:

   a. _____

   b. _____

   c. _____

4. **topic:** anger
   smaller, related topics:

   a. _____

   b. _____

   c. _____

Exercise 5 **Practice: Clustering Related Ideas**

Two topics, each with a list of ideas, follow. Mark all the related items on the list with the same number (1, 2, or 3). Not all items will get a number. When you've finished marking the list, write a title for each number that explains the cluster of ideas.

1. **topic:** my worst birthday celebration

   _____ my girlfriend gave me a shirt that I would never wear

   _____ my name was misspelled on the birthday cake

_____ celebrated my twenty-second birthday in May

_____ during the party, my best friend sent me a text saying he couldn't make it

_____ my dog knocked over the chips and salsa

_____ one friend gave me a gas card to help with my commute to school

_____ I hate surprise parties

_____ my girlfriend's best friend told an embarrassing story about me

The ideas marked _1_ can be titled _____

The ideas marked _2_ can be titled _____

The ideas marked _3_ can be titled _____

2. **topic:** when tears are a universal reaction

_____ a loved one dies

_____ the birth of a baby

_____ at a wedding

_____ your friend tells a string of hilarious jokes

_____ watching a funny YouTube video

_____ your employment is terminated

_____ attending a child's graduation

_____ carrying tissues to wipe away tears

_____ your parents announce that the family is going to move

The items marked _1_ can be titled _____

The items marked _2_ can be titled _____

The items marked _3_ can be titled _____

CRITICAL THINKING

As you plan the paragraph for your essay, you will need to distinguish between general and specific examples and understand how details support topic sentences.

PLANNING AN ESSAY

In the next stage of writing your essay, draft an outline. Use the thesis to focus your ideas. There are many kinds of outlines, but all are used to help a writer organize ideas. When you use a **formal outline**, you show the difference between a main idea and its supporting detail by _indenting_ the supporting detail. In a formal outline, Roman numerals (numbers I, II, III, and so on) and capital letters are used. Each Roman numeral represents a paragraph, and the letters beneath the numeral represent supporting details.

The Structure of a Formal Outline

first paragraph	I.	Thesis
second paragraph	II.	Topic sentence

details
{
  A.
  B.
  C.
  D.
  E.
}

| third paragraph | III. | Topic sentence |

details
{
  A.
  B.
  C.
  D.
  E.
}

| fourth paragraph | IV. | Topic sentence |

details
{
  A.
  B.
  C.
  D.
  E.
}

| fifth paragraph | V. | Conclusion |

Hints for Outlining

Developing a good, clear outline now can save you hours of confused, disorganized writing later. The extra time you spend to make sure your outline has sufficient details and that *each paragraph stays on one point* will pay off in the long run.

1. Check the topic sentences. Keep in mind that each topic sentence in each body paragraph should support the thesis sentence. If a topic sentence is not carefully connected to the thesis, the structure of the essay will be confusing. As mentioned previously, you can consider the thesis statement the sum of the topic sentences; if you create a strong group of topic sentences, they will help "add up" to your thesis. Here are a thesis and a list of topic sentences; the topic sentence that does not fit is crossed out:

thesis:	I.	A home-cooked dinner can be a rewarding experience for the cook and the guests.
topic sentences:	II.	Preparing a meal is a satisfying activity.
	III.	It is a pleasure for the cook to see guests enjoy the meal.
	IV.	~~Many recipes are handed down through generations.~~
	V.	Dinner guests are flattered that someone cooked for them.
	VI.	Dining at home is a treat for everyone at the table or in the kitchen.

Because the thesis of this outline is about the pleasure of dining at home for the cook and the guests, topic sentence IV doesn't fit: it isn't about the joy of cooking *or* of being a dinner guest. It takes the essay off track. A careful check of the links between the thesis and the topic sentences will help keep your essay focused.

2. Include enough details. Some writers believe that they don't need many details in the outline. They feel they can fill in the details later, when they actually write the essay. Even though some writers do manage to add details later, others who are in a hurry or who run out of ideas will have problems.

For example, imagine that a writer has included very few details in an outline, like this outline for a paragraph:

II. Meeting with a teacher after class can help students improve.

    A. Students can ask for clarification on an assignment.
    B. Teachers realize that the student is interested in the class.

The paragraph created from that outline might be too short, lack specific details, and look like this:

Meeting with a teacher after class can help students improve. First of all, students can ask for clarification on an assignment. Second, students show teachers that they are interested in succeeding.

If you have difficulty thinking of ideas when you write, try to tackle the problem in the outline. The more details you put into your outline, the more detailed and effective your draft essay will be. For example, suppose the same outline on the topic of meeting with teachers after class had more details, like this:

II. Meeting with a teacher after class can help students improve.

more details about how students can ask for clarification
    A. Students can ask for clarification on an assignment.
    B. They can ask the teacher to go over certain points discussed in class.
    C. They can bring an essay in to make certain they will improve on the next one.
    D. They can ask the teacher for advice about how to improve their grade.

more details about how students show teachers their interest in success
    E. In addition, students show teachers that they are interested in succeeding.
    F. Students can demonstrate that they are serious about learning.
    G. Students can discuss how the topics raised in class relate to their own lives and career goals.

You will probably agree that the paragraph will be more detailed, too.

3. Stay on one point. It is a good idea to check the outline of each body paragraph to see whether the paragraph stays on one point. Compare each topic sentence, which is at the top of the list for the paragraph, against the details indented under it. Staying on one point gives each paragraph unity.

The outline for a paragraph that has problems staying on one point follows. See if you can spot the problem areas.

III. Sonya is a kind person.

    A. She was the first to volunteer when our club had a car wash.
    B. She is always willing to share her lecture notes with me.

     C. She is a member of Big Sisters and spends every Saturday with
       a disadvantaged child.
     D. She can read people's minds when they are in trouble.
     E. She knows what they are feeling.

The topic sentence of the paragraph is about kindness. However, sentences D and E talk about Sonya's insight, not her kindness.

    When you have a problem staying on one point, you can solve the problem two ways:

1. Eliminate details that do not fit your main point.
2. Change the topic sentence to cover all the ideas in the paragraph.

For example, you could cut sentences D and E about Sonya's insight, getting rid of the details that do not fit. As an alternative, you could change the topic sentence in the paragraph so that it relates to all the ideas in the paragraph. A better topic sentence would be "Sonya is a kind and insightful person."

Revisiting the Prewriting Stage

Writing an outline can help you identify undeveloped places in your plan, places where your paragraphs will need more details. You can get these details in two ways:

1. Go back to the writing you did in the prewriting stage. Check whether items on a list or ideas from prewriting can lead you to more details for your outline.
2. Brainstorm for more details by a question-and-answer approach. For example, if the outline includes "My apartment is a mess," you might ask, "Why? How messy?" Or if the outline includes "I have no social life," you might ask, "What do you mean? No friends? No activities? Or what about school organizations?"

The time you spend writing and revising your outline will make it easier for you to write an essay that is well developed, unified, and coherently structured. The checklist that follows may help you to revise.

Checklist for Revising the Outline of an Essay

✓ **Unity:** Do the thesis and topic sentences all lead to the same point? Does each paragraph make one, and only one, point? Do the details in each paragraph support the topic sentence? Does the conclusion unify the essay?

✓ **Support:** Do the body paragraphs have enough supporting details?

✓ **Coherence:** Are the paragraphs in the most effective order? Are the details in each paragraph arranged in the most effective order?

A sentence outline on the problems of working and going to college follows. It includes the thesis in the first paragraph. The topic sentences have been created from the titles of the ideas clustered previously. The details have been drawn from ideas in the clusters and from further brainstorming. The conclusion has just one sentence that unifies the essay.

Outline for an Essay

paragraph 1 ——— I. Thesis: Students who work while going to college face problems at school, at work, and at home.

paragraph 2, topic sentence ——— II. Trying to juggle job and school responsibilities creates problems at school.

details about problems at school ———
  A. Early classes are difficult.
  B. I am too tired to pay attention.
  C. Once I slept in class.
  D. I have little time to do homework.
  E. I get behind in school assignments.

paragraph 3, topic sentence ——— III. Work can suffer when workers attend college.

details about problems at work ———
  A. I tried to study at work.
  B. I got caught by my boss.
  C. I was reprimanded.
  D. Sometimes I come to work very tired.
  E. When I don't have enough sleep, I can be impatient with customers.
  F. My impatience gets me in trouble.
  G. Another time, I had to cut work to take a makeup test.

paragraph 4, topic sentence ——— IV. Working students suffer outside of classes and the workplace.

details about problems at home ———
  A. I work nights during the week.
  B. The weekends are the only time I can study.
  C. My apartment is a mess since I have no time to clean it.
  D. Worse, my girlfriend is ready to kill me because I have no social life.
  E. We never even go to the movies anymore.
  F. When she comes over, I am busy studying.

paragraph 5, conclusion ——— V. I have learned that working students have to be very organized to cope with their responsibilities at college, at work, and at home.

Exercise 6 **Practice: Completing an Outline for an Essay**

Following is part of an outline that has a thesis and topic sentences, but no details. Add the details and write in complete sentences. Write one sentence for each capital letter. Be sure that the details are connected to the topic sentence.

I. Thesis: Many college students who live on their own do very little cooking.

II. For many students, fast-food restaurants are more popular than supermarkets.

A. _____

_____

B. _____

_____

C. _____

_____

D. _____

_____

E. _____

_____

III. A microwave or toaster is the only cooking device that students need.

A. _____

_____

B. _____

_____

C. _____

_____

D. _____

_____

E. _____

_____

IV. When hunger strikes college students, they can resort to delivery services.

A. _____

_____

B. _____

_____

C. _____

_____

D. _____

_____

E. _____

_____

V. College students may no longer enjoy home cooking, but they have plenty of choices.

Exercise 7   **Practice: Focusing an Outline for an Essay**

The outline that follows has a thesis and details, but it has no topic sentences for the body paragraphs. Write the topic sentences.

I. Thesis: Just once in my life, I would love the luxury of a new car.

II. _____

_____

A. No dirt would soil the floor.

B. There would be no scratches or tears on the upholstery.

C. I would own an elaborate car sound system that worked perfectly.

D. The only smell in the automobile would be the distinctive smell of a new car.

E. The interior of the car would be filled with gadgets I had never dreamed of.

III. _____

_____

A. The hubcaps and rims would shine.

B. There would be no scratches on the paint.

C. The paint would not be faded.

D. No dents would appear in the fenders or bumpers.

E. As for the tires, not a bit of wear would be evident.

IV. I have always dreamed of the day when I would drive a brand new car out of the car dealer's lot.

④ Write a multi-paragraph essay with sufficient supporting details and effective transitions.

DRAFTING AND REVISING **AN ESSAY**

When you are satisfied with your outline, you can begin drafting the essay. Start by writing a first draft of the essay, which includes these parts: introduction, body paragraphs, and conclusion.

WRITING THE INTRODUCTION

Where Does the Thesis Go?

The **thesis** should appear in the introduction of the essay, in the first paragraph. But most of the time, it should not be the first sentence. In front of the thesis, write a few (three or more) sentences of introduction. Generally, the thesis is the *last sentence* in the introductory paragraph.

Why put the thesis at the end of the first paragraph? First of all, writing several sentences in front of your main idea gives you a chance to lead into it, gradually and smoothly. This will help you build interest and gain the reader's attention. Also, by placing the thesis after a few sentences of introduction, you will not startle the reader with your main point.

Finally, if your thesis is at the end of the introduction, it states the main point of the essay just before that point is supported in the body paragraphs. Putting the thesis at the end of the introduction is like an arrow pointing to the supporting ideas in the essay.

Hints for Writing the Introduction

There are a number of ways to write an introduction.

1. **You can begin with an "agreeable" statement** that gradually leads to your thesis. An agreeable statement is, simply, a statement with which the vast majority of your audience would nod their head in agreement:

agreeable statements   Students face all kinds of problems when they start college. Some students struggle with a lack of basic math skills; others have never learned to write a term paper. Students who were stars in high school have to cope with being just another Social Security number at a large institution. Students with small children have to find a way to be good parents and good students, too. Although all these problems are common, I found an even more typical conflict. <u>My biggest problem in college was learning to organize my time</u>.

thesis at end

2. **You can begin with a quotation** that smoothly leads to your thesis. The quotation can be from someone famous, or it can be an old saying. It can be something your mother always told you, or it can be a slogan from an advertisement or the words of a song.

quotation   Everybody has heard the old saying, "Time flies," but I never really thought about that statement until I started college. I expected college to challenge me with demanding coursework. I expected it to excite me with the range of people I would meet. I even thought it might amuse me with the fun and intrigue of dating and romance. But I never expected college to exhaust me. I was

thesis at end   surprised to discover that <u>my biggest problem in college was learning to organize my time</u>.

3. **You can tell a story** as a way of leading into your thesis. You can open with the story of something that happened to you or to someone you know, a story you read about or heard on the news.

story   My friend Alexis is two years older than I am, and so she started college before I did. When Alexis came home from college for the Thanksgiving weekend, I called her with plans for fun, but Alexis told me she planned to spend most of the weekend sleeping. I didn't understand her when she told me she was worn out. When I started college myself, I understood her perfectly. Alexis was a victim of that old college ailment: not knowing how to handle

thesis at end   time. I developed the same disease. <u>My biggest problem in college was learning to organize my time.</u>

4. **You can explain why this topic is worth writing about.** Explaining could mean giving some background on the topic, or it could mean discussing why the topic is an important one.

explain   I do not remember a word of what was said during my freshman orientation, and I wish I did. I am sure somebody somewhere warned me about the problems I would face in college. I am sure somebody talked about getting organized. Unfortunately, I didn't listen, and I had to learn the

thesis at end   hard way. <u>My biggest problem in college was learning to organize my time.</u>

5. **Use one or more questions to lead into your thesis.** You can open with a question or questions that will be answered by your thesis. Or you can open with a question or questions that catch the reader's attention and move toward your thesis.

question	Have you ever stayed up all night to study for an exam, then fallen asleep at dawn and slept right through the time of the exam? If you have, then you were probably the same kind of college student I was. I was the student who always ran into class three minutes late, the one who begged for an extension on the term paper, the one who pleaded with the teacher to postpone the test. I just could not get things
thesis at end	done on schedule. <u>My biggest problem in college was learning to organize my time.</u>

6. **You can open with a contradiction of your main point** as a way of attracting the reader's interest and leading to your thesis. You can begin with an idea that is the opposite of what you will say in your thesis. The opposition of your opening and your thesis creates interest.

contradiction	People who knew me in my freshman year probably felt really sorry for me. They saw a girl with dark circles under her bloodshot eyes, a girl who was always racing from one place to another. Those people probably thought I was exhausted from overwork. But they were wrong. My problem in college was definitely not too much work; it was the way I handled
thesis at end	my work. <u>My biggest problem in college was learning to organize my time.</u>

Exercise 8 Practice: Writing an Introduction

Following are three thesis sentences. Pick one. Then write an introductory paragraph on the lines provided. Your last sentence should be the thesis sentence. If your instructor agrees, read your introduction to others in the class who wrote an introduction to the same thesis, or read your introduction to the entire class.

Thesis Sentences:

1. Being alone makes some people uncomfortable.

2. Three people have supported me in times when I was under stress.

3. Owning a dog taught me a lot about myself.

Write an introduction: _____

_____

_____

_____

_____

WRITING THE BODY OF THE ESSAY

In the body of the essay, the paragraphs *explain, support, and develop* your thesis. In this part of the essay, each paragraph has its own topic sentence. The topic sentence in each paragraph does two things:

1. It focuses the sentences in the paragraph.
2. It makes a point connected to the thesis.

The thesis and the topic sentences are ideas that need to be supported by details, explanations, and examples. You can visualize the connections among the parts of an essay like this:

Introduction with Thesis

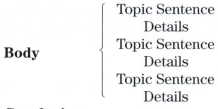

Body

    Topic Sentence
       Details
    Topic Sentence
       Details
    Topic Sentence
       Details

Conclusion

When you write topic sentences, refer to the following checklist to help you organize your essay.

Checklist for Topic Sentences of an Essay

✓ Does the topic sentence give the point of the paragraph?

✓ Does the topic sentence connect to or "echo" the thesis of the essay?

How Long Are the Body Paragraphs?

Remember that the body paragraphs of an essay are the place where you explain and develop your thesis. Those paragraphs should be long enough to explain your points, not just list them. To do this well, try to make your body paragraphs *at least seven sentences* long. As you develop your writing skills, you may find that you can support your ideas in fewer than seven sentences.

Developing the Body Paragraphs

You can write well-developed body paragraphs by following the same steps you used in writing single paragraphs for the previous assignments in this book. As you work through the stages of the writing process—whether gathering ideas and planning, drafting and revising, or editing and proofreading—you will gradually create detailed and effective paragraphs.

To focus and develop the body paragraphs, ask the questions in the following checklist as you revise.

> **Checklist for Developing Body Paragraphs for an Essay**
>
> ✓ Does the topic sentence cover everything in the paragraph?
>
> ✓ Do I have enough details to support the topic sentence?
>
> ✓ Do all of the details in the paragraph explain, develop, or illustrate the topic sentence?

Exercise 9 **Practice: Creating Topic Sentences**

Following are thesis sentences. For each thesis, write topic sentences (as many as indicated by the numbered blanks). The first one is done for you.

1. **thesis:** Cats make good pets.

   topic sentence 1: Cats are independent and don't mind being home alone.

   topic sentence 2: Cats are easy to litter train.

   topic sentence 3: Cats are fun to play with.

2. **thesis:** Most college students live on a tight budget.

   topic sentence 1: _____

   topic sentence 2: _____

   topic sentence 3: _____

3. **thesis:** The loss of a job can signal a time of crisis, but it can also be a time of opportunity.

   topic sentence 1: _____

   topic sentence 2: _____

   topic sentence 3: _____

   topic sentence 4: _____

WRITING THE CONCLUSION

The last paragraph in the essay is the **conclusion**. It does not have to be as long as a body paragraph, but it should be long enough to unify the essay and remind the reader of the thesis. You can use any of these strategies in writing the conclusion.

1. **You can restate the thesis in new words.** Go back to the first paragraph of your essay and reread it. For example, this could be the first paragraph of an essay:

    introduction

    thesis at end

    > Even when I was a child, I did not like being told what to do. I wanted to be my own boss. When I grew up, I figured that the best way to be my own boss was to own my own business. I thought that being in charge would be easy. I now know how difficult being an independent business person can be. <u>Independent business owners have to be smart, highly motivated, and hard-working</u>.

    The thesis, underlined in the previous example, is the sentence that you can restate in your conclusion. Your task is to *keep the point but put it in different words*. Then work that restatement into a short paragraph, like this:

    restating the thesis

    > People who own their own business have to be harder on themselves than any employer would ever be. Their success is their own responsibility; they cannot blame company policy or rules because they set the policy and make the rules. <u>If the business is to succeed, their intelligence, drive, and effort are essential</u>.

2. **You can make a judgment, valuation, or recommendation.** Instead of simply restating your point, you can end by making some comment on the issue you've described or the problem you've illustrated. If you were looking for another way to end the essay on owning one's own business, for example, you could end with a recommendation.

    ending with a recommendation

    > People often dream of owning their own business. Dreaming is easy, but the reality is tough. <u>Those who want to succeed in their own venture should find a role model</u>. Studying a role model would teach them how ambition, know-how, and constant effort lead to success.

3. **You can conclude by framing your essay.** You can tie your essay together neatly by *using something from your introduction* as a way of concluding. When you take an example, a question, or even a quotation from your first paragraph and refer to it in your last paragraph, you are "framing" the essay. Take another look at the introduction to the essay on owning your own business. The writer talks about not liking to be told what to do, being one's own boss, and believing that being in charge would be easy. The writer also mentions the need to

be smart, highly motivated, and hard-working. Now consider how the ideas of the introduction are used in this conclusion:

frame	Children who do not like to take directions may
frame	think that being their own boss will be easy. Adults who try to start a business soon discover that they must be totally self-directed; that is, they must be strong enough
frame	to keep learning, to keep pushing forward, and to keep
frame	working.

Exercise 10 Practice: Choosing a Better Way to Restate the Thesis

Following are three clusters. Each cluster consists of a thesis sentence and two sentences that try to restate the thesis. Each restated sentence could be used as part of the conclusion to an essay. Put *B* next to the sentence in each pair that is a better restatement. Remember that the better choice repeats the same idea as the thesis but does not rely on too many of the same words.

1. **thesis:** Drinking water instead of energy drinks can improve a person's health.

   restatement 1: _____ People can improve their health when they drink water instead of energy drinks.

   restatement 2: _____ Water is a healthy substitute for energy drinks.

2. **thesis:** One act of kindness can lead the way to many other good deeds.

   restatement 1: _____ One kind act can be like a seed that grows and spreads.

   restatement 2: _____ Several other good deeds can result from one act of kindness.

3. **thesis:** Regularly playing a sport or getting another form of exercise helps a person stay sane in a crazy world.

   restatement 1: _____ A person can stay sane in a world of craziness if he or she regularly plays a sport or gets another form of exercise.

   restatement 2: _____ When the world has gone mad, a person who exercises regularly can remain sane.

REVISING THE DRAFT

Once you have a first draft of your essay, you can begin revising it. The following checklist may help you to make the necessary changes in your draft.

Checklist for Revising the Draft of an Essay

✓ Does the essay have a clear, unifying thesis?

✓ Does the thesis make a point?

✓ Does each body paragraph have a topic sentence?

✓	Does the topic sentence "echo" the thesis?
✓	Is each body paragraph focused on its topic sentence?
✓	Are the body paragraphs roughly the same size?
✓	Do any of the words need to be changed?
✓	Are the ideas linked smoothly?
✓	Does the introduction catch the reader's interest?
✓	Is there a definite conclusion?
✓	Does the conclusion remind the reader of the thesis?

Transitions within Paragraphs

In an essay, you can use two kinds of transitions: those within a paragraph and those between paragraphs.

Transitions that link ideas *within a paragraph* are the same kinds you used previously. Your choice of words, phrases, or even sentences depends on the kind of connection you want to make. Here is a list of some common transitions and the kinds of connections they express.

INFO BOX   Common Transitions within a Paragraph

To join two ideas:

again	another	in addition	moreover
also	besides	likewise	similarly
and	furthermore		

To show a contrast or a different opinion:

but	instead	on the other hand	still
however	nevertheless	or	yet
in contrast	on the contrary		

To show a cause-and-effect connection:

accordingly	because	for	therefore
as a result	consequently	so	thus

To give an example:

for example	in the case of	such as	to illustrate
for instance	like		

To show time:

after	first	recently	subsequently
at the same time	meanwhile	shortly	then
before	next	soon	until
finally			

Transitions between Paragraphs

When you write something that is more than one paragraph long, you need transitions that link each paragraph to the others. There are several effective ways to link paragraphs and remind the reader of your main idea and of how the smaller points connect to it. Restatement and repetition are two of these ways:

1. **Restate an idea** from the preceding paragraph at the start of a new paragraph. Look closely at the two paragraphs that follow and notice how the second paragraph repeats an idea from the first paragraph and provides a link.

> If people were more patient, driving would be less of an ordeal. If, for instance, the driver behind me didn't honk his horn as soon as the traffic light turned green, both he and I would probably have lower blood pressure. He wouldn't be irritating himself by pushing so hard. Also, I wouldn't be reacting by slowing down, trying to irritate him even more, and getting angry at him. When I get impatient in heavy traffic, I just make a bad situation worse. My hurry doesn't get me to my destination any faster; it just stresses me out.

transition
restating an idea

> The impatient driver doesn't get anywhere; neither does the impatient customer at a restaurant. Impatience at restaurants doesn't pay. I work as a hostess at a restaurant, and I know that the customer who moans and complains about waiting for a table won't get one any faster than the person who makes the best of the wait. In fact, if a customer is too aggressive or obnoxious, the restaurant staff may actually slow down the process of getting that customer a table.

2. **Use synonyms and repetition** as a way of reminding the reader of an important point. For example, in the two paragraphs that follow, notice how certain repeated words, phrases, and synonyms all remind the reader of a point about facing fear. The repeated words and synonyms are underlined.

> Some people just <u>avoid</u> whatever they <u>fear</u>. I have an uncle who is <u>afraid</u> to fly. Whenever he has to go on a trip, he does anything he can to <u>avoid</u> getting on an airplane. He will drive for days, travel by train, take a bus trip. Because he is so <u>terrified</u> of flying, he lives with <u>constant anxiety</u> that some day he may have to fly. He is always thinking of the one emergency that could force him to <u>confront what he most dreads</u>. Instead of <u>dealing directly with his fear</u>, he lets it <u>haunt</u> him.
>
> Other people are even worse than my uncle. He won't <u>attack his fear</u> of something external. But there are people who won't <u>deal with their fear</u>. My friend Sam is a good example of this kind of person. Sam has a serious drinking problem. All of Sam's friends

know he is an alcoholic, but Sam <u>will not admit</u> his addiction. I think he is <u>afraid to face</u> that part of himself. So he <u>denies</u> his problem, saying he can stop drinking any time he wants to. Of course, until Sam has the courage to <u>admit what he is most afraid of</u>, his alcoholism, he won't be able to change.

A Draft Essay

A draft of the essay on working and going to college follows. As you read it, you'll notice many changes from the outline on page 238:

- An introduction has been added, written in the first person, "I," to unify the essay.
- Transitions have been added within and between paragraphs; many transitions are complete sentences.
- General statements have been replaced by more specific ones.
- Many new, specific details and examples develop the body paragraphs.
- Word choice has been improved.
- A conclusion has been added. Some of the ideas added to the conclusion came from the original list of ideas about the topic of work and school. They are ideas that do not belong in the body paragraphs but are useful in the conclusion.

You may also notice some careless errors in punctuation and spelling that can be corrected during the editing and proofreading stage.

Draft of an Essay

(Note: Changes from the outline are underlined; editing and proofreading is still necessary.)

introduction added that tells a story

I work thirty hours a week at the front desk of a motel in Riverside. When I first signed up for college classes I figured college would be fairly easy to fit into my schedule. After all, college students are not in class all day, as high school students are. So I thought the twelve hours a week I'd spent in class wouldn't be too much of a load. But I was in for a big

thesis statement at the end of the paragraph

surprise. <u>My first semester at college showed me that students who work while going to school face problems at school, at work, and at home</u>.

transition, topic sentence

<u>First of all, trying to juggle job and school responbilitys creates problems at school</u>. Early-

transition

morning classes, <u>for example</u>, are particularly difficult for me. <u>Because I work every weeknight from six to

added sentence of detail

midnight, I don't get home until 1:00 a.m., and I can't fall asleep until 2:00 a.m. or later</u>. I am too tired to pay

added detail

attention in <u>my 8:00 a.m.</u> class. Once, I even fell asleep

transitional sentence added

on that class. <u>My work hours create other conflicts</u>.

sentence added

<u>They cut into my study time</u>, so I have little time to do

added detail

<u>all the assigned reading and papers</u>. I get behind in these assignments, and <u>I never seem to have enough

added detail and transition

time to catch up. Consequently, my grades are not good as they could be</u>.

(Continued)

transitional sentences; topic sentence — <u>Because I both work and go to school, I have problems doing well at school. But work can also suffer when workers attend college.</u> <u>Students can bring school into the workplace.</u> One night I tried to study at work, but my boss caught me <u>reading my biology</u>

added detail — <u>textbook at the front desk</u>. I was reprimanded, and

added detail — <u>now my boss doesn't trust me</u>. Sometimes I come to work very tired. When I don't get enough sleep, I can

transition — be impatient with motel guests. <u>Then</u> the impatience can get me into trouble. <u>I remember on particular</u>

added example — <u>guest. She reported me because I was sarcastic to her.</u> <u>She had spent a half hour complaining about her bill,</u> and I had been too tired to be patient. Once again, my boss reprimanded me. <u>Another time,</u> school interfered

transition — with my job when I had to cut work to take a makeup test at school. <u>I know my boss was unhappy with me</u>

added detail — <u>then, too</u>.

transitional sentence and topic sentence — <u>As a working student, I run into trouble on the job and at college. Working students also suffer outside of classes and the workplace.</u> Since I work nights during the week the weekends are the only time I can study. <u>Because I have to use my</u>

transitional sentence — <u>weekends to do schoolwork, I can't do other things</u>. My apartment is a mess since I have no time to clean it. Worse, my girlfriend is ready to kill me because I have no social life. We never even go to the movies anymore. When she comes over, I am busy studying.

repeats focus of body paragraphs — With responsibilities at <u>home</u>, <u>work</u>, and <u>college</u>, I face a cycle of stress. I am constantly racing around, and I can't break the cycle. I want a college education, and I must have a job to pay my tuition. The only way I can manage is to learn to manage my time. <u>I have learned that working students have to be</u>

concluding sentence restates thesis in new words — <u>very organized to cope with their responsibilities at college, at work, and at home</u>.

Exercise 11 Practice: Identifying the Main Points in the Draft of an Essay

The draft of a five-paragraph essay follows. Read it, then reread it and underline the thesis and the topic sentences in each body paragraph and in the conclusion.

Until this year, I had never considered spending my free time helping others in my community. Volunteer work, I thought, was something retired folks and rich people did to fill their days. Just by chance, I became a volunteer for the public library's Classic Connection, a group that arranges read-a-thons and special programs for elementary school children. Although I don't receive a salary, working with some perceptive and entertaining third graders has been very rewarding in other ways.

Currently, I meet with a small group of four girls and three boys each Saturday morning from ten to eleven o'clock, and they have actually taught me more than I ever thought possible I usually assign the children various passages in an illustrated children's classic like *The Little Prince,* and I help them with the difficult words as they read aloud. When I occasionally read to them, they follow right along, but when it's their turn, they happily go off track. I've learned that each child has a mind of his or her own, and I now have much more respect for day-care workers and elementary school teachers who must teach, entertain, and discipline thirty rowdy children all day long. I'm tired after one hour with just seven children.

I have also learned the value of careful planning. I arrive at each session with a digital voice recorder and have the children record sound effects related to the story we'll be reading. At certain points during the session, we stop to hear the sound effects. They love to hear themselves and seem more focused on reading when I use this method. I feel more relaxed when I am well prepared and the sessions go smoothly.

I have enjoyed making several new friends and contacts through Classic Connection. I've become friendly with the parents of the kids in my reading group, and one of the fathers has offered me a good-paying job at his printing business. He even mentioned he could be flexible about my schedule. I asked him if he could help me put a collection together of the group's most outrageous original stories, and he said he'd be glad to do it in *his* free time. I've thus learned that the spirit of volunteerism is indeed contagious.

I plan to keep volunteering for Classic Connection's programs and look forward to a new group that should be starting soon. I don't know if I'm ready to graduate to an older group. After all, third graders still have much to teach me.

Exercise 12 **Practice: Adding Transitions to an Essay**

The following essay needs transitions. Add the transitions where indicated, and add the kind of transition—word, phrase, or sentence—indicated.

I am a fairly good student, but I have to work hard to earn decent grades. Most of that work is the long, sometimes boring time spent studying. Since I need to study as much as I can, I have found three places that offer me at least a little study time.

The first place isn't meant for studying. _____ (add a word) I have managed to slip a few minutes of cramming into the hours I spend there. This place is the supermarket where I work. Of course, work at a supermarket is constant, and I am always under supervision. _____ (add a word or phrase) I have found ways to incorporate a little mental work. When I have a test coming up, I write key terms, rules, or definitions on note cards. On my ten-minute breaks at the store, I sit outside and study my cards. When I return to the store, I try to repeat the information I have just learned. Of course, this repetition is silent _____ (add a word) I don't want to alarm the customers by muttering in the aisles.

The second place is more appropriate for studying. It is the college I attend. I try to find a quiet place like an empty bench where I can sit between classes. If I have a free hour or more, I go somewhere more private _____ (add a word or phrase) the library. Sometimes the library has too many students talking in the aisles or at the computers _____ (add a word or phrase), I find a spot under a tree and sit on the lawn.

_____

_____ (add a sentence). That place is my home. I am lucky to have my own bedroom, and when my family has finished dinner, I retreat to my room. First, I close the door. _____ (add a word) I spread out my books and notes on the bed. Sometimes I sit on the bed to study, but when I feel myself getting sleepy, I move to the floor. On the floor, I am less comfortable but more alert. My room is a quiet place. _____

(add a word or phrase) I do suffer one or two interruptions. Before she goes to bed, my little sister comes in to chat or kiss me goodnight. She can break my train of thought _____ (add a word or phrase) she is a sweet and affectionate visitor. Most of the time, my room gives me the peace that I need.

Studying for my college classes takes up more of my time than I had ever expected. _____ (add a word or phrase) it is more difficult than I had expected. _____ (add a word or phrase) my efforts are carrying me through the challenges of college. _____ (add a word or phrase) I am happy to spend the time on the work that will determine my future.

> **Exercise 13** **Practice: Recognizing Synonyms and Repetition Used to Link Ideas in an Essay**

In the following essay, underline all the synonyms and repetition (of words or phrases) that help remind the reader of the thesis sentence. (To help you, the thesis is underlined.)

We can make many changes in our lives. We can choose to move to a new town, to attend a certain college, or to train for a specific career. However, sometimes the changes in our lives are not our choices. In such cases, the changes can signal trouble. <u>Like everyone, I have felt the pain and the loss of control that can come with change, but I have also learned that loss can lead me to a better life.</u>

The first time that I suffered from a sudden change was when my best friend left the area. At the time, my friend and I were fourteen, and we spent most of our free time together. We confided in each other and created our private world of jokes, adventures, and pranks. When my friend's mother was offered a good job in a distant city, there was nothing I could do to keep my friend near me. At first, I was so upset that I became angry at my friend, and I refused to acknowledge that he was suffering, too. When the day came for him to leave, we were both resigned to the pain of separating.

My second experience of such misery came years later when my girlfriend announced that she was leaving me. One day she decided that she wanted to "move on" in her relationships. I was unprepared for the hurt of her blunt speech.

Nothing that I said could change her mind, and I could not escape the suffering that followed. When the shock wore off, I struggled to cope with the inevitable loneliness. The worst part of this conflict was my fear of getting hurt again. This fear kept me locked in misery.

A year later, my life changed again when the terror began to lose its grip on me. Slowly, I began to move closer to people who could be my friends. Each step was risky, but each step helped me to get stronger. When I began to trust again and feel that I had some value, I started to believe that other people might accept me. I admitted that I would never be able to control all my interactions with other people. I might be hurt again, but I might also find friends and even someone to love.

As I began to let go of my fears, I also gave up the past: I let go of the suffering and self-doubt that had come when I could not hold on to my friend or girlfriend. I made these changes by taking a risk. I stepped back into the real world where I could lose control of events again, but where I could also find fulfillment.

EDITING AND PROOFREADING AN ESSAY

Once you are satisfied with your latest draft, it is time to edit. You can begin by combining short sentences and refining word choice. Then check for spelling and punctuation errors. The following checklist may help you edit effectively:

Checklist for Editing the Draft of an Essay

✓ Should any of my sentences be combined?

✓ Are the verb forms correct and consistent?

✓ Are the word choices appropriate?

✓ Is the spelling correct?

✓ Is the punctuation correct?

Creating a Title

When you are satisfied with the edited version of your essay, you can begin to think of a short title that is connected to your thesis. Because the title is the reader's first contact with your essay, an imaginative title can create a good first impression. If you can't think of anything clever, try using a key phrase from your essay.

The title is placed at the top of your essay, about an inch above the first paragraph. Always capitalize the first word of the title and all major words such as nouns, pronouns, verbs, adjectives, and adverbs. Minor words such as articles (*the, an, a*), prepositions (*of, in, between*), and coordinating conjunctions (*and, but, so*) are not capitalized unless they are the first or last words of the title. *Do not* underline or put quotation marks around your title.

The Final Version of an Essay

As you know, careful editing and proofreading can lead to an error-free essay reflecting effective organization, refined style, and balanced, detailed paragraphs. When you compare the sample final version of an essay to the draft on pages 249–250, you may notice several improvements and corrections which include the following:

- In the first paragraph, the words *I thought* have been added to make it clear that the statement is the writer's opinion.
- One topic sentence, in paragraph two, has been edited to include the word *students* to make the meaning more precise.
- Words have been changed to sharpen the meaning (e.g., *registered* instead of *signed up*).
- Transitional words, phrases, and sentences have been added to link ideas smoothly.
- A title has been added.
- *Responsibilitys* has been corrected to *responsibilities*.
- The verb error *spent* has been corrected to *spend*.
- Sentences have been combined.

Final Version of an Essay

(Note: Changes from the draft are underlined.)

Problems of the Working College Student

I work thirty hours a week at the front desk of a motel in Riverside. When I first <u>registered</u> for college <u>classes</u>, I figured college would be fairly easy to fit into my schedule. After all, <u>I thought</u>, college students are not in class all day, as high school students are. So I <u>assumed</u> the twelve hours a week I'd <u>spend</u> in class wouldn't be too much of a load. But I was in for a big surprise. My first semester at college showed me that students who work while going to college face problems at school, at work, and at home.

First of all, <u>students who try</u> to juggle job and school <u>responsibilities</u> <u>find trouble at school</u>. Early-morning classes, for example, are particularly difficult for me. Because I work every weeknight from six to midnight, I don't get home until 1:00 a.m., and I can't fall asleep until 2:00 a.m. or later. <u>Consequently</u>, I am too tired to pay attention in my 8:00 a.m. class. Once, I even fell asleep <u>in</u> that class. My work hours create other conflicts. They cut into my study time, so I have little time to do all the assigned reading and papers. I get behind in the assignments, and I never seem to have enough time to catch up. <u>As a result</u>, my grades are not as good <u>as</u> they could be.

Because I both work and go to school, I have problems doing well at school. But work can also suffer when workers attend college. Students can bring school

(Continued)

into the workplace. <u>I've been guilty of this practice and have paid the price</u>. One night I tried to study at work, but my boss caught me reading my biology textbook at the front desk. I was reprimanded, and now my boss doesn't trust me. Sometimes I come to work very tired, <u>another problem</u>. When I don't get enough sleep, I can be impatient with <u>motel</u> guests who give me a hard time. Then my impatience can get me into trouble. <u>I remember one particular guest who reported me because I was sarcastic to her</u>. She had spent a half hour complaining about her bill, and I had been too tired to be patient. Once again, my boss reprimanded me. Another time, school interfered with my job when I had to cut work to take a makeup test at school. I know my boss was unhappy with me then, too.

As a working student, I run into trouble on the job and at college. Working students also suffer outside of classes and the workplace. <u>My schedule illustrates the conflicts of trying to juggle too many duties</u>. Since I work nights during the <u>week</u>, the weekends are the only time I can study. Because I have to use my weekends to do schoolwork, I can't do other things. My apartment is a mess since I have no time to clean it. Worse, my girlfriend is ready to kill me because I have no social life. We never even go to the movies anymore. When she comes over, I am busy studying.

With responsibilities at home, at work, and at college, I face a cycle of stress. I am constantly racing around, and I can't break the cycle. I want a college education, and I must have a job to pay my tuition. The only way I can manage is to learn to manage my time. <u>In my first semester at college, I've realized</u> that working students have to be very organized to cope with the responsibilities of college, work, and home.

Exercise 14   **Practice: Proofreading to Prepare the Final Version**

Following is an essay with the kinds of errors that are easy to overlook when you prepare the final version of an assignment. Correct the errors, writing above the lines. There are nineteen errors in the essay.

A Free Morning

Most morning's begin with responsibilities. A person has to work at a certain

time follow a specific routine, and rush to work, school, or to other commitments.

A morning without duties, chores, or schedules is rare. When someone has the gift

of a free morning, they can consider three of the best ways to spend it.

One of the most luxurious ways to enjoy a morning without chores is to turn

off the alarm clock, and go back to sleep. The irritating sound of the alarm makes

the freedom to stop the noise a pleasure. If someone turns off the clock the night

be fore the free morning, he or she will not enjoy the luxury of hearing the noise,

at first assuming that the sound signals another hectic morning, and then realize-

ing, that the clock is powerless on this day. Next, the sleeper can enjoy the plea-

sure of staying in bed, snuggling into the pillows, and slip into a long nap.

A morning without responsibilities can also be a time to wake up at a reasonable hour but to have nothing planned. A person can linger over a cup of coffee. On a free morning, he or she may have time to eat toast or cereal instead of rushing off, to begin another round of work and worry. The gift of time mean a chance to check phone messages sit calmly at a computer read a book, or listen to music. Without a plan, a person can choose to do nearly anything or nothing at all.

the best way to enjoy a free morning is to spend it out doors. Since their are many way to enjoy nature, a person can do as little or as much as he or she desires. An athlete can run, bike, or power-walk in the neighborhood. Someone less active can sit on a porch or patio, and enjoy the trees, the birds, or the squirrels. Parks, benches, lakes, and mountains may be nearby, and nature can be as calming or invigorating as someone wants it to be.

Most people are constantly short of time. They are behind in their responsibilities at work and at home. A free morning should be a time without responsibilities. Instead of using it to catch up on endless chores and duties, people should think of the morning as a gift with know strings attached.

Lines of Detail: A Walk-Through Assignment

Think of two careers that you believe would be right for you. They do not have to be careers for which you are studying or preparing now but can be the kind of work that you would choose if you had unlimited funds; time to study, train, or otherwise prepare; and the freedom to change your circumstances so that you could begin focusing on one of these two careers.

Step 1: Begin with some investigation. Even if you are extremely familiar with these two careers, do as much of the following as you can: talk to an expert in the college's career center and begin to investigate each career's required training/educational requirements as well as the necessary mental, psychological, and physical ability that this career demands. You can talk to a person who is presently working in this career field or to a student who is preparing for the field. Online research and time spent in the college or local public library will help you to become more informed.

Step 2: As you investigate, take notes. Keep in mind that your purpose is to discover what to expect if you were to work toward earning the qualifications for employment in this field.

Step 3: After your visit, survey your notes. Try to focus on a point that you can make about the two possible careers. Do they both require the same type of personality? What are the rewards of each? What are the drawbacks? What is the job market for those whose education or training prepares them for either of the two careers?

The answers to such questions can help you focus on a thesis.

Step 4: Once you have a thesis, you can begin to cluster the details you gathered in your visits.

Step 5: Once you have a thesis and clustered details, draft an outline. Revise your draft outline until it is unified, expresses the ideas in a clear order, and has enough supporting details.

Step 6: Write a draft of your essay. Revise the draft, checking it for balanced paragraphs, relevant and specific details, and a strong conclusion.

Step 7: Check to make certain your introduction is still accurate. Often, the writing process can take your ideas in a way that you had not planned. Make certain the introduction reflects your essay.

Step 8: Edit your latest draft to refine word choice, combine sentences, strengthen transitions, and correct any serious errors or omissions.

Step 9: Prepare a clean copy of your essay and proofread carefully to identify and correct any careless errors in spelling, punctuation, format, or typing.

Topics for Writing an Essay

When you write on any of these topics, be sure to work through the stages of the writing process in preparing your essay.

Collaborate

1. Take any paragraph you have already written for this class and develop it into an essay of four or five paragraphs. If your instructor agrees, read the paragraph to a partner or group, and ask your listener(s) to suggest points inside the paragraph that could be developed into paragraphs of their own.

2. Write an essay using one of the following thesis statements:

As I look back at my family history, I would characterize us with three words: _____, _____, and _____.

Making a few simple changes to your daily routine can save you a considerable amount of money each month.

I would love to live in _____ because _____.

I believe that listening is the most important gift that a person can give another person.

Three items that every college student needs are _____, _____, and _____.

3. Write an essay on first impressions of college. Interview three classmates to gather detail and to focus your essay. Ask each one to tell you about the first impression he or she has of those first couple of days of college. If possible, try to interview an array of people from different backgrounds and experiences. Be willing to ask follow-up questions that get to the strong details. Use the details collected at the interviews to write a five-paragraph essay with a thesis sentence like one of the following:

Collaborate

The first week of college can be an anxious time no matter who you are.

No matter what you have done in the past, starting college is going to be a challenge.

Some people adjust to college without a problem, but others take more time.

4. Freewrite for ten minutes on the two best days of your life. After you've completed the freewriting, review it. Do the two days have much in common? Or were they very different? Write a four-paragraph essay based on their similarities or differences, with a thesis like one of these:

The two best days of my life were both _____. (Focus on similarities.)

Although one of the best days of my life was _____, the other great day was _____. (Fill in with differences.)

5. Write a five-paragraph essay on one of the following topics:

Three Careers for Me	The Three Great Pets
Three Miserable Jobs	Three Joys of a Big Family
Three Hobbies I Love	Three Wishes
Three Relatives	Three Dating Mistakes I Will Never Make Again

6. Many people are turning to online dating services as a way to meet people and potential partners. Find an online dating service and investigate its methods, claims, and fees. Based on your research, write an essay that takes a stand on the following statement:

_____, an online dating service, is ethical/unethical (choose one) in its promises.

As an alternative, if you or someone you know has ever used an online dating service, write an essay based on the following statement:

Finding a suitable mate through an online dating service can be a(n) _____ experience.

7. Look closely at the photo on the next page and imagine the planning necessary to reach the top of the mountain, the experience itself of climbing the mountain, and the life lessons learned from the experience. Use these imaginings to write a five paragraph essay that clearly articulates each of the three phases. Be sure that your introduction identifies your topic and thesis and your final paragraph effectively concludes the entire experience.

Topics for Critical Thinking and Writing

1. Everyone has to make compromises. The father of a large family, for example, may have dreamed of buying a big house for his family. However, economic realities may have forced him to compromise by renting a small duplex. Your brother may have dreamed of becoming a professional athlete but settled for spending weekends playing on a city softball team. Write an essay about three compromises you have made, explaining what you dreamed of, what you settled for, and how you accepted these compromises.

2. Social media such as Twitter, Instagram, Facebook, and LinkedIn are popular among a wide spectrum of users for both personal and professional reasons. Freewrite about the ways in which social media improves the quality of life for its users, and then write an essay about the top three benefits of using social media.

or

If you feel that the drawbacks of social media outweigh the benefits, write about the three most significant negative aspects. Be sure to incorporate specific details and examples for each drawback.

Note: Additional writing options suitable for essay assignments can be found in the "Readings for Writers" appendix at the end of this book.

Different Essay Patterns: Part One

Jumping In

*Carpenters or mechanics might have access to many different tools, but what makes them experts at their craft is knowing which tool to use and when. Similarly, good writers know how to use tools like **the stages of the writing process** and **the basics of organizing essays** and apply them in a variety of rhetorical (writing) patterns.*

Learning Objectives

In this chapter, you will learn to:

1. Write an illustration essay with specific examples that support a general point.
2. Write a descriptive essay with specific details and a clear order.
3. Write a narrative essay that has a point and clear stages.
4. Write a process essay that makes a point and includes logical steps and detail.
5. Write a comparison or contrast essay that makes a statement and is supported by specific points.

You can write essays in a number of patterns, but any pattern will develop more easily if you follow the writing steps in preparing your essay. The examples in this chapter take you through the steps of preparing an essay in several patterns. Each sample essay expands on its related paragraph pattern in a previous chapter of this book.

① Write an illustration essay with specific examples that support a general point.

ILLUSTRATION

Hints for Writing an Illustration Essay

1. **Use specific examples to support a general point.** Remember that a *general* statement is a broad point, and a *specific* example is narrow.

    general statement: The weather was terrible yesterday.
    specific example: It rained for six hours.

    general statement: My car is not working.
    specific example: I need a new battery for my car.

2. **Be sure that you support a general statement by using specific examples** instead of merely writing another general statement.

    not this: general statement: The weather was terrible yesterday.
    more general statements: ~~It was awful outside.~~
       ~~Yesterday brought nasty weather.~~

    but this: general statement: The weather was terrible yesterday.
    specific examples: It rained for six hours.
       Several highways were flooded.

3. **Be sure that you have sufficient examples for each paragraph and that you develop the examples in each paragraph well.** If you do not develop your examples effectively, you will have one or more skimpy paragraphs in your essay. This will result in not only an undeveloped paragraph or two, but also an unbalanced essay. Your goal is to ensure that each paragraph in your essay is sufficiently and equally developed. You can use fewer examples and develop each one, or you can use more examples and develop them less extensively.

    not this: a skimpy paragraph:

    The weather was terrible yesterday. It rained for six hours. Several highways were flooded.

    but this: a paragraph with a few examples, each one well developed:

    The weather was terrible yesterday. It rained for six hours. The rain was heavy and harsh, accompanied by high winds that lashed the trees and signs on stores and restaurants. The downpour was so heavy that several highways were flooded. Drivers who usually take the Collins Road Expressway were diverted to a narrow city street and crawled home at 30 mph. Additionally, traffic on the interstate highway was at a standstill because drivers slowed to gawk at the numerous accidents caused by the lack of visibility and water-slicked roads.

> **CRITICAL THINKING**
>
> When evaluating topics, keep in mind that the purpose of an illustration essay is to show, explain, or prove a point through examples. These essays are specifically rich in detail.

WRITING THE ILLUSTRATION ESSAY IN STEPS

PREWRITING   ILLUSTRATION ESSAY

If you were asked to write an illustration essay about some aspect of preserving local resources, you might first freewrite.

Freewriting for an Illustration Essay

I'd like to be a better steward of my local environment. Where can I start? What about campus? The football team sponsors a yearly river clean-up event. They remove garbage and plant trees along the riverbed. There have also been efforts by other students to reduce food waste. Stewardship is about leaving a place better than you found it. Stewardship on campus has helped to create a real sense of community.

Some additional brainstorming might lead you to recognize that many groups at your school, including the Electrical Engineering Club, are stewards of your local resources. You might ask yourself some questions about what actions they take and what benefits result from their protecting and preserving local resources. Next, you are able to write a thesis sentence:

> *When student groups value stewardship and protect and preserve the school's resources, the entire college community benefits.*

This thesis contains three parts: it explains who values stewardship on campus ("student groups"), it explains the actions they take (to "protect and preserve the school's resources"), and who benefits (the "entire college community").

With a thesis statement and some of the ideas from your freewriting and brainstorming, you can begin to think about an outline.

PLANNING   ILLUSTRATION ESSAY

Following is an outline for an illustration essay on being a better steward of local resources. Study the outline carefully and be prepared to respond to the exercise that follows it.

Outline for an Illustration Essay

| paragraph 1 | — | I. | Thesis: When student groups value stewardship and protect and preserve the school's resources, the entire college community benefits. |
| paragraph 2, topic sentence | — | II. | <u>Stewardship is valued by many different groups on campus.</u> |

(Continued)

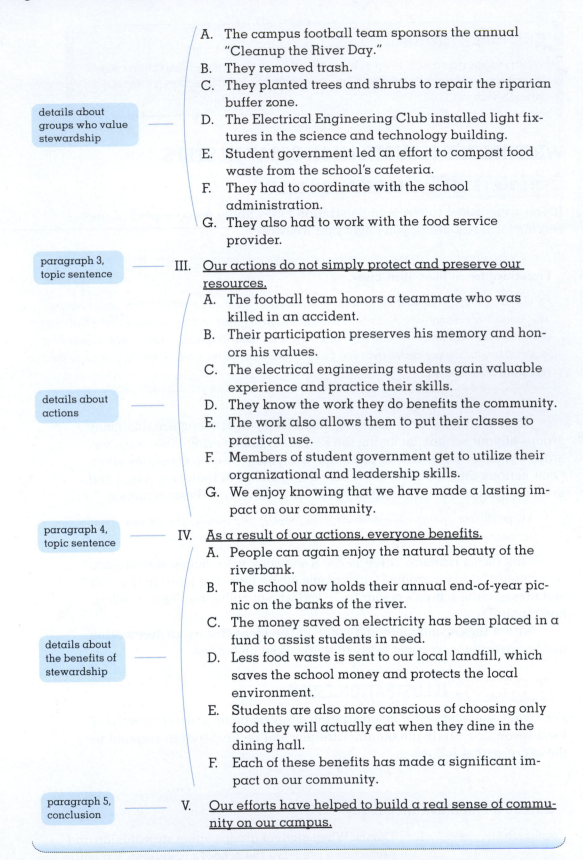

details about groups who value stewardship

A. The campus football team sponsors the annual "Cleanup the River Day."
B. They removed trash.
C. They planted trees and shrubs to repair the riparian buffer zone.
D. The Electrical Engineering Club installed light fixtures in the science and technology building.
E. Student government led an effort to compost food waste from the school's cafeteria.
F. They had to coordinate with the school administration.
G. They also had to work with the food service provider.

paragraph 3, topic sentence

III. Our actions do not simply protect and preserve our resources.

details about actions

A. The football team honors a teammate who was killed in an accident.
B. Their participation preserves his memory and honors his values.
C. The electrical engineering students gain valuable experience and practice their skills.
D. They know the work they do benefits the community.
E. The work also allows them to put their classes to practical use.
F. Members of student government get to utilize their organizational and leadership skills.
G. We enjoy knowing that we have made a lasting impact on our community.

paragraph 4, topic sentence

IV. As a result of our actions, everyone benefits.

details about the benefits of stewardship

A. People can again enjoy the natural beauty of the riverbank.
B. The school now holds their annual end-of-year picnic on the banks of the river.
C. The money saved on electricity has been placed in a fund to assist students in need.
D. Less food waste is sent to our local landfill, which saves the school money and protects the local environment.
E. Students are also more conscious of choosing only food they will actually eat when they dine in the dining hall.
F. Each of these benefits has made a significant impact on our community.

paragraph 5, conclusion

V. Our efforts have helped to build a real sense of community on our campus.

The outline combined some of the ideas from the freewriting and new details devised during the outlining process. As you write and revise your draft, you can continue to add details. Later in the writing process as you edit, you can combine sentences, strengthen transitions, and refine word choices.

| Exercise 1 | **Practice: Keeping the Examples in Order** |

In the outline for the essay on being a better steward of local resources, each body paragraph uses the same order in giving the examples of who values stewardship, their actions, and the benefits of protecting and preserving local resources. Survey the three body paragraphs and list that order.

_____

_____

_____

_____

DRAFTING AND REVISING   ILLUSTRATION ESSAY

Following is a revised draft of the essay on being a better steward of local resources. As you read it, you'll notice many changes from the outline on pages 263–264 (excluding some careless errors that can be corrected by careful editing and proofreading).

- An introduction has been added.
- Transitions have been added within and between paragraphs.
- Details have been added.
- A concluding paragraph has been added.

Study the draft carefully and be prepared to respond to the exercises that follow it.

Draft of an Illustration Essay

(Note: Thesis, topic sentences, and conclusion are underlined; editing and proofreading are still necessary.)

Students at my school spend hours studying in the library. They write essays for classes and prepare for the future. However, we are also stewards who find time to improve our school and local community. We believe in leaving this place better than we found it. When student groups value stewardship and protect and preserve the school's resources, the entire college community benefits.

Stewardship is valued by many different groups on campus. The campus football team sponsors the annual "Cleanup the River Day." This year they removed trash from the riverbank and also planted trees and shrubs to repair the riparian buffer zone. The Electrical Engineering Club used their newly learned skills in electrical engineering to install energy-efficient and cost-saving fixtures in the science and technology building. Another example of stewardship is the effort of student government to compost food waste from the school's cafeteria. This effort required coordination between student leaders, the school's administration, and the food service provider.

Our actions do not simply protect and preserve our resources. The football team began their participation three years ago after a teammate was killed in a car accident. He had been an avid fisherman and an environmental science major. The team uses their annual participation to preserve his memory and honor his values. The electrical engineering students use their environmental action to gain valuable experience and practice their skills. They know the work they do benefits the community while simultaneously allowing them to put their classes to practical use. Members of student government get to utilize their organizational and

(Continued)

leadership skills to better engage and serve their school community. We know that our school has been good to us. Moreover, we enjoy knowing that we have made a lasting inpact on our community.

<u>As a result of our actions, everyone benefits.</u> For instance, people can again enjoy the natural beauty of the riverbank. The school now holds their annual end-of-year picnic on the banks of the river. The money saved on electricity has been placed in a fund to assist students with tuition needs. This has allowed needy students to access the school's programs and classes. Finally, less food waste is sent to our local landfill, saving the school money and protecting the local environment. Students are also more conscious of choosing only food they will actually eat when they dine in the dining hall. Each of these benefits has made a significant impact on our local community.

Our school is well known for providing a good education, and that has always been a reason that people are proud to go to school here. Our students continue to study in the library and attend to their studies. Now the students at our school feel even more pride because we are stewards of our local community. We feel connected to each other because we all care about this place. <u>Our efforts has helped to build a real sense of community to our campus.</u>

Exercise 2   Practice: Using Framing to Conclude an Essay

Framing, which is discussed in Chapter 11 ("Writing an Essay"), is one way to tie an essay together neatly. It involves using something from the introduction as a way of concluding. You can take an example, a question, or even some general statement from the introduction and use that idea (though not necessarily the same words) in your conclusion. In the essay on being a good steward of local resources, the conclusion uses the framing device.

Reread the introduction, then reread the conclusion. Notice the repetition of certain ideas. Underline that repetition in the concluding paragraph.

EDITING AND PROOFREADING   **ILLUSTRATION ESSAY**

Once you are satisfied with your latest draft, it is time to edit. You can begin by combining short sentences, refining word choice, and checking for serious errors. You may even want to eliminate wordy or awkward phrases for more precise language. Then you can print a clean copy and proofread to catch any careless errors. The following checklist may help you with your refinements.

Checklist for Editing the Draft of an Essay

✓ Should any of my sentences be combined?

✓ Are the verb forms correct and consistent?

✓ Are the word choices appropriate?

✓ Is the spelling correct?

✓ Is the punctuation correct?

When you compare it to the draft on pages 265–266, you will notice some changes:

- A title has been added.
- Sentences have been combined.
- Verb form of *helped* has been corrected in the final paragraph.
- Spelling of *impact* has been corrected in Paragraph 3.
- Some of the word choices have been refined to make a description more precise or to eliminate an awkward phrase.
- Transitional words have been added throughout.
- A transitional sentence has been added to the first paragraph to introduce the readers to the hard work students do on campus. This transitional sentence leads to the essay's thesis sentence at the end of the first paragraph.
- New details have been added.
- Paragraphs 1 and 2 contain new examples of sentence combining.

Study the final version carefully and be prepared to respond to the exercise that follows it.

Final Version of an Illustration Essay

The Benefits of Being a Good Steward of Local Resources

Students at my school spend hours studying in the library, writing essays for classes, and preparing for the future. However, we are also stewards who find time to improve our school and local community. We believe in leaving this place better than we found it. When student groups value stewardship and protect and preserve the school's resources, the entire college community benefits.

Stewardship is valued by many different groups on campus. The campus football team sponsors the annual "Cleanup the River Day." This year they removed over two-hundred pounds of trash from the riverbank and planted trees and shrubs to repair the riparian buffer zone. A second example is the work of the Electrical Engineering Club. They used their newly learned skills in electrical engineering to install energy-efficient and cost-saving LED lighting fixtures in the science and technology building. Another example of stewardship is the effort of student government to compost food waste from the school's cafeteria, an effort that required a coordination between student leaders, the school's administration, and the food service provider.

Our actions do not simply protect and preserve our resources. The football team began their participation three years ago after a teammate was killed in a car accident. He had been an avid fisherman and an environmental science major. The team uses their annual participation to preserve his memory and honor his values. In contrast, the electrical engineering students use their environmental action to gain valuable experience and practice their skills. They know the work they do benefits the community while simultaneously allowing them to put their classes to practical use. Members of student government get to utilize their organizational and leadership skills to better engage and serve their school community. We know that our school has been good to us. Moreover, we enjoy knowing that we have made a lasting impact on our community.

As a result of our actions, everyone benefits. For instance, people can again enjoy the natural beauty of the riverbank. The school now holds their annual

(Continued)

end-of-year picnic on the banks of the river. The money saved on electricity has been placed in a fund to assist students in need. This has allowed needy students to access the school's programs and classes. Finally, less food waste is sent to our local landfill, saving the school money and protecting the local environment. Students are conscientious about serving size when they dine in the dining hall. Collectively, each of these benefits has made a significant impact on our local community.

Our school is well known for providing a good education, and that has always been a reason that people are proud to go to school here. Our students will continue to study in the library and attend to their studies. Now, however, the students at our school feel even more pride because we are stewards of our local community. We feel connected to each other because we all care about this place. Our efforts have helped to build a real sense of community to our campus.

> **Exercise 3** Practice: Identifying the Changes in a Final Version of an Illustration Essay
>
> To become more aware of the kinds of changes that can improve an essay, underline the following changes: (1) the transition sentence in Paragraph 1; (2) the added details in Paragraph 2; (3) the sentences combined in Paragraph 2; (4) transition words added in Paragraph 3; (5) wording improved in Paragraph 4; and (6) transition word added in Paragraph 5.

Topics for Writing an Illustration Essay

When you write on any of these topics, work through the stages of the writing process in preparing your essay.

1. Complete one of the following statements and use it as the thesis for an illustration essay.

   Starting a new job can be _____.

   Considering multiple perspectives of an issue is important because _____.

   Maintaining a healthy balance between work and play is vital for _____.

   My ability to organize my study time has allowed me to _____.

2. Choose one of the following topics. Narrow it to a more specific topic and then write a thesis statement about it. Use that thesis to write an illustration essay.

fast food	pets	fear
poverty	fatigue	sports
adoption	cereal	weather
traffic	music	ambition

Collaborate

3. To begin this assignment, brainstorm with a partner or a group. Together, write down as many types of weather as you can. For example, begin with the fairly obvious such as hot or cold or rainy. From there, refine the general types to more specific terms, such as humid or snowy or damp, or any other words that you might want to use. Because weather has a significant impact on how we dress and what we do, we are often controlled by the weather. Once you

have a strong list of types of weather, circle the three that you have some specific experiences with. Do a quick freewrite on some of those experiences. In a five-paragraph essay, discuss one type of weather in each body paragraph and how that type of weather influences a person's day. Clarify the three types of weather, include examples of how the weather impacts you or people you know.

4. To begin this assignment, look around your classroom. Now, write a general statement about some aspect of the classroom: the furniture, the condition of the room, the lighting, the number of windows, the time of day, and the way the seats are arranged. For example, if you observed that the lighting was too bright, there were no windows, and the desks were crammed together, you might conclude that "Class performance can be impacted by the physical atmosphere of a classroom." You could write a five-paragraph essay using that general statement as your thesis and support with specific examples and details from your observation.

Topics for Critical Thinking and Writing

1. In conversation, we often use expressions that are meant to hide what we really mean. We may want to conceal our motives, avoid hurting another person's feelings, or avoid taking responsibility. For instance, a statement from a boy- or girlfriend to a significant other may be, "I think it's time we started seeing other people." This may be coded, softer language for such messages as "I've found somebody I like better than you" or "I'm bored and need more excitement in my life." When talking to the parents of a badly behaved child, we may say, "He has a lot of energy" or "She certainly has a mind of her own, doesn't she?"

   Think of three situations in which people are likely to use less than frank expressions for a variety of reasons. For instance, people tend to be tactful at weddings, at dinners where they are guests, when they have to let an employee go, and so forth. Devote one body paragraph to each situation and illustrate your point with specific examples.

2. Most youth sports teams rely on volunteer coaches to organize and instruct the young players. For many young people, these coaches serve as important mentors and role models who volunteer for the benefit of the team or organization. From your experience with sports as a youth, illustrate the impact that a coach can have on a young person. Generate a list of some coaches that you recall. Then, make a list of memorable personality traits that each possessed. Write a five-paragraph essay either discussing the specific traits of a good coach, or simply write an essay illustrating three memorable coaches.

DESCRIPTION

Hints for Writing a Descriptive Essay

2 Write a descriptive essay with specific details and a clear order.

1. **Use many specific details.**   Because an essay is usually longer than one paragraph, you will need more details to develop an essay. To ensure that your details create an effective description, make them specific.

2. **Decide on a clear order.** Without a clear order, a descriptive essay will become a jumble of details spread over several paragraphs. Decide on a clear order (from inside to outside, from top to bottom, and so forth) and stick to it. Each body paragraph can focus on one part of that order.

CRITICAL THINKING

The purpose of a descriptive essay is to describe something or someone vividly. Think of the 5Ws and 1 H questions: *Who? What? When? Where? Why?* and *How?* Your goal is to paint a picture that the reader can imagine. Remember, using sensory language helps create strong descriptions.

WRITING THE DESCRIPTIVE ESSAY IN STEPS

PREWRITING DESCRIPTIVE ESSAY

If you were going to write an essay describing the contents of your garage, you might first brainstorm a list.

Brainstorming a List for a Descriptive Essay

Topic: The Contents of Our Garage
- *my husband*
- *Bradley's motorcycle*
- *his tools for the cycle, yard work, home repairs*
- *paint cans*
- *bulletin board with photos*
- *little plastic containers of nails, screws*
- *dusty shelves on the walls*
- *oil stains and smells on the floor*
- *Bradley's work bench*
- *musty smell of Bradley's junk on the floor*
- *noise of engine running*
- *garbage can smells*
- *Bradley's camping gear*
- *my collection of hand-painted pottery doesn't fit*

After surveying the list, you want to think about what point it makes. For this list, your thoughts might lead you to the idea that most of the details connect to Bradley. That main point is the *dominant impression*. For this list, the dominant impression could be this sentence:

The garage is my husband's territory.

This sentence could be the thesis statement of the descriptive essay.

PLANNING DESCRIPTIVE ESSAY

Following is an outline for a descriptive essay on Bradley's garage. Study the outline carefully and be prepared to respond to the exercise that follows it.

Outline for a Descriptive Essay

paragraph 1	I.	Thesis: The garage is my husband's territory.
paragraph 2, topic sentence	II.	The bare floor is a small space.

    A. It is an area by the garage door.

details about the bare floor

    B. It also includes enough space to enter the door to the house.
    C. The two spaces have oil stains.
    D. They are also gritty with dirt.
    E. The floor smells like gasoline.

paragraph 3, topic sentence — III. Most of the garage floor is filled.

    A. Boxes of Bradley's junk give off a nasty odor.
    B. Bradley's work bench is pushed into one corner and covers a large part of the floor.
    C. His camping gear stretches into the middle of the floor.

details about objects on floor

    D. His motorcycle, usually in pieces, lies on the floor.
    E. It fills one third of the space.
    F. Pieces of other cycles mingle with parts of Bradley's cycle.

paragraph 4, topic sentence — IV. The back and side walls seem to stagger because of the densely packed shelves.

    A. Dusty metal shelves are packed with tools.
    B. Old, crusty paint cans are on the shelves.
    C. Open bags of lawn fertilizer sit on a high shelf.

details about objects on shelves

    D. Dozens of small plastic containers of nails and screws are there.
    E. One shelf has a bulletin board.
    F. It leans against a mess of tools.

paragraph 5, conclusion — V. Bradley loves this part of our house.

The outline combined some of the details from the list with new details gathered during the outlining process. As you write and revise your drafts, you can continue to add details. Later, as you edit, you can combine sentences, add transitions, and work on word choice.

Exercise 4 **Practice: Recognizing Sense Descriptions**

A good description relies on many words that relate to the five senses of sight, sound, smell, taste, and touch (or texture). In the preceding outline, underline one example of a word or phrase that refers to each of the following: (1) sight, (2) smell, and (3) touch. Use 1, 2, or 3 to identify the type of sense description.

DRAFTING AND REVISING **DESCRIPTIVE ESSAY**

Following is a revised draft of the essay on Bradley's garage. As you read it, you'll notice many changes from the outline above.

- An introduction has been added.
- Transitions have been added within and between paragraphs.
- Details have been added.
- A concluding paragraph has been written.

Study the draft carefully and be prepared to respond to the exercises that follow it.

Draft of a Descriptive Essay

(Note: Thesis, topic sentences, and conclusion are underlined; editing and proofreading are still necessary.)

Everyone likes one part of his or her living space better than the other parts. Some people find pleasure in their comfortable living rooms. Others love a bedroom that reflects their tastes. My husband Bradley prefers a different part of our house. <u>The garage is my husband's territory</u>.

<u>The bare floor is a small space</u>. It is an area by the garage door and includes a small space near the door to the house. These two spaces are speckled with oil stains. They are also gritty with dirt. One good aspect of the grit is that it protects people from slipping on the oily patches on the floor. The floor smells like gasoline. Bradley doesn't mind the smell at all.

<u>Most of the garage floor is filled</u>. Boxes of Bradley's junk give off a nasty odor. These boxes contain lots of junk, but Bradley wants to save it all. Although the boxes take up space, Bradley's big work bench fills lots more space. It is pushed into one corner of the garage. In addition, his camping gear stretches into the middle of the floor. Bradley's motorcycle, which is usually in pieces, lies on the floor. Pieces of other cycles also mingle with parts of Bradley's cycle.

<u>The walls of the garage are also heavily loaded</u>. In fact, the back and side walls seem to stagger because of their densely loaded shelves. Some of these dusty metal shelves are packed with tools. Old, crusty paint cans are also on the shelves. Open bags of lawn fertilizer spill their contents on a high shelf. Dozens of small plastic containers of nails and screws are stacked between piles of cleaning rags and towels. One shelf contains a bulletin board that leans against a mess of tools.

The garage is not a showplace in a model home. It doesn't look like the clean, organized garages that appear in commercials for home improvement stores. However, it is a real garage. <u>Although I cannot imagine spending time in it, Bradley loves his garage.</u>

Exercise 5 Practice: Identifying the Type of Lead-In

Circle the type of lead-in used in this essay: (1) beginning with some general statements, (2) telling a story, or (3) explaining why this topic is worth writing about.

Exercise 6 Practice: Noticing How Contrast Is Used in the Conclusion

In the conclusion, several contrasts are used to lead to a rewording of the thesis. One of these contrasts, "Although I cannot imagine spending time in it," is used as a transition to "Bradley loves his garage." Underline one other use of contrast in the final paragraph (there are several).

EDITING AND PROOFREADING   DESCRIPTIVE ESSAY

Following is a final version of the essay on Bradley's garage. When you compare it to the draft, you will notice some changes:

- A new transition sentence opens one of the body paragraphs.
- Some repetitive words, such as the word *space*, have been replaced.
- Specific details have been added to all the body paragraphs.
- More sense words have been added.
- Two more sentences have been combined.
- Word choice, such as the replacement of the word *mess* in Paragraph 4 with a more specific word, has been improved.
- A title has been added.

Study the final version carefully and be prepared to respond to the exercise that follows it.

Final Version of a Descriptive Essay

One Person's Preference

Everyone likes one part of his or her living space better than the other parts. Some people find pleasure in their comfortable living rooms. Others love a bedroom that reflects their tastes. My husband Bradley prefers a different part of our house. The garage is my husband's territory.

The least noticeable part of the garage is the open floor. The bare floor is a small space. It is an area by the garage door and includes a small space near the door to the house. These two places are speckled with shiny, smelly oil stains. They are also gritty with dirt. One good aspect of the grit is that it protects people from slipping on the oily patches on the floor. The floor smells like gasoline, but Bradley doesn't mind the smell at all.

Most of the garage floor is filled. It is covered in boxes of Bradley's junk that give off a nasty odor. These boxes contain junk such as rags, cracked plastic flower pots, and rusted garden tools, but Bradley wants to save it all. Although the boxes take up space, Bradley's big work bench fills much more space. It is pushed into one corner of the garage. In addition, his camping gear, including a tent and a sleeping bag, stretches into the middle of the floor. In addition, Bradley's motorcycle, which is usually in pieces, lies on the floor. Pieces of other cycles also mingle with parts of Bradley's cycle.

The walls of the garage are also heavily loaded. In fact, the back and side walls seem to stagger because of their densely loaded shelves. Some of these dusty metal shelves are packed with tools such as wrenches, screwdrivers, and pliers. Old, crusty paint cans, some without any paint, are also on the shelves. Open bags of lawn fertilizer spill their contents on a high shelf. Dozens of small plastic containers of nails and screws are stacked between piles of cleaning rags and towels. One shelf contains a bulletin board that leans against a jumble of tools.

The garage is not a showplace in a model home. It doesn't look like the clean, organized garages that appear in commercials for home improvement stores. However, it is a real garage. Although I cannot imagine spending time in it, Bradley loves his garage.

Exercise 7 Practice: Recognizing the Changes in the Final Version of a Descriptive Essay

Compare the draft and the final version of the paragraph. Then, in the final version, underline and number these changes from the draft version: (1) an added transitional sentence; (2) a change in word choice to avoid too much repetition of the word *space*; (3) additional sense words; (4) two sentences that have been combined. All of these changes are in Paragraph 2.

Topics for Writing a Descriptive Essay

When you write on any of these topics, work through the stages of the writing process in preparing your essay.

1. Many people enjoy going to see live music. Some enjoy seeing the musicians in person, whereas others enjoy the communal aspect of enjoying music with a large audience. Consider a concert or performance you have attended. Then, describe the music or performance, the feelings it evokes in you, and why you react to it in a particular way.

Collaborate

2. Begin this essay with a partner. Describe a relative or a neighbor who is particularly interesting. Describe them physically (how he or she moves, speaks, looks, or acts). Ask your partner to (1) jot down the details of your description and (2) help you come up with specific details by asking you follow-up questions each time you run out of ideas. Work together for at least ten minutes. Then change roles. Let your partner describe his or her interesting relative or neighbor and take notes for your partner. Then split up and use the details you collected on your own relative or neighbor to write an essay.

3. Each year, multiple magazines rate the best places to live. Some base these rankings on the location's setting, its low crime rates, or its proximity to services like education and health care. Others base their rankings on the diversity of the population, its thriving arts community, and its cultural offerings. Consider your ideal place in which to live and the reasons for you selecting it. Then, write an essay that describes this place, specifically, describe the three qualities you used to select it.

Topics for Critical Thinking and Writing

1. Nature often provides us with an escape from our hectic schedule. Recall a spot in nature such as a park, wood, lake, beach, hill, or desert that you use as a spot to escape or "recharge." Recall some specific moments in that place and describe how the place can "fill you up" or refresh you. Consider why your choice of space appeals to you. As you revise your drafts, try to use as many vivid images as possible.

2. If you have fond memories of a particular holiday that you liked as a child, see if you can remember specific sights, sounds, smells, or emotions associated with it. Freewrite about these memories and then determine the most vivid images you want to include in your essay. For this descriptive essay, your details should focus on more of the atmosphere and/or appearance of the holiday rather than merely your activities there.

NARRATION

Hints for Writing a Narrative Essay

③ Write a narrative essay that has a point and clear stages.

1. **Give the essay a point and stick to it.** A narrative essay tells a story. A story without a point becomes a list of moments that lead nowhere. Once you have your point, check that your use of details does not lead you away from the point.

2. **Divide your narrative into clear stages.** In an essay, you divide your narrative into several paragraphs. Check that each body paragraph has a clear focus (in the topic sentence) and that you have a clear reason for your division. You may decide to divide your body paragraphs into (a) before, during, and after or (b) the first part of the story, the middle part, and the ending.

WRITING THE NARRATIVE ESSAY IN STEPS

PREWRITING   NARRATIVE ESSAY

If you were asked to write a narrative essay about something that changed you, you might begin by freewriting.

Freewriting for a Narrative Essay

Topic: Something That Changed Me

Something that changed me. I don't know. What changed me? Lots of things happened to me, but I can't find one that changed me. Graduating from high school? Everybody will write about that, how boring, and anyway, what was the big deal? I haven't gotten married. No big change there. Divorce. My parents' divorce really changed the whole family. A big shock to me. I couldn't believe it was happening. I was really scared. Who would I live with? They were real calm when they told me. I've never been so scared. I was too young to understand. Kept thinking they'd just get back together. They didn't. Then I got a stepmother. The year of the divorce was a hard time for me. Kids suffer in divorce.

Reviewing your freewriting, you decide to write on the topic of your parent's divorce. Once you have this topic, you begin to brainstorm about your topic, asking yourself questions that can lead to further details about the divorce.

With more details, you can decide that your essay will focus on the announcement of your parents' divorce and the emotions you felt. You devise the following thesis statement:

When my parents announced that they were divorcing, I felt confused by all of my emotions.

CRITICAL THINKING

A narrative tells a story, and all parts of the story must be present. Think again about the sequence of *who, what, where, when, why,* and *how.*

PLANNING   **NARRATIVE ESSAY**

Following is an outline for a narrative essay on the announcement of your parents' divorce and the emotions you felt. As you read it, note how it divides the announcement into three parts: (1) the background of the announcement, (2) the story of the divorce announcement, and (3) the emotions connected to the announcement. Study the outline carefully and be prepared to respond to the exercise that follows it.

Outline for a Narrative Essay

paragraph 1 ——————— I. Thesis: When my parents announced that they were divorcing, I felt confused by all my emotions.

paragraph 2, topic sentence ——————— II. I will never forget how one ordinary day suddenly became a terrible one.

> A. I was seven when my mom and dad divorced.
> B. My sister was ten.
> C. Both of my parents were there.

details about background of the announcement ———————
> D. They told us at breakfast, in the kitchen.
> E. I was eating toast.
> F. I remember I couldn't eat anything after they started talking.
> G. I remember a piece of toast with one bite out of it.

paragraph 3, topic sentence ——————— III. When my parents first spoke, I was in shock.

> A. They were very calm when they told us.
> B. They said they loved us, but they couldn't get along.
> C. They said they would always love us kids.

details about story of the announcement ———————
> D. It was an unreal moment to me.
> E. I couldn't believe it was happening.
> F. At first I just thought they were having another fight.
> G. I was too young to understand.
> H. I didn't cry.

paragraph 4, topic sentence ——————— IV. When the reality hit me, my emotions overwhelmed me.

> A. My sister cried.
> B. Then I knew it was serious.
> C. I kept thinking I would have to choose which parent to live with.

details about my emotions ———————
> D. I knew I would really hurt the one I didn't choose.
> E. I loved them both.
> F. I felt so much guilt about leaving one of them.
> G. I also needed both of them.
> H. I felt ripped apart.

paragraph 5, conclusion ——————— V. When my parents' marriage fell apart, so did I.

The outline combined some of the details from the freewriting with new details gathered through brainstorming and during the outlining process. As you write and revise your draft, you can continue to add details. As you edit later in the writing process, you can combine sentences, strengthen transitions, and refine word choices.

Exercise 8   **Practice: Recognizing New Details in the Outline**

Look at the writer's freewriting and note its details on the writer's emotions. Then compare those details to the details about emotions in Paragraph 4 of the outline. Underline the additional details in this section of the outline.

DRAFTING AND REVISING   **NARRATIVE ESSAY**

Following is a revised draft of the essay on an announcement of divorce. As you read it, you'll notice many changes from the outline on page 276.

- An introduction has been added.
- Transitions within the paragraphs have been added.
- Details have been added.
- Some dialogue has been added.
- A concluding paragraph has been added.

Study the draft carefully and be prepared to respond to the exercises that follow it.

Draft of a Narrative Essay

(Note: Thesis, topic sentences, and conclusion are underlined; editing and proofreading are still necessary.)

Divorce can be really hard on children. <u>When my parents announced that they were divorcing, I felt confused by all my emotions.</u>

<u>I will never forget how one ordinary day suddenly became a terrible one</u>. I was seven, and my sister was ten on that day. Both of my parents told us at breakfast, in the kitchen. I clearly remember that I was eating toast, but once they started talking, I couldn't eat anything. I can still recall holding a piece of toast with one bite out of it. I stared at the toast stupidly as I listened to what they had to say.

<u>When my parents first spoke, I was in shock</u>. They were very calm when they told us. "We love both of you very much," my dad said, "but your mother and I aren't getting along." "But we will always love you," my mother added. The announcement was such an unreal moment that I couldn't believe it was happening. My parents used to fight a lot, so at first I just thought they were having another fight. I was too young to understand. In fact, I didn't even cry.

<u>When the reality hit me, my emotions overwhelmed me</u>. My sister began to cry, and I suddenly knew it was serious. I kept thinking I would have to choose which parent to live with, and I knew I would really hurt the one I didn't choose. I loved them both. I was filled with guilt about hurting one. I also needed both parents so much that I dreaded separating from one of them. I believed that the one I didn't choose would hate me. I felt ripped apart.

In one morning, my world changed. One minute, I was an ordinary seven-year-old having breakfast with his family. The next, I was experiencing powerful emotions no child should feel. <u>When my parents' marriage fell apart, so did I.</u>

Exercise 9 Practice: Spotting Differences between the Outline and the Draft

Compare paragraph 2 in the outline to the same paragraph in the draft. The draft of the paragraph is better because it (1) combines sentences (twice) and (2) adds a sentence of new details. Underline and number these changes in the draft.

Exercise 10 Practice: Evaluating the Effectiveness of the Introduction and Conclusion

Compare the introduction to the concluding paragraph. Which do you think is more effective, and why? _____

_____

EDITING AND PROOFREADING **NARRATIVE ESSAY**

Following is the final version of the essay on an announcement of divorce. When you compare it to the draft, you will notice some changes:

- The introduction has been developed and improved.
- More specific details have been added.
- The word choice has been improved in several places to avoid repetition, to remove an overused phrase (*a lot*), and to change from an informal word for a parent (my *dad*) to a more formal one (my *father*).
- To improve the style in Paragraph 4, some sentences have been combined.
- A title has been added.

Study the final version carefully and be prepared to respond to the exercise that follows it.

Final Version of a Narrative Essay

An Emotional Morning

No childhood is perfect, and part of growing up is facing disappointment, change, and loss. However, there is one loss that can be overwhelming. Divorce can be really hard on children. When my parents announced that they were divorcing, I felt confused by all my emotions.

I will never forget how one ordinary day suddenly became a terrible one. I was seven, and my sister was ten on that day. Both of my parents told us at breakfast, in the kitchen. I clearly remember that I was eating toast, but once they started talking, I couldn't eat anything. I can still recall holding a piece of whole wheat toast with one bite out of it. I stared at the toast stupidly as I listened to what they had to say.

When my parents first spoke, I was in shock. They were very calm when they told us. "We love both of you very much," my father said, "but your mother and I aren't getting along." "But we will always love you," my mother added. The announcement was such an unreal moment that I couldn't believe it was happening. My parents used to fight often, so at first I just thought they were having another argument. I was too young to understand. In fact, I didn't even cry.

Then the reality hit me, and my emotions overwhelmed me. My sister began to cry, and I suddenly knew the situation was serious. I kept thinking I would have to choose which parent to live with, and I knew I would really hurt the one I didn't choose. Because I loved them both, I was filled with guilt about hurting one. I also needed both parents so much that I dreaded separating from one of them. I believed that the one I didn't choose would hate me. I felt ripped apart.

In one morning, my world changed. One minute, I was an ordinary seven-year-old having breakfast with his family. The next, I was experiencing powerful emotions no child should feel. When my parents' marriage fell apart, so did I.

Exercise 11   **Practice: Recognizing Changes in the Final Version**

Compare the draft version of this essay to the final version. Underline these changes in word choice: the word that replaced *a lot*; the word that replaced *fight*, so that *fight* no longer appears twice in one sentence; and the word that replaced *it* in the draft phrase *it was serious*.

Topics for Writing a Narrative Essay

When you write on any of these topics, work through the stages of the writing process in preparing your essay.

1. This assignment begins with an interview. Ask one (or both) of your parents or grandparents to tell you about the day you were born. Be prepared to ask questions. (For example, were you expected that day, or did you surprise your family? Was there a rush to the hospital?) Get as many details as you can. Then write a narrative essay about that day.

2. Write about a time you "missed out" on an important event. Use the details of the event to explain what you missed out on and why.

3. Write the story of your first day on your college campus. When was it? How did you feel?

4. Some people believe that some incidents in life are beyond their control and, therefore, decided by fate. Write about a specific incident that you believe was driven by fate. Recall the pattern of events that led up to this incident and how the resulting incident was beyond your control.

5. Write on any of the following topics:

your first date	your first big purchase
a dangerous event	your first time camping
the day you decided to attend college	a final goodbye

Topics for Critical Thinking and Writing

1. Write an essay about an incident involving you and a friend or family member. It can be a quarrel, a misunderstanding, a promise, a shared secret, or some other interaction between the two of you. In a five-paragraph essay, write one body paragraph on the way you perceived the incident and how you reacted to it. Then write another body paragraph imagining how the other person must have perceived the same incident based on his or her reactions. In the third body paragraph, include some valuable lessons you learned from these two perspectives.

2. Write about the first time you traveled far from home. Whether it was by car, bus, train, or plane, describe the events and your reactions to the travel. Consider how the experience changed or reaffirmed your perspective on the place(s) you visited and the value of traveling and leaving one's comfort zone.

④ Write a process essay that makes a point and includes logical steps and detail.

PROCESS

Hints for Writing a Process Essay

1. **Remember that there are two kinds of process essays:** A **directional** process essay tells the reader how to do something; an **informational** process essay explains an activity without telling the reader how to do it. Whether you write a directional or an informational process essay, be sure to make a point. That point is expressed in your thesis.

   When you write a process essay, it is easy to confuse a topic with a thesis.

   topic: How to change the oil in your car
   thesis: You don't have to be an expert to learn how to change the oil in your car.

   topic: How gardeners squirrel-proof their backyards
   thesis: Gardeners have to think like squirrels to keep the critters away from plants and trees.

2. **Find some logical way to divide the steps into paragraphs.** If you have seven steps, you probably don't want to put each one into a separate paragraph, especially if they are short steps. You would run the risk of having a list instead of a well-developed essay. To avoid writing a list, try to cluster your steps according to some logical division.

   If you are writing about how to prepare for a yard sale, you could divide your steps into groups such as (1) what to do a week before the sale, (2) what to do the day before the sale, and (3) what to do early on the day of the sale. Or if you are writing about how to cope with a bad cold, you could divide the steps into (1) recognizing the first signs of a cold, (2) assembling cold-fighting foods and vitamins, and (3) struggling through the days of misery.

3. **Develop your paragraphs by explaining each step thoroughly and by using details.** If you are explaining how to make a cake, you can't simply tell the reader to mix the combined ingredients well. You need to explain how long to mix and whether to mix with a fork, spoon, spatula, or electric mixer. Fortunately, an essay gives you the time and space to be clear, especially if you put yourself in the reader's place and anticipate his or her questions.

CRITICAL THINKING

A process essay provides instruction on how to do something (directional) or explains the steps of a procedure from start to finish, such as how a bill becomes a law (informational). It's important not to omit any steps. What may seem simple and logical to you may not seem as clear to your reader.

WRITING THE PROCESS ESSAY IN STEPS

PREWRITING   PROCESS ESSAY

If you were writing a process essay about finding an apartment, you might first freewrite your ideas on the topic. Brainstorming and listing your ideas might lead you to group your ideas into three categories, organized in time order:

Listing and Grouping Ideas for a Process Essay

Topic: Finding an Apartment

before the search

How many bedrooms?

Friends can help.

a good neighborhood

A convenient location can be more expensive.

can save you money on transportation

during the search

look around

don't pick the first apartment you see

look at a bunch

but not too many

after the search

Check the lease carefully.

How much is the security deposit?

After some more thinking, you could summarize these ideas in a thesis:

> *Finding the apartment you want takes planning and careful investigation.*

With a thesis sentence and some ideas clustered in categories, you can write an outline for your essay.

PLANNING   PROCESS ESSAY

Following is an outline for a process essay on finding an apartment. Study the outline carefully and be prepared to respond to the exercise that follows it.

Outline for a Process Essay

paragraph 1 ———— I.   Thesis: Finding the apartment you want takes planning and careful investigation.

(Continued)

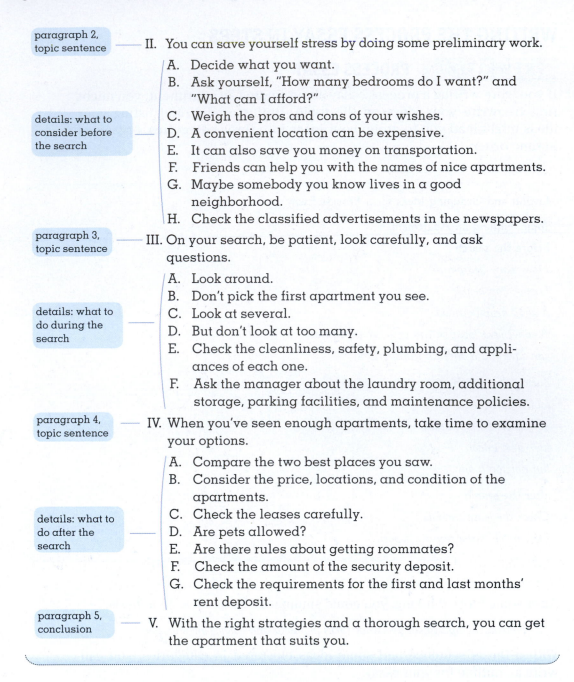

paragraph 2,
topic sentence —— II. You can save yourself stress by doing some preliminary work.

  A. Decide what you want.
  B. Ask yourself, "How many bedrooms do I want?" and "What can I afford?"

details: what to
consider before —— C. Weigh the pros and cons of your wishes.
the search   D. A convenient location can be expensive.
                  E. It can also save you money on transportation.
                  F. Friends can help you with the names of nice apartments.
                  G. Maybe somebody you know lives in a good neighborhood.
                  H. Check the classified advertisements in the newspapers.

paragraph 3,
topic sentence —— III. On your search, be patient, look carefully, and ask questions.

  A. Look around.
  B. Don't pick the first apartment you see.

details: what to
do during the —— C. Look at several.
search   D. But don't look at too many.
                  E. Check the cleanliness, safety, plumbing, and appliances of each one.
                  F. Ask the manager about the laundry room, additional storage, parking facilities, and maintenance policies.

paragraph 4,
topic sentence —— IV. When you've seen enough apartments, take time to examine your options.

  A. Compare the two best places you saw.
  B. Consider the price, locations, and condition of the apartments.
  C. Check the leases carefully.

details: what to
do after the   —— D. Are pets allowed?
search   E. Are there rules about getting roommates?
                  F. Check the amount of the security deposit.
                  G. Check the requirements for the first and last months' rent deposit.

paragraph 5,
conclusion   —— V. With the right strategies and a thorough search, you can get the apartment that suits you.

The outline used each cluster of steps as one body paragraph. A topic sentence for each body paragraph made some point about that group of steps. It also added many new details gathered during the outline process. As you write and revise your draft, you can continue to add details. Later, during editing, you can combine sentences, strengthen transitions, and refine word choices.

Exercise 12 **Practice: Recognizing Added Details in the Outline Stage**

Paragraph 2 of the outline is quite different from the list of ideas grouped for the same category ("before the search") on page 281. In the outline, a topic sentence and a number of new details have been added. Underline the added details in Paragraph 2.

DRAFTING AND REVISING   PROCESS ESSAY

Following is a revised draft of the essay on finding an apartment. As you read it, you'll notice many changes from the outline on pages 281–282.

- An introduction has been added.
- Transitions have been added within and between paragraphs.
- Details have been added.
- Direct questions have been turned into sentences.
- A concluding paragraph has been added.

Study the revised draft carefully and be prepared to respond to the exercises that follow it.

Draft of a Process Essay

(Note: Thesis, topic sentences, and conclusion are underlined; editing and proofreading are still necessary.)

Some people drive around a neighborhood until they see an apartment complex with a "Vacancy" sign. They talk to the building manager, visit the apartment, and sign a lease. Soon they are residents of their new apartment, and often they are unhappy with their home. These people went about their search the wrong way. They did not realize that finding the apartment you want takes planning and careful investigation.

You can save yourself stress by doing some preliminary work. First of all, decide what you want. Determine how many bedrooms you want and what you can afford. Weigh the pros and cons of your wishes. You may want a convenient location, but that can be expensive. On the other hand, that location can save you money on transportation. When you've decided what you want, rely on friends to help you with your search. They can help you with the names of nice apartments. Maybe somebody you know lives in a good neighborhood and can help you find an apartment. In addition, check the classified advertisements in the newspapers. They are full of possibilities.

In your search, be patient, look carefully, and ask questions. It's important to look around and not to pick the first apartment you see. Look at several so that you can get a sense of your options. However, don't look at so many apartments that they all become a blur in your memory. As you visit each apartment, check its cleanness, safety, plumbing, and appliances. You don't want an apartment that opens onto a bad area or one with a leaky refrigerator. Be sure to ask the apartment manager whether there are a laundry room, a storage area, and sufficient assigned parking and guest parking. Check to see if a maintenance person lives on the premises.

When you've seen enough apartments, take the time to examine your options. First, compare the two best places you saw. Now that you have narrowed your search, consider the price, location, and condition of each apartment. Check the leases carefully. If you have or are thinking of getting a pet, check to see if pets are allowed. Check the rules about roommates, too. Next, check to see how much money you will have to put up initially. Does the lease specify the amount of the security deposit? Does it require a payment of first and last months' rent? The answers to these questions can help you reach a decision.

Once you have followed the steps of the process, you are ready to make your choice. While these steps take more time than simply picking the first place you see on the street, they are worth it. With the right strategies and a thorough search, you can get the apartment that suits your needs. Finally, you are ready to settle into your new home.

> **Exercise 13**   **Practice: Recognizing How an Outline Can Be Developed into a Draft**

Study Paragraph 3 in its outline form. Then examine the same paragraph in draft form. The paragraph includes new details about (1) a reason to look at several apartments, (2) the danger of looking at too many apartments, (3) why it is important to check the safety of the apartment and the condition of the appliances, and (4) what to ask about maintenance. Underline these new details.

> **Exercise 14**   **Practice: Recognizing Effective Transitions**

The concluding paragraph carries the reader into the final step in the process of finding an apartment. Notice how effective time transitions lead the reader from the first part of the paragraph, then past the restatement of the thesis to the final sentence. Underline the time transitions.

EDITING AND PROOFREADING   PROCESS ESSAY

Following is the final edited version of the essay on finding an apartment. When you compare it to the draft on page 283, you will notice some changes:

- A transition has been added to the beginning of Paragraph 2 so that there is a smoother link from the thesis at the end of Paragraph 1 and the topic sentence of Paragraph 2.
- The words *nice*, *good*, and *bad* have been changed to more specific descriptions.
- More details have been added to the end of Paragraph 3.
- *Cleanness* has been corrected to *cleanliness* in Paragraph 3.
- A title has been added.

Study the final version carefully and be prepared to respond to the exercise that follows it.

Final Version of a Process Essay

How to Find a Suitable Apartment

Some people drive around a neighborhood until they see an apartment complex with a "Vacancy" sign. They talk to the building manager, visit the apartment, and sign a lease. Soon they are residents of their new apartment, and often they are unhappy with their home. These people went about their search the wrong way. They did not realize that finding the apartment you want takes planning and careful investigation.

When it comes to choosing an apartment, you can save yourself stress by doing some preliminary work. First of all, decide what you want. Determine how many bedrooms you want and what you can afford. Weigh the pros and cons of your wishes. You may want a convenient location, but that can be expensive. On the other hand, that location can save you money on transportation. When you've decided what you want, rely on friends to help you with your search. They can help you with the names of suitable apartments. Maybe somebody you know lives in an attractive neighborhood and can help you find an apartment. In addition, check the classified advertisements in the newspapers. They are full of possibilities.

In your search, be patient, look carefully, and ask questions. It's important to look around and not to pick the first apartment you see. Look at several so that you can get a sense of your options. However, don't look at so many apartments that they all become a blur in your memory. As you visit each apartment, check its cleanness, safety, plumbing, and appliances. You don't want an apartment that opens onto a dark and deserted area or one with a leaky refrigerator. Be sure to ask the apartment manager whether there are a laundry room, storage area, and sufficient assigned parking and guest parking. Check to see if a maintenance person lives on the premises or if a rental agency handles emergencies and repairs.

When you've seen enough apartments, take the time to examine your options. First, compare the two best places you saw. Now that you have narrowed your search, consider the price, location, and condition of each apartment. Check the leases carefully. If you have or are thinking of getting a pet, check to see if pets are allowed. Check the rules about roommates, too. Next, check to see how much money you will have to put up initially. Does the lease specify the amount of the security deposit? Does it require a payment of first and last months' rent? The answers to these questions can help you reach a decision.

Once you have followed the steps of the process, you are ready to make your choice. While these steps take more time than simply picking the first place you see on the street, they are worth it. With the right strategies and a thorough search, you can get the apartment that suits your needs. Finally, you are ready to settle into your new home.

Exercise 15 **Practice: Recognizing Small Improvements in the Final Version of a Process Essay**

Underline (1) the more specific descriptions that have replaced the words *nice*, *good*, and *bad* used in the draft and (2) the new detail added to the end of Paragraph 3.

Topics for Writing a Process Essay

When you write on any of these topics, work through the stages of the writing process in preparing your essay.

1. Write a directional or informational process essay about one of these topics:

   getting back into shape   childproofing a room
   improving your GPA   organizing a garage sale
   skateboarding tricks   applying for a loan
   buying a used car   making your favorite meal

2. You may work through some process at work. For example, you may have to open or close a store, clean a piece of machinery, fill out a report, use a specific computer program, or follow a process in making telemarketing calls. You may have to maintain the appearance of a work area (like aisles in a supermarket), or follow a procedure in dealing with complaints. If you follow a process at work, write an essay that teaches the process to a new employee.

3. What was the most physically challenging thing you have ever done? Tasks such as painting a house, fixing a car, walking or running a far distance, or trying to make a soccer team all require physical and mental focus. Discuss the challenge by describing the task, the process you used to succeed, why you had to accomplish it, and how you felt afterward.

Topics for Critical Thinking and Writing

1. Often when looking at the point a person is at in their personal or professional life, it is not always apparent how he or she arrived where they are. The same could be said about you. Trace the steps, minor and major, that have led to you being where you are in your personal or professional life. Write an essay about the series of steps you followed to get where you are today.

2. Your mother or father has asked you to help plan a birthday party for a family member. It could be for a sibling, an in-law, a parent, or a grandparent. Write an essay that describes the process that you would use to plan a memorable birthday party for a specific family member.

5 Write a comparison or contrast essay that makes a statement and is supported by specific points.

COMPARISON AND CONTRAST

Hints for Writing a Comparison or Contrast Essay

1. **Use the thesis of your comparison or contrast to make a statement.** Your essay must do more than explain the similarities or differences between two people, places, or things. It must make some statement about the two. For instance, if you are writing about the differences between your first and second semester of college, your thesis may be that a person can change radically in a short time.

2. **Use your points of comparison or contrast as a way to organize your body paragraphs.** A comparison or contrast essay needs points; each point focuses on a specific similarity or difference. For example, you might use three points to compare two dogs: their appearance, their temperament, and their abilities. You can write one body paragraph on each of these points of comparison.

3. **Use a point-by-point pattern.** That is, each body paragraph can explain one point of comparison or contrast. The topic sentence can summarize the point, and the details about the two subjects (people, places, or things you are comparing) can support the topic sentence. These details can be grouped so that you first discuss one subject, and then the other. You might, for example, compare the appearance of two dogs. An outline for one body paragraph might look like the following:

topic sentence	II. My German shepherd and my border collie are similar in appearance.
point: appearance **subject 1:** **my German shepherd**	A. Max, my shepherd, has long, shiny black and brown hair. B. His ears stand up as if he is always alert. C. His eyes are dark and intelligent.

subject 2: my border collie	D. Sheba, my collie, has glossy black and white hair.
	F. Her pointed ears make it seem as if she is always listening to something.
	G. Her black eyes are knowing and wise.

WRITING THE COMPARISON OR CONTRAST ESSAY IN STEPS

PREWRITING   COMPARISON OR CONTRAST ESSAY

One way to get started on a comparison or contrast essay is to list as many differences or similarities as you can on one topic. Then you can see whether you have more similarities (comparisons) or differences (contrasts), and decide which approach to use. For example, if you decide to compare or contrast two restaurants, you could begin with a list like this:

Listing Ideas for a Comparison or Contrast Essay

Topic: Two Restaurants: Victor's and The Garden

similarities

both offer lunch and dinner
very popular
nearby

differences

Victor's	The Garden
formal dress	*informal dress*
tablecloths	*placemats*
food is bland	*spicy food*
expensive	*moderate*
statues, fountains, fresh flowers	*dark wood, hanging plants*

Getting Points of Comparison or Contrast

Whether you compare or contrast, you are looking for points of comparison or contrast, items you can discuss about both subjects.

If you surveyed the list on the two restaurants and decided you wanted to contrast the two, you'd see that you already have these points of contrast:

dress	food
decor	prices

To write your essay, start with several points of comparison or contrast. As you work through the stages of writing, you may decide you don't need all the points you've jotted down, but it is better to start with too many points than with too few.

Once you have some points, you can begin adding details to them. The details may lead you to more points. If they do not, they will still help you develop the ideas of your essay. If you were to write about the differences in restaurants, for example, your new list with added details might look like this:

Listing Ideas for a Contrast Essay

Topic: Two Restaurants

Victor's	The Garden
dress—formal	*informal dress*
men in jackets, women in dresses	*all in jeans*
decor—pretty, elegant	*placemats, on table is a card listing specials*
statues, fountains, fresh flowers on tables, tablecloths	*lots of dark wood, brass, green hanging plants*
food—bland tasting, broiled fish or chicken, steaks, appetizers like shrimp cocktail, onion soup	*spicy and adventurous pasta in tomato sauces, garlic in everything, curry appetizers like tiny tortillas, ribs in honey-mustard sauce*
price—expensive	*price—moderate*
everything costs extra, like appetizer, salad	*price of dinner includes appetizer and salad*

Reading the list about restaurants, you might conclude that some people may prefer The Garden to Victor's. Why? There are several hints in your list. The Garden has cheaper food, better food, and a more casual atmosphere. Now that you have a point, you can shape a thesis statement contrasting the restaurants as follows:

> *Some people would rather eat at The Garden than at Victor's because The Garden offers better, cheaper food in a more casual environment.*

After you are satisfied with your thesis statement, you can begin the planning stage for your essay.

PLANNING   CONTRAST ESSAY

Following is an outline for a contrast essay on two restaurants. Study the outline carefully and be prepared to respond to the exercise that follows it.

Outline for a Contrast Essay

paragraph 1 —— I. Thesis: Some people would rather eat at The Garden than at Victor's because The Garden offers better, cheaper food in a more casual environment.

paragraph 2, topic sentence —— II. The menus at the two restaurants reveal significant differences.

details about food: Victor's
  A. Food at Victor's is bland tasting and traditional.
  B. The menu has broiled fish, chicken, and steaks.
  C. The spices used are mostly parsley and salt.
  D. The food is the usual American food, with a little French food on the list.

details about food: The Garden
  E. Food at The Garden is more spicy and adventurous.
  F. There are many pasta dishes in tomato sauce.
  G. There is garlic in just about everything.
  H. The Garden serves five different curry dishes.
  I. It has all kinds of ethnic food.
  J. Appetizers include items like tiny tortillas and hot honey-mustard ribs.

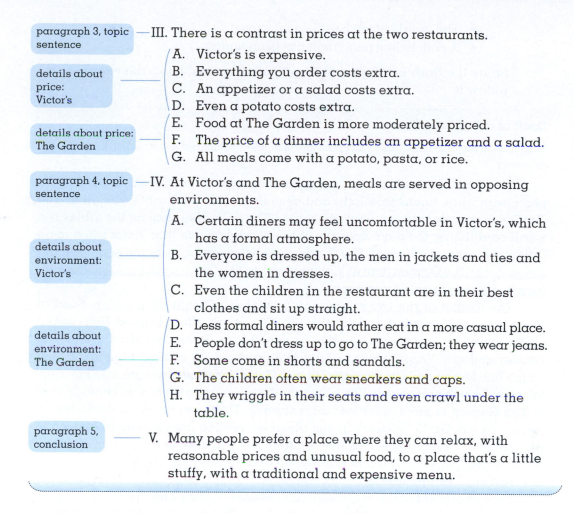

paragraph 3, topic sentence — III. There is a contrast in prices at the two restaurants.

details about price: Victor's
- A. Victor's is expensive.
- B. Everything you order costs extra.
- C. An appetizer or a salad costs extra.
- D. Even a potato costs extra.

details about price: The Garden
- E. Food at The Garden is more moderately priced.
- F. The price of a dinner includes an appetizer and a salad.
- G. All meals come with a potato, pasta, or rice.

paragraph 4, topic sentence — IV. At Victor's and The Garden, meals are served in opposing environments.

details about environment: Victor's
- A. Certain diners may feel uncomfortable in Victor's, which has a formal atmosphere.
- B. Everyone is dressed up, the men in jackets and ties and the women in dresses.
- C. Even the children in the restaurant are in their best clothes and sit up straight.

details about environment: The Garden
- D. Less formal diners would rather eat in a more casual place.
- E. People don't dress up to go to The Garden; they wear jeans.
- F. Some come in shorts and sandals.
- G. The children often wear sneakers and caps.
- H. They wriggle in their seats and even crawl under the table.

paragraph 5, conclusion — V. Many people prefer a place where they can relax, with reasonable prices and unusual food, to a place that's a little stuffy, with a traditional and expensive menu.

The outline added some new details gathered during the outlining process. The topic sentences of the body paragraphs are based on the points of contrast on the earlier list. One point of contrast, the decor of the restaurants, has been omitted. The details about decor may be useful in the introduction or conclusion of the essay.

As you write and revise your draft, you can continue to add details. During editing, later in the writing process, you can combine sentences, add transitions, and improve word choices.

Exercise 16   **Practice: Recognizing How an Outline Evolves from a List**

Compare the list of ideas on dress in the two restaurants to the outline section on the topic. Underline the ideas that have been added to the outline.

DRAFTING AND REVISING   **CONTRAST ESSAY**

Following is a revised draft of the essay on two restaurants. Compare it to the outline on pages 288–289, you may notice the following changes:

- An introduction has been added, and it contains some of the details on decor gathered previously.
- Transitions have been added within and between paragraphs.
- Details have been added.

- The word choice has been improved.
- A concluding paragraph has been added.

Study the draft carefully and be prepared to respond to the exercises that follow it.

Draft of a Contrast Essay

(Note: Thesis, topic sentences, and conclusion are underlined; editing and proofreading are still necessary.)

There are two well-known restaurants in town. One, Victor's, is an elegant place with white linen tablecloths and fresh flowers on each table. The other, The Garden, has paper placemats on the tables. The only other item on the tables is a small card listing the day's specials. While it might seem that Victor's is a more attractive setting for a meal, The Garden has its advantages. <u>Some people would rather eat at The Garden than at Victor's because The Garden offers better, cheaper food in a more casual environment</u>.

<u>The menus at the two restaurants reveal significant differences</u>. Food at Victor's is bland tasting and traditional. The menu offers broiled fish, baked chicken, and typical steaks like T-bone and sirloin. The spices used are mostly parsley and salt. Victor's serves standard American food with a little French food on the list; for example, the appetizers include an American favorite, shrimp cocktail, and French onion soup. While food at Victor's relies on old, safe choices, food at The Garden is more spicy and adventurous. There are many pasta dishes in tomato sauce. Garlic appears in just about everything from mashed potatoes to pork roasts. The Garden serves five different curry dishes. In fact, it has all kinds of ethnic food; tiny tortillas and ribs dipped in honey and hot Chinese mustard are the most popular appetizers.

Food choice is not the only difference between Victor's and The Garden; <u>there is also a contrast in prices at the two restaurants</u>. Victor's is expensive. Everything you order, such as an appetizer or a salad, costs extra. Even a baked potato costs extra. An entree like a steak, for example, comes on a platter with a sprig of parsley. If you want a potato or a vegetable, you have to pay extra for it. Food at The Garden is more moderately priced. The price of a dinner includes an appetizer and a salad; in addition, all meals come with a potato, pasta, or rice, so there are few pricey extras to pay for.

The cost of a meal at Victor's is different from one at The Garden, and the atmosphere in which the meal is enjoyed is different, too. <u>At the two places, meals are served in opposing settings</u>. Certain diners may feel uncomfortable in Victor's, which has a formal atmosphere. Everyone is dressed up, the men in jackets and ties, and the women in dresses. Even the children at Victor's are dressed in their best and sit straight up in their chairs. Less formal diners would rather eat in a more casual place, like The Garden. People don't dress up to go to The Garden; they wear jeans or shorts and sandals. The children often wear sneakers and baseball caps. They wriggle in their seats and even explore under the table.

Sometimes adults want to let go, just as children do. They want to sit back, not up, stretch their legs in casual clothes, not jackets and ties or dresses, and explore new food choices, not the same old standards. The Garden appeals to that childlike need for physical comfort and adventurous dining, at a moderate cost. <u>People</u> choose it over Victor's because they <u>prefer a place where they can relax, with reasonable prices and unusual food, to a place that's a little stuffy, with a traditional and expensive menu</u>.

Exercise 17 Practice: Spotting Synonyms

In an essay about food, the word *food* can be overused. One way around this repetition is to use synonyms. These synonyms can be general (such as "menu") or specific (such as "potato"). Search the essay and underline as many words or phrases as you can find that refer to specific things to eat or to spices.

Exercise 18 Practice: Recognizing the Power of Transitions

An essay that compares or contrasts needs effective transitions to keep the ideas flowing smoothly. Three paragraphs in this essay open with transitional sentences that link a new idea to a previous one. Underline this type of transition.

EDITING AND PROOFREADING **CONTRAST ESSAY**

Following is a final version of the essay on two restaurants. When you compare it to the draft on page 290, you will notice some changes:

- More specific details have been added.
- Two sentences in Paragraph 3 have been revised so that the shift to *you* is eliminated.
- The phrase *explore under the table* in Paragraph 4 has been changed to *explore the spaces under the table* for clarity.
- One sentence in the conclusion has been revised so that it has a stronger parallel structure.
- A title has been added.

Study the final version carefully and be prepared to respond to the exercise that follows it.

Final Version of a Contrast Essay

Victor's and The Garden: Two Contrasting Restaurants

There are two well-known restaurants in town. One, Victor's, is an elegant place with white linen tablecloths and fresh flowers on each table. The other, The Garden, has paper placemats on the tables. The only other item on the tables is a small card listing the day's specials. While it might seem that Victor's is a more attractive setting for a meal, The Garden has its advantages. Some people would rather eat at The Garden than at Victor's because The Garden offers better, cheaper food in a more casual environment.

The menus at the two restaurants reveal significant differences. Food at Victor's is bland tasting and traditional. The menu offers broiled fish, baked chicken, and typical steaks like T-bone and sirloin. The spices used are mostly parsley and salt; pepper, garlic, and curry are nowhere to be found. Victor's serves standard American food with a little French food on the list; for example, the appetizers include an American favorite, shrimp cocktail, and French onion soup. While food at Victor's relies on old, safe choices, food at The Garden is more spicy and adventurous. There are many pasta dishes, from linguini to lasagna, in a rich tomato sauce. Garlic appears in just about everything from mashed potatoes to pork roasts. The Garden serves five different curry dishes. In fact, it has all kinds of ethnic food; tiny tortillas and ribs dipped in honey and hot Chinese mustard are the most popular appetizers.

Food choice is not the only difference between Victor's and The Garden; there is also a contrast in prices at the two restaurants. Victor's is expensive. Everything a person orders, such as an appetizer or a salad, costs extra. Even a baked potato costs extra. An entree like a steak, for example, comes on a platter with a sprig of parsley. Anyone who wants a potato or a vegetable has to pay extra for it. Food at The Garden is more moderately priced. The price of a dinner includes an appetizer and a salad; in addition, all meals come with a potato, pasta, or rice, so there are few pricey extras to pay for.

The cost of a meal at Victor's is different from one at The Garden, and the atmosphere in which the meal is enjoyed is different, too. At the two places, meals are served in opposing settings. Certain diners may feel uncomfortable in Victor's, which has a formal atmosphere. Everyone is dressed up, the men in jackets and ties, and the women in fancy dresses. Even the children at Victor's are dressed in their best and sit straight up in their chairs. Less formal diners would rather eat in a more casual place, like The Garden. People don't dress up to go to The Garden; they wear jeans or shorts and sandals. The children often wear sneakers and baseball caps. They wriggle in their seats and even explore the spaces under the table.

Sometimes adults want to let go, just as children do. They want to sit back, not up, stretch their legs in casual clothes, not hold their breath in tight ties or fancy dresses, and explore new food choices, not settle for the same old standards. The Garden appeals to that childlike need for physical comfort and adventurous dining, at a moderate cost. People choose it over Victor's because they prefer a place where they can relax, with reasonable prices and unusual food, to a place that's a little stuffy, with a traditional and expensive menu.

Exercise 19 Practice: Correcting a Shift in Persons

A shift in persons is a grammar error that occurs when, for example, the third person (*he, she, it, they,* or *the name of a person, place,* or *thing*) suddenly shifts to another person such as the second person (*you*). In the draft version of the essay, there was a shift in persons from the third person (*people, food, it*) to the second person (*you*). The shift occurs <u>twice</u> in Paragraph 3. Read the draft version of Paragraph 3; note where the shifts occur, and then check the final version. Underline what replaced *you* and what replaced the verbs that followed *you* in the draft version.

Topics for Writing a Comparison or Contrast Essay

When you write on any of these topics, work through the stages of the writing process in preparing your essay.

1. Compare or contrast any of the following:

two video games	two teams
two types of pets	two foods
two cars	two places you've lived in
two music styles	two professors

2. Compare or contrast your life before having children and your life with children. You might consider such points of comparison as your worries, joys, responsibilities, fears, hopes, goals, or relationships.

3. Compare or contrast the way you drive when a parent is in the car and when you have friends in the car.

4. Compare or contrast your expectations of some aspect of college life (such as the instructors, the grading policies, and the classroom environment) with the reality you are now experiencing.

Topics for Critical Thinking and Writing

1. Compare or contrast the difference between a team sport and an individual sport. Consider some of the differences in terms of the mental and physical challenges that two different sports (such as soccer or tennis) require of an individual. As part of the essay, discuss which type of sport you prefer and why.

2. Lao Tzu, a sixth-century B.C. Chinese philosopher, once said, "A leader is best when people barely know he exists; when his work is done, his aim fulfilled, they will say: we did it ourselves." Consider this quotation about leadership. Then, write an essay that contrasts Lao Tzu's belief about leadership with another perspective on leadership. Be sure to provide clear examples to articulate each perspective and illustrate their differences. Consider using your concluding paragraph to identify which form of leadership resonates more with you.

CHAPTER 13

Different Essay Patterns: Part Two

Jumping In

Artists and designers often use interesting patterns in their work, but patterns can be seen all around us. The distinctive shapes in tile, carpet, or fabric combine and repeat to form patterns arranged to have a particular effect on viewers. Patterns help to organize what we see. In the same way, patterns of development in an essay organize what we write. Determining effective patterns of development can help you maintain the interest of your readers in the same way that patterns in art attract and hold the interest of viewers.

Learning Objectives

In this chapter, you will learn to:

1. Write a classification essay that has a clear basis (reason) for classifying (dividing) a topic into distinct types or categories.

2. Write a definition essay that explains a term, label, or phrase by providing distinguishing characteristics based on personal observations.

3. Write a cause or effect essay with developed body paragraphs that both explain and describe.

4. Write an argument essay that takes a stand, uses reason, and considers its audience.

5. Write a multipattern essay that has a clear topic and thesis, employs the same pattern within a paragraph, and uses transitions effectively.

CLASSIFICATION

Hints for Writing a Classification Essay

1. **Be sure to have a point in your classification.** Remember that you need to do more than divide something into three or more types, according to some basis, and explain and describe these types. You must have a reason for your classification. For example, if you write about three types of bicycles, you may be writing to evaluate them, and your point may state which type is the best buy for specific types of riding. If you are classifying weight-loss programs, you may be studying each type so that you can prove that two types are dangerous.

2. **A simple way to structure your classification essay is to explain each type in a separate body paragraph.** Then use the same kind of details to describe each type. For instance, if you describe the medical principles, food restrictions, and results of one type of weight-loss program, describe the medical principles, food restrictions, and results of the other types of weight-loss programs.

> **1** Write a classification essay that has a clear basis (reason) for classifying (dividing) a topic into distinct types or categories.

WRITING THE CLASSIFICATION ESSAY IN STEPS

PREWRITING   CLASSIFICATION ESSAY

First, pick a topic for your classification. The next step is to choose some basis for your classification. For example, if you were to write an essay classifying phone calls, you could write about phone calls on the basis of their effect on you. With this basis for classification, you can come up with three categories:

calls that please me
calls that irritate me
calls that frighten me

By brainstorming, you can then gather details about your three categories as follows:

CRITICAL THINKING

Think of classifying as a way of dividing a topic into groups to help the reader understand it more easily.

Added Details for Three Categories of a Classification Essay

Topic: Phone Calls

calls that please me
from boyfriend
good friends
catch-up calls—someone I haven't talked to for a while
make me feel close

(Continued)

calls that irritate me
sales calls at dinnertime
wrong numbers
calls that interrupt
invade privacy

calls that frighten me
emergency call in middle of night
break-up call from boyfriend
change my life, indicate some bad change

With these categories and details, you can write a thesis that (1) mentions what you are classifying and (2) indicates the basis for your classifying by listing all three categories or by stating the basis, or both. Here is a thesis that follows the guidelines:

> *Phone calls can be grouped into the ones that please me, the ones that irritate me, and the ones that frighten me.*

This thesis mentions what you are classifying: *phone calls*. It indicates the basis for classification, the effect of the phone calls, by listing the types: *the ones that please me*, *the ones that irritate me*, and *the ones that frighten me*. Here is another thesis that follows the guidelines:

> *I can classify phone calls according to their effect on me.*

This thesis also mentions what you are classifying, *phone calls*, but it mentions the basis for classification, *their effect on me*, instead of listing the types.

Once you have a thesis sentence and a list of ideas, you are ready to begin the planning stage of writing the classification essay.

PLANNING CLASSIFICATION ESSAY

Following is an outline for a classification essay on phone calls. Study the outline carefully and be prepared to respond to Exercise 1 which follows the sample outline.

Outline for a Classification Essay

paragraph 1 — I. Thesis: Phone calls can be grouped into the ones that please me, the ones that irritate me, and the ones that frighten me.

paragraph 2, topic sentence — II. Calls that please me make me feel close to someone.

A. I like calls from my boyfriend, especially when he calls to say he is thinking of me.

B. I like to hear from good friends.

C. My two best friends call me at least twice a day.

D. I like catch-up calls.

details about pleasing calls — E. These are calls from people I haven't talked to in a while.

F. A friend I hadn't seen in a year called me from Ecuador to say "Happy Birthday."

G. We talked for a long time.

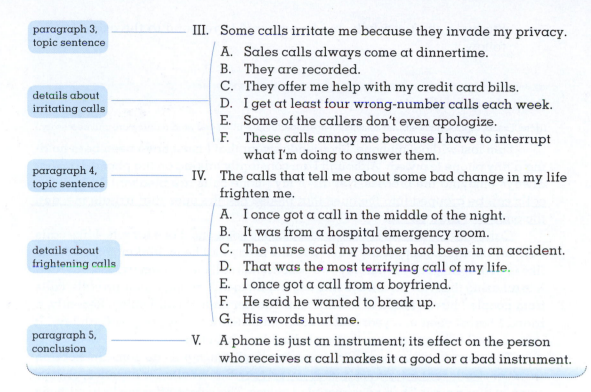

paragraph 3, topic sentence

III. Some calls irritate me because they invade my privacy.

   A. Sales calls always come at dinnertime.
   B. They are recorded.
   C. They offer me help with my credit card bills.

details about irritating calls

   D. I get at least four wrong-number calls each week.
   E. Some of the callers don't even apologize.
   F. These calls annoy me because I have to interrupt what I'm doing to answer them.

paragraph 4, topic sentence

IV. The calls that tell me about some bad change in my life frighten me.

   A. I once got a call in the middle of the night.
   B. It was from a hospital emergency room.

details about frightening calls

   C. The nurse said my brother had been in an accident.
   D. That was the most terrifying call of my life.
   E. I once got a call from a boyfriend.
   F. He said he wanted to break up.
   G. His words hurt me.

paragraph 5, conclusion

V. A phone is just an instrument; its effect on the person who receives a call makes it a good or a bad instrument.

The outline combined some of the details from the list with new details gathered during the writing process. It used the three categories as the basis for the topic sentences for the body paragraph. Each topic sentence has two parts: (1) the name of the category, such as pleasing calls, and (2) the effect of calls in this category. For example, here is one topic sentence:

   (1) the category   (2) the effect of calls in this category
   Calls that please me make me feel close to someone.

Because the point of the essay is to show the effect of different kinds of calls, this topic sentence is effective.

As you write and revise your draft, you can continue to add details and concentrate on your essay's organization. During the editing and proofreading stage, you can combine sentences, add or strengthen transition, refine word choice, and correct errors.

Exercise 1   Practice: Identifying the Added Details in Paragraph 2 of the Outline

Compare the list of details (under the heading "calls that please me") in the Prewriting section for the classification essay with the list of details in the outline. Underline the additional details.

DRAFTING AND REVISING   **CLASSIFICATION ESSAY**

Following is a revised draft of the essay on phone calls. As you read it, you'll notice many changes from the outline on pages 296–297.

- An introduction has been added.
- Transitions have been added within and between paragraphs.
- Details have been added.
- A concluding paragraph has been added.

Study the draft carefully and be prepared to respond to the exercises that follow it.

Draft of a Classification Essay

(Note: Thesis, topic sentences, and conclusion are underlined; editing and proofreading are still necessary.)

I am lost without a phone. My friends swear that I must have been born holding a tiny phone to my ear. Although I am constantly talking on the phone, I am not always enjoying the process. Not all of my phone calls are pleasant. In fact, <u>the calls can be grouped into the ones that please me, the ones that irritate me, and the ones that frighten me</u>.

<u>Calls that please me make me feel close to someone</u>. For example, I like calls from my boyfriend, especially when he calls to say that he is thinking of me. I also like to hear from good friends. My two best friends call me at least twice a day, and it is amazing that we can always find something to talk about. Catch-up calls, calls from people I haven't seen in a while, are another kind of call I enjoy. Recently, a friend I hadn't seen in a year called me from Ecuador to say "Happy Birthday." It was so good to hear from her that we talked for a long time.

The ring of a phone can bring me warm feelings, but it can sometimes bring irritation. <u>Calls that irritate me invade my privacy</u>. Sales calls, for instance, always come at dinnertime. They have recorded voices. The voices offer me help with my credit card bills. Also in this category are wrong-number calls. I get at least four of these a week, and some of the callers don't even apologize for bothering me. These calls annoy me because I have to interrupt what I'm doing to answer them.

Finally, there are the worst calls of all. <u>The calls that frighten me tell me about some bad change in my life</u>. I once got a call in the middle of the night. It was from a hospital emergency room; the nurse told me my brother had been in an accident. That was the most terrifying call of my life. Another time, a boyfriend called to say he wanted to break up. His cold words surprised and hurt me.

I rely on the telephone, but it is not always good to me. Ever since I received the call about my brother's accident, I tremble when the phone rings late at night. However, I have come to realize that <u>a phone is just an instrument; its effect on the person who receives a call makes it a good or a bad instrument</u>.

Exercise 2 **Practice: Examining the Introduction**

Look carefully at the introduction in the draft and notice how smoothly it moves from one idea to another. Underline the sentence that introduces the idea that the writer spends a great deal of time on the phone. Then underline the sentence that moves to another idea: that not all calls are pleasant. Finally, underline the transition that introduces the thesis.

EDITING AND PROOFREADING CLASSIFICATION ESSAY

Following is the final version of the essay on phone calls. When you compare it to the draft, you will notice some changes:

- Two sentences have been combined.
- Some of the word choices have been refined to make details more specific, to eliminate repetition, or to eliminate an awkward phrase.

- A final sentence has been added to Paragraph 4 to reinforce the point that both examples in the paragraph are about a life-changing phone call.
- The last sentence in the concluding paragraph has been revised to make a more precise statement about the basis for the classification: the effect of each type of phone call.
- A title has been added.

Study the final version carefully and be prepared to respond to Exercise 3 that follows it.

Final Version of a Classification Essay

Phone Calls: Good, Bad, and Ugly

I am lost without a phone. My friends swear that I must have been born holding a tiny phone to my ear. Although I am constantly talking on the phone, I am not always enjoying the process. Not all of the conversations are pleasant. In fact, the calls can be grouped into the ones that please me, the ones that irritate me, and the ones that frighten me.

Calls that please me make me feel close to someone. For example, I like calls from my boyfriend, especially when he calls to say that he is thinking of me. I also like to hear from good friends. My two best friends call me at least twice a day, and it is amazing that we can always find something to talk about. Catch-up calls, calls from people I haven't seen in a while, are another kind of call I enjoy. Recently, a friend I hadn't seen in a year called me from Ecuador to say "Happy Birthday." It was so good to hear from her that we talked for an hour.

The ring of a phone can bring me warm feelings, but it can sometimes bring irritation. Calls that irritate me invade my privacy. Sales calls that feature recorded voices always come at dinnertime. They offer help with my credit card bills. Also in this category are wrong-number calls. I get at least four of these a week, and some of the callers don't even apologize for bothering me. These calls annoy me because I have to interrupt what I'm doing to answer them.

Finally, there are the worst calls of all. The calls that frighten me tell me about some crisis in my life. I once got a call in the middle of the night. It was from a hospital emergency room; the nurse told me my brother had been in an accident. That was the most terrifying call of my life. Another time, a boyfriend called to say he wanted to break up. His cold words surprised and hurt me. Both of these calls brought me news that changed my life, and the news was totally unexpected.

I rely on the telephone, but it is not always good to me. Ever since I received the call about my brother's accident, I tremble when the phone rings late at night. However, I have come to realize that a phone is just an instrument; it conveys a message. Its effect on the person who receives that message makes it a welcome, annoying, or dreaded instrument.

Exercise 3   Practice: Evaluating the Concluding Sentence

Compare the last paragraph of the draft essay to the last paragraph of the final version. (1) Why did the final essay end by describing a phone as a "welcome, annoying, or dreaded instrument"? (2) How is this a more appropriate phrase than "good or bad instrument" in the draft version?

_____

_____

Topics for Writing a Classification Essay

When you write on any of these topics, work through the stages of the writing process in preparing your essay.

Collaborate

1. Write a classification essay on any of the following topics. If your instructor agrees, brainstorm with a partner or group to come up with a basis for your classification and categories related to the basis.

your friends	your favorite places	your mistakes
video games	your lunch options	your instructors
affordable tablets	discount stores	your social media apps

2. You may not know it, but you are probably an expert on something. For example, you may work in a coffee shop and know all about where coffees come from and how to best brew them. You may be a fanatical soccer fan and know all about the different leagues and teams worldwide. Consider what you know best through your work, hobbies, education, or leisure activities, and write a classification essay about a subject in that area. If you work in a coffee shop, you can classify types of drinks or coffee beans. If you are a soccer fan, you can compare the style of play in the different leagues or the style of play within a specific league.

3. Some topics follow and each one already has a basis for classification. Write a classification essay on one of the choices.

   Classify

   a. babysitters on the basis of how willing they are to engage children
   b. pets on the basis of how much they cost to maintain
   c. teens on the basis of their favorite types of music
   d. types of transportation based on affordability
   e. parents on the basis of how strict they are
   f. study areas on the basis of how quiet they are

4. There are a million types of pets to own. Dogs, cats, fish, snakes, and birds all have an upside and a downside. Select three different types of pets and categorize them in terms of maintenance. Consider such points as what the pets require in terms of the amount of time it takes to properly care for such a pet.

Topics for Critical Thinking and Writing

1. Think about the ways in which you may be classified. For example, if you are reading this book, you are probably classified as a college student. But are you classified as a part- or full-time student? Your racial or ethnic background may be difficult to categorize. Today there are so many ways each person can be classified—by income level, marital status, spending habits, and so forth—that most people defy simple classifications. In your body paragraphs, write about three ways in which you might be classified incorrectly. For each classification, include examples of how these terms do not truly describe you.

2. Over the course of your education, you have been exposed to many different types of teachers, some effective and some less so. Brainstorm about some of your most memorable teachers and classify them on the basis of how effective they were in teaching you new concepts or subject matter. As you make these judgments and draft your essay, include details about why certain teachers worked well or were largely ineffective for you.

DEFINITION

Hints for Writing a Definition Essay

2 Write a definition essay that explains a term, label, or phrase by providing distinguishing characteristics based on personal observations.

1. **Write a personal definition, not a dictionary definition.**   To develop a definition essay, you need to define a term that can be explained by more than the words in a dictionary. You can develop your essay with concrete terms and specific examples that help define the term.

   terms that won't work in a personal definition: photosynthesis, DNA, the Colt Revolver, the Renaissance
   terms that will work in a personal definition: self-pity, patience, courage, the optimist

2. **Include in your thesis (1) the term you are defining, (2) the broad class or category into which your term fits, and (3) the specific distinguishing characteristics that make the term different from all others in the class or category.**   Each of the following sentences could be the thesis for a definition essay.

   term   category   distinguishing characteristics
   Envy is the *desire for what others have.*

   term   category   distinguishing characteristics
   A *nit-picker* is a *person who worries excessively about minor details.*

3. **Form your body paragraphs from different aspects of your term.**   For example, if you defined *sarcasm,* you might write one paragraph on the times when sarcasm is appropriate but two other paragraphs on the times when sarcasm is inappropriate and hurtful. If you write about *anger,* you might write two paragraphs on ways in which to resist anger and a third body paragraph on when to give in to anger.

WRITING THE DEFINITION ESSAY IN STEPS

PREWRITING   DEFINITION ESSAY

To pick a topic for your definition essay, you can begin with some personality trait or type of person. For instance, you might define "the insecure person." If you listed your first thoughts, your list might look like this:

the insecure person
someone who is not emotionally secure
wants (needs?) other people to make him or her feel good
lack of self-esteem

Often, when you look for ideas to define a term, you get stuck with big, general statements or abstract words, or you simply cannot come up with enough to say. If you are having trouble getting ideas, think of questions about your term. Jot these questions down without stopping to answer them. One question can lead you to another question. Once you have five or more questions, you can answer them, and the answers will provide details for your definition essay.

If you were writing about an insecure person, for example, you could begin with questions like these:

> *What are insecure people like?*
> *What behavior shows a person is insecure?*
> *How do insecure people dress or talk?*
> *What makes a person insecure?*
> *Is insecurity a bad trait?*
> *How do insecure people relate to others?*

By scanning the questions and answering as many as you can, you can add details to your list. Once you have a longer list, you can review it and begin to group its items. Following is a list of grouped details on the insecure person.

Grouped Details for a Definition Essay

Topic: The Insecure Person

wants (needs?) other people to make him or her feel important
lack of self-esteem

insecure people have to brag about everything
a friend who brags about his car
they tell you the price of everything
a friend who talks about salary and money

they put others down
saying bad things about other people makes insecure people feel better

insecure people can never relax inside
can never enjoy being with other people
other people are always their competitors
must always worry about what others think of them

Grouping the details can help you arrive at several main ideas. Can they be combined and revised to create a thesis statement? Following is a thesis on the insecure person that meets the requirements of naming the term, placing it in a category, and distinguishing the term from others in the category:

> **term**   **category**   **distinguishing characteristics**
> The *insecure person* is *someone* who *needs other people to make him or her feel respected and important.*

Once you have a thesis statement, you can begin working on the planning stage of the essay.

PLANNING   **DEFINITION ESSAY**

Following is an outline for a definition essay on the insecure person. Study the outline carefully and be prepared to respond to Exercise 4 that follows it. The outline combined some of the details from the list with new details and examples gathered during the outlining process. As you write and revise your draft, you can continue to add details and work on the essay's organization. Later, during editing, you can combine sentences, add or strengthen transition, and refine word choice. You can also combine sentences, add transitions, and work on word choice.

Outline for a Definition Essay

| paragraph 1 | I. | Thesis: The insecure person is someone who needs other people to make him or her feel respected and important. |

| paragraph 2, topic sentence | II. | Insecure people have to brag about everything. |

A. An insecure friend may have to brag about his car.
B. He is sure to tell you if it is a popular car.
C. An insecure person talks about money and salary.
D. Insecure people wear expensive jewelry and tell what it cost.
E. A man will tell you what his ring cost; a woman will tell you what her boyfriend paid for her ring.
F. They make sure they wear clothes with trendy labels.
G. They have to have shirts with the designer's logo on the pocket and jackets with the designer's name spread across the front.
H. This is another kind of bragging.

details about bragging

| paragraph 3, topic sentence | III. | Insecure people put others down. |

A. They make mean remarks about other people's looks, clothes, or style.
B. Saying bad things about others makes insecure people feel better.
C. When some friends were talking about Susan's great new job, Jill had to make mean remarks about Susan.
D. Jill hated having Susan look like a winner.
E. Jill wanted all the attention and admiration for herself.
F. I work with a man who is always spreading cruel gossip.
G. His attacks on others are a cowardly way of making himself look good.

details about putting others down

| paragraph 4, topic sentence | IV. | Insecure people can never relax inside. |

A. They can never enjoy being with other people.
B. Other people are always their competition.
C. Luke plays pickup basketball games.
D. He can't enjoy any game of basketball unless he is the star.
E. When someone on his team scores, he is not pleased.
F. Instead, he becomes aggressive and selfish.
G. Another person I know is always loud and crude at parties.
H. He is so desperate to be liked that he turns himself into an obnoxious character that he thinks is the life of the party.

details about never relaxing

| paragraph 5, conclusion | V. | Insecure people must always worry about what others think about them. |

Exercise 4 **Practice: Recognizing Synonyms**

Section III of the outline focuses on insecure people's need to criticize others. Underline the phrases in this section that refer to hurtful comments.

DRAFTING AND REVISING   **DEFINITION ESSAY**

Following is a revised draft of the essay on the insecure person. As you read it, you'll notice many changes from the outline on page 303.

- An introduction has been added.
- Transitions have been added within and between paragraphs.
- Details have been added.
- A concluding paragraph has been added.

Study the draft carefully and be prepared to respond to the exercises that follow it.

Draft of a Definition Essay

(Note: Thesis, topic sentences, and conclusion are underlined; editing and proofreading are still necessary.)

Everybody knows at least one person who seems to feel so superior that no one could ever reach his or her status. Sometimes this person annoys others; at other times, this person hurts them. While it seems to be pride that motivates this person to irritate and belittle others, it is really insecurity disguised as ego. The insecure person is someone who needs other people to make him or her feel respected and important.

One sign of the insecure person is bragging. Insecure people have to brag about everything. An insecure friend may have to brag about his car and will be sure to tell everyone that he drives a Mercedes. He may talk about money and his salary. Some insecure people wear expensive jewelry and brag about what it cost. A man may boast about what his ring cost; a woman will mention what her boyfriend paid for her ring. Others filled with insecurity brag about their expensive clothes. They make sure they wear clothes with trendy labels. They have to have shirts with the designer's logo on the pocket or jackets with the designer's name spread across the front. This is another kind of bragging.

Insecure people not only like to build themselves up, but they also have to put others down. They make mean remarks about other people's looks, clothes, and style. Saying bad things about others makes insecure people feel better. Recently, some friends were talking about our classmate Susan's great new job. While most of us were happy for Susan, Jill had to add some comments about how lucky Susan had been to get the job since Susan was not qualified for it. Because she wants all the attention and admiration for herself, Jill hated having Susan looking like a winner. Another insecure person is a man I work with who is always spreading cruel gossip. His attacks on others are his cowardly way of making himself look good.

The constant need to shine in other people's opinion means that insecure people can never relax inside. Other people are always their competition for attention or approval. One such person is Luke, a college acquaintance who always plays on our pickup basketball games. Even though the games are just for fun, Luke can't enjoy any game of basketball unless he is the star. When someone on his team scores, he isn't pleased. Instead, he becomes aggressive and selfish. He wants to win every game singlehandedly. Another person who is eager to shine is always loud and crude at parties. He is so desperate to be liked that he turns himself into an obnoxious character that he thinks is the life of the party.

Insecure people can be mean and obnoxious, but they are mainly sad. <u>Insecure people must always worry about what others think of them.</u> Because they care so much about others' opinions, they cannot be spontaneous or open. They must get very tired of hiding their fears behind their bragging and criticizing. They must also be very lonely.

Exercise 5   Practice: Recognizing Variations in Wording

In Paragraph 2 of the preceding draft, each example of bragging uses a slightly different word or phrase to describe the insecure bragger. The first example refers to the "insecure person." The next refers to "insecure people." Underline the other synonyms or variations used in the paragraph.

Exercise 6   Practice: Spotting Added Details

The story of Susan, whose new job prompted some mean remarks, gets some added details in the draft of the essay. Underline these new details in Paragraph 3.

EDITING AND PROOFREADING   DEFINITION ESSAY

Following is the final version of the essay on the insecure person. When you compare it to the draft on pages 304–305, you will notice some changes:

- Sentences in Paragraph 2 have been combined for a smoother style.
- The word *this* in the last sentence of Paragraph 2 has been replaced with a more specific phrase: *This obsession with designer clothes.*
- Some of the word choices have been improved to avoid repetition or to be more precise.
- A specific example has been added to Paragraph 4.
- A title has been added.

Study the final version carefully and be prepared to respond to Exercise 7 that follows it.

Final Version of a Definition Essay

The Insecure Person

Everybody knows at least one person who seems to feel so superior that no one could ever reach his or her status. Sometimes this person annoys others; at other times, this person hurts them. While it seems to be pride that motivates this person to irritate and belittle others, it is really insecurity disguised as ego. The insecure person is someone who needs other people to make him or her feel respected and important.

One sign of the insecure person is bragging, for insecure people have to brag about everything. An insecure friend may have to brag about his car and will be sure to tell everyone that he drives a Mercedes sports car. He may talk about money and his salary. Some insecure people wear expensive jewelry and brag

(Continued)

about what it cost. A man may boast about what his ring cost; a woman will mention what her boyfriend paid for her ring. Others filled with insecurity show off their expensive clothes. They make sure they wear clothes with trendy labels. They have to have shirts with the designer's logo on the pocket or jackets with the designer's name spread across the front. This obsession with designer clothes is another kind of bragging.

Insecure people not only like to build themselves up, but they also have to put others down. They make mean remarks about other people's looks, clothes, and style. Making nasty comments about others makes insecure people feel better. Recently, some friends were talking about our classmate Susan's great new job. While most of us were happy for Susan, Jill had to add some comments about how lucky Susan had been to get the job since Susan was not qualified for it. Because she wants all of the attention and admiration for herself, Jill hated having Susan looking like a winner. Another insecure person is a man I work with who is always spreading cruel gossip. His attacks on others are his cowardly way of making himself look good.

The constant need to shine in other people's opinion means that insecure people can never relax inside. Other people are always their competition for attention or approval. One such person is Luke, a college acquaintance who always plays on our pickup basketball games. Even though the games are just for fun, Luke can't enjoy any game of basketball unless he is the star. When someone on his team scores, he isn't pleased. Instead, he becomes aggressive and selfish. He wants to win every game singlehandedly. Another person who is eager to shine is my cousin Jamie, a generally good-natured person, who is always loud and crude at parties. He is so desperate to be liked that he turns himself into an obnoxious character that he thinks is the life of the party.

Insecure people can be mean and obnoxious, but they are mainly sad. Insecure people must always worry about what others think of them. Because they care so much about others' opinions, they cannot be spontaneous or open. They must get very tired of hiding their fears behind their bragging and criticizing. They must also be very lonely.

Exercise 7   Practice: Distinguishing the Changes

In draft form, Paragraph 4 contains one example that names a specific person. In the final version of the essay, another example now includes a named person. Name the person and consider how a little added description makes him more human.

_____

_____

_____

Topics for Writing a Definition Essay

When you write on any of these topics, work through the stages of the writing process in preparing your essay.

1. What is the one quality you most admire in a mentor? Is it experience, kindness, a sense of humor, flexibility, or another character trait? Choose a quality and write an essay defining it in a mentor.

2. Define any of the terms that follow, using specific details and examples. You can begin by looking up the term in a dictionary to make sure you understand the dictionary meaning. Then write a personal definition.

devotion	satisfaction	shyness
boldness	wisdom	beauty
sympathy	grit	generosity

3. Write a personal definition of a specific type of person. Develop your definition by using specific details and examples. Following is a list of types, but you may write about another type of your choosing.

the pleaser	the rebel	the loner
the control freak	the class clown	the slacker
the good sport	the phony	the cynic

4. We often use terms that we understand and that we assume everyone knows. However, these terms may not have clear definitions. Write your definition of such a term. Examples of these terms are listed here, but you can also choose your own term.

people skills	politically motivated	personal issues
comfort zone	time crunch	alpha male

Topics for Critical Thinking and Writing

1. Think of a music style that is currently popular and then define it. In your essay, be sure to include several influences on the style and how the current version is both something old and new. Consider the age groups and backgrounds of the people who tend to enjoy this style of music.

2. As you have matured, your views about life and aging have probably changed numerous times. Today, what does the word *old* mean to you? You may need to examine your previous definitions or understandings of the word to compare it with your current definition to write this essay.

CAUSE AND EFFECT

Hints for Writing a Cause or Effect Essay

1. **Choose either causes or effects.** If you try to do both in a short essay, you will make your task more difficult. In addition, you need a longer and more complex essay to cover both causes and effects adequately.

2. **You can use each cause or effect as the focus of one body paragraph.** You can develop the paragraph by explaining and describing that cause or effect.

3 Write a cause or effect essay with developed body paragraphs that both explain and describe.

WRITING THE CAUSE OR EFFECT ESSAY IN STEPS

PREWRITING CAUSE OR EFFECT ESSAY

If you were thinking about writing a cause or effect essay on owning a car, you could begin by freewriting something like this:

Freewriting for a Cause or Effect Essay

Topic: Owning a Car

A car of my own. Why? I needed it. Couldn't get a part-time job without one. Because I couldn't get to work. Needed it to get to school. Of course I could have taken the bus to school. But I didn't want to. Feel like a grown-up when you have a car of your own. Freedom to come and go. I was the last of my friends to have a car. Couldn't wait. An old Ford. But I fixed it up nicely. Costs a lot to maintain. Car payments, car loan. Car insurance.

Then you could review the freewriting and write separate lists of causes and effects of owning a car:

causes (reasons)

needed to get a part-time job
needed to get to school
my friends had cars

effects (results)

feel like a grown-up
freedom to come and go
costs a lot to maintain
car payments
car loan
car insurance

If you had compiled more details on the effects of owning a car, you would then decide to write an effects essay.

After brainstorming questions to help you generate more effects and details, you would be ready to create another list:

List of Effects for an Effects Essay

Topic: Owning a Car

effect 1: I had to pay for the car and related expenses.

details: *costs a lot to maintain*
car payments
car loans
car insurance

effect 2: I had the adult freedom to come and go.

details: *didn't have to beg my father for his truck*
didn't have to get rides from friends
could go to the city when I wanted
could ride around for fun

effect 3: I became a more careful driver.

details: *worried about someone hitting the car*
worried about bad drivers
wanted to avoid the scratches cars get in parking lots

With at least three effects and some details for each effect, you could create a thesis. The thesis for this essay should indicate that the subject is the *effects* of getting a car. You can summarize all three effects in your thesis, or you can just hint at them. A possible thesis statement for the essay might be:

> *Owning my own car cost me money, gave me freedom, and made me more careful about how I drive.*

The thesis summarizes all three effects. Another possible thesis hints at the effects:

> *Once I got a car, I realized the good and bad sides of ownership.*

With a thesis statement, three effects, and a list of details, you would be ready to write an outline for your essay.

PLANNING   EFFECTS ESSAY

Following is an outline for an effects essay on owning a car. Study the outline carefully and be prepared to respond to the exercise that follows it.

Outline for an Effects Essay

paragraph 1 ——————— I. Thesis: Owning my own car gave me freedom, cost me money, and made me a more careful driver.

paragraph 2, topic sentence ——————— II. The wonderful part of owning a car was the adult freedom it gave me.

details about effect 1: freedom ———————
    A. I didn't have to beg my father for his truck.
    B. Every time I asked him, he seemed reluctant to lend it to me.
    C. He was always worried that I would get the interior dirty.
    D. I didn't have to get rides from my friends.
    E. I was really tired of begging rides from my buddies, and I am sure they were sick of driving me around.
    F. I could go to the city whenever I wanted.
    G. I could even ride around for fun.

(Continued)

paragraph 3,
topic sentence

III. I had to pay for the car and related expenses.

    A. A car costs a lot to maintain.

details about
effect 2: costs

    B. There are oil changes and tune-ups.
    C. My car needed new tires.
    D. I had car payments.
    E. I had a car loan to pay.
    F. I had car insurance.
    G. I had to work overtime to pay the insurance bills.

paragraph 4,
topic sentence

IV. I became a more careful driver.

    A. I worried about someone hitting the car.

details about
effect 3: caution

    B. I could see my beautiful car dented and dinged.
    C. I began to worry about bad drivers.
    D. I became more nervous on the road.
    E. I worried about parking lots.
    F. I wanted to avoid the scratches cars can get in parking lots.
    G. I parked at the end of the row, away from other cars.

paragraph 5,
conclusion

V. Owning a car gave me adult freedom, but it gave me adult responsibilities and worries, too.

CRITICAL THINKING

Notice that the thesis statement specifies the effects or results of owning a car. You will need to determine whether causes or effects will be better to use for your own thesis statement.

The outline categorized each effect as a separate body paragraph. It combined some of the details from the list with details gathered during the outlining process. As you write and revise your draft, you can continue to add details. During editing, you can also combine sentences, add transitions, and work on word choice. Remember that several drafts may be necessary before you feel ready to prepare the final version of your essay.

Exercise 8 **Practice: Changing the Order of Effects**

Review the order of the effects in the brainstorming list on the previous page, and then look closely at the order of effects in the outline. Why would a writer begin with the positive effect of owning a car (as in the outline) instead of leaving it in the middle of two effects about responsibilities? How does the thesis in the outline differ from the original one?

_____

_____

DRAFTING AND REVISING EFFECTS ESSAY

Following is a revised draft of the essay on owning a car. As you read it, you'll notice many changes from the outline on pages 309–310.

- An introduction has been added.
- Transitions have been added within and between paragraphs.

- Details have been added.
- A concluding paragraph has been added.

Study the draft carefully and be prepared to respond to the exercises that follow it.

Draft of an Effects Essay

(Note: Thesis, topic sentences, and conclusion are underlined; editing and proofreading are still necessary.)

Ever since I was six years old, I have dreamed of owning my own car. The day I got my driver's license was one of the happiest days of my life. All that was left, I thought, was having a car of my own. That day came, too, and it changed my life. <u>Owning my own car gave me freedom, cost me money, and made me a more careful driver.</u>

<u>The wonderful part of owning a car was the adult freedom it gave me</u>. First of all, I didn't have to beg my father for his truck anymore. Every time I asked him, he seemed reluctant to lend it to me. He was always worried that I would get the interior dirty. Second, I no longer had to get rides from my friends whenever I wanted to go somewhere. I was really tired of begging rides from my buddies, and I am sure they were sick of driving me around. With my own car, I could go to the city whenever I wanted. I could even ride around for fun.

On the more serious side, <u>I had to pay for the car and related expenses</u>. A car costs a lot to maintain. There are oil changes and tune-ups to keep the car in good running condition. Two months after I got my car, I had to buy four new and very expensive tires. Of course, I had monthly payments on my car loan. I also had to pay for car insurance, which, because of my young age, was unbelievably expensive. My insurance cost so much that I had to work overtime to pay it.

Now that I was paying for the car I drove, <u>I became a more careful driver</u>. I became worried about someone hitting the car; I could imagine my beautiful car dented and dinged. These thoughts made me worry about bad drivers and become more nervous on the road. Parking lots made me nervous, too. To avoid the scratches cars can get in parking lots, I parked at the end of the row, away from other cars.

<u>Owning a car gave me adult freedom, but it gave me adult responsibilities and worries, too</u>. Even with the stress of car payments, insurance payments, and car maintenance, I would never give up my car. My fear of dents and scratches can't keep me from the joy of driving whenever and wherever I want. I'm happy to accept the responsibilities that come with being on the road in my own car.

Exercise 9   **Practice: Seeing How the Essay Develops**

The draft of the essay is structured around a childhood wish for a car, the older phase of wanting to be independent, and the final phase of adult responsibility. Study each body paragraph and underline any words, phrases, or sentences (excluding the topic sentences) that show the stages of growth.

Exercise 10   **Practice: Recognizing the Role of Transitions**

1. Which body paragraph opens with a transition that shows a contrast from the subject of the previous paragraph?

2. Which body paragraph opens with a reference to the subject of the previous paragraph?

_____

_____

EDITING AND PROOFREADING   **EFFECTS ESSAY**

The final version of the essay about owning a car reflects careful editing and proofreading. When you compare it to the draft on page 311, you will notice the following:

- Some of the word choices have been improved, replacing a vague phrase like *costs a lot* with the more specific *costs hundreds of dollars*, and avoiding repetition of words like *worry* and *expensive*.

- Details have been added; for instance, in Paragraph 2 there are new details about what makes a car dirty and about how friends feel (*acting like a taxi service*) when they are constantly asked for rides.

- A sentence has been added to Paragraph 4 to support the topic sentence. The focus of the paragraph is on careful driving, and the body of the paragraph gives many examples of the fears of a new car owner, but it needed one more detail to show the change in the owner's driving.

- A title has been added.

Study the final version carefully and be prepared to respond to the exercise that follows it.

Final Version of an Effects Essay

Owning a Car: Driving into Adulthood

Ever since I was six years old, I have dreamed of owning my own car. The day I got my driver's license was one of the happiest days of my life. All that was left, I thought, was having a car of my own. That day came, too, and it changed my life. Owning my own car gave me freedom, cost me money, and made me a more careful driver.

The wonderful part of owning a car was the adult freedom it gave me. First of all, I didn't have to beg my father for his truck anymore. Every time I asked him, he seemed reluctant to lend it to me. He was always worried that I would dirty the interior with food wrappers and empty soda cans. Second, I no longer had to get rides from my friends whenever I wanted to go somewhere. I was really tired of begging rides from my buddies, and I am sure they were sick of acting like a taxi service. With my own car, I could go to the city whenever I wanted. I could even ride around for fun.

On the more serious side, I had to pay for the car and related expenses. A car costs hundreds of dollars to maintain. There are oil changes and tune-ups to keep the car in good running condition. Two months after I got my car, I had to buy four new and very expensive tires. Of course, I had monthly payments on my car loan. I also had to pay for car insurance, which, because of my young age, was unbelievably high. My insurance cost so much that I had to work overtime to pay the bill.

Now that I was paying for the car I drove, I became a more careful driver. I became worried about someone hitting the car; I could imagine my beautiful car dented and dinged. These thoughts made me fear bad drivers and become more nervous on the road. I began to drive more defensively, and instead of challenging aggressive drivers, I began to avoid them. Parking lots made me nervous, too. To avoid the scratches cars can get in parking lots, I parked at the end of the row, away from other cars.

Owning a car gave me adult freedom, but it gave me adult responsibilities and worries, too. Yet even with the stress of car payments, insurance payments, and car maintenance, I would never give up my car. My fear of dents and scratches can't keep me from the joy of driving whenever and wherever I want. I'm happy to accept the responsibilities that come with being on the road, in my own car.

Exercise 11 **Practice: Evaluating Changes in the Final Version**

Underline the details added to Paragraph 2. Would you have added these specific details? Defend your answer: _____

Underline the sentence added to Paragraph 4. Do you think it is necessary? Why or why not?_____

_____

Topics for Writing a Cause or Effect Essay

When you write on any of these topics, work through the stages of the writing process in preparing your essay.

1. Think of a time when you decided to end a relationship. Write an essay explaining the reasons for your choice. Your essay can include an explanation of the positive pieces of the relationship and the reasons you made your final decision.

2. Write an essay about how one of the following experiences changed you (or someone you know well).

   getting back into shape   quitting a comfortable job
   surviving an accident   moving away from home
   having a family   making a team
   a random act of kindness   spending time in the wilderness

3. Write an essay on one of the following topics:

   Why _____ is the best pizza in town.

   Why _____ is a better sport to play than to watch.

   Why _____ is a wonderful movie to watch in the summertime.

   Why my neighborhood needs better (law enforcement, fire service, roads, public transportation, schools, stores) (pick one).

4. Think of a sports team that is currently popular. Write an essay explaining the reasons for that team's popularity.

Topics for Critical Thinking and Writing

1. Many high school students dream of playing a sport in college. Although it is a realistic notion for some, many high school athletes look toward college with unrealistic visions of themselves as a college athlete. Think about why high school athletes dream of

playing sports in college, and write about three key reasons students are attracted to it. You may want to interview some college athletes, coaches, or just recall some notions from your personal experience to compile reasons and details behind this desire. To help you plan your essay, consider whether these reasons are practical, idealistic, or simply driven by unrealistic media images.

2. If you are unfamiliar with something, it is not uncommon to have an inaccurate understanding about a person, place, or thing. Consider something (a person, place, or thing) that you either had a bias against or an inaccurate view of. Brainstorm some of the reasons why you held those opinions and how they led to your views. As a second part of the essay, consider the specific event that helped to change your view on the person, place, or thing.

4 Write an argument essay that takes a stand, uses reason, and considers its audience.

ARGUMENT

Hints for Writing an Argument Essay

1. **Pick a topic based on your own experience and observation.** Although you may not realize it, you have a wide range of experience because you play many roles: consumer, student, parent, child, husband or wife, driver, pet owner, athlete. These and many other roles may fit you. In each of your roles, you may have noticed or experienced something that can lead to a topic.

2. **Be sure to take a stand in your thesis.** That is, don't merely state a problem, but make a point about how to solve or eliminate it.

   not this: Tree View Lane is dangerous.
   but this: The Department of Public Works needs to put guardrails up along Tree View Lane.

   not this: Surfers are losing the best beaches and it's terrible.
   but this: City zoning must take into account public access to the local surfing beaches or the surfers will have very limited options.

3. **Use the reasons in your argument as a way to focus your body paragraphs.** If you have three reasons, for instance, you can write three body paragraphs.

4. **Consider your audience's objections.** Always ask yourself who the audience is for your argument. If you are arguing that your office needs a new copier, you will probably be writing to your supervisor. If you are arguing for an after-school program at your child's elementary school, you will probably be writing to the school board. Consider why your audience should support your points and how they might object.

   There are several ways to handle objections and apply your critical thinking skills. If you can *refute* an objection (that is, you can prove that it isn't valid), you have removed a major obstacle. Sometimes you may have to admit the other side has a valid objection by *conceding* it. Even by conceding, however, you win confidence by showing that you know both sides of the argument and are fair enough to consider another point of view.

   Another way to handle an objection is to *turn an objection into an advantage.* Adopting this ploy, you admit the objection is valid but use it to reinforce your own point. If you are arguing for a new copier and your supervisor says it is too expensive, you can agree that it is expensive but that the office is losing time and money by constantly repairing the old copier. Turning an obstacle into an advantage shows that you are informed, open-minded, resourceful, and a *critical thinker*.

Even if you do not openly refer to objections in your argument essay, being aware of possible objections helps you frame your points effectively, with your audience in mind.

CRITICAL THINKING

If you know your argument (or proposal) will be controversial, show that you understand and acknowledge the opposition's views. Acknowledge that the issue is important to both sides. Use logic to refute opposing views and avoid emotionally loaded language.

WRITING THE ARGUMENT ESSAY IN STEPS

PREWRITING   ARGUMENT ESSAY

Imagine that your instructor has given you this assignment:

> Write a letter to the editor of your local newspaper. Argue for something in your town that needs to be changed.

One way to begin is to brainstorm for some specific issue that you can write about. You can ask questions such as these: Is there a part of town that needs to be cleaned up? Should the cafeteria change some of their policies to ensure student health and well-being? What could be improved in my neighborhood?

By answering these questions, you may come up with one topic, and then you can list ideas on it.

topic

Cleaning Up Roberts Park

ideas

dirty and overgrown
benches are all cracked and broken
full of trash
could be fixed up
people work nearby
they would use it

You can consider your audience and possible objections:

audience

local people of all ages who read the local paper

possible objections from this audience

would cost money
more important things to spend money on

answering objections

Money would be well spent to beautify the downtown.
Cleaning up the park will bring more people downtown.
City children could play there in the fresh air and in nature; workers could eat lunch there.

Once you have a list, you can start grouping the ideas on your list to develop an argument with clear reasons and supporting details. You should consider how your answers to possible objections help you to identify key reasons to be used in your argument. In other words, by answering objections, you can come up with the key reasons that best support your point.

It is also important to recognize that many strong arguments directly state and address their opponents' argument(s). They anticipate and explicitly mention their audience's possible objections and then respond to them. This is called *refutation*. You might consider when grouping your ideas which objection you might explicitly state and how you would refute it.

Following is a list with a point to argue, three supporting reasons, some supporting details about cleaning up Roberts Park, an objection to the point with supporting details, and an answer to that objection.

List for an Argument Essay

Topic: Cleaning Up Roberts Park

point:	*We should fix up Roberts Park.*
reason:	*Improving the park would make the downtown area more attractive to shoppers.*
details:	*Shoppers could stroll in the park or rest from their shopping.*
	Friends could meet in the park for a day of shopping and lunch.
reason:	*City children could play in the park.*
details:	*They could get fresh air.*
	They could play in a natural setting.
reason:	*Workers could eat lunch outdoors.*
details:	*Several office complexes are nearby.*
	Workers would take a break outdoors.
objection:	*The cost of fixing the park will impact the city's budget.*
details:	*The cost of fixing the park is too high.*
	There are other projects the city should spend its money on.
refutation:	*The money spent on beautifying the park will bring more people downtown.*
	People will spend money at local establishments.
	The city will experience more civic pride.

With your reasons and details, you can draft a thesis sentence:

Roberts Park should be cleaned up and improved.

With a thesis sentence, three reasons, and details, you are ready to move on to the planning stage of preparing an argument essay.

PLANNING ARGUMENT ESSAY

Following is an outline for an argument essay on cleaning up a park. Study the outline carefully and be prepared to respond to the exercise that follows it.

Outline for an Argument Essay

paragraph 1	I.	Thesis: Roberts Park should be cleaned up and improved.
paragraph 2, topic sentence	II.	Improving the park would make the downtown area more attractive to shoppers.

    A. If the city could clean, landscape, and refurnish the park, it would be a natural refuge for shoppers.

    B. It is located in the middle of the shopping district.

    C. Those who already shop in the city could stroll through the park or rest there after shopping.

details about reason 1: a place for shoppers

    D. Soon, shoppers would tell their friends about the attractive, new-looking park.

    E. Eventually, friends could agree to meet at the park for a day of shopping and lunch.

    F. City shops and department stores would see business improve.

    G. Business would be good for restaurants, too.

paragraph 3, topic sentence — III. Workers from nearby offices and stores could eat lunch outdoors.

    A. Several office buildings are nearby.

    B. During the lunch break, many people, even those who bring their lunch, want to get out of the office or store.

    C. Everyone wants to get up and forget the job for a little while.

details about reason 2: a place for workers

    D. Some want fresh air.

    E. Others want to read a book or magazine while they eat.

    F. Others want to get some exercise by walking a little.

    G. Others just want to observe nature and people.

    H. An improved park could meet all these needs.

paragraph 4, topic sentence — IV. City children could play there.

    A. City children live in apartments.

    B. They don't have backyards to enjoy.

    C. They are reduced to playing in dangerous streets or on narrow sidewalks.

details about reason 3: a place for children

    D. Many aren't allowed outside at all.

    E. They go from sitting all day at school to sitting at home.

    F. In the park, children could interact rather than sit alone inside, watching television and playing video games.

    G. They could play on grass, not asphalt.

    H. They would not have to play near traffic.

paragraph 5, topic sentence — V. The costs will negatively impact the city's budget.

    A. City government needs to be more fiscally responsible.

details about objection

    B. The costs for improving the park are too high.

    C. There are other projects the city should spend its money on.

    D. The money spent will attract visitors to downtown businesses.

refutation

    E. Visitors will spend more money at local establishments.

    F. These establishments will be more successful.

    G. The city will experience more civic pride.

paragraph 6, conclusion — VI. Roberts Park used to be the city's landmark, and it could be once again.

The outline combined some of the details from the list with new details devised during the planning process. It focused each body paragraph on one reason to clean up the park. It also includes an entire paragraph that explicitly acknowledges opposing arguments and offers a refutation to those arguments. As you write and revise your draft, you can continue to add details and arrange them in the most effective order to strengthen your argument. Later, as you edit, you can also combine sentences, add transitions, and refine word choice.

Exercise 12 **Practice: Recognizing Added Details in the Outline of an Argument Essay**

Many new details help to develop the body paragraphs of the outline. Paragraph 3, for example, contains four new items to support the topic sentence. Underline these items.

DRAFTING AND REVISING ARGUMENT ESSAY

Following is a revised draft of the essay on cleaning up a park. As you read it, you'll notice several changes from the outline on page 317.

- An introduction has been added.
- Transitions have been added within and between paragraphs.
- Details have been added.
- A concluding paragraph has been added.

Study the draft carefully and be prepared to respond to the exercises that follow it.

Draft of an Argument Essay

(Note: Thesis, topic sentences, and conclusion are underlined; editing and proofreading are still necessary.)

Roberts Park was once a pretty little park with a fountain, dark wood benches, carefully landscaped paths, and lush trees and flowers. Today, however, the fountain is cracked and dry, the benches are faded and splintered, and the paths are overgrown. Trash fills the flowerbeds. <u>Roberts Park should be cleaned up and improved</u>.

There are several reasons why a better park would make a better city. <u>First, improving the park would make the downtown area more attractive to shoppers</u>. If the city could clean, landscape, and refurnish the park, it would be a natural refuge for shoppers. It is right in the middle of the shopping district, making it convenient for those who already shop in the city to stroll through the park or rest there. Soon, shoppers might tell their friends about the attractive, new-looking park. Eventually, friends could agree to meet at the park for a day of shopping and lunch. City shops and department stores would see an increase in business, and restaurants would benefit, too.

Those who do business in the city would appreciate a renovated park as well. <u>Workers from nearby offices and stores could eat lunch outdoors</u>. Several high-rise office buildings are nearby, full of office workers. During their lunch break, many people, even those who bring their lunch, want to get out of the office or store. Everyone wants to get up and forget the job for a little while. Some want fresh air, and others want to read a book or magazine while they eat. The more ambitious want to get some exercise by walking a little; however, many people just want to observe nature and people. An improved park could meet all these needs.

The most important reason to clean up the park is to help children. <u>City children could play in Roberts Park</u>. City children, who live in apartments, don't have backyards to enjoy. If they go outside, they are reduced to playing in dangerous streets or on narrow sidewalks. Many aren't allowed outside at all. They go from sitting all day at school to sitting at home. In a restored park, children could interact rather than sit alone inside, watching television and playing video games. They could play on grass, not asphalt. Best of all, they would not have to play near traffic.

<u>Opponents argue the costs of cleaning and improving Roberts Park will impact the city's budget negatively</u>. They believe we should be more fiscally responsible. They think the expense of improving the park is too high and that money should be spent on other projects. However, the money spent on beautifying the park will bring more people downtown, who will, in turn, spend money at local establishments. These local establishments will be more successful and the city will experience more civic pride.

Today, the words "Roberts Park" describe a rundown, ragged plot of broken benches, weeds, and trash. But the place could be a haven for children, shoppers, and workers. Once the park was green, the fountain shimmered, and the benches shone. <u>Roberts Park used to be the city's landmark, and it could be once again</u>.

Exercise 13 **Practice: Identifying Time Contrasts in the Draft of an Argument Essay**

The introduction to the essay talks about the past of the park (what it "once" was), and its present ("Today" it is in bad shape). The conclusion also refers to time: past, present, and future. Underline the words or phrases in the conclusion that refer to each time.

_____

_____

Exercise 14 **Practice: Recognizing the Importance of Time Sequence Transitions**

Paragraph 2 also organizes its details with time transitions. Underline four time transitions in this paragraph, and consider why time is such an important part of this essay.

_____

_____

EDITING AND PROOFREADING **ARGUMENT ESSAY**

Following is the final version of the essay on cleaning up a park. When you compare it to the draft on pages 318–319, you will notice some changes:

- Paragraph 1, the introduction, needed a transitional sentence linking the description of the park to the thesis statement.

- In Paragraph 2, the fourth sentence has been revised to eliminate some wordiness.
- Also in Paragraph 2, the words *shop*, *shoppers*, and *shopping* became too repetitive, so one phrase, *these people*, replaced one use of *shoppers*.
- In Paragraph 4, a new sentence has been added.

- Also in Paragraph 4, a transition (*In addition*) has been added.
- In Paragraph 5, in the first sentence, a transition *There are those …* has been added.
- In Paragraph 5, the sentences *They believe* and *They think* have been combined to make a single sentence.
- A title has been added.

Study the final version carefully and be prepared to respond to the exercise that follows it.

Final Version of an Argument Essay

The Case for Renovating Roberts Park

Roberts Park was once a pretty little park, with a bubbling fountain, dark wood benches, carefully landscaped paths, and lush trees and flowers. Today, however, the fountain is cracked and dry, the benches are faded and splintered, and the paths are overgrown. Trash fills the flowerbeds. It is time to make this place park-like again. Roberts Park should be cleaned up and improved.

There are several reasons why a better park would make a better city. First, improving the park would make the downtown area more attractive to shoppers. If the city could clean, landscape, and refurnish the park, it would be a natural refuge for shoppers. Because it is right in the middle of the shopping district, those who already shop in the city would be likely to stroll through the park or rest there. Soon, these people might tell their friends about the attractive, new-looking park. Eventually, friends could agree to meet at the park for a day of shopping and lunch. City shops and department stores would see an increase in business, and restaurants would benefit, too.

Those who do business in the city would appreciate a renovated park as well. Workers from nearby offices and stores could eat lunch outdoors. Several high-rise office buildings are nearby, full of office workers. During their lunch break, many people, even those who bring their lunch, want to get out of the office or store. Everyone wants to get up and forget the job for a little while. Some want fresh air, and others want to read a book or magazine while they eat. The more ambitious want to get some exercise by walking a little; however, many people just want to observe nature and people. An improved park could meet all these needs.

The most important reason to clean up the park is to help children. City children could play in Roberts Park. City children, who live in apartments, don't have backyards to enjoy. If they go outside, they are reduced to playing in dangerous streets or on narrow sidewalks. Many aren't allowed outside at all. They go from sitting all day at school to sitting at home. In a restored park, children could interact rather than sit alone inside, watching television and playing video games. They would get some much-needed exercise. In addition, they could play on grass, not asphalt. Best of all, they would not have to play near traffic.

There are those who argue the costs of cleaning and improving Roberts Park will impact the city's budget negatively. They believe we should be more fiscally responsible. They think the expense of improving the park is too high and that money should be spent on other projects. However, the money spent on beautifying the park will bring more people downtown, who will, in turn, spend money at local establishments. These local establishments will be more successful and the city will experience more civic pride.

Today, the words "Roberts Park" describe a rundown, ragged site full of broken benches, weeds, and trash. But the place could be a haven for children, shoppers, and workers. Once the park was green, the fountain shimmered, and the benches shone. Roberts Park used to be the city's landmark, and it could be once again.

Exercise 15 **Practice: Spotting Changes in the Final Version of an Argument Essay**

Underline the transition sentence added to the introduction; then, in Paragraph 4, underline the new detail in sentence form and the new transitional phrase.

Topics for Writing an Argument Essay

When you write on any of these topics, work through the stages of the writing process in preparing your essay.

1. Write an essay for readers of your local newspaper, arguing for or against one of the following:

   a. free youth sports for neighborhood children

   b. creating community green spaces or gardens for people to congregate in

   c. establishing a bike lane on local roads

2. As a consumer, you purchase a number of products and services. Think of one product (like a meal, a pair of glasses, or camping gear) or a service (like an hotel stay, an insurance plan, or a meal in a restaurant) that you feel needs improvement. Write an essay in the form of a letter to the president of the company that produces the product or offers the service. Argue for the improvement you want. Be specific. For example, if you are dissatisfied with a stay at an hotel, you might want a lower rate, more amenities, or improvements made to their Web site in terms of accuracy.

3. Write to the president of a company whose advertising offends you. The advertising can be television, print, or online advertising. In an essay in the form of a letter, argue for removing that advertising.

4. Argue for one of the following college issues. Your audience will be the president, vice presidents, and deans at your college. Topics to argue:

   a. more affordable cafeteria options

   b. a twenty-four-hour study area with computers available

   c. better tutorial programs for how to access and submit online assignments

Topics for Critical Thinking and Writing

1. Argue for some change at your workplace. It must be a change that would not cost much money but would improve the product or the service the business offers.

2. Assume an anonymous donor has just given your college a gift of $250,000. The college has called for proposals on how to allocate the funds. Think about your experience at school and write an essay that discusses how that money could best benefit the students and instructors of your college.

⑤ Write a multipattern essay that has a clear topic and thesis, stays with the same pattern within a paragraph, and uses transitions effectively.

THE MULTIPATTERN ESSAY

Many essays rely on more than one essay pattern to make their point. For example, if you want to *describe* a city landmark, you might want to include a history (*narration*) of the place. If your goal is to convince a reader to take some action such as preserving the landmark, your essay might include sections on the benefits of keeping that landmark. In that case, your essay could use the patterns of *argument* (convincing a reader), *effects* (discussing what can happen if the landmark were to close), and *process* (tracing the steps of how the landmark can be saved).

Hints for Writing a Multipattern Essay

1. **Start with a topic, not with a concern about the patterns you use.** Most conversation and writing begin with a subject. You may tell your best friend about a game, for instance. When you start the conversation, you may be thinking about the story (*narrative*) of the game. However, you may soon find yourself *describing* a specific play or match-up within the game. Soon, you may be explaining why (*causes*) one team won and the other lost. In writing, as in conversation, the patterns you choose depend on what you want to say.

2. **When you write a multipattern essay, do not shift patterns within a paragraph.** Telling the story of a game and shifting to a description of a play in the same paragraph will be (1) confusing and (2) skimpy on development of either pattern.

   If you begin with a developed *story*, you tell the reader who the game was between, where it was played, what the conditions and crowd were like, and so on.

   If you intend to make the specific match-up a key part of the essay, you need a detailed *description* of each player in another paragraph. And in a separate paragraph, you need an explanation of the *reasons* one team won and another lost.

3. **Your thesis does not have to include a reference to each pattern you are using.** Your thesis is about the point of all your body paragraphs, but it can be short and focused.

   not this: Watching a college football game between two powerhouse teams, I noticed that a specific match-up between the quarterback and the linebackers played a big role in why one team won and the other lost.

   but this: A small match-up battle can tell the story of an entire game.

4. Be especially careful about transitions between paragraphs.
Transitions are always important in clear, smooth writing, but they are particularly important here. Because you are moving from one pattern to another, you need clear transitions that signal these moves.

WRITING THE MULTIPATTERN ESSAY IN STEPS

PREWRITING   MULTIPATTERN ESSAY ON PINE RIVER

Imagine that you are asked to write about a financial problem that affects you or people you know. You might begin by listing your first thoughts:

money is tight
unemployment in our area
our town relying on summer tourists
someone who left town after a foreclosure

You decide that the subject you know best is how much your town relies on summer tourism. To develop and focus the idea, you start listing questions:

What are summer tourists?
How do they bring money to our town?
Why do they visit here?
Do residents like tourists?
What do tourists do when they visit?
What are the attractions in this town?
Why is it only summer tourism?
How can the town survive or even grow?
What does the town need?

CRITICAL THINKING

When writing a multipattern essay, be sure you carefully determine the essay's organization and the most logical order of patterns. Be especially careful not to shift between ideas.

Organizing Your Ideas for a Multipattern Essay

By scanning the questions and answering as many as you can, you may realize that your writing is falling into three essay patterns. Following is a list of three patterns and details (formed by answering the questions). The list could be developed into a multipattern essay.

Grouped Details for a Multipattern Essay

Topic: Pine River

description: summer tourists love to visit
the weather is cool and sunny
area has much to do
town has camping, boating, fishing
small bed and breakfasts, a motel
friendly local restaurants, souvenir and crafts shops

(Continued)

effects: tourist economy is part time
after Labor Day, the town is empty
cold weather and storms discourage camping and boating
the bed and breakfasts struggle
the motel closes until spring
local stores suffer

argument: year-round businesses can save the town
a big-box store to employ people all year
store will bring customers from nearby towns all year
a local factory or plant is important
steady jobs mean better income

Grouping the details can help you shape your thesis. As you study your list, you realize that the town thrives in the summer but suffers in the winter. Tourists help to support the town, but because they are the main source of income, money dries up after Labor Day. You devise a thesis that makes this point and recommends a solution:

Pine River must grow beyond its reliance on tourist money.

Notice that the thesis includes the name of the town. This thesis can be supported three ways: by *describing* the summer prosperity, by writing about the *effects* on the community when tourist season ends, and by *arguing* for a solution to this problem.

PLANNING MULTIPATTERN ESSAY ON PINE RIVER

Following is an outline for a multipattern essay on helping Pine River to grow. Study the outline carefully and be prepared to respond to the exercise that follows it.

Outline for a Multipattern Essay

Topic: Pine River

paragraph 1 —— I. Thesis: Pine River must grow beyond its reliance on tourist money.

paragraph 2, topic sentence —— II. Pine River is a beautiful New England town that thrives when summer tourists visit.

    A. People who visit in the summer love the cool, sunny weather.

    B. There is much to do in Pine River.

    C. Boating and fishing attract many visitors to the river.

details: description of the town in summer ——

    D. Many people camp in the nearby hills.

    E. There are small bed-and-breakfast establishments.

    F. The one motel is always full in the summer.

    G. Downtown, friendly local restaurants, crafts shops, and souvenir stores charm people.

paragraph 3,
topic sentence

III. When summer ends and the tourists leave, Pine River's economy falls apart.

   A. Cold weather, rain, and storms mean the end of boating, fishing, and camping.
   B. Bed and breakfasts lose guests.
   C. The motel owners close their business until summer.

details: effects of the end of tourist season

   D. The small downtown area becomes nearly empty.
   E. Without a supply of tourists as customers, some restaurants close until late spring.
   F. Local people are not likely to buy souvenirs or craftwork.

paragraph 4,
topic sentence

IV. Pine River must save itself from this dangerous cycle by attracting year-round businesses.

   A. A big-box national store would create jobs.
   B. Constructing such a store would require local workers of all types.
   C. More permanent jobs would be available when the store opened.
   D. A large store would attract customers from nearby towns all year.

details: what should be done to save Pine River

   E. Big-box stores tend to be followed by smaller commercial businesses such as pizza restaurants.
   F. Another great addition to Pine River would be a factory or plant.
   G. Even a small manufacturing facility would mean more year-round jobs.
   H. Local people could have them.
   I. Workers at a superstore or factory earn money that can be spent in Pine River year round.

paragraph 5,
conclusion

V. Tourist towns suffer ups and downs, but a tourist town with other resources can enjoy steady prosperity.

The outline added many new details gathered during the planning process. The topic sentences indicate the pattern of each body paragraph: Paragraph 2 uses the descriptive word "beautiful" town; Paragraph 3 begins by discussing effects ("When the summer ends . . . Pine River's economy falls apart"); and Paragraph 4 opens by saying that the town "must save itself" (argument).

Exercise 16   **Practice: Noting the Development of Paragraph 4**

Compare the grouped details in the prewriting stage for Paragraph 4 to the same paragraph and details in outline form. Underline what is new in the outline.

DRAFTING AND REVISING MULTIPATTERN ESSAY ON PINE RIVER

Following is a revised draft of a multipattern essay on Pine River, its summer tourists, and the town's needs. As you read it, you will notice many changes from the outline on pages 324–325.

- An introduction has been added.
- Details have been added.
- The conclusion has been expanded.
- One sentence that was in the passive voice in Section IV of the outline has been revised so that it is now in the active voice (a better and less wordy choice).

Study the draft carefully and be prepared to respond to the exercises that follow it.

Draft of a Multipattern Essay

(Note: Thesis, topic sentences, and conclusion are underlined; editing and proofreading are still necessary.)

Many people like to visit a place that is known for its attractions in one special season. For example, Northerners love to visit Florida in the winter because Florida weather is sunny and warm. At the same time, other people head to Colorado for the snow-covered slopes of the skiing season. In the summer, many tourists go to New England for relaxation and natural beauty. <u>However, if Pine River is to find stability, it must go beyond its reliance on tourist money.</u>

<u>Pine River is a beautiful little New England town that thrives when summer tourists visit.</u> People who visit during the summer months love the cool but sunny weather. There is much to do in Pine River. Boating and fishing attract many to the river. Many people camp in the nearby hills. There are small bed-and-breakfast establishments. The one motel in town is always full in the summer. In the small downtown area, friendly local restaurants, crafts shops, and souvenir stores charm people.

<u>When the summer ends and the tourists leave, Pine River changes.</u> The town falls apart. Cold weather, rain, and storms mean the end of boating, fishing, and camping. Bed and breakfasts lose guests. The motel owners close their business until next summer. The small downtown area becomes nearly empty. Without a supply of tourists as customers, some restaurants close until late spring. Since local people are not likely to buy souvenirs or crafts, many small shops suffer.

<u>Pine River must save itself from this dangerous financial cycle by attracting year-round businesses.</u> For example, bringing a national superstore such as Target or Walmart would create jobs. Constructing such a store would require local workers of all kinds. Staffing the store would mean more year-round jobs, and a large store would attract customers from nearby towns all year. In addition, big-box stores tend to be followed by smaller businesses such as pizza restaurants, home improvement centers, and electronics stores. They, too, employ people year-round. Another great addition to Pine River would be a factory or plant. Even a small manufacturing facility would most likely hire local people. Best of all, workers employed at the new large or small stores could spend money in Pine River all year-round.

Pine River in the summer is a beautiful place for residents and tourists. However, when summer ends, life in Pine River changes. <u>Tourist towns suffer ups and downs, but a tourist town with other resources can enjoy economic prosperity.</u>

Exercise 17   Practice: Evaluating the Role of Contrasts in the Introduction

The introduction contains a number of contrasts (for example, winter and summer). Underline as many of these contrasts as you can and consider why they are important to the subject of the essay.

_____

_____

Exercise 18   Practice: Recognizing the Changes from Outline to Draft

Compare Paragraph 4 of the essay in outline and paragraph form. Underline the added specific details such as brand names and types of businesses.

EDITING AND PROOFREADING   MULTIPATTERN ESSAY ON PINE RIVER

Following is a final version of the essay on Pine River's summer tourists and the town's needs. As you read it, you will notice some changes:

- A title has been added.
- A sentence has been added to the introduction so that the link between the New England towns and one specific town, Pine River, is clear. (*Many of these tourists come to Pine River.*)
- In Paragraph 2, sentences have been combined.
- Also in Paragraph 2, the word choices have been improved; for example, the reference to shops and restaurants that *charm people* has been revised to *appeal to visitors* because *visitors* is more specific and refers to the town's dependence on tourists. (See end of Paragraph 2.)
- In Paragraph 4, a transition (*more important*) has been added to emphasize a point. (See line 5.)
- Also in Paragraph 4, what became one long sentence loaded with too much information has been divided into two. (See lines 5 and 6.)
- The conclusion has been revised and expanded so that it is more specific in describing how the year-round residents of Pine River can begin the work of transformation.
- A final sentence in the conclusion also links the title to the essay's point.

Study the final version carefully and be prepared to respond to Exercise 19 which follows it.

Final Version of a Multipattern Essay

The Two Pine Rivers

Many people like to visit a place that is known for its attractions in one special season. For example, Northerners love to visit Florida in the winter because Florida weather is sunny and warm. At the same time, other people head to Colorado for the snow-covered slopes of the skiing season. In the summer, many tourists go to New England for relaxation and natural beauty. Many of these tourists come to Pine

(Continued)

River. However, if Pine River is to find stability, it must go beyond its reliance on tourist money.

Pine River is a beautiful little New England town that thrives when summer tourists visit. People who visit during the summer months love the cool but sunny weather. There is much to do in Pine River. Boating and fishing attract many to the river. Many people camp in the nearby hills. There are small bed-and-breakfast establishments, and the one motel in town is always full in the summer. In the small downtown area, friendly local restaurants, crafts shops, and souvenir stores appeal to visitors.

When the summer ends and the tourists leave, Pine River changes. The town falls apart. Cold weather, rain, and storms mean the end of boating, fishing, and camping. Bed and breakfasts lose guests. The motel owners close their business until next summer. The small downtown area becomes nearly empty. Without a supply of tourists as customers, some restaurants close until late spring. Since local people are not likely to buy souvenirs or crafts, many small shops suffer.

Year-round residents of Pine River have seen this pattern develop each year. Pine River must save itself from this dangerous financial cycle by attracting year-round businesses. For example, bringing a national superstore such as Target or Walmart would create jobs. Constructing such a store would require local workers of all kinds. More important, staffing the store would mean additional permanent, year-round jobs. Such a large store would attract customers from nearby towns all year. In addition, big-box stores tend to be followed by smaller businesses such as pizza restaurants, home improvement centers, and electronics stores. They, too, employ people year-round. Another great addition to Pine River would be a factory or plant. Even a small manufacturing facility would most likely hire local people. Best of all, workers employed at the new large or small stores could spend money in Pine River all year round.

Pine River in the summer is a beautiful place for residents and tourists. However, when summer ends, life in Pine River changes. The leaders of the community such as the mayor and the members of the Chamber of Commerce must work with every citizen to find the ways and means to attract year-round businesses to Pine River. Tourist towns suffer ups and downs, but a tourist town with other resources can enjoy economic prosperity. Then Pine River could have two images: one as an attractive summer place and the other as a thriving year-round community.

Exercise 19   **Practice: Analyzing the Significance of an Essay's Title**

Explain the meaning of the essay's title. To understand its meaning, reread the essay's conclusion and also consider how the "two Pine Rivers" that currently exist could change if the town's economy is transformed.

_____

_____

_____

ANOTHER EXAMPLE OF THE MULTIPATTERN ESSAY

The essay on Pine River is just one example of an essay that relies on more than one pattern. There is no rule about how many patterns to choose or how to organize them. You can decide what kind of paragraphs will work best to support your thesis and what order works best for your topic.

The second multipattern essay is also shown from prewriting through the final version. It relies on narrative and on an analysis of effects to support a thesis.

PREWRITING   MULTIPATTERN ESSAY ON ONE FAMILY'S FIGHT AGAINST AGORAPHOBIA

Imagine that you are asked to write about a common psychological problem. You decide to write about *agoraphobia*, a fear of open spaces or of being alone in crowded spaces. Because the illness has affected a member of your family, you know something about its effects. You could begin by freewriting:

Freewriting for a Multipattern Essay on One Family's Fight Against Agoraphobia

I only know it from dealing with my sister. She wouldn't leave the house. Started with not going to crowded places like sports arenas or concerts. Later, Sarah didn't want to visit friends. Even family. We didn't know what to do. She lived in fear of everything. Family members get frustrated. Impatient. Insist on trying to drag her out. Then she's a prisoner. We worried about her. Finally, therapy starts. Kinds of therapy. Therapy and the family.

As you consider the freewriting, you decide that you will use two patterns to develop this essay: narrative and effects. You brainstorm and consider what details will help you develop the essay. With both the details from freewriting and additional details from brainstorming, you devise a possible grouping of the three body paragraphs:

Sarah's fall into fear (narration)

she wouldn't leave the house
started with not going to crowded places like sports arenas or concerts
later, Sarah didn't want to visit friends, even family
she lived in fear of everything
she's a prisoner

family panic (effects)

we didn't know what to do
family members get frustrated, impatient
insist on trying to drag her out
we worried about her

therapy helps (effects)

finally, therapy starts
Sarah seeks help
kinds of therapy
therapy and the family

With a topic for three body paragraphs and some details for each, you can think about a thesis for this multipattern essay. Your thesis does not have to refer to the patterns you will use, but it needs to make some point about Sarah's illness and the family's reaction. Here is a possible thesis statement:

My sister's battles with agoraphobia required the strength of an entire family.

This thesis will work well with the topics of your three body paragraphs because they will cover *the story* of Sarah's illness, its *effects* on the family, and the *effects* of therapy. With a thesis statement, three topic sentences for the body paragraphs, and a list of details, you are ready to write an outline for your essay.

PLANNING MULTIPATTERN ESSAY ON ONE FAMILY'S FIGHT AGAINST AGORAPHOBIA

Following is an outline for a multipattern essay on one family and its fight against agoraphobia. Study the outline carefully and be prepared to respond to the exercise that follows it.

Outline for a Multipattern Essay

Topic: A Family's Fight Against Agoraphobia

paragraph 1 —— I. Thesis: My sister's battles with agoraphobia required the strength of an entire family.

paragraph 2, topic sentence —— II. Agoraphobia slowly suffocated my sister.

details in narrative form about agoraphobia

A. The symptoms started a few months after Sarah's husband left her.
B. First, she would not go to crowded places such as sports arenas or concerts.
C. Then she didn't want to join me or her friends on our regular trips to the mall or other places.
D. She said the trips made her nervous.
E. Soon she was asking me to pick up items from the supermarket.
F. I realized that she was no longer leaving her house, even to buy food.
G. Later, she began to tremble when the doorbell or phone rang.

paragraph 3, topic sentence —— III. Sarah's loved ones suffered as well.

details about the effects of Sarah's illness on her family

A. Neither I nor my parents could persuade her to leave the house.
B. Our constant visits did not seem to help her.
C. My parents and I became fearful.
D. We could not help Sarah.
E. Our fear became frustration, impatience, and anger.
F. Sarah sensed these emotions.
G. We realized that she was dreading our visits.

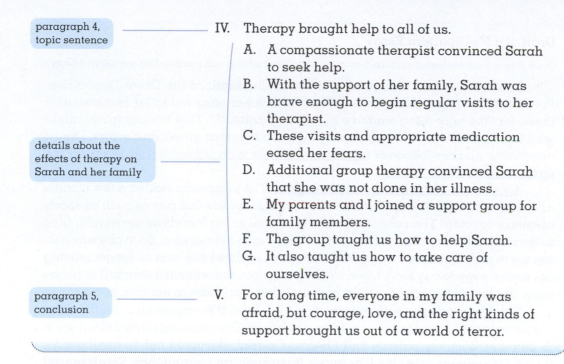

paragraph 4,
topic sentence

IV. Therapy brought help to all of us.

   A. A compassionate therapist convinced Sarah to seek help.
   B. With the support of her family, Sarah was brave enough to begin regular visits to her therapist.
   C. These visits and appropriate medication eased her fears.

details about the
effects of therapy on
Sarah and her family

   D. Additional group therapy convinced Sarah that she was not alone in her illness.
   E. My parents and I joined a support group for family members.
   F. The group taught us how to help Sarah.
   G. It also taught us how to take care of ourselves.

paragraph 5,
conclusion

V. For a long time, everyone in my family was afraid, but courage, love, and the right kinds of support brought us out of a world of terror.

Exercise 20 Practice: Adding Details to an Outline

How is Section IV of the outline different from the "therapy helps" grouping in the previous list of effects? Does it add more description of the same points or does it add new information? Give examples.

_____

_____

DRAFTING AND REVISING   **MULTIPATTERN ESSAY ON ONE FAMILY'S FIGHT AGAINST AGORAPHOBIA**

Following is a revised draft of a multipattern essay on one family and its fight against agoraphobia. As you read it, you will notice many changes from the outline on pages 330–331.

- An introduction has been added.
- A conclusion has been written.
- Details have been added, including one sentence at the end of Paragraph 2.
- Transitions have been added, especially in Paragraph 4 (*Later, meanwhile, also*).

Study the draft carefully and be prepared to respond to the exercises that follow it.

Draft of a Multipattern Essay

(Note: Thesis, topic sentences, and conclusion are underlined; editing and proofreading are still necessary.)

In his acclaimed inaugural address at the depth of the Great Depression, President Franklin Delano Roosevelt advised Americans not to let fear consume them, for "the only thing we have to fear is fear itself." This famous quote might well have been describing agoraphobia. It is a fear that grows and grows. I know about this disease because <u>my sister's battles with agoraphobia required the strength of an entire family</u>.

<u>Agoraphobia slowly suffocated my sister</u>. The symptoms started a few months after her husband left her. First, she would not go to crowded places such as sports arenas or concerts. Then she didn't want to join me or her friends on our regular trips to the mall and other places. She said the trips made her nervous. Soon she was asking me to pick up items from the supermarket. I realized she was no longer leaving her house, even to buy food. Later, she began to tremble when the doorbell or phone rang. Her fear of the outside world had made her a prisoner in her own home.

<u>Sarah's loved ones suffered when she did</u>. Even if we coaxed her, neither I nor my parents could persuade her to leave the house. Our constant visits did not seem to help her. Soon my parents and I became fearful. We could not do anything for Sarah. Our fear revealed itself as anger, frustration, and impatience. Sarah sensed these emotions. She began to dread our visits.

<u>Therapy brought help to all of us</u>. A compassionate therapist convinced Sarah to seek help. Accompanied by a family member, Sarah became brave enough to begin regular visits to her therapist. These visits and appropriate medication eased her fears. Later, additional group therapy convinced Sarah she was not alone. Meanwhile, my parents and I joined a support group for family members of agoraphobics. The group taught us how to encourage and support Sarah. It also taught us how to take care of ourselves.

<u>Agoraphobia caused our whole family to fight a battle against fear</u>. The war is not over, but Sarah and the rest of us are winning. Courage, love, and the right kinds of support brought us out of a world of terror.

Exercise 21 **Practice: Identifying the Type of Introduction Used in the Essay**

Circle the type of introduction used in this essay: (1) using one or more questions, (2) opening with a contradiction of your main point, or (3) opening with a quotation.

Exercise 22 **Practice: Recognizing the Frame in the Essay**

To understand how the essay opens and closes with words that refer to being afraid or enduring conflict, underline the synonyms for these words in the introduction and conclusion of the draft.

EDITING AND PROOFREADING   MULTIPATTERN ESSAY ON ONE FAMILY'S FIGHT AGAINST AGORAPHOBIA

Following is the final version of a multipattern essay on one family's fight against agoraphobia. As you read it, you may notice these changes:

- A title has been added.
- A transitional sentence has been added to the beginning of one paragraph.
- Sentences have been combined in Paragraph 3.

Study the final version carefully and be prepared to respond to the exercise that follows it.

Final Version of a Multipattern Essay

One Family's Fight Against an Enemy Within

In his acclaimed inaugural address at the depth of the Great Depression, President Franklin Delano Roosevelt advised Americans not to let fear consume them, for "the only thing we have to fear is fear itself." This famous quote might well have been describing agoraphobia. It is a fear that grows and grows. I know about this disease because my sister's battles with agoraphobia required the strength of an entire family.

Agoraphobia slowly suffocated my sister. The symptoms started a few months after her husband left her. First, she would not go to crowded places such as sports arenas or concerts. Then she didn't want to join me or her friends on our regular trips to the mall and coffee shop. She said the trips made her nervous. Soon she was asking me to pick up items from the supermarket. At that time, I realized she was no longer leaving her house, even to buy food. Later, she began to tremble when the doorbell or phone rang. Her fear of the outside world had made her a prisoner in her own home.

Sarah's loved ones suffered when she did. Even if we coaxed her, neither I nor my parents could persuade her to leave the house. Our constant visits did not seem to help her. Soon my parents and I became fearful because we could not do anything for Sarah. Our fear revealed itself as anger, frustration, and impatience. Sarah sensed these emotions. She began to dread our visits. When Sarah reacted to our visits with fear, we felt guilty.

Everyone seemed to be falling into despair, but therapy brought help to all of us. A compassionate therapist convinced Sarah to seek help. Accompanied by a family member, Sarah became brave enough to begin regular visits to her therapist. These visits and appropriate medication eased her fears. Later, additional group therapy convinced Sarah she was not alone. Meanwhile, my parents and I joined a support group for family members of agoraphobics. The group taught us how to encourage and support Sarah. It also taught us how to take care of ourselves.

Agoraphobia caused our whole family to fight a battle against fear. The war is not over, but Sarah and the rest of us are winning. Courage, love, and the right kinds of support brought us out of a world of terror.

Exercise 23 **Practice: Recognizing the Revisions in the Final Version**

Underline these revisions in the final version: (1) an additional sentence and (2) a paragraph that begins with an added transitional sentence.

Topics for Writing a Multipattern Essay

> **Note:** When you choose your own topic for writing an essay, you may decide which pattern (or patterns) are most appropriate to express your ideas. The topics that follow suggest patterns for a *specific* topic and are meant to give you some possibilities for writing a multipattern essay.

1. This topic requires you to write an essay that will be structured around two patterns. First, tell the story (narration) of a time when you failed at something. The choice could involve jobs, romantic partners, school, or a hobby. After you have told that story, write about the effects of that failure. (Note: You can write two paragraphs of narration and one of effects or vice versa.)

2. Write an essay that is structured around three patterns: process, contrast, and causes. First, write about the wrong way to perform a task (process); second, contrast the wrong way with the correct way; and third, discuss the reasons (causes) why many people choose the wrong way to perform the activity. Some possible topics could include studying, buying a car, selecting a roommate, or planning a wedding.

3. Write an essay that tells the story of an event that changed your life (narration) and also explains why this event affected you strongly (cause).

4. Write an essay that describes a place in your community where people are working together to create more family-friendly places. Then write about the effects of this environment on the residents of that place. They can be emotional, economic, political, physical, health related, personal, long range, or short range.

Topics for Critical Thinking and Writing a Multipattern Essay

1. Think of three common concerns that college students may face. Define each problem and classify it according to its severity, cause, or any other basis that works for you. Once you have completed the classification part of your essay, argue what could be done by the school community to aid students who face these challenges.

2. Write an essay about a time you observed or experienced unfair treatment by someone in authority. Relate what happened (narration), why you feel the person in authority acted inappropriately (causes), what resulted from his or her actions (effects), and what should be done to prevent or discourage someone in a similar position from acting so inappropriately (argument).

Using Research to Strengthen Essays

Learning Objectives

In this chapter, you will learn how to:

1. Search reliable print and online sources to strengthen essays.
2. Evaluate your sources to ensure their accuracy and validity.
3. Avoid plagiarism by properly incorporating and acknowledging sources.
4. Cite works in MLA documentation style.
5. Prepare a final version of an essay with research.
6. Cite works in APA documentation style.

THE ROLES OF RESEARCH

During your college experience, you will no doubt use research techniques in your coursework as well as in your daily life. Even if you have not yet written a formal paper involving research, you probably have already employed various research techniques to solve problems or make crucial decisions.

Most of the writing assignments you have completed thus far have probably been based on your own experiences, observations, or opinions. By writing regularly, you now know the importance of the writing process in producing a polished, final version of an essay. This chapter illustrates how you can strengthen an original essay by smoothly incorporating supporting material from outside sources.

Starting with a Basic Outline and Essay

The following outline and short essay about dog-rescue groups are based solely on the writer's own experience and knowledge about dog-rescue operations. You may notice that the outline is in the same format as the outlines you reviewed in Chapter 11, "Writing an Essay" previously.

Outline for an Essay without Research

I. Dog-rescue organizations perform a humane service by saving homeless dogs and matching responsible adopters with a devoted new family member.

II. Dog-rescue volunteers play several roles.
   A. Some volunteers are "spotters" who look for specific breeds at local shelters.
   B. Experienced rescue volunteers may become coordinators and arrange assistance from various sources.
   C. Volunteers work with national organizations such as Adopt-a-Pet and Petfinder, which maintain databases of adoptable dogs from rescue groups throughout the United States and Canada.
   D. Volunteers assist at rescue-dog "Adoption Days" hosted by pet supply chains such as Petco and PetSmart.

III. Rescue groups provide important information and benefits for prospective adopters.
   A. By viewing a rescue group's Web site, potential adopters can read about a dog's age, temperament, adoption fee, and any special medical conditions.
   B. If a potential adopter does not find a suitable dog, he or she can still complete an online application.
   C. On an application, a potential adopter can list his or her preferences for the age, gender, and size of the dog.
   D. Although some dogs are puppies rescued from abusive situations, most are adult dogs already socialized and housebroken.

IV. Careful screening often results in a successful adoption.
   A. Rescue groups routinely conduct home visits to check the living conditions and the neighborhood.
   B. The applicant must have access to veterinary care.
   C. The applicant must agree to return the dog to the rescue organization if he or she can no longer care for the animal.
   D. A foster parent can fully inform the adoptive parent about potential adjustment problems.
   E. Careful attention to such details leads to a winning adoption process.

V. Rescue groups not only provide care for homeless dogs; they also remind us of the joy made possible by compassionate adoption.

An Essay without Research

The following essay, written from the outline you have just reviewed, contains no research from outside sources; *it is based solely on the writer's own knowledge and experience.*

Draft of an Essay without Research

The Humane Work of Dog-Rescue Groups

Although the United States is generally regarded as a country that loves and pampers its pets, animal shelters are often filled to capacity with dogs that have been abandoned, abused, or surrendered by their owners. Sadly, some shelters routinely euthanize healthy dogs if no one claims or adopts them after a grace period ranging from just days to a few weeks. Fortunately, however, many shelters work closely with dog-rescue organizations that find loving, temporary homes where foster parents can provide care and, if necessary, rehabilitation. Staffed by dedicated volunteers, rescue groups perform a humane service by saving homeless dogs and enabling responsible adopters to gain a devoted new family member.

From rescuing retired greyhounds to saving mini "mutts," dog-rescue volunteers play several roles. For example, they often serve as "spotters" at local shelters, looking for dogs that can be fostered by individuals who specialize in specific breeds such as boxers and golden retrievers. Experienced volunteers may become coordinators who arrange for assistance from a variety of sources, including local veterinarians, groomers, transporters, and Web site designers. Many rescue groups work closely with national organizations such as Adopt-a-Pet and Petfinder, whose Web sites publish comprehensive lists of adoptable rescue dogs throughout the United States and Canada. On weekends, rescue volunteers can be seen helping out during "Adoption Days" sponsored by national chains, including Petco and PetSmart.

Rescue groups provide both crucial information and welcome benefits for potential adopters. When one becomes interested in a specific dog on a rescue group's Web site, he or she can read about the animal's medical needs, age, temperament, and adoption fee. Even if he or she does not spot a suitable dog but remains interested in adopting one from rescue, he or she can fill out an application and list preferences regarding a dog's age, gender, and size. Although rescue groups occasionally receive puppies and young dogs that have been picked up during police raids of abusive puppy mills and backyard breeders, the majority of dogs available for adoption are older ones. Any pet owner who has experienced the aggravation of sleepless nights and numerous house-training "accidents" can appreciate the benefits of adopting an older, socialized, and housebroken dog.

Although the adoption process may take several weeks or even months to find the best match, careful screening improves the chances for a successful adoption. Rescue groups routinely conduct home visits of prospective dog owners to see if both the living conditions and the neighborhood will be suitable for the dog's size, temperament, and exercise needs. In addition, the applicant must have access to veterinary care and agree to return the dog to the rescue organization if he or she can no longer properly care for it. A foster parent can fully inform the adoptive parent about a dog's potential adjustment problems because the animal's behavior has been observed over a period of weeks—if not months—in a home setting. Careful attention to such details leads to a winning adoption process.

(Continued)

Whichever way a dog comes to a rescue group—by an owner surrender, a good Samaritan, or even by a police raid of an illegal breeding operation—it will have an opportunity to live out the rest of its life free from harm and neglect. Rescue groups not only provide care for homeless dogs; they also remind us of the joy made possible by compassion, commitment, and unconditional love.

> **Note:** Later in this chapter, you will see how the outline for this essay and the essay itself are strengthened by research.

FINDING RESEARCH TO STRENGTHEN ESSAYS

1 Search reliable print and online sources to strengthen essays.

Locating Material in Your College Library

Online Catalog Your college library probably has an online catalog system that lists all of the library's books and major holdings. You can search the online catalog by a keyword related to your subject, or, if you already have information about authors who deal with your subject, you can search by the author's last name or the title of an author's book. An online catalog can provide you with a list of sources, the call number of each source (the number that will help you find the book on the library shelves), and information regarding the availability of the source.

Popular Subscription Services College libraries commonly subscribe to several subscription services that provide access to complete articles (called "full-text" articles) from periodicals (magazines, journals, and newspapers). Some of the most widely used subscription services include *EBSCOhost*, *InfoTrac*, *LexisNexis*, *JSTOR*, and *Reader's Guide to Periodical Literature*.

Always preview articles carefully to see if they contain useful information for your research essay. Scan articles online that will be useful for highlighting and note taking later. Be sure to note the date you accessed the article, the complete URL, or the digital object identifier (DOI) to ensure you can find the online article again. When previewing print copies of articles, consider copying the first and last page of the article, which include information you will need for giving credit to the author and the source of the article.

Internet Search Engines Search engines take a term or phrase and mine all of the data on the Internet to return potential sources of information you can then access for research purposes. Some of the most often used search engines include Google (*google.com*) and RefSeek (*refseek.com*).

Sometimes, outdated information may remain posted on a Web site indefinitely, so you will need to be cautious about using statistics or expert opinions that are several years old.

2 Evaluate your sources to ensure their accuracy and validity.

Checking for Validity of Sources

The writer of the dog-rescue essay decided to strengthen his paper by adding material from outside sources. The instructor required students to incorporate information from at least one print publication and two valid online sources. A short essay is enhanced by adding relevant material from experts.

The student began his Internet search by typing the key phrase "dog rescue organizations" into Google. This resulted in several hundred potential sources. The student was able to narrow his list to several dozen suitable sources.

Although the Internet is a valuable research tool, it is often tempting to use information from a Web site without checking for accuracy or validity. There is a large amount of questionable, biased, or misleading information available online today. It is critical that you check the author's credentials, such as educational background, and professional experience. In addition, you should locate any information about the background of the company or individuals responsible for a Web site. For example, if a you are investigating dog-rescue groups, the words of a veterinarian or background information from a nonprofit organization such as the Humane Society of the United States can generally be considered reliable.

Similarly, print sources need to be evaluated just as carefully. For example, a brochure advertising quick or foolproof dog-training programs would not be as reliable as an article from a magazine endorsed by the American Society for the Prevention of Cruelty to Animals (ASPCA).

The PAARC Test

PAARC is an acronym that stands for (P)urpose, (A)ccuracy, (A)uthority, (R)elevance, and (C)urrency. The PAARC test can be extremely helpful in evaluating the information you find online. Depending on the topic, certain criteria of the test may be more important than others. Some questions follow that will help you to better evaluate the research you find in the library or, more importantly, online.

Purpose Why does the information exist in the first place? Is it to explore an issue, explain a situation, or create something new?

> Is the information designed to inform, instruct, sell, persuade, or entertain?
> Is the information biased toward a particular political, ideological, or religious perspective?
> With regard to the topic, is the author objective or opinionated?
> Does the author or sponsor make their purpose or goals clear to their audience?

Accuracy How reliable, truthful, or correct is the content of the source? Is the generalization or claim made by the author accurate or is it overgeneralized?

> Where does the information come from? Is it opinion based or was it collected during a study?
> Has the information been peer reviewed or examined by experts in the field?
> Is the article supported by evidence and can this evidence be supported or corroborated by other sources?
> Is the author's tone or language use academic or professional in nature?
> Is the document carefully edited for errors or typos?

Authority Who is the source of the information? In scholarly, peer-reviewed literature authority is generally a no-brainer, but this criterion is important when evaluating online information, blogs, or opinionated pieces like editorials.

> Who is the author, sponsor, publisher, or source of information?
> What are the author's credentials? Does the author have vested interest?
> Does the author have anything to gain by providing this information?
> Is the author qualified to write about or comment on the topic?
> Does the URL reveal anything about the sources? .edu? .com? .gov? .org?

Relevance How important is this source to your research? Will it add credibility to your own claims and points you wish to make?

> Does the source directly answer your key research questions?
> Is this source written at an appropriate level for you to use in a college paper?

Currency Is the information still current, meaningful, and valid? In the humanities, information written hundreds of years ago is still valid. This is not true of the social sciences or STEM disciplines where recent publications are preferred over past studies.

> When was the information collected, published, or provided online?
> Does information on this topic change frequently?
> Does your topic require current information?

INCORPORATING AND ACKNOWLEDGING YOUR SOURCES

③ Avoid plagiarism by properly incorporating and acknowledging sources.

Gathering and Organizing Sources

Once you have selected the sources best suited for your topic, you will need printouts of any online article for highlighting and note taking. If you are using a book or a magazine in its original form, you will need to photocopy the relevant pages. There are, of course, many digital applications that will allow you to save and annotate PDFs, should you desire to keep your materials digital.

Your instructor may want to see a preliminary list of your potential sources. There are two great ways to organize your sources. One method is to use 4" × 6" note cards. Another, more popular method is to use a digital tool to store your research. Many of these tools are free and allow you to store digital sources, make notes, and organize. Such tools can be found at *zotero.org, evernote.com,* and *easybib.com. Be sure to follow your instructor's guidelines.*

Taking Notes and Acknowledging Your Sources

When you take notes from one of your sources and use the information in your paper, you must acknowledge the source. This acknowledgment is called **documentation**. When you provide documentation within a research essay, you are using an **internal citation**. At the end of your essay, you list all the sources you cited within the paper. This list is called the **Works Cited** (although some styles guides refer to it as the **Bibliography** or **References**). The list of works cited is on a separate page and is the last numbered page of the essay.

Using Sources

There are three different ways to incorporate sources into your writing.

1. A quote
2. A summary
3. A paraphrase

A **quote** repeats exactly what the source states. It is common to begin with the author's name, followed by a signal verb (also called a reporting verb). For example:

> Leigh and Geyer note that the "safest and most reliable identification is provided by a combination of an ID tag, which is easily visible, and a microchip, which is permanent" (2).

A **summary** includes only the scope or main idea(s) found in the source, and it should be written solely in your own words. When summarizing a work's overarching scope or argument as illustrated in the following example, you do not need to provide a specific page number because the entire work is used to establish that summarized point. If, however, you are summarizing a specific concept, idea, revelation, or passage from the work (as in the previous example), it is important to provide the specific location in the work.

Here is an example of a summary statement (no internal citation is necessary):

> In *One at a Time: A Week in an American Animal Shelter*, Leigh and Geyer describe the fate of seventy-five animals who passed through a local shelter in Northern California over a seven-day period.

A **paraphrase** can include main ideas, details, and even examples found in the source. A paraphrase is written in your own words, and it is approximately the same length as the original statement(s) from the source. Sentences or short passages are paraphrased.

> A clearly marked ID tag, along with a permanent microchip, provides an animal with the best and safest means of identification (Leigh and Geyer 2).

Deciding when to quote or paraphrase can sometimes be a difficult decision. It is best to quote when the source has a distinctive way of saying something. Although it may be easier to quote, a paraphrase demonstrates your understanding of the source.

Avoiding Plagiarism

Plagiarism occurs when you use a source's words or ideas and fail to give proper credit to the author or source of the work. Even if you paraphrase (state someone else's ideas in your own wording), you must give credit to the original source.

Whether you summarize material from an outside source, quote directly from it, or even paraphrase from it, you must acknowledge the source. Failure to do so is a form of academic theft. Penalties for plagiarism are severe, ranging from receiving a failing grade on the plagiarized paper or failing a course, to expulsion. Some departments now use special software programs to check all student papers for plagiarism.

④ Cite works in MLA documentation style.

Options for Acknowledging Your Sources: MLA Format

The **Modern Language Association (MLA) system of documentation** is preferred by English instructors. In the following discussion, you will see how MLA documentation is used for summarizing, paraphrasing, and directly quoting information from sources. *You will also see how sources should be listed on a Works Cited page.*

MLA In-Text Citations When using internal (or in-text) citations, you have several options. If you use a combination of techniques, your paper will read more smoothly. Notice that authors or page numbers appear in parentheses, and this form is called **parenthetical documentation**.

A Summary Statement of a Book's Subject or Scope

One at a Time: A Week in an American Animal Shelter describes the fate of seventy-five animals who passed through a local shelter in Northern California over a seven-day period (Leigh and Geyer).

No page numbers or other documentation are necessary for a summary statement because the work's entire scope is summarized. MLA style uses italics rather than underlining for all titles of published works and names of in-text Web sites (e.g., *Pet Finder*).

A Direct Quotation

According to Leigh and Geyer, "The safest and most reliable identification is provided by a combination of an ID tag, which is easily visible, and a microchip, which is permanent" (2).

If you do not introduce the author before you quote from his or her work, you must put the author's name in parentheses at the end of the quoted material. In this case, there are two authors. Both of their names could be placed in parentheses, as follows: (Leigh and Geyer 2). Notice that the period goes *after* the closing parenthesis.

A Paraphrase

A clearly marked ID tag, along with a permanent microchip, provides an animal with the best and safest means of identification (Leigh and Geyer 2).

A Combination of a Direct Quote and a Paraphrase

Leigh and Geyer emphasize that the best means of identification for an animal is "provided by a combination of an ID tag, which is easily visible, and a microchip, which is permanent" (2).

A Source Quoted in Another Author's Work

Kathy Nicklas-Varraso, author of *What to Expect from Breed Rescue*, notes that adopters will "most often get an adult whose chewing phase, housebreaking phase, and general puppy wildness are gone" (qtd. in Mohr).

Nicklas-Varraso is the author being quoted; her comment was found in an online magazine article by Mohr. Mohr is the source that the student writer found. Therefore, Mohr is the source cited in parentheses and in the Works Cited list. No page numbers are cited when the article comes from an online source.

Signal Verbs and Signal Phrases

Several preceding examples use either **signal verbs** or **signal phrases** (also called **reporting verbs** or **reporting phrases**) to introduce quoted or paraphrased material. Using signal verbs (such as "Leigh and Geyer *emphasize*") and signal phrases (such as "*According to* Leigh and Geyer") enable you to lead smoothly into documented information.

Each signal verb has a unique function, so choose carefully. For example, if you are using the source to persuade, you may use "Smith emphasizes" or "Smith argues." If you are using the source to show disagreement, you may use "Smith disputes" or "Smith refutes."

INFO BOX **Verbs in Signal Phrases**

acknowledges	comments	grants	rejects
adds	compares	implies	reports
admits	confirms	insists	responds
addresses	contends	illustrates	suggests
agrees	declares	notes	thinks
argues	denies	observes	writes
asserts	disputes	points out	
believes	emphasizes	reasons	
claims	endorses	refutes	

Documenting Information from a Source with an Unknown Author

If there is no author listed for a source, you can introduce the full title of the work after a signal phrase or place an abbreviation of the title in parentheses at the end of the information cited. For example, you can choose either of the following forms:

An Unknown Author

As the article "The Rules of Local Zoning Boards" notes, many counties prohibit businesses from operating out of garages in residential communities (C1).

or

Many counties prohibit businesses from operating out of garages in residential communities ("Rules" C1).

When your source is a newspaper article, as in the previous examples, give the section of the newspaper and the page number, as in C1, which stands for section C, page 1. Article titles are placed within quotation marks; book titles are placed in italics according to MLA style.

Exercise 1 **Practice: Paraphrasing from Sources**

Paraphrase each of the short excerpts that follow and include the appropriate parenthetical documentation. Use a signal phrase in at least one of the excerpts you paraphrase. The first excerpt is done for you and shows two options.

1. "A dog's sense of smell is not only exquisitely sensitive, but it communicates with a brain that can make fine discriminations among scents and learn new ones when they become important." (from *How Dogs Think*, by Stanley Coren, page 63)

   paraphrase (no signal phrase): Dogs have a keen sense of smell that enables the brain to distinguish between scents and remember new ones (Coren 63).

   or

   paraphrase (with a signal phrase): Coren notes that dogs have a very sensitive sense of smell that enables the brain to recognize and remember important scents (63).

2. "The world is full of damaged dogs who desperately need homes. Lots of wonderful people rescue them, and those people deserve our heartfelt appreciation. Patience and hard work can go a long way to rehabilitate dogs damaged in their youth by unstable environments." (from *For the Love of a Dog*, by Patricia O'Connelly, page 87)

   paraphrase: _____

   _____

   _____

3. "The sniffing ritual is designed in part to help dogs establish who has the more forceful personality and deserves extra respect. This is an

essential component of all of their introductions as well as the interactions that follow." (from *The Secret Lives of Dogs*, by Jane Murphy, page 64)

paraphrase (Use a combination of paraphrasing and direct quoting in your version.): _____

_____

_____

_____

WORKS CITED ENTRIES: MLA FORMAT (EIGHTH EDITION)

The Works Cited list of sources contains only the works you cited in your paper. This alphabetized list is the last page of your essay and is numbered accordingly. **On the Works Cited page, entries should be double spaced, and the second and subsequent lines of each entry should be indented five spaces.** This is called a hanging indentation. **Double-space between each entry.**

A General Primer

In 2016, the Modern Language Association changed their guidelines and created a new, more universal approach to citing sources in a research paper. The key reason for this change was the way in which we collect information in the twenty-first century. Student researchers still use their school's library for print resources, but today much of our research occurs online. As such, we use an array of search engines, subscription services, and other mediums from which to collect information. The MLA's streamlined approach to citation and documentation helps to create a uniform, universal, and flexible approach to documentation.

Containers One of the key facets of the new MLA approach to documentation is the concept of containers. A container is simply a place to hold things, and in the world of research, a container is a place that holds a source of information. For example, if you are citing a magazine article, the magazine itself is the container of that article. The same would hold true of a short story found in an anthology or an editorial found in a newspaper. The anthology and the newspaper would be containers.

There are also larger containers that hold multiple smaller containers such as journals, magazines, newspapers, and more. For example, you might locate a magazine article through a large subscription service like JSTOR. Although the original magazine in which the article was published is its first container, the larger subscription service like JSTOR represents a secondary, larger container.

Conceptually, these containers help a reader to locate a writer's source quickly. A general template to use when creating a Works Cited entry follows. When creating a works cited entry for your paper, the information must be provided in the prescribed order. Not every element, however, will be in every entry. Additionally, specific punctuation must be used with each piece of information.

Order of Information for Core Elements in a Works Cited Entry

1. Author
2. Title
3. Container 1 (first container such as a periodical, magazine, journal, Web site, or book or anthology)
   a. Other contributors
   b. Version
   c. Number
   d. Publisher
   e. Publication date
   f. Location
4. Container 2 (secondary, larger container, such as a subscription service)
   a. Other contributors
   b. Version
   c. Number
   d. Publisher
   e. Publication date
   f. Location

Basic Formatting of Core Elements in a Works Cited Entry

- **Author:** Author is listed last name first and followed by a period. When there are two authors, the second author is listed first name first. When there are three or more authors, the first author is listed last name first followed by et al., which means *and others*.
- **Title of the Source:** The title of the source is written in italics (for example, books, plays, pamphlets, periodicals, Web sites, films) or in quotation marks (for example, magazine articles, essays, stories, speeches, chapters of books, individual pages of a Web site) and followed by a period. When using quotation marks, the period goes inside of the final quotation mark.
- **Title of the First Container:** This container refers to the book, anthology, journal, magazine, or Web site in which the source appears. The title of the container is italicized and followed by a comma.
- **Other Contributors:** Sometime sources have additional editors, translators, illustrators, or other contributors. If this is the case, include this information first name first and follow it with a comma. Do not abbreviate terms like editor, contributor, or translator.
- **Version:** If your source is, for example, an abridged version or an updated version, be sure to provide this information. Follow the edition number with a comma. You may abbreviate edition.
- **Number:** Periodicals are often organized by volume and number. Volume refers to the circulation year of publication. Number (or issue) refers to the specific publication within a circulation year. Follow the number with a comma.
- **Publisher:** The publisher is the organization responsible for publishing, producing, or distributing the material. Follow the publisher with a comma. Please note that you no longer have to include the publisher city, as per older MLA guidelines.

- **Publication Date:** This is simply the date of publication, associated most frequently with printed materials. If no location is provided (see explanation of location below), then place a period after the publication date.
- **Location:** Location refers to the page number or range of page numbers, if provided.
- **Title of the Secondary Container:** Many periodicals and academic journals can be retrieved through online subscription services such as JSTOR, EBSCO, or Lexis Nexus. These subscription services are examples of larger containers that hold smaller containers.

  Please note that it is important to provide information about the original container before you provide information about the larger container.
- **Other Contributors:** See Other Contributors in Title of First Container, but apply to the larger container. Follow with a comma.
- **Version:** See Version in Title of First Container, but apply to the larger container. Follow with a comma.
- **Number:** See Number in Title of First Container, but apply to the larger container. Follow with a comma.
- **Publisher:** See Publisher in Title of First Container, but apply to the larger container. Follow with a comma.
- **Publication Date:** See Publication Date in Title of First Container, but apply to the larger container. Follow with a comma.
- **Location:** Unlike page numbers in printed material, with subscription services, location is a URL or a DOI.

COMMON EXAMPLES OF PRINT SOURCES IN WORKS CITED

Books

> **Book by One Author**
>
> Zheutlin, Peter. *Rescue Road: One Man, Thirty-Thousand Dogs, and a Million Miles on the Last Hope Highway*. Thorndike, 2016.

Thorndike is the publisher, and 2016 is the year of publication. Short forms of the publisher's name should be used, so "Inc.," "Co.," and "Books" can be omitted.

> **Book by Two Authors**
>
> Leigh, Diane, and Marilee Geyer. *One at a Time: A Week in an American Animal Shelter*. No Voice Unheard, 2003.

No Voice Unheard is the publisher, and 2003 is the year of publication.

Short Work in an Anthology

Wong, Edward. "A Long Overdue Apology." *Tales from the Times*, edited by Lisa Belkin, St. Martin's Griffin, 2004, 29–34.

An anthology is a book-length collection of short works such as articles, essays, poems, or short stories. It usually has at least one editor who compiles and organizes the short works by different authors. When you are citing from an anthology, begin with the author of the short work and its title; then list the name of the anthology and its editor. At the end of the entry, list the page numbers of the short work.

Introduction from a Book

Curtis, Jamie Lee. Foreword. *Second Chances: More Tales of Found Dogs*, by Elise Lufkin, Lyons, 2003, ix–x.

Foreword refers to the section, in this case an introduction, of the book cited. Curtis is the author of the book, *Second Chances: More Tales of Found Dogs*, and Lufkin is the author of the book's foreward.

Periodicals

Periodicals are newspapers, magazines, and scholarly journals. In Works Cited listings, all months except May, June, and July are abbreviated.

Newspaper Article

Caldwell, Tanya. "Boca Names Its New Dog Park." *South Florida Sun-Sentinel*, 10 Aug. 2005, B1+.

B1 refers to the section (B) and page number (1) of the article. The plus sign (+) means that the article was continued on another page.

Newspaper Editorial

"Disaster Aid." Editorial, *South Florida Sun-Sentinel*, 9 Aug. 2005, A10.

Newspaper editorials, if written by an editorial board, do not list an author.

Magazine Article (From a Monthly or Bimonthly Publication)

Richard, Julie. "The Lost Tigers of China." *Best Friends*, Mar. 2005, pp. 27–29.

Best Friends is the name of the monthly publication.

Magazine Article (From a Weekly Publication)

Boks, Ed. "The Dirty Little Secret in Your Community." *Newsweek*, 27 June 2005, p. 15.

Journal Article

Laderman-Jones, B.E., et al. "Survey of Animal Shelter Managers Regarding Shelter Veterinary Medical Services." *Veterinary Journal*, vol. 210, April 2016, pp. 68–76.

The number 210 is the volume number, and April 2016 is the publication date.

COMMON EXAMPLES OF ONLINE SOURCES IN WORKS CITED

Online sources can include professional Web sites and online periodicals. When you list a Web site as one of your sources, one component that you will need to add to your entry is the date you accessed the online source. This should be included at the end of the entry after the location. Make sure you end your date accessed with a period.

Web Sites

Entire Web Site

Humane Society of the United States. Humane Society of the United States, 2014, http://www.humanesociety.org. Accessed 20 Apr. 2017.

In this example, the sponsoring organization, the Humane Society of the United States, is also the group author of the site; 2014 is the date of the Web site's most recent update. The second date is the date of access by the user.

Article or Short Work

Mohr, Lori. "Adopting from a Breed Rescue Group." *Animal Forum*, June 2006, http://www.animalforum.com/forumdisplay.php/18-Adopt-A-Pet. Accessed 23 Apr. 2017.

In this example, the Web site, *Animal Forum*, is the first container for the article "Adopting from a Breed Rescue Group."

Online Periodicals

Article from an Online Journal

Van Eenennaam, Alison L. "GMOs in Animal Agriculture: Time to Consider Both Costs and Benefits in Regulatory Evaluations." *Journal of Animal Science*, vol. 4, no. 1, 2013, p. 1, https://doi.org/10.1186/2049-1891-4-37. Accessed 1 May 2017.

Although most journal articles are accessed via subscription services, you still might access some directly from the journal's Web site. In the example at the bottom of the previous page, notice that the article in its print form was on page 1. However, you also need to include a URL, as well as the access date.

Article from an Online Magazine

Woolf, Norma Bennett. "Getting Involved in Purebred Rescue." *Dog Owner's Guide*. Canis Major Publications, 18 May 2005, http://www.canismajor.com/dog/rescinv.html. Accessed 20 Apr. 2017.

Article from an Online Newspaper

Hoffman, Jan. "Is This Dog Dangerous? Shelters Struggle with Live-or-Die Tests." *New York Times*, 1 Aug. 2017, D1, https://nyti.ms/2udddst. Accessed 1 May 2017.

COMMON EXAMPLES OF SOURCES FROM SUBSCRIPTION SERVICES IN WORKS CITED

Subscription services such as JSTOR and EBSCO are useful because they provide users with access to articles from diverse periodicals, including everything from popular magazines to scholarly journals. Many subscription services are using DOIs to locate an online resource. However, many other subscription services are still using URLs to locate resources. When conducting research using a subscription service, it is important to note the DOI or URL for the source you will be using.

Journal Article from a Subscription Service Using a DOI

Gunter, Lisa M., et al. "What's in a Name? Effect of Breed Perceptions and Labeling on Attractiveness, Adoptions, and Length of Stay for Pit-Bull-Type Dogs." PLoS ONE, vol. 11, no. 3, 23 Mar. 2016, pp. 1–9. EBSCOhost, doi:10.1371/journal.prone.0146857.

If you use one of your library's online subscription services, you can first follow the same format as for a print periodical, but you will need to add the name of the subscription service (as the larger, secondary container), a DOI or URL, and the date you accessed the article. In the preceding example, PLoS ONE is the first container. EBSCOhost is the secondary container.

Periodical Article from a Subscription Service Using a URL

Boks, Ed. "The Dirty Little Secret in Your Community." *Newsweek*, vol. 145, no. 26. 27 June 2005, p. 15, EBSCOhost, search.ebscohost.com/login.aspx?direct=true&db=a9h&AN=17393041&site= ehost-live. Accessed 1 May 2017.

The preceding example is the same article originally published in *Newsweek*. The first container is *Newsweek*, and the larger container is EBSCOhost. Note that this example uses a URL rather than a DOI.

Exercise 2   **Practice: Creating Works Cited Entries**

Arrange the items in the source information provided in correct MLA format. Consult the "Works Cited Entries" section starting on page 345.

1. **Book**
   Publisher: Free Press
   Author: Stanley Coren
   Title of Source: How Dogs Think
   Publication Date: 2002

   _____

   _____

2. **Magazine Article** (from a monthly publication)
   Title of Source: The Pug Who Came to Dinner
   Author: Gail MacMillan
   Title of First Container: Bark
   Location: 67–69
   Publication Date: March 2007

   _____

   _____

3. **Article from a Web Site**
   Name of Web Site: Vet Street
   Author: Kim Campbell Thornton
   Title of Source: Shelter Intervention Programs: What Are They and How They Help Pets
   Publication Date: December 9, 2016
   Web Site Address: www.vetstreet.com/our-pet-experts/shelter-intervention-programs-what-they-are-and-how-they-help-pets?page=2&WT.mc_id=ETA
   Date of Access: October 17, 2017

   _____

   _____

   _____

4. **Article from an Online Newspaper**
   Name of Online Newspaper: Los Angeles Times
   Author: Veronica Rocha
   Title of the Source: L.A. Closer to 'No Kill' Animal Shelters as Euthanization Rates Drop
   Publication Date: April 26, 2016
   Location: www.latimes.com/local/lanow/la-me-ln-la-no-kill-animal-shelters-20160426-story.html
   Date of Access: August 7, 2017

   _____

   _____

   _____

5. Periodical Article from a Subscription Service
Name of Subscription Service: EBSCOhost
Author: Alisa Bowman
Title of the Source: The Adoption Option
Title of First Container: Prevention
Publication Date: May 2015
Number: Volume 67, Number 5
Location (First Container): pages 126–129
Location (Secondary Container): search.ebscohost.com/login.aspx
?direct=true&db=a9h&AN=102052079&site= ehost-live.

_____

_____

_____

6. Journal Article from a Subscription Service
Name of Subscription Service: JSTOR
Author(s) David S. Tuber and others
Title of the Source: Dogs in Animal Shelters: Problems,
Suggestions, and Needed Expertise
Title of First Container: Psychological Science
Publication Date: 1999
Number: Volume 10, Number 5
Location (First Container): pages 379–386
Location (Secondary Container): www.jstor.org/stable/40063451

_____

_____

_____

⑤ Prepare a final version of an essay with research.

INCORPORATING RESEARCH INTO YOUR OUTLINE

After you have compiled all of your notes from your sources, you need to determine what information you will use and where it best fits into your essay. The best way to do this is to work with your original outline before you draft a research version of your essay. Here again is the outline for the dog-rescue essay. This version now includes references to sources; *key information from these sources will be the research that strengthens the essay.*

Notice that the headings "Introduction" and "Conclusion" have been added to the outline. In this version, the writer wanted to include some relevant research in both the introductory and concluding paragraphs as well as in the body paragraphs, so he expanded his outline. By placing research references in the outline, the student writer will know where the new information will be included when he prepares the drafts and final version of his research essay.

> **Note:** The references to the added research appear in bold print so that you can compare this outline to the previous one on page 336.

Outline for an Essay with Research

I. Introduction
  A. Six to eight million dogs and cats are placed in shelters each year; three to four million are euthanized. **See Humane Society, source #2.**

B. Some shelters euthanize animals routinely. **See Leigh and Geyer, source #3.**

C. Some shelters work with rescue groups.
Thesis Statement: Dog-rescue organizations perform a humane service by saving homeless dogs and matching responsible adopters with a devoted new family member.

II. Dog-rescue volunteers play several roles.

A. Some volunteers are "spotters" who look for specific breeds at local shelters.

B. Experienced rescue volunteers may become coordinators and arrange assistance from various sources. **See Woolfe, source #5.**

C. Volunteers work with national organizations such as Adopt-a-Pet and Petfinder.com, which maintain databases of adoptable dogs from rescue groups throughout the United States and Canada.

D. Volunteers assist at rescue-dog "Adoption Days" hosted by pet supply chains such as Petco and PetSmart.

III. Rescue groups provide important information and benefits for prospective adopters.

A. By viewing a rescue group's Web site, potential adopters can read about a dog's age, temperament, adoption fee, and any special medical conditions.

B. If a potential adopter does not find a suitable dog, he or she can still complete an online application.

C. On an application, a potential adopter can list his or her preferences for the age, gender, and size of the dog.

D. Although some dogs are puppies rescued from abusive situations, most are adult dogs already socialized and housebroken. **See Nicklas-Varraso in Mohr, source #4.**

IV. Careful screening often results in a successful adoption.

A. Rescue groups routinely conduct home visits to check the living conditions and the neighborhood.

B. The applicant must have access to veterinary care.

C. The applicant must agree to return the dog to the rescue organization if he or she can no longer care for the animal.

D. A foster parent can fully inform the adoptive parent about potential adjustment problems.

E. Careful attention to such details leads to a winning adoption process.

V. Conclusion

A. Rescue groups provide an opportunity for a dog to live out the rest of its life free from harm and neglect.

B. We should "embrace non-lethal strategies" to show we are a humane society. **See Boks, source #1.**

Concluding Statement: Rescue groups not only provide care for homeless dogs; they also remind us of the joy made possible by compassionate adoption.

A Draft of an Essay with Research

The following is a rough version of the original essay strengthened with material from outside sources (underlined). The marginal annotations will alert you to (1) places where the information is directly quoted or paraphrased, and (2) places where editing is necessary to achieve a better style.

Draft of an Essay with Research

(Note: Blue marginal notes refer to underlined portions; editing and proofreading are still necessary.)

The Humane Work of Dog-Rescue Groups

statistic and paraphrased statement from online source as part of introduction

Although the United States is generally regarded as a country that loves and pampers its pets, animal shelters are often filled to capacity with dogs that have been abandoned, abused, or surrendered by their owners. Each year, six to eight million dogs and cats are placed in shelters, and three to four million of them are euthanized (*Humane Society*). Sadly, some shelters routinely euthanize healthy dogs if no one claims or adopts them after a grace period ranging from just days to a few weeks.

direct quotation from the preface of a book with two authors

These dogs have only "about a fifty percent chance of getting out alive" (Leigh and Geyer viii). Fortunately, however, many shelters work closely with dog-rescue organizations that find loving, temporary homes where foster parents can provide care and, if necessary, rehabilitation. Staffed by dedicated volunteers, rescue groups perform a humane service by saving homeless dogs and enabling responsible adopters to gain a devoted new family member.

From rescuing retired greyhounds to saving mini "mutts," dog-rescue volunteers play several roles. For example, they often serve as "spotters" at local shelters, looking for dogs that can be fostered by individuals who specialize in specific breeds such as boxers and golden retrievers. Experienced volunteers may become coordinators who arrange for assistance from a variety of sources, including local veterinarians, groomers, transporters, and Web site designers.

direct quotation from an online magazine; sentence combining needed

Norma Bennett Woolf writes for the online magazine *Dog Owner's Guide*. Woolf states, "There's always room for more foster homes, fund-raisers, dog spotters, kennels, public relations workers, and trainers." Many rescue groups work closely with national organizations such as Adopt-a-Pet and Petfinder.com, whose Web sites publish comprehensive lists of adoptable rescue dogs throughout the United States and Canada. On weekends, rescue volunteers can be seen helping out during "Adoption Days" sponsored by national chains, including Petco and PetSmart.

Rescue groups provide both crucial information and welcome benefits for potential adopters. When one becomes interested in a specific dog on a rescue group's Web site, he or she can read about the animal's medical needs, age, temperament, and adoption fee. Even if he or she does not spot a suitable dog but remains interested in adopting one from rescue, he or she can fill out an application and list preferences regarding a dog's age, gender, and size. Although rescue groups occasionally receive puppies and young dogs that have been picked up during police raids of abusive puppy mills and backyard breeders, the majority of dogs available for adoption are older ones.

a source quoted in another author's work; needs to blend more smoothly

Kathy Nicklas-Varraso wrote *What to Expect from Breed Rescue*. This writer says, "You'll most often get an adult whose chewing phase, housebreaking phase, and general puppy wildness are gone" (qtd. in Mohr).

Any pet owner who has experienced the aggravation of sleepless nights and numerous housetraining "accidents" can appreciate the benefits of adopting an older, socialized, and housebroken dog.

Although the adoption process may take several weeks or even months to find the best match, careful screening improves the chances for a successful adoption. Rescue groups routinely conduct home visits of prospective dog owners to see if both the living conditions and the neighborhood will be suitable for the dog's size, temperament, and exercise needs. In addition, the applicant must have access to veterinary care and agree to return the dog to the rescue organization if he or she can no longer properly care for it. A foster parent can fully inform the adoptive parent about a dog's potential adjustment problems because the animal's behavior has been observed over a period of weeks— if not months—in a home setting. Nicklas-Varraso states, "Borderline pets are offered for adoption within strict guidelines, such as no other pets or fenced yards only" (qtd. in Mohr). Careful attention to such details leads to a winning adoption process.

However a dog finds its way to a rescue group—by an owner surrender, a good Samaritan, or even by a police raid of an illegal breeding operation—it will have an opportunity to live out the rest of its life free from harm and neglect. Ed Boks is director of Animal Care and Control for New York City. He believes that we should "embrace preventive, non-lethal strategies that reveal that at our core we truly are a humane society" (15). Rescue groups not only follow Boks's advice by providing care for homeless dogs; they also remind us of the joy made possible by compassion, commitment, and unconditional love.

Margin note (left): direct quote; needs a transition

Margin note (left): print source is a magazine; sentence combining needed; put Boks's name in a signal phrase

Note: A Works Cited page will be included in the final version of this essay.

PREPARING THE FINAL VERSION OF AN ESSAY WITH RESEARCH

Making Final Changes and Refinements

The final version of the research essay includes the refinements suggested in the margins of the previous draft. The final essay reflects proper MLA format. Other improvements relate to the style of the essay. Changes include the following:

- The title has been changed to be more descriptive and appealing.
- Information from sources has been more smoothly blended by sentence combining and the use of signal phrases.
- An awkward repetition of *he or she* has been changed to the more specific term *a potential adopter* in the third paragraph.
- The word *humane* has been added in the last paragraph to reinforce the idea of compassionate care for animals.

- To conform to MLA format, the writer has placed his name, his instructor's name, the course title, and the date in the upper left-hand corner of the first page.
- Again following MLA style, the writer has placed his last name and page number in the upper right-hand corner of each page of the essay.
- A Works Cited page, in proper MLA format, is included and appears as the last page of the essay.

Note: Pages in the sample paper are not 8 ½ × 11 standard size. MLA format requires margins of at least one inch but no more than an inch and a half on all sides of the page. The last page of the sample paper (Works Cited page) has been abbreviated for space considerations.

Roberts 1

Jason Roberts

Professor Alvarez

English 100

7 May 2017

Crusading for Canines:

Dog-Rescue Groups and Winning Adoptions

Although the United States is generally regarded as a country that loves and pampers its pets, animal shelters are often filled to capacity with dogs that have been abandoned, abused, or surrendered by their owners. Each year, six to eight million dogs are placed in shelters, and three to four million of them are euthanized (*Humane Society*). Sadly, some shelters routinely euthanize healthy dogs if no one claims or adopts them after a grace period ranging from just days to a few weeks. These dogs have only "about a fifty percent chance of getting out alive" (Leigh and Geyer viii). Fortunately, however, many shelters work closely with dog-rescue organizations that find loving, temporary homes where foster parents can provide care and, if necessary, rehabilitation. Staffed by dedicated volunteers, rescue groups perform a humane service by saving homeless dogs and enabling responsible adopters to gain a devoted new family member.

From rescuing retired greyhounds to saving mini "mutts," dog-rescue volunteers play several roles. For example, they often serve as "spotters" at local shelters, looking for dogs that can be fostered by individuals who specialize in specific breeds such as boxers and golden retrievers. Experienced volunteers may become coordinators who arrange for assistance from a variety of sources, including local veterinarians, groomers, transporters, and Web site designers. As Norma Bennett Woolf suggests in the online magazine *Dog Owner's Guide*, "There's always room for more foster homes, fund-raisers, dog-spotters, kennels, public relations workers, and trainers." Many rescue groups work closely with national organizations such as Adopt-a-Pet and Petfinder, whose Web sites publish comprehensive lists of adoptable rescue dogs throughout the United States and Canada. On weekends, rescue volunteers can be seen helping out during "Adoption Days" sponsored by national chains, including Petco and PetSmart.

Rescue groups provide both crucial information and welcome benefits for potential adopters. When one becomes interested in a specific dog on a rescue group's Web site, he or she can read about the animal's medical needs, age, temperament, and adoption fee. Even if a potential adopter does not spot a suitable dog but remains interested in adopting one from rescue, he or she can fill out an application and list preferences regarding a dog's age, gender, and size. Although rescue groups occasionally receive puppies and young dogs that have been picked up during police raids of abusive puppy mills and backyard breeders, the majority of dogs available for adoption are older ones. Kathy Nicklas-Varraso, author of *What to Expect from Breed Rescue*, notes that adopters will "most often get an adult whose chewing phase, housebreaking phase, and general puppy wildness are gone" (qtd. in Mohr). Any pet owner who has experienced the aggravation of sleepless nights and numerous housetraining "accidents" can appreciate the benefits of adopting an older, socialized, and housebroken dog.

Although the adoption process may take several weeks or even months to find the best match, careful screening improves the chances for a successful adoption. Rescue groups routinely conduct home visits of prospective dog owners to see if both the living conditions and the neighborhood will be suitable for the dog's size, temperament, and exercise needs. In addition, the applicant must have access to veterinary care and agree to return the dog to the rescue organization if he or she can no longer properly care for it. A foster parent can fully inform the adoptive parent about a dog's potential adjustment problems because the animal's behavior has been observed over a period of weeks—if not months—in a home setting. Nicklas-Varraso stresses that the "borderline pets are offered for adoption within strict guidelines, such as no other pets or fenced yards only" (qtd. in Mohr). Careful attention to such details leads to a winning adoption process.

However a dog finds its way to a rescue group—by an owner surrender, a good Samaritan, or even by a police raid of an illegal breeding operation—it will have an opportunity to live out the rest of its life free from harm and neglect. Ed Boks, director of Animal Care and Control for New York City, urges us to "embrace preventive, non-lethal strategies that reveal that at our core, we truly are a humane society" (15). Rescue groups not only provide humane care for homeless dogs; they also remind us of the joy made possible by compassion, commitment, and unconditional love.

Roberts 4

Works Cited

Boks, Ed. "The Dirty Little Secret in Your Community." *Newsweek*, vol. 145,

no. 26. 27 June 2005, p. 15, EBSCOhost, search.ebscohost.com/login

.aspx?direct=true&db=a9h&AN=17393041&site =ehost-live. Accessed 1

May 2017.

Humane Society of the United States. Humane Society of the United States,

2014, http://www.humanesociety.org. Accessed 20 Apr. 2017.

Leigh, Diane, and Marilee Geyer. *One at a Time: A Week in an American*

Animal Shelter. No Voice Unheard, 2003.

Mohr, Lori. "Adopting from a Breed Rescue Group." *Animal Forum*, June

2006, http://www.animalforum.com/forumdisplay.php/18-Adopt-A-Pet.

Accessed 23 Apr. 2017.

Woolf, Norma Bennett. "Getting Involved in Purebred Rescue." *Dog Owner's*

Guide. Canis Major Publications, 18 May 2005, http://www.canismajor.

com/dog/rescinv.html. 20 Apr. 2017.

More Options for Acknowledging Your Sources: APA Format

6 Cite works in APA documentation style.

In the previous pages, we covered how to use the MLA system of documentation for papers in the humanities. But other major systems of documentation serve other fields of study, and you might be required to use a system other than MLA in some of your classes. The **American Psychological Association (APA) system of documentation** is the most commonly used format for papers in the social sciences (psychology, anthropology, social work, etc.).

Let's start with how APA documentation writers in the social sciences summarize, paraphrase, and directly quote information from their sources. In addition to understanding how to format these in-text citations using APA style, you will see how those sources are listed in a **References** list (similar to the Works Cited page in the MLA system) that gives the complete documentation for all the sources you cited in your paper.

APA In-Text Citations You'll find that both the APA and MLA documentation systems share a common feature: they both have in-text citations corresponding to a list of sources at the end of the paper. But the format of these in-text citations is not the same in APA format as it is in MLA format.

In APA format, an in-text citation has two main parts—the author or authors of a source and the publication year. For example, for a journal article written by Cornelia Guell and published in December 2019, the main elements to use in your in-text citation are *Guell* and *2019*. (Although you don't need to give the rest of the source information, such as the journal title, within the rest of your paper, you do need to provide it in a References list at the end of your paper.)

CRITICAL THINKING

Dates are important in APA format because much of the information conveyed in a research paper demands current, relevant information. One way writers convey the currency of the information they are using is by placing it in parentheses in the signal phrase introducing the information. You will see this in action in the first example of an in-text citation. If you are researching a topic in the field of psychology, you will want to communicate to your audience that you are using the most current research to support your claims.

APA in-text citations always include the author(s) and the year. The way you provide your readers with this information, however, depends on how you construct your sentences. Basically, you should include within parentheses any author or date information that you did not mention in your actual sentence. Here are some examples of APA in-text citations and how they can vary:

Author Name Included in Your Sentence

According to Kottak (2010), cultural notions of what a woman should look like can influence what competitive sport she chooses to pursue.

No Author Name(s) in Your Sentence

Cultural notions of what a woman should look like can influence what competitive sport she chooses to pursue (Kottak, 2010).

Notice that a comma is placed between the author and the year of the work's publication, unlike MLA format, which does not use the comma.

Two or More Sources Cited Within the Same Sentence

According to two similar studies of Brazilian culture (Kottak, 2010; Sanchez, 2014), body image can have far-reaching influences on women's lives.

If you cite more than one work in your sentence, list the sources in alphabetical order and separate them with semicolons.

Two Author Names Included in Your Sentence

Sanchez and Steinman (2014) argue that a desire to imitate the cultural ideal of female beauty causes young women to avoid physical activity, such as strenuous sports, that might develop their muscles in a way that is considered masculine.

Two Author Names Included in Your Parenthetical Citation

Because competitive swimming develops the upper body, parents consider it too masculine for girls (Sanchez & Steinman, 2014).

Combine two author names with an ampersand.

Three to Five Authors

Jolliffe, Klipfel, and Rice (2017) emphasize that conformity is a common feature of fads, fashion, mores, and custom.

or

Jolliffe et al. (2017) observed that individuals often imitate others without stopping to think about their own experiences.

Name all authors at first mention, and then give just the last name of the first author, followed by et al., which means *and others*. For six or more authors, give just the last name of the first author, followed by et al.

A Source without an Author

Women in college sports "have yet to reach parity with men," given that only about one-third of college athletes are women ("Empowering Women," 2014).

Use the first two or three main words of the title. In this case, the title is of a Web page, so it is in quotation marks.

REFERENCE LIST ENTRIES: APA FORMAT

Writers of papers in both MLA and APA documentation styles always include a list, placed at the end of the paper, that contains all of the sources cited in the paper. Like the MLA Works Cited page, the APA References list includes the complete publication information for each source. This information helps readers locate your original sources.

Key Components of a Reference List Entry

You will supply readers with the following key components:

- Author(s) full name(s)
- Date published (if none given, write *n.d.* in parentheses, without italics)
- Title of work

- Publication information (such as publisher name and location)
- Page numbers (as a range) for articles
- The APA style guide, *unlike* MLA, does not require database information (like EBSCOhost or JSTOR) as information and database holdings may change over time.
- For online sources, such as journal articles on the Internet, include either the URL for the source, or instead, if it is provided, the DOI (digital object identifier).

Basic Formatting of a Reference List Entry

Although the basic components of the MLA Works Cited list and the APA References list are the same, the way you arrange information within an entry is different. Take a look at the following guidelines for organizing your APA References list entries:

- Entries are alphabetical by author last name. (Use initials only for first and middle names.)
- If an entry has no author, arrange it alphabetically by the first main word of the title.
- Place the publication year in parentheses after the author names, followed by a period.
- Italicize titles, but capitalize only the first word of the title, the first word of the subtitle, and any proper nouns.
- All entries should be double-spaced.

Now that you know the key parts of an APA reference and some of the ways the entries can be arranged, take a look at the following examples of how you would enter specific types of sources in a References list.

COMMON EXAMPLES OF PRINT SOURCES IN A REFERENCE LIST

Book

Winzeler, R. L. (2012). *Anthropology and religion: What we know, think, and question* (2nd ed.). Lanham, MD: Altamira Press.

Book by Multiple Authors

Booth, W. C., Colomb, G. G., & Williams, J. M. (1995). *The craft of research.* Chicago, IL: University of Chicago Press.

Book with a Group Author

University of Chicago Press. (2010). *The Chicago manual of style* (16th ed.). Chicago, IL: Author.

The word *Author* in the publishing information part of the entry means that the author is the same as the publisher.

Journal Article, Print, One Author

Banks, J. A. (2006). Improving race relations in schools: From theory and research to practice. *Journal of Social Issues, 62,* 607–614.

Journal Article, Print, Two Authors

McGlynn, E. A., & Brook, R. H. (2001). Keeping quality on the policy agenda. *Health Affairs, 20*(3), 82–90.

The number in parentheses after the volume number is the issue number; it is not italicized. Note that the page numbers follow.

Journal Article, Print, Three to Five Authors

Cadinu, M., Maass, A., Frigerio, S., Impagliazzo, L., & Latinotti, S. (2003). Stereotype threat: The effect of expectancy on performance. *European Journal of Social Psychology, 33,* 267–285.

COMMON EXAMPLES OF ONLINE SOURCES IN A REFERENCE LIST

Unlike MLA style, APA does not require you to include information about subscription services in APA citations. You will not see reference to these larger containers. Additionally, APA does not require that you include information about retrieval or access dates. You do, however, need to include the retrieval URL or DOI. Unlike MLA style, you do not follow the URL or DOI with a period.

Journal Article, Web Source, DOI

Aronson, R. B., Macintyre, I. G., Lewis, S. A., & Hilbun, N. L. (2005). Emergent zonation and geographic convergence of coral reefs. *Ecology, 86,* 2586-2600. http://dx.doi.org/10.1890/05-0045

Web Source, URL

U.S. Department of Housing and Urban Development. (2005). *Discrimination in metropolitan housing markets: National results from phase 1, phase 2, and phase 3 of the Housing Discrimination Study (HDS).* Retrieved from http://www.huduser.org/publications/hsgfin/hds.html

Article found on a Subscription Service

Bemak, F., & Chung, R. C.-Y. (2017). Refugee trauma: culturally responsive counseling interventions. *Journal of Counseling and Development, 95*(3), 299+. Retrieved from http://go.galegroup.com/ps/i.do?p=STOM&sw=w&u=vol_s22s&v=2.1&it=r&id=GALE%7CA498130095&asid=36fd73e518cd1f33489a87267f7b13e7

The preceding example is from the subscription service Gale Group. Notice that the citation does not include information about this larger container, as MLA does. Instead it provides information about the print publication and then the URL from the site in which it was retrieved.

Exercise 3 Practice: Creating Reference List Entries

Create a References list entry in APA format for each of the following sources. Use the information provided about each source.

1. **Authors:** Frederick J. Gravetter and Lori-Ann B. Forzano
   Publication date: 2012
   Book title: Research Methods for the Behavioral Sciences, fourth edition
   Publication city and state: Belmont, California
   Publisher name: Wadsworth

   _____

   _____

2. **Authors:** P. Moyer, J. Bolyard, and M. Spikell
   Publication date: June 15, 2012
   Article title: What Are Virtual Manipulatives?
   Journal title: Teaching Children Mathematics
   Volume number: 8
   Issue number: 6
   Page numbers: 372 through 377

   _____

   _____

3. **Authors:** A. Raj and S. Bertolone
   Publication date: 2010
   Publication title: Sickle Cell Anemia
   URL: http://emedicine.medscape.com/article/958614-overview

   _____

   _____

4. **Authors:** Gueorgi Kossinets and Duncan J. Watts
   Publication date: 2009
   Article title: Origins of Homophily in an Evolving Social Network
   Journal title: American Journal of Sociology
   Volume number: 115
   Page number: 411
   DOI: 10.1086/599247

   _____

   _____

Jumping In

Your conversations with good friends no doubt cover a wide spectrum of topics. As you voice your opinions, ask questions, and respond to others' comments, you become actively engaged. Similarly, writing-from-reading assignments may require that you engage in active, focused "conversations" with authors. Whenever you summarize key points, question content, or react strongly to a reading selection's premise, you sharpen your critical-thinking skills and become an active learner.

Learning Objectives

In this chapter, you will learn to:

1. Apply prereading strategies to assigned readings.
2. Write an effective summary of a reading.
3. Use critical-thinking strategies to evaluate what you are reading.

WHAT IS WRITING FROM READING?

One way to find topics for writing is to draw on your ideas, memories, and observations. Another way is to write from reading you have done. You can *react* to it, or you might *agree* or *disagree* with something you have read. In fact, many college assignments or tests ask you to write about an assigned reading: an essay, a chapter in a textbook, or an article in a journal. This kind of reading is done in steps:

1. Preread
2. Read
3. Reread with a pen or pencil

After you have completed these steps, you can write from your reading. You can write about what you have read, or you can react to what you have read.

① Apply prereading strategies to assigned readings.

PREREADING

Prereading takes very little time, but it helps you immensely. Some students believe it is a waste of time to scan an assignment; they think they should jump right in and finish the reading quickly. However, spending just a few minutes on preliminaries can save hours later. Most importantly, prereading helps you become a *focused reader*.

If you scan the length of an assignment, you can pace yourself. Also, if you know how long a reading is, you can alert yourself to its plan. A short reading, for example, has to come to its point quickly. A longer essay may take time to develop its point and may use more details and examples. Any highlighted material, including subheadings, charts, graphs, boxes, or illustrations, is important enough that the author wants to emphasize it. A list of vocabulary words and their definitions that accompanies a reading selection is worth scanning too. Looking over that material *before* you read gives you an overview of the important points the reading will contain.

Introductory material or introductory questions will also help you know what to look for as you read. Background on the author or on the subject may hint at ideas that will come up in the reading. Sometimes even the title of the reading will give you the main idea.

You should preread so that you can start reading with as much knowledge about the writer and the subject as you can get. Then, when you read the entire assignment, you will be reading *actively* for more knowledge.

If you want to read with a focus, it helps to ask questions before you read. Form questions by using the information you gained from prereading. For example, if the title of the article is "Manners Matter Online," you may turn the title into a question: "What basic etiquette is required online?" You can jot down such questions, but it's not necessary. Just forming questions and keeping them in the back of your mind helps you read actively and stay focused.

Checklist for Prereading

✓ How long is this reading?

✓ Will I be able to read it in one sitting, or will I have to schedule several sessions to finish it?

✓ Are there any subheadings in the reading? Do they give any hints about the reading?

✓ Are there any charts? Graphs? Boxed information?

✓ Are there any photographs or illustrations with captions? Do the photos or captions give me any hints about the reading?

> ✓ Is there any introductory material about the reading or its author? Does the introductory material give me any hints about the reading?
>
> ✓ What is the title of the reading? Does the title hint at the point of the reading?
>
> ✓ Are any parts of the reading underlined, italicized, or emphasized in some other way? Do the emphasized parts hint at the point of the reading?

READING

The first time you read, try to get a sense of the whole piece you are reading. Reading with questions in mind can help you do this. If you find that you are confused by a certain part of the reading selection, go back and re-read that part. If you do not know the meaning of a certain word, check the list of vocabulary words if the article includes one. If there is no list or the word is not defined, try to determine the meaning from the way the word is used in the sentence.

If you find that you have to read more slowly than usual, don't worry. People vary their reading speed according to what they read and why they are reading it. If you are reading for entertainment, for example, you can read quickly; if you are reading a chapter in a textbook, you must read more slowly. The more complicated the reading selection, the more carefully you will read it.

REREADING WITH A PEN OR PENCIL

The second reading is the crucial one. At this point, you begin to *think on paper* as you read. In this step, you can make notes or write about what you read. Some students are reluctant to do this because they are not sure what to note or write. Think of these notes as a way of learning, thinking, reviewing, and reading. Reading with a pen or pencil in your hand keeps you alert. With that pen or pencil, you can do the following:

- Mark the main point (premise or thesis) of the reading.
- Mark other key points.
- Define words you don't know.
- Question parts of the reading that seem unclear to you.
- Evaluate the writer's ideas.
- React to the writer's opinions or examples.
- Add ideas, opinions, and examples of your own.

Some people like to use the margins to write comments such as "I agree!" or "Not true!" or "That's happened to me!" Sometimes readers put questions in the margins; sometimes they summarize a point in the margin next to its location in the essay. Some people make notes on the white space above the reading and list important points, and others use the space at the end of the reading. Every reader who writes while he or she reads has a personal system; what these systems share is an attitude. If you write as you read, you will concentrate on the reading selection, become familiar with the writer's ideas, and develop ideas of your own.

> ## CRITICAL THINKING
>
> You may find your professors asking you to *annotate* your text. This is another term for marking your text with a pen or pencil or for using post-it notes to make notes or add your insights. Annotations are extremely helpful because they promote engaged reading of a text and provide important markers to return to when writing about the text.

An Example of Rereading with a Pen or Pencil

Following is the article, "Manners Matter Online: Basic Etiquette Applies Even for E-Mail." It has been marked as if a student reader were rereading it after prereading and reading the selection.

Manners Matter Online: Basic Etiquette Applies Even for E-Mail

Amritha Alladi

Alladi wrote this article for the Gainesville Sun *(Florida), and she focuses on why students and other young people seeking employment need to sharpen their e-mail communication skills.*

Words You May Need to Know (Corresponding paragraph numbers are in parentheses.)

jargon (3): language used by a specific group or profession
indecipherable (3): impossible to understand
protocol (5): a formal procedure
hierarchical (5): organized by a person's rank or status
sublimated the role of the gatekeeper (6): eliminated the traditional, more rigid channels of communication
incoherent (6): not logically consistent
psychosocial implications (7): psychological and social effects
demeanor (9): behavior

1 Before you click "Send," reread the last line of that e-mail, will you?

2 After all, you wouldn't appreciate a message from your boss that read, "Dude, what's up with ur presentation? CU in my office ASAP," so it's best to extend him or her the same courtesy. When it comes to professional e-mails, business etiquette is no Laughing Out Loud matter.

3 Eric Hall, assistant director for employer relations at the University of Florida's Career Resource Center, says he has heard from job recruiters that *thesis* students are too casual when corresponding with prospective employers and professors. Many young professionals have become accustomed to *example* sending quick messages to friends and peers, and they sometimes forget that abbreviations and jargon may be inappropriate, or at times, even indecipherable. "In this day and age of text messaging, there are occasionally the LOLs," Hall says.

Meanwhile, communications professors feel the issue goes beyond e-mail etiquette. Professors at UF's Warrington College of Business say the problem is rooted more in the generation's behavioral trends rather than in technological ones.

4

<u>Jane Douglas</u>, associate professor of management communication, <u>says young people entering the workforce are generally unaware of protocol with regard to addressing people in higher positions</u>. "There is this illusion that communication is horizontal. They don't understand that it's hierarchical." Douglas says that during her twenty-five years of teaching, she has noticed a huge difference in the way students interact with faculty.

5

example

E-mail communication and the Internet have sublimated the role of the gatekeeper entirely, said Douglas. Last year, her college faced some "very problematic undergrads" <u>who took it upon themselves to address their complaints directly to the dean and provost</u>. "It's just one keystroke from the dean, and usually it's incoherent," she says. "Students seldom proofread or think of the entire impression."

6

Why is this so awful?

Basic etiquette teaches that you avoid the obvious ⬡improprieties⬡— abbreviations, slang, poor grammar, and informal greetings—no matter who you're sending an e-mail to. Formality is necessary anytime you are communicating with someone for the first time. However, Douglas, who has done extensive research in the psychosocial implications of communication, says she has noted some other major pitfalls that land this budding generation of professionals in hot water with future employers.

7

improper actions

"<u>You see a lot of unprofessional e-mail addresses like tequilagirl@aol. com,</u>" Douglas says. "They don't understand that when you're communicating with someone you don't know, you need to be somewhat formal."

8

example

Hall says UF's Career Resource Center tries to teach students appropriate business demeanor through <u>outreach programs</u> that focus on etiquette workshops, business attire, and interviewing tips. Experts at the center also review resumes and cover letters and give the students feedback for employment. Communication at all stages is important because managers are not just assessing your professional communication within the office. "They're also examining how you might work with potential clients," Hall says. "It's in a person's best interest to use formal language at all times."

9

no one has time

Of course, if you don't know whether your e-mail is appropriate, seek advice. "If you have any professional contacts, especially in the way of networking," Hall says, "they can be a good guiding force."

10

What the Notes Mean

In the sample above, the underlining indicates sentences or phrases that seem important. The words in the margin, such as *thesis* or *example*, can refer to important sections of the reading. Sometimes a word is circled in the selection itself and defined in the margin; for instance, *improprieties* is circled in Paragraph 7 and defined in the margin as "improper actions."

Sometimes, words in the margin are personal reactions. When a university administrator, Eric Hall, notes that his university offers outreach programs for teaching students about business demeanor and interviewing, the reader notes "no one has time" for such programs. The marked-up article is a flexible tool. If you are asked to write a summary of the article, you can use the thesis and the examples you noted as important components of the summary. A comment about students' lack of time for workshops or outreach programs may lead a reader to develop his or her own writing that agrees or disagrees with a point made in the article. Another underlined part, about some undergraduate students who went directly to high-level administrators instead of talking to their professors, could be the basis for writing on a related topic about student–faculty interaction.

The marked-up article is a flexible tool. You can go back and mark it further. Writing as you read involves you in the reading process. It can help you to write about or react to important points in the article. In addition, if you are to be tested on the reading selection or asked to discuss it, you can scan your markings and notations later for a quick review.

2 Write an effective summary of a reading.

A SAMPLE SUMMARY

A summary of a reading tells the important ideas in brief form. It includes (1) the writer's main idea, (2) the ideas used to explain the main idea, and (3) some examples used to explain the ideas. It also refers to the author and the title of the article you are summarizing. Following is a sample summary of "Manners Matter Online: Basic Etiquette Applies Even for E-Mail."

A Summary

"Manners Matter Online: Basic Etiquette Applies Even for E-Mail" by Amritha Alladi warns that college students tend to be "too casual when corresponding with prospective employers and professors." The article refers to concerned professors who believe that technology, which has made e-mail and texting so popular, is partly to blame. When younger people rely on such quick communication, they may forget that abbreviations and jargon can be out of place or confusing. Other professors believe that the cause of this violation of business etiquette is linked to this generation's belief that employee and employer, student and professor are equals. Alladi's research into business etiquette stresses that if today's students can learn correct communications skills, they can improve their relationships with faculty and employers.

> **Note:** When you refer to an author in something that you write, use the author's first and last name the first time you make a reference. For example, you write "Amritha Alladi" the first time you refer to this author. Later in the paragraph, if you want to refer to the same author, use only his or her last name. Thus, a second reference would be to "Alladi," as in the summary, which refers to "Alladi's research."

WRITING A REACTION TO A READING

A summary is one kind of writing you can complete after reading, but there are other kinds. You can react to a reading by agreeing or disagreeing with some idea within the reading or by writing on a topic related to the reading. The effectiveness of your reaction will depend on your careful evaluation of the reading selection.

THE ROLE OF CRITICAL THINKING

3 Use critical-thinking strategies to evaluate what you are reading.

When you start forming opinions based on what you observe, hear, read, or discuss, you are applying **critical-thinking skills**. Thinking critically as you read involves examining an issue from different sides as well as evaluating the validity, or truthfulness, of the information presented.

Applying the critical-thinking process to evaluate what you are reading requires that you ask yourself the following questions:

- What is the writer's main idea or proposal?
- Is the main idea supported by facts? Personal experience? Expert opinion(s)?
- Does the writer reach logical conclusions based on his or her evidence?

Sharpening your critical-thinking skills by using this type of questioning as you read can enable you to form reasonable opinions and express them confidently. Reading critically can help you succeed in all of your college classes, and it will be especially beneficial in your future composition courses.

DEVELOPING POINTS OF AGREEMENT OR DISAGREEMENT

One way to use a reading selection to lead you to a topic is to review the reading selection and jot down any statements that provoke a strong reaction in you. You will be looking for statements with which you agree or disagree. If you already marked "Manners Matter Online: Basic Etiquette Applies Even for E-Mail," you might focus your own writing on your disagreement with the point that outreach programs can change students' modes of communication with potential employers. The sample reaction paragraph that follows acknowledges that students need help in learning how to communicate with potential employers, but the student writer *disagrees* that outreach programs will reach everyone who needs them. Notice that the student writer not only disagrees that outreach programs are effective but also provides an alternative to outreach programs. This really strengthens the student's response to the reading selection.

Developing Points of Agreement or Disagreement: A Sample Reaction

One part of "Manners Matter Online: Basic Etiquette Applies Even for E-mail" by Amritha Alladi discusses college students' lack of the skills they need to communicate with employers. It also refers to one university that offers outreach programs that can teach students proper business etiquette, business attire, interviewing tips, and resume writing. Outreach programs are valuable, but I do not agree that they are an effective way to train many students who want to find jobs. Most students will not find time for these sessions because participating in any "outreach" means spending extra time and doing extra work. The realistic way to motivate students is to include lessons on interviewing, conducting job searches, and professional communications in a for-credit course. It could be a one-credit course tailored for different fields of study, or it could be part of a required course in such fields as business, education, science, and so forth. Students would get the information they need, and prospective employers would get the type of employees they need.

WRITING ON A RELATED IDEA

Another type of writing requires critical thinking and writing. Your instructor might ask you to react by writing about some idea connected to your reading. For example, your instructor might ask you to react to "Manners Matter Offline: Basic Etiquette Applies Even for E-Mail" by writing about whether every description of college students in the article is accurate.

Writing on a Related Idea: A Sample

In Amritha Alladi's article, "Manners Matter Online: Basic Etiquette Applies Even for E-Mail," the author refers to one university professor who was concerned when some undergraduate students "took it upon themselves to address their complaints directly to the dean and provost." This action seemed to create a problem because the students did not go first to their professors and other teaching staff. I understand why students should not skip steps in dealing with their problems, but I don't agree that all students who bring their problems directly to a dean or provost are being impatient or unreasonable. Sometimes, student concerns have been ignored so often that undergraduates become frustrated. Unfortunately, some professors do not respond to students' e-mails. When students try to talk to their instructors after class, most faculty are on their way to another class or an appointment. A few faculty do not always keep their office hours. Some part-time faculty do not have offices or are busy teaching at more than one campus. While people in high positions should not have to deal with everyday student concerns, students need to have their voices heard.

Writing from reading can develop your abilities to challenge others' ideas, widen your perspective, and help you build confidence in your critical-thinking skills.

Grammar for Writers

Overview

In this section, you'll be working with the basics of grammar that you need to master to be a clear writer. If you are willing to memorize certain rules and work through the activities here, you will be able to apply grammatical rules automatically as you write.

Using "Grammar for Writers"

Because this section of the textbook is divided into self-contained segments, it does not have to be studied in sequence. Your instructor may suggest you review specific rules and examples, or you may be assigned various segments as either a class or group assignment. Various approaches are possible, and thus you can regard this section as a "user-friendly" grammar handbook for quick reference. Mastering the practical parts of grammar will improve your writing, helping you become a more confident writer who is better prepared for future courses.

Contents

CHAPTER 16

The Simple Sentence

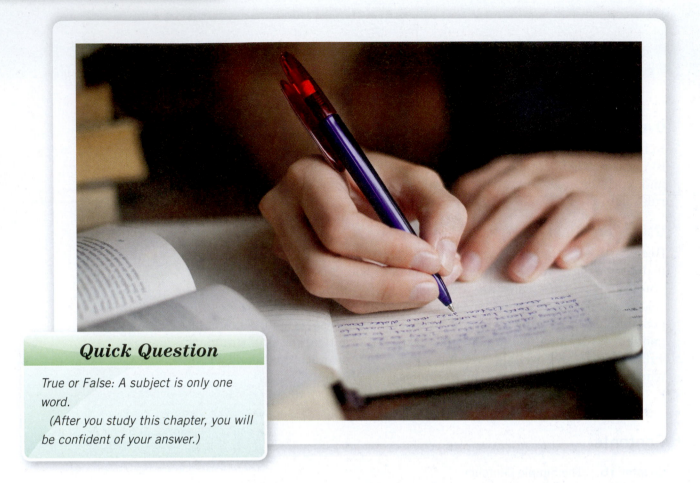

> ### *Quick Question*
>
> *True or False: A subject is only one word.*
>
> *(After you study this chapter, you will be confident of your answer.)*

Learning Objectives

In this chapter, you will learn to:

1 Identify subjects and verbs in sentences.

2 Identify prepositional phrases and correct word order.

3 Use verbs correctly in sentences.

Identifying the crucial parts of a sentence is the first step in many writing decisions: how to punctuate, how to avoid sentence fragments, and how to be sure that subjects and verbs "agree" (match). To move forward to these decisions requires a few steps back—to basics.

1 Identify subjects and verbs in sentences.

RECOGNIZING A SENTENCE

Let's start with a few basic definitions. A basic unit of language is a **word**.

> **examples:** *car, student, sun*

A group of related words can be a **phrase**.

> **examples:** *shiny new car; dedicated college student; in the bright sun*

When the group of words contains a subject and a verb, it is called a **clause**. When the word group has a subject and a verb and is a complete thought, it is called a **sentence** or an **independent clause**. When the word group has a subject and a verb but does not represent a complete thought, it is called a **dependent clause**.

If you want to check to see whether you have written a sentence, and not just a group of related words, you first have to check for a subject and a verb. Locating the verbs first can be easier.

RECOGNIZING VERBS

Verbs are words that express some kind of action or being. **Action verbs** tell what somebody or something *does*. **Being verbs** tell what somebody or something *is*. Verbs about the five senses (sight, sound, smell, taste, touch) are also part of the group called being verbs. Look at some examples of verbs as they work in sentences:

> **action verbs:**
> We *walk* to the store every day.
> The children *ran* to the playground.
> The baseball player *hit* a home run.

> **being verbs:**
> My mother *is* a good cook.
> The family *seems* unhappy.
> The soup *smells* delicious.

Exercise 1   **Practice: Recognizing Verbs**

Underline the verbs in each of the following sentences.

1. A loud cry woke me out of a sound sleep.

2. This game appears simple.

3. You are the hardest worker at the restaurant.

4. Two brave joggers run in the coldest weather.

5. The soldier saluted his mother.

6. Instructors give homework.

7. Vanessa and Chris were my neighbors in Providence.

8. Emilio sounds thrilled about the new baby.

9. My new instructor seems engaging.

10. My grandmother's food tastes spicy.

More on Verbs

The verb in a sentence can be more than one word. First of all, there can be **helping verbs** in front of the main verb, the action or being verb. Helping verbs are often a form of the verbs *be* (*is, am, are, was, were*) or *have* (*have, has, had*), or they can be **modals**. Modals include the words *can, could, will, may, might, should,* and *must.*

I *was watching* the Super Bowl. (The helping verb is *was*.)
You *should have called* me. (The helping verbs are *should* and *have*.)
The president *can select* his assistants. (The helping verb is *can*.)
Leroy *will graduate* in May. (The helping verb is *will*.)

Helping verbs can make the verb in a sentence more than one word long. However, there can also be more than one main verb, as shown:

Andrew *planned* and *practiced* his speech.
I *stumbled* over the rug, *grabbed* a chair, and *fell* on my face.

Exercise 2 **Practice: Writing Sentences with Helping Verbs**

Add at least one helping verb to the verb given. Then write two sentences using the main verb and the helping verb(s). The first one is done for you.

1. **verb:** named

   verb with helping verb(s): was named

   sentence 1: I was named after my father.

   sentence 2: Washington, D.C., was named after the first president.

2. **verb:** staring

   verb with helping verb(s): _____

   sentence 1: _____

   sentence 2: _____

3. **verb:** forget

   verb with helping verb(s): _____

   sentence 1: _____

   sentence 2: _____

4. **verb:** study

   verb with helping verb(s): _____

   sentence 1: _____

   sentence 2: _____

RECOGNIZING SUBJECTS

After you can recognize verbs, finding the subjects of sentences is easy because subjects and verbs are linked. If the verb is an action verb, for example, the subject will be the word or words that answer the question, "Who or what is doing that action?"

The truck stalled on the highway.

Step 1: Identify the verb: *stalled*

Step 2: Ask, "Who or what stalled?"

Step 3: The answer is the subject: The *truck* stalled on the highway.
Truck is the subject.

If your verb expresses being, the same steps apply to finding the subject.
Spike was my best friend.

Step 1: Identify the verb: *was*

Step 2: Ask, "Who or what was my best friend?"

Step 3: The answer is the subject: *Spike* was my best friend. *Spike* is the subject.

Just as there can be more than one word to make up a verb, there can be more than one subject.

examples:
David and *Leslie* planned the surprise party.
My *father* and *I* worked in the yard yesterday.

CRITICAL THINKING

Both dependent and independent clauses have subjects and verbs. If you have a sentence with an independent and a dependent clause, carefully identify the main verb of the sentence. It will be found in the independent clause. For example:

Because we were both early to class, we *studied* together.

The verb *studied* is the main verb of the sentence. It shows the action of the students who arrived early to class.

Exercise 3   **Practice: Recognizing the Subjects in Sentences**

Underline the subjects in the following sentences.

1. Nobody has been taking out the trash lately.

2. Something is happening at our neighbor's house.

3. After my last exam, worry and hope battled in my brain.

4. Sometimes, exercise offers an escape from my troubles.

5. Airports are becoming more crowded with holiday travelers.

6. Confidence can be an asset for a job seeker.

7. On Mondays, Chris, Bill, and I meet for coffee before class.

8. With great joy, Maria handed in her essay.

More about Recognizing Subjects and Verbs

When you look for the subject of a sentence, look for the core word or words; don't include descriptive words around the subject. The idea is to look for the subject, not for the words that describe it.

The dark blue *dress* looked lovely.
Dirty *streets* and grimy *houses* destroy a neighborhood.

The subjects are the core words *dress*, *streets*, and *houses*, not the descriptive words *dark blue*, *dirty*, and *grimy*.

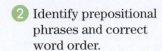 Identify prepositional phrases and correct word order.

PREPOSITIONS AND PREPOSITIONAL PHRASES

Prepositions are relatively short words that often signal a kind of position or possession, as shown in the following list:

> **INFO BOX** Common Prepositions
>
> | | | | | | |
> |---|---|---|---|---|---|
> | about | before | beyond | inside | on | under |
> | above | behind | during | into | onto | up |
> | across | below | except | like | over | upon |
> | after | beneath | for | near | through | with |
> | among | beside | from | of | to | within |
> | around | between | in | off | toward | without |
> | at | | | | | |

A prepositional phrase is made up of a preposition and its object. Here are some prepositional phrases. In each one, the first word is the preposition; the other words are the object of the preposition.

Prepositional Phrases

about the movie	of mice and men
around the corner	off the record
between two lanes	on the mark
during recess	up the wall
near my house	with my sister and brother

There is an old memory trick to help you remember prepositions. Think of a chair. Now, think of a series of words you can put *in front of* the chair:

around the chair	*with* the chair
behind the chair	*to* the chair
between the chairs	*near* the chair
by the chair	*under* the chair
of the chair	*on* the chair
off the chair	*from* the chair

Those words are prepositions.

You need to know about prepositions because they can help you identify the subject of a sentence. There is an important grammar rule about prepositions:

> **Nothing in a prepositional phrase can ever be the subject of the sentence.**

Prepositional phrases describe people, places, or things. They may describe the subject of a sentence, but they never include the subject. Whenever you are looking for the subject of a sentence, begin by putting parentheses around all the prepositional phrases.

> The restaurant (around the corner) makes the best fried chicken (in town).

The prepositional phrases are in parentheses. Because *nothing* in a prepositional phrase can be the subject, once you have eliminated the prepositional phrases, you can follow the steps to find the subject of the sentence:

> What is the verb? *makes*
> Who or what makes the best fried chicken? The *restaurant*
> *Restaurant* is the subject of the sentence.

By marking off the prepositional phrases, you are left with the *core* of the sentence. There is less to look at.

> (Behind the library), the *football field* was filled (with excited fans).
> **subject:** *football field*

> The *dog* (with the ugliest face) was the winner (of the contest).
> **subject:** *dog*

Exercise 4   **Practice: Recognizing Prepositional Phrases, Subjects, and Verbs**

Put parentheses around every prepositional phrase in the following sentences. Then underline the subject and verb and put an *S* above each subject and a *V* above each verb.

1. Alicia has been wondering about her chances for a job in nursing at a hospital near the military base.

2. An argument between my mother and father affected all the children in the family.

3. Elderly people in our neighborhood are becoming substitute grandparents to many children without older relatives in the area.

4. On the top of the essay, the teacher wrote comments about the student's work.

5. Nothing in the refrigerator except an apple looks edible to me.

6. Before dinner, I can run to the bakery and get some cookies for dessert.

7. The girl with the long dark hair sat near me during the pep rally inside the gym.

8. A couple of raindrops fell on Cody's newly waxed car and left tiny water marks.

WORD ORDER

When we speak, we often use a simple word order: first comes the subject; then comes the verb. For example, when someone says, "I am going to the store," *I* is the subject that begins the sentence; *am going* is the verb that comes after the subject.

But not all sentences are in such a simple word order. Prepositional phrases, for example, can change the word order:

sample sentence: Among the contestants was an older man.

Step 1: Mark off the prepositional phrase(s) with parentheses: *(Among the contestants)* was an older man. Remember that nothing in a prepositional phrase can be the subject of a sentence.

Step 2: Find the verb: *was*

Step 3: Who or what was? An older *man* was. The subject of the sentence is *man*.

After you change the word order of this sentence, you can see the subject (S) and verb (V) more easily:

       S   V
An older *man was* among the contestants.

Exercise 5 **Practice: Finding Prepositional Phrases, Subjects, and Verbs in Complicated Word Order**

Start by putting parentheses around the prepositional phrases in the following sentences. Then underline the subjects and verbs and put an *S* above each subject and a *V* above each verb.

1. Among my favorite pieces of clothing was an old baseball cap from my high school days.

2. Under my grandmother's bed is a box with old photographs of her and my grandfather in their wild teenage years.

3. Underneath the cold veneer of his personality is a warm and compassionate person.

4. Between my house on Daley Road and the corner was a huge old house behind a rusted iron fence.

5. From the back of the classroom came the soft snoring sound of a student in dreamland.

6. Beyond the layers of deception and intrigue was a simple answer to the mystery of the hero's death.

7. Among the most irritating programs on television are a talent show for deluded contestants and a comedy without any jokes.

8. Inside my backpack are class notes from last semester and an old

dictionary.

More on Word Order

The expected word order of subject first, then verb, changes when a sentence starts with *There is/are, There was/were, Here is/are, Here was/were*. In such cases, look for the subject after the verb.

        V   S   S

There *are* a *bakery* and a *pharmacy* down the street.

     V   S

Here *is* the *man* with the answers.

To understand this pattern, try changing the word order:

  S   S   V

A *bakery* and a *pharmacy* *are* there, down the street.

  S   V

The *man* with the answers *is* here.

You should also note that even if the subject comes after the verb, the verb has to "match" the subject. For instance, if the subject refers to more than one thing, the verb must also refer to more than one thing.

There *are* a *bakery* and a *pharmacy* down the road. (Two things, a bakery and a pharmacy, *are* down the road.)

Word Order in Questions

Questions may have a different word order. The main verb and the helping verb may not be next to each other.

question:	Do you like pizza?
subject:	*you*
verbs:	*do, like*

To understand this concept, think of answering the question. If someone accused you of not liking pizza, you might say, "I *do like* it." You would use two words as verbs.

question:	Will he think about it?
subject:	*he*
verbs:	*will, think*

question:	Is Maria telling the truth?
subject:	*Maria*
verbs:	*is, telling*

Exercise 6   **Practice: Recognizing Subjects and Verbs in Complicated Word Order: A Comprehensive Exercise**

Underline the subjects and verbs, putting an *S* above the subjects and a *V* above the verbs.

1. There were one hundred text messages and e-mails on my phone today.

2. Would you mind notifying our study group of the change in meeting times?

3. From the end of the long hall came the sound of laughter.

4. Was there anything in your coat pocket?

5. Have Emmie or Siri texted you yet about their arrival time?

6. Here are the most recent pictures of my nephew.

7. Among the healthy choices in the cafeteria was the vegetarian entree.

8. Can we think about a reasonable solution to the problem?

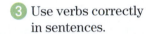 Use verbs correctly in sentences.

WORDS OFTEN CONFUSED AS VERBS

Words That Cannot Be Verbs

Sometimes there are words that look like verbs in a sentence, but they are not verbs. Such words include adverbs (words like *always, often, nearly, rarely, never, ever*). Adverbs are placed close to the verb, but they are not verbs. Another word that is not a verb is *not*. *Not* is placed between a helping verb and a main verb, but it is not part of the verb.

When you are looking for verbs in a sentence, be careful to eliminate words like *often* and *not*.

> He *will* not *listen* to me. (The verbs are *will listen*.)
> Althea *can* always *find* a bargain. (The verbs are *can find*.)

Be careful with contractions.

> They *have*n't *raced* in years. (The verbs are *have raced. Not* is not a part of the verb, even in contractions.)
> *Don't* you *come* from Arizona? (The verbs are *do come*.)
> *Won't* he ever *learn*? (The verbs are *will learn. Won't* is a contraction for *will not*.)

Recognizing Main Verbs

If you are checking to see if a word is a main verb, try the *pronoun test.* Combine your word with this simple list of pronouns: *I, you, he, she, it, we, they.* A main verb is a word such as *drive* or *noticed* that can be combined with the words on this list. Now try the pronoun test.

> For the word *drive:* I drive, you drive, he drives, she drives, it drives, we drive, they drive
> For the word *noticed:* I noticed, you noticed, he noticed, she noticed, it noticed, we noticed, they noticed

But words such as *never* cannot be used alone with the pronouns:

> ~~I never, you never, he never, she never, it never, we never, they never~~
> (Never did what?)

Never is not a verb. *Not* is not a verb either, as the pronoun test indicates:

~~I not, you not, he not, she not, it not, we not, they not~~
(These combinations do not make sense because *not* is not a verb.)

Verb Forms That Cannot Be Main Verbs

There are also words that are verbs, but they cannot be main verbs on their own. This includes *-ing* verbs. **An *-ing* verb, by itself, cannot be the main verb**, as the pronoun test shows.

For the word *voting:* ~~I voting, you voting, he voting, she voting, we voting, they voting~~

If you see an *-ing* verb by itself, correct the sentence by adding a helping verb.

Scott ~~riding~~ his motorcycle. (*Riding*, by itself, cannot be a main verb.)
correction: Scott *was riding* his motorcycle.

In addition to not being a main verb, *-ing* verbs sometimes do not act like verbs. For example, verbs with *-ing* can function as a **gerund**. Gerunds are formed from verbs but function as nouns. They can often be the subject of a sentence.

Texting can be dangerous when you are driving.
Volunteering your time is rewarding.
Because I live in Colorado, *hiking* is one of my favorite pastimes.

In these examples, the *-ing* verbs (*texting, volunteering, and hiking*) act as subjects of their sentences.

Infinitives are another verb form that cannot be a main verb. An infinitive is the form of the verb that has *to* placed in front of it.

INFO BOX **Some Common Infinitives**

to care	to vote	to repeat
to feel	to play	to stumble
to need	to reject	to view

Try the pronoun test, and you'll see that infinitives cannot be main verbs:

For the infinitive *to vote:* ~~I to vote, you to vote, he to vote, she to vote, we to vote, they to vote~~

So if you see an infinitive being used as a verb, correct the sentence by adding a main verb.

We ~~to vote~~ in the election tomorrow. (There is no verb, just an infinitive.)
correction: We *are going* to vote in the election tomorrow. (Now there is a verb.)

Like *-ing* verbs, infinitives can function as subjects.

To pay for textbooks is often difficult.
To tolerate rude people takes patience.
In Korea, *to touch* someone on the head is a sign of disrespect.

In these examples, the infinitives are subjects. Keep in mind, however, that using infinitives as subjects in your writing can be awkward in style. For example, "Tolerating" as a subject (gerund) is better style than "to tolerate" (infinitive).

Exercise 7   Practice: Correcting Problems with -ing or Infinitive Verb Forms

Most—but not all—of the sentences that follow are faulty; an -ing verb or an infinitive may be taking the place of a main verb. Rewrite the sentences with errors.

1. Behind the heavy purple curtains, a little girl in a nightgown hiding from the noise of the thunderstorm.

   rewritten: _____

   _____

2. After dinner, Mr. Stein wants to sit in front of his big-screen television until bedtime.

   rewritten: _____

   _____

3. The weeds around the stepping-stones creeping between the cracks and over the broken stones.

   rewritten: _____

   _____

4. After hours of negotiation, an escaped convict from Utah to surrender to police in New Mexico.

   rewritten: _____

   _____

5. At a high point in his career, the internationally known tennis star quitting for personal reasons.

   rewritten: _____

   _____

6. On weekends, my sisters to ride their bicycles to the park near our house.

   rewritten: _____

   _____

7. After the midterm exam, a few of the students in my science class were complaining about the grading scale.

   rewritten: _____

   _____

8. Without a second look, I turned my back on my former friend and walked calmly to my car.

   rewritten: _____

   _____

Exercise 8   **Practice: Finding Subjects and Verbs: A Comprehensive Exercise**

Underline the subjects and verbs in these sentences and put an *S* above each subject and a *V* above each verb.

1. There were a pen, a pencil, and a crumpled piece of paper in Sophie's book bag.

2. Melanie could have been waiting for you at the coffee shop.

3. At the front of the classroom is a large box with a stack of papers in it.

4. My computer does not offer quick access to the Internet.

5. You have suddenly developed an interest in our handsome neighbor on the third floor.

6. Won't you think about a career in mechanical engineering?

7. Alec is dreaming of making a return visit to Cancun.

8. At the top of my list of worries are the fear of missing an opportunity and the fear of failure.

Exercise 9   **Practice: Finding Subjects and Verbs: Another Comprehensive Exercise**

Underline the subjects and verbs in these sentences and put an *S* above each subject and a *V* above each verb.

1. Before my speech to the scholarship committee, I thought about my dream of higher education, looked into each person's eyes, and hoped for the best.

2. In any marriage, there will be a period of adjustment for both partners.

3. Here is the old scrapbook with the pictures of you in your Little League uniform.

4. Alicia would never ask for help from her brother.

5. Haven't you always wanted a house near the ocean?

6. With his giant television on the living room wall and his huge col-

lection of films, Todd rarely goes to a movie theater for
entertainment.

7. Can't the two of you ever think about anyone except yourselves?

8. In the bright light, the large dog seemed weird and dangerous.

Collaborate

Exercise 10 **Collaborate: Create Your Own Text**

Complete this activity with two partners. A list of rules you've just studied
follows. Each member of the group should write one example of each rule.
When your group has completed three examples for each rule, trade your
completed exercise with another group, and check their examples while they
check yours. The first rule has been done for you.

Rule 1: The verb in a sentence can express some kind of action.
examples:

a. Wanda sleeps late on the weekends.

b. On Monday I found a wallet in the street.

a. Melted snow covered the sidewalks and steps.

Rule 2: The verb in a sentence can express some state of being or one
of the five senses.
examples:

a. _____

b. _____

c. _____

Rule 3: The verb in a sentence can consist of more than one word.
examples:

a. _____

b. _____

c. _____

Rule 4: There can be more than one subject of a sentence.
examples:

a. _____

b. _____

c. _____

Rule 5: If you remove the prepositional phrases, it is easier to identify the subject of a sentence because nothing in a prepositional phrase can be the subject of a sentence. (Write sentences with at least one prepositional phrase and put parentheses around the prepositional phrases.)
examples:

a. _____

b. _____

c. _____

Rule 6: Not all sentences have the simple word order of subject first, then verb. (Give examples of more complicated word order.)
examples:

a. _____

b. _____

c. _____

Rule 7: Words like *not, never, often, always,* and *ever* are not verbs. (Write sentences using those words, but write *V* above the correct verb or verbs.)
examples:

a. _____

b. _____

c. _____

Rule 8: An *-ing* verb form by itself or an infinitive (*to* preceding the verb) cannot be a main verb. (Write sentences with *-ing* verb forms or infinitives, but write *V* above the main verb.)
examples:

a. _____

b. _____

c. _____

Exercise 11 Connect: Recognizing Subjects and Verbs in a Paragraph

Underline the subjects and verbs in this paragraph and put an *S* above each subject and a *V* above each verb.

My father could never have fit into his old U.S. Army uniform without a rigorous program of exercise and diet. In January, he received an invitation to a reunion of his army buddies. He was eager to attend. However, he wanted to look like the fit, trim soldier of long ago. He had six months for getting fit before the reunion. During those six months, my father joined a local gym and arrived faithfully at 6:00 a.m. on every day of the week. In the evening, he jogged through the neighborhood for two miles. On Saturdays, my father pushed me into walking long distances in the mountains near our house. In addition, he rarely drank beer or ate junk food in front of the television. Salads, broiled chicken, and grilled fish became frequent dinner choices. He stuck to his program for fitness and transformed himself from a typical middle-aged man with too little energy and too much flab into a perfect model of a former fighting man.

Chapter Test   **The Simple Sentence**

Underline the subjects and verbs in these sentences and put an *S* above each subject and a *V* above each verb.

1. The smell of freshly baked bread at the bakery near my apartment is making me hungry.

2. After a dental check-up, Dr. Talbott usually gives me a small bag with a new toothbrush and a small tube of toothpaste.

3. Inside the pancake restaurant are bright yellow booths and posters with photos of every kind of pancake and topping in the world.

4. Didn't you ever dream about living in a big city?

5. The warm wind in my hair and the sun in my eyes were a pleasant change from the sleet and snow at home.

6. Kyla never asked about my background or questioned my motives for leaving town suddenly.

7. Manny's nasty tantrum at dinner could have resulted in hurt feelings among the family members at the table.

8. Behind her carefree attitude and silly behavior is a woman with anxieties about her future.

9. Why didn't Steve invite Sonia to his graduation party?

10. Because she has a sparkling personality and strong people skills, May was encouraged to interview for the position in marketing.

CHAPTER 17

Beyond the Simple Sentence: Coordination

Quick Question

Which sentence(s) is(are) correct?

A. Edward owns a motorcycle, but he wants a car.

B. Edward owns a motorcycle but he wants a car.

(After you study this chapter, you will be confident of your answer.)

Learning Objectives

In this chapter, you will learn to:

1. Combine simple sentences using a comma and a coordinating conjunction.
2. Combine simple sentences using a semicolon.
3. Combine simple sentences using a semicolon and a conjunctive adverb.

AVOIDING SIMPLE SENTENCES

A group of words containing a subject and a verb is called a **clause**. When that group is a complete thought, it is called a sentence or an **independent clause**.

The kind of sentence that is one independent clause is called a **simple sentence**. If you rely too heavily on a sentence pattern of simple sentences, you risk writing choppy paragraphs like this:

> I am a college student. I am also a salesperson in a mall. I am always busy. School is time-consuming. Studying is time-consuming. Working makes me tired. Balancing these activities is hard. I work too many hours. Work is important. It pays for school.

Here is a better version:

> I am a college student and a salesperson at a mall, so I am always busy. School and study are time-consuming, and working makes me tired. Balancing these activities is hard. I work too many hours, but that work is important. It pays for school.

OPTIONS FOR COMBINING SIMPLE SENTENCES

Good writing involves sentence variety; it means mixing a simple sentence with a more complicated one, a short sentence with a long one. Sentence variety is easier to achieve if you can combine related, short sentences into one.

It is true that punctuation involves memorizing a few rules, but once you know them, you will be able to use them automatically and write with more confidence. Following are three options for combining simple sentences and the punctuation rules to follow in each case.

OPTION 1: USING A COMMA WITH A COORDINATING CONJUNCTION

1 Combine simple sentences using a comma and a coordinating conjunction.

You can combine two simple sentences with a comma and a coordinating conjunction. The coordinating conjunctions are *for, and, nor, but, or, yet,* and *so.*

To coordinate means to join equals. When you join two simple sentences with a comma and a coordinating conjunction (CC), each half of the combination remains an independent clause, with its own subject (S) and verb (V).

Here are two simple sentences:

> S   V   S   V
> *He cooked* the dinner. *She worked* late.

Here are the two simple sentences combined with a comma, and with the word *for*, a coordinating conjunction (CC):

> S   V   , CC S   V
> *He cooked* the dinner, *for she worked* late.

The combined sentences keep the form they had as separate sentences; that is, they are still both independent clauses, with a subject and a verb and with the ability to stand alone.

The word that joins them is the **coordinating conjunction**. It is used to join equals. Look at some more examples. These examples use a variety of coordinating conjunctions to join two simple sentences.

sentences combined with *and*:

> S   V   , CC   S   V
> *Maren likes* Italian food, *and Mark prefers* Korean dishes.

sentences combined with *nor*:

S V   V   , CC   V S V
I didn't like the book, nor did I like the movie made from the book.
(Notice what happens to the word order when you use *nor*.)

sentences combined with *but*:

S V   , CC S   V
I ran to the library, *but it was* already closed.

S   V   V   , CC S   V   V
She can write a letter to Jim, *or she can call* him.

sentences combined with *yet*:

S   V   , CC   S   V
James tried to please his sister, *yet she* never *seemed* appreciative of
his efforts.

sentences combined with *so*:

S   V   , CC S V
I was the first in line for the concert tickets, *so I got* the best seats in
the stadium.

> **Note:** One easy way to remember the coordinating conjunctions is to call them,
> as a group, **fanboys** (*for, and, nor, but, or, yet, so*).

Where Does the Comma Go?

Notice that the comma comes before the coordinating conjunction (*for,
and, nor, but, or, yet, so*). It comes before the new idea, the second independent clause. It goes where the first independent clause ends. Try this
punctuation check. After you've placed the comma, look at the combined
sentences. For example:

She joined the army, and she traveled overseas.

Then split it into two sentences at the comma:

She joined the army. And she traveled overseas. (The split makes sense.)

If you put the comma in the wrong place, after the coordinating conjunction,
your split sentences would be:

She joined the army and. She traveled overseas. (The split doesn't
make sense.)

This test helps you see whether the comma has been placed correctly—
where the first independent clause ends. (Notice that you can begin a sentence with *and*. You can also begin a sentence with *but, or, nor, for, yet,* or
so—as long as you're writing a complete sentence.)

> **Caution:** Do *not* insert a comma every time you use the words *and, but, or, nor,
> for, yet,* or *so*; use it only when the coordinating conjunction joins independent
> clauses. Do not use the comma when the coordinating conjunction joins words:
>
> blue and gold   tired but happy   hot or cold
>
> Do not use the comma when the coordinating conjunction joins phrases:
>
> on the chair or under the table
> in the water and by the shore
> with a smile but without an apology

The comma is used when the coordinating conjunction joins two independent clauses. Another way of expressing this same rule is to state that the comma is used when the coordinating conjunction joins two simple sentences.

Placing the Comma by Using Subject–Verb (S–V) Patterns

An independent clause, or simple sentence, follows one of these basic patterns:

> S   V
> *He ran.*

or

> S   S V
> *He* and *I ran.*

or

> S V   V
> *He ran* and *swam.*

or

> S   S V   V
> *He* and *I ran* and *swam.*

Study all four patterns for the simple sentence, and you will notice that you can draw a line separating the subjects on one side and the verbs on the other:

S	V
SS	V
S	VV
SS	VV

So whether the sentence has one subject (or more than one) and one verb (or more than one), in the simple sentence the pattern is subject(s) followed by verb(s)—one simple sentence.

When you combine two simple sentences, the pattern changes:

two simple sentences:

> S   V   S V
> *He swam. I ran.*

two simple sentences combined:

> S   V   S V
> *He swam,* but *I ran.*

In the new pattern, SVSV, you cannot draw a line separating all the subjects on one side, and all the verbs on the other. This new pattern, with two simple sentences (or independent clauses) joined into one, is called a **compound sentence**.

Recognizing the SVSV pattern will help you place the comma for compound sentences.

Here is another way to remember this rule. If you have this pattern:

> SV | SV

use a comma in front of the coordinating conjunction. Do not use a comma in front of the coordinating conjunction with these patterns:

S	V
SS	V
S	VV
SS	VV

For example, use a comma for this pattern:

S   V   ,   S   V

Jane followed directions, but *I rushed* ahead.

Do not use a comma for this pattern:

S   V   V

Carol cleans her kitchen every week but never *wipes* the top of the refrigerator.

You have just studied one way to combine simple sentences. If you are going to take advantage of this method, you have to memorize the coordinating conjunctions—*for, and, nor, but, or, yet,* and *so*—so that your use of them, with the correct punctuation, will become automatic.

Exercise 1 **Practice: Recognizing Compound Sentences and Adding Commas**

Add commas only where they are needed in the following sentences. Do not add any words.

1. The new night club downtown is very popular with the students so the line to get inside is always very long.

2. Claudia is looking for a two-bedroom apartment in a good neighborhood or a small house with a porch.

3. I will not attend my cousin's wedding nor will I be sending a gift.

4. Antonio seems worried about something but never confides in me or his sister.

5. My best friend can eat every item in the refrigerator yet he has maintained the same healthy weight for years.

6. The kitchen table is covered in scratches and dents for the family cuts and carves food on it every day.

7. Michelle rides her bicycle to class every day so she saves money on gas for her car.

8. We worked really hard on our presentation but we still didn't do very well.

Exercise 2   **Practice: Recognizing Compound Sentences and Adding Commas**

Add commas only where they are needed in the following sentences. Do not add any words.

1. The detective at the scene of the crime was neither thorough nor efficient in investigating the site.

2. This smartphone is beneficial for someone who needs to check e-mail frequently.

3. Next week we can go to the mall or I can come to your house for coffee.

4. Sam is always complaining about his job yet never has the initiative to look for a better position.

5. Mark and Melanie saved money and worked overtime to buy a new home.

6. Most horror movies rely on the same plots yet the films always attract big crowds.

7. You should drink eight glasses of water a day or you will get dehydrated in the summer heat.

8. There was a recall on the bagged spinach I had bought and I returned it to the store.

Exercise 3   **Practice: Combining Sentences Using Coordinating Conjunctions**

Combine each pair of sentences using a coordinating conjunction and the appropriate punctuation.

1. Jordan was a wonderful father to his three boys. He was not a great husband.

   combined: _____

   _____

2. Kevin made a reservation at the most popular restaurant in town. He wanted to please his new friends.

   combined: _____

   _____

3. Many of my friends are sick of the congestion of city life. They are looking for jobs in the country.

   combined: _____

   _____

4. He can buy a new car with great style and huge monthly payments. He can settle for a used car with less style and much smaller payments.

    combined: _____

    _____

    _____

5. William works really hard in calculus. William doesn't understand calculus.

    combined: _____

6. Ramon Ramirez played football in high school. Hector Ramirez attended college on a baseball scholarship.

    combined: _____

    _____

7. My grandfather always wanted to visit Barbados. He preferred to spend his money on his grandchildren's education.

    combined: _____

    _____

8. I got a concussion at the hockey game last weekend. I couldn't go to work yesterday.

    combined: _____

    _____

2 Combine simple sentences using a semicolon.

OPTION 2: USING A SEMICOLON BETWEEN TWO SIMPLE SENTENCES

Sometimes you may want to combine two simple sentences (independent clauses) without using a coordinating conjunction. If you want to join two simple sentences that are related in their ideas and you do not use a coordinating conjunction, you can combine them with a semicolon.

two simple sentences:

S   V   S   V
I cooked the turkey. *She made* the stuffing.

two simple sentences combined with a semicolon:

S   V   ; S   V
I cooked the turkey; *she made* the stuffing.

Here's another example of this option in use:

S   V   V   ; S   V
Rain can be dangerous; *it makes* the roads slippery.

Notice that when you join two simple sentences with a semicolon, the second sentence begins with a lowercase letter, not a capital letter.

You need to memorize the seven coordinating conjunctions so that you can make a decision about punctuating your combined sentences. Remember these rules:

- If a coordinating conjunction joins the combined sentences, put a comma in front of the coordinating conjunction.

  S   V   S   V
  Tom had a barbecue in his back yard, and the *food was* delicious.

- If there is no coordinating conjunction, put a semicolon in front of the second independent clause.

  S   V   S   V
  Tom had a barbecue in his back yard; the *food was* delicious.

OPTION 3: USING A SEMICOLON AND A CONJUNCTIVE ADVERB

> 3 Combine simple sentences using a semicolon and a conjunctive adverb.

Sometimes you may want to join two simple sentences (independent clauses) with a connecting word called a **conjunctive adverb**.

Here is a list of some conjunctive adverbs:

INFO BOX Common Conjunctive Adverbs			
also	furthermore	likewise	otherwise
anyway	however	meanwhile	similarly
as a result	in addition	moreover	still
besides	in fact	nevertheless	then
certainly	incidentally	next	therefore
consequently	indeed	now	thus
finally	instead	on the other hand	undoubtedly

You can use a conjunctive adverb (CA) to join simple sentences, but when you do, you still need a semicolon in front of the adverb.

two simple sentences:

S   V   S V
My *parents checked* my homework every night. *I did* well in math.

two simple sentences joined by a conjunctive adverb and a semicolon:

S   V   ; CA S V
My *parents checked* my homework every night; *thus I did* well in math.

S   V   ;   CA   S   V
She gave me good advice; *moreover, she helped* me follow it.

Punctuating after a Conjunctive Adverb

Notice the comma after the conjunctive adverb in the preceding sentence. Here is the generally accepted rule:

Put a comma after the conjunctive adverb if the conjunctive adverb is more than one syllable long.

For example, if the conjunctive adverb is a word such as *consequently*, *furthermore*, or *moreover*, you use a comma. If the conjunctive adverb is one syllable, you do not have to put a comma after the conjunctive adverb. One-syllable conjunctive adverbs are words such as *then* or *thus*.

> I saw her cruelty to her staff; *then* I lost respect for her.
> We worked on the project all weekend; *consequently*, we finished a week ahead of the deadline.

Exercise 4 Practice: Combining Simple Sentences with Semicolons and Conjunctive Adverbs

Some of the following sentences need a semicolon; others need a semicolon and a comma. Do not add, change, or delete any words; just add the correct punctuation.

1. Desmond likes insects in fact he has a pet spider at home.

2. At the end of dinner came a pleasant surprise it was a complimentary dessert for everyone at our table.

3. My first year in college is almost over then I'll be a sophomore with a fairly respectable academic record.

4. Professor Mackenzie talks too fast I can't keep up with her explanations of the math problems.

5. Shane never paid me back for the loan of twenty dollars instead he took me to the movies yesterday.

6. She always forgets to do her homework furthermore she rarely does well on her exams.

7. My hectic work schedule prevents me from having any fun on the other hand the extra hours at my job are paying my bills.

8. We must protect our planet we must conserve our natural resources.

Exercise 5 Practice: Combining Simple Sentences with Semicolons and Conjunctive Adverbs

Pairs of simple sentences follow. Combine each pair into one sentence. You have two options: (1) use a semicolon or (2) use a semicolon and a conjunctive adverb (with a comma if it is needed). Choose the option that makes the most sense for each sentence.

1. Green fuzz covered the leftover chicken and rice.

   The casserole had been in the refrigerator for two weeks.

   combined: _____

   _____

2. Natalie was three days late submitting her final paper.

   She finished the course with a B.

   combined: _____

   _____

3. Amanda bolted the apartment door.

   Connor frantically called an emergency number.

   combined: _____

   _____

4. She is not sure what she wants to study.

   She went to see an advisor.

   combined: _____

   _____

5. Tyler refused to speak to me yesterday at school.

   He even avoided eye contact.

   combined: _____

   _____

6. The first snow of the year began to fall.

   The white coating transformed the hills and trees into a strange scene.

   combined: _____

   _____

7. Hernando needs to renew his CPR certification.

   He will not be able to coach the youth soccer team.

   combined: _____

   _____

8. Skip is turning into a fine dog.

   He has learned all the essential skills of obeying commands and walking on a leash.

   combined: _____

   _____

Exercise 6   **Practice: Combining Simple Sentences Three Ways**

Add a comma, a semicolon, or a semicolon and a comma to the following sentences. Do not add, change, or delete any words; just add the correct punctuation.

1. It was very quiet no one was talking.

2. You should apologize to Sean moreover you should apologize sincerely and soon.

3. We will get to the trailhead early thus we will be the first ones at the summit.

4. Kelly buys a lottery ticket every week yet she has never won a penny.

5. Andrew regretted his angry words to his wife similarly his wife felt guilty about the cruelty of her responses.

6. I ran into your old girlfriend at the mall yesterday incidentally she is going to be in your biology class next semester.

7. My five-year-old son spent three hours at the beach now he is a tired but happy child with sand in his hair, toes, and ears.

8. She wanted to get the latest smartphone but the store was out of stock.

Collaborate

Exercise 7 **Collaborate: Using Three Options to Combine Simple Sentences**

Pairs of simple sentences follow. Working with a partner or partners, combine each pair into one sentence in two different ways. Remember, you have three options: (1) use a comma and a coordinating conjunction, (2) use a semicolon, or (3) use a semicolon and a conjunctive adverb (with a comma if it is needed). Pick the options that make the most sense for these sentences. The first one has been done for you.

1. Crystal ran out of money for her electric bill.
   I lent her enough to pay it.

   combinations:

   a. <u>Crystal ran out of money for her electric bill, so I lent her enough to pay it.</u>

   _____

   b. <u>Crystal ran out of money for her electric bill; therefore, I lent her enough</u>

   <u>to pay it.</u>

2. The museum is holding an exhibition.
   We want to go to it.

   combinations:

   a. _____

   _____

   b. _____

   _____

3. Luis can be an irritating person.
He deserves a little sympathy at this sad time.

combinations:

a. _____

_____

b. _____

_____

4. Uncle Scott could have gotten stuck in traffic.
Uncle Scott could have taken a wrong turn off the highway.

combinations:

a. _____

_____

b. _____

_____

5. My daughter refuses to eat broccoli.
My daughter will not eat cauliflower.

combinations:

a. _____

b. _____

6. We expected a delicious meal at the stylish and expensive
restaurant.
We got food poisoning.

combinations:

a. _____

_____

b. _____

_____

7. Allison will take me to school tomorrow.
She owes me a favor.

combinations:

a. _____

_____

b. _____

_____

8. Nelson Pinder was offered a great job in Boston.
   He decided to move there.

   combinations:

   a. _____

   _____

   b. _____

   _____

Connect

Exercise 8 **Connect: Editing a Paragraph for Errors in Coordination**

Edit the following paragraph for errors in coordination. You do not need to add or change words. Just add, delete, or change punctuation. There are seven errors in the paragraph.

   Maintaining a healthy weight is a challenge for Demetrius. He struggles with the temptations of junk food and his mother's ideas about nutrition. Demetrius has a busy schedule at school and at work consequently, he eats most of his meals on the run. He tries to focus on choosing healthy items but the choices are difficult. A salad at a salad bar can be loaded with fat in the choice of toppings such as croutons, meat, cheese, and thick, creamy, or even oily salad dressings. The special sauces on fatty burgers are a double temptation; even a serving of frozen yogurt, can be filled with sugar and fat. Demetrius's goal of eating healthy foods is challenged at home for his mother believes in large helpings of comfort food. Fried chicken, vegetables in creamy sauces, and homemade biscuits tempt him, moreover, his mother has strong feelings about food. To her, feeding people is part of her mission in life; so she pushes huge helpings of food on everyone at her table. In the fight against flab, Demetrius is trying hard but his battle is a tough one.

Chapter Test **Beyond the Simple Sentence: Coordination**

Add a comma, a semicolon, or a semicolon and a comma to the following sentences. Do not add, change, or delete any words; just add the correct punctuation.

1. At the end of the meeting, the president of the club stormed out of the room then the club members looked at each other and smiled.

2. LaShonda has never seen snow nor has she experienced the beauty of spring in a northern climate.

3. Archie is a good-natured person still he won't listen to his cousin's constant criticism.

4. I should have taken a class in yoga years ago now I am enjoying my Yoga for Beginners sessions.

5. The new student experienced culture shock for the classroom culture was new.

6. Rain began to pound the roof next the palm trees bent against the fierce winds.

7. I don't like to wear sweatpants when I run instead I wear running tights.

8. The destructive effects of global warming have been prevalent for years yet too many countries ignored the early warning signs.

9. The price of plane tickets is very high so our family will be driving to Florida.

10. We know that the roads in our town need to be repaired however no one wants to pay higher taxes.

CHAPTER 18

Avoiding Run-on Sentences and Comma Splices

Quick Question

True or False: Run-on sentences can always be corrected by adding a comma. (After you study this chapter, you will feel confident of your answer.)

Learning Objectives

In this chapter, you will learn to:

1 Recognize and correct run-on sentences.
2 Recognize and correct comma splices.

---

1 Recognize and correct run-on sentences.

RUN-ON SENTENCES

Run-on sentences are independent clauses that have not been joined correctly. This error is also called a **fused sentence**.

> **run-on sentence error:**
> Steve cleans his kitchen every week he shines every pot and pan.
> **run-on sentence error corrected:**
> Steve cleans his kitchen every week; he shines every pot and pan.
>
> **run-on sentence error:**
> I studied for the test all weekend I am well prepared for it.
> **run-on sentence error corrected:**
> I studied for the test all weekend, so I am well prepared for it.

run-on sentence error:
People crowded into the stadium they scrambled for seats.
run-on sentence error corrected:
People crowded into the stadium. They scrambled for seats.

Exercise 1 **Practice: Identifying Run-on Sentences**

Read each sentence. If the sentence is correct, write OK. If the sentence is a run-on, write an X.

1. _____ We worked on the project all day we went out at night.

2. _____ The college cafeteria is open all day on Saturdays, but it isn't open on Sundays.

3. _____ Driving and texting is very dangerous Bill does it all the time.

4. _____ Tickets to see *Hamilton* are difficult to obtain I managed to get two.

5. _____ My advisor works in the advising center during the day, and she teaches English in the evening.

6. _____ Working and studying isn't easy for Becky she has no free time to socialize with her friends.

7. _____ The science lab courses fill up quickly, and many students are unable to get the schedule they want.

8. _____ Don was late for work everyday he was fired.

STEPS FOR CORRECTING RUN-ON SENTENCES

When you edit your writing, you can correct run-on sentences by following these steps:

Step 1: Check for two independent clauses.

Step 2: Check that the clauses are separated by either a coordinating conjunction and a comma or by a semicolon.

Follow the steps in checking this sentence:

The meeting was a waste of time the club members argued about silly issues.

Step 1: Check for two independent clauses. You can do this by checking for the subject–verb, subject–verb pattern that indicates two independent clauses:

     S   V   S   V
The *meeting was* a waste of time the club *members argued* about silly issues.

The pattern indicates that you have two independent clauses.

Step 2: Check that the clauses are separated by either a coordinating conjunction (*for, and, nor, but, or, yet, so*) and a comma or by a semicolon.

There is no punctuation between the independent clauses, so you have a run-on sentence. You can correct it three ways:

run-on sentence corrected with a coordinating conjunction and a comma:
The meeting was a waste of time, *for* the club members argued about silly issues.

run-on sentence corrected with a semicolon:
The meeting was a waste of time; the club members argued about silly issues.

run-on sentence corrected with a period and a capital letter:
The meeting was a waste of time. The club members argued about silly issues.

Follow the steps once more as you check this sentence:

Working and studying isn't easy for Becky she has no free time to hang out with her friends.

Step 1: Check for two independent clauses. Do this by checking the subject–verb, subject–verb pattern:

$$\text{S} \qquad \text{V} \qquad\qquad\qquad \text{S} \quad \text{V}$$
*Working and studying is*n't easy for Becky *she has* no time to hang out with her friends.

Step 2: Check that the clauses are separated by either a coordinating conjunction (*for, and, nor, but, or, yet, so*) and a comma or by a semicolon.

There is no punctuation between the independent clauses, so you have a run-on sentence. You can correct the run-on sentence three ways:

run-on sentence corrected with a period and a capital letter:
Working and studying isn't easy for Becky. She has no time to hang out with her friends.

run-on sentence corrected with a coordinating conjunction and a comma:
Working and studying isn't easy for Becky, *so* she has no time to hang out with her friends.

run-on sentence corrected with a semicolon:
Working and studying isn't easy for Becky; she has no time to hang out with her friends.

Using the steps to check for run-on sentences can also help you avoid unnecessary punctuation. Consider this sentence:

The manager gave me my schedule for next week and told me about a special sales promotion.

Step 1: Check for two independent clauses. Do this by checking the subject–verb, subject–verb pattern.

$$\text{S} \qquad \text{V} \qquad\qquad\qquad\qquad\qquad \text{V}$$
The *manager gave* me my schedule for next week and *told* me about a special sales promotion.

The pattern is SVV, not SVSV. The sentence is not a run-on sentence. It does not need any additional punctuation.

Following the steps in correcting run-on sentences can help you avoid a major grammar error.

| Exercise 2 | Practice: Correcting Run-on (Fused) Sentences

Some of the sentences that follow are correctly punctuated. Some are run-on (fused) sentences; that is, they are two simple sentences run together without any punctuation. If the sentence is correctly punctuated, write *OK* in the space provided. If it is a run-on sentence, put an *X* in the space provided and correct the sentence above the lines.

1. _____ I can drive you to the clinic now or on Friday after my last class.

2. _____ Bill won't want to go to that restaurant he doesn't like Thai cuisine.

3. _____ Icy conditions were predicted for late afternoon the college decided to cancel evening classes.

4. _____ I had two cups of coffee after dinner now I can't get to sleep.

5. _____ A smile on your face encourages strangers to let go of their natural defensiveness and relax.

6. _____ Shopping online can be easy; it can also be addictive.

7. _____ The kitten grabs my hand with her front paws she puts her tiny teeth into my fingers.

8. _____ Driving on the highway and maneuvering in city traffic require different skills.

COMMA SPLICES

2 Recognize and correct comma splices.

A comma splice is an error that occurs when you punctuate with a comma but should use a semicolon instead. If you are joining two independent clauses without a coordinating conjunction (*for, and, nor, but, or, yet, so*) you must use a semicolon. A comma is not enough.

comma splice error:
The crowd pushed forward, people began to panic.

comma splice error corrected:
The crowd pushed forward; people began to panic.

comma splice error:
I forgot my glasses, thus I couldn't read the small print in the contract.

comma splice error corrected:
I forgot my glasses; thus I couldn't read the small print in the contract.

STEPS FOR CORRECTING COMMA SPLICES

When you edit your writing, you can correct comma splices by following these steps:

Step 1: Check for two independent clauses.

Step 2: Check that the clauses are separated by a coordinating conjunction (*for, and, nor, but, or, yet, so*). If they are, then a comma in front of the coordinating conjunction is sufficient. If they are not separated by a coordinating conjunction, you have a comma splice. Correct it by changing the comma to a semicolon.

Follow the steps to check for a comma splice in this sentence:

I dropped the glass, it shattered on the tile floor.

Step 1: Check for two independent clauses. You can do this by checking for the subject–verb, subject–verb pattern that indicates two independent clauses.

S   V   S   V

I dropped the glass, *it shattered* on the tile floor.

The pattern indicates that you have two independent clauses.

Step 2: Check that the clauses are separated by a coordinating conjunction.

There is no coordinating conjunction. To correct the comma splice error, you must use a semicolon instead of a comma.

comma splice error corrected:
I dropped the glass; it shattered on the tile floor.

Be careful not to mistake a short word such as *then* or *thus* for a coordinating conjunction. Only the seven coordinating conjunctions (*for, and, nor, but, or, yet, so*) with a comma in front of them can join independent clauses.

comma splice error:
Yuiko did her homework, then she checked her e-mail.

comma splice error corrected:
Yuiko did her homework; then she checked her e-mail.

Then is not a coordinating conjunction; it is a conjunctive adverb. When it joins two independent clauses, it needs a semicolon in front of it.

Also remember that conjunctive adverbs that are two or more syllables long (like *consequently, however, therefore*) need a comma after them as well as a semicolon in front of them when they join independent clauses:

Harry has been researching plane fares to New York; consequently, he knows how to spot a cheap flight.

(For a list of some common conjunctive adverbs, see Chapter 17.)

Sometimes writers see commas before and after a conjunctive adverb and think the commas are sufficient. Check this sentence for a comma splice by following the steps:

Jonathan loves his job, however, it pays very little.

Step 1: Check for two independent clauses by checking for the subject–verb, subject–verb pattern.

     S   V   S   V
Jonathan loves his job, however, *it pays* very little.

The pattern indicates that you have two independent clauses.

Step 2: Check for a coordinating conjunction.

There is no coordinating conjunction. *However* is a conjunctive adverb, not a coordinating conjunction. Because there is no coordinating conjunction, you need a semicolon between the two independent clauses.

comma splice error corrected:
Jonathan loves his job; however, it pays very little.

Exercise 3 **Practice: Identifying Independent Clauses and Coordination**

Read each sentence. Underline each independent clause(s) and circle the coordination.

1. Michele works in a hospital; she loves helping others.

2. Biology and chemistry aren't easy courses for Justin , yet he must take both of them.

3. Living in a new country isn't easy; therefore, it takes time to adjust.

4. Writing essays is a big part of this class, so it's important we do well on them.

5. Some people think big cities are exciting; however, others find them too congested.

6. I have a great app on my smartphone; it organizes all of my passwords.

7. Zachary takes only three courses a semester; therefore, he will take longer to graduate.

8. In the United States, students take general education courses first; on the other hand,in China, students only take courses in their major.

Exercise 4 **Practice: Correcting Comma Splices**

Some of the sentences that follow are correctly punctuated. Some contain comma splices. If the sentence is correctly punctuated, write *OK* in the space provided. If it contains a comma splice, put an *X* in the space provided and correct the sentence above the lines. To correct a sentence, do not add any words, just correct the punctuation.

1. _____ Anders changed the channel he couldn't watch any more celebrity gossip.

2. _____ Melinda and Tony were born in Taiwan and came to the United States as children, therefore, they speak two languages fluently.

3. _____ The bookstore was out of books, so I had to order mine online.

4. _____ We couldn't believe how expensive a new mattress set is, nevertheless, we had to purchase one.

5. _____ My dog loves to run in an open field, and I often take her to a huge dog park near the university.

6. _____ Most of my friends dress casually for work, a few wear business attire.

7. _____ The clothes at the discount clothing store are fashionable, but I hate that they fade after only a few washes.

8. _____ I tried to study the material meanwhile, my brother was yelling in the other room.

Collaborate

| Exercise 5 | Collaborate: Completing Sentences |

With a partner or group, write the first part of each of the following incomplete sentences. Make your addition an independent clause. Be sure to punctuate your completed sentences correctly. The first one is done for you.

1. The driver ignored the railroad warning signals, and his car was hit by the train.

2. _____ then I ran out of money.

3. _____ incidentally, you also told several lies about me to my friends.

4. _____ as a result, he was awarded a medal for his exemplary citizenship.

5. _____ otherwise, I won't be able to get a good job.

6. _____ but I didn't recognize the number.

7. _____ or someone will get hurt.

8. _____ now I am in a good position to graduate early.

9. _____ and I have a big test on Friday.

10. _____ besides, you can always change your mind.

Connect

| Exercise 6 | Connect: Editing a Paragraph for Run-on Sentences and Comma Splices |

Edit the following paragraph for run-on sentences and comma splices. There are six errors.

My girlfriend's car was stolen outside of her apartment we were both shocked. The apartment is in a safe neighborhood and many young people live in the area. Most of the residents are college students or people at the beginning of their careers. My girlfriend is usually careful about safety, however, one evening she was careless and left her car doors unlocked. On the next morning, she could not find her car in the parking lot. For half an hour she searched every section of the parking lot and the nearby parking areas. After her desperate search, she called the police and reported the crime. Two days later, the officers called with some news. Her car had been found in a wooded area near the local airport the auto had dented fenders and two smashed windows. First, my girlfriend was horrified by the damage, then she realized her good luck in getting her car back. In the future, she will be more vigilant about securing her car and keeping it safe from car thieves. One careless mistake had cost her money and misery so she doesn't want to make the same error again.

Chapter Test   **Avoiding Run-on Sentences and Comma Splices**

Some of the sentences that follow are correctly punctuated. Some are run-on sentences, and some contain comma splices. If a sentence is correctly punctuated, write *OK* in the space provided. If it is a run-on sentence or contains a comma splice, put an *X* in the space provided and correct the sentence above the lines. To correct a sentence, add the necessary punctuation. Do not add any words.

1. _____ Kristen loves to visit historical sites thus she has been to Philadelphia, Washington, D.C., and Charleston this year.

2. _____ Leon is nearsighted, as a result, he likes a seat near the front of the movie theater.

3. _____ The first quarter of the game was full of action but did not please the fans of the visiting team.

4. _____ Eddie was nosy, he bombarded me with personal questions.

5. _____ You're a good athlete, so you will enjoy the challenges of this game.

6. _____ I am finishing an important paper for class, otherwise, I would go out with you tonight.

7. _____ Our new puppy raced around the back yard for hours today; now he's sleeping.

8. _____ My smartphone was stolen, thus I am in a panic about keeping up with the news from my family and friends.

9. _____ I have read that book at least a dozen times, however, it always makes me happy.

10. _____ The students left the arena dejected, as their team had lost in overtime.

Beyond the Simple Sentence: Subordination

Learning Objectives

In this chapter, you will learn to:

1. Use a dependent clause to begin a sentence.
2. Use a dependent clause to end a sentence.
3. Generate and punctuate sentences correctly.

MORE ON COMBINING SIMPLE SENTENCES

Before you go any further, look back. Review the following:

- A clause has a subject and a verb.
- An independent clause is a simple sentence; it is a group of words, with a subject and a verb, that makes sense by itself.

There is another kind of clause called a **dependent clause**. It has a subject and a verb, but it does not express a complete thought. It cannot stand alone. That is, it *depends* on the rest of the sentence to give it meaning. You can use a dependent clause as another option for combining simple sentences.

> **Note:** Options 1–3 for sentence combining are explained in Chapter 17 on coordination.

OPTION 4: USING A DEPENDENT CLAUSE TO BEGIN A SENTENCE

❶ Use a dependent clause to begin a sentence.

Often, you can combine simple sentences by changing an independent clause from one sentence into a dependent clause and placing it at the beginning of the new sentence.

two simple sentences:

S V   S V
I was late for work. My *car had* a flat tire.

changing one simple sentence into a beginning dependent clause:

S V   S V
Because my *car had* a flat tire, *I was* late for work.

OPTION 5: USING A DEPENDENT CLAUSE TO END A SENTENCE

❷ Use a dependent clause to end a sentence.

You can also combine simple sentences by changing an independent clause from one sentence into a dependent clause and placing it at the end of the new sentence:

S V   S V
I was late for work because my *car had* a flat tire.

Notice how one simple sentence can be changed into a dependent clause in two ways:

two simple sentences:

S   V   S V
The *teacher explained* the lesson. *I took* notes.

changing one simple sentence into a dependent clause:

S   V   S V
The *teacher explained* the lesson while *I took* notes.

or

S   V   S V
While the *teacher explained* the lesson, *I took* notes.

3 Generate and punctuate sentences correctly.

USING SUBORDINATING CONJUNCTIONS

Changing an independent clause to a dependent one is called **subordinating**. How do you do it? You add a subordinating word, called a **subordinating conjunction**, to an independent clause, making it dependent—less "important," or subordinate—in the new sentence.

Keep in mind that the subordinate clause is still a clause; it has a subject and a verb, but it does not make sense by itself. For example, let's start with an independent clause:

> S   V
> *Caroline studies.*

Somebody (Caroline) does something (studies). The statement makes sense by itself. But if you add a subordinating conjunction to the independent clause, the clause becomes dependent and unfinished, like this:

> When Caroline studies. (When she studies, what happens?)
> Unless Caroline studies. (Unless she studies, what will happen?)
> If Caroline studies. (If Caroline studies, what will happen?)

Now, each dependent clause needs an independent clause to finish the idea:

> dependent clause   independent clause
> When Caroline studies, she gets good grades.

> dependent clause   independent clause
> Unless Caroline studies, she forgets key ideas.

> dependent clause   independent clause
> If Caroline studies, she will pass the course.

There are many subordinating conjunctions. When you put any of these words in front of an independent clause, you make that clause dependent. Here is a list of some subordinating conjunctions:

INFO BOX Common Subordinating Conjunctions

after	before	so that	whenever
although	even though	than	where
as	if	though	whereas
as if	in order that	unless	whether
as much as	provided	until	which
because	since	when	while

If you pick the right subordinating conjunction, you can effectively combine simple sentences (independent clauses) into a more sophisticated sentence pattern. Such combining helps you add sentence variety to your writing and helps to explain relationships between ideas.

simple sentences:

> S   V   V   S   V
> *Leo could* not *read* music. His *performance was* exciting.

new combination:

> dependent clause   independent clause
> Although Leo could not read music, his performance was exciting.

simple sentences:

   S   V   S   V

I forgot to do the English assignment. *I was* busy working and preparing for an algebra test.

new combination:

independent clause   *dependent clause*
I forgot to do the English assignment because I was busy working and preparing for an algebra test.

Exercise 1   **Practice: Identifying Subordinating Conjunctions**

Read each sentence. Circle the subordinating conjunction.

1. The movie had already started when we arrived.

2. Because her favorite actor is Chris Pratt, Cindy has seen all of his movies.

3. Unless we run into traffic, we will be at your house at 8:00 p.m.

4. Puri was studying literature before she moved to the United States.

5. Living in a new city can be difficult if you don't know anyone.

6. Whenever Jim plays games online, his mother gets angry.

7. The bookstore is really crowded since it's the first week of classes.

8. Although the weather is getting better, it still doesn't feel like summer.

Exercise 2   **Practice: Choosing the Right Subordinating Conjunction**

Read each sentence and then add the appropriate subordinating conjunction. Refer to the Info Box on common subordinating conjunctions on page 414.

1. Ben was working on his research paper_____his friends stopped by.

2. _____I finished the assignment, I reviewed for the test.

3. They went to the movies_____they had a lot of work to complete.

4. _____John visits, he brings some fresh vegetables from his garden.

5. _____I have to work all weekend, I must complete all of my class work.

6. Mary will be late for class_____she left her house late.

7. _____Bill took algebra in high school, he still doesn't completely understand it.

8. We plan to have the picnic outside_____or not it is warm.

PUNCTUATING COMPLEX SENTENCES

A sentence that has one independent clause and one (or more) dependent clause(s) is called a **complex sentence**. Complex sentences are very easy to punctuate. See if you can figure out the rule for punctuating by yourself. Look at the following examples. All are punctuated correctly.

dependent clause *independent clause*
Whenever the baby smiles, his mother is delighted.

independent clause *dependent clause*
His mother is delighted whenever the baby smiles.

dependent clause *independent clause*
While you were away, I saved your mail for you.

independent clause *dependent clause*
I saved your mail for you while you were away.

In these examples, look at the sentences that have a comma. Look at the ones that do not have a comma. Both kinds of sentences are punctuated correctly. Do you see the rule?

> **If the dependent clause comes at the beginning of the sentence, put a comma after the dependent clause. If the dependent clause comes at the end of the sentence, do not put a comma in front of the dependent clause.**

Although we played well, we lost the game.
We lost the game although we played well.

Until he called, I had no date for the dance.
I had no date for the dance until he called.

| Exercise 3 | **Practice: Punctuating Complex Sentences** |

All the sentences that follow are complex sentences; that is, they have one independent and one (or more) dependent clause(s). Add a comma to each sentence that needs one.

1. Until I can afford a new car I have to keep paying for repairs on my old one.

2. Give me a call if you want me to drive you to school tomorrow.

3. After my parents stopped arguing about my bad behavior I fell into a restless and troubled sleep.

4. I couldn't fall asleep after I watched the scary movie.

5. It is important to pack only the essentials when you are going backpacking.

6. Because my supervisor insists on punctuality I come to work early every morning.

7. My brother won't come to dinner unless I make his favorite banana cake.

8. The children made a mess of the kitchen while the babysitter was texting her friends.

Exercise 4   **Practice: Punctuating Complex Sentences**

All the sentences that follow are complex sentences; that is, they have one independent clause and one or more dependent clauses. Add a comma to each sentence that needs a comma, and circle the subject of the independent clause.

1. Gina struggled to hold on to her purse as the crowd around her began pushing forward.

2. The reception was moved to a larger location so that more guests could be invited.

3. Whether Al joins the U.S. Army or goes to flight school he will need the support of his friends.

4. Alicia was relieved because she found her missing wallet.

5. While the seniors decided to raise money to support a local animal shelter the juniors decided to spend their money on a local conservation project.

6. Since we had missed the first part of the movie we couldn't understand the plot.

7. When an aggressive driver follows my car too closely I pull over to let him pass.

8. I will pass chemistry even if I have to go to tutoring every day.

SUMMARY OF OPTIONS FOR COMBINING SENTENCES

Here are all five options for combining sentences:

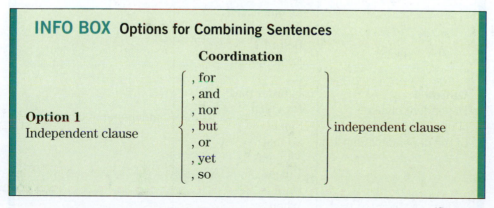

INFO BOX   Options for Combining Sentences

Coordination

Option 1
Independent clause
{
, for
, and
, nor
, but
, or
, yet
, so
}
independent clause

(Continued)

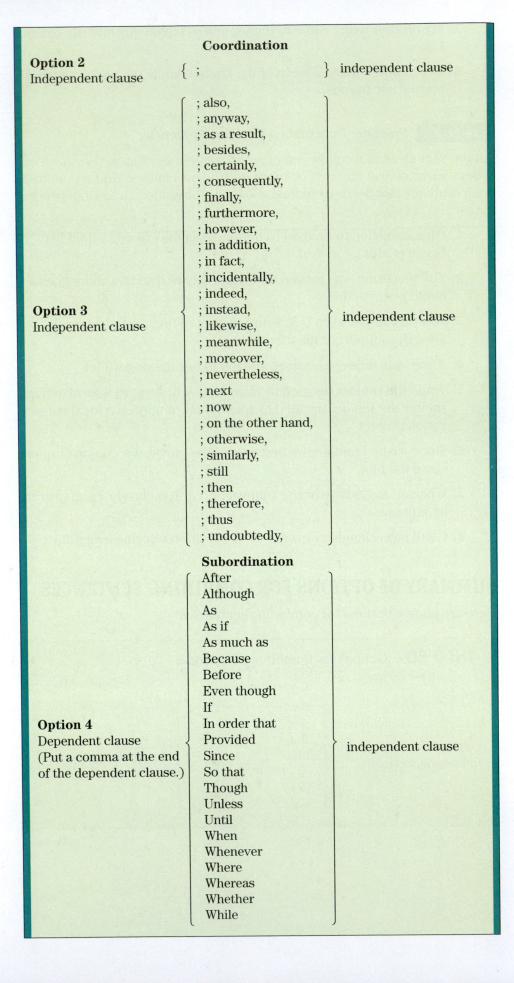

Coordination

Option 2
Independent clause { ; } independent clause

Option 3
Independent clause

; also,
; anyway,
; as a result,
; besides,
; certainly,
; consequently,
; finally,
; furthermore,
; however,
; in addition,
; in fact,
; incidentally,
; indeed,
; instead,
; likewise,
; meanwhile,
; moreover,
; nevertheless,
; next
; now
; on the other hand,
; otherwise,
; similarly,
; still
; then
; therefore,
; thus
; undoubtedly,

independent clause

Subordination

Option 4
Dependent clause
(Put a comma at the end
of the dependent clause.)

After
Although
As
As if
As much as
Because
Before
Even though
If
In order that
Provided
Since
So that
Though
Unless
Until
When
Whenever
Where
Whereas
Whether
While

independent clause

Subordination

Option 5 Independent clause	after although as as if as much as because before even though if in order that provided since so that than though unless until when whenever where whereas whether which while	dependent clause

Note: In Option 4, words are capitalized because the dependent clause will *begin* your complete sentence.

Exercise 5   Practice: Using the Five Options for Combining Sentences

Add the necessary commas and/or semicolons to the following sentences. Some are correct as they are.

1. After the rain stopped the plants in the garden looked fresh and new.

2. One of the puppies in the exercise pen began to bark at the visitor then all the puppies joined in the barking.

3. When the dress I bought online arrived it was stained with grease.

4. Caleb has a hot temper even though he seems easygoing and calm.

5. Whenever the phone rings in the middle of the night I expect bad news.

6. Unless Samantha gets a good night's sleep she is irritable the next day.

7. Give me your answer I need to know it now.

8. The candidate did not support his community's values consequently he lost the election.

Exercise 6   Practice: Using the Five Options for Combining Sentences

Add the necessary commas and/or semicolons to the following sentences. Some are correct as they are.

1. My brother turned my parents' wedding anniversary into something special he made a video out of their old, forgotten home movies.

2. Because I can't stand the smell of smoke on a person's clothing I avoid parties where people smoke.

3. My house is not the tidiest house in town but it is warm and comfortable.

4. My sister doesn't spend money on the latest toys for her children instead she takes them to the park, to the zoo, or to the library for new adventures.

5. Some parking lots were designed many years ago and the parking spaces in them are too small for many of today's large SUVs.

6. I always feel guilty when I gossip about a friend.

7. Although Raymond drives a tow truck at work his own car is a tiny Volkswagen.

8. The pot of spaghetti boiled over while I was distracted by my phone conversation with Eli.

Exercise 7 **Practice: Combining Sentences**

Pairs of sentences follow. Combine each pair of sentences into one clear, smooth sentence in two different ways. You can add words as well as punctuation. The first pair of sentences is done for you.

1. We always go to Country Ice Cream for a treat.
   The store has the best hot fudge sundaes in the world.

   combination 1: We always go to Country Ice Cream for a treat because the store has the best hot fudge sundaes in the world.

   combination 2: We always go to Country Ice Cream for a treat; the store has the best hot fudge sundaes in the world.

2. My cousin wouldn't drive me to the gym.
   I had to take the bus.

   combination 1: _____

   _____

   combination 2: _____

   _____

3. The snowstorm kept everyone inside.
   People were starting to feel restless.

   combination 1: _____

   _____

   combination 2: _____

   _____

4. The persistent salesperson followed me around the store.
   She referred to deals and special discounts.

   combination 1: _____

   _____

   combination 2: _____

   _____

5. Charlie wouldn't listen to Tommy's explanation for the delay.
   He wouldn't accept Tommy's apology.

   combination 1: _____

   _____

   combination 2: _____

   _____

6. I always wake Mark up in the morning.
   He sleeps through the sound of the alarm clock.

   combination 1: _____

   _____

   combination 2: _____

   _____

7. My dog has never caught a squirrel.
   She begins each day with the dream of catching one.

   combination 1: _____

   _____

   combination 2: _____

   _____

8. Bill wanted a career in music.
   He became a physician's assistant.

   combination 1: _____

   _____

   combination 2: _____

   _____

Exercise 8   **Connect: Editing a Paragraph for Errors in Coordination and Subordination**

Connect

Edit the following paragraph for errors in coordination and subordination. You do not have to add words to the paragraph; just add, delete, or change punctuation. There are ten errors.

My mother always dreamed about being a nurse finally, her dream will come true. When she was a young woman she wanted an education, so that she could enter the medical field. Poverty and other family struggles prevented her from finishing high school and she went to work at sixteen. My mother married at twenty, and had three children before she was twenty-four. She raised them, while she continued working at various low-paying jobs. After my father died she worked for fifty hours a week and put every penny into a college fund. The college fund began to grow but all of the money in it was spent on her children's education.

When her children were grown up and educated my mother remembered her lost dream of an education. A guidance counselor told my mother about earning a G.E.D. My mother studied hard, moreover, she often studied with the help of her college-educated children. She was proud of earning her high school diploma then she tackled college. Years of part-time enrollment and constant study passed, and today she is close to her longtime dream. At sixty-two, my mother will graduate from the nursing program at Roosevelt College.

Chapter Test **Coordination and Subordination**

Some of the following sentences need commas and/or semicolons. Write *OK* next to the correct sentences; write *X* next to the incorrect sentences and correct them above the lines.

1. _____ I began to feel ill after I ate a seafood dinner and had a piece of homemade key lime pie for dessert.

2. _____ On the plane, his complaining started at take-off and continued until landing finally the other passengers got some relief from the loud and constant whining.

3. _____ I packed my boxes of shoes and clothes in the trunk of my car and then stuffed every space inside the old Kia with pillows, blankets, and sporting goods.

4. _____ Trevor was always helpful and polite to the customers at the garden store for he was afraid of offending someone and losing his job in a time of high unemployment.

5. _____ My grandparents have lived in the same house for thirty years thus they haven't dealt with the ups and downs of the current real estate market.

6. _____ We can save enough money for a summer trip to Yellowstone if you will sacrifice your annual fishing trip with your cousin.

7. _____ Kira loves dance music yet rarely goes to any of the dance clubs in either of the nearby cities.

8. _____ As the water level in the basement began to rise and threaten the first floor of the house my brother frantically called the number of an emergency plumbing service.

9. _____ Natalie applied to three colleges in North Carolina however she decided to attend college in Nebraska.

10. _____ Since Javier introduced me to kickboxing, I have been going to classes each week at Central East Martial Arts.

Quick Question

True or False: These are both sentences:

A. While he was sitting in class.
B. Without a word, Ewan fainted.

(After you study this chapter, you will be confident of your answer.)

Learning Objectives

In this chapter, you will learn to:

1. Recognize and correct sentence fragments by checking for subject and verb.
2. Recognize and correct sentence fragments by making sure the group of words makes a complete statement.

AVOIDING SENTENCE FRAGMENTS

A **sentence fragment** is a group of words that looks like a sentence and is punctuated like a sentence, but it is *not* a sentence. Writing a sentence fragment is a major grammatical error because it reveals that the writer is not sure what comprises a sentence.

The following groups of words are all fragments:

Because customers are often in a hurry and have little time to look
    for bargains.
My job being very stressful and fast-paced.
For example, the introduction of salads into fast-food restaurants.

There are two easy steps that can help you check your writing for sentence fragments:

> **INFO BOX** Two Steps in Recognizing Sentence Fragments
>
> **Step 1:** Check each group of words punctuated like a sentence, looking for a subject and a verb.
>
> **Step 2:** If you find a subject and a verb, check that the group of words makes a complete statement.

① Recognize and correct sentence fragments by checking for subject and verb.

RECOGNIZING FRAGMENTS: STEP 1

Check for a subject and a verb. Some groups of words that look like sentences may actually have a subject but no verb, they may have a verb but no subject, or they may have no subject *or* verb.

> The puppy in the pet store window. (*Puppy* could be the subject of a sentence, but there is no verb.)
> Doesn't matter to me one way or the other. (There is a verb, *Does matter*, but there is no subject.)
> In the back of my mind. (There are two prepositional phrases, *In the back* and *of my mind*, but there are no subject and verb.)

Remember that an *-ing* verb by itself cannot be the main verb in a sentence. Therefore, groups of words like the ones that follow may look like sentences, but they lack a verb and are really fragments:

> Your sister having all the skills required of a good salesperson.
> The two top tennis players struggling with exhaustion and the stress of a highly competitive tournament.
> Peter being the only one in the room with a piece of paper.

An infinitive (*to* plus a verb) cannot be a main verb in a sentence, either. The following groups of words are also fragments:

> The manager of the store to attend the meeting of regional managers next month in Philadelphia.
> The purpose to explain the fine points of the game to new players.

Groups of words beginning with words like *also, especially, except, for example, in addition,* and *such as* need subjects and verbs, too. Without subjects and verbs, these groups can be fragments, like the ones that follow:

> Also a good place to grow up.
> Especially the youngest member of the family.
> For example, a person without a high school diploma.

Exercise 1 **Practice: Identifying Subjects and Verbs**

Read each sentence. Underline the subject of each sentence and circle the verb. Be sure to circle the complete verb form.

1. The manager closed the store early due to the storm.

2. Lena and Sadie were studying in the library Friday afternoon.

3. Playing soccer is his favorite activity.

4. I only need one more course to graduate.

5. Trying to work full time and attend classes isn't easy.

6. Unlike other classes, English requires extensive writing assignments.

7. Shopping and eating makes up her usual Saturday.

8. Anonymous bloggers often post hurtful comments.

> **Exercise 2**   **Practice: Checking Groups of Words for Subjects and Verbs**

Some of the following groups of words have subjects and verbs; these are sentences. Some are missing subjects, verbs, or both; these are fragments. Put an *S* by each sentence and an *F* by each fragment.

1. _____ Would consider changing the admission fee for the boxing match to be held on Friday night.

2. _____ No one at the house is answering the phone.

3. _____ My brother Jerome driving me to the Denver airport and my best friend meeting me at O'Hare Airport in Chicago.

4. _____ Two dogs with their noses sticking out of the car window and their ears flapping in the wind.

5. _____ Thai food may be too spicy for my mother.

6. _____ Should have asked me about spending our savings on an entertainment unit.

7. _____ Except one required course in sociology or psychology.

8. _____ When my smartphone vibrates.

RECOGNIZING FRAGMENTS: STEP 2

> **2** Recognize and correct sentence fragments by making sure the group of words makes a complete statement.

If a group of words has both a subject and a verb, check that it makes a complete statement. Many groups of words that have both a subject and a verb do not make sense by themselves. They are **dependent clauses**. How can you tell if a clause is dependent? After you have checked each group of words for a subject and a verb, check to see if it begins with one of the subordinating conjunctions that start dependent clauses. (Some common subordinating conjunctions are *after, although, as, as if, as much as, because, before, even though, if, in order that, provided, since, so that, than, though, unless, until, when, whenever, where, whereas, whether, which, while.*)

A clause that begins with a subordinating conjunction is a dependent clause. When you punctuate a dependent clause as if it were a sentence, you have a kind of fragment called a **dependent clause fragment**.

> After I woke up this morning.
> Because he liked football better than soccer.
> Unless it stops raining by lunchtime.

It is important to remember both steps in checking for fragments:

Step 1: Check for a subject and a verb.

Step 2: If you find a subject and a verb, check that the group of words makes a complete statement.

Exercise 3   **Practice: Checking for Dependent-Clause Fragments**

Some of the following groups of words are sentences. Some are dependent clauses punctuated like sentences, which are sentence fragments. Put an *S* by each sentence and an *F* by each fragment.

1. _____ After the interview at the bank was over.

2. _____ Without a word, Laura paid the dinner bill.

3. _____ Even though most students have their own computers.

4. _____ Near the administration building is a patio with stone tables and benches.

5. _____ Then my smartphone malfunctioned.

6. _____ Because no one told me about the nosy neighbors next door.

7. _____ Until Carl and Riggs can get some free time to work on restoring the car.

8. _____ Before Jose can choose his classes for the fall term.

Exercise 4   **Practice: Using Two Steps to Recognize Sentence Fragments**

Some of the following are complete sentences; some are fragments. To recognize the fragments, check each group of words by using the two-step process:

Step 1: Check for a subject and a verb.

Step 2: If you find a subject and verb, check that the group of words makes a complete statement.

Then put an *S* by each sentence and an *F* by each fragment.

1. _____ If my little boy can take swimming lessons at the community center.

2. _____ Regret was obvious in his tone of voice.

3. _____ One of my neighbors starting a project to send packages of goodies to American troops in foreign countries.

4. _____ Without my help, my five-year-old tied her own shoes.

5. _____ Around the front door was a string of holiday lights.

6. _____ Without a sign of regret for his actions.

7. _____ Whenever she tweets her thoughts online.

8. _____ As Gloria and Brian researched travel in India online.

Exercise 5   **Practice: Identifying Fragments in a Paragraph**

Read George's text message to his friend Barbara. There are five fragments. Circle the fragments.

Got your message. I can't finish by Friday. How is Monday? Kim and Jonathan will be back then, so I should be able to get it done by then. What about the party? Still on Saturday? Need to know so I can get a babysitter. I will text you later to confirm. Bringing chips.

CORRECTING FRAGMENTS

You can correct fragments easily if you follow the two steps for identifying them.

Step 1: Check for a subject and a verb. If a group of words is a fragment because it lacks a subject or a verb, or both, *add what is missing.*

fragment: My father being a very strong person. (This fragment lacks a main verb.)

corrected: My father is a very strong person. (The verb *is* replaces *being*, which is not a main verb.)

fragment: Need to know, so I can get a babysitter. (This fragment lacks a subject.)

corrected: I need to know, so I can get a babysitter. (A subject, *I*, is added.)

fragment: Especially on dark winter days. (This fragment has neither a subject nor a verb.)

corrected: I love a bonfire, especially on dark winter days. (A subject, *I*, and a verb, *love*, are added.)

Step 2: If you find a subject and a verb, check that the group of words makes a complete statement. To correct the fragment, you can turn a dependent clause into an independent one by removing the subordinating conjunction, *or* you can add an independent clause to the dependent one to create a sentence.

fragment: When the rain beat against the windows. (The statement does not make sense by itself. The subordinating conjunction *when* leads the reader to ask, "What happened when the rain beat against the windows?" The subordinating conjunction makes this a dependent clause, not a sentence.)

corrected: The rain beat against the windows. (Removing the subordinating conjunction makes this an independent clause, a sentence.)

corrected: When the rain beat against the windows, I reconsidered my plans for the picnic. (Adding an independent clause turns this into a sentence.)

Sometimes you can correct a fragment by linking it to the sentence before it or after it.

fragment (underlined): I have always enjoyed outdoor concerts. Like the ones at Pioneer Park.

corrected: I have always enjoyed outdoor concerts like the ones at Pioneer Park.

fragment (underlined): <u>Even if she apologizes for that nasty remark</u>. I will never trust her again.

corrected: Even if she apologizes for that nasty remark, I will never trust her again.

You have several choices for correcting fragments: you can add words, phrases, or clauses; you can also remove words or combine independent and dependent clauses. You can transform fragments into simple sentences or create compound or complex sentences. To punctuate your new sentences, remember the rules for combining sentences.

Exercise 6 Practice: Correcting Fragments

Correct each sentence fragment that follows in the most appropriate way.

1. I spent two hours waiting at the airport. Until Jessica's flight finally arrived.

   corrected: _____

   _____

2. To earn the money for my little sister's gymnastics lessons. My father took a second job.

   corrected: _____

   _____

3. Colin searched for candles and matches. After the electricity went off.

   corrected: _____

   _____

4. Because a severe drought has struck our area. We are not allowed to water our lawns.

   corrected: _____

   _____

5. Then took a sharp left turn across oncoming traffic and nearly caused a serious accident.

   corrected: _____

   _____

6. One reason Melinda is the valedictorian of the class being her willingness to rewrite her essays and seek help from her instructors.

   corrected: _____

   _____

7. Mosquitoes had bitten every exposed area of David's skin. Especially his neck and feet.

   corrected: _____

   _____

8. Choosing a difficult topic for her speech. Shawna researched her subject for hours.

corrected: _____

_____

Exercise 7 **Collaborate: Correcting Fragments Two Ways**

Collaborate

Working with a partner or group, correct each fragment that follows in two ways. The first one is done for you.

1. Whenever I am waiting for an important phone call.

corrected: I am waiting for an important phone call. _____

corrected: Whenever I am waiting for an important phone call, I am _____

extremely impatient and nervous.

2. While the children crowded around the aquarium.

corrected: _____

_____

corrected: _____

_____

3. On the other side of town, where Tyler lives.

corrected: _____

_____

corrected: _____

_____

4. Although he had never ridden a horse before.

corrected: _____

_____

corrected: _____

_____

5. After the returning soldier arrived home from the front.

corrected: _____

_____

corrected: _____

_____

Connect

Exercise 8 **Connect: Editing a Paragraph for Sentence Fragments**

Correct the sentence fragments in the following paragraph. There are seven fragments.

There is nothing in the world. Like sleeping under a soft, warm quilt. My grandmother had an old quilt on her guest room bed. I was always thrilled to sleep under that puffy covering. When I was a child. In fact, I always hoped for cold weather during my visits to her house. Then I could enjoy the nighttime comfort of the quilt. In addition, adult enjoyment of a good night's sleep under a quilt. My first purchase for my apartment was a big, warm quilt. To be used not only for my bed but also for napping on the sofa. With my own quilt covering me, a soothing, warm cocoon. I can reenter my childhood place. Everyone needing a quilt. Days of racing to work, sitting on hard plastic chairs, standing behind a counter, staring at a screen, or performing back-breaking labor difficult to endure. Sleeping under a quilt is a little reward for such days.

Chapter Test **Avoiding Sentence Fragments**

Some of the following are complete sentences; some are sentence fragments. Put an *S* by each sentence and an *F* by each fragment.

1. _____ A total stranger to assume the job now vacant as a result of the resignation of my supervisor.

2. _____ Unless someone can drive my mother to her doctor's appointment on Tuesday afternoon.

3. _____ The fumes in the basement giving Ellie a terrible headache during her two hours of work on the heating system.

4. _____ On the top shelf of the bookcase sits an old leather catcher's mitt from my father's high school days.

5. _____ While a group of happy children threw snowballs at each other.

6. _____ The reason for my lack of enthusiasm about the trip being my dislike for camping in the woods in winter.

7. _____ Unlike the birthday celebrations in my family, Jordan's birthday party was an elaborate and highly planned gathering.

8. _____ Because of their philanthropic work, the sorority was an important part of the college community.

9. _____ Although there were many reasons he was elected to the school's athletic hall of fame.

10. _____ The festival was held in mid-March as that was the height of the sugaring season in Vermont.

Using Parallelism in Sentences

Learning Objectives

In this chapter, you will learn to:
1. Recognize parallel structure in a sentence.
2. Use parallel structure to revise awkwardly worded sentences.

WHAT IS PARALLELISM?

1. Recognize parallel structure in a sentence.

Parallelism means balance in a sentence. To create sentences with parallelism, remember this rule:

Similar points should get a similar structure.

Often, you will include two or three (or more) related ideas, examples, or details in one sentence. If you express these ideas in a parallel structure, they will be clearer, smoother, and more convincing.

Here are some pairs of sentences with and without parallelism:

not parallel: Of all the sports I've played, I prefer tennis, handball, and playing golf.

parallel: Of all the sports I've played, I prefer *tennis, handball, and golf*. (Three words are parallel.)

not parallel: The professor said she needed to do all her work, on time, and study for the final exam.

parallel: The professor said she needed to *do all her work, get it in on time,* and *study for the final exam*. (Three verb phrases are parallel.)

not parallel: He is a good choice for manager because he works hard, he keeps calm, and well liked.

parallel: He is a good choice for manager because *he works hard, he keeps calm, and he is well liked*. (Three clauses are parallel.)

From these examples you can see that parallelism involves matching the structures of parts of your sentence. There are two steps that can help you check your writing for parallelism.

INFO BOX Two Steps in Checking a Sentence for Parallel Structure

Step 1: Look for the list in the sentence.

Step 2: Put the parts of the list into a similar structure. (You may have to change or add something to get a parallel structure.)

---

2 Use parallel structure to revise awkwardly worded sentences.

ACHIEVING PARALLELISM

Let's correct the parallelism of the following sentence:

sample sentence: The student government association met to decide on student activities, creating a budget, and for the purpose of reviewing the by-laws.

To correct this sentence, we'll follow the steps.

Step 1: Look for the list. The student government association met to do three things. Here's the list:

1. to decide on student activities
2. creating a budget
3. for the purpose of reviewing the by-laws

Step 2: Put the parts of the list into a similar structure:

1. *to decide* on student activities
2. *to create* a budget
3. *to review* the by-laws

Now revise to get a parallel sentence.

parallel: The student government association met *to decide* on student activities, *to create* a budget, and *to review* the by-laws.

If you follow Steps 1 and 2, you can also write the sentence like this:

> **parallel:** The student government association met to *decide* on student activities, *create* a budget, and *review* the by-laws.

But you cannot write a sentence like this:

> **not parallel:** The student government association met *to decide* on student activities, *create* a budget, and *to review* the by-laws.

Think of the list again. You can have:
The student government association met

1. to decide
2. to create   } parallel
3. to review

Or you can have:
The student government association met to

1. decide
2. create   } parallel
3. review

But your list cannot be:
The student government association met to

1. decide
2. create   } not parallel
3. to review

In other words, use the *to* once (if it fits every part of the list), or use *to* with every part of the list.

> **Caution:** Sometimes making ideas parallel means adding something to a sentence because all the parts of the list cannot match exactly.

> **sample sentence:** In his pocket the little boy had a ruler, rubber band, baseball card, and apple.

> **Step 1:** Look for the list. In his pocket the little boy had a
> 1. ruler
> 2. rubber band
> 3. baseball card
> 4. apple

Because they are all nouns, they will each need an article. The *a* goes with *a ruler, a rubber band, a baseball card,* and *a apple.* But *a* isn't the right word to put in front of *apple.* Words beginning with vowels (*a, e, i, o, u*) need *an* in front of them: *an apple.* So to make the sentence parallel, you have to change something in the sentence.

> **Step 2:** Put the parts of the list into a parallel structure.

> **parallel:** In his pocket the little boy had *a ruler, a rubber band, a baseball card,* and *an apple.*

Here's another example:

> **sample sentence:** She was amused and interested in the silly plot of the movie.

Step 1: Look for the list. She was

1. amused
2. interested in the silly plot of the movie

Check the sense of that sentence by looking at each part of the list and how it works in the sentence: "She was *interested in* the silly plot of the movie." That part of the list seems clear. However, when you look at the other part, problems arise: "She was *amused* the silly plot of the movie"? Or "She was *amused in* the silly plot of the movie"? Neither sentence is right. In the first example, a preposition is missing. When the preposition *in* is included in the second example, the sentence is still awkward. People are not *amused in*.

Step 2: The sentence needs a word added to make the structure parallel.

parallel: She was *amused by* and *interested in* the silly plot of the movie.

When you follow the two steps to check for parallelism, you can write clear sentences and improve your style.

Exercise 1 **Practice: Revising Sentences for Parallelism**

Some of the following sentences need to be revised so that they have parallel structures. Revise the ones that need parallelism.

1. Billy enjoys his job, especially helping people, working with computers, and because he earns a high salary.

   revised: _____

   _____

2. The wedding reception was the fanciest I have ever attended, also the most expensive, and the biggest of all.

   revised: _____

   _____

3. At my old school, the best teachers were the ones who listened to students, knew their subject matter, and they never gave tests without warning us.

   revised: _____

   _____

4. The car's price, size, and the condition it was in made it a good buy for a college student.

   revised: _____

   _____

5. After we studied for the test, we spent the rest of the afternoon watching TV, eat popcorn, and we chatted online.

   revised: _____

   _____

6. Cleaning out closets, having to throw away junk, and packing endless boxes are all part of moving out of your home.

   revised: _____

   _____

7. Put the money in the kitchen drawer or on the dresser.

revised: _____

_____

8. Every time I run into Katie, she talks so long that I wind up looking at my watch, making restless motions, and interrupt her before I can get away.

revised: _____

_____

Exercise 2 **Collaborate: Writing Sentences with Parallelism**

Collaborate

Complete this exercise with a partner or a group. First, brainstorm a draft list; then revise the list for parallelism. Finally, complete the sentence in parallel structure. You may want to assign one step (brainstorming a draft list, revising it, etc.) to each group member, then switch steps on the next sentence. The first one is done for you.

1. Three habits I'd like to break are

draft list	revised list
a. worry too much	a. worrying too much
b. talking on the phone for hours	b. talking on the phone for hours
c. lose my temper	c. losing my temper

sentence: Three habits I'd like to break are worrying too much, talking on the phone for hours, and losing my temper

2. Two reasons why people dislike public transportation are

draft list	revised list
a. _____	a. _____
b. _____	b. _____

sentence: _____

_____

3. Starting a new job can be stressful because (add three reasons)

draft list	revised list
a. _____	a. _____
b. _____	b. _____
c. _____	c. _____

sentence: _____

_____

4. When I finish college, I want to (add two goals)

draft list   **revised list**

a. _____   a. _____

b. _____   b. _____

sentence: _____

_____

5. Two things a smartphone can do are (add two things)

draft list   **revised list**

a. _____   a. _____

b. _____   b. _____

sentence: _____

_____

Exercise 3   **Practice: Combining Sentences and Creating a Parallel Structure**

Combine each cluster of sentences that follow into one clear, smooth sentence that includes parallel structure. The first one is done for you.

1. Before you buy a used car, you should research what similar models are selling for.
   It would be a good idea to have a mechanic examine the car.
   Also, how much mileage it has racked up is a consideration.

   combination: Before you buy a used car, you should compare prices of

   similar models, get a mechanic to examine the car, and think carefully about

   the mileage.

2. The qualifications for the job include some sales experience.
   Applicants also have to have good telephone skills.
   Another requirement is being trained in computers.

   combination: _____

   _____

3. Jake was the funniest friend I ever had.
   He was more generous than any other friend I ever had.
   His loyalty was the best, too.

   combination: _____

   _____

4. Hundreds of students waited in line to register for their classes.
   They also were paying their tuition fees.
   Their other goal was to see an advisor.

   combination: _____

   _____

5. My aunt started as a night security guard at Crescent Rehabilitation Center.
Then she was promoted to head of the night security shift.
Eventually she worked her way up to head of security for the center.

combination: _____

_____

_____

6. Shopping malls sell goods.
Contests are often held at shopping malls.
Early morning exercise for mall-walkers is offered.
Special events such as celebrity appearances are another sponsored feature at malls.

combination: _____

_____

_____

7. He was tall.
His skin was dark.
He looked muscular.
He dressed fashionably.
He was the new dean of students.

combination: _____

_____

_____

8. When I need advice, I go to Sean, who is a sensible person.
Sean has insight.
Perceptiveness is another one of his strengths.

combination: _____

_____

_____

Exercise 4   **Connect: Editing a Paragraph for Errors in Parallelism**

Connect

Correct any errors in parallelism in the following paragraph. There are five errors.

Most people get angry when they lose an argument or losing a game. For instance, my mother is usually a calm and polite individual. However, when she has a difference of opinion with me about my social life, she becomes a wild woman. Her eyes give off a fiery glint, her mouth stiffening into a pout, and her jaw juts out with rage if I make an intelligent observation. She does not like a challenge to her beliefs and opinions even if the challenge is polite. Similarly, my best

friend becomes very upset when he loses one of our neighborhood soccer games.

These games are supposed to be informal get-togethers where everyone can get

a little exercise, release some stress, and to enjoy each other's company. How-

ever, to my friend, these competitions are tests. Whenever he plays in a silly little

soccer game, he reacts as if he were in the World Cup and becoming an aggres-

sive fool. To him, losing means slinking away in disgrace, misery, and with fury.

I would love to advise my mother and my friend that their anger does not win an

argument nor change the outcome of a game.

Chapter Test Using Parallelism in Sentences

Some of the following sentences have errors in parallelism; some are correct.
Write *OK* next to the correct sentences; write *X* by the sentences with errors
in parallelism.

1. _____ The honors ceremony will celebrate the academic achievements of many scholars, the success of various sports teams, the ability of individual athletes, and award recognition of the many student clubs.

2. _____ Alonzo is a dear friend, a neighbor who is kind, a hard-working police officer, and a committed volunteer.

3. _____ The specialist in tropical diseases was puzzled by and afraid of the new form of malaria.

4. _____ My backpack has a chemistry book, a notebook to take notes, pencil, and energy bar for when I get hungry.

5. _____ Visiting my grandmother makes me nervous because she asks me personal questions, offers me strange food, and bores with long and pointless stories.

6. _____ If you get to the movie theater and I am not there yet, you can stand in the ticket line, buy the tickets, and waiting for me at the entrance.

7. _____ A whining worker can irritate the other employees, the boss, create a negative atmosphere, and take all the energy out of the room.

8. _____ I tried the front door, checked every window, and explored the entrance to the basement, but I could not find a way into the house.

9. _____ I decided to go to the store, buy some popcorn and soda, and head home to watch Netflix.

10. _____ Our new dog is a nuisance because he sheds, breaks dishes, and drooled on the couch.

Using Adjectives and Adverbs

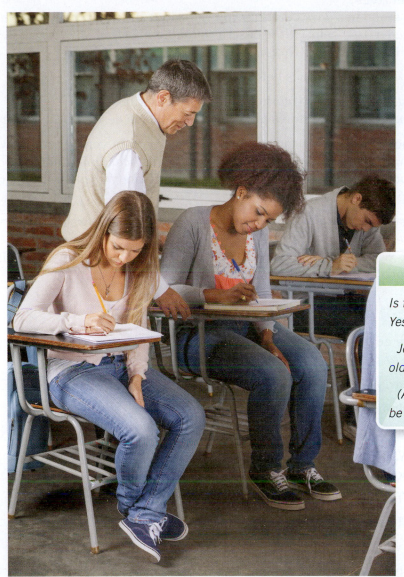

CHAPTER 22

Quick Question

Is the following sentence correct?
Yes/No

Jessica has two brothers, and the oldest brother is extremely handsome.

(After you study this chapter, you will be confident of your answer.)

Learning Objectives

In this chapter, you will learn to:

1. Identify adjectives.
2. Identify adverbs.
3. Use adjectives and adverbs correctly in your writing.

Identify adjectives.

WHAT ARE ADJECTIVES?

Adjectives describe nouns (persons, places, or things) or pronouns (words that substitute for nouns).

> **adjectives:**
> She stood in a *dark* corner. (*Dark* describes the noun *corner*.)
> I need a *little* help. (*Little* describes the noun *help*.)
> She looked *happy*. (*Happy* describes the pronoun *she*.)

An adjective usually comes before the word it describes.

> He gave me a *beautiful* ring. (*Beautiful* describes *ring*.)
> A *small* flash drive stores millions of files. (*Small* describes *flash drive*.)

Sometimes an adjective comes after a **being verb**, a verb that tells what something is. Being verbs are words like *is*, *are*, *was*, *am*, and *has been*. Words such as *feels*, *looks*, *seems*, *smells*, *sounds*, and *tastes* are also part of the group called being verbs.

> He seems *unhappy*. (*Unhappy* describes *he* and follows the being verb *seems*.)
> Alan was *confident*. (*Confident* describes *Alan* and follows the being verb *was*.)

Exercise 1 **Practice: Recognizing Adjectives**

Circle the adjective in each of the following sentences, and then underline the noun or pronoun it describes.

1. Larry got caught in a heavy rainstorm.

2. Mr. and Mrs. Salazar were kind neighbors.

3. A small mouse skittered across the floor.

4. When I go to the movies with Susan, we always share a large popcorn.

5. The enormous snake was curled inside a box.

6. The cough medicine smelled horrible.

7. I want your honest opinion of the performance.

8. TechCom sells innovative devices.

ADJECTIVES: MULTIPLE ADJECTIVE WORD ORDER

We often use more than one adjective to describe someone or something. For example:

> This is a *classic old American* classroom.
> Where are my *red Italian leather* shoes?
> *Large modern glass* buildings are common in this city.

When we use more than one adjective, we need to follow adjective word order. Adjective word order is based on category.

Look at the categories:

1. Opinion or evaluation (*beautiful, horrible, classic*)
2. Size/shape/condition (*small, triangular, broken*)
3. Age (*new, old*)

4. Color (*red, multicolored*)
5. Origin (*Italian, American*)
6. Material (*glass, leather*)

Commas are only placed between adjectives that are from the same category.

> **correct:** I live in a beautiful, friendly neighborhood. (Both *beautiful* and *friendly* are opinions or evaluations so a comma is needed.)
>
> **incorrect:** I have a large, black TV (The adjectives are from *different* categories, so no commas are needed.)
> **correct:** I have a large black TV.

> **Exercise 2** **Practice: Identifying and Correcting Adjective Word Order**

Some of the following sentences have errors with adjective word order, and others are correct. Put an X next to the incorrect sentences and then correct them.

1. _____ Ms. Taylor prefers modern busy cities over peaceful small towns.

2. _____ A new exciting British band will play in the park next week.

3. _____ A slimy green disgusting liquid was leaking from the pipes.

4. _____ Her favorite possession is her white lightweight useful reader.

5. _____ I decided to wear my old floppy red hat.

6. _____ Audra is an energetic, smart, and loyal employee.

7. _____ The homeowners wanted to redesign their circular huge concrete driveway.

8. _____ Isabel decided to sell her red new racing skates.

ADJECTIVES: COMPARATIVE AND SUPERLATIVE FORMS

The **comparative** form of an adjective compares two persons or things. The **superlative** form compares three or more persons or things.

> **comparative:** Your car is *cleaner* than mine.
> **superlative:** Your car is the *cleanest* one in the parking lot.
>
> **comparative:** Hamburger is *cheaper* than steak.
> **superlative:** Hamburger is the *cheapest* meat on the menu.
>
> **comparative:** Lisa is *friendlier* than her sister.
> **superlative:** Lisa is the *friendliest* of the three sisters.

For most adjectives of one syllable, add -*er* to form the comparative, and add -*est* to form the superlative:

> The weather is *colder* than it was yesterday, but Friday was the *coldest* day of the year.
> Orange juice is *sweeter* than grapefruit juice, but the *sweetest* juice is grape juice.

For adjectives that have two syllables and end in -y, drop the -y and add -ier for the comparative form, or -iest for the superlative form.

> She is *happier* today than she was yesterday, but she still isn't the *happiest* in class.
>
> This chapter is *easier* than the last chapter, but the first chapter was the *easiest*.

For adjectives with two or more syllables, use *more* to form the comparative and *most* to form the superlative:

> I thought algebra was *more difficult* than composition; however, physics was the *most difficult* course I ever took.
>
> My brother is *more outgoing* than my sister, but my father is the *most outgoing* member of the family.

The three forms of adjectives usually look like this:

Adjective	Comparative (two)	Superlative (three or more)
sweet	sweeter	sweetest
fast	faster	fastest
short	shorter	shortest

Or they may look like this:

Adjective	Comparative	Superlative
busy	busier	busiest
friendly	friendlier	friendliest
nasty	nastier	nastiest
easy	easier	easiest
pretty	prettier	prettiest

They may even look like this:

Adjective	Comparative (two)	Superlative (three or more)
confused	more confused	most confused
specific	more specific	most specific
dangerous	more dangerous	most dangerous

However, there are some *irregular* forms of adjectives:

Adjective	Comparative (two)	Superlative (three or more)
good	better	best
bad	worse	worst
little	less	least
many, much	more	most

> **Exercise 3**   Practice: Selecting the Correct Adjective Form

Write the correct form of the adjective in each of the following sentences.

1. Milk chocolate tastes _____ (good) than dark chocolate.

2. After my surgery, I had to make _____ (many) calls to my insurance company; in fact, I called the insurance company _____ (many) often than I called my boyfriend.

3. Nick's communications class requires _____ (little) public speaking than my communications class does.

4. Which of the four games would be the _____ (many) suitable for a four-year-old boy?

5. My brother did a _____ (good) job painting my bathroom, but he would have done a _____ (good) job if he had been painting his own bathroom.

6. My sister is learning to cook and has been trying out her creations on me; of the three dishes I've eaten, the broiled swordfish was the _____ (bad).

7. I love both my brothers, but Oscar is _____ (much) loveable than Malcolm.

8. *Pirates of the Caribbean*, *Fast and Furious*, and *X-Men* all produced sequels; I think *Pirates of the Caribbean* offers the _____ (good) of the sequels.

WHAT ARE ADVERBS?

2 Identify adverbs.

Adverbs describe verbs, adjectives, or other adverbs.

adverbs:
As she spoke, Steve listened *thoughtfully*. (*Thoughtfully* describes the verb *listened*.)
I said I was *really* sorry for my error. (*Really* describes the adjective *sorry*.)
The cook worked *very* quickly. (*Very* describes the adverb *quickly*.)

Adverbs answer questions such as "How?" "How much?" "How often?" "When?" "Why?" and "Where?"

| Exercise 4 | **Practice: Recognizing Adverbs**

Circle the adverbs in the following sentences.

1. The dog across the street is usually quiet, but he barks uncontrollably at cats.

2. Sometimes, Sarah Sanchez can be very irritable.

3. The burglar moved swiftly and silently through the house.

4. Ethan was extremely proud of his lovingly rebuilt motorcycle.

5. My friend could not clearly understand the directions I gave him.

6. Mr. Li regularly complains about the noise from the construction crew.

7. My English professor is genuinely interested in my stories about my childhood in Nigeria.

8. David Dowd's beautifully designed furniture won first prize at a decorator's showcase.

③ Use adjectives and adverbs correctly in your writing.

HINTS ABOUT ADJECTIVES AND ADVERBS

Do not use an adjective when you need an adverb. Some writers make the mistake of using an adjective when they need an adverb.

not this: Talk to me ~~honest~~.
but this: Talk to me *honestly*.

not this: You can say it ~~simple~~.
but this: You can say it *simply*.

Exercise 5 **Practice: Changing Adjectives to Adverbs**

In each pair of sentences, change the underlined adjective in the first sentence to an adverb in the second sentence. The first one is done for you.

1. **a.** She is a <u>graceful</u> dancer.

   b. She dances ___*gracefully*___.

2. **a.** Gloria gave an <u>impatient</u> response.

   b. Gloria responded _____.

3. **a.** Mrs. Goldstein was a <u>recent</u> visitor to Concord.

   b. Mrs. Goldstein _____ visited Concord.

4. **a.** As she drove to the emergency room, Abigail was <u>nervous</u>.

   b. Abigail _____ drove to the emergency room.

5. **a.** After the contestant conquered his stage fright, his singing was <u>magnificent</u>.

   b. After the contestant conquered his stage fright, he sang _____.

6. **a.** The team's second try for the title had <u>significant</u> differences from its first attempt.

   b. The team's second try for the title was _____ different from its first attempt.

7. **a.** When the student government president made a decision, she was <u>calm</u>.

   b. The student government president _____ made a decision.

8. **a.** Cristina made a <u>steady</u> advance to the finish line.

   b. Cristina _____ advanced to the finish line.

Do Not Confuse *Good* and *Well* or *Bad* and *Badly*

Remember that *good* is an adjective; it describes nouns. *Well* is an adverb; it describes verbs. (The only time *well* can be used as an adjective is when it means "healthy": *I feel well today.*)

not this: You ran that race ~~good~~.
but this: You ran that race *well*.

not this: I cook eggs ~~good~~.
but this: I cook eggs *well*.

Bad is an adjective; it describes nouns. It also follows being verbs such as *am, is, are, was,* and *has been.* Words such as *feels, looks, seems, smells, sounds,* and *tastes* are also part of the group called being verbs. *Badly* is an adverb; it describes action verbs.

> **not this:** He feels ~~badly~~ about his mistake.
> **but this:** He feels *bad* about his mistake. (*Feels* is a being verb; it is described by the adjective *bad.*)

> **not this:** He dances ~~bad~~.
> **but this:** He dances *badly.* (*Dances* is an action verb; it is described by the adverb *badly.*)

Exercise 6	Practice: Using *Good* and *Well, Bad* and *Badly*

Write the appropriate word in the following sentences.

1. Arthur sold his car to his sister Kathleen, who wanted it _____ (bad, badly).

2. Teresa skipped her math class yesterday because she didn't feel _____ (good, well).

3. A day after I had my smartphone repaired, it worked _____ (good, well), but a week later, it started working _____ (bad, badly) again.

4. Wen dropped his tablet, and the screen is _____ cracked. (bad, badly)

5. When Keith concentrates on his studies, he does _____ (good, well) on his exams.

6. My sister has never been a _____ (good, well) liar, but my brother has a gift for lying _____ (good, well).

7. No one wanted to buy the house because it was _____ (bad, badly) decorated.

8. How _____ (good, well) do you think the movie will be?

Not More + *-er* or Most + *-est*

Be careful. Never write both an *-er* ending and *more,* or an *-est* ending and *most.*

> **not this:** I want to work with someone ~~more smarter~~.
> **but this:** I want to work with someone *smarter.*

> **not this:** Alice is the ~~most richest~~ woman in town.
> **but this:** Alice is the *richest* woman in town.

Use *Than,* Not *Then,* in Comparisons

When you compare things, use *than. Then* means "at a later time."

> **not this:** You are taller ~~then~~ I am.
> **but this:** You are taller *than* I am.

> **not this:** I'd like a car that is more fuel-efficient ~~then~~ my old one.
> **but this:** I'd like a car that is more fuel-efficient *than* my old one.

When Do I Need a Comma between Adjectives?

Sometimes you use more than one adjective to describe a noun.

> I visited a cold, dark cave.
> The cat had pale blue eyes.

If you look at the preceding examples, one uses a comma between the adjectives *cold* and *dark*, but the other does not have a comma between the adjectives *pale* and *blue*. Both sentences are correctly punctuated. As explained previously in the chapter, adjective word order determines whether you need a comma, but to decide whether you need a comma, you can try one of these tests:

Test 1: Try to put *and* between the adjectives. If the sentence still makes sense, put a comma between the adjectives.

> **check for comma:** I visited a cold, dark cave. (Do you need the comma? Add *and* between the adjectives.)
> **add *and*:** I visited a cold *and* dark cave. (Does the sentence still make sense? Yes. You need the comma.)
> **correct sentence:** I visited a cold, dark cave.

> **check for comma:** The cat had pale, blue eyes. (Do you need the comma? Add *and* between the adjectives.)
> **add *and*:** The cat had pale *and* blue eyes. (Does the sentence still make sense? No. You do not need the comma.)
> **correct sentence:** The cat had pale blue eyes.

Test 2: Try to reverse the order of the adjectives. If the sentence still makes sense, put a comma between the adjectives.

> **check for comma:** I visited a cold, dark cave. (Do you need the comma? Reverse the order of the adjectives.)
> **reverse order:** I visited a dark, cold cave. (Does the sentence still make sense? Yes. You need the comma.)
> **correct sentence:** I visited a cold, dark cave.

> **check for comma:** The cat had pale, blue eyes. (Do you need the comma? Reverse the order of the adjectives.)
> **reverse order:** The cat had blue pale eyes. (Does the sentence still make sense? No. You don't need a comma.)
> **correct sentence:** The cat had pale blue eyes.

You can use Test 1 or Test 2 to determine whether you need a comma between adjectives.

Connect

Exercise 7 **Connect: Editing for Errors in Adjectives and Adverbs**

Edit the following paragraph, correcting all the errors in the use of adjectives and adverbs. Write your corrections above the errors. There are six errors.

When you see my new haircut, I want you to be honestly with me. Don't

try to cover up the truth with tactful remarks or badly disguised lies. The haircut

cost me more money then a week's groceries, so it should be more better than any other haircut I've ever had. In addition, I don't want to fool myself about my appearance. I need to know very quick whether I should cover my head with a cap for a few weeks. Of all the good friends in my life, you are my better friend, so I am relying on your judgment. Go ahead; breathe deep, and give me your opinion.

Chapter Test Using Adjectives and Adverbs

Some of the following sentences have errors in the use of adjectives and adverbs. Some are correct. Write *OK* next to the correct sentences; write *X* by each incorrect sentence.

1. _____ I have had three different phone plans; the first one looked like a bargain, but it turned out to be the worst deal.

2. _____ The tutor from the student learning center was more kinder to me than any of my math instructors in high school.

3. _____ She feels bad that she can't attend the wedding next month.

4. _____ When Maya left the hospital, she looked healthy, but she wasn't feeling well.

5. _____ On his trip to Savannah, Trevor saw three old friends; one had become a real successful cartoonist.

6. _____ My sister wants to meet a young, dark, and handsome man with a good job.

7. _____ After I gave her the giant teddy bear, my daughter gave me a great big kiss.

8. _____ Driving to Providence seems to be a more better idea than spending a great deal of money on plane tickets.

9. _____ The final exam was difficulter than I thought it would be.

10. _____ Madison heard that Natalie and Jason had been speaking bad about her to their friends.

Correcting Problems with Modifiers

Learning Objectives

In this chapter, you will learn to:

1️⃣ Identify modifiers within sentences.

2️⃣ Recognize and correct misplaced modifiers.

3️⃣ Recognize and correct dangling modifiers.

1️⃣ Identify modifiers within sentences.

WHAT ARE MODIFIERS?

Modifiers are words, phrases, or clauses that describe (modify) something in a sentence. Modifiers are often descriptive words, such as adjectives and adverbs, that modify other nouns and verbs. All the italicized words, phrases, and clauses that follow are modifiers.

> the *blue* van (word)
> the van *in the garage* (phrase)
> the van *that she bought* (clause)

foreign tourists (word)
tourists *coming to Florida* (phrase)
tourists *who visit the state* (clause)

In addition to describing something, sometimes modifiers limit another word or make another word (or words) more specific.

the girl *in the corner* (tells exactly which girl)
fifty acres (tells exactly how many acres)
the movie *that I liked best* (tells which movie)
He *never* calls. (tells how often)
The enemy retreated *hastily*. (tells the manner in which the enemy retreated)
Sam ate breakfast *in the car*. (tells where the breakfast was eaten by Sam)

Exercise 1 Practice: Recognizing Modifiers

In each of the following sentences, underline the modifiers (words, phrases, or clauses) that describe the italicized word or phrase.

1. A chocolate *sundae* with sprinkles on top makes my nephew smile with pleasure.

2. Walking confidently down the red carpet, the *celebrity* waved to his fans.

3. Ava searched through the racks for a new *dress* to wear to the party.

4. Smiling at me from the back row of the classroom, *my sister* applauded my speech.

5. Daniela carries her textbooks, notebooks, and tablet in an old green *backpack*.

6. The *passengers* waiting at the terminal for hours began to complain loudly.

7. The *woman* selected for the top job once worked at a local bank.

8. The *article* used by the student was unreliable and dated.

CORRECTING MISPLACED MODIFIERS

2 Recognize and correct misplaced modifiers.

Modifiers can make your writing more specific. Used effectively and correctly, modifiers give the reader a clear, exact picture of what you want to say, and they help you to say it precisely. However, modifiers have to be used correctly. The most common type of modifier error is called a **misplaced modifier**. As you edit your sentences, you can check for misplaced modifiers by following the three steps outlined in the Info Box.

INFO BOX Three Steps to Check for Misplaced Modifiers in Your Sentences

Step 1: Find the modifier.

Step 2: Ask, "Does the modifier have something to modify?"

Step 3: Ask, "Is the modifier in the right place, as close as possible to the word, phrase, or clause it modifies?"

If you answer no in either Step 2 or Step 3, you need to revise your sentence. Let's use the steps in the following example.

> **sample sentence:** I saw a girl driving a Mazda wearing a bikini.
>
> **Step 1:** Find the modifier. The modifiers are *driving a Mazda, wearing a bikini*.
>
> **Step 2:** Ask, "Does the modifier have something to modify?" The answer is yes. The girl is driving a Mazda. The girl is wearing a bikini. Both modifiers go with a *girl*.
>
> **Step 3:** Ask, "Is the modifier in the right place?" The answer is yes and no. One modifier is in the right place:
>
> I saw a *girl driving a Mazda*

The other modifier is *not* in the right place:

> a *Mazda wearing a bikini*

The Mazda is not wearing a bikini.

> **revised:** I saw a girl *wearing a bikini* and *driving a Mazda*.

Let's work through the steps once more:

> **sample sentence:** Scampering through the forest, the hunters saw two rabbits.
>
> **Step 1:** Find the modifier. The modifiers are *scampering through the forest*, and *two*.
>
> **Step 2:** Ask, "Does the modifier have something to modify?" The answer is yes. There are *two rabbits*. The *rabbits* are *scampering through the forest*.
>
> **Step 3:** Ask, "Is the modifier in the right place?" The answer is yes and no. The word *two* is in the right place:
>
> *two* rabbits

But *scampering through the forest* is in the wrong place:

> *Scampering through the forest*, the hunters

The hunters are not scampering through the forest, the rabbits are.

> **revised:** The hunters saw two rabbits *scampering through the forest*.

> **Caution:** Words such as *almost, even, exactly, hardly, just, merely, nearly, only, scarcely,* and *simply* are referred to as **limiting modifiers**. They impose restrictions on the word they immediately precede. They should be placed before the word they intend to modify. If you put them in the wrong place, you may write a confusing sentence.

> **sample sentence:** Etienne only wants to grow carrots and zucchini. (The modifier that creates confusion here is *only*. Does Etienne have only one goal in life—to grow carrots and zucchini? Or are these the only vegetables he wants to grow? To create a clearer sentence, move the modifier.)
>
> **revised:** Etienne wants to grow *only* carrots and zucchini.

The examples you have just reviewed involve **misplaced modifiers**, words that describe something but are not where they should be in the sentence. Here is the rule to remember:

> **Put a modifier as close as possible to the word, phrase, or clause it modifies.**

Exercise 2   Practice: Correcting Sentences with Misplaced Modifiers

Some of the following sentences contain misplaced modifiers. Revise any sentence that has a misplaced modifier by putting the modifier as close as possible to whatever it modifies.

1. Hanging from the ceiling, I noticed a giant spider.

   revised: _____

   _____

2. The village is well known for its giant garbage dump where I was born.

   revised: _____

   _____

3. Emma lent her handbook to a friendly classmate that she bought at the bookstore.

   revised: _____

   _____

4. Callie and Jeremy were surprised by the sudden appearance of two deer driving in the national forest.

   revised: _____

   _____

5. Painted a pale green, the old house looked new again.

   revised: _____

   _____

6. Dipped in chocolate, my aunt enjoyed the large, plump strawberries.

   revised: _____

   _____

7. Standing in line at the ticket counter, the children grew restless and bored.

   revised: _____

   _____

8. Right from the oven, Annie served the cinnamon cookies.

   revised: _____

   _____

③ Recognize and correct dangling modifiers.

CORRECTING DANGLING MODIFIERS

The three steps for correcting misplaced modifiers can help you recognize another kind of error. Let's use the steps to check the following sentence.

> **sample sentence:** Strolling through the tropical paradise, many colorful birds could be seen.

Step 1: Find the modifier. The modifiers are *Strolling through the tropical paradise*, and *many colorful*.

Step 2: Ask, "Does the modifier have something to modify?" The answer is yes and no. The words *many* and *colorful* modify birds. But who or what is *strolling through the tropical paradise?* There is no person mentioned in this sentence. The birds are not strolling.

This kind of error is called a **dangling modifier**. It is a modifier that does not have anything to modify; it just dangles in the sentence. To correct this kind of error, you cannot just move the modifier:

> **still incorrect:** Many colorful birds could be seen strolling through the tropical paradise. (There is still no person strolling.)

The way to correct this kind of error is to add something to the sentence. If you gave the modifier something to modify, you might come up with several different revised sentences:

> **revised sentences:** *As I strolled through the tropical paradise, I saw* many colorful birds.

or

> Many colorful birds could be seen *when we were strolling through the tropical paradise.*

or

> *While the tourists strolled through the tropical paradise, they saw* many colorful birds.

Try the process for correcting dangling modifiers once more:

> **sample sentence:** Ascending in the glass elevator, the hotel lobby glittered in the light.

Step 1: Find the modifier. The modifiers are *Ascending in the glass elevator*, and *hotel*.

Step 2: Ask, "Does the modifier have anything to modify?" The answer is yes and no. The word *hotel* modifies lobby, but *ascending in the glass elevator* doesn't modify anything. Who is ascending in the elevator? There is nobody mentioned in the sentence.

To revise this sentence, put somebody or something in it for the modifier to describe:

> *As the guests ascended in the glass elevator*, the hotel lobby glittered in the light.

or

> *Ascending in the glass elevator, she* saw the hotel lobby glitter in the light.

Remember that you cannot correct a dangling modifier just by moving the modifier. You have to give the modifier something to modify; you have to add something to the sentence.

Practice: Correcting Sentences with Dangling Modifiers

Some of the following sentences use modifiers correctly; some sentences have dangling modifiers. Revise the sentences with dangling modifiers. To revise, you will have to add words and change words.

1. Thoroughly cleaned and polished, I put the car back in the garage.

   revised: _____

   _____

2. While volunteering at an animal shelter on the weekends, Christopher met a beautiful woman.

   revised: _____

   _____

3. To find a house in a lower price range, looking farther from the city is necessary.

   revised: _____

   _____

4. Having trained as a paramedic in the army, Jose's skills would help him to find a job in civilian life.

   revised: _____

   _____

5. Unprepared for a hot day, people began shedding their coats and sweaters.

   revised: _____

   _____

6. He took a three-week camping trip after graduation from college in the Sierra Nevadas.

   revised: _____

   _____

7. With hard work and a positive attitude, many of the challenges and anxieties of a new job can be handled.

   revised: _____

   _____

8. At the age of five, my brother was born, and I had some difficulty being the older brother.

   revised: _____

   _____

REVIEWING THE STEPS AND THE SOLUTIONS

It is important to recognize problems with modifiers and to correct these problems. Modifier problems can result in confusing or even silly sentences. When you confuse or unintentionally amuse your reader, you are not making your point.

Remember to check for modifier problems in three steps and to correct each kind of problem appropriately. Use the following Info Box to help you remember the steps.

INFO BOX   A Summary of Modifier Problems

Checking for Modifier Problems

Step 1: Find the modifier.

Step 2: Ask, "Does the modifier have something to modify?"

Step 3: Ask, "Is the modifier in the right place?"

Correcting Modifier Problems

If the modifier is in the wrong place (a **misplaced modifier**), put it as close as possible to the word, phrase, or clause it modifies.

If the modifier has nothing to modify (a **dangling modifier**), add or change words so that it has something to modify.

Collaborate

Exercise 4   Collaborate: Revising Sentences with Modifier Problems

All of the following sentences have modifier problems. Working with a partner or group, write a new, correct sentence for each incorrect one. You may move words, add words, change words, or remove words. The first one is done for you.

1. Written in stone, the archaeologist could not understand the ancient message.

   revised: The archaeologist could not understand the ancient message
   written in stone.

2. Looking for a compatible mate, friends and family members may know several potential partners.

   revised: _____

   _____

3. Proudly carrying a large diploma, Belinda saw her friend emerge from the college auditorium.

   revised: _____

   _____

4. Exhausted after a long day at work, Tina only watched half an hour of television before she fell asleep.

   revised: _____

   _____

5. An angry man stormed into the police station covered in mud.

   revised: _____

   _____

6. Before buying a new home, the needs of all the family members should be considered.

   revised: _____

   _____

7. To restore the downtown plaza to its place as the center of the community, the support of all the citizens is necessary.

   revised: _____

   _____

8. Covered in fudge icing, I couldn't stop eating the brownies.

   revised: _____

   _____

Exercise 5   **Connect: Editing a Paragraph for Modifier Problems**

Connect

Correct any errors in the use of modifiers in the following paragraph. There are seven errors. Write your corrections above the line.

When two roommates and I moved into our first home, we were lucky to have my uncle checking the premises for safety hazards. First, my roommates and I would nearly have missed all the problems in the electrical system. My uncle found fire hazards in the wiring. I brought another danger into the house. Wanting to save on heating costs, an old space heater from a garage sale was brought into our new home. On its first use, the condition of the heater would have been a fire hazard. Heat became an issue in the kitchen, too. Without a fire extinguisher, there was danger in the kitchen. A pantry near the kitchen filled with stacks of old newspapers could ignite, and we would not see the fire until it spread past the pantry. My uncle also noticed cracked many windows that created security problems. Finally, my uncle explored our yard and installed bright lights at the front door. We were grateful for his careful inspection, although we had only wanted a quick survey of our home.

Chapter Test **Correcting Problems with Modifiers**

Some of the sentences that follow have problems with modifiers; some are correct. Write *OK* next to the correct sentences; write *X* by each sentence containing a modifier error.

1. _____ Stuck in an endless line of traffic and late for work, nothing seemed to be going well for me on Wednesday morning.

2. _____ At the age of nineteen, a beautiful baby entered my mother's life.

3. _____ To make money in a small business, patience and a realistic attitude about profit and loss are necessary.

4. _____ Racing through the airport, I nearly made the last flight to Puerto Rico but arrived at the gate as the doors of the plane closed.

5. _____ When cleaning the interior of a car, a portable vacuum cleaner, a brush, and a few soft cloths can be helpful.

6. _____ Caught in a lie, Sean and Mason tried talking fast as a way to cover their dishonesty.

7. _____ Whipped by strong winds, the beach cabana did not seem a safe place for us to to take shelter in a tropical storm.

8. _____ Josie got to know several kind and friendly classmates while taking the subway to school.

9. _____ The student submitted the essay to his teacher he had written the night before.

10. _____ Steve and Sonia decided to have three children on their wedding day.

Using Verbs Correctly: Standard Verb Forms, Irregular Verbs, Consistency, and Voice

Quick Question

Which sentence(s) is(are) correct?

A. My friend and I shared a cab ride, but I pay the entire fare.

B. My friend and I shared a cab ride, but I paid the entire fare.

(After you study this chapter, you will be confident of your answer.)

Learning Objectives

In this chapter, you will learn to:

1 Identify verbs.

2 Recognize errors in verb tense or consistency.

3 Distinguish between passive and active voice.

THE ROLE OF VERBS

1 Identify verbs.

Verbs are words that show some kind of action or being. The following verbs show action or being:

He *runs* to the park.
Melanie *is* my best friend.
The library *opens* at 8:00 a.m.

Verbs also tell about time.

He *will run* to the park. (The time is future.)
Melanie *was* my best friend. (The time is past.)
The library *opens* at 8:00 a.m. (The time is present.)

The time of a verb is called its **tense**. You can say a verb is in the *present tense*, *future tense*, or many other tenses.

Using verbs correctly involves knowing which form of the verb to use, choosing the right verb tense, and being consistent in verb tense.

2 Recognize errors in verb tense or consistency.

THE PRESENT TENSE

Look at the standard verb forms for the present tense of the word *listen*:

verb: listen

I listen	we listen
you listen	you listen
he, she, it listens	they listen

Take a closer look at the verb forms. Only one form is different:

he, she, it *listens*

This is the only form that ends in *s* in the present tense.

> ### INFO BOX
>
> In the present tense, use an *-s* or *-es* ending on the verb only when the subject is he, she, or it, or the equivalent, such as a proper name or a singular noun.

Take another look at the present tense.

I attend every lecture.
You care about the truth.
He visits his grandfather regularly.
She drives a new car.
The new *album sounds* great.
We follow that team.
You work well when you both compromise.
They buy the store brand of cereal.

Exercise 1   **Practice: Picking the Correct Verb in the Present Tense**

Underline the subject and circle the correct verb form in parentheses in each of the following sentences.

1. In the spring, my allergies (make, makes) me miserable.

2. This class (get, gets) more difficult every day.

3. My cousins in Puerto Rico (turn, turns) my visits into special occasions.

4. With a smile, my daughter's kindergarten teacher (welcome, welcomes) each child to class.

5. The construction workers across the street never (arrive, arrives) before 8:00 a.m.

6. Around the corner (stand, stands) an old house and a new apartment building.

7. Arriving quickly and without warning, thunderstorms (strike, strikes) the area on summer afternoons.

8. Our English class (require, requires) more writing than my math class.

Exercise 2 **Practice: Correcting the Form of the Verb in the Present Tense**

Read Eric's e-mail to his friend. You may spot several slang expressions, but just correct the verb tense errors. There are ten mistakes involving present-tense verbs.

Hey Tyler

I hope you are well. Things here is busy as usual. My weeks are filled with school and work. Every day I wakes up at 6:00 a.m. I take a shower, gets dressed, and grab a quick bite to eat before school. I catch a ride with my friend Judy. Judy and I has class together at 8:00 a.m. Sometimes Judy trys to talk me into stopping for a cup of coffee before school, but I don't like to because we be late to school. Once we get to school, we goes to English class. English class is pretty good. Our professor, Dr. Hubbard, is cool. She push us real hard to learn. After English, I have Algebra and History. They are okay. Judy go to work after English, so I usually take the bus home. At home I prepare a quick meal. After, I go to work. My job is really boring, but the people are nice. My coworker John and I laughs a lot. Sometimes after work we grab a bite to eat.

Well, look at the time! I have to go. Say hi to everyone.

Eric

THE PAST TENSE

The past tense of most verbs is formed by adding *-d* or *-ed* to the verb.

verb: listen

I listened	we listened
you listened	you listened
he, she, it listened	they listened

Add *-ed* to *listen* to form the past tense. For some other verbs, you may add *-d*.

The sun *faded* from the sky.
He *shouted* the answer.
She *crumpled* the paper into a ball.

Exercise 3 **Practice: Writing the Correct Verb Forms in the Past Tense**

Write the correct past tense form of each verb in parentheses in each sentence, and underline the noun or proper noun that represents the subject of the verb.

1. You _____ (ignore) the slow leak in the basement for months.

2. Last night, Ira _____ (play) cards for two hours.

3. In sixth grade, I _____ (earn) an award for perfect attendance.

4. For many years, my father _____ (talk) about coming to the United States.

5. The class _____ (visit) the writing center together last Monday.

6. On Friday, someone _____ (call) me in the middle of the night.

7. After the movie, my friends _____ (invite) me to a Chinese restaurant.

8. After getting lost on the highway, we finally _____ (discover) the correct exit to the Miami airport.

THE FOUR MAIN FORMS OF A VERB: PRESENT, PAST, PRESENT PARTICIPLE, AND PAST PARTICIPLE

When you are deciding which form of a verb to use, you will probably rely on one of four forms: the present tense, the past tense, the present participle, and the past participle. Most of the time, you will use one of these forms or add a helping verb to it. As an example, look at the four main forms of the verb *listen*.

Present	**Past**	**Present Participle**	**Past Participle**
listen	listened	listening	listened

You use the four verb forms—present, past, present participle, past participle—alone or with helping verbs, to express time (tense). Forms of regular verbs like *listen* are easy to remember. Use the present form for the present tense:

We *listen* to the news on the car radio.

The past form expresses past tense:

I *listened* to language tapes for three hours yesterday.

The present participle, or *-ing* form, is used with helping verbs to express an action in progress or an action that was in progress at a specific time:

He *was listening* to me.
I *am listening* to you.
You *should have been listening* more carefully.

The past participle is the form used with the helping verbs *have, has,* or *had* to express actions that began in the past and have continued to now, show a connection to the past, or were completed at an unspecified time in the past:

> I *have listened* for hours.
> She *has listened* to the tape.
> We *had listened* to the tape before we bought it.

Of course, you can add helping verbs (or modals) to the present tense:

> **present tense:**
> We *listen* to the news on the car radio.

> **add helping verbs:**
> We *will* listen to the news on the car radio.
> We *should* listen to the news on the car radio.
> We *can* listen to the news on the car radio.

When a verb is regular, the past form is created by adding *-d* or *-ed* to the present form. The present participle is formed by adding *-ing* to the present form, and the past participle form is the same as the past form.

IRREGULAR VERBS

Irregular verbs do not follow the same rules for creating verb forms that regular verbs do. Three verbs that we use all the time—*be, have, do*—are irregular verbs. You need to study them closely. Look at the present tense forms for all three:

verb: be	**verb:** have	**verb:** do
I am	I have	I do
you are	you have	you do
he, she, it is	he, she, it has	he, she, it does
we are	we have	we do
you are	you have	you do
they are	they have	they do

> **Caution:** Be careful when you add *not* to *does*. If you are writing a contraction of *does not*, be sure you write *doesn't*, not *don't*.

> **not this:** ~~The light don't work~~.
> **but this:** The light doesn't work.

Exercise 4   **Practice: Choosing the Correct Form of *Be, Have,* or *Do* in the Present Tense**

Circle the correct form of the verb in parentheses in each sentence.

1. If you (has, have) a free afternoon, you can spend some time with Karen and her children.

2. These directions (be, are) very clear.

3. The blue paint (has, have) the right tint of green to match your turquoise chairs.

4. Alicia won't come to the party because she (doesn't, don't) have a ride across town.

5. Dogs can be wonderful pets, but they (has, have) to be treated humanely.

6. Before I go on a blind date, I (do, does) a little investigating into my date's background.

7. Although she is very busy, she (do, does) take her time with her assignments.

8. Caroline (has, have) dreams of moving to Hawaii.

The Past Tense of *Be, Have,* and *Do*

Irregular past forms can be confusing because they often do not follow the same pattern as present forms. Take a look at the past tense forms below:

verb: be	**verb: have**	**verb: do**
I was	I had	I did
you were	you had	you did
he, she, it was	he, she, it had	he, she, it did
we were	we had	we did
you were	you had	you did
they were	they had	they did

Exercise 5 **Practice: Choosing the Correct Form of *Be, Have,* or *Do* in the Past Tense**

Circle the correct verb form in parentheses in each sentence that follows, and underline the subject of each sentence.

1. Years ago when my parents were working on their college degrees, my family (have, had) pizza for dinner three times a week.

2. I do not feel guilty about ignoring Todd's calls because he (done, did) nothing but argue with me for two days.

3. Yesterday, Shakira (had, have) to fix the broken screen of her smartphone.

4. After our senior year, Jamie Perez and I (was, were) best friends for a while.

5. Last Wednesday, several members of the local crime watch group (had, have) a meeting with residents in the Birch Glen area.

6. When I saw the grade on my psychology test, I (was, were) too surprised to say anything.

7. My sister bought the plants for a garden, but my brother-in-law (done, did) the planting, watering, clipping, and fertilizing.

8. The new library and student center (was, were) once vacant buildings.

More Irregular Verb Forms

Be, have, and *do* are not the only verbs with irregular forms. There are many such verbs, and everybody who writes uses some form of an irregular verb. When you write and are not certain if you are using the correct form of a verb, review the list of irregular verbs that follows.

For each irregular verb listed, the *present,* the *past,* and the *past participle* forms are given. The present participle isn't included because it is always formed by adding *-ing* to the present form.

Irregular Verb Forms

Present	Past	Past Participle
(Today I *arise*.)	(Yesterday I *arose*.)	(I have/had *arisen*.)
arise	arose	arisen
awake	awoke, awaked	awoken, awaked
bear	bore	born, borne
beat	beat	beaten
become	became	become
begin	began	begun
bend	bent	bent
bite	bit	bitten
bleed	bled	bled
blow	blew	blown
break	broke	broken
bring	brought	brought
build	built	built
burst	burst	burst
buy	bought	bought
catch	caught	caught
choose	chose	chosen
cling	clung	clung
come	came	come
cost	cost	cost
creep	crept	crept
cut	cut	cut
deal	dealt	dealt
draw	drew	drawn
dream	dreamed, dreamt	dreamed, dreamt
drink	drank	drunk
drive	drove	driven
eat	ate	eaten
fall	fell	fallen
feed	fed	fed
feel	felt	felt
fight	fought	fought
find	found	found
fling	flung	flung
fly	flew	flown
freeze	froze	frozen
get	got	got, gotten
give	gave	given
go	went	gone
grow	grew	grown
hear	heard	heard
hide	hid	hidden
hit	hit	hit

Present	Past	Past Participle
hold	held	held
hurt	hurt	hurt
keep	kept	kept
know	knew	known
lay (means to put)	laid	laid
lead	led	led
leave	left	left
lend	lent	lent
let	let	let
lie (means to recline)	lay	lain
light	lit, lighted	lit, lighted
lose	lost	lost
make	made	made
mean	meant	meant
meet	met	met
pay	paid	paid
ride	rode	ridden
ring	rang	rung
rise	rose	risen
run	ran	run
say	said	said
see	saw	seen
sell	sold	sold
send	sent	sent
sew	sewed	sewn, sewed
shake	shook	shaken
shine	shone, shined	shone, shined
shrink	shrank	shrunk
shut	shut	shut
sing	sang	sung
sit	sat	sat
sleep	slept	slept
slide	slid	slid
sling	slung	slung
speak	spoke	spoken
spend	spent	spent
stand	stood	stood
steal	stole	stolen
stick	stuck	stuck
sting	stung	stung
stink	stank, stunk	stunk
string	strung	strung
swear	swore	sworn
swim	swam	swum
teach	taught	taught
tear	tore	torn
tell	told	told
think	thought	thought
throw	threw	thrown
wake	woke, waked	woken, waked
wear	wore	worn
win	won	won
write	wrote	written

Exercise 6   **Practice: Choosing the Correct Form of Irregular Verbs**

Write the correct form of the verb in parentheses in each sentence. Be sure
to check the list of irregular verbs.

1. You have never _____ (swim) in a pool like this one.

2. She wore a necklace of glass beads _____ (string) on a silver
   chain.

3. Once Leila picked a major, she _____ (feel) more focused
   and motivated in college.

4. Marie Elena has _____ (swear) to organize her closet, so she
   can find her favorite jeans.

5. I _____ (lend) my pencil and calculator to her yesterday.

6. My mother _____ (wear) the same old coat for years.

7. The police found a warehouse full of electronic goods that the
   thieves had _____ (steal).

8. We are all very tired. His alarm clock has _____ (ring) every
   morning.

Exercise 7   **Collaborate: Writing Sentences with Correct Verb Forms**

Collaborate

With a partner or a group, write two sentences that correctly use each of the
following verb forms. In writing these sentences, you may add helping verbs
to the verb forms, but do not change the verb form itself. The first one is
done for you.

1. sent

   a. He sent her a dozen roses on Valentine's Day. _____

   b. I have sent him all the information he needs. _____

2. lie (means to recline)

   a. _____

   b. _____

      _____

3. shrank

   a. _____

   b. _____

4. meant

   a. _____

   b. _____

5. paid

   a. _____

   b. _____

6. lain

a. _____

b. _____

7. shined

a. _____

b. _____

8. seen

a. _____

b. _____

Connect

Exercise 8 **Connect: Editing a Paragraph for Correct Verb Forms**

Correct the errors in verb forms in the following paragraph. There are six errors.

My father should stop nagging me about my future. I has been in college for only a few weeks, and since my first day of class, he has been a nuisance. Last spring, he were thrilled when I received a grant and some other financial aid, and he burst with pride when I registered for my first semester. However, lately he has chose to lay a million questions on me whenever he sees me. For instance, he constantly asks me about my choice of a college major. Since I have not yet decided, I try to explain to him that at this time I do not need to select a major. He never lets me gets to the second part of my explanation when I patiently tell him that my current courses are useful and required for any major. Instead, he interrupts me and recites a list of possible careers for me. The list include everything from brain surgeon to accountant. I have grown to ignore his lists and simply remain silent. However, his constant quizzing has begun to wear me down. I know he means well, but his pressure don't help me to succeed in college.

Section Test **Using Verbs Correctly**

Some of the sentences that follow use verbs correctly; others do not. Put an *X* by each sentence with an error in using verbs correctly.

1. _____ We swum in the pool until sunset, when the water became too cold.

2. _____ My mother sewed like a professional but never teached me how to do anything as simple as threading a needle.

3. _____ She hasn't spoken to her lab partner since he blew up their science project.

4. _____ Yesterday morning I lay on the couch so I could rest my eyes until my headache medicine began to work.

5. _____ Chelsea will do well in her new position at the bank as long as she don't become impatient with rude customers.

6. _____ A social worker visited my uncle when he was in the hospital, and she been arranging home health care for him.

7. _____ Daniel and Lucy have chose to have a small wedding and have found a perfect place for the ceremony.

8. _____ During our class project, our group grew closer together.

9. _____ I knowed that I could trust him to always tell me the truth.

10. _____ Olivia and Gretchen, having passed calculus, has decided to take linear algebra.

Remember that your choice of verb form indicates the time (tense) of your statements. Be careful not to shift from one tense to another unless you have a reason to change the time.

CONSISTENT VERB TENSES

Tenses represent a time frame. It is important to keep the same time frame (unless you are making comparisons between two time frames). This is called **consistency of verb tense**.

> **incorrect shifts in tense:**
> The waitress *ran* to the kitchen with the order in her hand, *raced* back with glasses of water for her customers, and *smiles* calmly.
> He *grins* at me from the ticket booth and *closed* the ticket window.

You can correct these errors by putting all the verbs in the same tense.

> **consistent present tense:**
> The waitress *runs* to the kitchen with the order in her hand, *races* back with glasses of water for her customers, and *smiles* calmly.
> He *grins* at me from the ticket booth and *closes* the ticket window.

> **consistent past tense:**
> The waitress *ran* to the kitchen with the order in her hand, *raced* back with glasses of water for her customers, and *smiled* calmly.
> He *grinned* at me from the ticket booth and *closed* the ticket window.

Whether you correct the errors by changing all the verbs to the present tense or by changing them to the past tense, you are making the tenses consistent. Consistency of tense is important in the events you are describing because it helps the reader understand what happened and when it happened.

Exercise 9 **Practice: Correcting Sentences that are Inconsistent in Tense**

In each sentence that follows, one verb is inconsistent in tense. Cross it out and write the verb in the correct tense above the space.

1. My brother asked me to dinner, picked a fancy restaurant, and then leaves me with the entire bill.

2. Tanisha takes evening classes because they don't interfere with her work schedule, require attendance only once a week, attracted serious students, and offer a highly concentrated version of the course content.

3. As soon as Rick saved enough money, he packed up his car, drove across the country, and gets a job near a ski resort.

4. Because a new version of a popular phone was about to be introduced, people line up outside the local phone store and camped out overnight.

5. After Charlyce received her exam score, she slammed her book on the table and storms out of the classroom.

6. Yesterday, my boss didn't show up at the office; at the same time, major problems occur in the phone system, and no one knew how to handle the emergency.

7. Sometimes Matthew is good-natured and open, but occasionally he worries about minor problems, lost his temper, and hurts his closest friends.

8. At the courthouse, the police department made plans for the highly publicized trial; it increased the number of security guards, made room for members of the media to file reports, and blocks many entrances to the building.

Exercise 10   **Connect: Editing a Paragraph for Consistency of Tenses**

Connect

Read the following paragraph. Then cross out any verbs that are inconsistent in tense and write the corrections above. There are six errors.

My best friend Ryan tried college years ago but gave up after one wasted semester. He had no real purpose in going to college. He was a recent high school graduate and starts college because all his friends were going. Ryan has no of the demands of higher education. He took advantage of the freedom of college, skipped classes, avoids completing assignments, and relied on taking makeup tests instead of keeping up with the class. Ryan never thinks about the outcome. He just floated through the semester until he starts drowning. Unfortunately, he fails all his courses and dropped out of college. He swore that college was not right for him, but he was sad and a little defensive.

Exercise 11   **Collaborate: Writing a Paragraph with Consistent Verb Tenses**

Collaborate

The following paragraph has many inconsistencies in verb tenses; it shifts between past and present tenses. Working with a group, write two versions of the paragraph: *write it once in the present tense, then a second time in the past tense.* Divide your activity; half the group can write it in one tense while the other half can write it in the other tense.

After both rewrites are complete, read the new paragraphs aloud to both parts of the team as a final check.

My best friend took me for a ride in the country and tells me some bad news. He says that in two weeks he was moving to another state. This news is very sudden and shocks me to my core. My friend is more than a friend; he was a brother, a partner in pranks, a teammate in games, and a keeper of secrets. After he told me, we walk in the woods together. We find it hard to say much because we each knew what the other is feeling. After what seems like hours, he stops walking and faces me. He says the move wasn't what he wanted, but he added that his family needs him. I see sadness in his eyes, and I knew he saw the sorrow in mine.

Paragraph Revised for Consistent Tenses:

_____

_____

_____

_____

_____

_____

_____

_____

THE PRESENT PERFECT TENSE

When you are choosing the right verb tense, you should know about two verb tenses, the present perfect and the past perfect, that can make your meaning clear.

The **present perfect tense** is made up of the past participle form of the verb plus _have_ or _has_ as a helping verb. Use this tense to show an action that started in the past but is still going on in the present, or to state an action that was completed at an unspecified time in the past.

> **past tense:** My father _drove_ a truck for five months. (He doesn't drive a truck anymore, but he did drive one in the past.)
> **present perfect tense:** My father _has driven_ a truck for five months. (He started driving a truck five months ago; he is still driving a truck.)

> **past tense:** For years, I _studied_ ballet. (I don't study ballet now; I used to.)
> **present perfect tense:** For years, I _have studied_ ballet. (I still study ballet.)

> **past tense:** I _went_ to Miami Beach last year for spring break. (I am not in Miami now.)
> **present perfect tense:** I _have been_ to Miami. I _loved_ it! (I am not there now, but you don't know when I was there.)

Remember, use the present perfect tense to show that an action started in the past and is still going on.

> **Exercise 12**   **Practice: Distinguishing Between the Past Tense and the Present Perfect Tense**

Circle the correct verb in parentheses in each sentence. Be sure to look carefully at the meaning of the sentences.

1. Janet (sent, has sent) me a text message every morning for months now.

2. After heavy rain hit the area, the brakes on my car (felt, have felt) less efficient.

3. We (studied, have studied) the differences between the past and the present perfect for three days now.

4. Martina has a lot of life experience; she (traveled, has traveled) to eight different countries.

5. One of the instructors in the business department at the college (was, has been) a well-known banker but now teaches classes in finance.

6. My four-year-old son (was, has been) clinging to my leg for five minutes and is still begging me for ice cream.

7. Yesterday I finally confronted my roommate and (demanded, have demanded) an explanation for the unpaid light bill.

8. The academic advising office (moved, has moved) to the Student Center.

THE PAST PERFECT TENSE

The **past perfect tense** is made up of the past participle form of the verb and *had* as a helping verb. You can use the past perfect tense to show more than one event in the past—that is, when two or more things happened in the past but at different times.

> **past tense:** He *washed* the dishes.
> **past perfect tense:** He *had washed* the dishes by the time I came home. (He washed the dishes *before* I came home. Both actions happened in the past, but one happened earlier than the other.)

> **past tense:** Susan *waited* for an hour.
> **past perfect tense:** Susan *had waited* for an hour when she gave up on him. (Waiting came first; giving up came second. Both actions are in the past.)

The past perfect tense is especially useful because you write most of your essays in the past tense, and you often need to get further back into the past. Remember, to form the past perfect tense, use *had* with the past participle of the verb.

Exercise 13   **Practice: Distinguishing Between the Past Tense and the Past Perfect Tense**

Circle the correct verb in parentheses in each sentence. Be sure to look carefully at the meaning of the sentences.

1. Most of the audience (guessed, had guessed) the ending to the mystery before the movie was half-finished.

2. Melissa was not sure whether Jerry (tried, had tried) to call her earlier that morning.

3. On Mother's Day, my daughter (surprised, had surprised) me with a necklace she had made at her preschool arts and crafts class.

4. By the time Nelson remembered the soup, it (boiled, had boiled) over on the stove.

5. As Brianna brushed her hair, she (studied, had studied) her face in the mirror.

6. Jacob looked at the exam questions and wondered if he (read, had read) the right chapters in his textbook.

7. The defense attorney examined the transcripts of the trial that (took, had taken) place two years earlier.

8. On Sunday morning, I took part in a charity walk-a-thon because my sister (was, had been) nagging me about it for weeks.

Exercise 14   **Practice: Using the Past Perfect**

Complete each sentence with what happened before the first action.

1. Before I wrote my essay, _____.

2. When the power went out, _____.

3. Before I completed the homework assignment, _____.

4. By the time the professor arrived, _____.

5. Before Apple products were popular, _____.

6. By the time the movie was over, _____.

7. Before they finished the game, _____.

8. Before Bill and Emma went to the library, _____.

9. By the time all the students go to class, _____.

10. When I got to work, _____.

③ Distinguish between passive and active voice.

PASSIVE AND ACTIVE VOICE

Verbs not only have tenses, but they also have voices. When the subject in the sentence is doing something, the verb is in the **active voice**. When something is done to the subject—when it receives the action of the verb—the verb is in the **passive voice**.

active voice:
I painted the house. (*I*, the subject, did it.)
The people on the corner made a donation to the emergency fund.
    (The *people*, the subject, did it.)

passive voice:
The house was painted by me. (The *house*, the subject, didn't do anything. It received the action; it was painted.)
A donation to the emergency fund was made by the people on the corner. (The *donation*, the subject, didn't do anything. It received the action; it was given.)

Notice what happens when you use the passive voice instead of the active:

active voice:
I painted the house.

passive voice:
The house was painted by me.

The sentence in the passive voice is two words longer than the one in the active voice. Yet the sentence that uses the passive voice does not say anything different, and it does not say it more clearly than the one in the active voice.

Using the passive voice can make your sentences wordy, it can slow them down, and it can make them boring. The passive voice can also confuse readers. When the subject of the sentence is not doing anything, readers may have to look carefully to see who or what *is* doing something. Look at this sentence, for example:

A decision to fire you was reached.

Who decided to fire you? In this sentence, it is hard to find the answer to that question.

Of course, there will be times when you have to use the passive voice. For example, you may have to use it when you do not know who did something, as in these sentences:

Our house was broken into last night.
A leather jacket was left behind in the classroom.

But in general, you should avoid using the passive voice and rewrite sentences so they are in the active voice.

> **Exercise 15**   **Practice: Rewriting Sentences by Changing the Passive Voice to the Active Voice**

In the following sentences, change the passive voice to the active voice. If the original sentence does not tell you who or what performed the action, add words that tell who or what did it. An example is done for you.

> **example:** Sandy Adams was appointed chief negotiator last night.
>
> **rewritten:** The union leaders appointed Sandy Adams chief negotiator last night.

1. Harrison's reputation was ruined by the plagiarism episode.

   rewritten: _____

   _____

2. Questions are being asked about the missing funds at the health center.

   rewritten: _____

   _____

3. The bathroom was flooded by the overflowing toilet.

   rewritten: _____

   _____

4. Several paintings were donated to the museum by a wealthy woman.

   rewritten: _____

   _____

5. Once a month, the kindergarten class is entertained by a professional storyteller.

rewritten: _____

_____

6. Just before takeoff, an airline safety demonstration was conducted by a flight attendant.

rewritten: _____

_____

7. Because of the rising costs of energy, a slight increase in your cable bill has been instituted.

rewritten: _____

_____

8. Finally, the ringing phone was answered by the man behind the counter.

rewritten: _____

_____

Avoiding Unnecessary Shifts in Voice

Just as you should be consistent in the tense of verbs, you should be consistent in the voice of verbs. Do not shift from active voice to passive voice, or vice versa, without some good reason to do so.

        active   passive

shift: *I designed* the decorations for the dance; *they were put up* by Chuck.

        active   active

rewritten: *I designed* the decorations for the dance; *Chuck put them up.*

           passive   active

shift: Many *problems were discussed* by the council members, but *they found* no easy answers.

           active   active

rewritten: The council *members discussed* many problems, but *they found* no easy answers.

Being consistent in voice can help you to write clearly and smoothly.

Exercise 16 **Practice: Rewriting Sentences to Correct Shifts in Voice**

Rewrite the sentences that follow so that all the verbs are in the active voice. You may change the wording to make the sentences clear, smooth, and consistent in voice.

1. I enjoyed the party until red wine was spilled all over my silk shirt.

rewritten: _____

_____

2. If a window was broken by my son, I never knew about the incident.

   rewritten: _____

   _____

3. Esther screamed with rage when she was called a liar.

   rewritten: _____

   _____

4. My uncle used to be a pilot; airplanes and airports are loved by him.

   rewritten: _____

   _____

5. Today a local fisherman was honored by the city council; the fisherman had risked his life to save a drowning woman.

   rewritten: _____

   _____

6. The back roads were packed by frustrated drivers when flash floods closed two major highways.

   rewritten: _____

   _____

7. Because Paul is my old friend, he can be trusted by me.

   rewritten: _____

   _____

8. The schedule of summer classes is being posted online today; the college will also distribute paper copies of the schedule throughout the campus.

   rewritten: _____

   _____

OTHER COMMON MISTAKES WITH VERBS

There are a few errors that people tend to make with verbs, particularly in conversational settings. If you are aware of these errors, you'll be on the lookout for them as you edit your writing.

Used to: Be careful when you write that someone *used* to do, say, or feel something. It is incorrect to write *use to.*

   not this: Janine ~~use to~~ visit her mother every week.
              They ~~use to~~ like Thai food.
   but this: Janine *used to* visit her mother every week.
              They *used to* like Thai food.

Could Have, Should Have, Would Have: Using *of* instead of *have* is another error with verbs.

   not this: I ~~could of~~ done better on the test.
   but this: I *could have* done better on the test.

not this: He ~~should of~~ been paying attention.
but this: He *should have* been paying attention.

not this: The girls ~~would of~~ liked to visit Washington.
but this: The girls *would have* liked to visit Washington.

Would Have/Had: If you are writing about something that might have been possible, but that did not happen, use *had* as the helping verb.

not this: If I ~~would have~~ taken a foreign language in high school, I wouldn't have to take one now.
but this: If I *had* taken a foreign language in high school, I wouldn't have to take one now.

not this: I wish they ~~would have~~ won the game.
but this: I wish they *had* won the game.

not this: If she ~~would have~~ been smart, she would have called a plumber.
but this: If she *had* been smart, she would have called a plumber.

Collaborate

Exercise 17 Collaborate: Writing Sentences with the Correct Verb Forms

Do this exercise with a partner or a group. Follow the directions to write or complete each sentence that follows.

1. Complete this sentence and add a verb in the correct tense: My instructor explained the process before

   _____

   _____

2. Write a sentence that is more than eight words long and that uses the words *would have been happier* in the middle of the sentence.

   _____

   _____

3. Write a sentence that uses the past tense form of these words: *act* and *lose*.

   _____

   _____

4. Write a sentence in the passive voice.

   _____

   _____

5. Write a sentence in the active voice.

   _____

   _____

6. Write a sentence that uses *would have* and *had*.

   _____

   _____

7. Write a sentence that is more than six words long and that uses the words *had decided* and *before*.

_____

_____

8. Write a sentence of more than six words that uses the words *used to*.

_____

_____

| Exercise 18 | **Connect: Editing a Paragraph for Errors in Verbs: Consistency, Tense, and Voice** |

Connect

Edit the following paragraph for errors in verb consistency, tense, or voice. There are six errors.

My great aunt Emma Paluska has a pretty glass bowl that is a piece of family history. The bowl comes from Poland. Only one factory near Warsaw made this type of bowl, and during World War II, the Nazis bombed the factory. The bowl has been in the family for years. If my Aunt Emma's mother would not have brought the bowl to the United States in 1937, it could of been destroyed by the bombing near the Paluska home. Generations of Paluskas have cherished this bowl. I remember the bowl from the big Saturday night dinners of years ago. We use to eat the contents of the bowl, fruits and nuts, for dessert. Today the bowl is displayed by my great aunt on special occasions. She fills it with glittery pine cones in the winter; in spring, flowers are put in the bowl. I hope that one day, the bowl will be passed on to me by my great aunt.

Section Test   Verbs: Consistency and Voice

Some of the sentences that follow are correct; others have errors in verb consistency, correct tense, or correct voice. Put an *X* next to the sentences with errors.

1. _____ If I had checked the oil in my car, I would have been spared hundreds of dollars in car repairs and the misery of begging rides from family members.

2. _____ Hope for a better life came to the peasants of France and Spain when a treaty between the warring nations was signed.

3. _____ After the noise of the trucks at the dump site stopped, the workers can hear the thunder approaching from the western part of the woods.

4. _____   Amanda worked at the preschool for two years; then she left for a position at Memorial Hospital where she had enjoyed her interactions with the physical therapy patients.

5. _____   My sister had been nagging me about my hair until I finally agreed to get it cut before her wedding.

6. _____   Two of my cats ate a special treat of leftover turkey but had refused a small portion of sweet potatoes.

7. _____   I had finished my homework after I had spent two hours procrastinating and playing games on my computer.

8. _____   My vacation in South Carolina was terrible; for three days, I have done nothing but sweat and swat buzzing mosquitoes away from every part of my body.

9. _____   The tree had been decorated and my family will gather around it to open presents.

10. _____   After he refused the volunteers' request for a donation, he wished that he helped them.

Chapter Test   **Using Verbs Correctly: Standard Verb Forms, Irregular Verbs, Consistency, and Voice**

Some of the sentences that follow use verbs correctly; other have errors in standard verb forms, irregular verbs, consistency, and voice. Write *OK* next to the correct sentences; write *X* by each incorrect sentence.

1. _____   My grandparents are wonderful; every weekend, they takes me out to dinner at my favorite diner.

2. _____   The air conditioner in my bedroom is working, but it do make a strange noise every time I turn it on.

3. _____   Nathan is my oldest friend; therefore, he should be introduced by me at the sports banquet.

4. _____   If I had known about the surprise party, I would have dressed better and washed my hair.

5. _____   For five months, Marcy has worked as a receptionist at a dentist's office; unfortunately, the dentist plans to close his office next month.

6. _____   Olivia stared at her reflection in the mirror and wondered whether she had chosen the right haircut.

7. _____   By the time Caleb was in his early twenties, his tendency to borrow money and never repay it had caused his brother and sister to avoid Caleb's desperate calls and woeful stories.

8. _____   I will ask my sister-in-law to take care of my dog over the weekend; she have done this chore for me before.

9. _____   The members of the closing shift, Martha, Ken and Hector, goes through the same routine every evening.

10. _____   Three years of college had passed quickly, and Julio was ready to finish his degree.

Making Subjects and Verbs Agree

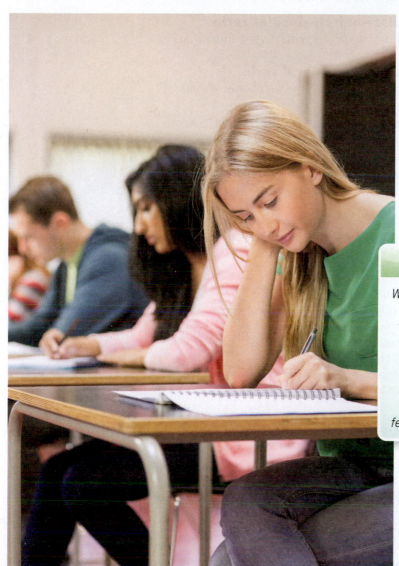

Learning Objectives

In this chapter, you will learn to:

1 Identify correct subject–verb agreement.

2 Recognize prepositional phrases.

3 Identify compound subjects, indefinite pronouns, and collective nouns.

① Identify correct subject–verb agreement.

SUBJECTS AND VERBS: SINGULAR VS. PLURAL

Subjects and verbs have to agree in number. That means a singular subject must be matched to a singular verb form, and a plural subject must be matched to a plural verb form.

singular subject, singular verb:
My *sister walks* to work every morning.

plural subject, plural verb:
Mary, David, and *Sam believe* in ghosts.

singular subject, singular verb:
Linguistics is the study of languages.

plural subject, plural verb:
The committee *members are* in the meeting room.

Caution: Remember that a regular verb has an *-s* ending in only one singular form in the present tense—the form that goes with *he, she, it,* or their equivalents:

He *makes* me feel confident.
She *appreciates* intelligent conversation.
It *seems* like a good buy.
Bo *runs* every day.
That girl *swims* well.
The machine *breaks* down too often.

Exercise 1   Practice: Subject–Verb Agreement: Selecting the Correct Verb Form

Circle the correct form of the verb in each sentence.

1. My nephew (is, are) a natural athlete with a great future.

2. The camera sometimes (give, gives) a false impression of the size of a room.

3. My classmates, John and Erin, rarely (go, goes) to the tutoring center.

4. That watch (cost, costs) more than I can afford.

5. By 10:00 p.m., my mother (want, wants) to go to bed.

6. People in the middle of meditation may become startled when a phone (ring, rings).

7. Reviewing the same chapter as last week (seem, seems) redundant.

8. Constantly blaming others (appear, appears) to be Siri's way of avoiding responsibility.

Exercise 2 Connect: Correcting Errors in Subject–Verb Agreement in a Paragraph

Connect

There are errors in subject–verb agreement in the paragraph that follows. If a verb does not agree with its subject, change the verb form. Cross out the incorrect verb form and write the correct one above. There are seven agreement errors in agreement in the paragraph.

Malcolm always bring a present when he visits his mother. He does not have much money but manage to find an appropriate gift every time. Sometimes he arrives with a bunch of flowers or some fresh fruit from a nearby fruit stand. His mother love his thoughtfulness; it make her feel valued. Occasionally, she scolds him for spending money on her. In addition, when he arrives with a small box of chocolates, she say, "Malcolm, you are tempting me to get fat." However, he know his mother too well to believe her complaints. She actually looks forward to his small surprises. Besides, he, too, like to eat a little of the fruit or chocolate.

PRONOUNS AS SUBJECTS

Pronouns can be used as subjects. Pronouns are words that take the place of nouns. When pronouns are used as subjects, they must agree in number with verbs.

The Info Box has a list of the subject pronouns and the regular verb forms that agree with them, in the present tense.

INFO BOX Subject Pronouns and a Present Tense Verb

pronoun	verb	
I	listen	
you	listen	all singular forms
he, she, it	listens	
we	listen	
you	listen	all plural forms
they	listen	

In all the sentences that follow, the pronoun used as the subject of the sentence agrees in number with the verb:

singular pronoun, singular verb:
I make the best omelet in town.

singular pronoun, singular verb:
You read very well.

singular pronoun, singular verb:
She performs like a trained athlete.

plural pronoun, plural verb:
We need a new refrigerator.

plural pronoun, plural verb:
They understand the situation.

SPECIAL PROBLEMS WITH AGREEMENT

Agreement seems fairly simple: If a subject is singular, you use a singular verb form, and if a subject is plural, you use a plural verb form. However, there are special problems with agreement that will come up in your writing. Sometimes, it is hard to find the subject of a sentence; at other times, it is hard to determine if a subject is singular or plural.

2 Recognize prepositional phrases.

Finding the Subject

When you are checking for subject–verb agreement, you can find the real subject of the sentence by first eliminating the prepositional phrases. To find the real subject, put parentheses around the prepositional phrases. Then it is easy to find the subject because nothing in a prepositional phrase is the subject of a sentence.

prepositional phrases in parentheses:

S   V
One (of my oldest friends) *is* a social worker.

S   V
A *student* (from one)(of the nearby school districts) *is* the winner.

S   V
The *store* (across the street) (from my house) *is* open all night.

S   V
Jim, (with all his silly jokes), *is* a nice person.

> **Note:** Words and phrases such as *along with*, *as well as*, *except*, *in addition to*, *including*, *plus*, and *together with* introduce prepositional phrases. The words that follow them are part of the prepositional phrase and cannot be part of the subject.

S   V   V
My *sister*, (along with her husband), *is planning* a trip to Bolivia.

S   V
Tom's *house*, (as well as his apartment), *is* part of a family inheritance.

Exercise 3   Practice: Finding the Real Subject by Recognizing Prepositional Phrases

Put parentheses around all the prepositional phrases in the sentences that follow. Put an *S* above each subject and a *V* above each verb.

1. Jealousy, in addition to lack of trust, threatens the stability

   of a marriage.

2. Cristina, along with her mother-in-law, is visiting Venezuela over the summer.

3. Without much thought, the student asked the instructor a question about the test.

4. In the early morning, a tall man with a Great Dane jogs through the park.

5. The truth behind Alison's perfect 4.0 GPA is a simple story of long hours studying.

6. Yogurt, as well as low-fat cheese, is a good source of calcium in any diet.

7. My best friend from high school arrived a day early for the reunion.

8. Today, weather cancelled two of my classes during the day.

Exercise 4   **Practice: Selecting the Correct Verb Form by Identifying Prepositional Phrases**

Put parentheses around all the prepositional phrases in the sentences that follow. Then circle the verb that agrees with the subject.

1. A motel with clean rooms, a small pool, and free breakfast (is, are) at the exit to Masonville.

2. Mr. Kelly's patience, in addition to his years of experience, (explain, explains) his popularity with students.

3. Madeline, with little thought for the consequences, (is, are) planning to drop out of school.

4. One of the most attractive men in town (is, are) my best friend, Tyler.

5. Under suspicion of murder, the young man, together with his fiancée, (was, were) the subject of a police search.

6. The house with the blue shutters (has, have) been sold to a family from Missouri.

7. Tennis players at summer tournaments often (compete, competes)

in dangerously hot weather.

8. One of the hosts on the early morning television show (go, goes) into

a fit of giggles during every episode.

Changed Word Order

You are probably used to looking for the subject of a sentence in front of the verb, but not all sentences follow this pattern. Questions, sentences beginning with words like *here* or *there*, and other sentences change the word order. So you have to look carefully to check for subject–verb agreement.

          V   S

Where *are* my *friends?*

      V S V

When *is he going* to work?

                             V   S

Behind the Adams Student Center *is* a *memorial* for fallen soldiers.

    V   S

There *are potholes* in the road.

    V   S

There *is* a *reason* for his impatience.

> **Exercise 5** **Practice: Making Subjects and Verbs Agree in Sentences with Changed Word Order**

In each of the sentences that follow, underline the subject; then circle the correct verb in parentheses.

1. Besides Scott's good looks, there (is, are) his sense of humor and kindness.

2. Across the courtyard in the Student Center (is, are) an area with concrete benches and tables.

3. Beneath the layers of dirt and grime (was, were) a beautiful marble bathtub in pale beige stone.

4. About an hour after dark, there (was, were) an ambulance with flashing lights and a police car in front of the house across the street.

5. Stuck in the small space between the refrigerator and the cabinet (was, were) the lost Super Bowl tickets.

6. On the walls of the waiting room at the dentist's office (was, were) a large collection of posters about dental hygiene.

7. Inside the flea market (is, are) an endless row of stalls with all kinds of merchandise from T-shirts to ten-foot artificial plants.

8. After a few awkward moments, there (was, were) smiles and laughter among the guests at the singles-only party.

COMPOUND SUBJECTS

A **compound subject** is two or more subjects joined by *and*, *or*, or *nor*.

When subjects are joined by *and*, they are usually plural.

3 Identify compound subjects, indefinite pronouns, and collective nouns.

    S   S   V

Jermaine and *Lisa are* bargain hunters.

    S   S   V

My *tablet* and *smartphone need* updating.

    S   S   V

A *bakery* and a *pharmacy are* down the street.

Caution: Be careful to check for a compound subject when the word order changes.

         V   S   S

There *are* a *bakery* and a *pharmacy* down the street. (Two things, a *bakery* and a *pharmacy*, *are* down the street.)

         V   S   S

Here *are* a *picture* of your father and a *copy* of his birth certificate. (A *picture* and a *copy*, two things, *are* here.)

When subjects are joined by *or*, *either ... or*, *neither ... nor*, *not only ... but also*, the verb form agrees with the subject closer to the verb.

                   singular S   plural S, plural V

Not only the restaurant *manager* but also the *waiters were* pleased with the new policy.

           plural S   singular S, singular V

Not only the *waiters* but also the restaurant *manager was* pleased with the new policy.

          plural S   singular S, singular V

Either the *instructors* or the *director makes* the tutoring schedule.

      singular S   plural S,   plural V

Either the *director* or the *instructors make* the tutoring schedule.

      plural S   singular S, singular V

Neither the *tenants* nor the *landlord cares* about the parking situation.

      singular S   plural S, plural V

Neither the *landlord* nor the *tenants care* about the parking situation.

Exercise 6   **Practice: Making Subjects and Verbs Agree: Compound Subjects**

Circle the correct form of the verb in parentheses in each sentence that follows.

1. Either the woman in the upstairs apartment or the men across the street (is, are) leaving garbage in the street.

2. Not only the fried chicken but also the vegetables (taste, tastes) homemade.

3. Neither the slipcovers on the sofa nor the huge pillow on the chair (hide, hides) the decrepit condition of the furniture.

4. Here (is, are) the baby's formula and his blanket.

5. There (was, were) a problem with the oil in my car and with a strange grinding sound in the engine.

6. After dinner, either my mother or my brother (clear, clears) the table while I do the dishes.

7. Anger and bitterness never (solve, solves) a problem.

8. Neither the textbook nor the handout (helps, help) me understand this new concept.

INDEFINITE PRONOUNS

Certain pronouns that come from a group called **indefinite pronouns** always take a singular verb as shown in the following Info Box.

INFO BOX   Indefinite Pronouns that Take a Singular Verb

one	nobody	nothing	each	other
anyone	anybody	anything	either	another
someone	somebody	something	neither	
everyone	everybody	everything		
no one				

If you want to write clearly and correctly, you must memorize these words and remember that they always take a singular verb. Using your common sense is not enough because some of these words seem plural; for example, *everybody* seems to mean more than one person, but in grammatically correct English, it takes a singular verb. Here are some examples of the pronouns used with singular verbs:

singular S   singular V
Everyone in town *is talking* about the scandal.

singular S   singular V
Each of the boys *is* talented.

singular S   singular V
One of their biggest concerns *is* crime in the streets.

singular S   singular V
Neither of the cats *is* mine.

> **Hint:** You can memorize the indefinite pronouns as the *one*, *thing*, and *body* words (every*one*, every*thing*, every*body*, and so forth) plus *each*, *either*, and *neither*.

Exercise 7   Practice: Making Subjects and Verbs Agree: Using Indefinite Pronouns

Circle the correct verb in parentheses in each sentence that follows.

1. (Was, Were) anybody from school at the club on Friday night?

2. Either of the smartphones (cost, costs) too much for my budget.

3. (Is, Are) someone taking photographs during the ceremony?

4. Each of my classes (has, have) an attendance requirement.

5. Neither of the boys (has, have) ever given me any trouble.

6. Beyond the college parking lot there (is, are) a tennis court and a soccer field.

7. After the party, (was, were) anyone talking to Michelle?

8. Everyone in my night classes (seem, seems) much more organized than I am.

COLLECTIVE NOUNS

Collective nouns refer to more than one person or thing:

team	company	council	majority
class	corporation	government	minority
committee	family	group	faculty
audience	jury	crowd	army

Most of the time, collective nouns take a singular verb.

singular S   singular V
The *committee is sponsoring* a fundraiser.

singular S   singular V
The *audience was* impatient.

singular S   singular V
The *faculty has reached* a decision.

The singular verb is used because the group is sponsoring, getting impatient, or reaching a decision, *as one unit*.

Collective nouns take a plural verb only when the members of the group are acting individually, not as a unit:

The sophomore *class are fighting* among themselves. (The phrase *among themselves* shows that the class is not acting as one unit.)

Exercise 8   **Practice: Making Subjects and Verbs Agree: Using Collective Nouns**

Circle the correct verb in parentheses in each sentence that follows

1. The Green Corporation (give, gives) all its full-time employees ten vacation days.

2. The family from Nevada (is, are) looking for a house to rent for at least one year.

3. Some members of the jury (was, were) falling asleep in the late afternoon sessions.

4. My son's kindergarten class (sing, sings) songs at the start of each day.

5. The Merrill College Student Council (was, were) determined to raise the issue of student fees.

6. The most popular team in baseball history (is, are) deeply divided on the issue of steroid use.

7. Although rain delayed the outdoor concert, the crowd at the park (was, were) patient and cheerful.

8. The committee (raise, raises) money for those less fortunate through its annual bake sale.

MAKING SUBJECTS AND VERBS AGREE: THE BOTTOM LINE

As you have probably realized, making subjects and verbs agree is not as simple as it first appears. But if you can remember the basic ideas in this section, you will be able to apply them automatically as you edit your own writing. A quick reference of subject–verb agreement principles is in the following Info Box.

INFO BOX **Making Subjects and Verbs Agree: A Summary**

1. Subjects and verbs should agree in number: singular subjects get singular verb forms; plural subjects get plural verb forms.

2. When pronouns are used as subjects, they must agree in number with verbs.

3. Nothing in a prepositional phrase can be the subject of the sentence.

4. Questions, sentences beginning with *here* or *there*, and other sentences can change word order, making subjects harder to find.

5. Compound subjects joined by *and* are usually plural.

6. When subjects are joined by *or, either … or, neither … nor,* or *not only … but also,* the verb form agrees with the subject closest to the verb.

7. Certain indefinite pronouns always take singular verbs. (See Info Box on p. 486.)

8. Collective nouns usually take singular verbs.

Exercise 9 **Practice: A Comprehensive Exercise on Subject–Verb Agreement**

Circle the correct verb form in parentheses in each sentence that follows.

1. Yesterday, there (was, were) a dining room table and four chairs on sale at Furniture Warehouse.

2. Around the back of the restaurant (is, are) a huge dumpster and a recycling bin.

3. Neither the child nor his parents (use, uses) the front porch very often because the house is on a busy street.

4. Before the semester begins, everyone (has, have) to register for classes.

5. When (was, were) your brothers planning to visit?

6. Everything in Jackie's room (seem, seems) dusty and grimy.

7. Either of my sisters (is, are) capable of handling a family emergency.

8. Axel George, as well as Mina Patel, (work, works) in the computer lab.

Exercise 10   **Collaborate: Create Your Own Text on Subject–Verb Agreement**

Collaborate

Working with a partner or a group, create your own grammar handbook. A list of rules on subject–verb agreement follows. Write one sentence that is an example of each rule. The first one is done for you.

Rule 1: Subjects and verbs should agree in number: singular subjects get singular verb forms; plural subjects get plural verb forms.

example: A battered old car stands in the front yard.

Rule 2: When pronouns are used as subjects, they must agree in number with verbs.

example: _____

Rule 3: Nothing in a prepositional phrase can be the subject of the sentence.

example: _____

Rule 4: Questions, sentences beginning with *here* or *there*, and other sentences can change word order, making subjects harder to find.

example: _____

Rule 5: When subjects are joined by *and*, they are usually plural.

example: _____

Rule 6: When subjects are joined by *or*, *either ... or*, *neither ... nor*, or *not only ... but also*, the verb form agrees with the subject closest to the verb.

example: _____

Rule 7: Indefinite pronouns always take singular verbs.

example: _____

Rule 8: Collective nouns usually take singular verbs.

example: _____

Connect

Exercise 11 **Connect: Editing a Paragraph for Errors in Subject–Verb Agreement**

Edit the following paragraph by correcting any verbs that do not agree with their subjects. Write your corrections above the lines. There are seven errors.

There is either thoughtlessness or cruelty in hurting someone's feelings. Spite, jealousy, and anger often prompt a person to lash out at another. Such behavior is deliberate and open. Children, who are less skilled in handling their emotions than adults are, can be cruel to another child. There is times when one four-year-old may call another "stupid" or "disgusting" while both children plays a game on the street. The speaker is simply venting his or her rage and soon forgets, but the victim shamed in front of other children may not forget. Adult cruelty are more sophisticated. This cruelty can be the critical remark a boss make to an employee or the constant sarcasm of a wife speaking to her husband. Habitual cruelty often turns into thoughtless cruelty. When one person constantly belittles another, the victim suffer with every repetition of the meanness, but the attacker feels very little. Another kind of thoughtless cruelty is the assignment of a nickname. A man often cringes for years because some childhood "buddies" was too eager to call him "Moose" or "Skinny," and the nickname stuck. Although adults may try to laugh about their nicknames, neither the intentionally cruel names or a thoughtlessly assigned name is a person's choice. In all stages of life, people need to show a little kindness and restraint. Not only the child on the playground but also adults in all their interactions deserves some of that kindness.

Chapter Test **Making Subjects and Verbs Agree**

Some of the sentences that follow are correct; others have errors in making subjects and verbs agree. Write *OK* next to the correct sentences; write *X* next to the incorrect ones.

1. _____ After the Safety Committee approves the new street signs, the signs will be placed in the school zones at the two elementary schools and the middle school.

2. _____ Everybody on the three highest floors of the skyscraper gets a wonderful view of Central Park.

3. _____ There is a certain taste and a special texture in the corn-bread from Ed's Barbecue Hut in Asheville, North Carolina.

4. _____ Neither a long day at work nor a long ride to our home in the suburbs keeps my father from maintaining a positive attitude.

5. _____ Something about seeing my son in a school play make me want to smile and cry at the same time.

6. _____ At the end of the dirt road in the dilapidated part of town was an old barn and a broken-down gate to the nearby pasture.

7. _____ Your concern about the price of car insurance make me worry about your ability to handle the costs of driving and maintaining your own car.

8. _____ What is the real causes of this massive forest fire?

9. _____ The team of high school lacrosse players was unanimous in their decision to elect Jack team captain.

10. _____ Wendy and her younger sister, Elizabeth, likes chili with hot sauce, jalapenos, and plenty of sour cream.

CHAPTER 26

Using Pronouns Correctly: Agreement and Reference

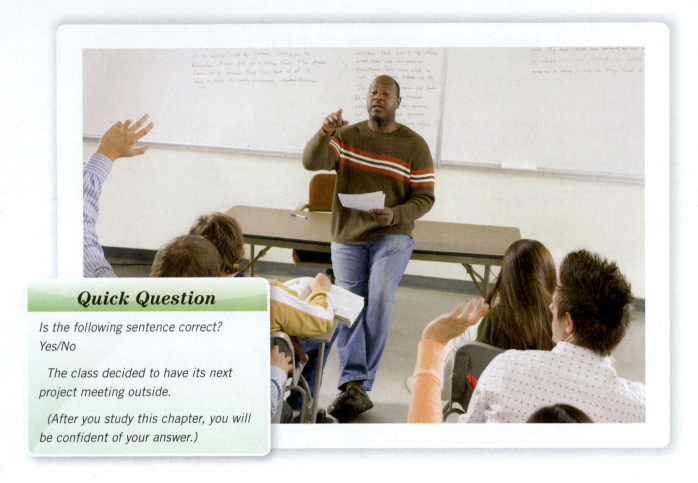

Quick Question

Is the following sentence correct?
Yes/No

The class decided to have its next project meeting outside.

(After you study this chapter, you will be confident of your answer.)

Learning Objectives

In this chapter, you will learn to:

1 Identify pronouns and make their antecedents agree.

2 Identify collective nouns.

3 Correct errors in pronoun agreement and reference.

---

1 Identify pronouns and make their antecedents agree.

NOUNS AND PRONOUNS

Nouns are the names of persons, places, or things.

> *Jack* is a good friend. (*Jack* is the name of a person.)
> The band is from *Orlando*. (*Orlando* is the name of a place.)
> We understood the *lecture*. (*Lecture* is the name of a thing.)

Pronouns are words that substitute for nouns. A pronoun's **antecedent** is the word or words it replaces.

antecedent   pronoun
Jack is a good friend; *he* is very loyal.

antecedent   pronoun

I hated *the movie* because *it* was too violent.

antecedent   pronoun

Playing tennis was fun, but *it* started to take up too much of my
    time.

antecedent   pronoun

Micah and Jessie are sure *they* understood the assignment.

antecedent   pronoun

Sharon gave away *her* old clothes.

antecedent   pronoun

The course's weekly assignments are posted on *its* Web site.

Exercise 1   **Practice: Identifying the Antecedents of Pronouns**

Underline the word or words that are the antecedent of the italicized pronoun in each of the following sentences.

1. A short walk is healthy for workers because *it* takes them away
   from the workplace and relieves stress.

2. Your brother called me yesterday; *he* seemed a little depressed.

3. Camille looked at two used cars this afternoon; *they* were overpriced and unattractive.

4. Some of my friends love sushi, but I hate *it*.

5. The baby can't go outside without *his* down jacket.

6. The television show lost *its* special charm a few episodes ago.

7. Luis, do *you* need a ride to work?

8. Please fill out the forms and take *them* to registration.

AGREEMENT OF A PRONOUN AND ITS ANTECEDENT

A pronoun must agree in number with its antecedent. If the antecedent is singular; the pronoun must be singular. If the antecedent is plural, then the pronoun must be plural.

singular antecedent   singular pronoun

Susan tried to arrive on time, but *she* got caught in traffic.

plural antecedent   plural pronoun

Susan and Ray tried to arrive on time, but *they* got caught in traffic.

plural antecedent   plural pronoun

The visitors tried to arrive on time, but *they* got caught in traffic.

There are some special problems with agreement of pronouns, and these problems will come up in your writing. If you become familiar with the explanations, examples, and exercises that follow, you will be ready to handle the special problems.

INDEFINITE PRONOUNS

As you know, certain indefinite pronouns always take a singular verb. Whenever one of these indefinite pronouns acts as an antecedent in a sentence, the pronoun that replaces it must also be singular. However, several indefinite pronouns always take a plural verb. If any of them acts as an antecedent, the replacement pronoun must be plural. Interestingly, some indefinite pronouns can be considered singular or plural depending on the sentence's meaning. The lists in the Info Box can serve as a quick reference guide and help you complete the exercises in this chapter on pronoun–antecedent agreement.

INFO BOX   **Common Indefinite Pronouns**

Indefinite Pronouns (Singular)		Indefinite Pronouns (Plural)	Indefinite Pronouns (Singular or Plural)
another	neither	both	all
anybody	no one	few	any
anyone	nothing	many	more
anything	one	others	most
each	other	several	none
either	someone		some
everyone	something		

(For a list of more indefinite pronouns that take a singular verb, see page 486.)

---

singular antecedent   singular pronoun
Everyone in the sorority donated *her* time to the project.

plural antecedent   plural pronoun
Several new students forgot to bring *their* IDs to registration.

Avoiding Gender Bias

Consider this sentence:

Everybody in the math class brought _____ own calculator.

How do you choose the correct pronoun to fill in the blank? If everybody in the class is male, you can write:

Everybody in the math class brought *his* own calculator.

Or if everybody in the class is female, you can write:

Everybody in the math class brought *her* own calculator.

Or if the class has students of both genders, you can write:

Everybody in the math class brought *his or her* own calculator.

In the past, most writers used the pronoun *his* to refer to both men and women. Today, many writers try to use *his or her* to avoid gender bias, but this solution is awkward. If you find using *his or her* is getting awkward or repetitive, you can rewrite the sentence and make the antecedent plural and avoid the gender issue completely:

correct: *The students* in the math class brought *their* own calculators.

But you cannot shift from singular to plural:

> **incorrect:** ~~Everybody in the math class brought their own calculators~~.

Exercise 2 **Practice: Making Pronouns and Antecedents Agree**

Write the appropriate pronoun in the blank in each of the following sentences. Look carefully for the antecedent before you choose the pronoun.

1. During the men's semifinals, one of the tennis players seemed to lose _____ confidence as the match went into its final minutes.

2. Everyone in the Women's Sculptors Association hopes to exhibit _____ best work at the Richardson Museum.

3. When the first snow falls, James and Bentley strap _____ skis on the car and head for the mountains.

4. Some of the players were upset about _____ new field assignments.

5. Most of the food from the catering truck was missing, but all of the guests enjoyed _____ time at the party anyway.

6. Once I visited the tiny set of a popular television comedy, everything about the show lost _____ glamour.

7. Yesterday, someone left _____ car keys in the restaurant.

8. Either of the politician's former aides could have leaked _____ personal stories about her to the media.

COLLECTIVE NOUNS

2 Identify collective nouns.

Collective nouns refer to a group of individuals:

team	faculty	council
class	corporation	government
committee	family	group
audience	jury	crowd

Most of the time, collective nouns take a singular pronoun.

> collective noun   singular pronoun
> The *team* that was ahead in the playoffs lost *its* home game.

> collective noun   singular pronoun
> The *corporation* changed *its* policy on parental leave.

Collective nouns are usually singular because the group is losing a game or changing a policy as one, as a unit. Collective nouns take a plural pronoun only when the members of the group are acting individually, not as a unit.

> The *class* picked up *their* class rings this morning. (The members of the class pick up their rings individually.)

Exercise 3 Practice: Making Pronouns and Antecedents Agree: Collective Nouns

Circle the correct pronoun in each of the following sentences and underline the corresponding noun.

1. The commissioners at the Sprucedale City Council gave (its, their) approval to the construction of a new teen center.

2. A group of my brother's army buddies met for (its, their) annual picnic at Still Waters Park.

3. Before the semester ended, the committee gave (its, their) recommendations to the academic dean.

4. A family from Georgia opened (its, their) second furniture company in Baton Rouge.

5. After the club meets, one of (its, their) members always suggests adjourning to a nearby restaurant.

6. Marilyn no longer orders pizzas from Henry's House of Pizza because of (its, their) poor delivery record.

7. Several of the drawing and design classes held (its, their) last class meeting outdoors because of the beautiful spring weather.

8. The team meets in (its, their) locker room before every game.

Collaborate

Exercise 4 Collaborate: Writing Sentences with Pronoun–Antecedent Agreement

With a partner or a group, write a sentence for each pair of words that follow, using each pair as a pronoun and its antecedent. The first pair is done for you.

1. parents ... their

   sentence: Parents who work outside the home have to plan their time

   carefully.

2. family ... its

   sentence: _____

   _____

3. anybody ... his or her

   sentence: _____

   _____

4. drivers ... they

   sentence: _____

   _____

5. security ... it

   sentence: _____

   _____

6. either ... her

sentence: _____

_____

7. everybody ... his or her

sentence: _____

_____

8. North America ... it

sentence: _____

_____

| Exercise 5 | Connect: Editing a Paragraph for Errors in Pronoun–Antecedent Agreement |

Connect

Read the following paragraph carefully, looking for errors in agreement of pronouns and their antecedents. Cross out each pronoun that does not agree with its antecedent and write the correct pronoun above it. Six pronouns need correcting.

My job at the reception desk at Millennium General Hospital can be challenging. My work is stressful when the hospital is busy. During visiting hours, I have to be helpful, cheerful, and alert because many people are in the hospital for the first time and don't know the layout of the place. They get anxious when they are faced with too many signs and hallways. In addition, each visitor is worrying about their loved one, sick and alone in a hospital bed. When the hospital is busy, time goes quickly for me. When visiting hours are over and nobody is with their family, time drags on. For example, in the quiet hours of the holidays, when patients want to be back in his or her homes, the staff works extra hard to cheer up patients and visitors. Fortunately, special events brighten up the atmosphere. Sometimes everyone in a local club visits the wards and does their best to entertain the staff, patients, and visitors in the hospital. At other times, the Steely Corporation, which owns Millennium General, brings a little brightness to their patients and staff. It lights up the corridors with bright lights, plays holiday music, and even brings clowns to the lounges. On Independence Day, the corporation has been known to celebrate by offering a small fireworks display on their front lawn.

3 Correct errors in pronoun agreement and reference.

PRONOUNS AND THEIR ANTECEDENTS: BEING CLEAR

Remember that pronouns are words that replace or refer to other words, and the words that are replaced or referred to are antecedents.

Make sure that a pronoun has one clear antecedent. Your writing will be vague and confusing if a pronoun appears to refer to more than one antecedent or if it doesn't have any specific antecedent to refer to. In grammar, such confusing language is called a problem with **pronoun reference.**

When a pronoun refers to more than one thing, the sentence becomes confusing or silly. The following are examples of unclear reference:

> Jim told Leonard his bike had been stolen. (Whose bike was stolen? Jim's? Leonard's?)

> She put the cake on the table, took off her apron, pulled up a chair, and began to eat it. (What did she eat? The cake? The table? Her apron? The chair?)

If there is no one clear antecedent, you must rewrite the sentence to make the reference clear. Sometimes the rewritten sentence may seem repetitive, but a little repetition is better than a lot of confusion.

> **unclear:** Jim told Leonard his bike had been stolen.
> **clear:** Jim told Leonard Jim's bike had been stolen.
> **clear:** Jim told Leonard, "My bike has been stolen."
> **clear:** Jim told Leonard that Leonard's bike had been stolen.
> **clear:** Jim told Leonard, "Your bike has been stolen."

> **unclear:** She put the cake on the table, took off her apron, pulled up a chair, and began to eat it.
> **clear:** She put the cake on the table, took off her apron, pulled up a chair, and began to eat the cake.

Sometimes the problem is a little more tricky. Can you spot what's wrong with this sentence?

> **unclear:** Bill decided to take a part-time job, which worried his parents. (What worried Bill's parents? His decision to work part time? Or the job itself?)

Be very careful with the pronoun *which*. If there is any chance that using *which* will confuse the reader, rewrite the sentence and get rid of *which*.

> **clear:** Bill's parents were worried about the kind of part-time job he chose.
> **clear:** Bill's decision to work part-time worried his parents.

Sometimes, a pronoun has nothing to refer to; it has no antecedent.

> **no antecedent:** When Eric got to the train station, they said the train was going to be late. (Who said the train was going to be late? The ticket agents? Strangers Eric met on the tracks?)

> **no antecedent:** Maria has always loved medicine and has decided that's what she wants to be. (What does "that" refer to? The only word it could refer to is *medicine*, but Maria certainly doesn't want to be a medicine. She doesn't want to be an aspirin or a cough drop.)

If a pronoun lacks an antecedent, add an antecedent or get rid of the pronoun.

add an antecedent: When Eric got to the train station and asked the ticket agents about the schedule, they said the train was going to be late. (*They* refers to the ticket agents.)

drop the pronoun: Maria has always loved medicine and has decided she wants to be a physician.

> **Note:** To check for clear reference of pronouns, underline any pronoun that may not be clear. Then try to draw a line from that pronoun to its antecedent. Are there two or more possible antecedents? Is there no antecedent? In either case, you will need to revise for clarity.

Exercise 6 **Practice: Rewriting Sentences for Clear Reference of Pronouns**

Rewrite the following sentences so that the pronouns have clear references. You may add, take out, or change words.

1. Leonard bought his mother a cat, which was kind.

2. Years ago, they believed that black cats were a sign of bad luck.

3. The heavy bowl fell on the tile floor, and it cracked.

4. Laura told her best friend Celia that she worried too much.

5. I'm glad I transferred to Emerson High School because they're all outgoing and friendly.

6. My brother has always been fascinated by space flight, and that's what he dreams of being.

7. Most of the conflicts between teenagers and their parents occur because they always think age makes people wiser.

8. Searching in his grandparents' attic, Tyler found some old love letters, which shocked him.

Exercise 7 **Connect: Editing a Paragraph for Errors in Pronoun Agreement and Reference**

Connect

Correct any errors in pronoun agreement or reference in the following paragraph. There are six errors. Write your corrections above the line.

Anyone with a strong will and enough motivation can change their attitude from negative to positive. I am living proof of this statement. Each day I used to focus on what could go wrong, which made me constantly anxious. I was also terribly self-conscious. Every time I entered a room or spoke in public, I was extremely nervous. I imagined everyone looking at me with their attention focused on my flaw. Each member of my family tried their best to brighten my moods and boost my confidence, but their efforts couldn't help. Fortunately, I signed up for a class in psychology and it led me to an important discovery. About halfway through the term, the assigned readings and class lectures helped me to realize that I was suffering from depression. I decided to do something about it. I began to see a counselor, and I am now learning to think of myself and my future in a new way. I am ready to focus on hope, not fear.

Chapter Test Using Pronouns Correctly: Agreement and Reference

Some of the sentences that follow are correct; others have errors in pronoun agreement or reference. Write *OK* next to the correct sentences; write *X* next to the incorrect ones.

1. _____ When Brendan came home, Colton announced that his dog had chewed up a leather sandal.

2. _____ I want to go to the University of Springfield because their business school has an excellent reputation for placing recent graduates in good jobs.

3. _____ Everyone in my old neighborhood wanted to sell their home before major road construction started nearby.

4. _____ Graham had always had a dream of musical stardom, which made him special.

5. _____ We desperately wanted the local football team to win, but it was no match for the opponents from out of town.

6. _____ After the argument, either of my sisters could have offered their apologies, but the feud continued for months.

7. _____ Marcia didn't understand her mathematics textbook; she feels frustrated when she reads them.

8. _____ After dinner, somebody took the leftover cookies from the kitchen counter and put them in his or her pocket.

9. _____ In the sports section of the paper, it describes last night's hockey game.

10. _____ We never let our children play with the neighborhood dogs because we know they bite.

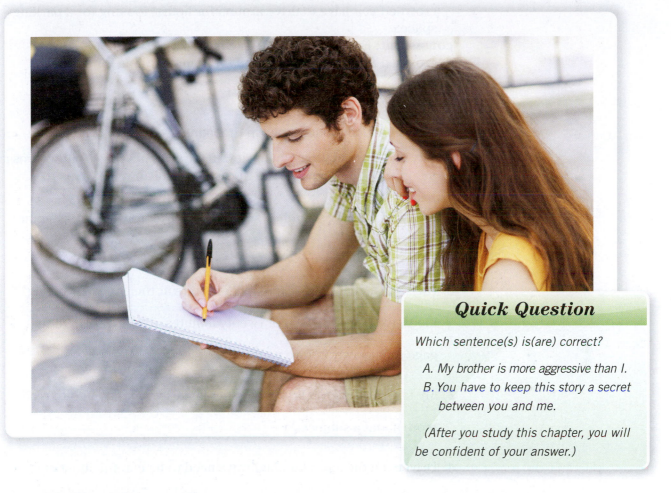

Learning Objectives

In this chapter, you will learn to:

1. Recognize first-, second-, and third-person points of view.
2. Identify and choose the correct pronoun case.
3. Correct errors in pronoun case.

POINTS OF VIEW AND PRONOUN CONSISTENCY

> 1. Recognize first-, second-, and third-person points of view.

When you write, you write from a point of view, and each point of view gets its own form. If you write from the first-person point of view, your pronouns are in the *I* (singular) or *we* (plural) forms. If you write from the second-person point of view, your pronouns are in the *you* form, whether they are singular or plural. If you write from the third-person point of view, your pronouns are in the *he, she,* or *it* (singular) or *they* (plural) forms.

Different kinds of writing may require different points of view. When you are writing a set of directions, for example, you may use the second-person (*you*) point of view. An essay about your childhood may use the first-person (*I*) point of view.

Whatever point of view you use, be consistent in using pronouns. That is, do not shift the form of your pronouns without some good reason.

not consistent: Every time *I* go to that mall, the parking lot is so crowded *you* have to drive around for hours, looking for a parking space.

consistent: Every time *I* go to that mall, the parking lot is so crowded *I* have to drive around for hours, looking for a parking space.

Exercise 1   **Practice: Consistency in Pronouns**

Correct any inconsistency in point of view in the sentences that follow. Cross out the incorrect pronoun and write the correct one above it.

1. Studying for long stretches doesn't work well for me; you become too tired to concentrate.

2. After the arriving airline passengers stare at the empty revolving luggage carousel for ten or twenty minutes, a long stream of luggage rolls slowly before you.

3. My favorite kind of class is one that makes you motivated to read more about a subject.

4. Drivers on the interstate highways need to be careful about entering the road; you have to be sure to gather enough speed to merge into traffic.

5. Hallie and I like to shop at the Dollar Bargain Bin because you can always find cheap cosmetics or jewelry there.

6. Sometimes I don't return Joe's calls; once I start talking to him, he keeps you on the phone for hours.

7. My boyfriend and I like camping near Lake Lion, but you have to be prepared for hordes of mosquitoes in the summer.

8. Whenever I visit the botanical gardens downtown, I realize how the sight of beautiful flowers can give you a lift to the mind.

Exercise 2   **Practice: Correcting Sentences with Consistency Problems**

Rewrite the following sentences, correcting any pronoun consistency errors.
To make the corrections, you may have to change, add, or eliminate words.

1. Unless a teenager is strong enough to resist peer pressure and
   smart enough to recognize true friends, you will not have an easy
   trip to adulthood.

   rewrite: _____

   _____

   _____

2. Pierre becomes aware of his mother's sadness whenever she tells
   you about her childhood in Haiti.

   rewrite: _____

   _____

3. Students registering for next semester must bring your ID and
   signed advisement form.

   rewrite: _____

   _____

4. Laura and I cannot trust her cousin George; if you tell him a secret,
   he reveals it to the whole neighborhood.

   rewrite: _____

   _____

5. Students who have never used the college library should not be
   nervous because, after their library tour, you will discover that
   everything is easy to find.

   rewrite: _____

   _____

   _____

6. Yolanda loves beginning a new semester; she likes seeing her old
   instructors, bumping into your old classmates, and meeting her
   new instructors.

   rewrite: _____

   _____

7. To me, Mrs. Carmichael is a strict teacher; you can give her a million excuses, but she will never let me out of class early.

   rewrite: _____

   _____

8. I try not to take Brian to the donut shop anymore; since he developed diabetes, you can't let him eat too much sugar.

   rewrite: _____

   _____

② Identify and choose the correct pronoun case.

CHOOSING THE CASE OF PRONOUNS

Pronouns have forms that show number and person, and they also have forms that show **case**. Case refers to the form a pronoun takes depending on its function in a sentence. Following in the Info Box is a list of the three cases of pronouns.

INFO BOX   **Pronouns and Their Case**

Singular Pronouns	Subjective Case	Objective Case	Possessive Case
1st person	I	me	my
2nd person	you	you	your
3rd person	he, she, it	him, her, it	his, her, its
	who, whoever	whom, whomever	whose
Plural Pronouns			
1st person	we	us	our
2nd person	you	you	your
3rd person	they	them	their
	who, whoever	whom, whomever	whose

Rules for Choosing the Case of Pronouns

The rules for choosing the case of pronouns are simple:

1. When a pronoun is used as a subject, use the **subjective case**.
2. When a pronoun is used as the object of a verb or the object of a preposition, use the **objective case**.
3. When a pronoun is used to show ownership, use the **possessive case**.

   pronouns used as subjects:

   He studies his sociology notes every day.
   Bill painted the walls, and *we* polished the floors.
   Who is making that noise?

   pronouns used as objects:

   Sarah called *him* yesterday.
   He gave his old computer science textbook to *me*.
   With *whom* did you argue?

   pronouns used to show possession:

   I am worried about *my* grade in Spanish.
   The nightclub has lost *its* popularity.
   I wonder *whose* tablet this is.

Pronoun Case in a Related Group of Words

You need to be careful in choosing case when the pronoun is part of a related group of words. If the pronoun is part of a related group of words, isolate the pronoun. Next, try out the pronoun choices. Then decide which pronoun is correct and write the correct sentence. For example, which of these sentences is correct?

Aunt Sophie planned a big dinner for Tom and *I*.

or

Aunt Sophie planned a big dinner for Tom and *me*.

Step 1: Isolate the pronoun. Eliminate the related words *Tom and*.

Step 2: Try each case:

Aunt Sophie planned a big dinner for *I*.

or

Aunt Sophie planned a big dinner for *me*.

Step 3: The correct sentence is

Aunt Sophie planned a big dinner for Tom and me.

The pronoun acts as an object, so it takes the objective case.

Try working through the steps once more to be sure that you understand this principle. Which of the following sentences is correct?

Last week, *me* and my friend studied in the library until midnight.

or

Last week, *I* and my friend studied in the library until midnight.

Step 1: Isolate the pronoun. Eliminate the related words *and my friend*.

Step 2: Try each case:

Last week, *me* studied in the library until midnight.

or

Last week, *I* studied in the library until midnight.

Step 3: The correct sentence is

Last week, I and my friend studied in the library until midnight.

The pronoun acts as a subject, so it takes the subjective case.

> **Note:** You can also write it this way for better style:
> *Last week, my friend and I studied in the library until midnight.*

COMMON ERRORS WITH THE CASE OF PRONOUNS

3 Correct errors in pronoun case.

Be careful to avoid these common errors:

1. *Between* is a preposition, so the pronouns that follow it are objects of the preposition: between *us*, between *them*, between *you and me*. It is never correct to write *between you and I*.

   not this: ~~The plans for the surprise party must be kept a secret between you and I.~~
   but this: The plans for the surprise party must be kept a secret between you and me.

2. Never use *myself* as a replacement for *I* or *me*.

   not this: ~~My father and myself want to thank you for this honor.~~
   but this: My father and I want to thank you for this honor.

> **not this:** ~~She thought the prize should be awarded to Arthur and myself~~.
> **but this:** She thought the prize should be awarded to Arthur and me.

3. The possessive pronoun *its* has no apostrophe.

> **not this:** ~~The car held it's value~~.
> **but this:** The car held its value.

> **not this:** ~~The baby bird had fallen from it's nest~~.
> **but this:** The baby bird had fallen from its nest.

4. Pronouns that complete comparisons can be in the subjective, objective, or possessive case.

> **subjective:** Christa speaks better than *I*.
> **objective:** The storm hurt Manny more than *her*.
> **possessive:** My car is as fast as *his*.

To decide on the correct pronoun, add the words that complete the comparison and say them aloud:

> Christa speaks better than I *speak*.
> The storm hurt Manny more than *the storm hurt* her.
> My car is as fast as his *car*.

5. *Who* and *whoever* are in the subjective case. *Whom* and *whomever* are in the objective case.

> **subjective:** *Who* came to the house?
> **subjective:** *Whoever* wants the books can take them.
> **objective:** *Whom* did Larry bring to the house?
> **objective:** You can bring *whomever* you like to the house.

If you have trouble choosing between *who* and *whom*, or *whoever* and *whomever*, substitute *he* for *who* and *whoever*, and *him* for *whom* and *whomever* to check the correctness of your choice.

Check this sentence:

> *Who* made the cake?

Is it correct? Change the sentence, substituting *he* in one version, and *him* in another version.

> *He* made the cake.
> *Him* made the cake.

If *he* is correct, then *who* is correct.

Check another sentence:

> With *whom* are you arguing?

Is it correct? Change the sentence, substituting *he* in one version, and *him* in another version. To make your choice simpler, write the sentence as a statement, not a question:

> You are arguing with *he*.
> You are arguing with *him*.

If *him* is correct, then *whom* is correct.

Exercise 3 Practice: Choosing the Correct Pronoun Case

Circle the correct pronoun in parentheses in each of the following sentences.

1. (She, Her) and Mr. Bergman were married in Yosemite Valley many years ago.

2. The mentoring program created a partnership between a senior and (me, myself).

3. Moving to Montana was the right decision for Josh and (I, me) because it offered a new beginning in a new place.

4. Although both Steve and Tabitha have Instagram accounts, Steve's feed is not updated as frequently as (her, hers).

5. Our long-awaited trip to the big city ended in disappointment for my parents and (I, me).

6. You and Tony both majored in business, but your skills in closing a deal are different from (him, his).

7. The advising center posted (its, it's) hours for summer advising.

8. Sometimes I become impatient with Joe and (she, her); they procrastinate about making even the smallest choices.

Exercise 4 Collaborate: Write Your Own Text on Pronoun Case

Collaborate

With a partner or with a group, write two sentences that could be used as examples for each of the following rules. The first one is done for you.

1. **Rule 1:** When a pronoun is used as a subject, use the subjective case.

   examples: He complained about the noise in the street.

   Tired and hungry, they stopped for lunch.

2. **Rule 2:** When a pronoun is used as the object of a verb or the object of a preposition, use the objective case.

   examples: _____

   _____

3. **Rule 3:** When a pronoun is used to show ownership, use the possessive case.

   examples: _____

   _____

4. **Rule 4:** When a pronoun is part of a related group of words, isolate the pronoun to choose the case. (For your examples, write two sentences in which the pronoun is part of a related group of words.)

   examples: _____

   _____

Connect

| Exercise 5 | Connect: Editing a Paragraph for Errors in Pronoun Consistency and Case |

In the following paragraph, correct any errors in pronoun consistency and case. There are seven errors. Write your corrections above the line.

I am very grateful for this award from the Community Cares Club. Many people encouraged, supported, and even changed me in my work with local homeless children. One is my mother, whom introduced me to the organization several years ago. At that time, I thought of my mother's work in the club as worthy but depressing. I never realized how mistaken I was until you actually met the children. Because of my mother's involvement in the club, I had a chance to learn about the spirit, courage, and strength of disadvantaged boys and girls. Interacting with these children created a bond between them and I. I gave them the stability of regular attention, academic support, and physical activity. Around them, I became a more positive person. They were a good influence on I. Them and me were a good combination. Therefore I have to thank the Community Cares Club. They brought me and the children together.

Chapter Test   Using Pronouns Correctly: Consistency and Case

Some of the sentences that follow are correct; others have errors in pronoun consistency or case. Write *OK* next to the correct sentences; write *X* next to the incorrect ones.

1. _____ Who did you gossip about after I left the party?

2. _____ Sometimes I get angry at Claudia and he; they take advantage of my generosity.

3. _____ It was difficult for my parents and I to leave our house in the suburbs and move to a small apartment in a decrepit part of the city.

4. _____ Whoever gets to the restaurant first needs to find a table for six.

5. _____ I am a little upset with my brother; he always gets better grades in English than me.

6. _____ How to use the file-sharing site is unclear to everyone except me and Alexia.

7. _____ After the blizzard, Kate and myself were grateful for the emergency vehicles that rescued us from the huge drifts of snow around the cabin.

8. _____ Whom do you expect at the farewell party for your supervisor?

9. _____ They wanted my friend Hasan and I to represent the students at the Collegiate Forum.

10. _____ We believe the writer of the anonymous post to be she.

Punctuation

CHAPTER 28

Quick Question

Which sentence(s) is(are) correct?

A. *Brew and Chew, a popular coffee shop near campus, is offering a discount to students.*

B. *Brew and Chew a popular coffee shop near campus is offering a discount to students.*

(After you study this chapter, you will feel confident of your answer.)

Learning Objectives

In this chapter, you will learn to:

1. Use the period and question mark correctly.
2. Identify the four main ways to use a comma in a sentence.
3. Use the comma correctly with quotations, dates and addresses, numbers, tags, and interjections.
4. Use the semicolon and colon correctly within a sentence.
5. Use the apostrophe correctly in contractions and to show possession.
6. Use the exclamation mark, dash, parentheses, and hyphen correctly.
7. Use quotations and capital letters correctly.
8. Use numbers and abbreviations correctly.

THE PERIOD

Periods are used two ways:

1. Use a period to mark the end of a sentence that makes a statement or gives a command.

   We invited him to dinner at our house.
   When Richard spoke, no one paid attention.

1 Use the period and question mark correctly.

Don't be late for class.
Leave your paper on your desk.

2. Use a period after abbreviations.

Mr. Ryan
James Wing, Sr.
10:00 p.m.

> **Note:** If a sentence ends with a period marking an abbreviation, do not add a second period.

Exercise 1　**Practice: Using Periods**

Add periods where they are needed in each of the following sentences.

1. Oscar bought about fifteen lbs of special food for his sick terrier

2. When the elementary school children went on field trips, they were nervous around people like Mr Carlson, the principal

3. Isaac wants to get a BS degree in Biology, and his friend, Dr Hamilton, told him to prepare by taking many science classes in high school

4. Tell Ms Marko or Mr Scanlon about the parking problems in the gymnasium parking lot.

5. Last night I studied for my psychology test until 1:00 am but had to be alert to take the test at 8:00 am

6. Nicholas Anderson, Sr is a better businessman than his son

7. Someday, I want to be known as Cecilia Knowles, RN, so I am going to college to study nursing.

8. You can purchase snacks and drinks at the South St Mini Mart

THE QUESTION MARK

Use a question mark after a direct question, a tag question, or a request.

Isn't she adorable?
We have homework tonight, don't we?
Could you lend me a sheet of paper?

If a question is not a direct question, it does not get a question mark.

They asked if I thought their grandchild was adorable.
She questioned whether I had car insurance.

Exercise 2　**Practice: Punctuating with Periods and Question Marks**

Add any missing periods and question marks to each sentence that follows.

1. Are the people upstairs moving out of their apartment

2. Have you ever thought about getting a BA in graphic design

3. I plan on interning at the local hospital at the end of the semester

4. She didn't explain that clearly, did she

5. I'm not certain that the meeting will take place as scheduled

6. Don't you think 4:00 am is a little early to start driving to Ocean City, MD

7. Would you tell Prof Thomas that I may be late

8. I wonder why you never call me on Saturdays

| Exercise 3 | Connect: Editing a Paragraph for Errors in Periods and Question Marks |

Connect

In the following paragraph, correct errors in punctuating with periods and question marks. The errors may involve missing or incorrect punctuation. There are eight errors.

Last Tuesday, a simple errand started me wondering if I had lost my mind?

First, I visited my allergy doctor for a routine check of my sinuses and bronchial

tubes. Then I went to my local pharmacy to refill a prescription for an antihista-

mine. This is a regular prescription for me; I have been taking the medicine since

I developed seasonal allergies several years ago. After I received the bag with the

vial of pills in it, I ran several more errands. I returned to my house at about

6:30 pm. for dinner and a good night's sleep. The next morning, I opened the plastic

container with my allergy pills inside. Suddenly I noticed a problem with the pills.

The pills were large and blue. My allergy pills are always small and pink. I didn't

know what to do. First, I asked myself whether I had paid enough attention to Dr

Kasabian during my visit a day earlier? Had he changed my medication. Or had

the pharmacist given me the wrong pills? What would happen if I took one of the

new pills? I needed my allergy medicine, and I was slipping into a state of panic.

After obsessing for a few more minutes, I decided not to take an allergy pill until

I called the pharmacist. My heart beat wildly as I waited to be connected to the

pharmacy department at the drug store. The woman who answered the phone was

Ms Patel, and she seemed very calm. I wondered how she could be so calm when

my life might be at stake? Soon, I learned the real story. My prescription medicine

was now being manufactured by a new company. The company was producing the same pill in the same dose, but the pill was now large and blue. I began to feel calm, and my voice lost its hysterical tone I swallowed my pill, smiled, and vowed never again to create a crisis out of nothing.

Section Test   **Punctuation: The Period and the Question Mark**

Some of the sentences that follow are correct; others have errors in the use of periods and question marks. Put an *X* next to the sentences with errors.

1. _____ After I got to know Dr Stefanovic, I trusted her with my medical care.

2. _____ Parker was not sure whether the computer lab was open on Saturdays.

3. _____ The officer could have asked Kate Gomez about the time of the break-in.

4. _____ Now that Eddie has finished medical school, he has become Edward Obara, MD

5. _____ This book must weigh three lbs more than my laptop.

6. _____ Will Abraham ever finish restoring his old Ford Mustang?

7. _____ My roommate woke me up at 6:00 am yesterday so that we could study for our botany test.

8. _____ Could you let me see your notes from yesterday?

9. _____ The weather forecaster predicted more than 12 inches of snow tonight.

10. _____ That was the most most interesting film we have seen in a long time, wasn't it.

2 Identify the four main ways to use a comma in a sentence.

THE COMMA

There are four main ways to use a comma, as well as other, less important ways. *Memorize the four main ways.* If you can learn and understand these four rules, you will be more confident and correct in your punctuation. That is, you will use a comma only when you have a reason to do so; you will not be scattering commas in your sentences simply because you think a comma might fit, as many writers do.

The four main ways to use a comma are as a lister, a linker, an introducer, or an inserter (use two commas).

Use a Comma as a Lister

Commas support items in a series. These items can be words, phrases, or clauses.

comma between words in a list: She has enrolled in literature, history, and art classes this semester.

comma between phrases in a list: I looked for my ring under the coffee table, between the sofa cushions, and behind the chairs.

comma between clauses in a list: In the past month, she has completed a marathon, climbed a 14,000-foot mountain, and biked across the state.

> **Note:** In a list, the comma before *and* is optional, but many writers use it to avoid ambiguity. For clarity's sake, it is generally best to include the comma before *and*.

Exercise 4   Practice: Using a Comma as a Lister

Add commas only where they are needed in the following sentences. Do not add any other punctuation or change existing punctuation.

1. Meat fish cheese beans and dairy products are sources of protein.

2. Nicole can do the laundry Mike can vacuum the house and I can clean the kitchen.

3. The thief caught with the money was silent snarling and slippery.

4. Bargain prices for rugs pillows and curtains drew online shoppers to the House Goods Web site.

5. I will wash dry and fold your dirty clothes when you take them off the floor and put them in the laundry basket.

6. My aunt knew she was spending too much time and money on television shopping channels when boxes of glittering jewelry expensive makeup and household gadgets started piling up in her house.

7. Eric is self-centered lacks any sense of responsibility and lies to his friends.

8. Working full time going to school part time and managing a household keep Jenna quite busy.

Use a Comma as a Linker

A comma and a coordinating conjunction link two independent clauses. The coordinating conjunctions are *for, and, nor, but, or, yet,* and *so.* The comma goes in front of the coordinating conjunction:

> I have to get to work on time, or I'll get into trouble with my boss.
> My mother gave me a beautiful card, and she wrote a note on it.

Exercise 5   Practice: Using a Comma as a Linker

Add commas only where they are needed in the following sentences. Some sentences do not need commas. Do not change words or add any other punctuation.

1. Dr. Pinsky used to clean my teeth and he would give me a new toothbrush afterward.

2. My daughter can spend the weekend with her father or she can stay at her grandmother's house.

3. A day with my best friend lets me escape from my worries and act like a child again.

4. Marsha wouldn't take her professor's advice nor would she listen to her academic advisor.

5. Sophie must be sick for she has missed every class this week.

6. George had planned a perfect holiday party but something went wrong.

7. Jerry has tried several diets and exercise plans yet can't seem to lose weight.

8. My art and photography classes are enjoyable but I know that jobs are scarce in those fields.

Use a Comma as an Introducer

Put a comma after introductory words, phrases, or clauses in a sentence.

a comma after an introductory word:
Yes, I agree with you on that issue.
Generally, students prefer electronic textbooks, or e-books.

a comma after an introductory phrase:
In the long run, you'll be better off without him.
Before the anniversary party, my father bought my mother a necklace.

a comma after an introductory clause:
If you call home, your parents will be pleased.
When my smartphone buzzes, I am always in the shower.

> **Exercise 6**   **Practice: Using a Comma as an Introducer**

Add commas only where they are needed in the following sentences. Some sentences do not need commas. Do not change words or add any other punctuation.

1. Across the aisle from me stood the woman of my dreams.

2. Unless the weather improves we won't be able to hunt tomorrow.

3. Absolutely I can help you with that assignment.

4. Courtney do you have an extra pencil or pen?

5. On my little brother's birthday I took him to a water park.

6. While the professor explained the problem I took careful notes.

7. Behind the curtains are two children playing hide-and-seek.

8. After a few days Luisa got used to the traffic in the city.

Use a Comma as an Inserter

When words or phrases that are *not* necessary are inserted into a sentence, put a comma on *both* sides of the inserted material:

The game, unfortunately, was rained out.
My test score, believe it or not, was the highest in the class.
Potato chips, my favorite snack food, are better-tasting when they're fresh.
James, caught in the middle of the argument, tried to keep the peace.

Using commas as inserters requires that you decide what is essential to the meaning of the sentence and what is nonessential. Here is a good rule to remember:

If you do not need material in a sentence, put commas around the material. If you need material in a sentence, do not put commas around the material.

For example, consider this sentence:

The girl who called me was selling magazine subscriptions.

Do you need the words *who called me* to understand the meaning of the sentence? To answer that question, write the sentence without those words:

The girl was selling magazine subscriptions.

Reading the shorter sentence, you might ask, "Which girl?" The words *who called me* are essential to the sentence. Therefore, you do not put commas around them.

correct: The girl who called me was selling magazine subscriptions.

Remember that the proper name of a person, place, or thing is always sufficient to identify it. Therefore, any information that follows a proper name is inserted material; it gets commas on both sides.

Carlton Furniture, which is nearby, has the best prices on futons and sofa beds.
Sam Harris, the man who won the marathon, lives on my block.

Note: Sometimes the material that is needed in a sentence is called **essential** (or **restrictive**), and the material that is not needed is called **nonessential** (or **nonrestrictive**).

Exercise 7   **Practice: Using Commas as Inserters**

Add commas only where they are needed in the following sentences. Some sentences do not need commas.

1. A house full of toys will not always make a troubled child happy.

2. My best friend his eyes red and swollen mourned the loss of his cousin.

3. Mr. Murdock could of course decide to raise the rent.

4. Drivers who take the shortcut to the airport can save at least ten minutes and avoid the congestion at the toll plaza.

5. Our neighbor an enthusiastic gardener has transformed his yard into a small park.

6. *The Polar Express* which both children and adults enjoy was created with an experimental animation process.

7. The little girl at the end of the line has dropped the ice cream out of her cone.

8. Ultimate Books the bookstore in the Midland Mall has the biggest collection of manga and graphic novels.

Remember the four main ways to use a comma—as a lister, a linker, an introducer, and an inserter—and you'll solve many of your problems with punctuation.

Exercise 8 **Practice: Punctuating with Commas: The Four Main Ways**

Add commas only where they are needed in the following sentences. Do not add any other punctuation, and do not change any existing punctuation. Some sentences do not need commas.

1. As Philip turned the key in the front door he heard a strange noise coming from the second floor.

2. The sweet potato casserole the best item on the Thanksgiving day table disappeared in about five minutes.

3. Anyone who loves art will want to visit the new exhibit at the Student Center.

4. I had to work overtime at the hospital of course and couldn't go to the lake with Martin.

5. A house with a fireplace seems more appealing to me than a house with a pool.

6. Well you can do whatever you want and I'll just stay home and watch television.

7. Although we went on vacation to rest, we rode bikes every morning swam at the beach during the day and danced late into the evenings.

8. Shelley would you like a mango cake from the Cuban bakery for your birthday?

3 Use the comma correctly with quotations, dates and addresses, numbers, tags, and interjections.

Other Ways to Use a Comma

There are other places to use a comma. Reviewing these uses will help you feel more confident as a writer.

1. Use commas with quotations. Use a comma to set off a direct quotation from the rest of the sentence.

> My father told me, "If you can't be on time, be early."
> "Let's take the scenic route," Raymond said.

Note that the comma that introduces the quotation goes before the quotation marks. But once the quotation has begun, commas or periods go inside the quotation marks.

2. Use commas with dates and addresses. Use commas between the items in dates (specifically separating the month and day from the year) and addresses (separating street address from the city and separating the city from the state). Please note, however, that a comma is not used if only the month and year are provided (January 2016).

> August 5, 1992, is Chip's date of birth.

> We lived at 133 Emerson Road, Lake Park, Pennsylvania, before we moved to Florida.

> August 2016 was one of the hottest months on record.

Notice the comma after the year in the date, and the comma after the state in the address. These commas are needed when you write a date or address within a sentence.

3. Use commas in numbers. Use commas in numbers of one thousand or larger.

> The price of the new tires and rims was $1,115.

4. Use commas with tags. Place the commas after the statement and before the question.

> You aren't going to major in two subjects, are you?
> Professor Jones is giving us the test on Monday, isn't she?

5. Use commas with yes, no, and other interjections.

> Yes, I'll meet for coffee after class.
> Oh, did I forget to take the garbage out again?

Exercise 9 **Practice: Punctuation: Other Ways to Use a Comma**

Add commas wherever they are needed in the following sentences. Do not add any other punctuation, and do not change any existing punctuation.

1. "There isn't any milk in the refrigerator" my little boy complained.

2. On January 1 2002 Suzanne and Colin moved into a small house in Clifton New Jersey.

3. Be sure that anything you do you do for the right reasons.

4. She wasn't in class yesterday was she?

5. "I have lived at 535 Orchid Place Denver Colorado for more than six years" Alex told me.

6. Kevin graduated from college on June 15 2017 and soon started work as a landscape architect in Sante Fe New Mexico.

7. Melissa stood in front of the clothes in her closet and muttered "I have got to clean out this mess."

8. No I cannot tell William that you do not want to date him anymore.

Exercise 10 **Practice: Punctuating with Commas: A Comprehensive Exercise**

Add commas only where they are needed in the following sentences. Do not add any other punctuation, and do not change any existing punctuation. Some of the sentences do not need commas.

1. The tired little boy refused to eat any of his chicken nuggets nor would he touch his French fries.

2. My old sneakers are in bad shape yet they are more comfortable than any other shoes I own.

3. Cough syrup in tasty flavors should be kept out of children's reach because they might drink the syrup for its taste.

4. Media Literacy II the hardest class to get into has another section added for next semester.

5. People who enter the theater after a movie has started should stay in one place until their eyes adjust to the darkness.

6. Tim can meet me at the coffee shop or call me when he gets home.

7. Running as fast as he could the fire fighter shouted "Get out of the building!"

8. Dr. Levin the famous psychiatrist has written a book about depression, anxiety, and teenagers.

Connect

Exercise 11 **Connect: Editing a Paragraph for Errors in Commas**

In the following paragraph, correct any errors related to punctuating with commas. The errors may involve missing or incorrect use of commas. There are nineteen errors.

My grandparents live in an old but very sturdy home. Whoever built it built it well. They bought it in 1970 for $35450 and it was a bargain even in those days. The house has survived several blizzards and my grandfather has never had to make major repairs for heating problems or burst pipes. When a huge hurricane hit the area the house suffered only minor roof damage. The home a two-story wooden house is strong solid, and stable. Part of the story of the house is of course a story of luck. Cable Road where the house sits on several acres of land is full of old houses. Many, have survived bad times and bad weather but most have been hit by a falling tree or flooded by melting snow. My grandparents have watched their neighbors pump the water out of basements cut tree limbs away from the roof or tape broken windows on the storm side of a house. My grandfather and grandmother have helped the other residents of Cable Road deal with the effects of time and weather. On the other hand the neighbors have never had to come to my grandparents' rescue. "We're just grateful for our home" my grandfather says and I envy his good luck.

Section Test **Punctuation: The Comma**

Some of the sentences that follow are correct; others have errors in punctuating with commas. Put an *X* next to the sentences with errors.

1. _____ Christina Roberts, my best friend since high school was born in Fort Lauderdale, during a powerful hurricane.

2. _____ The damage to the empty house was senseless, and whoever did it, did it out of pure meanness.

3. _____ No I don't want your old computer, printer, or digital camera.

4. _____ English has borrowed words from many languages, and many languages have borrowed words from English.

5. _____ Super Foods, which is open twenty-four hours a day, is the best place for last-minute grocery shopping.

6. _____ "No one will criticize you for telling the truth," my brother told me.

7. _____ Ella, her face beaming with happiness, graduated from college on May 22, 2007 with a degree in physical therapy.

8. _____ Getting my truck repaired cost me $1214, but it was cheaper than making enormous car payments on a new truck.

9. _____ The school's hockey team, winless in their previous eight games won in overtime.

10. _____ Although I sometimes go to parties on weekends I really prefer some quiet time with my friends.

THE SEMICOLON

There are two ways to use semicolons:

④ Use the semicolon and colon correctly within a sentence.

1. Use a semicolon to join two independent clauses:

Michael loved his old Firebird; he worked on it every weekend.
The situation was hopeless; I couldn't do anything.

> **Note:** If the independent clauses are joined by a conjunctive adverb, you will still need a semicolon. You will also need a comma after any conjunctive adverb that is more than one syllable long. Conjunctive adverbs are discussed in more depth in Chapter 17.

conjunctive adverb

He was fluent in Spanish; *consequently*, he was the perfect companion for our trip to Venezuela.

conjunctive adverb

I called the hotline for twenty minutes; *then* I called another number.

> **For your information:** A list of common conjunctive adverbs is in an Info Box in Chapter 17.

Independent clauses joined by coordinating conjunctions (the words *for, and, nor, but, or, yet,* and *so*) do not need semicolons. Use a comma in front of the coordinating conjunction:

coordinating conjunction

Michael loved his old Firebird, *and* he worked on it every weekend.

coordinating conjunction

He was fluent in Spanish, *so* he was the perfect companion for our trip to Venezuela.

2. Use semicolons to separate the items on a list that contains commas. Adding semicolons will make the list easier to read:

The contestants came from Rochester, New York; Pittsburgh, Pennsylvania; Trenton, New Jersey; and Boston, Massachusetts.
(The semicolons show that Rochester is a city in the state of New York, Pittsburgh is a city in the state of Pennsylvania, and so forth.)

The new officers of the club will be Althea Bethell, president; Francois Riviere, vice-president; Ricardo Perez, secretary; and Lou Phillips, treasurer. (The semicolons link the person, Althea Bethell, with the office, president, and so forth.)

Exercise 12 **Practice: Punctuating with Semicolons**

Add any missing semicolons to the following sentences. In some sentences, you may have to change commas to semicolons.

1. The noise of construction workers outside the building grew louder meanwhile, I was trying to finish an end-of-the-year project for my literature class.

2. Two years ago, I was terrified of water now I love to swim in the ocean.

3. The campus tour allowed us to see classes in action in addition, we were able to speak to a few professors.

4. Stacey is smart, attractive, and outgoing, yet she longs to be more like her younger sister.

5. Mario, my father, Mark, my older brother, Michael, my younger brother, and Michelle, my sister, all have first names that begin with *M*.

6. The research paper is due Tuesday the final exam is on Wednesday.

7. Sarah will call the cell phone company or stop by one of its customer locations for an explanation of the latest bill.

8. I have to pack my suitcase tonight otherwise, I might forget something in the morning rush to the airport.

THE COLON

A colon is used at the end of a complete statement. It introduces a list or an explanation:

> **colon introduces a list:** When I went grocery shopping, I picked up a few things: milk, eggs, and coffee.

> **colon introduces an explanation:** The room was a mess: dirty clothes were piled on the chairs, wet towels were thrown on the floor, and an empty pizza box was tossed in the closet.

Remember that the colon comes after a complete statement. What comes after the colon explains or describes what came before the colon. Look once more at the two examples, and you'll see the point.

> When I went grocery shopping, I picked up a few things: milk, eggs, and coffee. (The words after the colon—*milk, eggs, and coffee*—explain what few things I picked up.)
>
> The room was a mess: dirty clothes were piled on the chairs, wet towels were thrown on the floor, and an empty pizza box was tossed in the closet. (In this sentence, all the words after the colon describe what the mess was like.)

Some people use a colon every time they put a list in a sentence, but this is not a good rule to follow. Instead, remember that a colon, even one that introduces a list, must come after a complete statement.

not this: ~~When I go to the beach, I always bring: suntan lotion, a big towel, and a cooler with iced tea.~~

but this: When I go to the beach, I always bring my supplies: suntan lotion, a big towel, and a cooler with iced tea.

A colon may also introduce long quotations.

On December 8, 1941, the day after the Japanese attacked Pearl Harbor, President Franklin Delano Roosevelt summed up the situation: "Hostilities exist. There is no blinking at the fact that our people, our territory, and our interests are in grave danger." *(Note that what comes after the colon explains what came before it and is a complete statement.)*

Exercise 13 **Practice: Punctuating with Colons**

Add colons where they are needed in the following sentences. Some sentences do not need a colon.

1. When you go to the cabin for the weekend, be sure to fill your car with groceries, extra blankets, insect repellent, books, binoculars, and fishing gear.

2. My brother did a superb job of cleaning the bathroom a shining bathtub, a spotless sink, a gleaming toilet, and even a floor free of footprints.

3. Since I had twenty dollars left over at the end of the week, I bought some small surprises for my husband a can of cashews, a bottle of wine, and his favorite magazine.

4. Until we cleaned out the garage, we had a collection of tools, ladders, empty boxes, lawn chairs, broken appliances, and rags crowded into the space.

5. Be sure to bring the following to the next class a dictionary, five sheets of paper and a blue-ink pen.

6. Our neighborhood has several Fourth of July traditions flags flying in people's yards, a parade of small children on their bikes or in strollers, and a community barbecue on a dead-end street.

7. If you want to contribute to the food drive for victims of the storm, you can bring canned food, bread and rolls, bottled water, and paper plates and towels.

8. My grandmother believes that there are two kinds of children the ones who behave and the ones who don't.

Exercise 14 **Practice: Using Semicolons and Colons**

Add semicolons and colons where they are needed in the following sentences. You might have to change a comma to a semicolon.

1. I will never go to a sushi restaurant the thought of eating raw fish makes me nauseous.

2. You need floor mats for your car, and be sure to look for the usual auto supplies motor oil, car wax, and windshield wiper fluid.

3. All the students passed the exam, they had worked hard on this unit.

4. If you go to the drug store, get me some toothpaste, hair gel, and aspirin.

5. Patrick Henry, American patriot, is known for a memorable phrase "Give me liberty or give me death."

6. There has been a shake-up in the managerial staff of Tompkins Motors, so the new leaders are Karen Killian, manager, Pierre La-Valle, assistant manager, Ron Jessup, service manager, and Lorena Robles, business manager.

7. Because I am majoring in hotel and hospitality management, I have enrolled in classes in accounting, customer relations, restaurant management, and business law.

8. We take notes on our tablets however, our professor makes us send them to her.

Connect

Exercise 15 **Connect: Editing a Paragraph for Errors in Semicolons and Colons**

In the following paragraph, correct any errors related to punctuating with semicolons or colons. The errors may involve missing or incorrect use of semicolons or colons. There are nine errors.

On one subzero day in Minnesota, my friend and I dreamed of a tropical vacation, but we did not exactly find our dream. We started by listing all the warm places we craved Miami; Florida; Cancun; Mexico; Honolulu; Hawaii; and Kingston; Jamaica. Of course, we soon discovered that the price of traveling to and staying at any of these four places was well beyond our means. We were ready to give up our dreams, then we thought of another way to enjoy fun in the sun without spending thousands of dollars. My sister and her husband had recently returned from a bargain cruise in the Bahamas. The reasonable price included the following round-trip airfare to the port of departure, accommodations in a double cabin, all meals, and all entertainment. Our ship would stop at two ports and also spend a day at a private island where we could swim, snorkel, and soak up the sun. This trip sounded like a perfect way for us to spend our spring break. Of course, nothing is perfect, and we soon experienced many small and large snags. Just as we flew into the city where we would board the ship, a rare winter rain storm hit the tropics. As we left the port of departure, we stood on deck and held giant umbrellas over our heads. The storm followed us to the ports we visited it also hit the private island. Dancing the limbo on a rain-swept patio is not exciting even when the steel drums play. Snorkeling in the rain is not much fun even when the setting

is a private island. By the time we returned to Minnesota, we had learned one hard

lesson; pack more than sunscreen and swimsuits when you prepare for any cruise.

Section Test   **Punctuation: The Semicolon and the Colon**

Some of the following sentences are correct; others have semicolon or colon errors. Put an *X* next to the incorrect sentences.

1. _____ Drawn by the famous country singer's last concert, people came from all over the southern states: Gainesville, Florida; Savannah, Georgia; Huntsville, Alabama; and Jackson, Mississippi.

2. _____ I am firm in my decision; I will continue to work at the restaurant until I graduate.

3. _____ Amanda forgot to pack her medication; so we had to turn around and drive fifty miles back to her house.

4. _____ Chris will eat just about any cookie in the world: stale cookies, cookie crumbs, half-eaten cookies, even cookies that have fallen on the floor.

5. _____ My cousin got stuck in traffic: then his car overheated.

6. _____ If you go to the islands, be sure to enjoy the natural beauty: the turquoise water, the powdery white beaches, and the amazing undersea creatures.

7. _____ The college debate team won tournaments in Jacksonville, Florida, Athens, Georgia, and Charleston, South Carolina.

8. _____ Charlie won't talk to me about his worries; nor will he share them with his mother.

9. _____ There is much to like about Steven he is thoughtful and kind, smart and industrious, and creative and innovative.

10. _____ Siri has learned many new tricks in gymnastics this past season: the double back, the giant, and a triple back hand-spring.

THE APOSTROPHE

Use the apostrophe in the following ways:

1. Use an apostrophe in contractions to show that letters have been omitted.

do not	= don't
I will	= I'll
is not	= isn't
she would	= she'd
will not	= won't

Also use the apostrophe to show that numbers have been omitted:

the summer of 1998 = the summer of '98

⑤ Use the apostrophe correctly in contractions and to show possession.

Exercise 16 **Practice: Using Apostrophes in Contractions**

Add apostrophes where they are necessary in each sentence that follows.

1. Dr. Fanelli is a great veterinarian; shell tell you whats wrong with your potbellied pig.

2. My grandfather never stops talking about the blizzard of 84 and how he didnt think hed live through it.

3. The trip wasnt what Id expected, but Ill never forget it.

4. Hows your new job?

5. Terry wont tell you that theres a problem with his health.

6. Henry and Lori couldnt make the trip this week; theyll come next month when theyve got more time.

7. If youre sick, youd better stay home and drink plenty of fluids.

8. Its wonderful to see dolphins in their natural habitat.

2. **Use an apostrophe to show possession.** If a word does not end in *s*, show ownership by adding an apostrophe and *s*.

the ring belongs to Jill	= Jill's ring
the wallet belongs to somebody	= somebody's wallet
the books are owned by my father	= my father's books

If two people jointly own something, put the *'s* on the name of the second person listed.

Ann and Mike own a house = Ann and Mike's house

If a word already ends in *s* and you want to show ownership, just add an apostrophe.

the ring belongs to Frances	= Frances' ring
two boys own a dog	= the boys' dog
the house belongs to Ms. Jones	= Ms. Jones' house

> **Caution:** Be careful with apostrophes. These words, the possessive pronouns, do not take apostrophes: *his, hers, theirs, ours, yours, its.*

not this: ~~The pencils were their's.~~
but this: The pencils were theirs.

not this: ~~The steak lost it's flavor.~~
but this: The steak lost its flavor.

Exercise 17 **Practice: Using Apostrophes to Show Possession**

Add apostrophes where they are needed in the following sentences. Some sentences do not need apostrophes.

1. Mrs. Noriko promised to improve the companys marketing division and expand its overseas office.

2. I went to Charles and Agnes wedding yesterday, and I thought their wedding cake tasted better than yours.

3. I have been looking for a new smartphone case because my cases design has worn off.

4. Catherine and Anthony are creative people, and the credit for reno-
vating the pediatric wing of the hospital is all theirs.

5. I hope that, when I mentioned the changes at the womens club, I
did not hurt anyones feelings.

6. Be careful with Saras laptop; she just bought it.

7. I miss San Diegos weather, but I love Bostons college life and its
sense of history.

8. My sister Allisons musical ability is all hers; no one else in the family can sing, play an instrument, or read music.

3. Use the apostrophe for special uses of time, and to create a plural of
numbers mentioned as numbers, letters mentioned as letters, and words
that normally do not have plurals.

> **special uses of time:** It will take a week's work.
> **numbers mentioned as numbers:** Take out the 5's.
> **letters mentioned as letters:** Cross your *t*'s.
> **words that normally do not have plurals:** I want no more *maybe*'s.

> **Caution:** Do not add an apostrophe to a simple plural.

> **not this:** ~~He lost three suitcase's~~.
> **but this:** He lost three suitcases.

Exercise 18 Practice: Special Uses of Apostrophes

Add apostrophes where they are needed in the following sentences. Some
sentences do not need apostrophes. Do not change or add any words.

1. I have *B*s on all my science quizzes, so I feel confident about the test.

2. Alice is going to New Zealand for three weeks; she will stay with
relatives who live there.

3. Jennifer deserves a days pay for all the time she spent on cleaning
up your office.

4. The winner of the lottery won an amount of money with six *0*s at
the end, so it has to be at least one million dollars.

5. It will be several months before I can save up enough vacation days
for a trip to Wyoming.

6. My mother writes very fancy capital *A*s because she used to study
calligraphy.

7. The down payment on my new house is less than a years worth of
rent on my old one.

8. Dont forget your "*excuse me*s" and "*please*s" when you visit Aunt
Claudia.

Exercise 19 Practice: Using Apostrophes: A Comprehensive Exercise

Circle the correct form in parentheses in each sentence that follows.

1. Could the white rabbit in our yard be (someones, someone's) pet?

2. (Theres, There's) nothing wrong with your computer.

3. A new (mens, men's) store just opened in the Palms Plaza.

4. The advisor handed back the registration cards to English II, but they were (ours, our's).

5. I fell in love for the first time in the spring of (99, '99).

6. Tell me if you like (Laura's and Kim's, Laura and Kim's) new roommate.

7. Lamont's answers to my requests are too full of (*nos*, *no*'s).

8. Staying out late began to lose (its, it's) appeal for me when I became a father.

Connect

Exercise 20 Connect: Editing a Paragraph for Errors in Apostrophes

In the following paragraph, correct any errors related to punctuating with apostrophes. The errors may involve missing or incorrect use of apostrophes. There are eleven errors.

Watching the Super Bowl in Aunt Kathleen's and Uncle Manny's basement lounge is almost as good as being in the stadium. First of all, the room is huge, and its filled with sports memorabilia, comfortable chairs, and a giant television screen. A big refrigerator is packed with food and beverages that are all our's. This basement is soundproof, so the crowd in front of the screen can cheer or cry loudly. Everyone can look at this years most outrageous commercials and wait for the surprise's of the halftime show. Enjoying the Super Bowl while we sit in my aunt and uncles basement has become a tradition for me, my cousin Anthony, my parent's, and my fathers' best friend, Patrick. Also, new faces appear at the party each year. After some games, it takes me a weeks worth of family calls to identify newcomers such as the woman sitting with my cousin or the old man who kissed my aunt. I know that I would love to sit in the seat's at the Super Bowl, but I also love game day with my aunt and uncle. That special Sunday has it's own pleasures.

Section Test Punctuation: The Apostrophe

Some of the sentences that follow are correct; others have errors in using punctuation. Put an *X* by each sentence with an error.

1. _____ Morris is sure to say his "*thank yous*" when he visits his grandfather's house.

2. _____ I'm not sure if Mark and Maria left behind the serving bowls, but I know the platters are theirs.

3. _____ The stray kitten has to be somebodys pet, so we'll post the kitten's photo throughout the neighborhood and keep the little cat safe until it's owner shows up.

4. _____ Although the two data-sharing sites look similiar, the site's are completely different.

5. _____ We'll go to Rita's and Carlos' party after we've had dinner.

6. _____ Tammy got a months salary as a bonus after she'd broken the company's record for sales.

7. _____ I'd like to see a few more *0*'s at the end of my income tax refund check.

8. _____ There's no one under the bed; the monster is a product of Charles imagination.

9. _____ Its been more than a month since someone has cleaned the dogs bowl.

10. _____ Although it's nice to ride again, I found the horse uncooperative and its saddle uncomfortable.

THE EXCLAMATION MARK

The exclamation mark is used at the end of sentences that express strong emotion:

> **appropriate:** You've won the lottery!
> **inappropriate:** ~~We had a great time!~~ (*Great* already implies excitement.)

Be careful not to overuse the exclamation mark. If your choice of words is descriptive, you should not have to rely on the exclamation point for emphasis. Use it sparingly, because it is easy to rely on exclamations instead of using better vocabulary.

THE DASH

Use a dash to interrupt a sentence. Dashes are used for emphasis, to further explain or define something, or to make a dramatic shift.

> I picked up the crystal bowl carefully, cradled it in my arms, walked softly—and tripped, sending the bowl flying.

Two dashes set off dramatic words that interrupt a sentence.

> Ramon took the life preserver—our only one—and tossed it far out to sea.

> Everyone at the university—faculty, students, and administration—was in shock when the power went out.

Because dashes are somewhat dramatic, use them sparingly.

PARENTHESES

Use parentheses to enclose extra material and afterthoughts.

> I was sure that Ridgefield (the town I'd just visited) was not the place for me.
> Her name (which I have just remembered) was Celestine.

6 Use the exclamation mark, dash, parentheses, and hyphen correctly.

> **Note:** Commas in pairs, dashes in pairs, and parentheses are all used as inserters. They set off material that interrupts the flow of the sentence. The least dramatic and smoothest way to insert material is to use commas.

THE HYPHEN

Use a hyphen to join two or more descriptive words that act as a single-word adjective or **phrasal adjective**.

> Bill was a smooth-talking charmer.
> The stadium had state-of-the-art scoreboards.

Also, use a hyphen in the written form of compound numbers from twenty-one to ninety-nine.

| Exercise 21 | Practice: Punctuating with Exclamation Marks, Dashes, Parentheses, and Hyphens |

Add any exclamation marks, dashes, parentheses, and hyphens that are needed in the sentences that follow.

1. Larry took the airline ticket my last chance at freedom and threw it into the incinerator.

2. There's someone hiding in the closet

3. Lenny Montalbano the boy who used to live next door grew up to start his own medical research company.

4. Mr. Okada is a caring, competent, and good natured supervisor.

5. Mr. Thompson is known for his eccentric ways; one day he came to work in a handsome blue blazer, striped silk tie, gray flannel slacks and believe it or not bright orange sneakers.

6. Get out of the middle of the road

7. The salesperson said the radio was a top of the line product.

8. Amanda was a trend setting dresser; she always looked fantastic.

QUOTATION MARKS

7 Use quotations and capital letters correctly.

Use quotation marks for direct quotes, for the titles of short works, and for other special uses.

   1. Put quotation marks around direct quotes, a speaker or writer's exact words:

> My mother told me, "There are plenty of fish in the sea."
> "I'm never going there again," said Irene.
> "I'd like to buy you dinner," Peter said, "but I'm out of cash."
> My best friend warned me, "Stay away from that guy. He will break your heart."

Look carefully at the preceding examples. Notice that a comma is used to introduce a direct quotation, and that at the end of the quotation, the comma or period goes inside the quotation marks:

> My mother told me, "There are plenty of fish in the sea."

Notice how direct quotes of more than one sentence are punctuated. If the quote is written in one unit, quotation marks go before the first quoted word and after the last quoted word:

> My best friend warned me, "Stay away from that guy. He will break your heart."

But if the quote is not written as one unit, the punctuation changes:

> "Stay away from that guy," my best friend warned me. "He will break your heart."

> **Caution:** Do *not* put quotation marks around indirect quotations.

> **indirect quotation:** He asked if he could come with us.
> **direct quotation:** He asked, "Can I come with you?"

> **indirect quotation:** She said that she wanted more time.
> **direct quotation:** "I want more time," she said.

  2. Put quotation marks around the titles of short works. If you are writing the title of a short work like a short story, an essay, a newspaper or magazine article, a poem, or a song, put quotation marks around the title:

> In middle school, we read Robert Frost's poem "The Road Not Taken."
> My little sister has learned to sing "Itsby Bitsy Spider."

If you are handwriting the title of a longer work like a book, movie, magazine, play, television show, or CD, underline the title:

> Last night I saw an old movie, <u>The Godfather</u>.
> I read an article called "Campus Changes" in <u>Newsweek</u>.

In typed papers and printed publications such as books or magazines, titles of long works are italicized:

> Last night I saw an old movie, *The Godfather*.
> I read an article called "Campus Changes" in *Newsweek*.

  3. There are other, special uses of quotation marks. You use quotation marks around words mentioned as words in a sentence.

> When you said "never," did you mean it?
> People from the Midwest pronounce "water" differently than I do.

If you are using a quotation within a quotation, use single quotation marks.

> My brother complained, "Every time we get in trouble, Mom has to say 'I told you so.'"
> Kyle said, "Linda has a way of saying 'Excuse me' that is really very rude."

CAPITAL LETTERS

There are ten main situations in which you capitalize:

  1. Capitalize the first word of every sentence:

Yesterday we saw our first soccer game.

2. Capitalize the first word in a direct quotation if the word begins a sentence:

My aunt said, "This is a gift for your birthday."
"Have some birthday cake," my aunt said, "and have some more ice cream." (Notice that the second section of this quote does not begin with a capital letter because it does not begin a sentence.)

3. Capitalize the names of persons:

Nancy Perez and Frank Murray came to see me at the store.
I asked Mother to feed my cat.

Do not capitalize words like *mother*, *father*, or *aunt* if you put a possessive in front of them. Only capitalize these words if they are proper nouns.

I asked my mother to feed my cat.

4. Capitalize the titles of persons:

I spoke with Dr. Wilson.
He has to see Dean Johnston.

Do not capitalize when the title is not connected to a name:

I spoke with that doctor.
He has to see the dean.

5. Always capitalize countries, cities, languages, nationalities, religions, races, months, days of the week, documents, organizations, holidays, and historical events or periods:

In high school, we never studied the Vietnam War.
The Polish-American Club will hold a picnic on Labor Day.

Use small letters for the seasons:

I love fall because I love to watch the leaves change color.

6. Capitalize the names of particular places:

We used to hold our annual meetings at Northside Auditorium in Montpelier, Vermont, but this year we are meeting at Riverview Theater in Bellows Falls.

Use small letters if a particular place is not given:

We are looking for an auditorium we can rent for our meeting.

7. Use capital letters for geographic locations:

Jim was determined to find a good job in the West.

But use small letters for geographic directions:

To get to my house, you have to drive west on the turnpike.

8. Capitalize the names of specific products:

I always drink Minute Maid Orange Juice for breakfast.

But use small letters for a kind of product:

I always drink orange juice for breakfast.

9. Capitalize the names of specific school courses (and do not abbreviate the course):

I have to take Child Psychology next term (*not* "Child Psych").

But use small letters for a general academic subject:

My advisor told me to take a psychology course.

10. Capitalize the first and last words in the titles of long or short works, and capitalize all other significant words in the titles:

I've always wanted to read *For Whom the Bell Tolls*.
Whenever we go to see the team play, my uncle sings "Take Me Out to the Ballgame."

> **Note:** Remember that the titles of long works, like books, are italicized (unless these titles are handwritten; then they are underlined). The titles of short works, like songs, are placed within quotation marks.

Exercise 22 **Practice: Using Quotation Marks, Underlining, and Capital Letters**

Add any missing quotation marks, underlining, and capital letters to the following sentences. You can assume that all these sentences are in printed form.

1. When I was growing up, uncle Richard was my favorite relative, but I later discovered my uncle had a dangerous temper.

2. When Melanie signed up for her winter term at college, she registered for classes in social science, writing, and music.

3. I can't stand it, my girlfriend said, when you say maybe instead of giving me a definite answer.

4. I finally found a good preschool for my son; it's the Madison school for early childhood education, and dr. Howard of Miller university is the director.

5. One night, my brother Jason was watching a television show called Dirty Jobs; I watched it for a minute and said, Ugh! Turn off that disgusting program."

6. David is looking for a job in the midwest because he wants to be near his parents, who live north of Chicago.

7. Whenever Mimi says the word love, she means the word infatuation.

8. There is nothing funnier than listening to my grandfather sing

Marvin Gaye's old song, heard It Through the Grapevine.

8 Use numbers and abbreviations correctly.

NUMBERS

Spell out numbers that take one or two words:

> Alice mailed two hundred brochures.
> I spent ninety dollars on car repairs.

Use the numbers themselves if it takes more than two words to spell them out.

> We looked through 243 old photographs.
> The sticker price was $16,397.99.

Also use numbers to write dates, times, addresses, and parts of a book.

> We live at 24 Cambridge Street.
> They were married on April 3, 1993.
> Chapter 3 had difficult maps to read, especially the one on page 181.

ABBREVIATIONS

Although you should spell out most words rather than abbreviate them, you may abbreviate *Mr.*, *Mrs.*, *Ms.*, *Jr.*, *Sr.*, and *Dr.* when they are used with a proper name. You should abbreviate references to time and to organizations widely known by initials.

> The moderator asked Ms. Steinem to comment.
> The bus left at 5:00 p.m., and the trip took two hours.
> He works for the FBI.

You should spell out the names of places, months, days of the week, courses of study, and words referring to parts of a book:

> **not this:** ~~I missed the last class, so I never got the notes for Chap. 3.~~
> **but this:** I missed the last class, so I never got the notes for Chapter 3.

> **not this:** ~~He lives on Chestnut Street in Boston, Mass.~~
> **but this:** He lives on Chestnut Street in Boston, Massachusetts.

> **not this:** ~~Pete missed his psych. test.~~
> **but this:** Pete missed his psychology test.

Exercise 23 **Practice: Using Numbers and Abbreviations**

Correct any errors in the use of numbers or abbreviations in the following sentences. Some sentences may not need corrections.

1. Ellen came into our soc. class last Mon., carrying her research

   paper, which looked about three in. thick.

2. Mr. and Mrs. Chang sent one hundred fifty five invitations to their

   daughter's wedding in Minneapolis, Minn.

3. My parents' apartment on Sunset Ave. had 4 rooms.

4. Matthew left Fla. on Mar. third, 2014, to begin a job with the

Abraham and Braun Co. in N. Dakota.

5. My phys. ed. teacher starts class promptly at 8:30 a.m. every Fri.

6. It took me two hrs. to finish Chap. 3 of my sociology textbook.

7. Gregory charges twenty-five dollars an hour to help people with

their computer problems.

8. Sam Khan, Jr., was a sports reporter for the *Houston Chronicle* for

six years before he took a job with ESPN.

Note: Exercises incorporating concepts from all punctuation sections follow
the section test.

Section Test Other Punctuation

Some of the sentences that follow are correct; others have errors in using
quotation marks, capital letters, numbers, and abbreviations. Put an *X* next
to the sentences.

1. _____ My mother warned, "Before you do anything impulsive,
think about your future".

2. _____ Carlotta spent one thousand and eighty dollars on new curtains for her house even though she owes her brother thousands of dollars for fixing her roof.

3. _____ At my aunt's wedding reception, my sister sang "I Will
Always love You" as the bride and groom danced.

4. _____ Dr. Gillespie is teaching an online course in Intro. to
Psychology in the summer term.

5. _____ In our elementary school library, there was a framed copy of
the Declaration of Independence on the wall.

6. _____ Mike always says "eventually" when I ask him when he will
graduate.

7. _____ "Give me a few minutes," Father said, "and I'll take you to
the park."

8. _____ I used to walk down the fashionable streets in Chicago, Ill.,
and stare at the the expensive cars and luxury stores.

9. _____ The British Poet, Gerald Manly Hopkins, wrote a poem titled
"Spring and Fall."

10. _____ Yosemite National Park in the Sierra Nevadas of California
is one of the Nation's finest parks.

Exercise 24   **Practice: A Comprehensive Exercise on Punctuation**

Add any missing punctuation to the following sentences. Also, correct any errors in capitalization and in the use of numbers or abbreviations. Assume that all the sentences are in printed or typed form.

1. We had a second rate meal at Frank and Maries house of Ribs last Sat. night we can't recommend the place to you.

2. I'm looking for a book called the rule of four my friend recommended it.

3. The five year old boy began to pour chocolate syrup on the kitchen floor meanwhile the babysitter dozed on the living room couch.

4. Lance took 2 spanish courses at National H.S. so he does not have to take a foreign language class at Centenary college.

5. The star athlete wanted to know if she could miss a days practice.

6. The star athlete asked Can I miss a days practice

7. I love a whole new world, the song from the movie Aladdin.

8. Now that we live in Buffalo N.Y. I need some warm clothes sweaters, gloves, hats, and a coat with a heavy lining.

Connect

Exercise 25   **Connect: Editing a Paragraph for Errors in Punctuation**

In the following paragraph, correct any errors related to punctuation or mechanics. The errors may involve missing or incorrect punctuation, capitalization, use of numbers, or abbreviations. There are nineteen errors.

When I agreed to do some work at a dirty old house I was not prepared, for the consequences. The house had belonged to my Mothers second cousin. When he died, he left it to my mother. She persuaded me and my brother to clean the house for her. After it was cleaned, she planned to sell the property. As my brother Sam and I approached the decrepit house we noticed that a dark, blue sky covered us. Beneath the brooding sky, the roof of the house had lost many of it's shingles. The rickety gate creaked ominously when we entered the yard. I reached the front entrance, and grabbed the rusty doorknob. Almost immediately, a hairy spider crawled across my hand. The atmosphere did not improve when we entered the house. Spider webs, and dust covered each room, then a horrible smell repelled us as we moved toward the basement stairs. The stairs to the basement were creaky. Some were missing. My brother stumbled and had to grab my hand, after he put his foot into an open space where a stair should have been. Soon we saw more horror. At least 100 rats were crawling around the dark basement spaces. Racing back to the smelly safety of the upper floor's, I wondered, "What else was waiting for us in this miserable place?" We decided not to explore any more of this crazy place. Our short time in the house had made us feel like ready made victims in a movie like *Dawn Of The Dead.*

Chapter Test Punctuation

Some of the sentences that follow are punctuated correctly; others have errors. Write *OK* next to the correct sentences; write *X* next to the incorrect sentences.

1. _____ I wonder if you would like me to bake a cake for your birthday.

2. _____ Andrew tried to fit in with his brother's friends, but never felt at ease around them.

3. _____ At the back of the house was a large patio surrounded by palm trees.

4. _____ Burgers and More, the most popular restaurant near campus, is closing its doors.

5. _____ Lisa warned her sister, "Stay away from people who love to gossip."

6. _____ Lightning struck the old school; fortunately no one was hurt.

7. _____ I would never drive a long distance without: my phone, water, and snacks.

8. _____ The credit for Jan and Jimmy's success in business is all theirs.

9. _____ Using so many ifs and buts was unusual for him.

10. _____ During my freshman composition class, I read two works: A Tale of Two Cities and War and Peace.

CHAPTER 21

Quick Question

Does the following sentence contain a spelling error? Yes/No

A week in the mountains appealled to me because I could find relief from the city's heat.

(After you study this chapter, you will be confident of your answer.)

Learning Objectives

In this chapter, you will learn to:

1. Know the difference between vowels and consonants.
2. Apply basic spelling rules to determine correct word endings.
3. Recognize when a one- or two-word spelling applies to certain terms.

No one is a perfect speller, but there are ways to become a better speller. If you can learn a few spelling rules, you can answer many of your spelling questions.

1 Know the difference between vowels and consonants.

VOWELS AND CONSONANTS

To understand the spelling rules, you need to know the difference between vowels and consonants. **Vowels** are the letters a, e, i, o, u, and sometimes y. **Consonants** are all the other letters.

The letter y is a vowel when it has a vowel sound.

silly (The y sounds like ee, a vowel sound.)

cry (The y sounds like i, a vowel sound.)

The letter *y* is a consonant when it has a consonant sound.

yellow (The *y* has a consonant sound.)
yesterday (The *y* has a consonant sound.)

SPELLING RULE 1: DOUBLING A FINAL CONSONANT

2 Apply basic spelling rules to determine correct word endings.

When you add an ending, double the final consonant of a word if all three of the following are true:

1. The word is one syllable, or the accent is on the last syllable.
2. The word ends in a single consonant preceded by a single vowel.
3. The ending you are adding starts with a vowel.

begin	+	ing	=	beginning
shop	+	er	=	shopper
stir	+	ed	=	stirred
occur	+	ed	=	occurred
fat	+	est	=	fattest
pin	+	ing	=	pinning

Exercise 1   Practice: Doubling a Final Consonant

Add *ed* to the following words by applying the rules for double consonants.

1. stammer _____   5. admit _____

2. swat _____   6. cram _____

3. trick _____   7. stop _____

4. order _____   8. excel _____

SPELLING RULE 2: DROPPING THE FINAL *e*

Drop the final *e* before you add an ending that starts with a vowel.

observe	+	ing	=	observing
excite	+	able	=	excitable
fame	+	ous	=	famous
create	+	ive	=	creative

Keep the final *e* before an ending that starts with a consonant.

love	+	ly	=	lovely
hope	+	ful	=	hopeful
excite	+	ment	=	excitement
life	+	less	=	lifeless

Exercise 2   Practice: Dropping the Final *e*

Combine the following words and endings by following the rule for dropping the final *e*.

1. imagine + able _____

2. care + less _____

3. arrange + ment _____

4. resource + ful _____

5. behave + ing _____

6. expense + ive _____

7. intense + ly _____

8. refuse + ing _____

SPELLING RULE 3: CHANGING THE FINAL *y* TO *i*

When a word ends in a consonant plus *y*, change the *y* to *i* when you add an ending:

try	+ es	=	tries
silly	+ er	=	sillier
rely	+ ance	=	reliance
tardy	+ ness	=	tardiness

When you add -*ing* to words ending in *y*, always keep the *y*.

| cry | + ing | = | crying |
| rely | + ing | = | relying |

Exercise 3 **Practice: Changing the Final *y* to *i***

Combine the following words and endings by applying the rule for changing the final *y* to *i*.

1. happy + er _____

2. apply + ing _____

3. penny + less _____

4. marry + ed _____

5. deny + es _____

6. ally + ance _____

7. comply + ant _____

8. ready + ness _____

SPELLING RULE 4: ADDING *s* OR *es*

Add *es* instead of *s* to a word if the word ends in *ch*, *sh*, *ss*, *x*, or *z*. The *es* adds an extra syllable to the word.

box	+ es	=	boxes
witch	+ es	=	witches
class	+ es	=	classes
clash	+ es	=	clashes

Exercise 4   **Practice: Adding *s* or *es***

Apply the rule for adding *s* or *es* to the following words.

1. polish _____
2. defeat _____
3. march _____
4. stock _____

5. fix _____
6. pass _____
7. back _____
8. tax _____

SPELLING RULE 5: USING *ie* OR *ei*

Use *i* before *e*, except after *c*, or when the sound is like *a*, as in *neighbor* and *weigh*.

i before *e*:
relief   convenience   friend   piece

e before *i*:
conceive   sleigh   weight   receive

Exercise 5   **Practice: Using *ie* or *ei***

Add *ie* or *ei* to the following words by applying the rule for using *ie* or *ei*.

1. dec _ _ t
2. fr _ _ ght
3. conc _ _ t
4. bel _ _ f

5. perc _ _ ve
6. ch _ _ f
7. n _ _ ce
8. f _ _ ld

Exercise 6   **Practice: Spelling Rules: A Comprehensive Exercise**

Combine the following words and endings by applying the spelling rules.

1. blur   + ed   _____
2. carry   + ed   _____
3. fizz   + s or es   _____
4. tidy   + er   _____
5. perch   + s or es   _____
6. harass   + s or es   _____
7. plan   + ed   _____
8. ready   + ness   _____
9. ply   + able   _____
10. concur   + ed   _____

Connect

<table>
<tr><td>**Exercise 7**</td><td>**Connect: Editing a Paragraph for Spelling**</td></tr>
</table>

Correct the spelling errors in the following paragraph. Write your corrections above each error. There are nine errors.

Buying store-brand products, which are usually cheaper than national-brand products, is a good way to save money. I used to think that buying national brands of items such as cereal or peanut butter meant getting food of better quality. However, I have stoped beleiving in that distinction. For example, how much difference can there be in two boxs of raisin bran from different companys? In addition, I have learned that many of the store brands are produced in the same mills or factorys as the national brands. It is quite possible that Kellogg's raisin bran and Publix raisin bran were made with the same bran, sugar, raisins, and other ingredients and were made in the same place. The only difference between a can of peachs sold by a national brand and one sold by a store brand may be the price. The national brand usually costs more because nationally known companies have to pay more for their expensive national advertising campaigns. Recently, I have tryed to be a smarter shoper, and I have concentrated on buying store brands of such items as bottled water, English muffinns, ice cream, and peanuts. In most cases, I cannot tell the difference between the national and the store brands. Now, when I visit my nieghborhood supermarket, I am a little smarter than I used to be.

③ Recognize when a one- or two-word spelling applies to certain terms.

DO YOU SPELL IT AS ONE WORD OR TWO?

Sometimes you can be confused about certain words. You are not sure whether to combine them to make one word or to spell them as two words. The following lists show some commonly confused words.

Words That Should Not Be Combined

a lot	each other	high school	every time
even though	good night	all right	no one
living room	dining room	in front	

Words That Should Be Combined

another	newspapers	bathroom
bedroom	playroom	good-bye, goodbye, or good-by
bookkeeper	roommate	cannot
schoolteacher	downstairs	southeast, northwest, etc.
grandmother	throughout	nearby
worthwhile	nevertheless	yourself, himself, myself, etc.

Words Whose Spelling Depends on Their Meaning

one word: *Already* means "before."
He offered to do the dishes, but I had *already* done them.
two words: *All ready* means "ready."
My dog was *all ready* to play Frisbee.

one word: *Altogether* means "entirely."
That movie was *altogether* too confusing.
two words: *All together* means "in a group."
My sisters were *all together* in the kitchen.

one word: *Always* means "every time."
My grandfather is *always* right about baseball statistics.
two words: *All ways* means "every path" or "every aspect."
We tried *all ways* to get to the beach house.
He is a gentleman in *all ways*.

one word: *Anymore* means "any longer."
I do not want to exercise *anymore*.
two words: *Any more* means "additional."
Are there *any more* pickles?

one word: *Anyone* means "any person at all."
Is *anyone* home?
two words: *Any one* means "one person or thing in a special group."
I'll take *any one* of the chairs on sale.

one word: *Apart* means "separate."
Liam stood *apart* from his friends.
two words: *A part* is "a piece or section."
I read *a part* of the chapter.

one word: *Everyday* means "ordinary."
Tim was wearing his *everyday* clothes.
two words: *Every day* means "each day."
Sam jogs *every day*.

one word: *Everyone* means "all the people."
Everyone has bad days.
two words: *Every one* means "all the people or things in a specific
   group."
My father asked *every one* of the neighbors for a donation to the
   Red Cross.

Exercise 8   **Practice: Do You Spell It as One Word or Two?**

Circle the correct word in parentheses in each sentence that follows.

1. Jason apologized to me yesterday; he said he wanted to make
   everything (all right, alright) between us.

2. Terry would be happy to own (any one, anyone) of the beautiful
   houses being built on Pinewood Avenue.

3. If you have (all ready, already) seen the new Jamie Foxx movie,
   let's go see the one with Jennifer Lopez and Matt Damon.

4. Robin is thinking of moving back to the (North East, Northeast); she misses her friends in Vermont.

5. Being snowed in at the airport was an (all together, altogether) horrible experience.

6. My father sold insurance, and my mother was a (school teacher, schoolteacher) in an elementary school.

7. (Every time, Everytime) I hear that song, I think of Luis.

8. My math professor says he doesn't want to hear (any more, anymore) complaints about the homework.

Connect

Exercise 9 **Connect: Do You Spell It as One Word or Two? Correcting Errors in a Paragraph**

The following paragraph contains errors in word combinations. Correct the errors in the space above each line. There are ten errors.

My friends all ways want to go to a club on Saturday nights, but I am not

willing to go with them any more. Like many women, I want to meet people, but I

don't think I want to meet men in a bar. Everytime I go to a bar, I meet two kinds

of men: drunk men or arrogant men. Of course, most of my girlfriends and I drink

too much at a bar or a club, too. Perhaps we also appear to be arrogant. I have

begun to think that, a part from putting men and women under the same roof,

bars don't do much to help people get to know eachother. Loud music, crowded

spaces, and role-playing don't help anyone make a new friend. Worth while

relationships are likely to begin in a more natural environment such as a class-

room, snack bar, gym, workplace, or place of worship. I can not put myself in the

same situation of dressing up, trying to look cool, and scanning the crowd for

any one who might become a friend. The night all ways ends in a headache, a

disappointment, or a mistake. I am saying goodby to my Saturday night routine

and looking for something healthier.

A LIST OF COMMONLY MISSPELLED WORDS

Following is a list of words you use often in your writing. Study this list and use it as a reference.

1. absence	5. ache	9. advertise
2. absent	6. acquire	10. again
3. accept	7. across	11. a lot
4. achieve	8. actually	12. all right

13. almost
14. always
15. amateur
16. American
17. answer
18. anxious
19. apparent
20. appetite
21. apology
22. appreciate
23. argue
24. argument
25. asked
26. athlete
27. attempt
28. August
29. aunt
30. author
31. automobile
32. autumn
33. avenue
34. awful
35. awkward
36. balance
37. basically
38. because
39. becoming
40. beginning
41. behavior
42. belief
43. believe
44. benefit
45. bicycle
46. bought
47. breakfast
48. breathe
49. brilliant
50. brother
51. brought
52. bruise
53. build
54. bulletin
55. bureau
56. buried
57. business
58. busy
59. calendar
60. cannot
61. career
62. careful
63. catch
64. category

65. caught
66. cemetery
67. cereal
68. certain
69. chair
70. cheat
71. chief
72. chicken
73. children
74. cigarette
75. citizen
76. city
77. college
78. color
79. comfortable
80. committee
81. competition
82. conscience
83. convenient
84. conversation
85. copy
86. cough
87. cousin
88. criticism
89. criticize
90. crowded
91. daily
92. daughter
93. deceive
94. decide
95. definite
96. dentist
97. dependent
98. deposit
99. describe
100. desperate
101. development
102. different
103. dilemma
104. dining
105. direction
106. disappearance
107. disappoint
108. discipline
109. disease
110. divide
111. doctor
112. doesn't
113. don't
114. doubt
115. during
116. dying

117. early
118. earth
119. eighth
120. eligible
121. embarrass
122. encouragement
123. enough
124. environment
125. especially
126. etc.
127. every
128. exact
129. exaggeration
130. excellent
131. except
132. exercise
133. excite
134. existence
135. expect
136. experience
137. explanation
138. factory
139. familiar
140. family
141. fascinating
142. February
143. finally
144. forehead
145. foreign
146. forty
147. fourteen
148. friend
149. fundamental
150. general
151. generally
152. goes
153. going
154. government
155. grammar
156. grateful
157. grocery
158. guarantee
159. guard
160. guess
161. guidance
162. guide
163. half
164. happiness
165. handkerchief
166. heavy
167. height
168. heroes

(Continued)

169. holiday	219. nickel	269. restaurant
170. hospital	220. niece	270. ridiculous
171. humorous	221. ninety	271. right
172. identity	222. ninth	272. rhythm
173. illegal	223. occasion	273. sandwich
174. imaginary	224. o'clock	274. Saturday
175. immediately	225. often	275. scene
176. important	226. omission	276. schedule
177. independent	227. once	277. scissors
178. integration	228. operate	278. secretary
179. intelligent	229. opinion	279. seize
180. interest	230. optimist	280. several
181. interfere	231. original	281. severely
182. interpretation	232. parallel	282. significant
183. interrupt	233. particular	283. similar
184. irrelevant	234. peculiar	284. since
185. irritable	235. perform	285. sincerely
186. iron	236. perhaps	286. soldier
187. island	237. permanent	287. sophomore
188. January	238. persevere	288. strength
189. jewelry	239. personnel	289. studying
190. judgment*	240. persuade	290. success
191. kindergarten	241. physically	291. surely
192. kitchen	242. pleasant	292. surprise
193. knowledge	243. possess	293. taught
194. laboratory	244. possible	294. temperature
195. language	245. potato	295. theater
196. laugh	246. practical	296. thorough
197. leisure	247. prefer	297. thousand
198. length	248. prejudice	298. tied
199. library	249. prescription	299. tomorrow
200. loneliness	250. presence	300. tongue
201. listen	251. president	301. tragedy
202. lying	252. privilege	302. trouble
203. maintain	253. probably	303. truly
204. maintenance	254. professor	304. twelfth
205. marriage	255. psychology	305. unfortunately
206. mathematics	256. punctuation	306. unknown
207. meant	257. pursue	307. until
208. measure	258. quart	308. unusual
209. medicine	259. really	309. using
210. million	260. receipt	310. variety
211. miniature	261. receive	311. vegetable
212. minute	262. recognize	312. Wednesday
213. muscle	263. recommend	313. weird
214. mysterious	264. reference	314. which
215. naturally	265. religious	315. writing
216. necessary	266. reluctantly	316. written
217. neighbor	267. remember	317. yesterday
218. nervous	268. resource	

* *judgement* is an alternate spelling

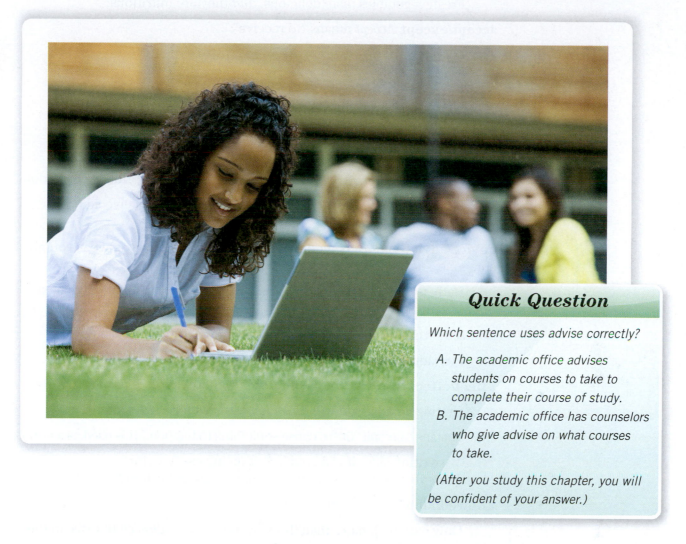

Learning Objectives

In this chapter, you will learn to:

1️⃣ Distinguish between sound-alike and look-alike words.

2️⃣ Use sound-alike and look-alike words correctly in writing.

WORDS THAT SOUND ALIKE/LOOK ALIKE

Words that sound alike or look alike (often called **homonyms**) can be confusing. Here is a list of some of the confusing words. Study this list, and make a note of any words that give you trouble.

1️⃣ Distinguish between sound-alike and look-alike words.

a/an/and *A* is used before a word beginning with a consonant or consonant sound:

> Jason bought *a* car.

An is used before a word beginning with a vowel or vowel sound:

> Emma took *an* apple to work.

545

And joins words or ideas:

> Psychology 101 *and* English Literature are my favorite courses.
> Fresh vegetables taste delicious, *and* they are nutritious.

accept/except *Accept* means "to receive":

> I *accept* your apology.

Except means "excluding":

> I'll give you all my books *except* my research guide.

addition/edition An *addition* is something that is added:

> My father built an *addition* to our house in the form of a porch.

An *edition* is an issue of a newspaper or one of a series of printings of a book:

> I checked the latest *edition* of the *Daily News* to receive an update
>   on the election.

advice/advise *Advice* is an opinion offered as a guide; it is what you give someone:

> Beth asked for my *advice* about which classes she should take next
>   semester.

Advise is what you do when you give an opinion offered as a guide:

> I couldn't *advise* Beth about the courses.

affect/effect *Affect* means "to influence something." It is used as a verb:

> Getting a bad grade will *affect* my chances for a scholarship.

Effect means "a result" or "to cause something to happen." It is used as a noun:

> My writing class had a great *effect* on my essay writing.
> The *effects* were evident throughout the neighborhood.

allowed/aloud *Allowed* means "permitted":

> Only cars with more than three occupants are *allowed* to drive in the
>   carpool lane.

Aloud means "out loud":

> I love to read *aloud* to my son at night.

all ready/already *All ready* means "ready":

> The dog was *all ready* to go for a walk.

Already means "before":

> David had *already* made plans for the weekend.

altar/alter An *altar* is a table or place in a church:

> They were married in front of the *altar*.

Alter means "to change":

> My plane was delayed, so I had to *alter* my plans for the evening.

angel/angle An *angel* is a heavenly being:

> I often feel as if a guardian *angel* is looking out for me.

An *angle* is the space within two lines:

> The road turned at a sharp *angle*.

are/our *Are* is a verb, the plural of *is:*

> We *are* friends of the mayor.

Our means "belonging to us":

> We have *our* writing workshop in Ranger Hall today.

beside/besides *Beside* means "next to":

> He sat *beside* me at the concert.

Besides means "in addition":

> I would never lie to you; *besides*, I have no reason to lie.

brake/break *Brake* means "to stop" or "a device for stopping":

> That truck *brakes* at railroad crossings.
> When he saw the moose on the road, he hit the *brakes*.

Break means "to come apart," or "to make something come apart":

> He *broke* a long standing deal.
> I can *break* the seal on that package.

breath/breathe *Breath* is the air you take in, and it rhymes with *death:*

> I was running so fast, I lost my *breath*.

Breathe means "to take in air":

> He found it hard to *breathe* in high altitudes.

buy/by *Buy* means "to purchase something":

> Sylvia wants to *buy* a new laptop.

By means "near," "by means of," or "before":

> He sat *by* his sister.
> I learn *by* taking good notes in class.
> *By* ten o'clock, Nick was tired.

capital/capitol *Capital* means "city" or "wealth":

> Albany is the *capital* of New York.
> Jack invested his *capital* in real estate.

A *capitol* is a building where a legislature meets:

> The city has a famous *capitol* building.

cereal/serial *Cereal* is a breakfast food or type of grain:

> My favorite *cereal* is Cheerios.

Serial means "in a series":

> Look for the *serial* number on the appliance.

choose/chose *Choose* means "to select." It rhymes with *snooze:*

> Today I am going to *choose* a dress for my first interview.

Chose is the past tense of *choose:*

> Yesterday I *chose* a new rug.

close/clothes/cloths *Close* means "near" or "intimate." It can also mean "to end or shut something":

> We live *close* to the subway station.
> James and Marnie are *close* colleagues.
> Noreen wants to *close* her eyes for ten minutes.

Clothes are wearing apparel:

> Eduardo has new *clothes.*

Cloths are pieces of fabric:

> I clean the silver with damp *cloths* and a special polish.

coarse/course *Coarse* means "rough" or "crude":

> The top of the table had a *coarse* texture.
> His language was *coarse.*

A *course* is a direction or path. It is also a subject in school:

> The hurricane took a northern *course.*
> In my freshman year, I took a *course* in drama.

complement/compliment *Complement* means "complete" or "make better":

> The colors in that room *complement* the style of the furniture.

A *compliment* is praise:

> Susan gave me a *compliment* about my new haircut.

conscience/conscious Your *conscience* is your inner, moral guide:

> His *conscience* bothered him when he told a lie.

Conscious means "aware" or "awake":

> The accident victim was not fully *conscious.*

council/counsel A *council* is a group of people:

> The Student Government *Council* meets this afternoon.

Counsel means "advice" or "to give advice":

> I need your *counsel* about my investments.
> My father always *counsels* me about my career.

decent/descent *Decent* means "suitable" or "proper":

> I hope Mike gets a *decent* job.

Descent means "going down, falling, or sinking":

> The plane began its *descent* to the airport.

desert/dessert A *desert* is dry land. To *desert* means "to abandon":

> To survive a trip across the *desert*, people need water.
> He will never *desert* a friend.

Dessert is the sweet food we eat at the end of a meal:

> I want tiramisu for *dessert.*

do/due *Do* means "perform":

> I have to stop complaining; I *do* it constantly.

Due means "owing" or "because of":

> The rent is *due* tomorrow.
> The class was canceled *due* to low enrollment.

does/dose *Does* is a form of *do:*

> My father *does* the laundry.

A *dose* is a quantity of medicine:

> Whenever I had a cold, my mother gave me a *dose* of cough syrup.

fair/fare *Fair* means "unbiased." It can also mean "promising" or "good":

> I received a *fair* grade for my project.
> Jose has a *fair* chance of winning the title.

A *fare* is the amount of money a passenger must pay:

> I couldn't afford the plane *fare* to Miami.

farther/further *Farther* means "a greater physical distance":

> His house is a few blocks *farther* down the street.

Further means "greater" or "additional." Use it when you are not describing a physical distance:

> My second French class gave me *further* training in French
>   conversation.

flour/flower *Flour* is ground-up grain, an ingredient used in cooking:

> I use whole-wheat *flour* in my muffins.

A *flower* is a blossom:

> She wore a *flower* in her hair.

forth/fourth *Forth* means "forward":

> The pendulum on the clock swung back and *forth*.

Fourth means "number four in a sequence":

> I was *fourth* in line for tickets.

hear/here *Hear* means "to receive sounds in the ear":

> I can *hear* the music.

Here is a place:

> We can have the meeting *here*.

heard/herd *Heard* is the past tense of *hear:*

> I *heard* you talk in your sleep last night.

A *herd* is a group of animals:

> The farmer has a fine *herd* of cows.

hole/whole A *hole* is an empty place or opening:

> I see a *hole* in the wall.

Whole means "complete" or "entire":

> Silvio gave me a *whole* steak.

isle/aisle An *isle* is an island:

> We visited the *Isle* of Capri.

An *aisle* is a passageway between sections of seats:

> The flight attendant came down the *aisle* and offered us a beverage and snack.

its/it's *Its* means "belonging to it":

> The car lost *its* hubcap after hitting a pothole.

It's is a shortened form of *it is* or *it has:*

> *It's* a beautiful day.
> *It's* been a pleasure to meet you.

knew/new *Knew* is the past tense of *know:*

> I *knew* Teresa in high school.

New means "fresh, recent, not old":

> I want some *new* shoes.

know/no *Know* means "to understand":

> They *know* how to play soccer.

No is a negative:

> Carla has *no* fear of heights.

Exercise 1 **Practice: Words that Sound Alike/Look Alike**

Circle the correct words in parentheses in each sentence that follows.

1. I need to look (farther, further) into the circumstances of the crime before I can (advice, advise) you about possible suspects.

2. Although car companies offer limited (additions, editions) of their luxury vehicles, I think it is best to (buy, by) a more modest, practical car.

3. Edward must have no (conscience, conscious), for he was willing to (desert, dessert) his children to satisfy his own desires.

4. Whenever Kim (compliments, complements) me, I (hear, here) a hint of insincerity in her voice.

5. It is clear that Henry (does, dose) not know if he can drive us to New Orleans, so we should (alter, altar) our plans.

6. I spent a (hole, whole) lot of money on dresses and other (close, clothes, cloths) last month, and now payment is (do, due).

7. When I had to speak in front of the town (council, counsel), I was so nervous I could hardly (breath, breathe).

8. In (are, our) algebra course, the professor reviewed how to find the correct (angel, angle) of different shapes.

Exercise 2   **Connect: Editing a Paragraph for Errors in Words that Sound Alike/Look Alike**

Connect

The following paragraph has errors in words that sound alike/look alike. Correct each error in the space above it. There are ten errors.

Driving an old truck presented several challenges for me recently. I usually ride my bike to school and sometimes drive my girlfriend's car. However, one afternoon she called me and asked for help. She was stranded on a country road about ten miles from home. Her car had broken down, and she needed me to pick her up. I couldn't leave her desperate and desserted, waiting alone for a tow truck. Since I had no car, I borrowed my friend's old truck. I had never driven a truck before; beside, I was nervous about driving on strange roads. Nevertheless, I set fourth bravely. As soon as I started the engine, I was conscience of weird sounds. They seemed to be coming from the engine. A few minutes later, I hit a whole in the road. I imagined the worst consequences. Maybe I had broken something important under the truck. Perhaps I had lost the ability to steer. Nervously, I drove further down the rough road. My next challenge was a steep decent down a hill. At that moment, I feared a loss of break power, but fortunately, I made it safely down the hill. Several miles later, I saw my girlfriend and her car at the side of a wooded area. After a long wait, we managed to get her car towed and to return safely to town. The series of mishaps involved in driving that truck led me to make a promise to myself: I will never drive that truck again. I would rather pay bus or even taxi fair, hitchhike, or even stay home. I will do anything accept get behind the wheel of that decrepit vehicle.

MORE WORDS THAT SOUND ALIKE/LOOK ALIKE

2 Use sound-alike and look-alike words correctly in writing.

lead/led When *lead* rhymes with *need*, it means "to give directions, to take charge." If *lead* rhymes with *bed*, it is a metal:

> The tutor will *lead* our study group this afternoon.
> Your book bag is as heavy as *lead.*

Led is the past form of *lead* when it means "to give directions, to take charge":

> The cheerleaders *led* the parade last year.

lessen/lesson *Lessen* means make less or reduce:

> I took an aspirin to *lessen* the pain of my headache.

A *lesson* is something to be learned or studied:

> I had my first guitar *lesson* yesterday.

loan/lone A *loan* is something you give on the condition that it be returned:

> When I was broke, I got a *loan* of fifty dollars from my aunt.

Lone means "solitary, alone":

> A *lone* shopper stood in the checkout line.

loose/lose *Loose* means "not tight":

> In the summer, *loose* clothing keeps me cool.

To *lose* something means "to be unable to keep it":

> I'm afraid I will *lose* my car keys.

medal/meddle/metal A *medal* is a badge of honor or a coinlike piece of bronze, silver, or similar substance used to commemorate an event:

> Mandy won a *medal* for swimming at the regional competition.
> At the Revolutionary War museum, visitors could buy souvenir
>   *medals* depicting famous battles.

To *meddle* means to interfere when the interference is not justified:

> Ben didn't think his mother should *meddle* in his romantic attachments.

Metal is an element such as gold or silver that often has a particular luster:

> Her bracelet was a thick cuff of a beaten *metal*.

moral/morale *Moral* means "upright, honorable, connected to ethical standards":

> I have a *moral* obligation to care for my children.

Morale is confidence or spirit:

> After the victory, the team's *morale* was high.

pain/pane *Pain* means "suffering":

> I had very little *pain* after the surgery.

A *pane* is a piece of glass:

> A bird flew into the window and broke a *pane*.

pair/pear A *pair* is a set of two:

> Mark has a *pair* of antique swords.

A *pear* is a fruit:

> In the autumn, I like a *pear* for a snack.

passed/past *Passed* means "went by." It can also mean "handed to," or received a successful score:

> The happy days *passed* too quickly.
> Janice *passed* me the mustard.
> I *passed* my driving test on the first try.

Past means "the time that has gone by":

> Let's leave the *past* behind us.

patience/patients *Patience* is calm endurance:

> When I am caught in a traffic jam, I should have more *patience*.

Patients are people under medical care:

> There are too many *patients* in the doctor's waiting room.

peace/piece *Peace* is calmness:

> Looking at the ocean brings me a sense of *peace*.

A *piece* is a part of something:

> Norman took a *piece* of coconut cake.

personal/personnel *Personal* means "connected to a person." It can also mean "intimate":

> Whether to lease or own a car is a *personal* choice.
> That information is too *personal* to share.

Personnel are the staff in an office:

> The Digby Electronics Company is developing a new health plan for
>   its *personnel*.

plain/plane *Plain* means "simple, clear, or ordinary." It can also mean "flat land":

> The restaurant serves *plain* but tasty food.
> Her house was in the center of a windy *plain*.

A *plane* is an aircraft:

> We took a small *plane* to the island.

pray/prey A person who *prays* is speaking to a spiritual being:

> Every night, my mother *prayed* for my safe return from the war.

Prey is a victim, whether it is an animal killed for food or a person. It can also mean to make another person into a victim:

> Small animals such as rabbits are often the *prey* of larger carnivores.
> The robber *preyed* on those who walked alone at night.

presence/presents Your *presence* is your attendance, your being somewhere:

> We request your *presence* at our wedding.

Presents are gifts:

> My daughter got too many birthday *presents*.

principal/principle *Principal* means "most important." It also means "the head of a school":

> My *principal* reason for returning to school is to prepare for a better
>   job.
> The *principal* of Crestview Elementary School is popular with
>   students.

A *principle* is a guiding rule:

> Betraying a friend is against my *principles*.

quiet/quit/quite *Quiet* means "without noise":

> The library has many *quiet* corners.

Quit means "stop":

> Will you *quit* complaining?

Quite means "truly" or "exactly":

> Victor's speech was *quite* convincing.

rain/reign/rein *Rain* is wet weather:

> We have had a week of *rain*.

To *reign* is to rule; *reign* is royal rule:

> King Arthur's *reign* in Camelot is the subject of many poems.

A *rein* is a leather strap in an animal's harness:

> When Charlie got on the horse, he held the *reins* very tight.

residence/residents A *residence* is a place to live:

> For years, my *residence* was a one room apartment downtown.

Residents are the people who live in a certain place:

> *Residents* of the Florida Keys are used to the uncertainty of hurricane season.

right/rite/write *Right* is a direction (the opposite of left). It can also mean "correct":

> To get to the gas station, turn *right* at the corner.
> On my sociology test, I got nineteen out of twenty questions *right*.

A *rite* is a ceremony:

> I am interested in the marriage *rites* of other cultures.

To *write* is to set down in words:

> Brian has to *write* a research paper.

sight/site/cite A *sight* is something you can see:

> The Grand Canyon was an amazing *sight*.

A *site* is a location:

> The city is building a courthouse on the *site* of my old school.

Cite means "to quote an authority." It can also mean "to give an example":

> In her term paper, Christina wanted to *cite* several computer experts.
> When my father lectured me on speeding, he *cited* the story of my best friend's car accident.

soar/sore To *soar* is to fly upward. It can also mean to rise higher:

> We watched the eagle *soar* from its perch in the tree.
> Sam sang at the audition and *soared* above the competition.

Sore means "painful."

> After I spent the afternoon raking leaves, I had a *sore* back.

sole/soul A *sole* is the bottom of a foot or shoe:

> As a result of my marathon training, I have worn a hole in the *sole* of my shoe.

A *soul* is the spiritual part of a person:

> Some people say meditation is good for the *soul*.

stair/stare A *stair* is a step:

> The toddler carefully climbed each *stair*.

A *stare* is a long, fixed look:

> I wish that woman wouldn't *stare* at me.

stake/steak A *stake* is a stick driven into the ground:

> The gardener put *stakes* around the tomato plants.

A *steak* is a piece of meat or fish:

> I like my *steak* cooked medium rare.

stationary/stationery *Stationary* means "standing still":

> As the speaker presented his speech, he remained *stationary*.

Stationery is writing paper:

> For my birthday, my uncle gave me some *stationery* with my name printed on it.

steal/steel To *steal* means "to take someone else's property without permission or right":

> Last night, someone tried to *steal* my car.

Steel is a form of iron:

> The door is made of *steel*.

than/then *Than* is used to compare things:

> Composition I was much easier *than* Composition II.

Then means "at that time":

> I studied Spanish I in high school; *then* I took Spanish II my first year of college.

their/there/they're *Their* means "belonging to them":

> My grandparents donated *their* car to charity.

There means "at that place." It can also be used as an introductory word:

> Sit *there*, next to Simone.
> *There* is a reason for his happiness.

They're is a contraction of *they are:*

> Jaime and Sandra are visiting; *they're* my cousins.

thorough/through/threw *Thorough* means "complete":

I did a *thorough* cleaning of my closet.

Through means "from one side to the other." It can also mean "finished":

We drove *through* Greenview on our way to Lake Western.
I'm *through* with my studies.

Threw is the past tense of *throw*:

I *threw* the ball to him.

to/too/two *To* means "in a direction toward." It is also a word that can go in front of a verb:

I am driving *to* Miami.
Selena loves *to* write poems.

Too means "also." It also means "very":

Anita played great golf; Adam did well, *too*.
It is *too* kind of you to visit.

Two is the number:

Mr. Almeida owns *two* clothing stores.

vain/vane/vein *Vain* means "conceited." It also means "unsuccessful":

Victor is *vain* about his dark, flowing hair.
The doctor made a *vain* attempt to revive the patient.

A *vane* is a device that moves to indicate the direction of the wind:

There was an old weather *vane* on the barn roof.

A *vein* is a blood vessel:

I could see the *veins* in his hands.

waist/waste The *waist* is the middle part of the body:

He had a leather belt around his *waist*.

Waste means "to use carelessly." It also means "thrown away because it is useless":

I can't *waste* my time watching trashy television shows.
We need to reduce the amount of *waste* we produce.

wait/weight *Wait* means "to hold yourself ready for something":

I can't *wait* until my check arrives.

Weight means "heaviness":

He tested the *weight* of the bat.

weather/whether *Weather* refers to conditions outside:

If the *weather* is warm, I'll go swimming.

Whether means "if":

Whether you help me or not, I'll paint the hallway.

were/we're/where *Were* is the past form of *are*:

Only last year, we *were* scared freshmen.

We're is the contraction of *we are:*

Today *we're* confident sophomores.

Where refers to a place:

Show me *where* you used to play basketball.

whined/wind/wined *Whined* means "complained":

Polly *whined* about the weather because the rain kept her indoors.

Wind (if it rhymes with *find*) means "to coil or wrap something" or "to turn a key":

Wind that extension cord, or you'll trip on it.

Wind (if it rhymes with *sinned*) is air in motion:

The *wind* blew my cap off.

If someone *wined* you, he or she treated you to some wine:

My brother *wined* and dined his boss.

who's/whose *Who's* is a contraction of *who is* or *who has:*

Who's driving?
Who's been leaving the door unlocked?

Whose means "belonging to whom":

I wonder *whose* dog this is.

woman/women *Woman* means "one adult female person":

A *woman* in the supermarket gave me her extra coupons.

Women means "more than one woman":

Three *women* from Missouri joined the management team.

wood/would *Wood* is a hard substance made from trees:

I have a table made of a polished *wood*.

Would is the past form of *will:*

Albert said he *would* think about the offer.

your/you're *Your* means "belonging to you":

I think you dropped *your* wallet.

You're is the short form of *you are:*

You're not telling the truth.

Exercise 3   **Practice: More Words that Sound Alike/Look Alike**

Circle the correct words in each sentence that follows.

1. During the (rain, reign) of King George III of England, the American colonies lost (patience, patients) with the king's restrictive laws and fought for (their, there, they're) freedom.

2. (Moral, Morale) at the fraternity has declined since the group was criticized for its reckless initiation (rights, rites, writes).

3. The poor and trusting are often the (pray/prey) of con artists who offer get-rich-quick schemes such as fake overseas lotteries and worthless (medal/meddle/metal) disguised as gold.

4. It was (quiet, quit, quite) noisy in the library today until the librarian asked the three elderly men to (quiet, quit, quite) laughing and chatting at the computers.

5. We thought we were lost at first, but eventually Diane's directions (lead, led) us to a large red barn with a (weather, whether)(vain, vane, vein).

6. The (whined, wind, wined) swept the rain against the car with such force that we hardly knew (were, we're, where) we (were, we're, where) going.

7. I want to know (who's, whose) responsible for making that (woman, women) wait for an hour and (than, then) giving her the wrong prescription.

8. If (your, you're) looking for a (loan, lone) to start your business, you will have to (site, cite) other, similar projects that have been successful.

Connect

| Exercise 4 | **Connect: Editing a Paragraph for Errors in More Words that Sound Alike/Look Alike** |

The following paragraph has errors in words that sound alike or look alike. Correct each error in the space above it. There are sixteen errors.

Silvio hated his job. He didn't know how he would make it threw another day at work. Yet he was afraid to loose his job. Moral at the party and costume store was low. Months of misery had past. Silvio didn't know if he could endure many more days of dissatisfaction. The principle problem was the assistant manager. He had no idea how to deal with personal and had no patients. Most of the staff worked in quite despair, but Silvio's days past in a silent, growing anger. Then the horrible rain of the assistant manager ended. He resigned when the owner of the store discovered a discrepancy between the sales records and the bank deposits. Soon the assistant manager was identified as the one who had been steeling money. Rumors spread. Supposedly, the assistant manager had pleaded in vane for another chance. As the news of the assistant manager's departure spread, Silvio and the other employees we're relieved. Surely a new boss wood have to be better then there old one, they felt. At last, Silvio was able to let go of his anger.

Exercise 5 **Practice: Words that Sound Alike/Look Alike: A Comprehensive Exercise**

Circle the correct words in parentheses in each sentence that follows.

1. As the officer began to (advice, advise) Lucy of her (rights, rites, writes), Lucy remained (stationary, stationery).

2. Mrs. Kowalski is such a good (sole, soul) that I sometimes feel she is an (angle, angel) (hear, here) on earth.

3. (Its, It's) a sad day when a science fiction movie loses (its, it's) power to entertain me, but this movie is a (waist, waste) of my time.

4. The color in the foreground of that painting (complements, compliments) the colors in the background, and it (wood, would) look attractive in my apartment, (to, too, two).

5. I was not (conscience, conscious) of Anita's bad temper until she jerked hard on her horse's (rains, reigns, reins) and (than, then) kicked the poor animal.

6. It was so cold that I could see my (breath, breathe) on the window (pane, pain) and (knew, new) that winter had arrived.

7. Sam was not willing to (accept, except) his brother's (council, counsel) about applying for financial aid.

8. (Your, You're) behavior in court can (affect, effect) the outcome of the trial, no matter how (fair, fare) the jury tries to be.

9. As I walked down the (isle, aisle) with my bride, I suddenly realized that we were about to go (forth, fourth) into a (knew, new) life.

10. My doctor is encouraging his (patience, patients) to try a (does, dose) of an over-the-counter cold medicine instead of overusing antibiotics.

11. My brother's class is taking a trip to Tallahassee, the (capital, capitol) of Florida, as part of a (coarse, course) in political science.

12. I hope that the loss of his home will have no (farther, further) (affect, effect) on the (all ready, already) unhappy child.

13. Larry doesn't follow fashion trends; when he needs (close, clothes, cloths), he buys (plain, plane) old jeans and flannel shirts from discount stores.

14. My first goal is to find a (decent, descent) apartment; (then, than) I want to meet someone (who's, whose) (principals, principles) are the same as mine.

15. I (wander, wonder) if I should go to the (personal, personnel) department of Satellite Services and apply for a job; I've (heard, herd) that (moral, morale) is high among the staff.

Collaborate

Exercise 6   Collaborate: Words that Sound Alike/Look Alike:
             A Comprehensive Exercise

Working with a partner or group, write one sentence for each of the words
that follow.

1. **a.** loose   _____

    b. lose   _____

2. **a.** accept _____

    b. except _____

3. **a.** it's   _____

    b. its   _____

4. **a.** passed _____

    b. past   _____

5. **a.** plain   _____

    b. plane   _____

6. **a.** thorough _____

    b. through _____

    c. threw   _____

7. **a.** affect _____

    b. effect _____

8. **a.** course _____

    b. coarse _____

Connect

Exercise 7   Connect: Editing a Paragraph for Errors in Words that Sound
             Alike/Look Alike: A Comprehensive Exercise

The following paragraph has errors in words that sound alike or look alike.
Correct each error in the space above it. There are eleven errors.

A family tradition in are house was celebrated every Sunday when we

enjoyed homemade pancakes. Although many advertisements show woman

cooking, a man made our Sunday breakfast. I wood stand beside my father as he

stirred the batter and carefully poured spoonfuls into a buttered pan. I learned to

weight for him to flip each pancake at the rite time. A pancake cannot be too soft

or too solid when it is flipped, he said. My father new the right way to make them:

he showed patients. Whether he made plane or blueberry pancakes, he made delicious ones. My memories of this ritual came to me recently when I was far from home. I was in the U.S. Army, and I woke to the sight of the sun rising in the dessert. Suddenly I thought of my father's pancakes. I wanted to be in the family kitchen, watching my father make breakfast. Someday I will enjoy the quite pleasure and piece of such a day.

CHAPTER 31

Word Choice

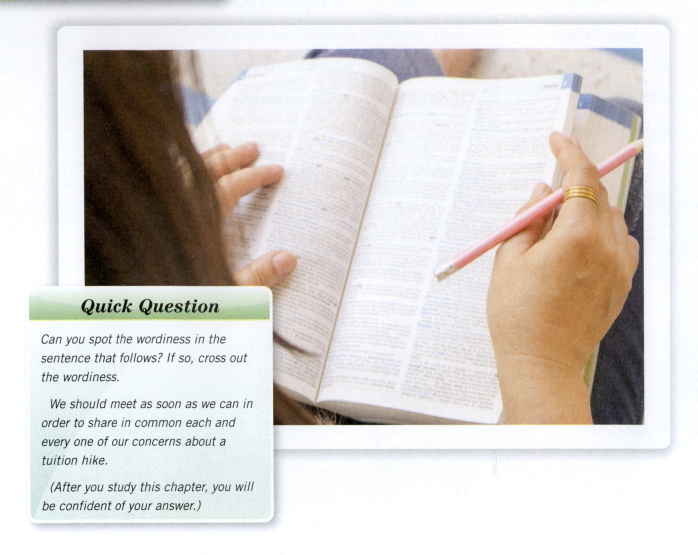

Quick Question

Can you spot the wordiness in the sentence that follows? If so, cross out the wordiness.

We should meet as soon as we can in order to share in common each and every one of our concerns about a tuition hike.

(After you study this chapter, you will be confident of your answer.)

Learning Objectives

In this chapter, you will learn to:

1 Write precisely.

2 Avoid wordiness, clichés, and slang in your writing.

1 Write precisely.

PRECISE LANGUAGE

One way to improve your writing is to pay close attention to your choice of words. As you revise and edit, be careful to use precise language and avoid wordiness, clichés, and slang.

Try to be as specific as you can in explaining or describing. Replace vague, general words or phrases with more precise language.

> **not this:** Yesterday, our English instructor assigned ~~a lot of~~ reading.
> **but this:** Yesterday, our English instructor assigned *twenty-five pages* of reading.

> **not this:** He gave me a ~~nice~~ smile.
> **but this:** He gave me a *friendly* smile.
> **or this:** He gave me a *reassuring* smile.
> **or this:** He gave me a *welcoming* smile.

not this: Maggie is a ~~good~~ friend.
but this: Maggie is a *loyal* friend.
 or this: Maggie is a *devoted* friend.

Exercise 1 **Practice: Using Precise Language**

In the following sentences, replace each italicized word or phrase with a more precise word or phrase. Write your revisions above the lines.

1. I had a *nice* weekend with my folks.

2. You need to buy *a lot* of paper for the printer.

3. I think about you *often*.

4. Take Mr. Benson for English; he's *nice*.

5. Mitchell had another *bad* day at work.

6. This time, let's go to an *interesting* movie.

7. I am going to need *a lot* of pasta for the party.

8. I tried to practice my speech, but it sounds *stupid*.

WORDINESS

② Avoid wordiness, clichés, and slang in your writing.

As you revise and edit your work, check for *wordiness*: the use of extra words. If you can convey the same idea in fewer words, do so. You can be precise *and* direct.

not this: After the accident, I thought ~~in my mind that~~ I was to blame.
but this: After the accident, *I thought* I was to blame.

not this: ~~In my opinion~~, I think children should exercise daily.
but this: *I think* children should exercise daily.

not this: Jorge bought a CD for ~~the price of~~ $10.95.
but this: Jorge bought a CD *for* $10.95.

Here is a list of some wordy expressions and possible substitutes:

Wordy Expressions	Possible Substitutes
alternative choices	alternatives, choices
asset group	assets
at a later date and time	later
at a future date	later
at that time	then
at the present moment	now, presently
at the present time	now, presently
at this point in time	now, today
attach together	attach
basic essentials	essentials
blend together	blend

(Continued)

Wordy Expressions	Possible Substitutes
bring together	unite
by means of	by
by the fact that	because
change out (or swap out)	replace
combine together	combine
consider the fact that	consider
continue on	continue
day in and day out	daily
deep down inside he believed	he believed
due to the fact that	because
each and every one	each one
end result	result
for all intents and purposes	realistically
for the reason that	because
gather together	gather
have a need for	need
have a realization of	realize
I felt inside	I felt
I personally feel	I feel
I thought in my head	I thought
in the field of art (music, etc.)	in art (music, etc.)
in the near future	soon
in this day and age	today
in this modern world	today
in my mind, I think	I think
in my opinion, I think	I think
in order to	to
in today's society	today
join together	join
maximum amount	maximum
mix together	mix
of a remarkable kind	remarkable
on a daily basis	daily
on and on	endlessly
on a regular basis	regularly
past experience	experience
point in time	time
reached a decision	decided
really and truly	really
reason why	reason
refer back	refer
reflect back	reflect
repeat again	repeat
separate out	separate
shadow of a doubt	doubt
share in common	share
short in stature	short
small in size	small
skills set	skills
start off	start
switch out	replace

Wordy Expressions	Possible Substitutes
the reason being	because
the shape is a circle	circular
things of that nature	similar traits/objects
top priority	priority
true facts	facts
two different kinds	two kinds
unite together	unite
until and unless	until, unless
very unique	unique

Exercise 2 **Practice: Revising for Wordiness**

Revise the following sentences, eliminating the wordiness. Write your revisions in the space above the lines.

1. At this point in time, I personally feel that smartphones are the best technological devices.

2. I cannot approve a promotion for Walter Ford because in my opinion I think that his skills set would not be adequate in the new position.

3. By means of researching the alternatives, our committee has reached a decision to continue the office's contract with the Info-Fix computer maintenance company due to the fact that Info-Fix offers us the maximum amount of service at a reasonable price.

4. In this day and age, consumers are willing to spend their money on some computer products of a remarkable kind.

5. I thought to myself that I had better start studying on a regular basis if I really and truly wanted to finish college.

6. Todd asked me to repeat my refusal again because deep down inside he believed that I would never say "no" to him.

7. Christina is small in size and short in stature, yet she has a powerful personality and a very unique ability to motivate others.

8. Past experience has taught me that in today's society we can blend together two different kinds of music and create a popular and profitable sound.

CLICHÉS

Clichés are worn-out expressions. Once they were a new way of making a point, but now they are old and tired. You should avoid them in your writing.

not this: I know that Monica will always ~~be there for me~~.
but this: I know that Monica will always *support me*.

not this: Alan experienced the ~~trials and tribulations~~ of late registration.
but this: Alan experienced the *difficulties* of late registration.

Following are some common clichés. If you spot clichés in your writing, replace them with more direct or thoughtful statements of your own.

Some Common Clichés

acting like there's no tomorrow	in the blink of an eye
all in all	in the final analysis
all the time in the world	information superhighway
at the end of the day	I wouldn't be where I am today
avoid like the plague	it is what it is
beat around the bush	kick the bucket
between a rock and a hard place	let bygones be bygones
break the ice	light as a feather
break new ground	live and let live
breathtaking	live life to the fullest
by the same token	make ends meet
can't hold a candle to	on the same page
climb the ladder of success	on top of the world
cold as ice	one day at a time
cry my eyes out	over the hill
cutting edge	pure as the driven snow
dead as a doornail	quick as a wink
dead tired	ready on day one
down in the dumps	rock solid
down on his luck	shoulder to cry on
a drop in the bucket	sick as a dog
few and far between	smooth as silk
first and foremost	state of the art
free as a bird	the ball's in your court
give it your best shot	the sky's the limit
go the distance	through thick and thin
go the extra mile	trials and tribulations
good as gold	tried and true
grass is always greener	up at the crack of dawn
hard as a rock	when all is said and done
he (she) is always there for me	worked and slaved
hit the ground running	worked like a dog
hit the nail on the head	
hot under the collar	
hustle and bustle	

Exercise 3 **Collaborate: Revising Clichés**

The following sentences contain clichés (italicized). Working with a partner or a group, rewrite the sentences, replacing the clichés with more direct or thoughtful words or phrases. Write in the space above the lines.

1. When I lost my best friend, I was ready to *cry my eyes out.*

2. An accident can change a person's life *in the blink of an eye.*

3. *I wouldn't be where I am today* without Professor Miyori's inspiring classes.

4. Since I lost my weekend job at the hospital, I am struggling to *make ends meet.*

5. Hank has a *tried and true* method of repairing leaky windows.

6. When I take my dog for a walk, she acts like she is *on top of the world.*

7. On the first day of registration, I woke up *at the crack of dawn.*

8. Tanika has been *down in the dumps* ever since she had an argument with her sister.

Exercise 4 **Practice: Identifying Clichés**

Underline all the clichés in the following paragraph. There are nine clichés.

Since first grade, you and I have been best friends. Our disagreements have been few and far between. Thinking about our shared history, our talents, and our goals, I have come to an important conclusion. If we can maintain our friendship through thick and thin, then the sky's the limit if we want to start a small business together. However, we have to be on the same page about our goals and financial arrangements. Once we have learned to go the distance in the early days of building our business, we will break new ground in our cutting-edge technology lab. It may be a challenge to climb the ladder of success as quickly as we would like. However, in the final analysis, our achievements will be great if we can become just as loyal business partners as we are friends.

Connect

Exercise 5 **Connect: Editing for Imprecise Language, Wordiness, and Clichés**

Edit the following paragraph for imprecise language and clichés. Cross out wordiness and write your revisions above the lines. There are nine places that need editing.

A few years ago, my boyfriend Jimmy had a hard time finding work by the-fact that he never finished high school and had no clear goals. At this point in time, he is studying for his GED and at a future date wants to study law enforcement at a community college. Without a shadow of a doubt he has changed dramatically from the teenager with no direction and no self-esteem. After a long struggle with dead-end jobs and family conflicts, Jimmy has reached a decision to look forward with determination and things. Now he needs to work on his skills set and stay patient and focused through the trials and tribulations of testing, training, and preparing for a career. When I look at the hardships he has already survived, I really and truly believe in Jimmy's future.

SLANG

Slang is an informal vocabulary frequently used during conversations among friends. It is also used by fiction writers when they try to create realistic dialogue. Slang expressions and their meanings can change frequently. "Cool" and "hot" can both mean "popular," whereas "bad" as a slang term can mean "good." Today, "guys" as slang refers to males and females. Slang expressions change often, and because they can easily be misunderstood, you should avoid them in formal writing assignments that require precise word choice.

The following list may contain slang that you use in everyday conversation, but you may also notice several expressions that are now considered outdated. See how many you recognize from your own daily conversations.

Slang	**Standard English**
a slam dunk	a certainty
All bets are off.	The future is uncertain.
awesome	terrific
back in the day	in the past (or when I was younger)
been there for me	supported me
bent out of shape	upset
big time	major
blowback	harsh reaction
bounce (verb)	leave
Bring it on.	Challenge me.
bummed	disappointed
call him or her out	criticize (or shame him or her)
chill (or chill out)	relax (or calm down)

Slang	Standard English
creeps me out	makes me uneasy
Don't do me like that.	Don't treat me that way.
don't have a clue	have no idea
Don't mess with me.	Don't bother me.
Dial it back.	Be less intense.
ditch (verb)	throw away
Do you know what I'm saying?	Do you understand?
Don't go there.	Don't talk about it.
Feel me?	Do you understand?
For real?	Really?
for sure	certainly
from the get go	from the beginning
get his or her act together	become more organized or focused
get his or her groove on	regain momentum or confidence
get (or wrap) my head around	understand (or imagine)
Get real.	Be realistic.
gets me down	upsets me, saddens me
give it up for; give a shout out	applaud for; recognize
Give me a break.	Be more lenient with me.
got game	has excellent skills
He bailed on us.	He quit on us.
he or she goes	he or she says
he's all about	he's very interested in
Here's the thing (or here's the deal).	Here's what's important.
Hold up.	Wait.
I freaked.	I became upset.
I got your back.	I'll protect you.
I'm down with that.	I agree with that; I accept that.
I'm into	I'm interested in
I'm not buying it.	I don't believe it.
I'm with you.	I agree with you.
It's all good.	Everything is fine.
It's on you.	It's your fault.
stoked	excited
keeping it real	being realistic
Lighten up.	Be less serious.
mess up	make a mistake
mix it up	fight (or use a variety of tactics)
my bad	my mistake
my ride	my car
No worries. (after "Thank you.")	Don't worry; you're welcome.
not feelin' it	don't like it
party (verb)	socialize (or celebrate)
pushback	resistance
seal (or close) the deal	reach an agreement (or win)
set of wheels	automobile
Show me some love.	Be considerate (or kind) to me.
That's how we roll.	That's what we do.
That's on you.	That's your fault.
That's sick.	That's the best. (or That's terrific.)
That's what I'm talkin' about.	That's what I like.

(Continued)

Slang	**Standard English**
They got served.	They were soundly defeated/insulted.
They're tight.	They are close friends.
This is huge.	This is very important.
totaled	destroyed
tripping	acting strangely (or irrationally)
True story?	Is it true?
true that	definitely
wasted	inebriated
What's the deal?	Why (or How) did that happen?
What's up with that?	What does that mean?

Collaborate

Exercise 6 **Collaborate: Revising Slang**

Working with a partner or group, revise each sentence to eliminate slang. For smoother style, you can change the word order as well as wording that is not slang.

1. My brother was really bummed about ditching on me; I told him to show me a little love next time.

   _____

   _____

   _____

2. Driving down a dark, deserted road creeps me out at times, but my sister can't even lighten up enough to drive anywhere.

   _____

   _____

   _____

3. Kesha hopes to win a lead role in our civic center's production of *Rent*, but she knows that all bets are off if professional actors are allowed to audition.

   _____

   _____

   _____

4. Back in the day, my father was all about being the starting quarterback for his high school, and he often brags that he's still got game.

   _____

   _____

   _____

5. In my speech at the academic awards ceremony, I gave a shout out to my parents because they had always been there for me. Their support was huge for me.

   _____

   _____

   _____

6. Whenever Jenna drinks too much, she starts tripping and shouting at strangers, "Bring it on!"

_____

_____

_____

7. My little brother and I are tight, so I told him that he should get real about living on his own since he works only part time and barely has enough money for the security deposit on a small apartment.

_____

_____

_____

8. Sometimes it gets me down when my parents argue, but I know that's just how they roll and they'll always have each other's back.

_____

_____

_____

| Exercise 7 | **Connect: Editing for Imprecise Language, Wordiness, Clichés, and Slang** |

Connect

Edit the following paragraph for imprecise language, wordiness, clichés, and slang. Cross out problem areas and write any necessary revisions above the lines. There are thirteen places that need editing.

Nina and I stopped seeing each other because she didn't know how to dial it back, and I couldn't find a way to get her to chill. We never seemed to be on the same page in our emotional responses. She expressed a lot of anger and anxiety if I did things with other people. I began to feel funny about having a girl-friend who acted as if we were married. At the present moment she is not speaking to me, and I feel relieved of stress and guilt. Nina and I are two different kinds of people, and I am not crying my eyes out about the situation. I only hope that Nina can learn to lighten up. I personally feel that she is a nice person who needs to change out her emotional dramas with a little self-confidence.

CHAPTER 32

Sentence Variety

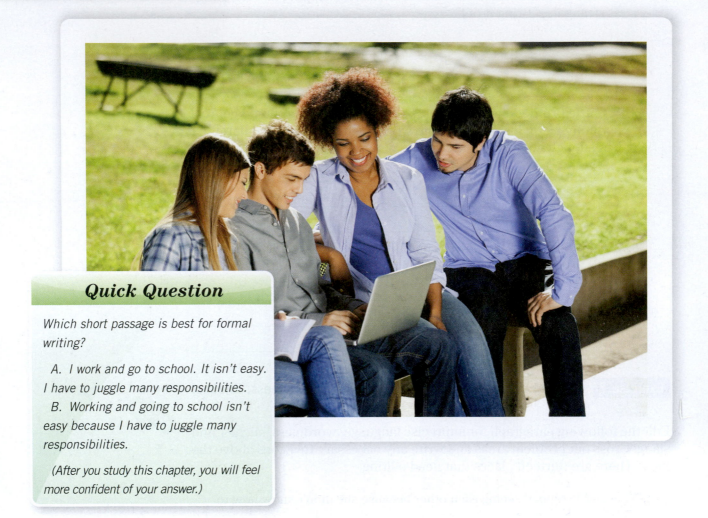

Quick Question

Which short passage is best for formal writing?

A. I work and go to school. It isn't easy. I have to juggle many responsibilities.

B. Working and going to school isn't easy because I have to juggle many responsibilities.

(After you study this chapter, you will feel more confident of your answer.)

Learning Objectives

In this chapter, you will learn to:

1 Incorporate a mix of long and short sentences into your writing.

2 Use word order to add variety to your writing.

3 Combine sentences by converting short sentences into phrases or clauses.

1 Incorporate a mix of long and short sentences into your writing.

BALANCING LONG AND SHORT SENTENCES

One way to improve your writing is to work on *sentence variety*, the use of different lengths and kinds of sentences. You can become skilled in sentence variety by (1) revising your writing for a balance of short and long sentences and for a mix of sentence types and (2) being aware of the kinds of sentences you can use.

There are no grammar errors in the following paragraph, but it needs revision for sentence variety.

I have a routine for getting ready for classes. First, I turn on the coffee pot. I start the shower. I turn on some music. I jump in the shower. I get out of the shower. I have a cup of coffee. Then I review my class notes. Afterward, I usually text my friend. She takes me to school.

The paragraph is filled with short sentences. Read it aloud, and you will notice the choppy, boring style of the writing. Compare it to the following revised paragraph, which contains a variety of short and long sentences:

> I have a routine for getting ready for classes. First, I turn on the coffee pot and start the shower. Next, I turn on some music as I jump in the shower. When I get out of the shower, I have a cup of coffee while I review my class notes. Afterward, I usually text my friend who takes me to school.

The revised paragraph balances short and long sentences. Read it aloud, and you will notice the way the varied lengths create a more flowing, interesting style.

> Some writers rely too heavily on short sentences; others use too many long sentences. The following paragraph contains too many long sentences.

> Randall wanted to make new friends because his old friends had become a bad influence. Randall loved his old friends, especially Michael, but they had begun to be involved in some dangerous activities, and Randall didn't want to be part of these crimes because Randall wanted to apply to the police academy, and he knew that having a record would destroy his chances of admission. Consequently, Randall was honest with Michael, and Randall told him that Randall couldn't risk his future by mixing with people who liked to joyride in stolen cars or steal from neighborhood stores. Soon Randall's friends stopped asking him out, and for a while Randall felt lonely and isolated, but eventually, Randall formed some new friendships, and he was happy to be part of a new group and happy it was one that didn't break the law.

Read the previous paragraph aloud, and you will notice that the sentences are so long and complicated that part of their meaning is lost. Piling on one long sentence after another can make a paragraph boring and difficult to follow. Compare the previous paragraph to the following revised version.

> Randall wanted to make new friends because his old friends had become a bad influence. Randall loved his old friends, especially Michael. However, his old friends had begun to be involved in some dangerous activities, and Randall didn't want to be a part of these crimes. He wanted to apply to the Police Academy and knew that having a record would destroy his chances of admission. Consequently, Randall spoke honestly to Michael. Randall explained that he couldn't risk his future by mixing with people who liked to joyride in stolen cars or steal from neighborhood stores. Soon Randall's friends stopped asking him out, and for a while, Randall felt lonely and isolated. Eventually, he formed some new friendships and was happy to be part of a new, law-abiding group.

Read the revised paragraph aloud, and you will notice the combination of long and short sentences makes the paragraph clearer and smoother. Careful revision helps you achieve such a mix.

Connect

Exercise 1   Connect: Revising Short Sentences

The following paragraph is composed entirely of short sentences. Rewrite it so that it contains a mix of short and long sentences. Write your revisions above the lines.

My great aunt leads an active life for a woman of seventy-five. She works at a drug store. She has worked there for thirty years. She works five days a week. Every Friday night she meets her friends. They drink coffee and play cards. They also gossip about their neighbors. Each weekend, she sings in a choir. Afterward, the members of the choir go out for brunch. My great aunt also keeps up with the latest fashions. She is well known for her style. It is clearly expressed in her elaborate hats. She is a young woman of seventy five. I'd like to be like her someday.

Connect

Exercise 2   Connect: Revising Long Sentences

The following paragraph is composed entirely of long sentences. Rewrite it so that it contains a mix of short and long sentences. Write your revisions above the lines.

Yesterday I heard a conversation that hurt me deeply. I am still upset about it because I cannot figure out why people would be so unkind about me when they hardly know me or have any right to assess me so negatively. It all began at work as I was about to enter the break room and I heard two people I considered to be my friends talking. All I heard was my name, and then someone laughed as if I were a joke of some kind, and by this point I decided to stay outside the door and listen. Soon I heard one of my so-called friends say, "Jerome? He's not invited." I decided to walk away from the room so the two wouldn't notice me outside and since I couldn't walk in without them wondering what I might have heard. I have spent hours trying to understand why they laughed at me and, even worse, why I'm being left out of some party or other event. I know I'm being silly, and I tell myself I heard only part of a conversation that could be interpreted in a different way, but I still feel that hearing others discuss me was a terrible experience.

2 Use word order to add variety to your writing.

USING DIFFERENT WAYS TO BEGIN SENTENCES

Most of the time, writers begin sentences with the subject. However, if you change the word order, you can break the monotony of using the same pattern over and over.

Begin with an Adverb

One way to change the word order is to begin with an adverb, a word that describes verbs, adjectives, or other adverbs. (For more on adverbs, see Chapter 22.) You can move adverbs from the middle to the beginning of the sentence as long as the meaning is clear.

> **adverb in the middle:** Ricky opened the package *carefully* and checked the contents.
> **adverb at the beginning:** *Carefully*, Ricky opened the package and checked the contents.
>
> **adverb in the middle:** The policewoman *calmly* issued a ticket to the aggressive driver.
> **adverb at the beginning:** *Calmly*, the policewoman issued a ticket to the aggressive driver.

> **Exercise 3** Practice: Writing Sentences that Begin with an Adverb

In the following sentences, move the adverb to the beginning of the sentence.

1. Isabel smiled slyly at the unsuspecting new team member.

2. Emilio searched frantically for his lost tablet.

3. My sister responded angrily when I told her I dropped her smartphone.

4. Ernie beat the drum rhythmically to keep the beat.

5. My mother frequently spends her Saturdays at garage sales.

6. Amber walked carefully between the shelves filled with antiques.

7. The evil scientist in the film laughed cruelly at his victim.

8. Andrew thoughtlessly borrowed my car without asking.

Begin with a Prepositional Phrase

A prepositional phrase contains a preposition and its object. (For more on prepositions, see Chapter 16.) You can change the usual word order of a sentence by moving a prepositional phrase from the end of a sentence to the beginning. You can do this as long as the meaning of the sentence remains clear.

> **prepositional phrase at the end:** A gleaming silver convertible suddenly passed me *in the left lane.*
> **prepositional phrase at the beginning:** *In the left lane*, a gleaming silver convertible suddenly passed me.
>
> **prepositional phrase at the end:** She completed the cross-fitness class *with fierce intensity.*
> **prepositional phrase at the beginning:** *With fierce intensity*, she completed the cross-fitness class.

> **Note:** Usually, you should put a comma after a prepositional phrase that begins a sentence. However, you do not need a comma if the prepositional phrase is short.

Exercise 4 **Practice: Writing Sentences that Begin with a Prepositional Phrase**

Rewrite the following sentences, moving a prepositional phrase to the beginning of the sentence. Write your revisions above the lines.

1. Oscar was in bed with the flu during most of spring break.

2. The white van with a dented rear panel remained abandoned in the alley.

3. Daniel's schedule is busier on the weekends.

4. You can get homemade lemon cake at the Superior Bakery.

5. Autumn can't write a letter or an essay without using spell check.

6. I'll do the laundry before I go to work.

7. The heroic soldier received letters and gifts from hundreds of strangers.

8. An old letter was concealed inside a dusty leather book.

USING DIFFERENT WAYS TO JOIN IDEAS

3 Combine sentences by converting short sentences into phrases or clauses.

Another way to create sentence variety is to try different methods of combining ideas. Among these methods are (1) using an -*ing* modifier, (2) using an -*ed* modifier, (3) using an appositive, and (4) using a *who, which,* or *that* clause.

Use an -*ing* Modifier

You can avoid short, choppy sentences by using an -*ing* modifier. This way, one of the short sentences becomes a phrase. (For more on modifiers, see Chapter 23.)

> **two short sentences:** Sarah was talking on her cell phone. She drove into a tree.
> **combined with an -*ing* modifier:** *Talking on her cell phone,* Sarah drove into a tree.

> **Note:** If the modifier begins the sentence, be sure that the next word is the one the modifier describes.

two short sentences: Mr. Martinez loves to read travel books. He plans his next vacation.

combined with an *-ing* modifier: Mr. Martinez loves to read travel books, *planning his next vacation.*

Exercise 5   **Practice: Using *-ing* Modifiers**

Following are pairs of sentences. Combine each pair by using an *-ing* modifier.

1. Carlos was texting his friend. He sat in the back of the room.

   combined: _____

   _____

2. My friends smiled warmly. They invited me to join the conversation.

   combined: _____

   _____

3. Tonya wiped her little boy's tears. She struggled to comfort the child.

   combined: _____

   _____

4. The poison ivy I developed on my hands itched a lot. It irritated me all weekend.

   combined: _____

   _____

5. One of my friends hoped to get good tips. She took a job at a popular restaurant.

   combined: _____

   _____

6. Aggressive drivers tailgate at high speeds. They risk their own and others' lives.

   combined: _____

   _____

7. My mother worried about my first job away from home. She called me three times a day.

   combined: _____

   _____

8. Jennifer needed to ask my advice. She called me last night at ten o'clock.

   combined: _____

   _____

Use an -*ed* Modifier

You can also avoid short, choppy sentences by using an -*ed* modifier. This way, one of the short sentences becomes a phrase. (For more on modifiers, see Chapter 23.)

> **two short sentences:** The text was filled with equations and problems. It was difficult.
> **combined with an -*ed* modifier:** *Filled with equations and problems,* the text was difficult.

Note: If the modifier begins the sentence, be sure that the next word is the one the modifier describes.

> **two short sentences:** Sam gave me a jewelry box. It was painted with silver and blue flowers.
> **combined with an -*ed* modifier:** Sam gave me a jewelry box *painted with silver and blue flowers.*

Exercise 6 **Practice: Using -*ed* Modifiers**

Following are pairs of sentences. Combine each pair, using an -*ed* modifier.

1. The chicken was stuffed with herb dressing. The chicken was delicious.

   combined: _____

   _____

2. Armand's boat was a total loss. Armand's boat was wrecked in a fierce storm.

   combined: _____

   _____

3. Alan followed every rule. Alan was motivated by fear of his supervisor.

   combined: _____

   _____

4. I lost a beautiful bracelet. The bracelet was studded with coral beads.

   combined: _____

   _____

5. My new belt had a large silver buckle. The buckle was engraved with an elaborate design.

   combined: _____

   _____

6. Sergeant Thomas Levy was named "Officer of the Year." He risked his life to save a woman drowning in a canal.

   combined: _____

   _____

7. The old house was designed for a large family. It was converted into three spacious apartments.

   combined: _____

   _____

8. Patrick is inspired by his famous mother. He is studying to become a child psychologist.

   combined: _____

   _____

Use an Appositive

Another way to combine short, choppy sentences is to use an appositive. An **appositive** is a phrase that renames or describes a noun. Appositives can go in the beginning, middle, or end of a sentence. Use commas to set off the appositive.

> **two short sentences:** Chocolate milk contains calcium and vitamins. It is a favorite of children.
> **combined with an appositive:** Chocolate milk, *a favorite of children*, contains calcium and vitamins.

> **two short sentences:** Jollof is a famous dish from Nigeria. It is also very spicy.
> **combined with an appositive:** Jollof, *a famous dish from Nigeria*, is very spicy.

> **two short sentences:** I am looking forward to Thanksgiving. It is my favorite holiday.
> **combined with an appositive:** I am looking forward to Thanksgiving, *my favorite holiday*.

Exercise 7   **Practice: Using Appositives**

Following are pairs of sentences. Combine each pair by using an appositive.

1. Inez is an accountant. She is helping me with my taxes.

   combined: _____

   _____

2. Island Theaters is an old movie house. It is being sold to a restaurant chain.

   combined: _____

   _____

3. You should buy your new smartphone from Phones 'R Us. It is the cheapest store in the area.

   combined: _____

   _____

4. My friends and I decided to go to Meridian. It is the newest club in the city.

   combined: _____

   _____

5. Kima is a warm-hearted person. She adopted a shelter cat last week.

   combined: _____

   _____

6. Arrogance and impatience are my brother's worst qualities. They show up whenever he is under stress.

   combined: _____

   _____

7. Yesterday, I heard the song of the ice cream truck. It is a sure sign of summer.

   combined: _____

   _____

8. Dr. Harjo dresses like a college student. He is a world-renowned scientist.

   combined: _____

   _____

Use a *Who, Which,* or *That* Clause

Clauses beginning with *who, which,* or *that* can combine short sentences.

> **two short sentences:** Jacob is my favorite cousin. He won the golf tournament.
> **combined with a *who* clause:** Jacob, *who is my favorite cousin,* won the golf tournament.

> **two short sentences:** Good running shoes can be expensive. They make running easier.
> **combined with a *which* clause:** Good running shoes, *which can be expensive,* make running easier.

> **two short sentences:** The cinnamon buns were delicious. I tasted them.
> **combined with a *that* clause:** The cinnamon buns *that I tasted* were delicious.

Punctuating *who, which,* or *that* clauses requires some thought. Decide whether the information in the clause is *essential* or *nonessential*. If the information is essential, do not put commas around it:

> **essential clause:** Students *who like history* will love the movie. (Without the clause *who like history*, the sentence would not have the same meaning. Therefore, the clause is essential and is not set off by commas.)

> **nonessential clause:** Mel, *who has been singing for years*, deserves to win. (The clause *who has been singing for years* is not essential to the meaning of the sentence. Therefore, it is set off by commas.)

If you have to choose between *which* and *that*, *which* usually begins a nonessential clause, and *that* usually begins an essential clause.

> **essential clause:** The car *that he was driving* is expensive.
> **nonessential clause:** The car, *which I've had for years*, needs a new muffler.

Note: Essential and nonessential clauses are also referred to as *restrictive* and *nonrestrictive* clauses.

Exercise 8   **Practice: Using *Who, Which*, or *That* Clauses**

Following are pairs of sentences. Combine each pair by using a *who, which,* or *that* clause.

1. Elizabeth bought a new car. The car had a bright yellow paint job.

   combined: _____

   _____

2. Belgian chocolate is available in the United States. Some consider it the best chocolate in the world.

   combined: _____

   _____

3. Clara works with a young man. The young man teaches yoga in the evenings.

   combined: _____

   _____

4. Tyler Nelson is married to my sister. He used to play baseball on a minor league team.

   combined: _____

   _____

5. People love their pets. They will spend a great deal of money to keep their animals healthy and happy.

   combined: _____

   _____

6. Hannah was the class valedictorian. She was the first member of her family to graduate from high school.

   combined: _____

   _____

7. Joanna bought a new coffeemaker. The coffeemaker brews one cup of coffee at a time.

   combined: _____

   _____

8. Selena wants to go back to Albuquerque. Albuquerque is her favorite vacation spot.

   combined: _____

   _____

Connect

Exercise 9 **Connect: Revising for Sentence Variety: A Comprehensive Exercise**

Rewrite the following paragraph, combining each pair of underlined sentences using one of the following: an -*ing* modifier, an -*ed* modifier, an appositive, or a *who*, *which*, or *that* clause. Write your revisions in the spaces above the lines.

Jealousy is like a poison. My last girlfriend was a beautiful woman. She swore she had not a drop of jealous blood. At first, she was understanding and tolerant of the time I spent without her. Then I noticed a slight change. She would check my eyes carefully. She tried to detect any lies about my social activities. This subtle surveillance made me somewhat uneasy. Antonio was my best friend. He advised me to break off the relationship. Antonio said I would soon see my girlfriend become more possessive. I was blinded by my infatuation. I hoped that my girlfriend would change. She did, but the change made me jealous. She left me when she found someone she liked better.

Appendix: Readings for Writers

READINGS FOR WRITERS: THE WRITING PROCESS

Getting Carded

David Migoya

"Getting carded" usually means getting checked for identification at bars, restaurants, or clubs, but Denver Post *writer David Migoya uses it to mean getting one's first credit card, a milestone for many college students. He warns that the card, a symbol of maturity, has its dangers.*

Lexile Measure/Words: 1160L/1036W

Words You May Need to Know (Corresponding paragraph numbers are in parentheses.)

bombard (1): attack
entice (1): draw on by exciting hope or desire
"maxed out" (3): slang for "used to the maximum amount allowed"
rescinded (4): taken back
droves (5): herds
savvy (6): knowledgeable
jalopy (6): an old car that is falling apart

travesty (6): grotesque imitation (in this case, of graduating with a bright future)
cavalier (7): free and easy
pitfalls (8): hidden dangers
vulnerable (8): liable to be hurt
ultimately (9): eventually
perks (10): slang for "perquisites" (extra payments or rewards)

They remember their first love, their first car, and, if financial institutions have it right, their first credit card. Because the result could be a commitment that outlasts the first two, banks bombard college students with credit offers designed to entice them to sign up and start charging. And the unsuspecting will be lured by methods ranging from free tee shirts and university-logo coffee mugs to inconceivably low interest rates and high spending limits. "Every year, there's a fresh pack of prospects called freshmen," said Kim McGrigg of Consumer Credit Counseling Services in Denver. "College students are the largest identifiable segment of new customers." 1

It didn't take long for the credit-card offers to land at Jeffrey Kaczmarek's feet. "It seemed like they showed up the moment I moved into the dorm," said Kaczmarek, an Iowa State University graduate. "Most of the problems I created have been behind me for only two years." The thirty-three-year-old computer programmer recalls a freshman year filled with important purchases—"pizza, beer, cigarettes, and other really useful things for college," he said with sarcastic tone—all of them on a $500-limit credit card, his first. 2

3   With one card "maxed out," Kaczmarek said, getting a second card was easy. "It was a chain reaction," the Denver resident said. "And when all was said and done, I was into it for $4,500." Not only did the debt follow him, but the creditors did, too. "When you're in school and the creditors are calling all the time, it's stress you don't need," he said. "I turned off my phone; I screened calls; it was a terrible way to live."

4   The time after college wasn't any better because a poor credit history affected interest rates Kaczmarek was offered on car loans. He said he even suspects a job offer was rescinded because of it. "As a freshman, I had no way to pay the $500 card," he said, "but it looked soooo good."

5   As colleges and universities begin the new school year, the credit offers come in droves. More than fifty-eight percent of college students said they saw credit-card marketers on campus for two or more days at the beginning of a semester, and seventy-eight percent of all students say they have a card, according to the U.S. Public Interest Research Group. "There's significant data supporting the theory that if you can be the first card in their wallet, they'll remain loyal," said John Ulzheimer, president of education services at Credit.com. "Some issuers mail over a billion pieces a year."

6   The savvy student will use the new card to build credit responsibly so that it later comes in handy to rent an apartment, get a car loan, obtain a mortgage, or even land a job. Used improperly, though, a credit card can cause more heartache to a student than a breakup and cost a lot more than a tune-up. In the end, some students learn it's easier to part ways with a jalopy than with the bad credit they got from buying it. "That low credit score is the grade they never thought about or wanted to earn," Ulzheimer said. "The students spend their time working on an impressive GPA, and they get a degree in one hand and a bad credit score in the other. It's a sad travesty."

7   The worst problems occur not from overspending or maxing out credit limits—which typically are kept low to start—but from fees associated with late payments or interest rates. Put simply, a student who consistently pays only the monthly minimum is likely to hit financial ruin quickly. In fact, the number of eighteen-to-twenty-four-year-olds who filed for bankruptcy has ballooned by ninety-six percent in the past decade, according to the Richmond Credit Abuse Resistance Education Program. "The biggest issue is in the attitude toward using the card, and it's usually very cavalier," McGrigg of Consumer Credit Counseling said. "It's a tool of convenience, not an extension of your income."

8   Problems come from a lack of understanding about how credit cards work and the everlasting pitfalls of abuse. Some students just aren't ready for them, said Judy McKenna, a Fort Collins–based financial planner. "It's a particularly vulnerable population that may not come from much money, or it's a group of the temporarily poor," McKenna said. "The pulls to use the cards can be very strong." The average college student has a credit-card balance of $552, according to the Credit Research Center at Georgetown University.

Yet forty-five percent of students say they're in serious debt with balances averaging $3,000, Jumpstart Coalition reports.

Despite the possible long-term association, why do credit card issuers   9 pursue students if they pose such a financial risk? The answer, according to experts, is Mom and Dad. "Ultimately, the cards get paid by parents who swoop in and save them," said Susan Black, director of financial planning at eMoney Advisor. Said Ulzheimer, "It's actually a safer bet to sign up a student than what common sense tells you."

The experts offer several approaches to avoiding problems. The easiest,   10 McKenna said, is simply to avoid problems, at least until a student gets a full-time job. "Living on a checkbook or cash is smarter," she said. If a student must have a card, he or she should shop around for the best offer, including a competitive interest rate, low or no annual fee, a payment grace period, and user perks such as bonus points or cash back. Sometimes, the perks can pay for a student's trip home or a spring break destination. "Credit isn't for you if you're not serious enough about your financial future to take the time and research which card is best," McGrigg said.

Alternatives to credit cards and good ways to build a student's credit history   11 include secured cards—those that require a deposit equaling the credit limit— and charge cards, which require full payment for all purchases each month. Prepaid cards, known as "stored-value cards," are popular because they limit spending. They are accepted like a credit card but are more like a gift certificate. The owner buys an amount on the card and spends it down, either by purchases or cash advances. "They're easy to control and can't be abused," Ulzheimer said.

Reading Comprehension

1. What is the thesis (main point) of this essay? How does the author's description of former student Jeffrey Kaczmarek in Paragraphs 2 through 4 help support his thesis? What other examples from Kaczmarek's essay effectively support the thesis?

2. In Paragraphs 10 and 11, Migoya offers the reader alternatives to credit-card reliance in college. Which suggestion do you feel would be most effective for preventing you or your college friends from accumulating too much debt? Why do you think this suggestion is most effective?

Discussion Prompts/Writing Options

If you write on any of the following topics, work through the stages of the writing process in preparing your assignment.

1. "Getting Carded" discusses the dangers that shadow a student getting his or her first credit card. Write a summary of the article. Describe the short-term and long-term dangers, and explain how a student bombarded with credit-card offers can avoid "maxing out" or can find a better alternative to a credit card.

2. Discuss or write about three items (small or large) that college students typically purchase with a credit card but that, in your opinion, should be bought only with cash or a check. Explain why college students are tempted to purchase these items on a credit card and how they might curb these temptations to avoid credit-card debt.

3. Although college students must cope with the dangers and temptations of credit cards, students also enjoy the advantages of owning at least one credit card. Working with a partner or group, research some examples of these advantages. Be sure to use reputable sources. When you have at least five examples, share your list with the class or work individually on writing about these advantages.

Topics for Critical Thinking and Writing

If you write on any of the following topics, work through the stages of the writing process in preparing your assignment.

1. William Shakespeare's character Polonius in the play *Hamlet* imparts the following advice to his son, Laertes:

   Neither a borrower nor a lender be;

   For loan oft loses both itself and friend,

   And borrowing dulls the edge of husbandry.

   Imagine you are a parent composing a letter to a son or daughter beginning college. The topic of your letter is financial responsibility and living within a budget. What would you say to your child about the temptations of credit cards and debt? What advice would you share? What would you recommend, particularly to your child, an incoming freshman, with regard to credit cards?

2. According to the College Board's report, "Trends in College Pricing, 2016," the average cost of in-state tuition in 2016–2017, including room and board, was $20,060.

   Seen through your lens as a student, does the increased cost of college tuition play a role in the growth of credit-card applications and debt? How are college students using credit cards to help pay for costs associated with college? Should credit cards be used to pay for these expenses? Write an editorial to your student newspaper that articulates your position on whether or not students should use credit cards to pay for expenses associated with attending college.

3. As you read "Getting Carded," did you notice some of the phrases that revealed the attitudes of some financial experts? For example, Judy McKenna, a Fort Collins–based financial planner, called first-year college students "a particularly vulnerable population that may not come from much money," or "a group of the temporarily poor." Do you believe these are valid descriptions? Another expert, Susan Black, director of financial planning at eMoney Advisor, said that credit-card issuers pursue student business even when the companies expect many students to fall into debt because "the cards get paid by parents who swoop in and save them." In your experience, do parents save their college-aged children from credit-card debt? Are these experts creating an accurate picture of the freshman student population?

READINGS FOR WRITERS: ILLUSTRATION

Fake News, Echo Chambers, and Filter Bubbles: Under-Researched and Overhyped

William Dutton

William H. Dutton is a professor of media and information policy at Michigan State University. Dutton's research focuses on the social and political implications of Internet communications and the larger implications of regulating and creating policy for online activities. He has published multiple books on these topics. The following essay was originally published by The Conversation, *an online, independent source of news and information from the academic, research-based community.*

Lexile Measure/Words: 1330L/896W

Words You May Need to Know (Corresponding paragraph numbers are in parentheses.)

inherently (1): an inseparable part
algorithms (2): a set of rules used to solve a problem
undermining (2): weakening or destroying through secret means
unwittingly (3): unconsciously
irrelevant (6): not important
regulators (6): people or entities that create standards or
requirements, in this case for the Internet
validity (12): how truthful something is
omnivores (14): in this case, someone who takes in everything, including multiple perspectives

In the early years of the Internet, it was revolutionary to have a world of information just a click away from anyone, anywhere, anytime. Many hoped this inherently democratic technology could lead to better-informed citizens more easily participating in debate, elections and public discourse.

Today, though, many observers are concerned that search algorithms and social media are undermining the quality of online information people see. They worry that bad information may be weakening democracy in the digital age.

The problems include online services conveying fake news, splitting users into "filter bubbles" of like-minded people and enabling users to unwittingly lock themselves up in virtual echo chambers that reinforce their own biases.

These concerns are much discussed, but have not yet been thoroughly studied. What research does exist has typically been limited to a single platform, such as Twitter or Facebook. Our study of search and politics in seven nations—which surveyed the United States, Britain, France, Germany, Italy, Poland and Spain in January 2017—found these concerns to be overstated, if not wrong. In fact, many Internet users trust search to help them find the best information, check other sources and discover new information in ways that can burst filter bubbles and open echo chambers.

Surveying Internet Users

5   We sought to learn directly from people about how they used search engines, social media and other sources of information about politics. Through funding from Google, we conducted an online survey of more than 14,000 Internet users in seven nations.

6   We found that the fears surrounding search algorithms and social media are not irrelevant—there are problems for some users some of the time. However, they are exaggerated, creating unwarranted fears that could lead to inappropriate responses by users, regulators and policymakers.

The Importance of Searching

7   The survey findings demonstrate the importance of search results over other ways to get information. When people are looking for information, they very often search the Internet. Nearly two-thirds of users across our seven nations said they use a search engine to look for news online at least once a day. They view search results as equally accurate and reliable as other key sources, like television news.

8   In line with that general finding, a search engine is the first place Internet users go online for information about politics. Moreover, those Internet users who are very interested in politics, and who participate in political activities online, are the most likely to use a search engine like Bing or Google to find information online about politics.

9   But crucially, those same users engaged in search are also very likely to get information about politics on other media, exposing themselves to diverse sources of information, which makes them more likely to encounter diverse viewpoints. Further, we found that people who are interested and involved in politics online are more likely to double-check questionable information they find on the Internet and social media, including by searching online for additional sources in ways that will pop filter bubbles and break out of echo chambers.

Internet-savvy or Not?

10   It's not just politically interested people who have these helpful search habits: People who use the Internet more often and have more practice searching online do so as well.

11   That leaves the least politically interested people and the least skilled Internet users as most susceptible to fake news, filter bubbles and echo chambers online. These individuals could benefit from support and training in digital literacy.

12   However, for most people, Internet searches are critical for checking the reliability and validity of information they come across, whether online, on social media, on traditional media or in everyday conversation. Our research shows that these Internet users find search engines useful for

checking facts, discovering new information, understanding others' views on issues, exploring their own views and deciding how to vote.

International Variations

We found that people in different countries do vary in how much they **13** trust and rely on the Internet and searches for information. For example, Internet users in Germany, and to a lesser extent those in France and the United Kingdom, are more trusting in TV and radio news, and more skeptical of searches and online information. Internet users in Germany rate the reliability of search engines lower than those in all the other nations, with 44 percent saying search engines are reliable, compared with 50 to 57 percent across the other six countries.

In Poland, Italy and Spain, people trust traditional broadcast media less **14** and are more reliant on, and trusting of, Internet and searching. Americans are in the middle; there were greater differences within European countries than between Europe as a whole and the U.S. American Internet users were so much more likely to consult multiple sources of information that we called them "media omnivores.'"

Internet users generally rely on a diverse array of sources for political **15** information. And they display a healthy skepticism, leading them to question information and check facts. Regulating the Internet, as some have proposed, could undermine existing trust and introduce new questions about accuracy and bias in search results.

But panic over fake news, echo chambers and filter bubbles is exagger- **16** ated, and not supported by the evidence from users across seven countries.

Reading Comprehension

1. William Dutton is a researcher. Consider the essay's first four paragraphs. What concerns or problems does Dutton's research hope to address? What are the results, or findings, of Dutton's study?

2. The author uses the terms *fake news*, *filter bubbles*, and *echo chambers* in his title and throughout his essay. Define these terms in your own words.

3. Consider the new understanding about online searches that Dutton reaches upon completing his study. What specific details or evidence does he highlight to support his claim?

Discussion Prompts/Writing Options

If you write on any of the following topics, work through the stages of the writing process in preparing your assignment.

1. Dutton's article provides a summary or synopsis of his research method and findings. He claims that "through funding from Google, [he and his researchers] conducted an online survey of

more than 14,000 Internet users in seven nations." What type of questions do you think Dutton included in his survey? If you were to create a survey, how would you ensure a valid sample size? Is it appropriate in your opinion for a company like Google to sponsor Dutton's research? Is there a conflict of interest? Consider these questions and report your thoughts to the class as a whole.

2. With a group of peers, identify and discuss current controversial issues in society. Agree to focus on one issue. Then find online news sites that report and publish articles or opinions on this topic. What sites do you and your peers find most trustworthy and why? Which sites to you find least trustworthy and why? Discuss the parameters your group used to judge a news source's credibility. Then, write an essay that illustrates the way in which you evaluated the trustworthiness of the site, how you determined some sites were less reliable than others, and how you determined which sites were most credible.

3. Because of the widespread perception that fake news and echo chambers undermine democracy, some critics are calling for new policies and regulation of social media and online news outlets. With your peers, discuss the benefits or pitfalls of potential new policies and regulations. Then, write an essay that illustrates your position on developing policies and regulations on social media and online news sources.

Topics for Critical Thinking and Writing

If you write on any of the following topics, work through the stages of the writing process in preparing your assignment.

1. Dutton claims, "Nearly two-thirds of users across our seven nations said they use a search engine to look for news online at least once a day." How do you seek out news and information on the Internet? What means other than search engines do you use to read the daily news or gather information? With a group of peers, brainstorm ways to ensure the reliability of these other sources. How do you ensure the information from these sources is accurate, unbiased, and reliable? Consider creating a presentation or an informational essay illustrating ways to ensure accuracy, objectivity, and reliability in online information.

2. Dutton claims, "The least politically interested people and the least skilled Internet users as most susceptible to fake news, filter bubbles and echo chambers online. These individuals could benefit from support and training in digital literacy." What might this support and training look like in the college setting? Should digital literacy be offered as a stand-alone required course or should skills necessary for digital literacy be implemented in core classes? Research multiple perspectives on this issue and write a letter voicing your opinions to your school's administration. In your letter, illustrate the need, an implementation plan, and credible evidence to support your position.

READINGS FOR WRITERS: DESCRIPTION

Coming Home Again

Chang-rae Lee

Chang-rae Lee is a Korean-American novelist. His works have received multiple accolades, and his most recent work, On Such a Full Sea, *was a 2014 finalist for the National Book Award. In this excerpt from a longer essay titled "Coming Home Again," Lee relates a story from his youth that captures the deep connection he had with his mother, a connection that was highlighted by their interactions in the kitchen.*

Lexile Measure/Words: 1200L/540W

Words You May Need to Know (Corresponding paragraph numbers are in parentheses.)

deprecating (1): expressing disapproval

crook (2): the bend or flex (in this case, of the arm)

beheld (2): witnessed or saw

kalbi (2): a traditional Korean barbecued beef ribs dish

embedded (2): inserted

opaque (2): not transparent

methodically (2): in a systematic manner

butterflied (2): to split a piece of meat in two and spread it out flat

minced (2): to chop finely

gingerroot (2): literally a root used for spice

scallions (2): small onions

marinade (2): a sauce in which to soak meat to tenderize and flavor

julienne (3): cutting into small strips

aromatic (3): fragrant and perfumed

When I was six or seven years old, I used to watch my mother as she prepared our favorite meals. It was one of my daily pleasures. She shooed me away in the beginning, telling me that the kitchen wasn't my place, and adding, in her half-proud, half-deprecating way, that her kind of work would only serve to weaken me. "Go out and play with your friends," she'd snap in Korean, "or better yet, do your reading and homework." She knew that I had already done both, and that as the evening approached there was no place to go save her small and tidy kitchen, from which the clatter of her mixing bowls and pans would ring through the house. 1

I would enter the kitchen quietly and stand beside her, my chin lodging upon the point of her hip. Peering through the crook of her arm, I beheld the movements of her hands. For *kalbi*, she would take up a butchered short rib in her narrow hand, the flinty bone shaped like a section of an airplane wing and deeply embedded in gristle and flesh, and with the point of her knife cut so that the bone fell away, though not completely, leaving it connected to the meat by the barest opaque layer of tendon. Then she methodically butterflied the flesh, cutting and unfolding, repeating the action until the meat lay out on her board, glistening and ready for seasoning. She scored it diagonally, then sifted sugar into the crevices with her pinched fingers, gently rubbing in the 2 crystals. The sugar would tenderize as well as sweeten the meat. She did this with each rib, and then set them all aside in a large shallow bowl. She minced a half-dozen cloves of garlic, a stub of gingerroot, sliced up a few scallions, and spread it all over the meat. She wiped her hands and took out a bottle of sesame oil, and, after pausing for a moment, streamed the dark oil in two swift circles around the bowl. After adding a few splashes of soy sauce, she thrust her hands in and kneaded the flesh, careful not to dislodge the bones. I asked her why it mattered that they remain connected. "The meat needs the bone nearby," she said, "to borrow its richness." She wiped her hands clean of the marinade, except for her little finger, which she would flick with her tongue from time to time, because she knew that the flavor of a good dish developed not at once but in stages.

3   Whenever I cook, I find myself working just as she would, readying the ingredients—a mash of garlic, a julienne of red peppers, fantails of shrimp— and piling them in little mounds about the cutting surface. My mother never left me any recipes, but this is how I learned to make her food, each dish coming not from a list or a card but from the aromatic spread of a board.

Reading Comprehension

1. In the second paragraph, the author describes an experience watching his mother prepare *kalbi*, a traditional Korean barbecue beef rib dish. Reread the short essay. Then, considering the essay as a whole, describe the significance of this experience to the author.

2. The author concludes in the final paragraph: "My mother never left me any recipes, but this is how I learned to make her food, each dish coming not from a list or a card but from the aromatic spread of a board." In your own words, what did Lee learn from his mother?

Discussion Prompts/Writing Options

If you write on any of the following topics, work through the stages of the writing process in preparing your assignment.

1. Successful descriptive writing uses specific details that engage the senses. With your classmates, consider how Lee uses specific details to appeal to multiple senses in this excerpt from his essay. Which details appeal to the sense of sight? Smell? Taste? Touch? Sound? Create a chart that lists specific details that appeal to each of the senses. Which sense does Lee engage in the most? What is the primary effect of this?

2. Good descriptive writing leaves a dominant impression (the main point). What do you think is the dominant impression of the essay? What details are critical to its development? Does Lee order descriptions in time sequence, spatial position, or by similar types?

Topics for Critical Thinking and Writing

If you write on any of the following topics, work through the stages of the writing process in preparing your assignment.

1. Consider Lee's essay as a model. Think about a specific memory of an experience with a loved one. Brainstorm details from this experience, being sure to recall specific details that appeal to multiple senses. Then, consider the greater meaning of this experience to your life. Is the experience simply nostalgic, reminding you of a time of joy earlier in your life? Is it an early indicator of the type of person you are today? Was the experience transformative? Did it change you and your outlook in life in a significant way?

   After brainstorming details about your experience, write a descriptive essay about the experience, making sure to provide specific details that leave a dominant impression. Make sure to consider the organization of details, specifically whether they should be organized by time sequence, spatial position, or by similar types.

2. Advertisements online and in newspapers depend heavily on images and text to appeal to customers. However, radio advertising has to rely on descriptions alone. Imagine you work for a local advertising company and have been hired by a local restaurant, nightclub, or coffee shop to write a script for a 60-second radio commercial to be aired during the evening rush hour.

   The dominant impression you want to leave is to encourage potential customers to visit your client's place of business. Brainstorm the specific details of your client's business, make the client's product appealing to potential consumers, and compose a compelling, detail-driven advertisement. If you have the capability, use technology to record your advertisement, complete with appropriate sounds and music.

READINGS FOR WRITERS: NARRATION

Field of Dreams: From Farm Work to Medical Work

Alfredo Quiñones-Hinojosa

Alfredo Quiñones-Hinojosa grew up outside Mexicali, Mexico, and entered the United States at age nineteen. He received a scholarship to the University of California, Berkeley, and completed an honors thesis in neuroscience. Subsequently, he gained admission to Harvard Medical School and graduated with honors in 1999. "Dr. Q," as he calls himself, is internationally known for his work as a neurosurgeon at Johns Hopkins Hospital in Baltimore, Maryland.

Lexile Measure/Words: 1120L/1760W

Words You May Need to Know (Corresponding paragraph numbers are in parentheses.)

commencement (1): beginning, graduation ceremony
novel (3): new
migrant (4): moving from place to place

terra firma (9): solid ground
primed (14): prepared
inculcated (16): installed, implanted

1   My father used to tell me when I was a little kid that "aunque no tengas buena punteria, si le tiras al cielo, a lo mejor le pegas a una estrella" (even if you do not have good aim, if you shoot at the sky, you may hit a star). Well, I am not known for my baseball abilities, so Pedro Martinez does not have to worry about his job. I am better known for my perseverance. I am thankful and honored to have the opportunity to give this commencement speech. Please, let me echo what was told to me by many of my friends and classmates graduating today from Harvard Dental and Medical School. It was the support of our loved ones and mentors, our determination, discipline, and dreams that have taken us here today.

2   "Con trabajo, deterrninación, y apoyo, puedes llegar a ser el arquitecto de tu propio destino" (With hard work, determination, and support, you can become the architect of your own destiny), my family constantly told me. Growing up in Mexicali, Mexico, I developed self-confidence and a sense of independence at an early age. In order to help my parents financially, as the oldest child, I was simultaneously attending elementary school and pumping gas in my parents' small gas station at the age of five. Helping to shoulder the financial burdens we carried developed my determination and inner strength while I was quite young—qualities for which I continue to be thankful today.

3   The idea that our dreams are within our reach is not novel. I am no different from any of my classmates graduating today. We are all here with incredible and interesting stories. The only difference, perhaps, is that I am in front of you willing to share my own.

My story in the United States began one night in January 1987. As an   4
eager, ambitious young Mexican, I crossed the border illegally, landed in the
fields of California, and became a migrant farm worker. I packed the little I
had, and with $65 in my pocket, decided to explore "El Norte." I migrated to
the United States to fulfill a dream: the dream that many people, like myself,
have of escaping poverty and one day returning "triumphant" to our countries.

The reality was a stark contrast. I spent long days in the fields picking   5
fruits and vegetables, sleeping under leaky camper shells, my hands bloodied
from pulling weeds, eating anything I could. My only comfort was that I had
a good tan and I was in top shape.

One day in the fields, while I was talking with a coworker, I told him   6
that I wanted to learn English and go to school. He laughed and said, "This
is your fate; you will spend the rest of your life working in the fields." Those
words were painful to hear. I realized that without English language skills,
without an education, and without support, this predicted fate of being a
migrant farm worker for the rest of my life seemed very likely.

I wish I could tell you what inspired me to leave the fields of the San   7
Joaquin Valley that day. What possessed me to move without a job, the ability to speak English, and knowledge of what was going to happen next? I
do not know, but I did it. I think that my dream, although it was fogged by
uncertainty, was more powerful than the fear of the unknown. It was one of
those decisions that changed my life entirely since, miraculously, four years
later, I ended up at the University of California at Berkeley.

This experience has always reminded me of what Henrik Ibsen once   8
said: "Rob a man of his life-illusion, and you rob him also of his happiness."

The Importance of Mentoring

After the fields, I began to work in a rail car repair company in Stock-   9
ton, California. I first cleaned railroad cars. Then I was a welder, a painter,
and a high-pressure valve specialist, and within sixteen months, a supervisor.
On April 14, 1989, an event took place that made me reevaluate my direction
and my life. I fell into a tank carrying liquified petroleum gas—I almost died!
I woke up in the hospital and saw a person dressed all in white; I felt assured
to know that a doctor was taking care of me. I had a feeling of being on *terra
firma*. This brush with death gave me the strength to continue pursuing my
dreams with a rejuvenated force.

I constantly daydreamed. I have learned that if our minds can conceive a   10
dream and our hearts can feel it, it will be much easier to achieve that dream.
At night, I attended community college. I started out taking English as a Second Language courses. Less than three years of hard work later, I was a member of the track and field team and captain of the debate team. As a member of
the track team, I found that a race does not end once you reach the finish line;
rather, every time you reach the end, a new race begins. During my speech

class, a mentor who believed in me made me the captain of the debate team. I began to appreciate that the ability to work as part of a team is vital to succeed.

11   Everything went well in community college; my life in academia was beginning to take off. My mentors helped me to get to my next stop, the University of California–Berkeley. I met more important role models and mentors. I learned from them that "knowledge is better learned by action than by contemplation." I also learned that it takes much more than intelligence to succeed; it also takes discipline, dedication, determination, and a dream. Without knowing it, I was being prepared for medical school. When one of my mentors told me that I should apply to Harvard, I thought that he was a very nice man but clearly *living la vida loca* (or a little insane in the brain).

12   After my acceptance to Harvard Medical School, I hesitated to attend. I was not sure it was the institution where a poor student who grew up in a small rural community in Mexico, like I did, would thrive. My mentors at Berkeley insisted that I travel to Boston and visit Harvard. During that visit, I met two distinguished professors, Drs. Edward A. Kravitz and David D. Potter. From them and other important mentors at Harvard, I have learned to see academic medicine as an opportunity to understand and treat human diseases better, but more, as an opportunity to provide leadership and support to future physicians-scientists in order to serve our communities the best possible way. These outstanding professors embody the words of Plutarch: "The mind is not a vessel to be filled but a fire to be ignited."

13   Like many others here today, I realized long ago the great extent to which I have depended on the help received from my mentors in pursuing my dreams of being a physician-scientist. Henry Brooke Adams once said that "A teacher affects eternity; he can never tell where his influence stops." I, like many of us, hope that I can begin to have the same impact as a mentor to future medical students and graduate students—to change their lives for the better.

Our Dreams Have No Barriers, No Borders, and No Limits

14   It is no secret that minority communities have the highest dropout and lowest educational achievement rates in the country. The "pipeline" to higher education and especially in professional programs is not fully "primed" for minority students. Although members of minority groups make up about 18 percent of the U.S. population, in 1994, they accounted for only 3.7 percent of the M.D. faculty at the nation's medical schools.[*] Recent investigations found that Black and Hispanic physicians are much more likely to serve minority communities and to include minorities and poor people among their patients. Minority physicians are twice as likely to work in locations designated as health workforce shortage areas by the federal government.

---

[*]According to the 2010 U.S. Census, about 36 percent of the U.S. population belonged to a racial or ethnic minority group. In 2010, minority representation in medical school faculty members was 8 percent.

Minority patients are more than four times as likely as Whites to receive their regular care from a minority physician. I have been very fortunate in my involvement in education to meet outstanding minority role models—the quality of the role models is high, but the numbers are low.

Drs. Willam Bowen and Derek Bok, in their book, *The Shape of the River*, point out that a "healthy society in the 21st century will be one in which the most challenging, rewarding career possibilities are perceived to be, and truly are, open to all races and ethnic groups." The effort to recruit underrepresented minority students in selective institutions has come under "heavy fire." Changes in admissions policies in places such as California and Texas have occurred recently. The astounding effects that a "race-neutral admissions policy" has had in decreasing the number of Blacks, Hispanics, and Native Americans being admitted to institutions in these states indicate that the time is "ripe" for re-evaluating how race-sensitive admissions policies have been applied and what their consequences have been during the past thirty years.

Recently, while having dinner with some of my friends, we spoke about Harvard's contributions and commitment to making our institution a leader in science, in community service, and in recruitment of underrepresented students. We felt privileged and honored to be part of this family that has demonstrated dedication, discipline, love, and passion for everything it has done. Many of us have constantly commented that we hope one day as future physicians we can all embody the value that this institution and its dedicated faculty has inculcated in us—the value of being a role model, a mentor, an outstanding physician, a colleague, and a friend.

Like many other illegal immigrants, I arrived able only to contemplate what my dreams might be. Now, due to the support I have from my family; my wife, Anna; and our dear daughter, Gabriella; the support of my friends and mentors; and the backing of vital organizations such as our institution, I feel that I can contribute greatly to our community as a physician-scientist.

Today, we graduate from this fine institution, happy, ready to take on the world, perhaps also slightly nervous about starting residency. Let us not forget that thanks to our loved ones and our mentors, and the determination we all carry, we have been able to fulfill our dreams.

I now can welcome and accept my fate of "working in the fields" for the rest of my life—but in the "field of academic neurosurgery."

Reading Comprehension

1. Referring to Paragraph 1, identify the author's specific audience and thesis for this commencement address.

2. In your own words, what is the main point of Quiñones-Hinojosa's narrative? Which line(s) serve as the narrative's thesis statement? List several examples from the reading that support this claim.

Discussion Prompts/Writing Options

If you write on any of the following topics, work through the stages of the writing process in preparing your assignment.

1. Discuss or write a short essay about a time when you achieved a goal that was important to your future success. Did you reach your goal through hard work, a determined attitude, support from others, or some combination of these? Incorporate some dialogue in your narrative, include specific details, and be sure your sequence of events is easy to follow.

2. In Paragraph 15, the author elaborates on the notion that a "healthy society in the 21st century will be one in which the most challenging, rewarding career possibilities are perceived to be, and truly are, open to all races and ethnic groups." Do you agree? Why or why not? Provide reasons and specific examples to support your view.

3. Quiñones-Hinojosa uses multiple maxims in his speech. Maxims are short, memorable statements that impart advice or express general truths. Identify the maxims the author uses in the reading. Then with your classmates discuss how the maxims help to develop Quiñones-Hinojosa's narrative and establish his main point.

Topics for Critical Thinking and Writing

If you write on any of the following topics, work through the stages of the writing process in preparing your assignment.

1. Quiñones-Hinojosa emphasizes the positive impact that mentoring can have on young people's lives. Have you ever acted as someone's mentor or been mentored yourself? Based on your own experiences or observations, write a short essay on the benefits of being mentored or serving as a mentor.

2. Imagine that you have agreed to deliver a motivating speech to high school seniors about overcoming one's fears about adjusting to college life. Plan to incorporate some specifics about the challenges you faced when you started college and how you dealt with them successfully. Brainstorming about financial, social, and time-management pressures, as well as how you learned to cope with them, can help you generate ideas for your speech. You might also consider adding maxims into your speech, as Quiñones-Hinojosa did in his.

READINGS FOR WRITERS: PROCESS

How to Tell a Story: An Essay on Humorous Storytelling

Mark Twain

Mark Twain was born Samuel Langhorne Clemens on November 30, 1835. Twain, American humorist (comic writer) and novelist, captured a world audience with stories of boyhood adventure and with commentary on man's faults. His writing is often humorous even while it probes, often bitterly, at the roots of human behavior. In "How to Tell a Story," written in 1895 and published in a collection of essays in 1897, Twain explains that the difference between a humorous story and a comic one lies in the techniques employed by the respective storyteller.

Lexile Measure/Words: 1000L/568W

Words You May Need to Know (Corresponding paragraph numbers are in parentheses.)

gravely (5): in a serious manner
dimly (5): in a faint or soft manner
nub (5): the heart, crux, or central point of the matter; in this case, the punchline
snapper (6): another name for a nub or punchline
pretense (6): in this case, to pretend
belated (7): late or delayed
renounce (8): to give up

1   I do not claim that I can tell a story as it ought to be told. I only claim to know how a story ought to be told, for I have been almost daily in the company of the most expert story-tellers for many years.

2   There are several kinds of stories, but only one difficult kind—the humorous. I will talk mainly about that one. The humorous story depends for its effect upon the manner of the telling; the comic story and the witty story upon the matter.

3   The humorous story may be spun out to great length, and may wander around as much as it pleases, and arrive nowhere in particular; but the comic and witty stories must be brief and end with a point. The humorous story bubbles gently along, the others burst.

4   The humorous story is strictly a work of art—high and delicate art—and only an artist can tell it; but no art is necessary in telling the comic and the witty story; anybody can do it. The art of telling a humorous story—understand, I mean by word of mouth, not print—was created in America, and has remained at home.

5   The humorous story is told gravely; the teller does his best to conceal the fact that he even dimly suspects that there is anything funny about it; but the teller of the comic story tells you beforehand that it is one of the funniest things he has ever heard, then tells it with eager delight, and is the first person to laugh when he gets through. And sometimes, if he has had good success, he is so glad and happy that he will repeat the "nub" of it and glance

around from face to face, collecting applause, and then repeat it again. It is a pathetic thing to see.

6   Very often, of course, the rambling and disjointed humorous story finishes with a nub, point, snapper, or whatever you like to call it. Then the listener must be alert, for in many cases the teller will divert attention from that nub by dropping it in a carefully casual and indifferent way, with the pretense that he does not know it is a nub.

7   Artemus Ward* used that trick a good deal; then when the belated audience presently caught the joke he would look up with innocent surprise, as if wondering what they had found to laugh at. Dan Setchell used it before him, Nye and Riley and others use it to-day.

8   But the teller of the comic story does not slur the nub; he shouts it at you—every time. And when he prints it, he italicizes it, puts some whooping exclamation points after it, and sometimes explains it in a parenthesis. All of which is very depressing, and makes one want to renounce joking and lead a better life.

Reading Comprehension

1. Explain in your own words the process Twain outlines for the telling of a humorous story. How is this process different from the telling of a comic story?

2. Although the author never specifically condemns the "comic" or "witty" story, it is evident that he does not think highly of this type of story. What problems does Twain associate with the comic story?

3. Twain seems to suggest that the real craft of a humorous story is to deny that there is anything humorous going on within the story. It almost seems that the teller is unaware that there is something funny occurring. According to Twain, why is this strategy humorous?

Discussion Prompts/Writing Options

If you write on any of the following topics, work through the stages of the writing process in preparing your assignment.

1. There are many people who make a living narrating humorous stories. Consider the stand-up comic or the late-night talk show host. Select a comedian or late-night talk show host who you view as humorous. Search for some of his or her video clips online and view a few monologues. Discern the process by which he or she tells humorous stories. Is the process similar to or different from Twain's?

---

*Note: Artemus Ward, Dan Setchell, Nye, and Riley are all humorists. Ward and Setchell rose to fame prior to Twain. Nye and Riley were late contemporaries.

2. Are there additional steps to the process that could have been inserted into the essay? Brainstorm these additional steps with your peers. Then compose a paragraph that adds a step to Twain's process. Try to capture the tone and humor of Twain's writing in composing your paragraph.

3. Tone is best described as the general attitude or mood of a piece of writing. Consider the tone of Twain's essay. What contributes to this tone? What role does the subject matter of the essay, as well as its mode of writing, process, play in contributing to the essay's tone? How would you classify Twain's tone?

Topics for Critical Thinking and Writing

If you write on any of the following topics, work through the stages of the writing process in preparing your assignment.

1. Often humorous writing makes light of or mocks real-life issues or problems. What do you believe the writer is mocking in this essay? What is his real subject matter? Is the writer justified in mocking this issue? Why or why not? Using Twain's essay as a model, select another everyday occasion and write a humorous process essay that addresses a real-life issue.

2. Although Twain's essay uses humor to describe the process of telling a humorous story, process essays sometimes provide directions or information about other complex processes. Think of a topic different from telling a humorous story (for example changing the oil in your car, maximizing your savings, or initiating a job search). Then write a multiparagraph process essay that helps to direct or inform your audience about the process one should follow in undertaking such a task.

3. Twain states that writing a humorous story is the most difficult thing to write. Although you might not know many funny writers, you probably have some friends or family members who are funny. Select a specific person and reflect on his or her humor. Write an essay that specifically examines the approach or process that this person uses to create laughter.

READINGS FOR WRITERS: COMPARISON AND CONTRAST

A New Game Plan

Lisa Bennett

High school football coach Bill Miller says he "was a jerk" during the years he was an All-American football player and college coach. He insulted opponents, treated women badly, and drank heavily. Now he's a different man, "teaching players to be accountable on and off the field."

Lexile Measure/Words: 1000L/912W

Words You May Need to Know (Corresponding paragraph numbers are in parentheses.)

strides (1): walks with long steps
adorned (2): decorated
convert (2): a person who has been persuaded to change his or her beliefs
taunting (3): insulting, provoking
belittling (3): treating as if others have little value
accountable (4): responsible
mandatory (5): required

pre-empt (5): prevent
CEOs (6): chief executive officers, usually a title given to people who head large businesses
ushered (6): led
anticipated (7): prevented
monitoring (8): observing, checking
sexist (8): biased in favor of a particular gender
progressive (12): improving

1   At Brattleboro Union High School, in the southeastern corner of Vermont, football coach Bill Miller sips a Pepsi from an oversized plastic cup as he strides about his office, rarely pausing to sit during a two-hour conversation. Miller is a former All-American football player and Gettysburg College coach. Young people are drawn to him like fans to a rock star. They stop in his office to talk about a game, a relationship, a drug problem, or anything that concerns them.

2   When they're not stopping in, as on this cold November morning, Miller stands outside his office and watches them walk by on the way to class: "Did you get a part in the play this semester?" he asks a student at his locker. "Wow, new hairstyle—looks great!" he calls to a girl as she turns the corner, her head newly adorned in braids. "What are you going to do about college?" he asks another. His voice is loud, his posture confident, his dress impeccable. Miller is a man with a mission—a convert, as it were, to the idea that school sports should be about something more than just winning.

3   "In the old days, I was a jerk," he says, referring to his years as a player and college coach. Miller recalls taunting opponents on the field, belittling women off the field, and drinking heavily between games. This, he explains, was what he thought it meant to be a "cool" athlete. But time made Miller see things differently. By his mid-thirties, he recognized not only that his behavior was insulting and beside the point of academic competition, but that it got in the way of his being a good player and coach.

He took the coaching job at Brattleboro eight years ago, armed with a   4
new philosophy: "There's more to football than just playing. Players have
to be accountable for their mistakes, on and off the field. And they have to
know that everything doesn't revolve around them."

At the beginning of every season, Miller calls a mandatory meeting   5
for players and their parents in which he announces his rules of the game.
He asks parents to be present, he says, because he wants their support.
He also wants to pre-empt complaints if one of their sons or daughters is
suspended from a game because of a violation of the rules. In some cases,
he also wants parents present because whatever they teach their children
at home, when it comes to football, he wants them to know, "It's my way
or the highway."

Among Miller's rules: Any player who puts down a teammate, taunts an   6
opponent, argues with an official, or scores a touchdown and does anything
but hand the ball to an official *will be pulled from the game.* Further, any
player who gets into a fight will be pulled from that game, plus the next two.
Even parents who engage in disruptive taunting as spectators at a game will
be asked to leave. "We've even had CEOs in this town ushered out of a game
for their behavior—and after a warning!" says Brattleboro soccer coach and
health teacher Steve Holmes.

But not everything in football can be anticipated by a rule, as Miller   7
discovered six years ago when his juniors and seniors taped some sophomore players' legs together and taped another to the locker room bench. In
the spirit of the movie "Scared Straight," he took the offending students on a
field trip to the county courthouse, introduced them to the district attorney,
and required them to observe a full day of court proceedings. Miller recalls
their reaction to sentence after sentence that the judge handed down: "It was
a shell-shocker. They kept saying, 'You can go to *jail* for that?'"

To be sure, Miller takes a broad view of coaching, monitoring his play-   8
ers' behavior off the field as well as on it. If they drive too fast out of the
parking lot, he makes them run laps after practice. If they are caught drunk,
he requires them to sit out the next two games. If he hears his male players
making sexist put-downs—especially to their girlfriends—he confronts both
players and girlfriends.

"Athletes get away with that because everybody thinks that's the way   9
they're supposed to be," he says. "But I ask the girl, 'Why do you allow him
to talk that way to you? Don't you want him to respect you? Walk away. Tell
him you won't put up with it anymore until he cleans up his act.'"

Recently, Miller required a number of his worst offenders to view a one-   10
woman play and discussion about a teenage victim of dating violence. "You
want to talk about eyes opening?" he says. "They got the message because,
deep-down, they know it's wrong."

11   Jason Houle, an eighteen-year-old senior who has been on the team for three years, believes that Miller's message is something most athletes want to hear. "It makes me feel respected," he says, "to think that somebody cares about what others think about us. I don't want to be thought of as a bad person."

12   For all his progressive efforts, Miller is the first to admit that old habits die hard. "I'm spoiled," he says. "I lose my temper sometimes and yell and swear and get caught up in the moment. And when I first came here, I was called into the office for my language more than the kids. But," he adds, "I've gotten better."

Reading Comprehension

1. What are some of the examples Lisa Bennett provides to contrast with Bill Miller's former behavior that "got in the way of his being a good player and coach" (Paragraph 3)? Why are these examples effective in developing this contrast?

2. Why did student athlete Jason Houle respond positively to Miller's message (Paragraph 11)? Do you agree with his statements? Why or why not?

Discussion Prompts/Writing Options

If you write on any of the following topics, work through the stages of the writing process in preparing your assignment.

1. In his mid-thirties, Miller changed from an arrogant bully to an empathetic mentor. Have you or has someone you know experienced a change of attitude as dramatic as Miller's? Was the change for better or worse, and what caused it? Write an essay that contrasts a new attitude with a former one. Be sure to explain how the new attitude is better (or worse) than the former one and identify the event or catalyst that contributed to the change.

2. Lisa Bennett refers to "the idea that school sports should be about something more than just winning." What can happen to high school or college athletes, coaches, and programs when winning becomes everything? As you formulate an answer, support your point(s) with specific examples from your own school experiences or observations.

Topics for Critical Thinking and Writing

If you write on any of the following topics, work through the stages of the writing process in preparing your assignment.

1. Is there a better solution to holding high school athletes accountable for their own behavior than the "tough love" disciplinary tactics Miller uses? In a paragraph or short essay, explain how you would handle unacceptable behavior by athletes—drunkenness, sexism, violence—if you were the coach at Brattleboro Union High

School. Explain why your method would be more effective than Coach Miller's approach.

2. At the beginning of every football season, Coach Miller calls a mandatory meeting of players and their parents "to announce his rules of the game." What is his motivation for holding this meeting? Do you think his strategy could be effective at other schools? Write a short essay describing at least three realistic ways teachers and parents could work together to enrich academic programs or provide support for students who need more structure or discipline in their lives.

READINGS FOR WRITERS: CLASSIFICATION

First Generation? Second? For Immigrants and Their Children, a Question with Meaning

Rupa Shenoy

Rupa Shenoy is creator and host of Public Radio International's podcast Otherhood. *The producers of* Otherhood *describe its reporting as "part personal narrative, part old-school reporting, and part sound-rich storytelling." The podcast focuses on the dynamics that arise as the United States becomes a majority-multicultural country. This specific essay, written for a January 2016 podcast, addresses the awkwardness faced by multigenerational immigrant families when asked where they are from.*

Lexile Measure/Words: 1020L/673W

Words You May Need to Know (Corresponding paragraph numbers are in parentheses.)

conventional (2): the normal or the regular way in which something is done

clinical (4): impersonal or detached

intrusive (4): causing a disruption into one's personal life

minimize (5): reduce

malicious (6): hateful or mean-spirited

privileged (6): having special rights or advantages

femme fatal (8): an enchantress or temptress; an attractive woman who brings about the downfall of a man

courtesan (8): a prostitute

morphed (8): changed into

sociologists (9): professionals who study society

1   "Where are you from?"

2   Children of immigrants, maybe those with funny names or who don't look like what people think of as a "conventional" American—we get that question a lot. Maybe everyone does. But they probably don't get the follow-up question.

3   "No, where are you *from*?"

4   This happens sometimes when your answer to the first question was something like "Iowa." What they really want to know is "what's your ethnic background?" But maybe that seems like a strangely clinical and intrusive question to ask right off the bat. Still, they want to know. So you say something like, "Oh, my parents are from India."

5   After years of confronting this same situation again and again, you make conscious decisions about how you want to respond. You might decide to minimize the awkwardness and just say to the first "where are you from," "I'm from Iowa, my parents are from India." Or, you can go the opposite way—make the questioner ask a second time so everyone's clear about what's going on—they want to know what you are, ethnically.

That's not to say people have any malicious intent in asking the "where are you from" question. Abdul El-Sayed, Detroit's new director of public health, gets it a lot when he speaks at community meetings. "I think people are genuinely curious; they want to know about the person they're talking to," he says. "I often ask. And it's funny because I feel more privileged to ask, because the question is often asked of me."

Another popular question we ask: "what do you call yourself?" But the answer to that question is more difficult, and perhaps even more telling, because of the general disagreement on what the term "first generation" means.

Eliza Dushku—the femme fatal vampire hunter of *Buffy the Vampire Slayer*—calls herself "second generation," because her father was the American-born child of Albanian immigrants. Dushku just put out a documentary, *Dear Albania*, about her trip back to that country, and her father's roots there. "I think that finding out who we are, and where we came from, and how we're different, and how we're alike—all that exploration is what makes life interesting," says Dushku, who starred in another Joss Whedon show, *Dollhouse*, as a courtesan who morphed into different women with different accents and backgrounds. Albanians reached out to Dushku as she got famous. She learned more about Albania's culture and realized how much of it spoke to her own beliefs and spirit. Dushku now claims Albanian culture proudly.

But, according to academics, she is not "second generation." That term, and other words we still use to describe immigrants, their children, and their grandchildren, were created by sociologists more than a century ago. Van C. Tran, a Columbia University professor whose research focuses on post-1965 immigrants and their children, told me their correct definitions. "First generation" means the people who come to this country and become Americans, he says. The second generation is their American-born children, and so forth. And, according to what Tran says, Dushku is following the pattern academics have recognized in the first, second and third generations of Americans who came out of the immigration wave a century ago. The first generation, Dushku's grandparents, tried to blend in. The second generation, her father, did too. Dushku says he just didn't talk about it much. The third generation—Dushku herself—discovers their roots, recovers what they can and claims the culture proudly.

But Van Tran argues that's not how it's working out for members of the contemporary first and second generations in the U.S. The first generation is returning to home countries, and taking their children. Those children are the first to grow in multiple cultures, taking summer or winter trips to other sides of the world and living a very different reality. "And," Van Tran says, "that makes it more likely that the raw material of cultural differences persist."

Perhaps that's why Dushku asks: "What is American now?" Her conclusion: "America is now so many different cultures."

Reading Comprehension

1. According to the essay, what is the correct definition of first-, second-, and third-generation immigrants? How is Eliza Dushku classified according to this definition? How does the author use Dushku to introduce a general disagreement about such a classification?

2. Shenoy's essay discusses the classification not only of first-, second-, and third-generation immigrants, but also the differences between waves of immigrants to the United States, specifically members of contemporary first- and second-generation families and members from previous waves of immigration. What patterns have academics recognized about each wave that make them uniquely different from one another?

Discussion Prompts/Writing Options

If you write on any of the following topics, work through the stages of the writing process in preparing your assignment.

1. Reflect on your own family. What are the different ways in which you might classify each generation and their attitudes toward a particular issue? How might you classify how each generation views education, work and professional responsibilities, family and traditions, and culture? You may want to consider how to classify each generation's answer to Dushku's question, "What is American now?"

2. Abdul El-Sayed, one of Shenoy's cited experts in the essay, stated, "I think people are generally curious; they want to know about the person they are talking to." Do you agree with this sentiment? Why or why not?

Topics for Critical Thinking and Writing

If you write on any of the following topics, work through the stages of the writing process in preparing your assignment.

1. Oral historians collect and study information using sound recordings of interviews with people who have personal knowledge of past events. Consider a past event of significance to a group of people (perhaps your classmates). This past event could be one of historical significance like September 11, 2001, or a common experience like falling in love, getting married, raising children, or losing a loved one. Conduct interviews of at least five people, being sure to record your questions and their responses. When you have completed your interviews, replay the recordings and find ways to classify the responses. Write a multiparagraph essay that classifies the different ways in which your interviewees responded to your questions.

2. Consider the attitudes that members of different generations of your own family have toward issues like parenting, social media, technology and smartphones, saving or investing money, and education (or an issue of your choice). Then compose a multiparagraph essay that classifies these members' different attitudes on the issue.

READINGS FOR WRITERS: DEFINITION

Be Cool to the Pizza Dude

Sarah Adams

Sarah Adams is a professor of writing at Olympic College in Bremerton, Washington. Her essay, "Be Cool to the Pizza Dude," was originally submitted in 2005 to "This I Believe," a personal essay contest. The essay has also been featured on NPR's All Things Considered. Adams, reportedly, has never delivered pizzas for a living, despite holding many different jobs in her life.

Lexile Measure/Words: 1100L/493W

Words You May Need to Know (Corresponding paragraph numbers are in parentheses.)

principles (1): truths or essential information

harried (2): harassed

encroach (2): to trespass upon

empathy (3): to understand and share the feelings of other people

fickle (3): change beliefs or feelings frequently

brethren (6): brothers

bestow (6): to present or to award

f I have one operating philosophy about life it is this: "Be cool to the pizza delivery dude; it's good luck." Four principles guide the pizza dude philosophy.   1

Principle 1: Coolness to the pizza delivery dude is a practice in humility   2
and forgiveness. I let him cut me off in traffic, let him safely hit the exit ramp from the left lane, let him forget to use his blinker without extending any of my digits out the window or towards my horn because there should be one moment in my harried life when a car may encroach or cut off or pass and I let it go. Sometimes when I have become so certain of my ownership of my lane, daring anyone to challenge me, the pizza dude speeds by me in his rusted Chevette. His pizza light atop his car glowing like a beacon reminds me to check myself as I flow through the world. After all, the dude is delivering pizza to young and old, families and singletons, gays and straights, blacks, whites and browns, rich and poor, vegetarians and meat lovers alike. As he journeys, I give safe passage, practice restraint, show courtesy, and contain my anger.

Principle 2: Coolness to the pizza delivery dude is a practice in empathy.   3
Let's face it: We've all taken jobs just to have a job because some money is better than none. I've held an assortment of these jobs and was grateful for the paycheck that meant I didn't have to share my Cheerios with my cats. In the big pizza wheel of life, sometimes you're the hot bubbly cheese and sometimes you're the burnt crust. It's good to remember the fickle spinning of that wheel.

4   Principle 3: Coolness to the pizza delivery dude is a practice in honor and it reminds me to honor honest work. Let me tell you something about these dudes: They never took over a company and, as CEO, artificially inflated the value of the stock and cashed out their own shares, bringing the company to the brink of bankruptcy, resulting in 20,000 people losing their jobs while the CEO builds a home the size of a luxury hotel. Rather, the dudes sleep the sleep of the just.

5   Principle 4: Coolness to the pizza delivery dude is a practice in equality. My measurement as a human being, my worth, is the pride I take in performing my job—any job—and the respect with which I treat others. I am the equal of the world not because of the car I drive, the size of the TV I own, the weight I can bench press, or the calculus equations I can solve. I am the equal to all I meet because of the kindness in my heart. And it all starts here—with the pizza delivery dude.

6   Tip him well, friends and brethren, for that which you bestow freely and willingly will bring you all the happy luck that a grateful universe knows how to return.

Reading Comprehension

1. In your own words, summarize the overall message of the essay. How is this message enriched by the author's definition of being cool?

2. What specific terms does the author identify as the principles that guide the "pizza dude philosophy"? What distinguishing characteristics does the author use to make each term unique from one another?

3. What is the speaker's attitude toward the pizza guy? What reason does the author give "for being cool to the pizza delivery dude"? Where is this reason stated in the essay? Where is this reason repeated? What is the effect of repeating it?

Discussion Prompts/Writing Options

If you write on any of the following topics, work through the stages of the writing process in preparing your assignment.

1. With a classmate, discuss Adams's overall message. Do you and your partner agree or disagree with the author's message that small kindnesses are returned in the future? What aspects of the message do you agree with? What aspects do you disagree with? What would you change, if anything? Report out your discussion to the larger class and take note of areas of general agreement and disagreement.

2. The idea of "coolness" is discussed repeatedly in the essay's first five paragraphs. How would you define the concept of coolness? In a paragraph or short essay, define coolness and then illustrate a type of person who displays the characteristics of this type of coolness.

Topics for Critical Thinking and Writing

If you write on any of the following topics, work through the stages of the writing process in preparing your assignment.

1. How do you define a happy life? What key terms would use to describe this life? What specific and concrete examples would you use to define these terms? Write your own essay on living a happy life, being sure to define your key terms with specific, concrete examples.

2. Select a term to define that falls under the category of sadness or sorrow. Show how such a term helps to contrast, and by contrasting, strengthen a definition of happiness.

READINGS FOR WRITERS: DEFINITION

Mysterious Connections that Link Us Together

Azar Nafisi

Azar Nafisi is the Iranian-born author of the bestselling book, Reading Lolita in Tehran. *As a result of refusing to wear a veil, she was fired from her job as a professor at the University of Tehran in Iran. Nafisi immigrated to the United States in 1997 and became a United States citizen in 2008. She is currently a professor of English at the Johns Hopkins School for Advanced International Studies. This essay was published as a part of NPR's "This I Believe" essay series.*

Lexile Measure/Words: 1120L/533W

Words You May Need to Know (Corresponding paragraph numbers are in parentheses.)

empathy (1): the ability to understand and share the feelings of others

intimate (1): close

rapport (1): relationship

transcend (1): to go above

contemplating (2): thinking about deeply

self-righteousness (3): the state in which one feels morally superior to others

vividly (3): clearly

staunchest (3): strongest or firmest

ideological (3): deeply held beliefs or ideas

segregated (4): separated and isolated

1   I believe in empathy. I believe in the kind of empathy that is created through imagination and through intimate, personal relationships. I am a writer and a teacher, so much of my time is spent interpreting stories and connecting to other individuals. It is the urge to know more about ourselves and others that creates empathy. Through imagination and our desire for rapport, we transcend our limitations, freshen our eyes, and are able to look at ourselves and the world through a new and alternative lens.

2   Whenever I think of the word empathy, I think of a small boy named Huckleberry Finn contemplating his friend and runaway slave, Jim. Huck asks himself whether he should give Jim up or not. Huck was told in Sunday school that people who let slaves go free go to "everlasting fire." But then, Huck says he imagines he and Jim in "the day and nighttime, sometimes moonlight, sometimes storms, and we a-floating along, talking and singing and laughing." Huck remembers Jim and their friendship and warmth. He imagines Jim not as a slave but as a human being and he decides that, "alright, then, I'll go to hell."

3   What Huck rejects is not religion but an attitude of self-righteousness and inflexibility. I remember this particular scene out of *Huck Finn* so vividly today, because I associate it with a difficult time in my own life. In the early 1980s when I taught at the University of Tehran, I, like many others, was expelled. I was very surprised to discover that my staunchest allies

were two students who were very active at the University's powerful Muslim Students' Association. These young men and I had engaged in very passionate and heated arguments. I had fiercely opposed their ideological stances. But that didn't stop them from defending me. When I ran into one of them after my expulsion, I thanked him for his support. "We are not as rigid as you imagine us to be Professor Nafisi," he responded. "Remember your own lectures on Huck Finn? Let's just say, he is not the only one who can risk going to hell!"

This experience in my life reinforces my belief in the mysterious connections that link individuals to each other despite their vast differences. No amount of political correctness can make us empathize with a child left orphaned in Darfur or a woman taken to a football stadium in Kabul and shot to death because she is improperly dressed. Only curiosity about the fate of others, the ability to put ourselves in their shoes, and the will to enter their world through the magic of imagination, creates this shock of recognition. Without this empathy there can be no genuine dialogue, and we as individuals and nations will remain isolated and alien, segregated and fragmented.   4

I believe that it is only through empathy, that the pain experienced by an Algerian woman, a North Korean dissident, a Rwandan child or an Iraqi prisoner, becomes real to me and not just passing news. And it is at times like this when I ask myself, am I prepared—like Huck Finn—to give up Sunday school heaven for the kind of hell that Huck chose?   5

Reading Comprehension

1. In your own words, summarize Nafisi's definition of the term *empathy*.

2. Consider the essay as a whole. What specific examples does Nafisi use to explain her definition? How would you classify her use of examples?

3. In defining empathy, Nafisi uses antonyms such as self-righteousness and inflexibility. How do these antonyms help Nafisi to define her key term?

Discussion Prompts/Writing Options

If you write on any of the following topics, work through the stages of the writing process in preparing your assignment.

1. Definition essays often do more than just define key terms. They use these definitions to send a message or make a greater point. What is Nafisi's message in her essay? How does her definition of empathy help to establish this point?

2. In a single word, how would you describe Nafisi's attitude toward her subject matter? What words, phrases, or examples from her essay help to express this attitude? Discuss your description of

Nafisi's attitude with your classmates. Try to reach some consensus through the examination of examples from the text and words selected by your classmates to describe her attitude.

Topics for Critical Thinking and Writing

If you write on any of the following topics, work through the stages of the writing process in preparing your assignment.

1. In the fourth paragraph, Nafisi comments on her expulsion from the University of Tehran and the support she received from two of her staunchest allies, students who had challenged her frequently in class. She states that the experience "reinforces [her] belief in the mysterious connections that link individuals to each other despite their vast differences." Think of a similar experience in which a person who has a vast difference in opinion from you empathized with or supported you. Write an essay about this mysterious connection and define your experience with another's empathy.

2. There are many words from the Words You May Need to Know list that might spark a definition essay. Consider words like *intimacy*, *rapport*, *transcendence*, or any other fitting word you can describe. Using Nafisi's essay as a model, define your term in a multiparagraph essay using examples from your personal life; fiction, literature, or history; and current issues.

READINGS FOR WRITERS: CAUSE AND EFFECT

Why Do We Binge-Watch Television Shows?

Alia Al-Chalabi

Alia Al-Chalabi is a student at Boston University and a regular contributor and staff member of The Daily Free Now, *the news, opinion, arts, sports, and lifestyle blog of* The Daily Free Press, *the independent student newspaper of Boston University.*

Lexile Measure/Words: 1020L/619W

Words You May Need to Know (Corresponding paragraph numbers are in parentheses.)

binge-watching (1): watching multiple episodes of a television series, often one after another

accessibility (2): the ability to access or obtain something, in this case, episodes of a television series

instantaneous (3): done without delay

nostalgia (5): a longing for something in the past

stationary (6): remaining still; not moving

indulging (6): to give in to one's desires or wants

We have entered the era of one episode never being enough. We live in a time where we can never be satisfied with not knowing what happens next, but how has this constant yearning for knowledge developed into such an extreme case of binge-watching? Netflix, Hulu and other streaming services have let us into the world of nonstop television. We can watch when we want, how we want and what we want. But what is it about these TV shows that make us watch entire seasons in one sitting?   1

The easy accessibility of just picking up your laptop, phone, tablet or watch has increased our constant desire for content, now. I always wanted to figure out the answer to things immediately, partially because I'm curious and partially because of the generation I'm a part of. The constant access to search engines has bred an era of "the now," which seems to have translated into the same concept for TV shows. Just pick up a device of your choice and start watching wherever you are. Not only is it immediate, but it's also satisfying.   2

The need for everything to be instantaneous does not end with starting a show. It continues into watching the entire show. I have yet to meet a person with enough self-control to stop a show on Netflix after one episode. So why do we do this? Is it our thirst for knowledge, our investment in these shows or are we just too lazy to keep up with a show on a regular basis? After speaking with my sister, I found out that she binge-watches because she feels like she's part of the show. For her, binge-watching means being a part of something, and if you stop watching it's like breaking that connection.   3

4   Along these lines, another one of my friends said that he wants to complete the story line. For me, I only have infrequent bursts of free time, which means that the convenience of watching as much as possible on a particular work-free Sunday may be my only option. However, I also hold the belief that I love binge-watching because it makes me feel closer to the story. Binge-watching comes from the need to be satisfied with the amount you have watched and how passionately you feel toward the show.

5   Binge-watching seems to be woven into the fabric of our generation, but my mom has also become a part of this trend. For her, staying up until 3:00 a.m. comes from her homesickness. She watches Turkish TV shows in binges because it makes her feel closer to her home country of Turkey. Perhaps binge-watching also has an emotional aspect to it as well. When I watch "House," I keep watching because it reminds me of my childhood. When I was young, I wanted to be a doctor and I watched "House" quite frequently with my family. Restarting the show made me feel connected to my childhood dreams and the fondness I felt for all of the characters on the show. While my dreams have shifted, it's always nice to be reminded of your past. Sometimes these waves of nostalgia need to go a little past one episode.

6   Binge-watching may not be the healthiest thing. After all, you're stationary for an extended period of time watching a screen, but sometimes it's necessary. Binge-watching seems to be a satisfying and emotional time for almost everybody I spoke to, but it's important to remember that a little goes a long way. Netflix is great, but not when used in excess. By definition, binge-watching means indulging yourself, but perhaps if we do this less frequently, we can be more productive and still look forward to the occasional binge.

Reading Comprehension

1. What are the reasons the author provides for the increase in binge-watching? Highlight the reasons within the reading selection.

2. How does the author differentiate between immediate causes for increased binge-watching and more remote causes?

3. What is the author's attitude toward binge-watching television? Where in the essay is this attitude most apparent? What words, expressions, or examples best illustrate this attitude?

Discussion Prompts/Writing Options

If you write on any of the following topics, work through the stages of the writing process in preparing your assignment.

1. With a classmate, backward-map the essay by recreating its outline. When you backward-map an essay, you begin with the finished product—the essay—and then recreate its outline, including its thesis, subtopics, and supporting details. Discuss the order that the author used in presenting his reasons for the increase in

binge-watching televisions shows. Does he order them by time, for emphasis, or for logic reasons? Reach consensus and then discuss how the essay would be different if the author had chosen another organizational approach.

2. Although the author primarily focuses on reasons people binge-watch television shows, the effects of too much binge-watching are addressed in the concluding paragraph. Consider the negative effects that Al-Chalabi presents in the essay's conclusion. Then, write your own essay that explores more thoroughly the negative effects of too much binge-watching of television shows.

Topics for Critical Thinking and Writing

If you write on any of the following topics, work through the stages of the writing process in preparing your assignment.

1. With your peers, brainstorm other cultural phenomena similar to binge-watching television. Think about our culture's fascination with selfies, tweets, the 24/7 news cycle, or even app-based reality games like *Pokeman Go*. What are the causes of these phenomena? Write an essay in which you explore the causes of a cultural phenomenon.

2. In the fifth paragraph, the author mentions our human need to connect to "childhood dreams" and experience "waves of nostalgia." Think about some of your childhood experiences, particularly ones you remember fondly. What power do these memories have on you in the present? Write an essay that explores your positive childhood memories and the effects they have on you today. Be sure to include specific details to clearly communicate the effect these memories have on you in the present.

READINGS FOR WRITERS: ARGUMENT

How Not to Be Alone

Jonathan Safran Foer

Jonathan Safran Foer is an acclaimed American novelist. His novels, which include Everything Is Illuminated *and* Extremely Loud and Incredibly Close, *have received numerous awards and accolades. The following essay, published in* The New York Times, *is adapted from the author's 2013 commencement address at Middlebury College. "Safran Foer, Jonathan. "How Not to Be Alone." From* The New York Times, *June 8 © 2013 The New York Times. All rights reserved. Used by permission and protected by the Copyright Laws of the United States. The printing, copying, redistribution, or retransmission of this content without express written permission is prohibited."*

Lexile Measure/Words: 1020L/1161W

Words You May Need to Know (Corresponding paragraph numbers are in parentheses.)

interject (5): to insert between other things
affluent (5): wealthy or well-off
empathy (7): having feelings for the welfare of others
miserly (8): stingy
telephonic (9): relating to a telephone system

burdensome (9): troublesome and oppressively heavy
declension (9): in this case, a variation or a variety
to schlep (10): to move unwillingly
inflection (11): in this case, tone
finite (14): having limits or bounds
corporeal (16): relating to the body

1   A couple of weeks ago, I saw a stranger crying in public. I was in Brooklyn's Fort Greene neighborhood, waiting to meet a friend for breakfast. I arrived at the restaurant a few minutes early and was sitting on the bench outside, scrolling through my contact list. A girl, maybe 15 years old, was sitting on the bench opposite me, crying into her phone. I heard her say, "I know, I know, I know" over and over.

2   What did she know? Had she done something wrong? Was she being comforted? And then she said, "Mama, I know," and the tears came harder.

3   What was her mother telling her? Never to stay out all night again? That everybody fails? Is it possible that no one was on the other end of the call, and that the girl was merely rehearsing a difficult conversation?

4   "Mama, I know," she said, and hung up, placing her phone on her lap.

5   I was faced with a choice: I could interject myself into her life, or I could respect the boundaries between us. Intervening might make her feel worse, or be inappropriate. But then, it might ease her pain, or be helpful in some straightforward logistical way. An affluent neighborhood at the beginning of the day is not the same as a dangerous one as night is falling. And I was me, and not someone else. There was a lot of human computing to be done.

It is harder to intervene than not to, but it is vastly harder to choose   6
to do either than to retreat into the scrolling names of one's contact list,
or whatever one's favorite iDistraction happens to be. Technology celebrates connectedness, but encourages retreat. The phone didn't make
me avoid the human connection, but it did make ignoring her easier in
that moment, and more likely, by comfortably encouraging me to forget
my choice to do so. My daily use of technological communication has
been shaping me into someone more likely to forget others. The flow of
water carves rock, a little bit at a time. And our personhood is carved,
too, by the flow of our habits.

Psychologists who study empathy and compassion are finding that   7
unlike our almost instantaneous responses to physical pain, it takes time
for the brain to comprehend the psychological and moral dimensions of a
situation. The more distracted we become, and the more emphasis we place
on speed at the expense of depth, the less likely and able we are to care.

Everyone wants his parent's, or friend's, or partner's undivided   8
attention—even if many of us, especially children, are getting used to far
less. Simone Weil wrote, "Attention is the rarest and purest form of generosity." By this definition, our relationships to the world, and to one another,
and to ourselves, are becoming increasingly miserly.

Most of our communication technologies began as diminished substi-   9
tutes for an impossible activity. We couldn't always see one another face to
face, so the telephone made it possible to keep in touch at a distance. One is
not always home, so the answering machine made a kind of interaction possible without the person being near his phone. Online communication origi-
nated as a substitute for telephonic communication, which was considered,
for whatever reasons, too burdensome or inconvenient. And then texting,
which facilitated yet faster, and more mobile, messaging. These inventions
were not created to be improvements upon face-to-face communication, but
a declension of acceptable, if diminished, substitutes for it.

But then a funny thing happened: we began to prefer the diminished   10
substitutes. It's easier to make a phone call than to schlep to see someone
in person. Leaving a message on someone's machine is easier than having a
phone conversation—you can say what you need to say without a response;
hard news is easier to leave; it's easier to check in without becoming entangled. So we began calling when we knew no one would pick up.

Shooting off an e-mail is easier, still, because one can hide behind the   11
absence of vocal inflection, and of course there's no chance of accidentally
catching someone. And texting is even easier, as the expectation for articu-
lateness is further reduced, and another shell is offered to hide in. Each step
"forward" has made it easier, just a little, to avoid the emotional work of
being present, to convey information rather than humanity.

12   THE problem with accepting—with preferring—diminished substitutes is that over time, we, too, become diminished substitutes. People who become used to saying little become used to feeling little.

13   With each generation, it becomes harder to imagine a future that resembles the present. My grandparents hoped I would have a better life than they did: free of war and hunger, comfortably situated in a place that felt like home. But what futures would I dismiss out of hand for my grandchildren? That their clothes will be fabricated every morning on 3-D printers? That they will communicate without speaking or moving?

14   Only those with no imagination, and no grounding in reality, would deny the possibility that they will live forever. It's possible that many reading these words will never die. Let's assume, though, that we all have a set number of days to indent the world with our beliefs, to find and create the beauty that only a finite existence allows for, to wrestle with the question of purpose and wrestle with our answers.

15   We often use technology to save time, but increasingly, it either takes the saved time along with it, or makes the saved time less present, intimate and rich. I worry that the closer the world gets to our fingertips, the further it gets from our hearts. It's not an either/or—being "anti-technology" is perhaps the only thing more foolish than being unquestioningly "pro-technology"—but a question of balance that our lives hang upon.

16   Most of the time, most people are not crying in public, but everyone is always in need of something that another person can give, be it undivided attention, a kind word or deep empathy. There is no better use of a life than to be attentive to such needs. There are as many ways to do this as there are kinds of loneliness, but all of them require attentiveness, all of them require the hard work of emotional computation and corporeal compassion. All of them require the human processing of the only animal who risks "getting it wrong" and whose dreams provide shelters and vaccines and words to crying strangers.

17   We live in a world made up more of story than stuff. We are creatures of memory more than reminders, of love more than likes. Being attentive to the needs of others might not be the point of life, but it is the work of life. It can be messy, and painful, and almost impossibly difficult. But it is not something we give. It is what we get in exchange for having to die.

Reading Comprehension

1. Why does the author believe it is so important to be "attentive"? What does he mean when he states, "Being attentive to the needs of others might not be the point of life, but it is the work of life"? Do you agree or disagree with this point of view?

2. The author uses different types of evidence in the essay. Identify the main reasons Foer gives to support his argument (identify at least three). In your opinion, which reason is the most convincing? Which is the least? Why?

3. Good argument essays often appeal to the emotions of the audience. What examples does Foer use that appeal to the emotions of his audience? What emotions are they arousing in the audience? Do these emotional appeals help or hurt Foer's argument in your opinion?

Discussion Prompts/Writing Options

If you write on any of the following topics, work through the stages of the writing process in preparing your assignment.

1. The introduction to the author's argument recalls an incident in which he sees a stranger crying in public. Following this introduction, he comments that "technology celebrates connectedness, but encourages retreat." Explain how the incident described in the first four paragraphs introduces the author's argument about technology. Then discuss the effectiveness of such an example with your classmates. Can you and your classmates think of alternative ways of introducing the audience to the issue?

2. Foer states in the twelfth paragraph, "The problem with accepting—with preferring—diminished substitutes is that over time, we, too, become diminished substitutes. People who become used to saying little become used to feeling little." In a small group, discuss this quotation. Come up with examples from your own experiences that both support and challenge this statement. Did your group come up with more examples in support of the quotation or did you find more reasons to challenge it? Consider having an in-class debate or divide the class and construct competing arguments.

Topics for Critical Thinking and Writing

If you write on any of the following topics, work through the stages of the writing process in preparing your assignment.

1. In the essay's fourteenth paragraph, Foer imagines a reality in which people will live forever. Consider the implications of living forever. In your opinion, will this possibility enhance the human condition and make our lives more "intimate and rich," or will it have the opposite effect? Take a position on this issue and write an argument essay. Consider researching advancing technologies (such as cloning organs, for example) to provide researched-based evidence as context for your argument.

2. Write a counter-argument to Foer's position. Consider the many ways in which technology has enriched human connectedness and communications. You might consider how social media and other forms of technology connect families separated by distance, how they bring about social justice, or how they inspire peaceful protest. Be sure to identify reputable sources in the research and planning of your response.

READINGS FOR WRITERS: THE MULTIPATTERN ESSAY

Grit, Determination, and Four Friends Laughing

Robin Vincent

Robin Vincent is a student at Middlebury College in Middlebury, Vermont. Vincent wrote this essay in 2013 and submitted it to the Calvin Coolidge Presidential Foundation's Calvin Prize Essay Contest. It was inspired by a Calvin Coolidge quotation that reads, "Industry, thrift, and self-control are not sought because they create wealth, but because they create charac- ter." She was selected as a finalist in the contest. The essay blends many of the modes of writing discussed in this book.

Lexile Measure/Words: 1070L/958W

Words You May Need to Know (Corresponding paragraph numbers are in parentheses.)

antithesis (2): the opposite
unsustainable (2): not able to be maintained at the current levels
conviction (2): a belief or strongly held opinion
fend (2): to provide for oneself
self-sufficient (2): independent
whitewash (3): a solution used for painting walls white
butternuts (3): a type of squash
counters (3): to speak in opposition
discourse (4): conversation and dialogue
discord (4): conflict

horde (4): to store away for later use
amicably (4): in a friendly fashion
petty (5): trivial or not meaningful
irrelevant (5): not important
default (5): a failure to meet an obligation
status quo (5): current situation
consigned (5): assigned or placed
tawny (6): yellowish brown
meandering (6): winding (as in a winding stream)
monetary (6): relating to money

1   A small homestead overlooks the rural hillside of Sheffield, Vermont. Four friends huddle together, cooking beet soup, steaming barley, and eating fresh goat cheese, laughing over a mishap on the farm that brought them together as workers. One of the friends built the house with his own two hands: every plank, every daub of clay, every insulating blade of straw. I sit here on a rough-hewn bench next to the roaring woodstove, listening to the conversation. I've worked in the garden all afternoon, as I have all summer long, and my mind wanders. It skims the mason jars rest- ing on the counter, the homemade sourdough bread rising on the battered tin plate, the farm butter with its musty, honeyed scent. As my eyes travel the room, I think: why would someone live here? What on earth does that weathered contraption in the corner do? Why does my friend choose to live such an existence? There is something independent, even liberating, about a cabin in the woods.

2   I learned early in life that the culture in America mandates that you acquire all you can before it's too late. Invest early! Plan for the worst! Make

money fast! Buy this or that before the SALE ends. We have become the antithesis of this little gathering of friends in the woods of Sheffield. We live in a free country, but its guiding spirit of Liberty has fallen prey to irresponsible and unsustainable habits. In their wake, our conviction has been swept away. No longer are we able to fend for ourselves, no longer are we as self-sufficient as we once were. But here, in the Northeast Kingdom of Vermont, is a reminder, a link to our nobler past.

This link can be found in our conversation thread, which has tied itself in a knot over food. The potatoes are not roasting very fast, and our host swears and stuffs them back into the oven. The powdery smell of toasted rosemary mixes with the smoke from the woodstove and fills the room where we sit. We trade stories over buttered sourdough: *this* is the right way to dry beans; *this* is how you whitewash a wall; *this* is the proper way to crack butternuts. Actually, that's not true, our host declares: you ruin the nutmeat and your hammer if you do it that way. No, I've done it like that before and it works, counters my neighbor to the left. Well, I disagree, chimes in another friend, stirring pepper into the barley.   **3**

Our difference in opinion means less than the sound a water droplet makes when it falls to the surface of Lake Champlain. Across the stove, we look at one another and shrug. Friendship welcomes contrasting perspectives. Discourse only becomes discord when participants horde ideas like material objects. It is difficult to live detached from modern conveniences, and still more difficult to disagree amicably, but this is the Vermont way. The differences in conviction under the roof of this cabin may carry less weight than formal controversy under the dome of the Capitol Building, but I have learned that intelligent debate enlarges our minds and improves our ideas. These four walls enclose the keys to happiness as Vermonters have defined them for generations: self-sufficiency, goodwill, and hard work.   **4**

Outside of this cabin, I fear we have lost sight of what is important. We go to war over oil rights, we shut down the government in a petty clash of egos, and we waste time debating those aspects of life that are not only private, but irrelevant to everyone but individuals making choices. We are afraid of failure, of default, of any act of individuality that jeopardizes the status quo. A bitter nervousness haunts the hearts of those in the rat race: someone will make more money; someone will outrank or outthink or outdo me. Single-minded ambition has replaced levelheaded focus. The values this country was founded on—diligence and hard work and personal sacrifice—have been consigned to the backcountry.   **5**

The beet soup is ladled into wooden bowls, tinting the tawny maple a faint red. I look at the work represented in this food, this house, these gardens surrounded by the meandering brook and the fence to deter deer, and long for the value of a country to be measured in sweat and happiness   **6** instead of monetary triumphs. The contraption in the corner—I know now that it grinds grain—whirrs rhythmically, cranked by my friend's hand. The beans on the stove boil over, sending up clouds of steam that send us running for rags and potholders. The *effort* to live this way is unrivaled. Cutting and stacking wood, hauling water for washing and food preparation, planting, harvesting, and saving every seed—it does not end. Each season follows the last. I finally leave at twilight, running through the rustling leaves to my car, clutching three homemade oatmeal cookies. Admittedly, I will return to a house with electricity, running water, and modern conveniences. As I grow older, I will not always pursue the solitary life of a homesteader. Its values, though, are my own. Wherever I eventually live, in a small town like the one I have grown up in, or in a much larger area, these principles will enable me to hold on to my individual ideals while taking part in shaping the greater community.

7   In this small corner of a small state, there is nothing more important than this grit, this special brand of determination conceived in the satisfaction of a hard day's work, and this achingly beautiful stubbornness shut up in a one-room house with a roaring fire and four friends laughing.

Reading Comprehension

1. Vincent's essay contrasts life outside the "small homestead" with the life inside. What "life" does she prefer? Why? What specific details does she provide to create this contrast? Do you agree with Vincent's preferred life? Why or why not?

2. The author defines the keys to happiness as self-sufficiency, goodwill, and hard work. What details does she provide to support this argument? Do you agree with Vincent's definition of the keys to happiness? Why or why not?

Discussion Prompts/Writing Options

If you write on any of the following topics, work through the stages of the writing process in preparing your assignment.

1. In the fourth paragraph of Vincent's essay, she comments, "Friendship welcomes contrasting perspectives. Discourse only becomes discord when participants horde ideas like material objects." Discuss the validity of this statement with your peers. Then, consider your own experiences with friends. Do you welcome contrasting perspectives or do they create discord with others? Does friendship grow as a result of contrasting perspectives or wither? Write about a personal experience that either confirms or challenges Vincent's assertion.

2. Vincent argues that American culture "mandates" that people "acquire all [they] can before it's too late." Do you agree or

disagree with this position? What evidence can you provide to support Vincent's argument? What evidence can you provide to challenge Vincent's argument? Create a T-chart in which you compare the evidence for both arguments. Share your T-chart with your classmates and add any examples they might have that you have not considered to your chart. Develop a multiparagraph essay that defends, challenges, or qualifies Vincent's claims.

Topics for Critical Thinking and Writing

If you write on any of the following topics, work through the stages of the writing process in preparing your assignment.

1. Vincent's essay combines a number of modes of writing discussed in this book. She uses descriptive writing to describe the homestead, her friends, and the smells of the food they are cooking. She narrates a story about a singular day when her friends gathered around a woodstove to share food and conversation. She also builds an argument about friendship, work ethic, and the keys to happiness.

    Consider how these modes of writing come together into a coherent essay in which Vincent reflects on a singular experience to gain a greater understanding of the world around her. Using Vincent's essay as a model, think about a singular experience you have had that sparked a greater understanding of friendship, the value of work, or the keys to happiness (or any issue or greater understanding of the world around you). Then, write a multiparagraph essay that uses multiple modes of writing to capture the experience and its greater understanding.

2. Vincent's essay was inspired by President Coolidge's claim, "Industry, thrift, and self-control are not sought because they create wealth, but because they create character." Research other famous quotations about character. Identify one that speaks to you personally and write an essay that illustrates its central argument.

READINGS FOR WRITERS: THE MULTIPATTERN ESSAY

Roaring Waves of Fire

Christi Lester

Christi Lester won second place in the 2012 Pearson Education Writing Rewards Contest, a national competition for college students enrolled in basic composition classes. Lester wrote "Roaring Waves of Fire" when she was enrolled in Developmental English at Palm Beach State College (Palm Beach Gardens Campus) in Florida. The essay is about an experience that changed her life. Note that the essay employs strategies associated with both the descriptive and narrative writing modes.

Lexile Measure/Words: 920L/745W

Words You May Need to Know (Corresponding paragraph numbers are in parentheses.)

drought (1): period of dry weather
veld (1): grassland
traumatic (1): psychologically painful
frantically (2): desperately or wildly
massive (2): huge
drenching (2): soaking, flooding
dreaded (4): feared

tractor (5): high-powered, low-speed vehicle, often used for pulling farm machinery
soot (5): black dust given off by fire
pessimism (6): tendency to expect the worst
motto (6): rule to live by
strive (6): try, struggle

1   Many would think that living on a calm, peaceful farm would be perfect aside from the occasional dry season. However, with dry seasons come droughts, and with droughts come fires. We call these fires veld fires in South Africa. I had never experienced anything quite so scary until I moved to my grandparents' beautiful farm outside a small town called Bronkhorstspruit. *Until* that day, August 3, farm life had been absolutely serene. This *traumatic* day changed everything.

2   "Look at the strange yellow light," yelled Megan as we walked down the winding dirt road. "It's getting bigger as we walk." We continued down the path and soon arrived at our grandparents' house. Granny was frantically filling up massive buckets of water and drenching as much of the ground around her beautiful brick house as she could. It seemed very strange for a second, but it suddenly struck us. That light that reminded us so much of the beautiful sun, that we so often took for granted, was actually an unwanted, raging fire. It was moving faster than any human could ever run, and it would soon overtake us if we did not take action.

3   Megan, one of my four cousins living on the same farm, quickly made her way to her house, as did I. As soon as I got home, I found my mother doing just what my grandmother had been doing. The only difference between the two was that my mother looked a lot more panicked. The fire was now nearing us way too fast and would reach our little brick house first. I joined her

in making sure that all areas of the garden were drenched. We hoped that the water would keep the fire from coming too close to our house.

Before I knew it, I was pouring one last bucket of water out onto the dry grass. Glancing over my shoulder as I ran inside, I noticed that the fire was about seven feet away from me. As soon as I got inside, I locked the door (as anyone trying to escape something would do) but then realized that doing so was useless. Fire could destroy wood; it could destroy *me*. Next, my mother, sister, and I started running a bath in case we needed to escape the flames. If the fire were to reach into our house with its merciless flames, a bath full of water would be our only hope for staying alive. We were taking sensible steps to protect ourselves, but at the same time, they generated many awful images of what would happen in the next few minutes. I pictured everything belonging to me slowly crackling and then melting away completely—total destruction. I envisioned my two adorable cats and my bulldog trying to escape. I tried to call my friends to say my last goodbyes but felt sick to my stomach when I found I had no signal on my phone. Everything seemed hopeless.

Minutes later, as the fire reached my bedroom window, I was on my knees, praying, when my grandfather and Uncle Alan appeared on a big red tractor. On it was a tank of water that we hoped would save our house and our lives. For a time, it seemed that we were helplessly watching them frantically spray the fire. Just when it seemed that the flames would overtake my grandfather and uncle, their hard work began to pay off. It seemed that my prayers had been heard in that moment. They were finally gaining control of the fire; they were winning the battle. Soon, the fire was all out except for a few little flames that were too small to spread. Calm was in the air. Although we were surrounded by black soot, and our lungs were filled with smoke, we were safe.

The evidence of the fire remained for months. Everything was completely black; still we saw only the beautiful blue sky that reminded us how beautiful life can be. I realized that for years, I had been too pessimistic about life. My outlook changed on the day I was surrounded by roaring flames of fire. I finally appreciated the beauty of life; I live by the motto that one should always focus on the positive. I will admit that on some days, I find it difficult not to submit to negativity; I strive to think positively. After the fire, I was alive. To this day, that is enough for me.

Reading Comprehension

1. What actions did the women take to prevent the house from burning down? In your own words, describe Lester's emotions during this ordeal.

2. At the end of Paragraph 4, Lester states, "Everything seemed hopeless." Summarize the sequence of events that occurred next that restored her hope.

3. What is the climactic moment of the essay? What descriptions or language choices does Lester use in order to build tension in achieving this climactic moment?

Discussion Prompts/Writing Options

If you write on any of the following topics, work through the stages of the writing process in preparing your assignment.

1. Lester states that before her home was saved from burning, she had often felt pessimistic about life and maintained a negative attitude (Paragraph 6). But after the family was able to save their home, Lester says that she tries hard to stay positive. Can chance events permanently change a person's outlook on life? If not, what else needs to happen? Discuss these questions with your peers. Then write an essay that explains your position on whether or not chance events can permanently change one's outlook on life. Support your ideas with specific examples from your observations and experience.

2. Consider the behavior of Lester and her family as they joined forces to fight the fire. What positive traits did they exhibit? Write a paragraph or develop an essay about the strength of character exhibited by a friend or someone in your family during an emergency. Be sure your sequence of events is easy to follow and that you incorporate sensory details to capture the interest of your readers or listeners if you are asked to share your experience with the class.

Topics for Critical Thinking and Writing

If you write on any of the following topics, work through the stages of the writing process in preparing your assignment.

1. Imagine how you would handle yourself in a life-threatening situation similar to the Lester family. Compare or contrast your potential behavior with theirs.

2. Write a narrative essay about an event that gave you a more positive outlook on life. Incorporate specific reasons for your new perspective and include specific details about how your life has changed. Conclude your essay by imagining how your story might help others.

3. Consider the role that a minor incident has had in your life. Write an essay that uses both the descriptive and narrative modes to show how a minor incident set off a series of events that have contributed to your current attitude or outlook on life, college, or your future.

READINGS FOR WRITERS: THE MULTIPATTERN ESSAY

Lines of Spines: What Is a Library?

Tim Gorichanaz

Tim Gorichanaz is a doctoral candidate in information studies at Drexel University. His research focuses on "the question of building understanding with information and documents." His essay, "Line of Spines: What Is a Library," examines how the traditional library has been redefined in the information era and argues that libraries are needed more than ever as places in which to build community and foster relationships. When reading the essay, you should consider how Gorichanaz blends aspects of definition, compare and contrast, and argument modes to develop his essay and its message. The essay was originally published via The Smart Set, *Drexel University's online magazine of arts and culture.*

Lexile Measure/Words: 1000L/794W

Words You May Need to Know (Corresponding paragraph numbers are in parentheses.)

equivalents (1): in the case, the same words—or equal words—in Latin or Greek

respectively (1): in the same order as mentioned previously

Indo-European (1): relating to the family of languages that make up Europe and Asia

conceptualized (1): to make a concept of something

relevant (2): pertinent or important to the issue at hand

yore (2): times past or long ago

proliferate (2): to grow or produce, often rapidly

sloughing (3): discarding or shedding off

informatics (3): the study of information processing, like computer science

impoverished (5): lacking, poor or having little strength or vitality

If you ask Google Images what a library is, you'll get a very clear answer: books on shelves in a column-faced building. Like Google, most of us think of the library as a storehouse for books. We can be forgiven for thinking so. Our word *library* comes from the Latin *librarium*, meaning bookcase. It's the same for the Latin and Greek equivalents for library—*bibliotheca* and *bibliothiki*, respectively—which led to the word for library in most modern Indo-European languages. It's also notable that the Latin word for book, *liber*, originally referred to the kind of bark that was used in book construction. All this is to say that, through and through, we have conceptualized the library in terms of physical objects. Bark, books, shelves, buildings.   1

If a library is just where a society keeps its books, then it's easy to see   2
why many people no longer perceive libraries as relevant. In the days of yore, a building full of books was a clear metaphor for collective knowledge. But today, knowledge is no longer bound to the printed page, and electronic and non-textual forms of media proliferate. Our cultural knowledge is no longer

represented primarily as text within books. Moreover, with the Internet, we can access our multimedia cultural knowledge from virtually anywhere.

3   It's no secret that libraries are struggling. Funding is down in many public library systems across the country as the public no longer has much use for centralized storehouses of books. People say things like, "Why do we need libraries anymore when we've got Google?" Even the academic discipline dedicated to studying libraries seems to be backing away: A century ago, it was called library science; after World War II, it became better known as library and information science; over the past few decades, it's been sloughing the L word (and often picking up words like computer and data). At my institution, for instance, the School of Library and Information Science was renamed to the College of Information Studies in 1985—and today it's the College of Computing and Informatics.

4   But libraries are still important, and that's because they are *not* fundamentally storehouses for books—despite the name and our longstanding cultural assumptions.

5   We have undervalued the library all this time, I think, in part because we have overvalued the written word. In the modern scientific tradition, we have come to consider knowledge to be only that which is communicable via text. But that is a terribly impoverished view of what human knowing can be.

6   Part of the reason for this is the way we conceptualize reading. We tend to think of books as things that hold information, and we think that when you read, the information jumps into your brain. If that were really how it worked, how could two people read the same text and get different information from it? It happens all the time, both in science and in life. Clearly there's more to knowing than just getting information. As Emilio says in the novel *The Sparrow*, by Mary Doria Russell, reflecting on a failed mission to space, "We had all the information, really. It was all there. We just didn't understand."

7   In the age of print we have been held sway to what books can do and forgotten what they cannot do. To the extent that information from texts equates to knowledge, it is only knowledge-that, not knowledge-how or knowledge-of-what-it-is-like. For information to unfold as these ways of knowing, to lead to understanding, we must think of information as a process rather than a thing, and certainly not a process that is bound up in any particular object.

8   What is fundamental about the library is not that it holds objects, or even the nature of those objects, but rather how those objects are used. And though books are the first objects that come to mind, libraries hold far more than just books. To be sure, libraries also have objects like CDs, DVDs, magazines, newspapers, maps, artwork, electronic databases, computers, and printers. But they also offer things we're less quick to identify as objects: space, relationships, trust, understanding, and opportunities. We must recognize that libraries speak to the whole person, not just the intellect.

9   What is a library? In the 21st century, more than ever, a library is a place that helps us realize that we are all part of each other.

Reading Comprehension

1. In your own words, summarize the overall message of the essay. How has this message been enhanced by the author's definition of a 21st century library?

2. What does the author see as the fundamental misconceptions associated with the written word and the reading of texts?

3. How does the author distinguish past definitions of libraries from those definitions in which they might be defined today?

Discussion Prompts/Writing Options

If you write on any of the following topics, work through the stages of the writing process in preparing your assignment.

1. In the past, information found in the library had been carefully curated by librarians. Now, however, much information can be found electronically. With a group of peers, discuss the problems associated with relying too heavily on "electronic and non-textual forms of media." Consider the following questions: Is information always reliable? How do you ensure the information is credible? How do you ensure you are examining an issue from multiple perspectives? How do you wade through vast quantities of information readily available via an online search? Categorize the problems into three groups. Then write an essay in which you illustrate these problems for your audience.

2. With a classmate, discuss Gorichanaz's overall message. Do you and your partner agree or disagree with the author's argument that libraries are still important? What aspects of the message do you agree with? What would you change, if anything? Report out your discussion to the larger class and take notes of areas of general agreement or disagreement. Then write an essay in which you illustrate these areas of general agreement.

Topics for Critical Thinking and Writing

If you write on any of the following topics, work through the stages of the writing process in preparing your assignment.

1. How might your campus library be redesigned, as Gorichanaz suggests, to "speak to the whole person, not just the intellect"? Brainstorm ways in which your campus library's physical space might be better utilized to foster "relationships, trust, understanding, and opportunities." Find or create a blueprint for the library and be prepared to defend your design decisions to your instructor, the head librarian, trustees, or school administers.

2. Recent research has shown a decline in e-books and a consumer return to print books. What are the advantages or disadvantages, in your opinion, of print books? Write an essay in which you both compare and contrast the advantages and disadvantages of e-books and print books and argue a preference for either e-books or print books.

Text Credits

Page 359: Alladi, Amritha. "Manners Matter Online: Basic Etiquette Applies Even for E-mail." *Gainesville Sun* (FL), © June 2, 2008. Reprinted with permission.

Page 521: Roosevelt, Franklin D. "Pearl Harbor Address to the Nation." December 8, 1941.

Page 583: Migoya, David. "Getting Carded at College." *Denver Post*, August 23, 2007. http://www.denverpost.com/headlines/ci_6692541. Copyright 2007. Used by permission.

Page 587: Dutton, William H. "Fake News, Echo Chambers, Filter Bubbles." *The Conversation, Salon.* May 13, 2017. Used with permission.

Page 591: Lee, Chang-rae. "Coming Home Again." *The New Yorker.* October 16, 1995 pg 164. Used with permission.

Page 594: Quinones-Hinojosa, Alfredo. "Field of Dreams." Copyright *Hispanic Outlook Magazine.* Used with permission.

Page 599: Twain, Mark. "How to Tell a Story." Written in 1897.

Page 602: Bennett, Lisa. "A New Game Plan." *Teaching Tolerance,* Number 14, Fall 1998. Copyright 1998. Used with permission of Teaching Tolerance, a project of the Southern Poverty Law Center.

Page 606: Shenoy, Rupa. "First Generation? Second? For Immigrants and Their Children, A Question with Meaning." Public Radion International. Used with permission.

Page 609: Adams, Sarah. "Be Cool to the Pizza Dude." Copyright © 2005 by Sarah Adams. From the book *THIS I BELIEVE: The Personal Philosophies of Remarkable Men and Women* edited by Jay Alison and Dan Gediman. Copyright © 2006 by This I Believe, Inc. Reprinted by permission of Henry Holt and Company. All rights reserved.

Page 612: Nafisi, Azar. "The Art of Being a Neighbor: The Mysterious Connections that Link Us Together." Copyright © 2005 by Azar Nafisi. From the book *THIS I BELIEVE: The Personal Philosophies of Remarkable Men and Women* edited by Jay Alison and Dan Gediman. Copyright © 2006 by This I Believe, Inc. Reprinted by permission of Henry Holt and Company. All rights reserved.

Page 615: Al-Chalabi, Alia. "Why Do We Binge-Watch TV Shows?" *Daily Free Press* blog, Boston University Student Newspaper, October 16, 2016. Used with permission from *The Daily Free Press.*

Page 622: Vincent, Robin Brooke. "Grit, Determination, and Four Friends Laughing." Copyright © 2014. Used with permission.

Page 626: Lester, Christi. "Roaring Waves of Fire." Pearson Writing Rewards student essay winner, 2012. Used with permission.

Page 629: Gorichanaz, Tim. "Line of Spines." Copyright Tim Gorichanaz. This essay was originally published in *The Smart Set.* The author is grateful to Professor Denise Agosto for her feedback on an earlier draft. Used with permission.

Photo Credits

Index

Note: Reading selections are listed under "Readings for Writers." Each selection contains vocabulary definitions, comprehension questions, discussion prompts, writing options, and topics for critical thinking and writing.